THE LINCOLNS

THE LINCOLNS

PORTRAIT OF A MARRIAGE

DANIEL MARK EPSTEIN

BALLANTINE BOOKS

New York

Published in the United States by Ballantine Books, an imprint of
The Random House Publishing Group, a division of
Random House, Inc., New York.

BALLANTINE and colophon are registered trademarks of
Random House, Inc.

Acknowledgment is gratefully made to the Collection of
Keya Morgan, LincolnImages.com, NYC, for photographs
used in the insert.

LIBRARY OF CONGRESS CATALOGING-IN-PUBLICATION DATA
Epstein, Daniel Mark.
The Lincolns : portrait of a marriage / Daniel Mark Epstein.
p.   cm.
Includes bibliographical references and index.
ISBN 978-0-345-47799-6
1. Lincoln, Abraham, 1809–1865.   2. Lincoln, Mary Todd, 1818–1882.
3. Lincoln, Abraham, 1809–1865—Marriage.   4. Lincoln, Mary Todd, 1818–1882—
Marriage.   5. Presidents—United States—Biography.   6. Presidents' spouses—
United States—Biography.   I. Title.
E457.25.E67 2008
973.7092'2—dc22
[B]   2008004471

Printed in the United States of America on acid-free paper

www.ballantinebooks.com

2 4 6 8 9 7 5 3 1

FIRST EDITION

Book design by Simon M. Sullivan

FOR OREM AND HARRIET ROBINSON

Marriage resembles a pair of shears,
so joined that they cannot be separated;
often moving in opposite directions, yet
always punishing anyone who comes
between them.

—REV. SYDNEY SMITH

CONTENTS

ROMANCE

JOURNEYS AND DISCOVERIES

THE RISING STAR

ROMANCE

THE TRYST: SPRINGFIELD, 1842

WALKING EAST ON JEFFERSON STREET with the setting sun behind him, Abraham Lincoln followed his shadow toward the house on Sixth Street where he had arranged to meet his love in secret.

The tall man cast a long shadow in the November light. The October rains and wind had nearly stripped the trees of their leaves—the maple, the walnut, the oak of the prairie. He liked the trees without their foliage, "as their anatomy could then be studied." The outline of a silver maple against the sky was delicate but firm; the network of shades the branches cast upon the ground seemed to him a virtual "profile" of the tree.

"Perhaps a man's character is like a tree, and his reputation like its shadow; the shadow is what we think of it; the tree is the real thing." This idea, which would attend the young man on an eventful journey into middle age, might now provide small comfort. For he had gone and made a fool of himself, during the previous two years of his life, a very public sort of fool at the age of thirty-three.

Now, strolling the wooden planks of a makeshift sidewalk laid along the mud ruts of Jefferson Street, past the new state capitol building with its stately columns and dome upon the square, Lincoln followed his shadow and his reputation toward the home of his friend Simeon Francis, where he could pursue his folly behind closed doors. If a man's character is like the tree and one's reputation like the shadow, he had begun, by trial and error, to understand his character, his virtues and weaknesses; but he still had little sense of what the world might make of his reputation.

He was a secretive man, who kept his own counsel. He was an ambitious man of humble origins, with colossal designs on the future. And it would always be advantageous not to be closely known, never to be transparent. Passing a farmer on a dray, he would tip his hat and grin. Everybody knew him. Nobody knew him. He would play the fool, the clown, the melancholy poet dying for love, the bumpkin. He would take the world by stealth and not by storm. He would disarm enemies by his apparent naïveté, by seeming pleasantly harmless. He would go to such lengths in making fun of his own appearance that others felt obliged to defend it.

On this November afternoon in 1842 it would hardly seem necessary to argue that he was appealing to women, this lanky, clean-shaven fellow, seeing as how one of the most attractive, nubile ladies of Springfield had singled him out, pursued him, and was now waiting for him in the parlor of that house on the northeast corner of Jefferson and Sixth streets.

The friend who owned the house, Simeon Francis, editor of the *Sangamo Journal*, and his wife, Eliza, were childless. They made their large home available for Lincoln and his beloved as a trysting place, where they had been meeting since the summer. The inhibitions that attend lovers when they first are alone, speechless, had gradually given way until they found themselves in a situation where marriage was, if not obligatory, inevitable.

LINCOLN KNEW HE had made a spectacle of himself on a grand scale recently, in the newspapers, caught up in a scandalous duel—there were rumors the cause of it was Miss Mary Todd. And now walking on his way to what might be greater imprudence, he could reflect that only a few years earlier he had resolved never again to get into such a scrape.

In 1838, on April Fool's Day, he had written a letter to Eliza Browning, wife of his lawyer friend Orville Hickman Browning, in which he had reached the following conclusion: "Others have been made fools of by the girls; but this can never be with truth said of me. I most emphatically, in this instance, made a fool of myself. I have now come to the conclusion never again to think of marrying; and for this reason; I can never be satisfied with any one who would be block-head enough to have me." Perhaps he was only joking. He had more masks and poses than Hamlet. This letter explaining his failed courtship of the tall, matronly Miss Owens is scathing comedy, in which he gives vent to feelings of distaste he could not quite conceal in sardonic billets-doux he wrote to the lady herself.

"Although I had seen her before, she did not look as my immagination [*sic*] had pictured her. I knew she was oversize, but she now appeared a fair match for Falstaff; I knew she was called an 'old maid,' and I felt the truth of at least half of that appellation; but now when I beheld her, I could not for the life avoid thinking of my mother; and this, not from withered features, for her skin was too full of fat, to permit its contracting into wrinkles." When he had first glimpsed Miss Owens, she had been twenty-four and pretty, but if Lincoln is to be trusted, the years had not been kind. "From her want of teeth, weather-beaten appearance in general, and from a kind of notion that ran in my head, that *nothing* could have commenced at the size of infancy, and reached her present bulk in less than thirty-five or forty years; and in short, I was not all pleased with her. But what could I do? I had told her sister that I would take her for better or worse."

The match had been made in a playful spirit, on both sides, at the instigation of Miss Owens's sister, Mrs. Bennett Able. But after a while no one could be sure just how serious the agreement had become. Lincoln made it a point of honor to keep his word, "especially if others had been induced to act on it," which in this case he thought they had.

"I was now fairly convinced, that no man on earth would have her, and hence the conclusion that they were bent on holding me to my bargain." Well, they were not, and he had been mistaken. Miss Mary Owens would marry an excellent husband and have four children—but not Lincoln's. Knowing his ambivalence, exasperated by his stalling and his convoluted avowals, not of his love but of some deep concern that she might come to grief if he declined to marry her, she relieved him of his suffering by informing him the wedding was not to be.

When he was sure he had heard her correctly, Lincoln was stunned.

"I verry unexpectedly found myself mortified almost beyond endurance. . . . My vanity was deeply wounded by the reflection, that I had so long been too stupid to discover her intentions, and at the same time never doubting that I understood them perfectly; and also, that she whom I had taught myself to believe no body else would have, had actually rejected me with all my fancied greatness; and to cap the whole, I then, for the first time, began to suspect that I was really a little in love with her. But let it go. I'll try and outlive it."

That courtship—if one could call it that—had ended. But if he had appeared foolish in his approach to Mary Owens, he made himself look like a lunatic with Mary Todd. He had made a fool of himself not by thinking

himself the last chance for a woman he found unattractive, but by falling
in love so deeply he lost his wits. He was a romantic figure in a romantic
age, regarding himself as a poet and a politician. A follower of Byron and
Burns, he had, at thirty, not wholly outgrown his illusions. Who could be
more outrageous, more fantastical than an impetuous young man, in love
or out, who trusts his heart for guidance rather than his reason?

The first round of his courtship of Mary Todd was played out in public, in 1840. She was a bright-eyed, buxom maiden of twenty-one with
glowing skin, abundant auburn hair, and shapely arms and shoulders,
which she displayed to the limit the fashion would allow. She was more
than a foot shorter than Lincoln, and a friend told her, "You'll have to take
a ladder to get to Abraham's bosom, Mary," a remark that made her indignant. He called her Molly. She was widely admired for her beauty and vivacity. "The very creature of excitement," one man said of her, and "one
who could make a bishop forget his prayers," said another, while even her
worst enemy admitted that, until middle age, she remained "a brilliant
woman."

From the day in 1835 when she arrived in Springfield from Kentucky,
the fiery seventeen-year-old might have had any bachelor or widower in
town, including the charismatic young judge Stephen A. Douglas and the
wealthy lawyer Edwin B. Webb, a widower with two children. She might
have had the gallant, swashbuckling Irishman James Shields, the state auditor who was destined for military glory. She lived with her sister Elizabeth, the wife of the governor's son, Ninian Edwards, Jr., in one of the
finest houses in Springfield. Yet she chose the tousled Abraham Lincoln
in his Conestoga boots. Despite his poverty, his humble origins, her sister's disapproving frowns—despite his moods and vacillations, his perplexity in love—she had clung to him.

Why? No better answer can be found than in a letter of July 23, 1840,
explaining her rejection of one distinguished suitor, "the grandson of
Patrick Henry—what an honor!" She wrote: "My hand will never be
given, where my heart is not."

And her heart—as she had confided to several women and at least one
suitor—would only go to a man who would someday be president. It was
a fairy-tale notion that fused ambition and sentiment. She was as much a
romantic in her way as Lincoln was in his, with his idealism, his tormented, melancholy soul, his bittersweet fatalism, and his hunger for

glory. In season, Molly wore blossoms—Sangamon phlox, sky-blue asters, wild indigo—prairie flowers invisible to him until he saw them crowning her hair. She danced with him, although he was no good at it; she drew him out in conversation, despite his innate shyness with women. Late in the year 1840 they became engaged.

Despite her flattering attentions, notwithstanding the passion on both sides and the public display of it, they had broken off their engagement in the winter of 1840–41. Then, too, he had played the halfwit by appearing to have fallen in and out of love with two, or three, women almost simultaneously, depending upon who was counting (and everyone in the neighborhood seemed to be counting). This was the first of several demonstrations of Lincoln's folly, not to say madness, that were well known to Springfield society and deplorably documented in the newspapers and private letters of the time.

According to Mary Todd's brother-in-law Ninian Edwards, Lincoln went "crazy as a loon." Lincoln went crazy and broke off their engagement, or the couple broke off the engagement and Lincoln went crazy, depending upon who was telling the story. The principal players in the drama let no one know the truth. Indeed, the more gossip spread, the more these lovers, Lincoln in particular, went to some lengths to see that the folks in Springfield, not to mention posterity, might never know the truth of the matter. People will talk, and there would be no end to the gossip about this tortuous affair, but the gossip mattered little to Lincoln so long as it was just talk. In their own good time and space, they would resume their courtship.

If the gray-eyed man had become a cipher or an enigma; if the silhouette of reputation rapidly lengthening were to become an impenetrable mystery to the town of Springfield, the states of Illinois, Kentucky, and Missouri, and eventually to the nation—for generations time out of mind—it was all very well to him. Mystery is an element of romance.

The story of a rich girl and a poor boy who fall in love, and whose plight is brought to melodramatic ruin by a scheming father, was a tale told in a popular ballad that Lincoln loved—and it bore just enough resemblance to Lincoln's courtship of the aristocratic Mary Todd for Lincoln to see himself in it. The ballad "William Riley," with its haunting minor melody, was one Lincoln was known to sing aloud, a cappella, although its range of more than an octave was a challenge:

A wealthy squire, he lived in our town,
And he was a man of high renown.
He had a daughter, a beauty bright,
And the name he called her was his heart's delight.

Oh, many a young man for to court her came,
And none of them could her favor gain.
And then there came one of a low degree
And of all of them, she did fancy he.

The plaintive English ballad had come down from Canada in the 1830s in several versions. It was all the rage in taverns and inns and genteel parlors, wherever folks gathered by the fireside with pennywhistles and fiddles and squeezeboxes to tell stories and sing.

Lincoln's memory was a wonder to all who heard him give speeches or tell fables or recite Shakespeare, Byron, Burns, and Poe. The dark side of this gift is the interior echo that goes on involuntarily, waking and sleeping, even after the original desire to learn the verses has passed. So the song of the poor man who falls in love with the rich man's daughter obsessed him, and he would sing or hum it aloud as he walked the streets of Springfield:

One day this couple they were left alone;
The truth to him she did make known.
Said he, "Fair lady, put no trust in me,
For you are a lass of a high degree."

Molly's rich father, far away in Lexington, Kentucky, was not the one to raise objections; it was instead the snobbish Ninian Edwards, Jr., the governor's son, who had married Mary's older sister Elizabeth. They were Molly's guardians in Springfield. Of course they would never know the suspicion that was Lincoln's secret pride and shame, that his own mother was the bastard child of a Virginia planter, "of the highest and best blood of Virginia." From her he had derived his genius. If he appeared to the world as a plowboy, like Robert Burns, he was no less, in breeding and quality, a blueblood, like Lord Byron.

Perhaps the melody of "William Riley" and its woeful story ran in his head as he pursued his shadow east on Jefferson Street to the corner house where his beloved waited for him.

MARY TODD ALSO knew the importance of discretion. It was not easy keeping a secret in such a small town, a town of no more than four thousand, especially a matter of such titillating interest as a love affair. To get to her assignation, she would have to walk nine full blocks alone in the fading light of day, passing carpenters, shopkeepers, and busybodies who wished to know her destination and agenda. Lincoln had only to walk around the corner from the law office that he shared with Stephen Logan on Fifth Street.

She came down from "Aristocracy Hill," where she lived in a large two-story brick house with the Edwardses. The mansion stood on an eminence overlooking, to the northeast, the burgeoning state capital, and, to the south, the groves and rivulets along the Sangamon riverbanks, beyond which lay the prairie. A merchant who had failed at politics, Edwards was part owner of a general store in Huron, north of town on the Sangamon River. Exactly Lincoln's age, thirty-three, Ninian junior, having already inherited considerable property, lived beyond his means—and would always live beyond his means—while looking down on those, like Lincoln, who were born without his privileges.

Making her way downhill along Third Street and then east on Adams, the twenty-three-year-old woman held her skirt in a fist to lift it above the mud. Hogs rooted and rolled at the crossways, as if this were still a frontier hamlet and not the new capital of Illinois. The southwest corner of town had been covered over with impressive houses and yards, most of them built within the last year. Still, in spring and autumn, mud was everywhere, and the hogs spread it, even up to Aristocracy Hill.

Mary Todd was astonished by how much Springfield had grown in the six years since her first visit to Elizabeth and Ninian in the spring of 1835. She recalled the journey from Lexington, Kentucky, by coach and riverboat in the company of her older sister Frances.

The sisters, then seventeen and twenty, were Southern aristocrats, daughters of the Honorable Robert Todd and his first wife, the late Elizabeth Parker. She had died in childbirth when Mary was six. Robert owned a mill that made cotton yarn; he was a state senator and the president of the

Lexington Branch Bank of Kentucky. From the Parkers, Robert had inherited farmland and slaves. He remarried quickly, taking Elizabeth (Betsy) Humphreys as his second wife in 1826. In 1832, they moved their brood of children (five from the first marriage, two from the second) into an L-shaped brick mansion on West Main Street, with its stables, coach house, slave quarters, and a garden in back, through which a brook ran.

That luxurious house in the bluegrass country proved insufficiently large for the growing family, especially the older children, who believed their stepmother slighted them. From the time Mary was nine years old, she had felt more at home at boarding school than in her stepmother's house. Perhaps this is one reason she had stayed on beyond the age of all but a few women at Madame Mentelle's school, studying French, geography, and history.

The same year Robert Todd's family moved to the larger house, Mary's eldest sister, Elizabeth, just seventeen, had married Ninian Edwards, Jr., twenty-two, a law student at Transylvania University in Lexington. Moving with her new husband to the most fashionable residence in Springfield, Elizabeth formed a plan to rescue her three younger sisters from their stepmother's home. As soon as Mary and Frances were old enough to make the journey, she made them welcome in her new house. Anne Marie, the youngest, would arrive four years later.

So Mary remembered Springfield as it had looked in the spring of 1835, when the town had fewer than two thousand inhabitants and the air rang and clattered with the sound of hammers and saws and talk that this was soon to be the capital of Illinois. As Springfield boomed, so did the price of real estate. On May 16, 1835, Mary and Frances accompanied Ninian and Elizabeth to the new courthouse on the square, an imposing brick building with a hip roof crowned with a cupola. The girls stood as witnesses to the sale of a plot of Edwards's land to a Cincinnati banker for $200. Frances signed the record book, then handed the quill to Mary to add her signature.

Thus Mary, at seventeen, became a certified party to the business life of the capital-to-be, and got a glimpse of the character of her brother-in-law, in whose spacious home she was lodging. Somewhere in that house, hidden away in a drawer or a trunk, was a letter from former governor Edwards to his son that would have fascinated the younger sisters had they come upon it, while proving an embarrassment to Ninian junior, newly appointed attorney general of the state of Illinois.

This letter was written in the winter before Elizabeth's marriage to Ninian; the engagement came as an unwelcome surprise to the governor.

My dear son,

If you have been inconsiderate, the past cannot be recalled. The only thing that remains is to act with all practicable prudence hereafter. I am not the least dissatisfied with you, have no objections to the lady you wish to marry, & would gladly assist in facilitating that want, if I could command the means of enabling you to support a family.

Ninian junior wanted to get married *right away*, although he had not finished college and had no means of support. He wanted to get the old man's blessing; furthermore, he had asked for enough money and/or income-producing property to underwrite his marriage venture. And his father, with what now seems almost saintly forbearance, did not scold or ridicule his impulsive son. The boy had gotten caught, and it was too late to chastise him. Rather, he explained that the best he might do is offer him a good house and farm and some other odd lots of real estate. "You should well consider what I can do & act accordingly as far as you can honorably do so."

He advised his son to postpone the marriage if possible until he had finished his studies, at which time he, the governor, might be sufficiently liquid that he could give his son what he had asked for: a cash allowance.

Now if I were in your place I would like to receive such a letter, and would lay it before her [Elizabeth] supporting the propriety of a postponement, and leave the decision to herself. I may in the meantime be able to supply you with money enough to keep you at Lexington till after a second course of lectures, when you might be ready to commence the practice [of law].

But if before the proposed time I should be able to raise money enough to set up housekeeping I would be willing, & far rather do it, under the existing circumstances.

The circumstances may have included that Ninian and Elizabeth had gotten themselves in the family way; in any case, there can be little doubt that the lovers had been imprudent, and either had to rush to the altar on February 18, 1832, or thought that they must. This was not the sort of secret that could be kept from the impressionable younger sisters, Frances and Mary.

But sex and marriage were not the themes in the air of the courthouse where Mary signed the 1835 indenture conveying Edwards's land for $200. It was about money. Shrewd investors were snatching up land lots in Springfield, not selling them at such prices, unless they needed cash. Ninian Edwards, who lived like a prince—who indeed looked like a prince in a fairy tale, with his perfect features, wide-set blue eyes, and shock of wavy hair—needed money, would always need money. Perhaps his father had spoiled him. As a born aristocrat, he felt entitled to a standard of living not accessible to men born in log cabins, by and large. He was described by one of Lincoln's legal associates as hating "democracy as the devil is said to hate holy water."

If Ninian Edwards, Mary's "guardian" in 1842, had understood that his ward had resumed her designs on the plebeian lawyer Abraham Lincoln, or known her destination on this November afternoon, he would not have approved of it. She moved with a natural grace constrained by the wish to go unnoticed—lightfooted and prim at once, like someone balancing a book on her head, avoiding the mud on Fourth Street.

In defiance of Ninian and Elizabeth's opinion, driven by a passion she herself only partly understood, Mary Todd advanced upon the north end of town, passing under signs that swung on little gallows from storefronts and taverns—the dry goods store, the grocer's, the drugstore. On Adams Street stood the noisy Globe Tavern, where sister Frances had boarded for a while in 1839 as a newlywed with her bridegroom, Dr. William Wallace. A block farther east stood Torrey's Temperance Hotel, which made up for its lack of "spirits" by providing the best meals in Springfield.

She would smile and curtsy if accosted. She might say she was on her way to visit her friend Mercy Conkling, until the moment she had passed her home on Fourth Street and was walking away from it. Then she would have to say she was on her way to visit Eliza Francis up on Jefferson, which was too close to the truth for comfort.

Mary did not want to talk about her love affair and she did not want to hear any more about it. People had been gossiping about Mary Todd and Abraham Lincoln ever since the cotillion party at the American House on December 16, 1839, in honor of the opening of the first legislature. The American House was an enormous new hotel on the southeast corner of

Sixth and Adams whose interiors, carpets, and furniture evoked "a Turkish splendor." There, in the great columned ballroom, all of Springfield society had gathered to dance that evening from seven until four the following morning—the polka, the schottische, and country rounds. Mary knew all the dances and would not go wanting for partners.

Abraham Lincoln, serving his fourth term in the state House of Representatives, was one of sixteen "managers" of the cotillion. His name appeared on the printed invitation, under the spreading wings of an eagle holding a banner in its beak with the motto *E Pluribus Unum*. Lincoln's was the last name on a distinguished list that included Mary's brother-in-law Ninian; James Shields, the state auditor—who would challenge Lincoln to a duel; Dr. Elias H. Merryman, who took Lincoln's side in that affair of honor; and Lincoln's friend Joshua Speed, the shopkeeper. Opposite Lincoln's name was that of Stephen A. Douglas, secretary of the state of Illinois, soon to be a judge of the state supreme court, a man marked for greatness and a suitor for the hand of Mary Todd.

The girl from Lexington had many suitors here, but she preferred the tall, amusing legislator with the thick, unruly black hair, "a rising man" who was her cousin John Todd Stuart's law partner. After the cotillion, during the winter of 1839–40, Mr. Lincoln began calling upon "Molly" in the forty-foot parlor of the Edwards house, with its marble fireplace, astral lamps, and columns of dark polished walnut.

He came on Sundays. There was a fine piano, and Lincoln liked to hear the sisters play it. He and Molly loved poetry and could recite it by the canto.

> *Prometheus-like, from heaven she stole*
> *The fire, that through those silken lashes*
> *In darkest glances seems to roll,*
> *From eyes that cannot hide their flashes:*
> *And as along her bosom steal*
> *In lengthened flow her raven tresses,*
> *You'd swear each clustering lock could feel,*
> *And curl'd to give her neck caresses.*
> —BYRON, "THE GIRL OF CADIZ"

Each was adept at mimicry, of voices, gestures, and facial expressions. Molly could render her sister Elizabeth perfectly, the drooping eyes, the tight, wide mouth, the Southern accent striving to lose itself in an upper-class, British inflection. Mr. Lincoln could capture the haughty scowls of Ninian, the tone of condescension in his voice as he grudgingly welcomed Mary's suitor.

Molly had studied French at Madame Mentelle's school, so she was adept at playing the Parisian courtier or dressmaker; she could assume the Irish brogue and "take off" the swaggering James Shields, who came courting her and her friend Julia Jayne at once, shamelessly—Shields with all his blarney. Then there was the slave's dialect, which they both had mastered, and the Scots brogue with which Lincoln recited his Burns:

> *O Lord!—yestreen,—thou kens—wi'Meg—*
> *Thy pardon I sincerely beg;*
> *O! may't ne'er be a livin' plague,*
> *To my dishonor!*
> *An' I'll ne'er lift a lawless leg*
> *Again upon her.*

Elizabeth would enter the room and find them seated together on the horsehair couch talking quietly: "Mary led the conversation—Lincoln would listen and gaze on her as if drawn by some Superior power . . ." That is how Elizabeth viewed them. They kept their irreverent humor to themselves.

Each had the power to hold up the mirror to the other, these two oddly matched lovers, the one tall and rawboned, the other small and plump. He was usually delighted to be in her company. But he had a melancholy streak that he could not conceal in that first year they were courting. During the late 1830s, during an economic depression, Lincoln, as Whig "floor leader," had led his party and the legislature deeply into debt, and now his leadership was under fire.

He was absorbed in politics, struggling to keep his place. In 1840, he traveled all over Illinois making speeches in favor of General William Henry Harrison for president and against the Democrats. This took him away from Mary Todd and his law practice, so that he could not pay off the mountain of debt that made him feel unworthy of such a potential bride. Perhaps this mattered less to her than to him. But he would come through the door of the Edwards house on a Sunday afternoon steeped in melancholy, and she would mimic his sighs and frowns and downcast glances until he would grin and laugh in spite of himself. Then they could speak of the canvass, the raucous debates in villages where farmers cheered and hooted and dogs howled. They talked of the Whig newspaper Lincoln had started with his friend Dr. Anson Henry; they could discuss their possible future together.

No one then, in the summer and fall of 1840, objected to the match, at least not openly, despite the disparity in the couple's breeding—not even Ninian Edwards or Mary's father, Robert Todd. As far as Mary was concerned, it had all been decided. But her lover was a man of temperament, of moods and curious scruples and deep meditations. She did not know quite what to think. She might as well have gone and plucked petals from a daisy—*he loves me, he loves me not*—as to fathom the man's emotions, now full of high ambition and confidence, then plunged into self-doubt, despair, and the fear that he was unworthy of her.

In the autumn of that year, Mary shared her room with Ninian's niece from Alton, a blond, willowy girl of seventeen. "A lovelier girl I never saw," Mary told her friend Mercy Levering, after hearing Mr. Lincoln himself confess that he would not alter a feature of Matilda Edwards's perfect face if it were in his power. Like other society girls, Matilda was looking for a husband in this town that was teeming with promising politicians, lawyers, and other enterprising men, while noticeably short of marriageable women. Matilda quickly found herself very popular, surrounded by suitors like handsome Joshua Speed, who fell in love with her, and admirers like Lincoln, who said that he thought he had.

His talk of Matilda seemed to Mary a small detail in the larger picture of his ambivalence that year, no matter how much he made of it. Lincoln also was known to admire Sarah Rickard, the younger sister of Mrs. William Butler, with whom he had boarded for several years. There would be rumors about Sarah and Mr. Lincoln, too, but there was nothing to it: The girl had been like a sister to him, no more. As for Matilda, she and Mary shared a bed and many confidences; she knew Matilda better than Mr. Lincoln ever would, and was sure there could be no romance between them.

Far more damaging to their hopes was Mr. Lincoln's sense, real or imagined, that his family, his character, or his income made him unworthy of her love, unworthy therefore to love her. He was a romantic then and an idealist, afraid that he did not love her as he ought. No sooner were they engaged, late in 1840, than he broke off the engagement—it had all happened so quickly that few but the lovers knew of it. Now her knowledge of Lincoln's former doubts and ambivalence accompanied the young woman like the profile of her figure that the sun cast beside her as she walked downtown.

MUD OR NO mud, Mary would avoid the corner of Fourth and Adams, where Ninian's brother Benjamin's house stood across the street from the Second Presbyterian Church. She did not wish to be seen by Benjamin Edwards or his wife, Helen, who might be suspicious.

The church spire called to mind a curious memory. Nearly two years earlier, on December 5, 1840, Mr. Lincoln and several other Whigs had leaped from the second-story window of this very church, where the legislature was temporarily meeting. True, the Democrats had barred the door. But the escape was an ill-conceived maneuver to disrupt a quorum that would allow the session to adjourn. Adjournment would ruin the Whiggish bank in Springfield that had been allowed dispensations that would expire with the session. This was frontier politics at its most colorful. Folks went to watch the legislature in session as they went to wrestling matches and horseraces, expecting action—outrageous vituperation, fistfights, furious exits. The "jumping scrape" got Lincoln bad publicity, furthering his reputation in the widely Democratic state as a Whig extremist beholden to the bank, an ill-bred rustic, and a clown.

Two weeks later Ninian Edwards, Jr., dressed in fine black broadcloth and sporting a gold-headed cane, took a seat in the freshly painted hall of the new statehouse. Swelled with his own dignity, scowling, he was on a mission from the governor. His words were meant for Lincoln, the Whig leader, who sat just to the right of center in the semicircle of the great hall. Edwards held in his hand a bill to repeal every law that had authorized the building of railroads, canals, and roads in Illinois. He stood before the assembly.

"Without censuring the patriotism of the legislature that created it," Edwards declared, with a nod to his future brother-in-law, "I disapprove of the whole system as too vast in its extent for the means of the state. In view of the present financial condition of the state, an immediate suspension of all work and expenses of every description is recommended, and the sale of all the timber, and the railroad iron, if it should bring 70 per cent on its cost."

This was a terrible blow to Lincoln and his party. The bank so important to Lincoln and other Whigs, the bank that was to make possible the railroads and canals they had bartered away in return for the Springfield statehouse where they now assembled—that could go to the devil, for all Ninian Edwards cared. At that time the Democratic party was the party of fiscal conservatism, while the Whigs believed in liberal government investment in internal improvements, paper currency, and the efficacy of central banks. The party was not destined for a long life: Founded in 1832, it would not survive the slavery controversies of the 1850s. Ninian was an ambivalent Whig who would eventually become a Democrat.

Mary Todd's guardian may have tolerated Lincoln as a suitor for a while, but by Christmas of 1840 Ninian Edwards and Abraham Lincoln were at loggerheads—at least over the future of Illinois—and Lincoln's career was in trouble. Nearing the winter solstice, as the days grew shorter, his courage and his spirits faded with the sunlight; he questioned everything, including his commitment to Mary Todd.

At last, at the year's end, Mr. Lincoln came to Molly, during Yuletide, when the nights were long and the parlor was fragrant with Christmas greens and bayberry candles. He was gloomy, distraught, disheveled; his long coat, silk vest, and satin stock looked as if he had slept in them. She invited him to come and sit and tell her his trouble. That is when he told her things that she could not ever believe.

He said that he did not love her. Did he mean he did not love her at all, or that he did not love her in the way an idealist imagined a man was supposed to love the woman he proposed to marry?

She rose from his side, turning away. Regretting all past coquetry, with him and Douglas and her other suitors, she said:

"The deceiver shall be deceived. Woe is me."

It was then he began to speak like a man not right in his mind, telling her that he loved Matilda Edwards, and so he could not love her. Meanwhile his actions contradicted his speech, for he drew her down on his knee and kissed her in a way that definitely did not mean good-bye. Matilda had no interest in him; if he wished to think the girl was the reason for his change of mind, then so be it. Molly would release him, heart and hand, from the bond of their engagement, until such time as he might come to his senses.

They kissed and parted, and it would be a year and a half until they would reconcile and embrace again, a long time before they would be ready for each other. Meanwhile those words she had spoken to him in anguish, in tears that brought tears to his own eyes, would resonate, take on a spectrum of meanings. This man—already so widely known for his honesty—how could he have deceived her, and why?

Nearing the Capitol square in the changeable light of November 1842, she would avoid the sunshine, hoping to arrive at the Francises' as invisibly as a shadow among shadows.

REMEDIES

THE RECIPE WAS so simple that any druggist or doctor with a mortar and pestle could roll the pills: licorice root, rose water, honey, sugar, a confection of rose petals—and mercury, also known as quicksilver.

The doctor's pestle ground and compounded the mixture in the stone mortar until it was the consistency of thin dough. He would lay narrow strips of the compound on a ruled ceramic pill tile, six centimeters each, then roll the dark mass into a ball the size of a peppercorn. In an hour this would harden. Each of the "blue mass" pills contained about sixty-five milligrams of elemental mercury.

Lincoln took one of the pills three times a day. No one, with the possible exception of Dr. Anson Henry, Lincoln's "indispensable" friend, and William H. Herndon, who roomed with Speed and Lincoln above the general store, knew exactly when Lincoln began taking the mercury pills. The antibacterial effect of mercury had made it the foremost treatment for syphilis since the sixteenth century. Lincoln confided to Herndon that about the year 1836 he "went to Beardstown and during a devilish passion had connection with a girl and caught the disease." Either Lincoln caught it, or he feared he had. In those days diagnosing syphilis, in its early stages, was difficult.

Despite warnings about the dangers of mercury poison exceeding its curative powers, milder mercury compounds became an occasional treatment for the mental distress syndrome known as hypochondriasis, and a less common treatment for constipation (for that complaint the harmless rhubarb would do, or chittam bark). The popular textbook of the day, William Buchan's *Domestic Medicine,* which was on every doctor's shelf and available to Lincoln if he wished to study it, described hypochondriasis as "a disease attacking men of melancholy temperament and brought

on by long and serious attention to abstruse subjects, grief, the suppression of customary evacuations, excess of venery. . . ."

If Lincoln had not been a man "of melancholy temperament" before
his trouble with his fiancée Mary, he certainly had become one thereafter.
Friends said he was suicidal. And in every other particular, he served
as Buchan's exemplary hypochondriac—grief-stricken, self-obsessed,
bound up.

Shortly after breaking his engagement he sought medical advice, but
not from any local doctor at first. Thinking his case was beyond the scope
of the local medical faculty—or fearful that diagnosis and treatment might
shame him if it were known—he wrote to Dr. Daniel Drake of Cincinnati.
Lincoln wanted the most expert medical advice, and Drake, raised in a log
cabin in Kentucky and largely self-educated, was at fifty-five years of age
one of the most famous physicians in America. They called him "the Benjamin Franklin of the West." He had been on the first medical faculty of
Transylvania University in Lexington, Kentucky; he later founded the
medical department of Cincinnati College.

Before posting the letter to Dr. Drake, Lincoln showed it to Joshua
Speed. The letter was a long one. Speed, who also suffered periodically
from "hypo," as folks called it, read all but two of the pages, which Lincoln declined to share with his best friend, without explaining why. Speed
wondered if the passages and Lincoln's crazy spell might have something
to do with Ann Rutledge, a girl he had loved who had died in 1835, but
this does not seem like the sort of story he would conceal from Speed, to
whom he confided intimate matters. The suppressed pages "had reference to his disease and not his crazy spell, as Speed supposes," Herndon
insisted, that is, the venereal disease that Lincoln would confess to Herndon only after Lincoln was convinced that the affliction was a thing of
the past.

Dr. Drake replied by letter "that he would not undertake to prescribe
for him [Lincoln] without a personal interview." But there would never be
a personal interview with the distant Dr. Drake. Lincoln had to put his
trust in the local medical community, to diagnose, and to prescribe treatment, and to be discreet about it.

There was no physician, and perhaps no one in all of Springfield in
1840, that Lincoln trusted more than his fellow Whig, Dr. Anson Henry.
Only five years older than Lincoln, Henry had streaks of gray in his thick

hair and the fringe of Scots whiskers that framed his square jaw. His deep-set eyes twinkled merrily, and his wide mouth smiled easily at his friend's jokes. He was not tall, but broad-shouldered, with large, strong hands. Born in New York, the thirty-six-year-old doctor had already lived in eight states pursuing half a dozen professions. He had completed his medical training in Cincinnati in 1826 (where he would have encountered "the Benjamin Franklin of the West" himself), and then practiced in Indiana, Kentucky, and Tennessee until 1828, when he decided to make his fortune mining in the Michigan Territory. When luck failed him, he went back to practicing medicine in Louisville, Kentucky.

He married Eliza D. Bradstreet in 1830, and the first of their children, Margaret, was born later that year. The doctor planned to augment his income by becoming a druggist, so he set up a storefront with scales in the window, and colored jars, and laid in a supply of mercury, iodine, camphor, and paregoric. No sooner was the store open for business than a flood swept it away. So Dr. Henry moved to Springfield in 1831. He had visited once before, and he must have admired the village of seven hundred in the Sangamon Valley. There the soil was so rich it was "scarcely necessary to do more than hoe the ground," according to a newsman. The population soon doubled, and there was plenty of work for a new physician.

In the spring of 1832, while Dr. Henry was setting up his practice in Springfield, Lincoln was serving in the Black Hawk War against the Sauk and Fox Indians. Far away in Lexington, Kentucky, Elizabeth Todd married Ninian Edwards, Jr., and Mary Todd, fourteen years old, finished the preparatory course at Doctor Ward's Academy. She proved herself "far in advance over girls of her age in education," according to her cousin Elizabeth Humphreys. Mary entered Madame Mentelle's finishing school. Being driven to school in a carriage, living in a brick mansion with slave servants, Mary moved in a world of privilege unknown to the soldier and the doctor. The force that would unite them in spirit was Whig politics: The spiritual father of the Whigs, Henry Clay, was the Todds' neighbor. Little Mary thought he was handsome. She used to sit upon Clay's knee, and offered to marry him if he became president.

Abraham Lincoln, mustered out of the army in July, returned to the failing grocery he owned in New Salem; when the business "winked out," he worked as a surveyor in order to dig himself out of debt. He ran for a seat in the legislature and lost. But he gave an impressive speech in Springfield on August 4, 1832, advocating the national bank, a high tariff, and internal improvements—the main planks of the Whig platform. Anson Henry shared Lincoln's anti-Jackson politics.

For most of Dr. Henry's life he was torn between the demands of his family and medical career, and his passion for politics. The executive tyranny of "King Andrew" Jackson and the Democratic party gave rise to fierce opposition, and the formation of the Whigs in the early 1830s, under the leadership of Kentucky senator Henry Clay. Like Abraham Lincoln and Mary Todd, Anson Henry idolized Clay, the Great Compromiser, who had fought for the National Bank and a reasonable tariff law in 1833.

Lincoln won his seat in the Illinois General Assembly in 1834, about the time that Anson Henry started to campaign for General Thomas M. Neal, an anti-Jacksonian candidate for the legislature. When Neal won, he made Henry the inspector of the Illinois militia in Sangamon and Tazewell counties, with a payment of $90 per year for five years. The family needed every penny of it. Eliza gave birth to their first son, Gordon, in 1835, and several more children would soon follow.

In June of 1835, Anson Henry and Lincoln both supported Whig Hugh L. White in his bid for the Whig nomination for president. Sangamon County had become a cradle of Whiggery, and Lincoln, twenty-seven, was the youngest of the nine Whig legislators from the county. Under his leadership they fought for railroads and canals, and the relocation of the capital from the disease-ridden backwater of Vandalia to Springfield. Meanwhile Dr. Henry was lobbying for the bank, writing editorials to support Lincoln's agenda. Democrat Stephen Douglas masterminded the $10 million in bonds to finance the railroads and canals that Lincoln, as Whig floor leader, used as bait to buy votes to make Springfield the capital. After the logrolling and scheming won the prize for Springfield on February 28, 1837, there was a drunken celebration in the square. Five days later, Henry was named one of the commissioners entrusted to engage contractors for the new capitol building. This was a lucrative appointment, promising to keep Henry in Springfield for a while.

In mid-April of 1837, Abraham Lincoln, known and lauded for moving the capital to Springfield, moved there too. Nine months earlier he had passed the bar exam, and had come to join John Todd Stuart in his distinguished law practice. Stuart was a cousin of Mary Todd, who, in a few weeks, would be arriving to stay with her sister Elizabeth and Ninian Edwards in the house on the hill. Stuart had known and admired Lincoln since they had served together in the Black Hawk War—Stuart as a major, Lincoln as a captain. In 1834, when both men served in the legislature, the captain became Stuart's protégé. The senior member had encouraged Lincoln to study the law, giving him free access to his library, and three years later he invited him to join his firm.

In those days Lincoln shared a room with Joshua Speed above Speed's general store on the corner of Fifth and Washington streets, facing the vacant square where the new capitol would soon rise upon its columns. Speed, five years younger than Lincoln, was also from Kentucky. He had come to Springfield in 1835 to seek his fortune, and bought a partnership in the store.

Across the street, just to the north, stood Hoffman's Row, six adjoining brick buildings with storefronts below and offices above. Dr. William Wallace, who was courting Frances Todd, had an office and drugstore on the street level. Upstairs was Stuart and Lincoln's law office, suite number 4, with windows looking east. Dr. Henry's office was next door. It was here, at 109 North Fifth Street, that the thirty-three-year-old physician and statehouse commissioner came to know the whimsical, hypochondriacal poet/lawyer Abraham Lincoln.

They had been acquainted for some time; now they became friends. Like other friends of Lincoln, the doctor was charmed by the Southern lawyer's humility, his honesty and sense of humor. But Henry—more than others, perhaps—was troubled by the young man's Byronic moods of melancholy, the sense of doom that darkened his features when, in a world of his own, thinking himself unnoticed, one noticed him. Dr. Henry observed his friend with some concern, and with professional curiosity.

Henry, like most readers in Springfield, had read the remarkable poem "The Suicide's Soliloquy" in the *Sangamo Journal* the week of August 25, 1838. It was published with a note that the unsigned verses "had been found near the bones of a man supposed to have committed suicide, in a deep forest, on the Flat Branch of the Sangamon* sometime ago." The poem begins with the hooting of owls in a desolate setting where the suicide is sure "No fellow-man shall learn my fate," and then describes the state of mind that has led him to plunge a dagger into his heart, "Though I in hell should rue it!"

---

* the river that flows north of Springfield

Hell! What is hell to one like me
Who pleasures never knew;
By friends consigned to misery,
By hope deserted too?

To ease me of this power to think,
That through my bosom raves,
I'll headlong leap from hell's high brink,
And wallow in its waves.

Though devils' yells, and burning chains
May waken long regret;
Their frightful screams, and piercing pains,
Will help me to forget.

Yes! I'm prepared, through endless night,
To take that fiery berth!
Think not with tales of hell to fright
Me, who am damn'd on earth!

Sweet steel! Come forth from out your sheath,
And glist'ning, speak your powers;
Rip the organs of my breath,
And draw my blood in showers!

No such bones had been discovered. The anonymous stanzas remained unclaimed, but most people in the know suspected that Abraham Lincoln had written the poem. The town was too small to keep this sort of secret. Who else had the temperament and skill to write such a thing? And no one had more open access to Simeon Francis's newspaper than his good friend Lincoln.

"The Suicide's Soliloquy" lays bare the thoughts and agonies of a man tormented by an obsession or idée fixe so painful that he would prefer the hell of the next world with its "devils' yells and burning chains" to the torments of this one. What has caused a man in the prime of life to abandon hope?

Fifteen years of medical practice had taught Dr. Henry that such emotional crises are sometimes symptoms of underlying pathology.

• • •

WHATEVER HIS INFIRMITIES by 1840, Lincoln was fit to woo—and win—the hand of Mary Todd. But no sooner had Joshua Speed, Dr. Henry, and the Edwards clan gotten used to the idea of the marriage than the wooer came down with a severe case of the "hypo."

Later Lincoln looked back on these events with wonder, embarrassment, and shame. After informing his Molly that he did not love her, he staggered down Fifth Street in the cold and groped his way upstairs to his room above the general store. He threw himself on the bed and sank down in the mattress, staring at a candle flame, or up at the eaves. He may not have had the pox, but he certainly had hypochondriasis, which doctors believed was one of its symptoms.

The first symptoms of syphilis, the venereal sores, are usually obvious—although the pox was not called "the great imitator" for nothing. The most experienced doctors occasionally failed in the diagnosis. But the lesions of primary syphilis eventually vanish, with or without treatment, and in the early nineteenth century a man might think he was cured until months, or a year, later he would notice a rash, lesions on his hands and feet, on his back. The doctor would have then shaken his head sadly and told him: *It is as I feared. You are not yet cured. The disease lingers. And if it is not vanquished by mercury or a miracle, you may look forward to persistent headaches and fever; degeneration of the heart and digestive system; crumbling bones; deafness; blindness;* and by an inexorable calculus the "devil in the neck"—tabes dorsalis, paroxysmal pain in the spine, madness, and merciful death.

One might have any or all of the symptoms, in no predictable order, or none of them for many years. As a result, syphilis was a nightmare for hypochondriacs—even those who did not have the disease. There was even a medical term for the obsession: syphilophobia.

In early January 1841, Lincoln suffered the torments vividly described in the verses of "The Suicide's Soliloquy." The moon waxed full on January 7, an ominous sign for a superstitious man. As the moonlight shone upon the town, Joshua Speed found Lincoln thrashing and raving in their room upstairs. "Lincoln went crazy," Speed told Herndon, "I had to remove razors from his room—take away all Knives and other such dangerous things—it was terrible." Lincoln told Speed he might put an end to his life but for the fact that "he had done nothing to make any human being remember that he had lived." In the depths of his despair, he clung to the dream of linking "his name with something that would redound to the interest of his fellow man."

Lincoln could not eat or sleep. He appeared at the statehouse irregularly, hollow-eyed, unshaven, emaciated—an object of pity to his friends and of derision to others. After a week of this he took to his bed and failed to appear for roll calls from January 13 until the nineteenth. Mary Todd's cousin Martinette wrote to her brother John Hardin, Lincoln's colleague in the House, "We have been very much distressed, on Mr. Lincoln's account; hearing he had two Cat fits, and [a] Duck fit since we left [for Jacksonville]. Is it true?"

It was true, and Lincoln readily confessed it. On January 20, he wrote to his law partner John T. Stuart, who had gone to Washington to serve in the U.S. Congress: "I have, within the past few days, been making a most discreditable exhibition of myself in the way of hypochondriasism and thereby got an impression that Dr. Henry is necessary to my existence." Indeed, Lincoln had written the letter to persuade Stuart to give Henry the postmastership—fearing that if the doctor did not get it he would leave Springfield. Henry needed Lincoln as much as Lincoln needed Henry, for the doctor's patronage had dried up: His term as inspector of the militia was done, and his lucrative job as building commissioner was soon to be turned over to the secretary of state and the treasurer. He now had three children, and Eliza was pregnant again. "Unless he gets that place he leaves Springfield," Lincoln wrote.

Why was Lincoln so desperate to keep Dr. Henry with him? One reason could be that Lincoln was about to lose Joshua Speed, his former roommate and the closest friend he ever had. Just a few months after taking Lincoln's razors and knives away, Speed, bored with his career as a merchant and perhaps frustrated by his rumored attempts at courting Matilda Edwards, packed up his belongings and returned to his family's plantation in Kentucky. Lincoln would sorely miss him.

Speed's departure alone could not explain Lincoln's insistence upon keeping Dr. Henry in town. After all, Lincoln had many friends left to keep him company when Speed was gone. There was James Matheny, the legislator with whom he played handball behind the court clerk's office and who shared Lincoln's reverence for Henry Clay. "Jim" had known Lincoln for six years and had become a close observer of his friend's changing personality. There was also the sympathetic James Conkling, a lawyer slightly older than Lincoln, who was engaged to Mary Todd's best friend, Mercy Levering. "Poor L.[incoln]!" he wrote to Mercy on January 24.

> How are the mighty fallen! He was confined about a week, but though he now appears again he is reduced and emaciated in appearance and seems scarcely to possess strength enough to speak above a whisper. His case at present is truly deplorable but what prospect there may be for ultimate relief I cannot pretend to say. I doubt not but he can declare "That loving is a painful thrill, And not to love more painful still" but would not like to intimate that he has experienced "That surely 'tis the worst of pain To love and not be loved again."

Conkling knew this detailed summary of Lincoln's plight would reach Mary Todd via Mercy Levering, perhaps providing his friend some prospect of "ultimate relief."

Then there was Orville Browning, who also roomed at William Butler's house, where the abstemious Lincoln boarded. The Butlers did not charge Lincoln for his meals—he ate little. According to Browning, Lincoln was so disturbed "as to talk incoherently and to be delirious to the extent of not knowing what he was doing." Finally there was Butler, clerk of the Sangamon Circuit Court, forty-three years old, and his wife, Elizabeth, who did Lincoln's laundry and took him into their spacious home after Speed departed for Kentucky. They had treated Lincoln like a son since the winter of 1836–37 when they all lived in Vandalia. Without Lincoln's knowledge, Butler had even paid off some of his friend's bank debts from New Salem so that he might start anew in Springfield.

SNOW FELL. FREEZING rain beat against the windows. Lincoln never had to be alone, but no one seemed to him so vital to his survival as Dr. Henry, who lived around the corner on Jefferson Street (between Fifth and Sixth) with his wife and children. During the time Lincoln was too sick to attend the legislature, he spent hours of every day at home with Anson Henry.

As his letter to Dr. Daniel Drake had indicated, Lincoln wanted a physician to diagnose and dose him, not for constipation or "the blues" but for something far more serious, something that he thought was already laying waste to his mind and body. He wrote to Stuart on January 23: "I am now the most miserable man living. If what I feel were equally distributed to the whole human family, there would not be one cheerful face on the earth. Whether I shall ever be better I can not tell; I awfully forbode that I shall not. To remain as I am is impossible; I must die or be better, it appears to me." If Herndon is correct, it had been several years since the lesions first appeared; sometime during 1840, while Lincoln was on the path to the altar, worrisome symptoms recurred. Now marriage to Molly, or anybody, was out of the question until such a time as he might be reasonably certain the mercury had cured him. In the meantime, any excuse would serve him better than the truth.

Dr. Henry was a trusted friend and a man of the world. A veteran physician, he had seen and treated every sort of illness from cholera-ridden hospitals in Cincinnati and Louisville to mining towns like Dodgeville, where the pox was as common as baldness. He was an experienced druggist who could provide his friend with blue mass pills. In a year or two, with luck and sobriety and a spartan diet, Lincoln might be cured.

A YEAR OF WAITING

D URING THAT WINTER of 1840–41, when Lincoln was so unbalanced, Mary Todd bided her time, in no apparent distress over her broken engagement. She and Matilda Edwards dominated the coterie of politicians and socialites who gathered in the house on the hill. James Conkling reported to Mercy Levering, "Swarms of strangers who had little else to engage their attention hovered around them, to catch a *passing smile*. By the way, I do not think they were received, with even ordinary attention, if they did not obtain a *broad grin* or an *obstreperous laugh*."

A broad grin and obstreperous laugh were about the most that Mary Todd was willing to offer her suitors that year. She was quick and graceful in her movements, gliding and turning on ballroom slippers that flashed beneath the fluffed overskirt. Her chestnut-colored hair shone with bronze highlights. She was brilliant, but she was unattainable as the moon.

"And L.[incoln] poor hapless simple swain," James Conkling continued, in his familiar doggerel rhyme, "who loved most true but was not loved again—I suppose he will now endeavor to drown his cares among the intricacies and perplexities of the law."

Conkling did not have it quite right. Mary Todd was still in love with Lincoln; and Dr. Anson Henry, acting as a go-between, had conveyed assurances to the invalid that Mary's heart was still open to him. She loved him, said Dr. Henry, "as women of her nervous, sanguine temperament only can love." Orville Browning, who spent a great deal of time at the Edwards mansion while the legislature was in session, would linger after others had gone, and sit with Mary, "sometimes till midnight," and talk "about this affair of hers with Mr. Lincoln." Browning knew, as did Henry, that she still longed to be Lincoln's wife.

While she put on a show of gaiety to encourage suitors, she was secretly melancholy. The giddiness of her joyful hours gave way to periods of terrible gloom. She wrote to her friend Mercy Levering in June that she wished Mercy were not so far away, in Baltimore. "Were you aware of the delight given by hearing from you, dearest Merce, surely you would more frequently cheer my sad spirit—the last two or three months have been of *interminable* length, after my gay companions of last winter departed, I was left much to the solitude of my own thoughts, and some *lingering regrets* over the past, which time can alone overshadow with its healing balm."

There had been gossip of her flirtation with "Mr. [Edwin] Webb, a widower of modest merit," who "last winter is our principal lion," and "dances attendance very frequently," Mary admitted to Mercy. Webb was twenty years older, a widower with two children whom Mary called "his two *sweet little objections*," by way of conveying to Merce that the flirtation would come to nothing more than that, despite Webb's fortune.

She missed James Conkling, who was too busy to visit, "e'en for your loved sake." She missed Joshua Speed, "our former most constant guest," although Speed still wrote to her, but most of all she missed "His worthy friend [Lincoln who] deems me unworthy of notice, as I have not met *him* in the gay world for months." Misery loves company; and so "with the usual comfort of misery" she imagined "that others were as seldom gladdened by his presence as my humble self," that is, that her former lover had become a recluse. "Yet I would that the case were different, that he would once more resume his Station in Society, that 'Richard should be himself again' [alluding to the Shakespeare play—*Richard II*—that they both loved], much, much happiness would it afford me—."

Lincoln would "be himself again" when she next saw him, yet it would not be quite the same self. His personality changed significantly during the ensuing two years. With strained humor he had written to John Stuart in February 1841: "You see by this I am neither dead nor quite crazy yet." In March, Congressman Stuart wrote to Daniel Webster, then secretary of state, recommending Lincoln as chargé d'affaires at Bogotá, Colombia, thinking a change of scene might lift his partner's spirits. The position did not materialize, but the recommendation suggests that Stuart might have grown impatient with his partner's troubles and erratic behavior. When he returned to Springfield in April 1841, the men dissolved the partnership, and Lincoln joined the wild-haired, brilliant Stephen Trigg Logan in his law practice across the street. Logan, forty-two, was a better match for Abraham Lincoln, as a friend and business partner. Lincoln would learn a great deal from this methodical, hardworking lawyer, whose command of the law, in both theory and precedents, was unsurpassed in that time and place.

As Conkling had predicted, the lovelorn attorney would seek to "drown his cares among the intricacies . . . of the law." Work was therapeutic, and so were the blue mass pills. Lincoln was almost constantly on the circuit, trying cases: Tremont, Bloomington, Springfield, Clinton, Urbana, Danville, Petersburg. In a buggy with Stephen Logan, or alone, Lincoln followed a horse over thousands of miles of bumpy roads through the rolling prairie, attending the various county sessions. Sometimes the lawyers had made arrangements with clients; sometimes claimants or defendants hired them on the spot. In country inns and courtrooms where he was welcomed and cheered for his jokes and stories, he ran a step ahead of his heartache.

Perhaps nothing was more helpful in lifting Lincoln's spirits than his visit with his old friend Joshua Speed. In early August 1841, Lincoln took a vacation with Speed and his family on their plantation, Farmington, in Jefferson County, Kentucky. Speed's mother gave Lincoln a Bible, saying it was the best cure for the blues. Together the men read books and took long walks in the woods and meadows, and talked by the hour. They were so similar in temperament that Lincoln felt he was addressing a second self. And what was the topic that most consumed them during their walks in the field before breakfast, or rocking on the porch after supper in the twilight? Love. A vast and probing dialogue on love occupied them that summer, during the six weeks Lincoln stayed at Farmington; and they carried the conversation with them in mid-September when Speed returned with Lincoln to Springfield to stay until Christmas with the Butlers.

"I now have no doubt that it is the peculiar misfortune of both you and me, to dream dreams of Elysium far exceeding all that anything earthly can realize," Lincoln wrote to Speed in February 1842. This was the crux of the matter. They were full-blown romantics besotted with Byron; their notions of love owed more to "The Bride of Abydos" and the "dark-eyed girl of Cadiz" than to the vows in the *Book of Common Prayer*. True love was rare, divine, doom-driven. Marriage was forever, and children to be expected. In that day, if half of one's offspring survived adolescence, the couple was blessed. Grown children were hostages to fortune. If one's wife survived her seventh labor, her seventh child was hailed as a prodigy with supernatural powers. The churchyards were crowded with head-stones of women who perished in childbirth. It was terrifying to think that marital sex was often a death sentence for women; it must have given sensitive men pause.

Speed had fallen deeply in love with a frail, sloe-eyed beauty named Fanny Henning. Meeting her that summer, Lincoln found her "one of the sweetest girls in the world," with only a slight "tendency to melancholy ... a misfortune not a fault" familiar to both men. As Speed courted Fanny that fall and winter, 1841–42, Lincoln advised, consoled, and encouraged his hesitant friend. His letters often appear to be reflections of his own feelings for Mary Todd:

"I think it reasonable that you will feel verry badly some time between this and the final consummation of your purpose. . . . let me, who have some reason to speak with judgment on such a subject, beseech you. . . ." He cautions Speed to remember that they both suffer from a rare "nervous debility" that causes them to magnify petty doubts and fret over trifles.

> I know what the painful point with you is, at all times when you are un-happy. It is an apprehension that you do not love her as you should. What nonsense!—How came you to court her? Was it because you thought she desired it; and that you had given her reason to expect it?
>
> Did you court her for wealth? Why, you know she had none. But you say you *reasoned* yourself *into* it. What do you mean by that? Was it not, that you found yourself unable to *reason* yourself *out* of it?

He invokes the principle of love at first sight: "Whether she was moral, amiable, sensible, or even of good character, you did not, nor could not then know. . . . All you then did or could know of her, was her *personal ap-pearance and deportment;* and these, if they impress at all, impress the heart and not the head."

Lincoln counseled his friend to conquer his doubts and get on with loving and marrying Fanny Henning, but Speed panicked over some minor weakness in his fiancée's constitution. He wrote that he could not bear it if his wife were to fall ill and die. Lincoln patiently reassured him that this "intense anxiety about her health, if there were nothing else, would place this [your complete devotion] beyond all dispute in my mind. I incline to think it probable, that your nerves will fail you occasionally for a while; but once you get them fairly graded now, that trouble is over forever."

The letter announcing Speed's betrothal came too late for Lincoln to attend the wedding. The day after Valentine's Day 1842, Joshua married Fanny. The groom arose from the marriage bed the next morning, ecstatic, to write to his friend that Fanny and he "are no more twain, but one flesh." Lincoln replied, "I feel somewhat jealous of both of you now."

On Easter Sunday, Lincoln, at full leisure (the time others took for prayer he would spend on reading and writing), penned a long letter to Speed. He had received one from the newlyweds three days before. A violet that Fanny had pressed in the letter had crumbled to dust, leaving a purple stain that Lincoln would "preserve and cherish." He was thrilled with joy "to hear you say you are *far happier than you ever expected to be.* That much I know is enough. I know you too well to suppose your expectations were not, at least sometimes, extravagant; and if the reality exceeds them all, I say, enough, dear Lord."

In fact the news from Speed had given him "more pleasure than the total sum of all I have enjoyed since that fatal first of Jany. '41 [a day that found the friends consoling each other for loves lost—Lincoln's Molly, Speed's Matilda Edwards, or Sarah Rickard, so some said]. "Since then, it seems to me, I should have been entirely happy, but for the never-absent idea, that there is one still unhappy whom I have contributed to make so. That still kills my soul. I can not but reproach myself, for even wishing to be happy while she is otherwise."

"She," of course, was Mary Todd.

That summer, Speed, who knew Lincoln's heart, advised him to resume his courtship of Mary Todd or banish her from his thoughts, and he accepted this as good advice. Yet on July 4 he replied that "before I resolve to do the one thing or the other, I must regain my confidence in my own ability to keep my resolves . . . in that ability, you, know, I once prided myself as the only, or at least the chief, gem of my character; that gem I lost—how, and when, you too well know. I have not yet regained it; and until I do, I can not trust myself in any matter of much importance."

That gem of his character—how would he regain it? He had always been, and would remain, superstitious. "As part of my superstition, I believe God made me one of the instruments of bringing your Fanny and you together, which union, I have no doubt He had fore-ordained." A similar sense of fate now ruled this man who many constant churchgoers considered an infidel. "Whatever he designs he will do for me yet. 'Stand *still* and see the salvation of the Lord,' is my text just now."

MARY HAD WATCHED him from a distance for more than a year and a half. Although spring found Lincoln the lawyer on the circuit, away from Springfield, the tall politician was never long out of sight or out of mind. Her brother-in-law and guardian, Ninian Edwards, was frequently in contact with Lincoln in the conduct of Whig political party business. If she was not hearing Abraham Lincoln's name at the breakfast or dinner table from Ninian's lips, or from Orville Browning, James Conkling, Edward Dickinson Baker, or a dozen other Whigs who gathered at the Edwards mansion, then she was reading his name, or his eloquent speeches, in the newspapers.

With Logan and Baker, he defended William Trailor in a sensational murder trial, during the course of which the victim was discovered to be alive. At noon on Washington's birthday 1842, in the Second Presbyterian Church—the same building he had infamously escaped by leaping from the window—he gave a speech to the Washington Temperance Society. It was full of common sense about the drinker and the dram-seller, an eloquent address with touches of poetry. Simeon Francis had filled the pages of the *Sangamo Journal* with his friend's speech, so there Mary Todd could read her lover's thoughts. Success in saving drunkards, he said, came not from denouncing them but rather through "kind, unassuming persuasion." He quoted the maxim that a "drop of honey catches more flies than a gallon of gall":

> If you would win a man to your cause, *first* convince him that you are his sincere friend.... On the contrary, assume to dictate to his judgment, or to command his action, or mark him as one to be shunned and despised, and he will retreat within himself, close all avenues to his head and his heart; and tho' your cause be naked truth itself, transformed to the heaviest lance, harder than steel ... and tho' you throw it with more than Herculean force and precision, you shall no more be able to pierce him, than to penetrate the hard shell of a tortoise with a rye straw.

His name was being bandied about as a candidate for the governorship, and there was even talk among the Springfield Whigs about whether Edward Baker or Lincoln should go to the United States Congress from the district. A few cynics whispered that neither Lincoln nor his friend Baker would have spoken a word on the subject of whiskey had the temperance movement not been so popular. Perhaps this was true. Mr. Lincoln did not take a drop of spirits himself, but Mary had never known him to speak ill of those who did.

On March 21, she went with a party of friends, serenaded by a band, on the new railroad cars to Jacksonville. Fifteen miles west over the thawing prairie they traveled under the clear, wide sky. Her older cousin, the handsome John J. Hardin, thirty-one, and his wife, Sarah, liked to arrange these jaunts to Jacksonville, where both he and Stephen Douglas had started up their law practices. Only a year earlier, when Mary had made the same pleasure trip, Matilda Edwards and Abraham Lincoln had added to their merriment. Now Matilda had gone to Alton to marry Mr. Newton D. Strong, and Lincoln was keeping his distance for reasons only he seemed to understand.

John Hardin, who led the party to Jacksonville, had mustered in Lincoln's company in the Black Hawk War in 1832, and they had been friends ever since. Hardin and Edward D. Baker led the Whig party in Illinois. Conversation never strayed too far from politics in this coterie, and when Whig politics came up for discussion, on the rattling train or on the street corner, Mary heard Mr. Lincoln's name.

Among several friends, perhaps her favorite companion now was the clever Julia Jayne, daughter of Springfield's first physician, old Gershom Jayne. Julia, who had a dignified profile, with large noble features that belied her sense of humor and mischief, was six years younger than Mary. The younger girls looked up to Mary Todd, a twenty-three-year-old woman of rare refinement, education, and wit, although she wavered precariously on the verge of spinsterhood by the standards of the time. Why did she resist the overtures of Stephen A. Douglas and Edwin B. Webb, either of whom would have married her? Of course it was barely whispered that she was holding out for Lincoln. No one knew her heart, really, or her intentions, unless it was Dr. Henry, who served the couple as a go-between. Since she was a child, she had dreamed of marrying a man who would be president. In moments of excitement—half in jest—she had blurted this out, this vainglorious plan to marry a man who would occupy the White House. Her girlfriends, less experienced in courtship and the ways of the world, must have thought Mary Todd extremely romantic and grand. They looked up to her anyway, and it always pleased her to be looked up to.

Mr. Lincoln, despite his difficulties, was the man of her dreams; and he would never be—she would never allow him to be—long out of her thoughts. He knew this. "On her return [she] spoke, so that I heard of it, of having enjoyed the trip exceedingly," Lincoln wrote to Speed. Mary spoke, pointedly, so that he *would* hear of it, if not directly from her, then through one of the friends she might trust to remind Lincoln he was in her thoughts, that she was well, and that he might join her in thinking of their shared past even if they did not meet. Inevitably they would.

Mary Todd and Abraham Lincoln both had friends who would be happy to know they had renewed their courtship, and might wish them luck on this November afternoon in 1842. Mary passed by the clock in a store window that caught her reflection, showing her face, at once joyful and anxious. She might detour around Seventh Street and approach the house from the east, knock at the back door. They must be cautious. It would be bad luck to meet Mr. Lincoln on the street. Suppose Ninian's friend James Shields saw them together? He disliked her almost as much as he despised Mr. Lincoln.

Still single at thirty-six, the dashing Irishman with the Winchester mustache behaved among women as if he had no competition—and the competition for ladies here was fierce. Shields flirted with all the women; he danced attendance upon blond Matilda Edwards and dark-haired Anna Rodney; he made eyes at Mary Todd and Julia Jayne. For Miss Jayne, it seems, he had an ungovernable passion, which she did not welcome. Julia had set her cap for Lyman Trumbull, the lean, bespectacled Illinois secretary of state, and she was not a year away from marrying him.

Trumbull was courting Julia Jayne that summer, while another Illinois congressman, the handsome widower William Cushman, was soon to marry Anna Rodney; Mary Todd alone remained without a declared suitor. She and Julia had ridiculed the persistent James Shields, and Lincoln had joined in the fun. Then the short Irishman and the tall man from Kentucky had agreed to fight each other to the death with broadswords, and some folks whispered that Mary Todd had provoked the seriocomic duel.

That summer of 1842, Mary Todd was intrigued when Eliza Francis invited her, with mysterious urgency, to visit her home down on Jefferson Street, the house where she was now headed again in November, among fallen leaves.

She had entered the warm parlor then to find Lincoln there, pleased to see her as she swept into the room in her hoop skirt and crinolines. Her former lover was, if somewhat shy, hardier than she remembered him. Whatever malady had afflicted him a year and a half before, and made a hash of their marriage plans, had passed. Eliza told them to be friends. Taking seats in the parlor, they resumed their conversation about politics and society, who was courting whom and who was likely to be wed, who would win and lose at the next election. They read the verses of Burns and Shakespeare—but no more Byron. He had had enough of Byron and that poet's pact with darkness.

Yet Lincoln had not altogether shed the Byronic attitude and sentiment. There were codes of behavior by which gentlemen of John Stuart's and Ninian Edwards's class maintained their honor. If Abraham Lincoln were ever to find himself welcome as Edwards's brother-in-law (as certainly he was not now), the ex-plowman and rail-splitter would have to keep his linen and honor in better repair than he had during the eighteen months previous. As he had confessed to John Stuart, he had made "a most discreditable exhibition of myself in the way of hypochondriaism" and had so failed in his legislative duties that John Hardin had to cover for him. Lincoln was sensitive on this point, and no one could assure him of how to restore his honor.

The feisty Irishman would unwittingly provide him with an opportunity. James Shields was a short man with a square jaw, jutting chin, and deep-set eyes under a broad brow. Nevertheless, he got one's attention when he walked into a room, limping slightly, pressing on as if against a headwind on the deck of a ship. He had shipped out of Belfast as a boy, leaving his home in the mill town of Dungannon in the 1820s. Shields found plenty of adventures sailing the seas, until he fell from the topmast rigging to the deck of a merchant ship in New York Harbor at age twenty, breaking both of his legs.

He adopted the country in which he had "landed" so precipitously, and where he had slowly healed. The man of action temporarily became a man of reflection, studying law in Kaskaskia, Illinois. Shields took up the practice of law in 1832. Never a man to miss a war, when the Black Hawk

War broke out that year he went to it, and mustered out with the rank of colonel.

In those days it was natural that a man of such various talents would seek public office, and perhaps inevitable that an immigrant with martial instincts should become a Jacksonian Democrat. In 1836, he was elected to the Illinois legislature, where he served with Stephen Douglas across the aisle from Abraham Lincoln. By 1839, he was made state auditor of public accounts; he signed Lincoln's paychecks "for his services as a member of the General Assembly," $292.00 for sessions 1840 and 1841. The two men agreed upon almost nothing, and became bitter opponents over the question of the State Bank, which Shields hated with a Jacksonian vehemence.

IN THE HEAT of August, few flowers were left but the sky-blue asters and the foxgloves, which Molly picked to adorn her hair. She and Lincoln met in the heavily draped parlor of Simeon Francis's house, while Simeon and Eliza left them alone to find their way in love's labyrinth. What they must overcome in order to be married was substantial and unmistakable. There was the difference in their breeding that had caused sister Elizabeth to warn her "that they had better not Ever marry—that their natures, mind— Education—raising &c were So different they could not live happy as husband & wife—had better never think of the Subject again . . ."

Lincoln was still struggling under the burden of the Salem debt and wasn't making enough money to support Molly in the way he wanted. Then the tension between Ninian Edwards and himself had hardened into an unpleasant rivalry. Edwards was jealous of the upstart Lincoln's charm and power, and would never fully accept him; Lincoln feared that Elizabeth, and perhaps the whole Todd family, would dismiss him as Ninian had.

Curiously, it was because Lincoln ran afoul of the combustible James Shields that he managed—at least partly—to overcome Edwards's condescension. Sometimes the actions that lead to profound and far-reaching results begin with small, negligible acts. Looking back on the event, it seems inconceivable that Lincoln, knowing "Jimmie" Shields as he did— the little Irishman's pride and short fuse, his vanity, and his handiness with pistol and rapier—could have laughed at him and mocked him in print without knowing what would come of it. There was probably not a man in Springfield with honor worth defending who could be counted upon to defend it as readily as James Shields. But the whole affair began as a private joke.

To be fair to Shields, he had been through a trying several months before Lincoln got to him. The State Bank of Illinois had failed despite the efforts of Lincoln and others to bail it out, and now its promissory notes were nearly worthless. As state auditor, Shields had made an unpopular decision not to accept devalued banknotes from the State Bank in payment of taxes. The auditor could not accept this funny money in lieu of silver for the state's coffers. But the Whigs, including Lincoln, attacked him as a scourge of widows and orphans and the source of every failure of the government and economy of Illinois.

Months before this affront to his integrity, Shields had made a rabble-rousing speech in Springfield, declaiming, "Strike for social equality, for the Mechanic's Union. Raise the banner for labor," which Simeon Francis published in the *Sangamo Journal* on November 26. Then for weeks thereafter Francis published responses damning and ridiculing the speech, which was about a hundred years ahead of its time. A town that was raising itself brick by brick on the hard principles of capitalism, and where there was an insufficient labor supply, had little patience with this sort of rhetoric. For half a year Shields had found himself the butt of abuse.

And sometime that summer—after Lincoln and Mary had been reunited by Eliza Francis in her parlor—the couple happened to be seated opposite Julia Jayne and her unrelenting suitor James Shields at a dinner party. He importuned Julia and would not take no for an answer. Julia was out of patience with Shields's uninvited attention, his pressing next to her at dinner parties, his hand perhaps wandering under the table, seeking hers.

Mary Todd must have known what was coming, and tipped off Lincoln, or he would not have reacted the way he did. In those days when every girl spent hours at the sewing table, many as pretty as Julia and Mary kept a pin or two tucked at the waistband as a defense in case a gentleman might cross the line. The barbarous custom was known as "pinning," and evidently Julia had told Mary that if Colonel Shields squeezed her one more time, she meant to pin him.

Well, he did, and she did. If he did not cry out in pain, the auditor must have shown his amazement, injury, and embarrassment in a grimace anyone could read across the table. And Lincoln laughed. Surely he did not mean to laugh at this proud and bellicose Irishman who had more than one reason to hate him, but Lincoln's sense of humor, then and later, was not always under strict control.

Molly and Lincoln liked to talk about Shields, who made them laugh. Shields became the perfect focus and emotional escape, providing for them a political scapegoat and an ideal subject for ridicule. They were keen mimics, these two, and they began to lampoon James Shields in the voice of backwoods yeomen and farmers' wives, fed up with corrupt state government and officials.

Their merriment over the vain auditor seemed too rich to keep to themselves. When their host Simeon Francis overheard it, he knew immediately this was just the sort of satire that would regale the readers of his *Journal,* and sell newspapers. Spurred by Francis, Lincoln spent the weekend of August 27 and 28 completing a twenty-five-hundred-word "Letter from the Lost Townships," signed "Yours truly, Rebecca." Rebecca was not Lincoln's invention but Francis's, the character of a semiliterate farm woman the editor had used for years to criticize Shields and others. But now the device had been taken up by a master of vituperation. Lincoln, inspired by uncharacteristic animus against James Shields, love for Mary Todd, and a desire to impress and delight Molly and Julia, unleashed a ferocious and trenchant attack against the unsuspecting Democrat. It included a sidesplitting take on Shields based on the pinning incident that had occurred recently with Julia Jayne at the dinner party.

I seed him when I was down in Springfield. . . . They had a sort of gatherin there one night, among the grandees, they called a fair. All the galls about town was there, and all the handsome widows, and married women, finickin about, trying to look like galls, tied as tight in the middle, and puffed out at both ends like bundles of fodder that hadn't been stacked yet, but wanted stackin pretty bad. . . .

They wouldn't let no democrats in, for fear they'd disgust the ladies, or scare the little galls, or dirty the floor. I looked in at the window, and there was this same fellow Shields floatin about on the air, without heft or earthly substance, just like a lock of cat-fur where cats had been fightin.

He was paying his money to this one and that one . . . and sufferin great loss because it wasn't silver instead of State paper; and the sweet distress he seemed to be in,—his very features, in the exstatic agony of his soul, spoke audibly and distinctly—"Dear girls, *it is distressing,* but I cannot marry you all. Too well I know how much you suffer; but do, *do* remember, it is not my fault that I am *so* handsome and *so* interesting."

This letter that took up so many columns of the newspaper the first week of September included all of the dialogue quoted above, and a great deal more that Shields found offensive. "Rebecca" calls Shields a liar, citing his proclamation suspending the acceptance of bank paper for taxes:

"I say its a lie, and not a well told one at that. It grins out like a copper dollar. Shields is a fool as well as a liar. With him truth is out of the question, and as for getting a good bright passable lie out of him, you might as well try to strike fire from a cake of tallow."

Lincoln's reference to the pinning incident is so thinly disguised that it must have caused poor Shields to relive the moment all over again, feeling the pain and mortification in front of an audience of a thousand other readers.

Do remember, it is not my fault that I am so handsome—

"As this last was expressed by a most exquisite contortion of his face, he seized hold of one of their hands and squeezed, and held on to it about a quarter of an hour. O, my good fellow, says I to myself, if that was one of our democratic galls in the Lost Township, the way you'd get a brass pin let into you, would be about up to the head [of the pin]."

Mary Todd and Julia Jayne thought this was marvelous fun, and had a good laugh over it when the columns appeared that Friday, September 2, 1842. It was just too rich, and no more than the audacious Irishman deserved for his terrible monetary policies and his romantic pretensions. To their minds, it might not be quite enough, although they had heard that Shields was already so offended that he had sent his friend, General John D. Whiteside—a fellow Democrat and former senator—to editor Francis to demand the name of the author. Shields wanted a formal apology, or "satisfaction" from the perpetrator of this humiliation. Francis waited at least forty-eight hours before giving up Lincoln's name, wanting that much time to confer with his friend about the matter, knowing that bloodshed was not out of the question.

Serious damage had been done, and the young women knew it. Yet they audaciously added fuel to the fire, picking up where Lincoln had left off, writing their own "Rebecca" letter that very week. Mary Todd's Rebecca finds herself in receipt of a note from Shields "that had demanded the author of my letters, threatenin' to take personal satisfaction of the writer. . . .

"You say that Mr. S— is offended at being compared to cats' fur, and is as mad as a March hare (that ain't fur), because I told about the squeezin'. Now I want to tell Mr. S— that, rather than fight, I'll make any apology; and if he wants personal satisfaction, let him only come here, and he may squeeze my hand as hard as I squeezed the butter. . . ."

In short, Mary Todd's Aunt 'Becca offers her hand in marriage to the furious auditor: "Wouldn't he—may be sorter let the old grudge drap if I was to consent to be—be—h-i-s w-i-f-e? I know he's a fightin' man, and would rather fight than eat; but isn't marryin' better than fightin', though it does sometimes run in to it?"

Julia Jayne got credit for collaborating in this salty epistle, but at age sixteen, she could not have done much more than chuckle over Mary's shoulder as the older woman dipped her pen and scratched these lines of prophecy. Fighting does sometimes run into marriage, just as matrimony sometimes runs into fighting.

"But after all, maybe I'm countin' my chickens before they are hatched, and dreamin' of matrimonial bliss when the only alternative reserved for me may be a lickin'."

Clearly, this letter written the first week of September recognizes an impending duel, and taunts Shields at every turn of phrase. Only gentlemen fought proper duels; if nothing else could confirm her lover's standing as a gentleman among Stuarts and Todds and Edwardses, then a mock duel might do it. (Most duels were mere posturing—but accidents did happen.) Dueling was still most common as a means of settling political differences, although no one had been killed dueling in twenty years. As the challenged party, Rebecca would choose as weapons "broomsticks or hot water or a shovelful of coals," which she likens to a shillelagh, poking fun at Shields' Irishness. "I will give him a choice, however, in one thing, and that is, whether when we fight, I shall wear breeches or petticoats, for, I presume that change is sufficient to place us on an equality. Yours, etc., Rebecca—"

During the legislative session of 1840–41, animosity between Whigs and Democrats ran so high that senators and assemblymen were frequently moved to defend their honor after real or imagined offenses. In fact, so many "affairs of honor" hung over the capitol, darkening the lawmakers' vision, that at last "one honorable member, Mr. Hacker, solemnly moved" that the Illinois ban on dueling be suspended for two weeks, "to accommodate all the doughty and chivalrous gentlemen who desired to settle their personal differences on the field."

Anticipating a duel, Lincoln began preparing for it in late August. When he was not practicing law—filing affidavits and praecipes—or wooing Mary in the shuttered parlor, he was mastering the positions, cuts, and guards of the broadsword exercise. The former rail-splitter knew that rapiers were made for thrusting, broadswords for cutting. Who knew when a man might be called upon to defend his honor?

James Shields had sent General Whiteside to Simeon Francis to demand that the editor "give up" the author of the Rebecca letter. Shields let it be known that he would "have satisfaction" from the perpetrator of this slander. Whiteside, to his credit, wanted this affair peaceably settled, and the sooner the better. Lincoln told Francis to go ahead, the week of September 5, and tell Whiteside to inform Shields that he, Abraham Lincoln, was the sole author of the Rebecca letters.

When Shields's formal challenge arrived in September, Lincoln chose broadswords.

FAME

WHAT HAD STARTED as a giddy prank in the late summer had become a matter of life and death by early autumn. It had also become a public event. As dueling was illegal in Illinois, to even pretend to settle their affair of honor on the field, Lincoln and Shields would have to travel eighty miles south of Springfield, to Missouri. There, near the town of Alton on a sandbar called "Bloody Island" after the countless duels that had been staged there, the dueling party convened, on September 22, 1842, to the delight of a crowd that came from many miles around. Hardin, Merryman, and Whiteside wrangled over terms and conditions, trying to reach an "adjustment." Shields sat on a log in a murderous rage, and Lincoln stood ostentatiously swinging his broadsword, lopping twigs off a tree at a height no other man could hope to reach, so his short-armed opponent could see that if it came to blows, he would get the worse of it.

From the hour Lincoln left Springfield on Tuesday, September 20, until his return that weekend, Mary Todd was in a state of high anxiety verging on panic. Wild rumors preceded the dueling party's return: Lincoln or Shields was dead or wounded; both had come away unscathed; the last-minute diplomacy of John Hardin or the stern hand of a constable had relieved the enemies of their terrible duty. As Mary's thoughts leaped from one to another of these possibilities, she found herself increasingly enamored of Lincoln the more she perceived that he was in danger. She could share these thoughts and her guilt in the matter with Julia Jayne, who had witnessed the writing of the second Rebecca letter. She might confide in Eliza Francis or in Anson Henry, who was covering for his partner in the medical practice, Dr. Elias H. Merryman, while he was riding around the prairie with Lincoln. Merryman, an authority on dueling, had volunteered to be Lincoln's second.

Mary would get no sympathy from her sister Elizabeth, or that proud man Ninian Edwards. Lincoln had been a thorn in Edwards's side for too long, and Mary's guardian cared little how the duel turned out. One thing was clear to Edwards, in this age when the memory of Jackson's glory was still fresh: Whoever survived this affair would be none the worse for it in the public eye. As a governor's son, he understood this at least as well as Lincoln did.

If Molly could have saddled up a horse and hurried south, she would have done so. She stayed within shouting distance of Eliza Francis, as her husband would be among the first to get the news from the lone rider posting ahead of the dueling party. Simeon Francis, sharp-featured and bespectacled, stroked the thick black whiskers that shaded his square jaw and left his lips bare, frowning ironically. He had the austere, kindly face of a Quaker elder. This would be a big news story in Illinois, especially in the capital, so the editor meant to make the most of it, whether it should mean writing a eulogy for his fallen friend, or feeding the Springfield reader's insatiable desire for details about an old-fashioned affair of honor between a popular Whig and a vilified Democrat.

In the long newspaper accounts by Whiteside and Merryman that filled the newspapers during the next two weeks, there was a disagreement between the seconds over the manner in which peace was made. But if either Lincoln or Shields risked a loss of honor in the transaction, it was clearly the fault of Whiteside and Merryman, who had—within their rights—made concessions unknown to the duelists. The seconds, each laying blame upon the other, diverted the public's attention from the principals to their own petty quarrel. Whiteside, half in earnest, soon challenged Merryman to a duel.

The news, thankfully, was the best possible: no bloodshed, honor preserved all around. At least that was the understanding before the parade arrived. Soon after Shields drove up Sixth Street with Whiteside, he was welcomed at Ninian Edwards's mansion, to regale the company—excepting Mary Todd—with his Irish version of the opera. Lincoln, Merryman, Butler, and Bledsoe would be welcome for whiskey at Simeon Francis's home, where Mary Todd was reunited with her hero. She would approach shyly, uncertain whether she should be proud or ashamed, whether he would reproach her for precipitating the affair or simply be glad to see her.

She was a woman of powerful and ungovernable passions. He deserved a hero's welcome. Left alone with him at last in the guttering candlelight of the parlor, she would embrace him with the fervor born of fear that he had been lost forever, and the hope that she might never lose him again.

THE YELLOW LEAVES of the cottonwoods and sycamore, the scarlet leaves of the maples, signaled autumn in its glory. And Simeon Francis gave a column to some prose poet who effused: "October has come—the sweetest, saddest month of all the year. Its sunsets and its gorgeous forests, how beautiful—and brief as beautiful their gorgeous dyes. There is a pensive beauty in October days—autumn is now clothed in her loveliest drapery; the forest leaves are not yet dry and crisp; nature has not yet put on her frigid aspect, but the sighing breeze and the falling leaf is nature's knell for her fallen glories; soon all these beautiful things will have lost their beauty—all these bright things their brightness."

Such calm evenings, when Venus shone, seemed made for lovers, and such skies: "It is the very gate of heaven—and that lone star seems a beacon light, hung out from his golden portals, to guide us erring wanderers, home." Perhaps Mr. Lincoln himself had written the lines—he certainly would have appreciated the sentiment, and had the gift to express it, as well as the editor's indulgence.

The prairie landscape and the peaceful sky stood in contrast to the turmoil that had erupted in Springfield. "The town is in a ferment and a street fight somewhat anticipated," Lincoln wrote to Joshua Speed on October 5. Speed had heard about the duel a few days after the Alton confrontation; news had spread to Kentucky and through Missouri, where the affair was reported in *The Missouri Republican* (St. Louis) on October 3. A bitter editorial in the *Alton Telegraph* on October 1 denounced the duelists, lamenting "that these gentlemen have both violated the laws of the country" and demanding that they be arrested and called to account.

"Both of them are lawyers; both have been legislators of the State and aided in the construction of laws for the protection of the society; both exercized no small influence in the community—all of which, in our estimation, aggravates, instead of mitigates, their offense. . . . Wealth, influence and rank can trample upon the laws with impunity, while poverty, scarcely permitted to utter a word in its defense, is charged with crime in our miscalled temples of justice." The editor called for Attorney General Josiah Lamborn to bring the miscreants to justice.

But the attorney general, himself infamously corrupt, would do nothing of the kind. Wealth, influence, and rank would flourish, magnified by the timeworn tradition of the Code Duello, which the lawmakers had outlawed before they were quite ready to let go of it in their hearts.

To most of the citizens of Springfield, where the laws were made, these figures Lincoln and Shields were heroes, and there was no talk of jailing anybody for dueling. On the contrary, Mr. Lincoln was acting as second to Dr. Merryman, who had challenged General Whiteside to a duel on October 4, the day after Shields challenged Butler. How could he decline? "The dueling business still rages in this city," Lincoln reported to Speed. And just as soon as Simeon Francis could gather the correspondence and set the type, he would begin filling the columns of the *Sangamo Journal* with as much eyewitness detail about all these affairs of honor as he could find.

Dueling news dominated the *Sangamo Journal* for two weeks, beginning with Whiteside's account of Lincoln and Shields's duel, and Merryman's account of his own with Whiteside, both published on October 7. There had been nothing like it in recent memory. The death of a steeplejack, "a young man of good character" who got struck by lightning and fell seventy-two feet from the steeple of the new Presbyterian Church, got eleven lines of type on October 17, while Merryman's response to Whiteside filled many columns.

Public opinion was divided roughly along party lines, excepting the curious alliance between the Democrat Shields and the aristocratic, reluctant Whig Ninian Edwards. Perhaps it was Edwards's agreement with Shields on monetary policy that united them. More likely, to Mary Todd, it was her guardian's contempt for Lincoln, which made her feel uncomfortable in that house on the hill where he was not welcome despite his new fame. She felt more at home with the Francises on Sixth Street.

As Lincoln's friend, the editor planned the newspaper columns to the Whig's advantage. Whiteside fired the first salvo on October 7, insinuating that Lincoln had surprised him with the dueling preliminaries, that in the end the seconds agreed to "withdraw all papers," and that Lincoln's friends offered a full apology on his behalf. On October 14, Dr. Merryman took four thousand words to defend Lincoln against Whiteside's attack, and Francis led the issue with the comment: "The last publication closes the correspondence in this paper between these gentlemen on that subject."

Mary Todd and her friends read and reread the newspaper stories with excitement and some degree of sentimental pride. These "two distinguished gentlemen of the City of Springfield," as the *Alton Telegraph* called Lincoln and Shields on October 1, were celebrities by the end of the month. Her beloved had used the old code of chivalry to demonstrate his valor as a gentleman. The duel was so famous that Mary's father, Robert Todd, heard of it in Kentucky, and he was properly impressed. People would not be so quick to question Lincoln's standing as a gentleman or his fitness to marry a Todd on that score.

Still they carried on their courtship in secret. As Mary soon afterward explained to her sister Elizabeth, "the Cause why it was—that the world— woman & man were uncertain & slippery and that it was best to keep the secret Courtship from all Eyes & Ears." This was a thing that Elizabeth recalled from her own courtship: that women, and men in particular, were uncertain and slippery and not easily caught. Mary wanted to make sure she had her man for good and all, and was more confident she could do it behind closed doors.

DURING JOSHUA SPEED'S courtship, Lincoln had acted as his confidant and adviser, and now that he and Molly had achieved a degree of intimacy whereby the talk of marriage, if not the thing itself, was imminent, Lincoln turned to Speed for advice. "You have now been the husband of a lovely woman nearly eight months. That you are happier now than you were the day you married her I well know . . . I have your word for it. . . . But I want to ask a closer question—'Are you now, in *feeling* as well as *judgement*, glad you are married as you are?' From any body but me, this would be an impudent question not to be tolerated; but I know you will pardon it in me. Please answer it quickly as I feel impatient to know."

He was about to leave Molly for two weeks of practicing law on the circuit: Clinton, Urbana, and Danville, then another week in Charleston. Visits to Molly from these eastern towns between court cases would be hasty, surreptitious, and, in all likelihood, very intense. Absence is a powerful incentive for lovers to put aside inhibitions when reunited for an hour or a night. *Feeling* might get the upper hand of *judgment*—perhaps it had already. Now it had become a matter of some urgency to know if he had made a mistake; if, caught up in his emotions, he might have lost his judgment. Speed was happy in wedlock, no doubt about it. Lincoln could depend upon him to provide the answer that he needed and wanted to hear.

What else could Speed say after eight months of increasing happiness but that he was glad to be married and that his head had followed his heart? That letter has been lost, but if it covered the post roads from Louisville with due dispatch, Lincoln would receive the answer he wanted by October 23, during a weekend with Molly before riding off to Charleston, Illinois, for a week, to argue cases on the Coles County Circuit. Up until now, neither dueling nor courtship had interfered much with Lincoln's growing law practice.

On Sunday, October 30, the lawyers would begin the hundred-mile journey home from Charleston to Springfield, arriving on Halloween.

Above the little wooden church on Adams and Third, St. Paul's Episcopal, a bell summoned the Anglicans to mass on All Saints' Day. The congregation, led by the Reverend Charles Dresser, included Eliza and Simeon Francis and Mr. and Mrs. Ninian Edwards. While Mary Todd was not an Anglican, she often went to church with them, honoring custom in attending the church of her hosts. This Hallowmass she would not likely be joining them.

That day in early November, Lincoln arrived at the Francis home as soon as possible so as not to keep her waiting. But she was eager likewise, as she turned the corner of Washington and Sixth Street and knocked softly at the side door, eager to embrace him, longing to converse in the curtained parlor and reach a decision. There could no longer be any doubt. The time had come for them to be married.

On the west side of the public square stood the new C. W. Chatterton & Brother jewelry store (established October 27, 1842), purveyors of gold and silver watches and fobs, gold spectacles, silver pencils, shell combs, and golden lockets. These "and many others in their line will be sold twenty-five percent less than ever before offered in Springfield," said their ad in the *Journal*. There Lincoln purchased the wide-band ring of Etruscan gold, within which he had ordered engraved the words "A. L. to Mary, Nov. 4, 1842. Love Is Eternal." She would have to try it on first, if not there in the shop, then in some private place.

The couple might have eloped, gone to Jacksonville and taken their vows before the justice of the peace. Lincoln belonged to no religious denomination; his bride-to-be had been raised a Presbyterian. Yet in this town full of Presbyterians and Methodists, Mary and Abraham chose an Episcopal minister, the Reverend Charles Dresser, pastor of Ninian and Elizabeth Edwards, as well as the Francises.

With breathtaking spontaneity Lincoln knocked on Dresser's door the morning of Friday, November 4, calling the parson from the breakfast table and curtly informing him, "I want to get hitched tonight."

In those days, Friday was considered an unlucky day to be married, and the notoriously superstitious Lincoln was, in his mad dash to the altar, tempting fate. In the meantime, Mary announced to her sister that she was to be wed that very night by Reverend Dresser in the parsonage over on the corner of Jackson and Eighth streets. Elizabeth was livid. Harsh words passed between the sisters, who had clashed before over Mr. Lincoln, but now Mary presented the marriage to her sister as a fait accompli, a necessity not to be negotiated or delayed. Elizabeth quickly sized up the situation for what it was and moved swiftly to make the best of it for appearances' sake. Only necessity could have reconciled Elizabeth to such haste.

"Mary, if you insist on being married today, we will make merry, and have the wedding here this evening," said Elizabeth Todd Edwards between clenched teeth. "I will not permit you to be married out of my house."

The choice of Dresser had been strategic, a firm bridge between the impetuous lovers and the house that had hitherto been closed to them. Ninian Edwards, hearing the news from Lincoln on a street corner—that he meant to marry his ward in the parsonage—quickly reached the same conclusion as his wife, and told him, "No, I am Mary's guardian and if she is married at all, it must be from my house."

Ninian and Elizabeth had no choice but to invite Lincoln to come and marry Mary Todd in their parlor. This was just the thing that Mary had wanted all along.

To the Springfield community that had grown to expect the unexpected from Lincoln, this was nonetheless a profound shock to their sense of order and ceremony. Now it was remarkable how quickly the arrangements came together. Friends and family of this couple appear to have had little to do that Friday but wait for the call to witness and cater the nuptials. No doubt Lincoln would have chosen Anson Henry as best man if that fiery Whig had been welcome in the Edwards home. Instead Lincoln wanted young James Matheny, the court clerk, but he couldn't be found until a few hours before the wedding. Meanwhile, Mr. Beverly Powell, a dapper dry-goods clerk and friend of Speed's, agreed to stand up for Lincoln. When at last he found Matheny, Lincoln unburdened himself, saying, "Jim, I shall have to marry that girl"; and Matheny would always believe that Lincoln had been caught up in a tide of emotional events that had swept him away to the altar before he was ready. Matheny was proud to stand by Lincoln, and so he would have two best men to support him in the crucial moment.

While Mary's sisters, Elizabeth and Frances, scrambled to put the house in order and prepare a ham and a wedding cake for the party, Mary recruited her bridesmaids: Julia Jayne, Lina Lamb, and Anna Rodney.

Twilight came early on that cloudy Friday. Lincoln bathed and dressed for the wedding in his little bedroom at William Butler's house, and was about to put on his black silk stock when he heard someone at his door. It was his friend Elizabeth Butler, dressed in her best gown of yellow silk, come to see if the nervous bridegroom was properly dressed and shaved, combed and brushed for the wedding. Behind her were her children, Salome and five-year-old Speed. Lincoln bent down and allowed Mrs. Butler to knot his black tie in a bow.

He joked and chatted with the children, who had never seen him quite so dapper and handsome.

"Where are you going, Mr. Lincoln?" asked the little boy.

From the Butler house on the southwest corner of Madison and Third it was six long blocks up the hill to the Edwards mansion, where he had not been invited for two years.

"To Hell, I suppose," Lincoln answered, before starting out up Second Street in the rain.

AT LEAST THIRTY people gathered in the parlor to witness the nuptials of Abraham Lincoln and Mary Todd as they faced the Reverend Charles Dresser in his cassock and tippet. He stood with his back to the marble fireplace, holding the *Book of Common Prayer*.

The bride wore a dress of pale yellow silk embroidered with flowers. There were the three bridesmaids and two best men. Attending were the Butlers, and Simeon and Eliza Francis; there stood Mary's twenty-seven-year-old sister, Frances Todd Wallace, and her husband, Dr. William Wallace, and little William Jayne, Julia's brother. And of course the occasion would not have been complete without Lincoln's friend Dr. Merryman, who had stood up with him on a less dangerous occasion, and the lawyers: John Stuart, Stephen Logan (both cousins to the bride), James Conkling, Edward D. Baker, and Albert Bledsoe, and their wives and children.

Ninian Edwards and his wife listened while the clergyman's sonorous voice filled the parlor that had been cleverly hijacked by the determined lovers:

> Dearly beloved, we are gathered here in the sight of God, and in the face of this company, to join together this Man and this Woman in holy Matrimony . . . not by any to be entered into unadvisedly or lightly; but reverently, discreetly, advisedly, soberly, and in the fear of God.

Lincoln had never before been asked to carry on his business *in the fear of God,* and the words, if he heard them (and many nervous bridegrooms do not), he might have found perplexing.

> Into this holy estate, these two persons present come now to be joined. If any man can show just cause, why they may not lawfully be joined together, let him speak, or else hereafter forever hold his peace.

In Elizabeth's mind there were reasons enough that this couple ought not be married, but none having to do with the law.

> Who giveth this Woman to be married to this Man?

Ninian alone held the responsibility to give her away, here in this house where she had lived as his ward for five years, so far from her father, Robert Todd.

Few would forget the solemnity of the occasion or the tension that suffused the wedding party until the golden ring appeared from Matheny's pocket; he held it in readiness for the moment the minister would call for Lincoln "to put it upon the fourth Finger of the Woman's left Hand."

Matheny and Powell stood behind Lincoln. Behind them stood the stout supreme court judge Thomas C. Browne. At forty-eight years of age, the judge was probably the oldest man in the house. He had seen and endured much in his quarter of a century on the bench, and was accustomed to speaking his mind regardless of the occasion. Now his eyes narrowed. He had heard just about all of this Anglican rigmarole he could stand and wanted to get on to the gingerbread and beer that had come from Dickey's bakery. As he listened to the minister drone on through the legalistic formula, "With this ring I thee endow with all my goods and chattels, lands and tenements," Judge Browne, by right of seniority, was moved to break up the god-awful solemnity and nervous tension that racked the humid parlor.

"Lord Jesus Christ, God Almighty, Lincoln, the Statute fixes all that," the judge bellowed in his Kentucky accent. And there was hardly a man in the room who could keep from laughing, including the parson, who paused just long enough to collect himself before pronouncing the bride and the bridegroom man and wife.

God the Father, God the Son, God the Holy Ghost, bless preserve and keep you. The Lord mercifully with his favour look upon you, and fill you with all spiritual benediction and grace; that ye may live together in this life, that in the world to come ye may have life everlasting. Amen.

NEWLYWEDS

THEIR ROOM ON THE SECOND FLOOR of the wood-frame boardinghouse was no more than eight feet wide by fourteen feet long. It was
dominated by the marriage bed, which was in turn overwhelmed by the
bridegroom, who had to lie on the bias or curled around his bride if he
wished to be in the bed altogether. He held his shapely wife, who referred
to herself as a "ruddy pineknot" and an "exuberance of flesh," struck by
the wonder of it all, as they discovered each other by candlelight and then
by touch in the dark.

The excitements, fears, and joys of the wedding night can be just as intense for the man and woman who have already known a measure of intimacy. To undress for the first time in a room legally shared and find
oneself at the beginning of an eternity of nights and days, *till death us do
part,* is a ritual as sacred as any in the marriage ceremony, "a matter of
profound wonder," as Lincoln put it.

The little room in the Globe Tavern, which stood on Adams Street between Third and Fourth, across from the Episcopal church, had recently
been occupied by Mary's sister Frances and her new husband, Dr.
William Wallace. So it was considered an appropriate lodging for newlyweds. When the Lincolns had unpacked their worldly goods and stowed
what would fit in the clothing press or a walnut wardrobe, the room
would still be strewn with garments and paraphernalia curious to one or
the other: panniers, camisoles, long johns and shaving gear, mysterious
vials and jars on the night table, objects of curiosity, topics of idle or hilarious conversation. *What's this, and what's this?*—conversation that readily leads to foreplay between a man and woman in a close space, and in the
bloom of health.

The word "honeymoon" was unknown to folks in those days, and this couple hardly expected a luxurious vacation in that ramshackle tavern, where they took their meals downstairs in the common dining room beyond the parlor, good country fare served up by the widow landlady, Sarah Beck. There was much traffic in the halls and common rooms. A porter pulled a rope attached to a bell on the rooftop every time a carriage or stagecoach drew up to the door, day or night. The bell rang whenever someone stopped for a meal or a glass of ale or for lodging.

Lincoln was familiar with the Globe as a watering hole for Whig politicians. It also served as a polling place. The hostelry was "respectable," but it did not have the prestige of the American House on the far side of the square, known for its "Turkish Splendor" and high-ceilinged ballroom. And then the Globe parlor was haunted by the memory of the Methodist minister and physician Jacob Early, murdered by Henry Truett in 1838. Truett had inquired whether the minister had authored a resolution to remove him from the legislature, and when Early refused to answer, Truett aimed a pistol at him. Early picked up a chair to shield himself, and Truett shot through it, killing him. Lincoln the lawyer got Truett acquitted of the murder charge on the grounds that the chair was a lethal weapon and Truett had fired in self-defense.

Sarah Beck charged $4 a month for room and board for both of the newlyweds.

They had neither the time nor the money for a romantic getaway. They would make do with such comforts as the Globe could provide, but it must be temporary; a woman who was raised in a mansion could not be expected to live in a room in which she could hardly turn around, even if it were with the man she loved. Lincoln would have to work hard to dig himself out of the old Salem debt while saving enough money to rent or purchase a home.

Not forty-eight hours after the wedding, Lincoln was up and gone. On Sunday he and Logan headed south on the road to Taylorville, fifty miles away on the far side of Edinburg, where the Christian County Court was in session. The lawyers stayed at the Long Tavern. In the one-day term the partners had nine cases called, so Lincoln could not return to his bride until Tuesday night at the earliest. He was with her for the rest of the week, then gone again, this time in the company of Albert Taylor Bledsoe, who also lived at the Globe, to try cases up in Petersburg at the Menard Circuit Court.

So at the very time Molly was learning the joys of intimacy, she was also learning the sorrows and ennui of being left behind in a room grown smaller by her husband's absence when Mr. Lincoln was on the road.

When court was in session in Springfield, as it was from November 19 until spring, the newlyweds finally settled into a daily rhythm of waking and sleeping, lovemaking and conversation. He would rise early and wash at the pump, and as she lay in the bed and stretched, she could watch him shave, scraping his skin before the little portable swivel mirror with the dark wooden frame.

His office with Logan was just north of the capitol, at 106 North Fifth. If Molly were up early she might walk with him on a chilly morning in December east on Adams Street with the slant winter sunlight in their eyes, turning north on Fifth Street in the shadow of the imposing capitol. At last they could stroll down the streets together arm in arm, where they had not dared to go together in years, and wave to the merchants opening their doors, and the doctors and lawyers going to work. She left him at the office door to go about the work that she understood as much as he could explain it to her. Trespass for false imprisonment. Bankruptcy. A forged note. Divorces. The divorces were mysterious, confidential, difficult to explain.

Mary returned to the Globe Tavern and made up the bed, tidying the room where there was no place to put anything. It was cold in the bedroom, so she would go downstairs and sit by the fire, perhaps with Harriet Bledsoe, twenty-seven, and her little girl, Sophie, age five. Mary enjoyed children. Little Sophie was excited because Christmas was coming, and the three could decorate the door and chimneypiece with pinecones and pine-branch wreaths and red ribbons.

A porter carried wood and poked the fire. The widow Beck hurried to do her chores—checking out lodgers, minding the till, baking, cooking meals, and doing laundry. She did not allow the lodgers to help her; the reputation of the house depended upon their comfort and ease. So there was not much for Molly to do except sew and read books and journals, chat with the other ladies, and play with the little girl. There was mending to do, because Mr. Lincoln was hard on his few articles of clothing. She could not shop in earnest, because they had so little money. She might visit Eliza Francis, a few blocks away; it would be good to attend church with Eliza, who might act as a buffer in the presence of Ninian Edwards and Mary's sister Elizabeth. The hasty marriage had caused a rift in the family that would be slow to mend.

Mr. Lincoln worked hard every day of the week, and often on Saturdays. But he would not work on Tuesday, December 13; it was Molly's birthday. On Monday, after a day in the circuit court, he went to Robert Irwin's store across from the capitol square and spent $2 on a pair of martingales—straps to steady the horses' heads—a practical purchase that might also double as a birthday gift. The ring around the gibbous moon called for snow. There would be snow on Molly's birthday, and if it lay right, he might hitch the horses to a sleigh so the two of them could ride out over the prairie covered in its blanket of white.

MARRIAGE IS A state of mysterious paradoxes and contradictions that unfold rapidly in a small room. Bride and groom find themselves naked as never before, and vulnerable, with perhaps greater need for cover. They begin in awe of each other's perfections, only to be dismayed when they discover flaws. The man who longed for comfort in a woman's arms suddenly feels suffocated, oppressed, wanting air. Lincoln had been a private and secretive man, always preferring to remain apart. How could he love this woman as he meant to love her while preserving the core of his being? And what is she to make of this man who, like an infinity of Chinese boxes, opens one after another to her in the effort to reveal his heart, and uncovers only one more box locked as tight as the one before? She is an open book, her emotions visible to all. Needing love, she finds herself one night ecstatic in the prospect of it, seeming to hold it for a joyful hour, only to awaken and find it insufficient, or that her need in response to his giving is redoubled.

Lincoln had night terrors. He woke in the middle of night trembling, talking gibberish. Suppressing her own fear, she tried to comfort him. But in that nightmare between waking and sleeping, he was in another world, far removed from her, as he was sometimes in broad daylight when he would fall into an impenetrable reverie.

Molly was passionate and impetuous. He had known this all along—it was part of her allure. Now he began to see the depths of her emotions, how the intensity of her love was matched by a savage hatred or anger—not for him, but for some shape-shifting demon that might take the form of the landlady, or Ninian Edwards, or Poverty, or a ragged petticoat past mending. Some terrible moments, her animus was directed at her husband himself, and she would look at him with strange, piercing eyes. Her fury could be terrible. Her capacity for joy had a counterpart in her disposition to misery and wrath. Her bravery in defying convention, or in personal ambition—perhaps greater even than her husband's—was curiously complemented by childish fears of thunder and lightning, mice and burglars. He sometimes called her his child wife. She called him Mr. Lincoln until she began to call him Father.

"She was very highly strung," recalled her cousin, Mrs. Margaret Woodrow, "nervous, impulsive, irritable, having an emotional temperament much like an April day, running all over with laughter one moment, at the next crying as though her heart would break."

She found his moodiness profound and troubling. He could be— especially in company, at the dinner table where he had an audience—full of high spirits, his eyes twinkling, taking as much pleasure in telling his jokes and yarns as in hearing her laughter. But he could sink into fits of melancholy that could drain the light from a room. More often it was his silence that worried or exasperated her. He sat staring into space as if he were dead or time traveling—who knew?—in a trance or catatonic state. She could not reach him though he sat within a few feet of her.

Perhaps it was after one such performance that she learned, to her horror, the limits of her endurance, and he discovered, to his unending dismay, her lack of self-control. The boarders were seated at the breakfast table. Mr. Lincoln was staring into the middle distance, without a thought of the wife who had fathomless needs and uncharted impulses. When she came down the stairs she was furious. If she could not get his attention before, in the privacy of their little room, perhaps she would command it in the larger theater of the dining room where there was an audience.

Mr. Lincoln was drinking his coffee as she sat down near him and coffee was poured for her. According to one source, he chided her for being late. It was too much. In a moment of rage Mary Lincoln raised her coffee cup, and, as if a devil had seized her wrist, she threw the hot coffee into her husband's face.

The source of this terrible story is worthy but not unimpeachable; the retailed anecdote has sometimes been challenged since it surfaced in the 1930s. Perhaps it was not hot coffee but bitter words she flung at him. Yet the act cannot be discarded as "out of character." It is in keeping with other memories of the young woman's fiery temper and the need for Lincoln quickly to come to terms with it. Molly was horrified by what she had done. While someone went for towels and cold water, she covered her eyes with her hands and retreated in shame to that room that had come to seem now a refuge and at other times a prison.

After her outbursts she was tearfully repentant, mortified, and begged for forgiveness, and there was nothing for him but to forgive her. She would try to make it up to him, with a pint of honey to drown a dram of gall. Swings of the pendulum, once recognized, can be accommodated, as marriage—that most forgiving of institutions—was intended to accommodate all things, sickness and health, poverty and riches, madness and equanimity. "If you make a bad bargain, hug it the tighter," Lincoln had learned in his youth, an adage of his father's. He would hug her tightly. Never having been married, and being a man of precise and careful definitions, he was not even prepared yet to say this was a bad bargain, only a transaction whose profit had yet to be measured.

She was pregnant. And, as the busybodies in town would be eager to confide, she must have suspected it soon after the marriage or soon before, given the mad rush to the altar. Charitable gossips were willing to attribute her infamous rages to her condition, explain them away by the unpredictable power of gestation and morning sickness; and then there were Mary's agonizing migraine headaches, especially in springtime, when the light of day was a torment.

Having done all he could to mend the breach between them, he went to work, the alternate heat and chill of his scalded cheek reminding him, in the courtroom, of the unpredictable and perilous journey of the marriage ahead of him.

SHE WAS NOT housebound that winter. If she felt up to it, she might go for a stroll, or even to the courthouse to sit with other ladies in the gallery watching their husbands at the bar. During much of January 1843, Lincoln was defending his friend Judge Thomas Browne against charges of incompetence by the Galena bar. The lawyers complained, "The only charge which we call upon the house to notice, involves nothing derogatory to his character, as a man of integrity, but is founded on the natural infirmity and feebleness of his intellect, and over which he has no control." Bride and bridegroom had enjoyed many a good laugh over the judge's lack of control at the wedding (*"God Almighty, Lincoln, the Statute fixes all that!"*). But evidently Lincoln held a different opinion of Browne's intellect and whether or not it was sufficient to the juridical needs of the Sixth Judicial Circuit.

The trial opened on January 3, and it was a raucous affair conducted in the statehouse, where the indignant judge incited a chorus of friends and rowdies to hurl invective at his accusers, four lawyers from Galena. The galleries were packed; the doorkeepers could keep order only by great exertions. The poor jury (rather, the "committee appointed to conduct" the legislative trial) repeatedly begged to be discharged. The request was finally granted on January 5, by which time Lincoln and Springfield had fairly routed the heartless attorneys of Galena. Eventually charges against Judge Browne were dropped, and he held his seat until 1848, shouting verdicts and swearing ungodly oaths and banging his gavel.

That was great fun. And then the Mormon prophet Joseph Smith showed up in the circuit court on Wednesday, January 4, to appeal for a writ of habeas corpus. Joseph Smith and his saints and apostles, with their reputation for polygamy and rumors of treason swirling about them, caused a stir wherever they appeared. After being driven out of Missouri in 1838, they had crossed the Mississippi into Illinois and made a settlement in the river town of Nauvoo in Hancock County, a hundred miles west of the capital. For four years they were a source of contention, as a threat to the Christian establishment and the state. Smith became a lightning rod for the debate over individual freedom and the law's authority; and politicians sought to capture Mormon votes by granting them liberal charters, or to gather anti-Mormon votes by attacking the saints when they had worn out their welcome.

The Lincolns had been talking about Joseph Smith since after Christmas. The Mormon prophet had been indicted back in May as accessory in the attempted murder of the ex-governor of Missouri, Lilburn W. Boggs. Boggs persuaded Governor Thomas Carlin of Illinois to arrest Smith and extradite him to Missouri, where he could be tried. But Smith went on the lam for six months, vanishing before giving himself up to the authorities in Springfield, where his lawyers demanded a local writ of habeas corpus—so he would not be wrongfully imprisoned. He charmed everyone in the capital, and the press enthusiastically followed his appearances at social functions at the American House and elsewhere.

Lincoln's friend Justin Butterfield had taken Smith's case; Mary's brother-in-law Benjamin S. Edwards assisted him. Simeon Francis had given the Mormons' adventures many columns in the *Sangamo Journal*. Lincoln was interested in the Smith hearing because the prophet was in himself a fascinating specimen of charisma, and because Butterfield was fighting for the sacred right of habeas corpus. Smith could not be extradited and tried for a murder in Missouri if in fact he had been in Illinois while the alleged crime was committed.

As Lincoln was that day laboring to bring some dignity to the political circus that Judge Browne had summoned up in the statehouse, he could not watch the proceeding in the circuit court. But his wife would dress in her finest and go with twenty-five-year-old Ben Edwards, and his wife, Helen, exactly Mary's age, to attend the hearing in the courthouse where Josiah Lamborn, attorney general of the state of Illinois, would try to deprive Joseph Smith of the right to a writ of habeas corpus.

The presiding judge was the honorable Nathaniel Pope, a droopy-eyed walrus of a gentleman, highly regarded by all. It seemed that everyone in town who was not engrossed in Lincoln's defense of Judge Browne had lined up at the door of the courthouse to get a glimpse of the handsome Joseph Smith and his twelve apostles. When the doors opened, the multitude rushed the benches. There were not enough seats in the room, so a few of the ladies—including Mrs. Lincoln, Mrs. Edwards, and one of Pope's daughters—squeezed in on either side of the black-robed judge.

Mary watched and listened closely so that she might report to her husband all that transpired. That night, as they lay together in their room, she would recall how the chattering crowd grew hushed as Justin Butterfield stood tall in a long blue coat with brass buttons, his gold watch chain hooked in a yellow waistcoat, and swept his eyes around the courtroom before fixing them upon her and the other young ladies, some in muslin and some in silk.

"May it please the court," said Butterfield. "I appear before you today under circumstances most novel and peculiar. I am to address the Pope [bowing to the judge] surrounded by angels [with a very low bow to Mrs. Lincoln], in the presence of the Holy Apostles, on behalf of the Prophet of the Lord!"

The husband was learning that his bride was indeed a she-devil at times and an angel at others. On his thirty-fourth birthday, February 12, she made a little speech at the dinner celebration in the tavern parlor that included a few close friends. The speech concluded: "I am so glad you have a birthday. I feel so grateful to your mother." His birthday that year fell on a Sunday, so they could spend the entire day together, reading aloud to each other, sharing their hopes and dreams, walking out in the cold air arm in arm, lying in bed in the light of a nearly full moon. As much joy as they had shared in the little room, Molly was nevertheless eager to get out of it. As graciously as her temperament would allow, she had accepted her reduced circumstances. She had come from a mansion on the hill to lodge in a low boardinghouse, and from being a fixed star in the Edwards "coterie" to being the idle wife in the chimney corner.

Lincoln was working day and night at his law practice earning the money to lift them out of this noisy lodging house, but she was impatient for change. She dreamed that the two of them might occupy a place in society that would transcend everything that she and her more snobbish sisters had ever known. The key to this was politics. In her own lifetime she had seen humble men ascend in the social order by the ladder of politics. Politics had done its part to draw him to her—they were both ardent Whigs who idolized Henry Clay. If Mr. Lincoln still had any doubts about his desire to rise in the ranks of the Whig party, or his innate ability to attain the highest offices, she would do everything in her considerable power to persuade him.

A RUN FOR CONGRESS

MONDAY MORNING, FEBRUARY 13, 1843, Lincoln was busy in court with his fellow lodger Albert Taylor Bledsoe. First the men took opposite sides of a replevin action, and then they teamed up to challenge an injunction in a banking case. The rest of that day, filing affidavits and writing a bill in chancery, Lincoln's mind was never far from the subject that also absorbed his wife: his political prospects.

He had not sought reelection to the legislature since his term ended in 1841; he needed to concentrate on his law practice and retiring his debts. And as leader of the Whig party in the House, the opposition leader in an overwhelmingly Democratic state, Lincoln had accomplished as much as a local politician ever could. The next step for him had to be a seat in the U.S. Congress, representing the Seventh Congressional District— Sangamon County, Tazewell, and other Whig strongholds where Lincoln was respected as a lawyer. John Stuart was about to give up his seat in Congress. If Lincoln wished to replace him, he would find himself in an intense competition with two friends: cousin John J. Hardin and Edward Dickinson Baker, thirty-two, a blue-eyed, sandy-haired father of five.

Tall and muscular, Baker was known for his good looks and impassioned speech-making. According to the *Sangamo Journal*, June 5, 1840, Baker performed his oration flanked by a caged eagle that piped when the speaker prophesied that General William Henry Harrison would be president. Born in England, Baker studied law in Carrollton, Illinois, in the 1820s before serving bravely in the Black Hawk War, where he made first lieutenant. He got to know Lincoln well when they sat together in the state legislature in the late 1830s. Baker had been a state senator since 1840. Meanwhile, he was practicing law in partnership with Benjamin Edwards, Ninian's brother. Lincoln and Baker's intimacy had probably culminated in 1838–39 while they were fellow assembly members in Vandalia; now Baker appeared as a formidable opponent with similar principles.

Regardless of the competition, Lincoln, encouraged by his wife, wrote two letters on Valentine's Day to prominent Whigs expressing his desire for the office. To Richard S. Thomas, a lawyer and active party member, he wrote, "Now if you should hear any one say that Lincoln don't want to go to Congress, I wish you as a personal friend of mine, would tell him you have reason to believe he is mistaken. The truth is, I would like to go very much."

The same Tuesday, Lincoln wrote to his friend Alden Hull, who had served alongside him in the legislature in 1838–41: "Your county and ours are almost sure to be placed in the same congressional district. I would like to be its Representative; still circumstances may happen to prevent my even being a candidate." Besides the ambitions of Hardin and Baker, did the Lincolns know of any other circumstance, domestic or other, that might sideline him? "If, however," he continued, "there are any Whigs in Tazewell who would as soon I should represent them as any other person, I would be glad they would not cast me aside until they see and hear further what turn things take.

"There is nothing new here now worth telling," he concludes, omitting any reference to his wife's pregnancy. They would keep the secret as long as they could.

The winter of 1843 was harsh. The Illinois River was frozen, closed to merchant traffic, and there was difficulty crossing the Mississippi at St. Louis. The wheat was "winter killed." Even with both chimney fires blazing at opposite ends of the double parlor of the Globe, it was terribly cold. Yet there were diversions even in the dead of winter, occasions for Molly to change from woolen day dress to full skirt smartly flared with lots of petticoats. She might still draw in her waistband and wear the blouse with scooping neckline she had worn as a maiden, for she was not yet "showing." With gloves and bonnet and woolen coat she could go with Mr. Lincoln to the Senate chamber on Saturday evening, where the Springfield band played to a full house by oil light. The brass and strings performed stately marches and lilting waltzes. Male trios and quartets sang exuberant "glees."

On Monday evening, February 20, she did not even have to leave the house for entertainment, as one of Mr. Lincoln's friends, General William

Fitzhugh Thornton, gave a big party at the Globe Tavern. A Democrat who cultivated the Whigs, Thornton had served as president of the Board of Canal Commissioners until 1842, when canal work was abandoned for lack of funding. Lincoln himself had drafted a petition in 1837 pleading for Thornton to maintain that embattled post. Thornton was director of the State Bank, and showed his gratitude to Whigs and Democrats alike by bringing all together to drink and eat in the candlelit parlors of the Globe. It was an opportunity for Mary to shine once more in the presence of Douglas, Shields, Baker, and so many others she had entertained with her ready wit and graceful moves on the dance floor only a year earlier in the house on the hill.

A reporter from the Peoria *Democratic Press* wrote of the occasion: "There was a sound of revelry by night, and Springfield's capital had gathered then—her beauty and her chivalry—and bright the lamps shone o'er fair women and brave men."

As MOLLY LONGED for a home, her waistline swelling to reveal their "secret," Lincoln toiled not on lucrative legal actions, but on the "Campaign Circular from the Whig Committee." He wanted to be recognized as the most eloquent spokesman of the minority party.

On Wednesday, March 1, 1843, Whigs from all over the state met in the Representatives Hall. The purpose of that meeting was to formulate a concise party platform; up until then, Whig principles were too vague. High on the agenda was to "recommend to the Whigs of all portions of this state to adopt, and rigidly adhere to, the Convention System of nominating candidates." Politicians had learned that the convention system consolidated a party's power. Such a district convention, Mary Lincoln well knew, would favor a man with her husband's personal popularity. As the convention system had been largely Lincoln's idea, it was *"Resolved, that A. T. Bledsoe, S. T. Logan, and A. Lincoln, be appointed a committee to prepare an address to the People of the State."* Neither Lincoln's housemate Bledsoe nor his law partner Logan had political ambitions or a vision of the party platform to match Lincoln's. The Whigs knew that the campaign circular would be chiefly Lincoln's handiwork; the members of the Whig central state committee—Ninian Edwards, Anson Henry, James Matheny, and others—understood this. Yet it must appear to the public that they spoke as one.

Bledsoe and Lincoln toiled over the ten-page "Address to the People of Illinois" in their adjacent law offices at 106 Fifth Street, across from the circuit court, and by candlelight in the Globe parlor, in their shirtsleeves, while their wives waited for them to come to bed. The purpose of this campaign circular was to show why the various resolutions of the Whig meeting must be adopted. These included "a tariff of duties upon foreign importations," which was to be the main source of revenue for the government, as the Whigs held "Direct Taxation for a National Revenue to be improper."

A Whig by birth and breeding, raised in the shade of Ashland, Henry Clay's estate, Mary Lincoln shared the principles her husband set forth in the eloquent circular. It is hardly to be supposed that this woman who was fascinated by everything that had to do with Lincoln's career—and who had so much time on her hands in March of 1842—was not an avid reader of his prose. She delighted in his wit and admired the forcefulness of his common sense as he attacked the Democratic opponents who "boldly advocate direct taxation" and "refuse to adopt the tariff."

He did not mean to censure the Whigs who had opposed the convention system, only to persuade them by an appeal to the highest authority:

> That "union is strength" is a truth that has been known, illustrated and declared, in various ways and forms in all ages of the world. The great fabulist and philosopher, Aesop, illustrated it by his fable of the bundle of sticks; and he whose wisdom surpasses that of all philosophers, has declared that "a house divided against itself cannot stand."

Although the young couple did not yet have a house of brick and mortar, or even a house of wood, they were united, as united as they would ever be: in their anticipation of a child, and in the prospect of Mr. Lincoln's congressional candidacy. The woman who had written the Whiggish "Lost Townships" letter had not put off her passion for politics when she put on her wedding gown. She was proud of her husband and intensely interested in what he wrote, what he wore, and what he had to say in public. Mary was not prepared—by temperament or by education—to play the role of the silent, submissive helpmeet. She would influence him insofar as she could. And he would listen to her whenever he could summon the attention after a long day of work. She wanted him to read to her what he had written, in his gentle voice, and it was always his pleasure to read aloud.

The "Campaign Circular from the Whig Committee" was copied in a fair hand, signed A. Lincoln, S. T. Logan, and A. T. Bledsoe, and dated March 4, 1843, a Saturday. If Lincoln was still polishing his prose all day on Sunday while the deacon Bledsoe, his wife, their little girl, and Molly attended mass in Dr. Dresser's church across Adams Street, he would not flaunt his iconoclasm by dating the address on the Lord's Day. His status as a Christian was already a question mark that hung over his political future despite his wife's regular church attendance. She did not presume to convert him, but she was ever vigilant that he make no display of his free thinking.

On Monday morning the circular was read aloud to the Springfield Whigs, who "agreed to hold the convention at Tremont in Tazewell County" in early April. That evening Molly welcomed her husband home with pride in his leadership and his party's approval of the eloquent Address to the People, which was to be published in the *North Western Gazette and Galena Advertiser* on March 17, and in the *Quincy Whig* on the twenty-second. Mr. Lincoln's own candidacy was strong, and his prospects for representing his district in the U.S. Congress were as good as any man's if he could simply get the Sangamon delegation pledged to him.

This support was more difficult to muster than he supposed. March can be a harsh month on the Illinois prairie, and this March brought a bitter wind, with ice and snow that closed the roads and shops for a full week before St. Patrick's Day. The courts and the legislature were shut down. In their idleness certain Whigs brought their own unkind wind, a "whispering campaign" that favored the appealing younger candidate Edward Dickinson Baker, the state senator. Lincoln was not a man with many enemies, but something was in the air that year that favored the smooth-talking, fiery, churchgoing Baker, a Disciple of Christ. The young Whigs somehow perceived him as more of a self-made man of the people than Abraham Lincoln.

The situation perplexed and vexed Lincoln and his wife, who felt partly responsible for it. Writing to a delegate from Menard County who preferred Lincoln to Baker, the frustrated candidate wrote: "It would astonish if not amuse the older citizens of your county who twelve years ago knew me as a strange, friendless, uneducated, penniless boy, working on a flat boat—at ten dollars per month to learn that I have been put down here as the candidate of pride, wealth, and aristocratic family distinction. Yet so chiefly it was."

Lincoln also refers to "the strangest combination of church influence against me." Baker, a longtime Christian, got the support of the Campbellites (Disciples of Christ) and related groups like the Baptists. Mary Lincoln, who had relatives in the Episcopalian as well as the Presbyterian churches, made the most of her connections there, "whilst," her husband observed, "it was everywhere contended that no Christian ought to go for me, because I belonged to no church, was suspected of being a deist, and had talked about fighting a duel." Molly did not reproach him for his "deism," though she was grateful for his company on the occasions when he went to church with her. As for the duel, it remained a source of mingled pride and embarrassment, a curious incident that had briefly ennobled her lover, and then to her dismay was used against her husband the candidate.

Perhaps the greatest irony to the expectant mother—who had suffered such a decline in her circumstances, moving from the Edwards mansion to a cramped room in a second-rate inn—was the characterization of her husband "as the candidate of pride, wealth, and aristocratic family distinction." In this she and her sister (who had cautioned her against marrying a man of inferior breeding) were implicated. Yet now the very office that would confer upon them a true distinction might be lost for no better reason than that Mr. Lincoln had married her. And where was the wealth? Unlike Edward Baker, who had married a rich widow with a mansion, the Lincolns lived very modestly. Yet the Todd name evoked images of wealth and privilege.

Mary's cousin John J. Hardin, who had once helped to reconcile the estranged lovers, made a third strong candidate for the congressional seat that Lincoln and Baker sought. Hardin, of nearby Morgan County, had been visiting Kentucky when Lincoln and the Whig central committee fixed upon April 5 as the date for the district convention. The date surprised Hardin. He had assumed the Whigs would wait at least until May 1, so as to give candidates like himself—outside the Sangamon clique folks called the "Junto"—more time to gather support in good weather. Mary, familiar with local politics and her cousin's power, sensed that the Springfield Whigs had overplayed their hand when the central committee swiftly acted—on March 15—to placate Hardin. They postponed the convention until the first Monday in May "to secure party harmony." Lincoln knew that a three-way race is often less predictable than a "two-hander," and in the weeks to come he would hope against hope that Hardin would even his odds against Edward Baker.

On March 17, the democratic *Illinois State Register* reported: "Our ears are stunned here, just now, by the din of the Whigs, concerning Lincoln and Baker, as to which shall go to Congress from this district.... The Junto are organized here—they have their secret agents ready to visit the several counties.... They will choke down the throats of the Whigs of Tazewell, Morgan, Scott, ... whatever candidate they please.... Next Monday ... the Whigs of Sangamon are to make a choice between Lincoln and Baker. Whichever candidate is defeated, is to withdraw.... This is done in order to give Sangamon the candidate...."

The weekend before the convention, the Lincolns, holding each other for warmth, watched a comet on the western horizon. Its head was nearly as brilliant as Venus, and the tail "3 degrees in length," according to the newspapers. The weather was bitter; for a week the mercury rarely rose above zero. It was too cold to snow, so folks could watch the comet in the clear blue sky and marvel upon the prodigy, wondering what it might portend.

The convention of the Sangamon County Whigs in the statehouse on March 20, 1843, was the largest meeting ever held in the county. For weeks the newspapers had been raising the pitch of excitement, harping on the competition between Lincoln and Baker, as well as the conspiracy of the Springfield "Junto" to force one of its own candidates upon the district.

The high curved Representatives Hall, bathed in light from the tall windows on the western wall either side of the speaker's platform, quickly filled with the animated Whigs in their dark woolen overcoats and capes and stovepipe hats. It was a space fit for great speeches, momentous occasions, and courageous acts. The white paint had yet to be dulled by the smoke from the coal stoves. Looking up from the ranks of slanted desks with their inkwells, quills, and candlesticks, a man might shift his focus to gaze upon the coffered ceiling, which looked like a huge cockleshell supported at the rear by fluted Corinthian columns.

From the balcony, the ladies looked down through the columns upon the raised wooden platform where the American flag hung to the left of the low balustrade rail, behind which the orators stood. Though the stoves were stoked to the limit, it was still so cold that March day that one might see a man's breath as he rose to speak on behalf of one candidate or the other, Edward Baker or Abraham Lincoln—what each had done for the Whig party and how each might best represent their interests in the coming election. In accord with the custom of the time, neither man spoke for himself. They sat in respectful silence—the broad-browed, sharp-featured Baker, with his hyperextended military posture, and the loose-limbed, rawboned Lincoln, with his unruly hair and bemused expression. Now and then the men would glance at each other, or cast their eyes up to the balcony where the ladies watched and waited hopefully. Anson Henry spoke glowingly of Lincoln, as did others; Ninian Edwards had little if anything to say about his brother-in-law, but lauded young Baker, as did James Kierschner and many others. The candidates were friends, it was well known, so no bitterness marred the proceeding. Yet it was with a heavy heart that, after much debate and seven ballots, Lincoln withdrew. According to the *Sangamo Journal,* "About 800 ballots [votes] were taken, of which E. D. Baker, Esq. had a majority."

As Albert Bledsoe stood up to offer the resolution to appoint convention delegates, Lincoln struggled to imagine the phrases with which he would congratulate Baker without permanently and irrevocably conceding to him; beyond this present county meeting there would be others where the outcome might be different. But the resolution, formed in caucuses he did not control, was worse news than he and Mary could have guessed.

> Resolved, That the following persons be appointed Delegates to the Convention, to be held at Pekin, to nominate a candidate for Congress for the Seventh Congressional District, and that they be instructed to vote for E. D. Baker, as their first choice, and have power to fill vacancies—A. Lincoln, N. W. Edwards, J. A. Hough, Joseph Smith, S. G. Jones, Dr. E. S. Frazier, Eden Lewis and James Kierschner.

In vain had he attempted to decline the honor of serving as a delegate. His ambition was transparent, and the county Whigs' desire to squelch it was inexorable. They liked Lincoln, they admired him, but they wanted Baker to run for them.

That evening the comet that shone in the western sky held no joyful auguries for Mr. and Mrs. Lincoln. At dinner, Albert Bledsoe, a loyal Whig as well as Baker's partner, had few words of consolation for the loser or for Mary Lincoln, who was never known to conceal her anger effectively. Bledsoe was proud and pleased to see "the spirit of 1840 again rising" (the year the Whig Harrison was elected president), and Lincoln had little choice but to feign delight if he did not actually feel it, commending his friend Edward Baker and trying to soothe Mary. This was the first of many lessons they would learn, together, about the cruel and capricious ways of politics.

Only later in the privacy of the bedroom, lit by candlelight, they might share their emotions about the day's events. As Lincoln wrote to his old roommate Joshua Speed: "The meeting, in spite of my attempt to decline it, appointed me one of the delegates; so that in getting Baker the nomination, I shall be 'fixed' a good deal like a fellow who is made groomsman to the man what has cut him out, and is marrying his own dear 'gal.' "

If he had been allowed to attend the convention as a free agent, without obligation, a deadlock between Baker and Hardin might have thrown the nomination into his lap. But the Whigs counted upon his loyalty to Baker and the party. They all relied on his good humor to keep solidarity and peace within the ranks. Yet as the Lincolns lay in bed, before and after embracing, neither would let the other's ambition rest nor let the other give up hope. He counted votes per candidate, county by county. The stammering Hardin would get Morgan, Scott, and Cass—fourteen votes. Baker had Sangamon, "and he or someone else not the Morgan [County] man will get Putnam, Marshall, Woodward, Tazewell & Logan—which with Sangamon make 16," Lincoln wrote to Martin S. Morris on March 26, 1843. That "someone else" might still be Lincoln. Menard County and Mason County had three votes committed to him. "If any thing should happen (which however is not probable) by which Baker should be thrown out of the fight, I would be at liberty to accept the nomination if I could get it." Discreetly he would approach Morris of the Menard County delegation. Anything was possible, if not probable.

They put out the candle and in the cold darkness drew together, refusing to give way to despair.

His few days riding the circuit in November had offered Lincoln no more than a narrow preview of the intermittencies of the married life to come: the sadness of frequent farewells, the anxiety and longings of

drawn-out separations, the sudden and often unexpected ecstasies of reunion. Perhaps at first the forced absences may have lent a certain pi-
quancy to the passion of the newlyweds. If so, that sweet novelty would
not survive the spring of 1843.

On April 4 Lincoln hitched up his horse and buggy and headed north
on the muddy road to Tremont. On the seventy-mile journey the horse
pulled Lincoln across the Sangamon River, Salt Creek, and Mackinaw
River with their rickety bridges, and innumerable rills and bogs occasioned by the season. If a bridge was broken, he had to ford the river. Arriving at nightfall in Tremont he trusted his horse to the tavern livery,
joined the lawyers and judges at the table for supper and conversation,
and turned in for a night's sleep.

On that Wednesday, April 5, in Tazewell Circuit Court, Logan and Lincoln appeared for William L. May in a lawsuit concerning the ownership
of a strip of land along the Illinois River at Peoria, which the defendants—
L. M. Green and J. B. Loose—claimed they had patented before May did.
May plied a horse ferry back and forth across the river, tying up on the
disputed bank. It was a complicated proceeding that at last was "continued," that is, left unresolved at the end of a long day, probably to the frustration of the defendants and to May's satisfaction: The lack of a decision
meant he might continue making his living by operating his horse ferry
unencumbered by ground rent.

For this the young attorney had left his wife for three days, a day in
court, and two muddy days in transit, returning to their bed the evening
of April 6. Upon his return she showed him an intriguing item about him
in the newspaper:

A WORD TO OUR FRIENDS.—We have understood that our political enemies are endeavoring to produce the impression in the neighboring counties, that the friends of Mr. Lincoln are dissatisfied with the result of the
great whig county meeting held in this city on the 20th ult. for the elections
of delegates to the Congressional Convention. We assure those who feel an
interest on this subject, that no such dissatisfaction exists. The whigs of
this county, as we believe, will support Mr. Baker with hearty good will:
and our friends in the counties in this district, could not do Mr. Lincoln or
his friends greater injury, than to listen to and sanction the rumors and reports referred to, and which we again repeat, are unfounded. Having been,
throughout the late canvass, and being at this time, one of Mr. Lincoln's

friends, we cannot justly be charged with any design to mislead the public in giving the facts embraced in this paragraph.

The gossip had followed quickly upon news that the Whig convention in Menard County had charged its delegates to vote first for Lincoln. So he was not yet wholly out of the race! But he would have to diffuse the suspicion that he was engineering a mutiny.

The Lincolns had the weekend together, although Lincoln must work, sending out bills to clients, writing and filing affidavits; for there was much of this paperwork to be done in the law office of Logan and Lincoln. On Wednesday he would be leaving Springfield for three weeks. For Mary it was rather like being married to a sea captain—except the lawyer kept coming home at shorter intervals. No sooner had the wife become accustomed to her solitude, insofar as she could, than she must again adjust to having the man in her room and her bed.

Mary was now "showing," and they could no longer keep up any pretense that a baby was not on the way. "The ruddy pineknot," as she called herself, the "exuberance of flesh," was rounder and more exuberant than ever. It seemed cruel that he must leave her now, but they needed money. Soon, in keeping with the custom, she must begin her confinement. This seemed an unfair punishment—with good weather on the way at last—especially since she had to stay in the Globe Tavern.

On April 12, Lincoln left his wife again, departing early to travel nearly seventy miles due east to Versailles, where the Woodford Circuit Court met for a two-day session. There the lawyers spread rumors of division in the Whig party, with a new twist. Baker had been trying to get Menard County delegates "to violate the instructions of the meeting," and instead of voting for Lincoln as they had been charged, to vote for Baker instead. Hearing this story, as soon as he could take time, on April 14, Lincoln dashed off a note to his friend Martin Morris of Menard. While attending to his duties at the courthouse, Lincoln never lost sight of the potential of party politics to make or break his fortune.

"I have insisted, and still insist, that this can not be true. Surely Baker would not do the like. . . . Upon the same rule, why might I not fly from the decision against me in Sangamon and get up instructions to their delegation to go for me. *There are at least twelve hundred whigs in the county, that took no part.* And yet I would as soon put my hand in the fire as to attempt it. I should feel myself strongly dishonored by it."

He would not stand for anyone accusing himself or Edward Baker of undermining party harmony in the district. Yet at the same time, in this urgent letter to Morris, he means to claim his rights as a candidate who might count upon the support of twelve hundred Whigs that took no part in Baker's Springfield victory. "I repeat, such an attempt on Baker's part can not be true. Write me, at Springfield, how this matter is. Don't show or speak of this letter," he wrote, binding his advocate to silence.

He posted the letter before leaving Versailles on April 15.

Lincoln was due to attend the opening of a weeklong term of the McLean court on April 17, convening in Bloomington, a journey of 135 miles from Versailles. Passing through Springfield on April 15, the weary traveler had the Saturday night before Easter to spend with his wife. They woke to the sound of church bells tolling the resurrection of the Lord. But she went to church without him, having kissed her husband good-bye at dawn.

Lincoln was a very clever navigator of the treacherous April terrain. To give some idea of how difficult traveling was, at the time, on the road north to Bloomington, we have James Conkling's account of the journey— which he started a day earlier than Lincoln—in a letter to his wife: "A mile or two beyond the Sangamon River I plunged into a bad mudhole when the horse fell and broke a shaft. Such an unfortunate accident at the very commencement of my trip made me think very seriously of returning, particularly as a young man who had just traveled over the road I wished to go, represented it as almost impassable."

The hapless traveler pried the buggy out with a rail and went on. He "jogged on slowly, and after jumping over the sloughs and wading through bogs in order to relieve the horse," he arrived at Elk Heart Grove, only nine miles from Springfield, at dusk.

Conkling slept in an inn at Elk Heart Grove, and "about seven next morning I started again, crossed an eight mile prairie tolerably well— passed through a narrow strip of timber and came upon another prairie which is generally impassable in the Spring by the usual route." So he took "a circuitous road a short distance from the timber and parallel to it, on a ridge of land and found it very fine." When the road washed out he "struck into the prairie, starting up deer and prairie hens and shaking gopher settlements." At noon he stopped at a log cabin to rest and feed his horse, and there dined on corndodger, eggs, and ham. By five o'clock he had arrived at Waynesville, fifteen miles from Bloomington as the crow flies. And he must have wished he were a crow, for the swollen Kickapoo River lay between him and his destination, a nightmare of "miserable roads, deep slough, execrable bridges, swollen streams, drenching rains, high winds. . . ."

Sometime that tempestuous Easter Sunday, Abraham Lincoln in his buggy had passed him. That night Conkling slept in a farmhouse somewhere below the river; it would take him most of the next day, "jumping fences and wading mudholes—fine sport," before reaching Bloomington near three o'clock in the afternoon of the seventeenth, Easter Monday.

James Conkling wrote to his wife that upon arriving in Bloomington he had "found Lincoln desperately homesick and turning his head frequently toward the south."

Lincoln had so many good friends in Bloomington, including David Davis and Jesse Fell, he once considered moving there himself. He was welcome to stay in any of their homes when he was attending the McLean court on the square, and the lawyers cleared workspace for him in the brick office building nearby on North Main and East Front Street. He was as much at home here as he could be anywhere save Springfield. But he missed his wife and their little room at the Globe Tavern sorely.

A HOME AT LAST

L INCOLN AND SPEED had talked of naming their sons for each other. He had written to Speed in early spring, during that cold equinox: "About the prospect of your having a namesake at our house can't say, exactly yet." Speed must have inquired, in order to have prompted this imprecise confirmation. Lincoln did not know the sex of his unborn child; furthermore he and Mary had not yet agreed to share the news even with their dearest friends. But Joshua Speed could read between the lines. He was in touch with William Butler and his wife, who did know.

In mid-May, after Butler wrote to Speed that a baby was expected, Speed informed Lincoln, prompting this droll response: "In relation to the 'coming events' about which Butler wrote you, I had not *heard* one word before I got your letter; but I have so much confidence in the judgment of a Butler on such a subject, that I incline to think there may be some reality in it. What *day* does Butler appoint? By the way, how do 'events' of the same sort come on in your family? Are you possessing houses and lands, and oxen and asses, and men-servants and maid-servants, and begetting sons and daughters?" Joshua and Fanny were to have all of these blessings except sons and daughters, so Lincoln would get no namesake of the Speeds. Perhaps this was one reason no son of the Lincolns would be named Joshua, although four times the opportunity offered. In any case, for the child on the way, there was no more talk of naming him Joshua. The rest of this long letter of May 18 is taken up with business concerns and a surprising report on "our congress matter here."

Lincoln writes, "You were right in supposing I would support the nominee. Neither Baker nor I, however, is the man; but *Hardin.* So far as I can judge from present appearances, we shall have no split or trouble about the matter; all will be harmony." Hardin had managed to trump the Sangamon County Whigs, and the best Lincoln could do was engineer an accord whereby he would work with Hardin and Baker; they would campaign for one another with the understanding they would "take turns" running for Congress.

Lincoln concludes his letter with a cordial invitation for the Speeds to visit them since "poverty, and the necessity of attending to business, those 'coming events' " would make it impossible for them to go to Kentucky. Molly leaned over his shoulder as he wrote in the twilight, asking to be remembered. "Mary joins in sending love to your Fanny and you. Yours as ever, A. Lincoln."

Indeed they were poor. As hard as Lincoln worked at the law, he was not yet making enough money to pay off his old debts and move into a new house. The Speeds did not visit them for many years.

THE GLOBE TAVERN, like many boardinghouses the world over, was a close community of families and individuals compelled to tolerate and learn to appreciate one another as needs arose and opportunities offered.

Albert Bledsoe was a curious, brilliant man of many talents. He had been a soldier, a minister, and a lawyer; later he became a noted professor of mathematics. He was short of stature, with thinning hair grown long over his ears, so blond it was almost white. His wide-set blue eyes seemed to lack eyelashes. His wife, Harriet, was so good-natured that somehow she managed to be a good companion to the volatile Mary, even though— according to Harriet's daughter, Sophie—her mother "never cared personally for Mrs. Lincoln." Sophie herself, at six years old, was tiny but resourceful, a lively and intelligent sprite.

The Bledsoes made good company at dinner, but they also exerted a strange influence over the other residents of the Globe. There was Mrs. Beck, the landlady, and a widow now only known as "Mrs. B——," an expert pianist who boarded at the Globe. Often in the evenings they enjoyed the sound of Mrs. B—— at the keyboard "in another story of the house and some distance away, but near enough for her playing to be heard" in the parlor while folks were talking.

Mrs. B—— had a nervous tic that made her blink and squint in an unseemly manner (tic douloureux). In those days, in fashionable parlors in Paris, London, New York, and Boston, hypnotism (known until 1842 as mesmerism and animal magnetism) was all the rage. And Albert Bledsoe "was found to have uncommon power in this line." Sophie recalled that her father was able to relieve Mrs. B——, the pianist, of her suffering by inducing trances through eye fatigue, waving a spoon or a flashing watch before her face. "Mr. Lincoln was profoundly interested in these experiments." Both of the Lincolns were curious about occult and spiritual phenomena; both were quite suggestible, if not credulous, when it came to such things. Perhaps Bledsoe, with the spin and glitter of a gold watch, might cure Molly of her infernal headaches.

As Hamlet tells his friend, "There are more things in heaven and earth, Horatio, / Than are dreamt of in your philosophy." The uncanny talent of Albert Bledsoe—a man with boundless confidence in his abilities—was not unlike the magic of orators like Daniel Webster and Henry Clay, or the authority of certain statesmen such as Thomas Jefferson, Andrew Jackson, and the living legend John Quincy Adams. All of them employed the power of will to change the world.

If an act of will could transport the pregnant woman out of that noisy tavern where the bell on the roof rang day and night to announce the arrival of strangers with their muddy boots and coarse manners—if Mary Lincoln could have any influence upon their circumstances—she would not shrink from exercising it. She was willful and bold, no ordinary woman who would passively follow her husband wherever he led her.

She certainly had Mr. Lincoln's attention—his affection as well as his sense of duty as a provider. During the rest of that spring and summer during Mary's confinement, Lincoln stayed close to home, traveling only to nearby Taylorville on May 22 for a one-day term of the Christian County Circuit Court, and to a two-day term at Petersburg only a few hours north on June 5. On July 15, he trotted over firm roads to Hillsboro on a hot Saturday morning to give a stump speech for the Whig congressional ticket. But mostly Mr. Lincoln stayed nearby. Mary also had the support of her father, Robert Smith Todd, a merchant, banker, and lawyer, a man of robust passions and a sly Southern ruthlessness in looking out for his own.

The oil portrait of Robert Todd that hung in the great house on West Main Street in Lexington—the home Mary had left to come north—shows a round, handsome face that looks out from the dark oval background, with wide-set eyes, a broad, well-formed nose, and a sensual mouth, determined yet flickering with humor. Mary resembled him physically, and somewhat in her passionate temperament.

By the age of fifty, Todd had fathered fifteen children by two wives, and of the first brood—born to Elizabeth Parker—the lively, feisty Mary, his third daughter, was his favorite. Devastated by her mother's death, seven-year-old Mary did not take to her stepmother, Elizabeth Humphreys, when her father remarried only months later. Naturally drawn to her handsome father, she sought his attention and got it. She distinguished herself from her pretty sisters—Elizabeth, Frances Jane, and Ann Marie—by her uncommon scholarship, intellect, and eventually her interest in Whig politics. Few girls of her generation could have engaged their fathers in a discussion of Henry Clay's prospects for the presidency, or the tariff, or a national bank.

Mary left home to follow her sisters to Springfield not because of love lost between her and her father, but because her stepmother, "Betsy" Humphreys (who had five of her own babies), was out of patience with her headstrong stepdaughter. Yet Mary had found a constant place in her father's affections, and over the years she would not let him forget her. None of the Springfield Todds held Abraham Lincoln in such high esteem as did Robert Todd of Lexington, who said, "I only hope that Mary will make as good a wife as she has a husband."

The Lincolns were in touch with Robert Todd in early June. He engaged his son-in-law to sue a Mr. Ware, in order "to compel defendant to accept Bank of Illinois money in payment of notes." Ware wanted harder cash to pay off a debt, and Todd preferred to pay in the less stable bank-notes. It was the first time Robert Todd had hired Lincoln. While he had not met his son-in-law, Robert had confidence in Lincoln's legal skill, as well as reliable knowledge that his daughter was in straitened circumstances. A banking action would send much-appreciated funds in his daughter's direction.

Perhaps it was in June, two months before the child was due, that the expectant parents took up the happy subject of the naming. If it were a girl, it would please Lincoln to name her Nancy after his natural mother, who died of milk sickness at thirty-eight, when he was nine; or Sarah, the name of his beloved sister, who had died in childbirth when he was nineteen. His stepmother, Sarah Bush, whom he adored, was still living, and she would be delighted with the honor of having a Lincoln namesake.

As for Mary, there was hardly a woman in her family upon whom it would please her as much as it would the Lincoln family to bestow this honor. So it would make sense, if the baby were a girl, for Mr. Lincoln to do the naming. If it were a boy, the shrewd daughter of the wealthy Robert Todd knew she would be a fool to name the baby anything other than Robert Todd Lincoln.

She liked Joshua Speed very well, and his was a proud biblical moniker, but there was more at stake here than honoring her husband's friendship or his friend's vanity. Surely they shared this feeling. One day Lincoln would remark that he had nothing to do with the naming of his children, but this was an evasion, a public pose, part of a larger disclaimer that Mary held dominion over the home while he dealt with the demands of the greater world. It was not so simple. The naming of a child and the acceptance or rejection of a political or career opportunity were—from the beginning—decisions the couple usually made together.

ON TUESDAY, THE first of August, 1843, there was a great bustling and rushing to and fro of women—Mrs. Beck and Mrs. Bledsoe and the midwife—in the Globe Tavern, as Mary Lincoln's water broke, and her cries could be heard from the window of her room. This nativity was of more than usual interest to gossips in the small town, who had been counting, buzzing, and ciphering (three days less than nine months!) since the hasty wedding, and who wondered why the poor relation of two wealthy sisters living nearby had not been invited at last into one home or the other to have her baby, instead of moaning and screaming through labor in a common hostelry while her husband paced in the parlor below stairs. For all the comfort and privacy she had there, Mary Lincoln might as well have been laboring in a manger.

The pain would have been about the same anywhere, and the outcome could not have been happier. Mrs. Lincoln gave birth to a healthy boy without any injury to herself, and promptly named him Robert Todd. Mr. Lincoln, his heart pounding, his eyes welling with emotion, entered the little room as soon as the women would let him. Mary would never forget the sight of her "darling husband . . . bending over me, with such love and tenderness," or the joy of seeing the baby at her breast. Robert Todd Lincoln was strong-limbed and hearty, with a cry that could be heard throughout the Globe Tavern, to the dismay of the other boarders. The baby was perfect except that his left eye turned inward, a minor defect in the larger scheme of things, in an era when so many infants and mothers died in childbirth.

Lincoln remained close to home, doting on mother and son during the hot days of August, helping "Mother" as soon as he could get away from work. They could not afford a maidservant for the nursing mother, but Harriet Bledsoe "went every day to her room in the hotel, washed and dressed the baby," according to Sophie Bledsoe, "and made the mother comfortable and the room tidy, for several weeks, till Mrs. Lincoln was able to do these things for herself."

Mary was grateful for these attentions because on September 6 her husband must be off again on the circuit, traveling sixty miles north to Tremont, leaving her alone with that strong-lunged infant in the less and less hospitable, clamorous tavern. This time he would be working in Hanover, Bloomington, Clinton, Urbana, Charleston, and Danville for the next two months. In mid-October he would return briefly to see his wife and child, and to get his buggy repaired at Obed Lewis's carriage shop.

The young mother was so desperate for rest that if she could find no other help she would have the precocious Sophie mind the baby. "I was very fond of babies," Sophie recalled, "and I remember well how I used to lug this rather large baby about to my great delight, often dragging him through a hole in the fence between the tavern grounds and an adjacent empty lot, and laying him down in the high grass, where he contentedly lay awake or asleep, as the case might be." Sophie later had cause to wonder "how Mrs. Lincoln could have trusted a particularly small six-year-old with this charge."

In the autumn, when the roads were packed firm, Robert Todd traveled up from Kentucky to visit his four Springfield daughters and their husbands and six grandchildren. He was particularly eager to meet his new son-in-law, Abraham Lincoln, about whom he had heard and read so much, and the baby boy, the only one of his grandchildren that had been named for him.

The reunion of Robert Todd with his favorite daughter was a happy one for all, despite the humble setting of the Globe Tavern. Dressed in their Sunday best, the family must have made a proud and affecting impression upon the Kentucky banker. "May God bless and protect my little namesake," said the grandfather. Knowing how providence works in the real world, the kindly gentleman pressed a twenty-dollar gold piece into Mary's hand. With tact, persistence, and a sense of tradition, the Kentucky gentleman addressed his daughter and her deferential husband in the low-ceilinged bedroom of the tavern.

Mary's father insisted on helping them. While Mary welcomed his help (indeed had solicited it indirectly by naming her firstborn Robert Todd), her husband was a proud and capable man. Lincoln had not married this woman for a dowry, and in fact he had married her over the objections of every Todd in Springfield. Even now he was laboring under the spurious charge that he had married a Todd for the good it might do his career—when Ninian Edwards did not turn a finger to help him in any way. What would people think if they knew of Robert Todd's offer now to advance his daughter $120 per year until Mr. Lincoln was making enough money to support a Todd lady in the manner to which she had been born? She could not refuse. And soon after this, the gentleman banker deeded eighty acres of land to the Lincolns, a few miles southwest of town, which provided a tidy income for them until long after they needed it.

Mr. Lincoln was earning about $1,200 per year: $400 went to the landlady for room and board, some $250 to Irwin & Company for goods; it cost another $100 per year to keep the horse fed and shod and the buggy in good repair. No one knows how much money he was sending home to his family, how much he spent on room and board when he was on the road, the cost of blue mass pills or other medicines, or exactly how much was going to pay off the New Salem debt.

The money his father-in-law granted would have two immediate effects, and others more subtle and far-reaching. First, it would enable Mary to hire a maid to help her when Mr. Lincoln was out of town. Second, it would permit them to move out of the Globe Tavern. There were more indirect results of these cash infusions, which it would have been ungracious for Lincoln to refuse. Todd's money altered the balance of power between husband and wife, and her relations with her sisters. Insofar as Lincoln's pride could suffer such charity (for he wished to make their living on his own), he appreciated that Robert Todd was giving the money to his daughter for her use, not to him. But now she had a stronger voice in family expenditures, from yard goods to lending money to needy relatives. Mr. Lincoln would never be able to say to her that he had "made it" entirely on his own. As for her sisters, Elizabeth, Frances, and Anne, none had ever received such largesse from their father. None had needed it, which hardly justified their condescension to Mary, who must have seen her father's gifts as an affirmation of her worth, or perhaps reparation for her sisters' neglect.

Before Lincoln departed on Sunday, October 15, for Charleston and the fall term of the Coles County Court, Mrs. Lincoln had hired a maid-servant and sent her to buy herself a pair of shoes for a dollar at Robert Irwin's store. On Friday the twentieth, Mary stepped out on her own in a day dress, greeting the passersby on Adams street (*How's the baby, Mrs. Lincoln!*), turning north on Fifth and Washington, where Lincoln had once lived above Speed's store. That general store at the southeast corner had been purchased by Robert Irwin & Co. Irwin sold everything from leghorn straw hats, mittens, and children's socks to combs and mirrors, whalebones, and corset lace. They had every kind of yard goods: calico, tweed, cambric, beaver cloth, muslin, flannel, silk, and cassimere, a fancy twilled wool.

Now Mary entered Irwin's store and beheld all these treasures, and the barrels of tea leaves and coffee beans and nails, sacks of feathers, a bucket of flowers, a cluster of umbrellas, a pair of brass candlesticks—and there on top of a dress dummy, a pretty bonnet. For once she might have bought what she pleased with the bright gold in her fist. *What can we do for you, Mrs. Lincoln?*

She chose carefully: two and a quarter yards of checked gingham, six yards of calico, a few wooden buttons, a paper of tacks, and a pair of black lamb's wool hose. The hose, at seventy-five cents a pair, were something of an extravagance, but she wanted them for the coming winter. She paid Irwin the total, $2.31, and left the store pleased with her first purchases there and looking forward to what she might buy there in the future. The Neapolitan bonnet? The parasol? The kid slippers? The brass candle-sticks?

They would move out of the Globe Tavern before December, and on January 16, 1844, they would sign a contract to purchase their own home.

For a few months they rented a three-room cottage around the corner from the Globe, on the east side of Fourth Street, between Adams and Monroe. The two main rooms fronted Fourth Street and were built out to the sidewalk, so visitors stepped right from the unpaved street to the front door. In the back there was a kitchen ell where Mary could begin to learn to cook. This looked out onto a garden that had only started to bloom when at last they moved to their own home at the south edge of town in April of 1844.

They had much to be thankful for: a healthy child, Lincoln's thriving law practice, and the generosity of Robert Todd, which had released them from the cramped quarters of the Globe Tavern and allowed such comforts as occasional maidservants, cut flowers, and three yards each of beaver cloth and cassimere wool to make the lawyer a new suit for $25.56.

She missed him on Easter Sunday, April 7, the second Easter since their wedding that they had been apart. He was away in Peoria, where he had detoured while riding the Tazewell circuit in order to give a political speech to the Clay Club on the evening of April 6. His career as an attorney ran together with his political ambitions. As his friend David Davis wrote that week: "Politics rage hereabouts. . . . The first day of every court is occupied with political speaking, usually by an elector on each side of politics, each person generally taking some three or four hours. . . . Lincoln is the best stump speaker in the State."

She understood that his absence on Easter morning had as much to do with politics as with moneymaking. The year before, when John Hardin secured the Whig party's nomination for Congress at the Pekin convention, Lincoln had masterminded what was later called the "Pekin Agreement" to assure party unity. Hardin, Baker, and Lincoln agreed as follows: Baker and Lincoln would back Hardin's candidacy and stump for him in 1844; when Hardin's term was up, he and Lincoln would support Baker in 1846; and in 1848 it would be Abraham Lincoln's turn to go to Washington. "Turn about is fair play," Lincoln argued. If the Whigs campaigned as a unit, they would always defeat the Democrats in Central Illinois.

So Lincoln's barnstorming for Whig candidates and principles during the next three years was not purely altruistic and unselfish. He was setting a good example for Baker and Hardin, who must, in their turn, deliver him to Washington as the Whig representative in Congress.

By April 1844, the Lincolns had much to look forward to: a seat for Lincoln in the Thirtieth U.S. Congress, an honor for him, and for her an eminence beyond anything her sisters had achieved. The Pekin Agreement was no secret in the community. By April of 1844, Abraham Lincoln, Edward Baker, and John Hardin were a team pulling in harness.

• • •

MARY LINCOLN STOOD in the mud of Eighth Street surveying the brown cottage that was soon to become their home. The front of the house measured about forty feet across, framing four louver-shuttered windows, two on either side of the stately front door of walnut wood, with its sidelights, inset within the simple Greek Revival porch. Three red-brick chimneys rose out of the pitched roof, one on each end coming from the fireplaces in the parlor and the sitting room, and one from the kitchen in the rear.

She looked up at the western elevation, which began seven or eight steps above the rutted street. The house was not grand, but the parlor rooms on either side of the little stair hall were spacious, and the three bedrooms under the pitched roof were adequate for husband, wife, baby, and maidservant. The house was almost new, and like the new owners, had bright prospects. It would grow with them.

The man who built the house in 1839 and sold it to them in 1844 was the Reverend Charles Dresser, who had married them. His family had outgrown the cottage, and now he was pleased to convey to Lincoln and his wife "a clear title in fee simple" to the house, barn, and outbuildings, on an eighth of an acre of grounds at the south edge of town. That winter, as she sat in the rented cottage on Fourth Street sewing clothing or window curtains, her foot rocking the cradle where the baby slept, Mary Lincoln dreamed of the new house and the comfortable home she would make for them there when it was finally theirs.

She would begin with a few lamps in the parlor and the sitting room, knowing that Mr. Lincoln sometimes came home late, wanting a light by which to read and eat and converse with her at night. Astral oil lamps were preferable to candles, casting a steadier light, and they did not spatter grease as tallow candles did. If she could not afford the finest oil at first, the clear and colorless spermaceti whale oil, then lard was a good substitute, cheap and plentiful in Springfield. She knew how to melt it in a pitcher each morning and keep it fresh.

On April 16, she purchased the lamps in Irwin's store. Keeping them clean and fueled was a homemaker's ritual described in detail by the domestic economist Catherine Beecher, requiring "so much attention and discretion, that many ladies choose to do this work themselves rather than trust it with domestics." One needed a tray to hold all the implements: a lamp-filler with a small upturned spout, a ball of wickyarn in a basket, a lamp-trimmer, sharp scissors, a broad-mouthed bottle of pearlash for cleansing the vessels and oil cans, soft cloths and towels to wipe them. "Wash the shade of an astral lamp, once a week, and the glass chimney oftener. Take the lamp to pieces, and cleanse it, once a month," Mrs. Beecher advised. To raise the wick, turn it to the right; to lower, turn to the left. After it has once been used, trim it; and in lighting it, raise to the proper height or it will either smoke or form a crust. Dipping the wick in vinegar makes it burn the clearer. Light the lamp with a strip of rolled paper kept on the mantelpiece.

Lincoln admired the sound carpentry of the new home, the sturdy oak that made the frame and floorboards, the hand-split hickory laths, the rich black walnut of the window frames. There was plenty of black walnut wood in the doors, door frames, and weatherboarding, and the carpenters had used handmade wooden pegs instead of nails that rust. The house was built to last. Out back, twenty yards east, was the barn where he would keep his horse and cow, and next to that the slant-roofed privy with three seats.

When the violet sheep sorrel and Sangamon phlox were blooming on roadsides in the bright May light, the family moved the five blocks from Fourth and Monroe, taking along their clothing and belongings. It took many trips in the buggy. Robert Lincoln, now called "Bobbie," nine months old, was at his mother's breast for comfort. She would hand him over to a nurse or a friend when time came to show a drayman where to put a bed, chair, or table. At first they had only the bare essentials that Lincoln could afford: a bedstead, a cot, a drop-leaf table of walnut, a few rush-bottom chairs, the bed linens and counterpanes. "Mother" must supply the rest of the furnishings over time—though lawyers were known to accept tables, chairs, and copper kettles when cash fees were not forthcoming. Piece by piece she acquired the utensils for cooking and baking, and then carpets and curtains, glasses and crockery. He no longer called her Molly—only "Mother" and sometimes, playfully, "Puss." She called him "Father" at home and in private—otherwise, it was Mr. Lincoln.

She climbed the stairs with clean sheets and blankets folded over her arm to make up their bed in the north bedroom under the eaves. Like maintaining the astral lamps, this task was not to be left to the help. She draped the bedding on a chair at the foot of the bed and opened the little windows on either side of the brick chimney. When the bed was well aired, Mary shook the feathers from each corner to the middle, shook the mattress well, and turned it over. Pushing the feathers into place, she made the head higher than the foot, the sides even and as high as the middle. She put down the bolster and the undersheet, tucking it in neatly all around. She put on the pillows, then spread the upper sheet, wrong side up to face the blankets, marked end at the head. Then she laid down the cotton comforter, tucking it in all around and turning down the upper sheet at the head, so the pillows showed. The pillowcases were so smooth and bright outside the cover. She drew her hand along the side of the pillows and tenderly smoothed and shaped them.

Now the bed was ready for her husband, for a night's sleep or an hour of lovemaking.

Soon the maid's bedroom on the east side of the house over the kitchen must be fitted out like theirs, with a washstand, pitcher and bowl, and washbucket under the stand to receive slops. It needed only a narrow bed and a little towel horse by the washstand. In the summer, Harriet Hanks, eighteen, was coming from Coles County to stay with them—to help with the chores and attend the Springfield Female Seminary, a finishing school.

Until Bobbie was born, Mary Lincoln had always lived where there were servants to do the cooking, laundry, housecleaning, and child care. The new house with all its comforts came with burdens she was ill prepared to shoulder alone, so the Lincolns soon began to look for a live-in maid. In those days when honest and able-bodied young women were soon betrothed, such help was hard to find and costly. So when Harriet Hanks, a distant cousin of Lincoln's, showed an interest in coming to Springfield from Coles County to study and improve herself, the Lincolns began to discuss an accommodation that would be beneficial to all.

Harriet was a distant blood relative, and the Hanks connection to the Lincolns evokes a tangle of family history. She was the fourth of seven children born to Dennis Hanks—Lincoln's mother's cousin—and Sarah Johnston, Lincoln's stepsister. Sarah Johnston was the daughter of Sarah Bush; in 1818 Sarah Bush had become the second wife of Thomas Lincoln (Abraham's father), and Abraham Lincoln's stepmother. Lincoln was ten years younger than Dennis Hanks, who had come to live with him in 1818, after Lincoln's mother and Dennis's foster parents died of milk sickness. The boys grew up like brothers in southern Indiana, and Lincoln remained loyal to Hanks all his life.

Now Dennis, a poor, semiliterate cobbler in Charleston, and his wife, Sarah, had too many mouths to feed, and Mrs. Lincoln needed help. By letter, the families reached an agreement that was incompletely understood or narrowly appreciated by the young women. The Lincolns would provide room and board for Harriet and pay her tuition at Reverend Brooks's finishing school; in return, Harriet Hanks was to serve as a housemaid and babysitter. There ought to have been a detailed contract, for it was a situation fraught with possibilities of high hopes and dashed expectations on both sides.

Harriet considered the invitation to live with her relatives in their new home as a golden opportunity. It delivered her from the squalor of the crowded Hanks homestead so she might begin life anew among people of education and refinement in the social mecca of Springfield, where women like Mary Todd had gone to find husbands.

She failed to take into account Mrs. Lincoln's class consciousness and the young mother's current state of mind, which was understandably self-absorbed. Only a few months earlier, Mrs. Lincoln, with her father's help, had escaped the embarrassment of living in a boardinghouse. Now that Mrs. Lincoln at last had arrived in a freestanding house, she meant to transform it into a home fit for a future congressman. She wanted a maid-servant, not a social-climbing poor relation in the parlor. She was not about to treat this milkmaid as an equal. She simply could not. Harriet Hanks would have to earn her board and keep; she would have to follow orders. For her husband's sake, Mary Lincoln would be civil to the girl if she could not be kind.

Cases on the circuit and Whig meetings took Lincoln away to Petersburg on June 3 and 4, and to Peoria on June 19, but for most of that month he was practicing law in Springfield and helping his wife set up housekeeping—hauling furniture, chopping wood for the coming winter, and hanging pictures. In mid-July he was gone for a full week to the statewide Whig convention in Vandalia, some five thousand men and one thousand women backing Henry Clay for president. Lincoln was a principal speaker there, as were Albert Bledsoe and Simeon Francis. Lincoln left Springfield on July 15 with his wife's blessing. While he was taking further steps upon the road to the nation's capital, she was putting the house in order for the celebration of Bobbie's first birthday on August 1. She certainly needed help.

One of Harriet's first tasks for the mistress was going uptown to Irwin's store in early July to pick up thirty yards of calico cloth. The material, which came in two bolts, was heavy, so she may have made more than one trip up Seventh Street. The calico was for curtains to cover the eight double-hung sash windows at the front and sides of the house, four parlor windows, and four looking out of the sitting room, which counterbalanced the parlor on the opposite side of the stair hall.

There was much that Mary Lincoln had still to learn about "domestic economy," as housekeeping was called in the women's manuals of the time. Eliza Leslie's *Lady's House Book* (which Mrs. Lincoln would soon own) drew heavily upon Catherine Beecher's best-selling *Treatise on Domestic Economy*, whose instructions on cleaning, sewing, and cooking were known in 1844 by word of mouth even to wives who had not actually read the book.

Mary Lincoln had grown up in a Kentucky mansion with slaves who did the hard work of boiling and washboarding soiled clothing and bedsheets; ironing men's shirts; making soap, lye, and candles; and baking bread and preparing meals. The servants did this work in spaces separate from family life, so it might seem virtually invisible to most children. Mary probably knew less about firing the kitchen stove and scouring kettles than did Harriet Hanks, who grew up poor.

Sewing was a different matter altogether. Needlework and dressmaking were considered suitable occupations for young ladies, and Mrs. Lincoln had become a proficient seamstress. This would be one of the chief means by which she could practice domestic economy while expressing her affection for her husband—making curtains to keep out the cold, sheets to keep them warm, and shirts he would be proud to wear in any courtroom on the Eighth Circuit or in speaking before a crowd of six thousand in Vandalia, as he did at the Whig convention on July 19, 1844.

Mary Lincoln laid the baby in the cradle. She and Harriet Hanks unrolled the bolts of calico on the floor of the parlor and measured the lengths with a yardstick to make sure they had gotten what they had paid for, $2.40 worth of good fresh calico all of a piece, with a well-marked pattern of curves. She scored the cloth with chalk. And then, with the largest of three sets of scissors she kept in a drawer, she began cutting.

To Mary, during that year, the girl was almost more trouble than she was worth, being neither a common servant nor a houseguest. Harriet Hanks was a student with social ambitions who became, during Mr. Lincoln's long absences in 1845, Mrs. Lincoln's ward. It was the older woman's responsibility to see to it that the teenager attended to her household chores and studies and stayed out of trouble. When she made friends among the young folk of Springfield, she must have some degree of liberty; and insofar as men found her attractive, so much greater would be the burden on her guardians.

Married only a year and a half, Mary and Abraham Lincoln found themselves sharing their modest new home with a nubile woman who sat down to dine with them and made herself at home in the parlor and the sitting room. They forfeited precious privacy. Her status as a relation (however distant) made it unthinkable that she could be restricted to the kitchen and the maid's room upstairs. It is a considerable adjustment for a husband and wife to make room in their lives for a child, however much they desire it. Adding Harriet Hanks to the family mix so soon after Robert's birth, when Mary was working so hard to transform the plain cottage into a respectable home, created an additional tension.

Harriet adored Mr. Lincoln, and as much as she loved and admired her gentle benefactor, she resented his wife. When asked about Mrs. Lincoln years later, Harriet replied, "[I] would rather *Say nothing* about his Wife, as I Could Say but little in her *favor* I Conclude it best to Say nothing, and I presume it is not really necessary that I Should." She would anyway, at length, in a letter to William Herndon in 1866. If Mary ever expressed an opinion of Harriet, it is not recorded. Let it suffice to say that the women got along with each other for most of a year and a half during which Mrs. Lincoln had far more to give Harriet than Harriet was ever to repay. If the situation had proved intolerable, she would have hurried back to Coles County.

From 1844 to 1845, Harriet got to observe Abraham Lincoln at home in his shirtsleeves. In fact, one day when people came to call, Mr. Lincoln answered the door and "in shirt sleeves invited visitors in and stated that he would 'trot the women folks out' [meaning Mary and Harriet]" as if they had been two fillies, chuckling as he did at the barnyard metaphor. Mrs. Lincoln failed to see the humor in it. And she did not like the way Lincoln would answer his own door at any hour with or without his coat, vest, or shoes. "This made Mrs. Lincoln mad," Harriet recalled, for "Abraham's wife was high strung" at that time, what with her concerns about house-keeping and Mr. Lincoln's manners and her boy's crossed eye.

After the last day of the summer term of the circuit court there in Springfield, and just before the election that would send Baker to Congress, the baby would be one year old. On August 1, there would be a party to which the Todd family members would be invited: the Wallaces, the Edwardses, and Mary's uncle, Dr. John Todd, who lived in the finest house in Springfield, a mansion over on Washington Street. He had entertained them the year before when his brother Robert Todd came to celebrate the birth of his namesake. Now the Lincolns would be having a party for the first time in their new home. But, as Harriet Hanks recalled, Mrs. Lincoln conspicuously disinvited a daughter of Dr. Todd "because the cousin had intimated that Robert L. who was a baby was a sweet child but not good looking."

Harriet and the Lincolns watched the toddler take his first shaky steps on the oaken floor in that house and heard him speak his first words sometime that winter. He was precocious, "one of the little rare-ripe sort, that are smarter at about five than ever after," as his father wryly remarked.

Sometime before Robert turned two, his father thought the boy was smart enough to have his manners corrected. Maybe Bobbie had pulled the cat's tail or the tablecloth, or threatened to overturn a lamp or run into the fireplace. But on that day, Harriet Hanks remembered, "he undertook to correct his child and his wife was determined that he should not, and attempted to take it from him . . . but in this she failed . . . She then tried tongue lashing but met with the same fate, for Mr. Lincoln corrected his Child as a Father ought to do, in the face of his Wife's anger and that too without even Changing his Countenance, or making any reply to his wife."

Because the Lincolns eventually became notoriously indulgent parents—chided and ridiculed for failing to discipline their children—Hanks's story is of great interest. Much later, explaining his leniency, Lincoln would say that "love is the chain whereby to bind a child to its parents." But it may well be that Lincoln, after an early effort to force his children to mind their manners, soon realized he was fighting a losing battle. With no control over domestic matters when he was traveling, he would have to defer to his wife's laissez-faire parenting while he concentrated on his career.

. . .

NOW THAT HE was able to turn his full attention to the law, Lincoln was making good money, and his wife could afford the furniture, carpets, and dishes to make the house a comfortable home. They had begun to discuss building improvements, adding a master bedroom to the first floor beyond the parlor, and a bedroom/nursery with a new fireplace. They would also build a back staircase from the hired girl's room to the kitchen as soon as possible, in order to preserve their privacy.

Mr. Lincoln's smooth advancement in his profession had come with a wrinkle or two that made his wife uncomfortable. As political rivalry developed between Lincoln and Stephen Logan—both wanted to run for Congress—Lincoln slowly disengaged himself from his old law partner. The separation appeared amicable enough, as Logan wished to make room in the firm for his son David, and the partners remained colleagues and good friends. In any case, Mary was not so much troubled that Lincoln was leaving Logan (to whom he had been the "junior" partner) as she was with his new partner, a twenty-six-year-old fledgling lawyer named William Henry Herndon.

She never liked him. "Billy" Herndon had been a clerk in Joshua Speed's store in 1837 and roomed above it with Speed and Lincoln and Mr. Beverly Powell. Herndon stood five foot nine, with black hair and dark, close-set eyes. At a ball in 1839, the twenty-year-old Herndon had danced with the pretty Mary Todd, and made the mistake of offering her the overwrought compliment that "she seemed to glide through the waltz with the ease of a serpent." To this the young lady icily replied: "Mr. Herndon, comparison to a serpent is rather severe irony, especially to a newcomer." And she turned her back on him.

Relations between the two never improved much after that. Herndon liked pretty women, yet they too easily wounded his vanity. Mary did not like Herndon's style of dress: his ruffled shirts, his tall silk hats, his patent leather shoes. He was a big talker, issuing a flow of chatter on all topics ancient and contemporary, from Kant to Clay, from Emerson to Whig politics, from sex and mesmerism to phrenology. Herndon's father had kept a saloon. Billy took spirits, and Mary heard that sometimes he drank too much. In 1840, he had married Mary Maxcy, a pretty girl from a humble family, daughter of the town marshal.

Regardless of Mary Lincoln's feelings about Herndon, he had become a good friend to Lincoln, and he had been reading law in the Logan and Lincoln office for a year and a half. In December, Herndon was admitted to the bar, and on March 18, 1845, the week before Easter, Lincoln and Herndon appeared as partners in their first case, a debt action in circuit court. Lincoln was now so widely respected that he might have chosen a more experienced lawyer for his partner, someone like Orville H. Browning or Albert Bledsoe. But he picked Herndon because he liked him. Despite Mary's objections, he explained that he believed Herndon "had a system and would keep things in order."

Easter came early that year, March 23, 1845, while the Sangamon Circuit Court was still in session, and Mary was pleased to have her husband at home for the first time on that holiday. Henceforth, he would make a point of it. Easter was one day people could expect to see the Lincolns in the pew together in the new Presbyterian church, a beautiful brick building on the corner of Third and Washington streets.

The Judas trees had shed their purple blossoms weeks before, and now the wild plums and the masses of flowers on the crab apple trees were strewing their petals on the fresh grass. The cornfields had been plowed and planted. The road to and from Petersburg, where Lincoln attended the circuit court with Herndon and Baker, was "tolerable, fine where much travelled" in June.

Mr. Lincoln came through the door at twilight when supper had been on the stove for some time. He hung his coat on a hook in the stair hall. The little boy, almost two years old now, clung to his knees, and Father lifted him up on his shoulder. "One of his greatest pleasures," Hanks remembered, "was that of nursing and playing with his little boy." He embraced his wife and greeted his cousin warmly. It was past time for supper, and Mr. Lincoln had a hearty appetite in those days, so they sat right down in the kitchen, at the drop-leaf walnut table across from the fireplace. Mr. Lincoln drank cold water with his food, so the women carried water through the door that led to the backyard pump.

He sat down to eat in his shirtsleeves. In mid-June this seemed natural enough to Harriet Hanks, but it displeased Mrs. Lincoln. The "practice annoyed his wife very much . . . who by the way loved to put on *Style*." Since April, after purchasing seven yards of gingham, a yard of lawn, hooks and eyes, and whalebones for her skirts, Mary had been busy with

needle and thread. On April 13, she paid $7.50 (a tidy sum) for a Neapoli-
tan bonnet, three yards of ribbon to trim it, and a new parasol—all perhaps to make up in style what she must concede to Harriet in youth.

The women watched the man at the table. "Mr. Lincoln was what I call
a hearty eater and enjoyed a good meal of victuals as much as any one I
ever knew," his cousin recalled. "I can eat corn cakes as fast as two women
can make them," said Mr. Lincoln proudly, knowing that it took two
women, each with a hot iron skillet on the fire, to keep the hotcakes coming fast enough to serve a hungry family. Corn cakes and molasses cost little, so it was fortunate he liked them. "Mrs. Lincoln was very *economical*,"
Harriet recalled. "So much so that by some she might have been pronounced stingy." Although Harriet Hanks would not herself call her
benefactress stingy, she did remark that the "table at home was usually set
very sparingly"; more so when Lincoln was out riding the circuit—all the
more reason for Harriet to rejoice in his return.

After the dinner dishes were cleared away and washed, and the baby
was quiet in his cradle, Mr. Lincoln would read to the women in the parlor. Sometimes he sensed that Harriet or Mary, or both of them, were out
of sorts, so first he would do his best to clear the air. "He often told laugh-
able Jokes and Stories when he thought we was looking gloomy."

The women would climb the stairs first to bed because they must be
up with the chickens and the baby, while Mr. Lincoln was not, in those
days, an early riser. He lay on the floor in the light of the astral lamp his
wife had filled and trimmed for him and read the newspaper. The lamp
had a new shade she had bought just weeks before when someone had
knocked it over and shattered it. He loved the hours before midnight
when the house was silent except for the clock ticking and the wind
whistling in the chimney and owls hooting in the sycamore trees. Then he
could read the papers and think about the day's work and what he might
do in the future. John Hardin had gone to Washington, and if he and
Baker kept their word, then Lincoln would be the Whig candidate a year
from now. Following Baker, he would be elected to the U.S. Congress on
August 3, 1846, and go to Washington in December of 1847. Meanwhile he
must make money, lots of it, and pay off his debts so Mary could furnish
the house and hire a maid who was not a relation—he must do this before
politics consumed his legal career and his livelihood.

The house still had only one stairway. On her way down the curving
stairwell and out the back door to answer a call of nature, Harriet saw him

reading late at night by the light of the lamp. Passing by in her nightgown, going and returning, she saw him lying there.

The moon was full on June 19, rising near midnight. On a clear night when it shone in the windows, one could go about from room to room without a candle. Mary Lincoln lay in the bed on the broad straw matting. Waking and dozing and dreaming as the toddler nearby was fretful or still, waiting for her husband, waiting in the moonlight for tomorrow and the rest of their life, she thought some of the thoughts and dreamed some of the dreams her husband shared below. But she was always more fearful.

He extinguished the lamp and came upstairs. He took off his clothing and lay down beside her. He was always a great comfort. They made love under the eaves in the soft fragrant air of June, and soon she was pregnant again.

THE LINCOLNS' SECOND child was born on Tuesday, March 10, 1846.

Mary did not name the baby Joshua, or Anson after her husband's loyal friend Dr. Henry; she did not name him Thomas after Abraham's father, or Henry after the illustrious Henry Clay. With Mr. Lincoln's approval she named the child Edward Baker Lincoln, after the Illinois politician who had taken a seat in Congress on December 1, three months earlier. Baker had just decided to go on military leave to fight the Mexicans, and Lincoln was supposed to replace him.

The so-called Pekin Agreement of 1843 was a slippery knot that threatened to fall apart with the passage of time and the complacency of the incumbents. Hardin, Baker, and Lincoln had agreed that turnabout was fair play; but the man whose turn came last, Mr. Lincoln, would have the greatest interest in keeping the agreement alive. John Hardin, who sat first in the gilded Hall of Representatives, already had begun to challenge it when Mary was seven months pregnant.

Edward Dickinson Baker, who now occupied the seat in Congress that Lincoln was to have next, was wavering in his commitment to the pact. His military leave would muddy the waters. By the time Baker had left Springfield for Washington, in November 1845, the succession was sufficiently in doubt that Lincoln was grateful for Baker's assurance "that the track for the next congressional race was clear to me, so far as he was concerned," and that when the time came "he would say so publicly in any manner."

But when Mary found her husband and her cousin John Hardin engaged in a heated conflict over the convention system and the Pekin Agreement, it clouded her view of the future. Hardin wanted to do away with the convention system and their plan to take turns in office, and suddenly condemned these ideas as undemocratic and unfair. He wanted to return to the days when any Whig could run for office as he pleased. Lincoln was alarmed by Hardin's vacillation.

High office is intoxicating. Power corrupts, and an imbalance of it can be corrosive to the best of friendships. Hardin had told Lincoln twice, years ago, "that if Baker succeeded he would most likely hang on as long as possible," but with himself "it would be different." It *was* different with Hardin—it was far worse. "It seems," Lincoln recalled, "you *then* thought a little more favorably of 'turn about' than you seem to now."

"There is a fact as fatal to your claims as mine, which is, that neither you nor I, but *Baker* is the jockey now in the stirrups," Lincoln wrote on February 7, 1846, after Baker had served two months of his first session in the Twenty-ninth U.S. Congress, with more than a year to go. If Lincoln was going to get to Congress, he *had* to get Edward Baker not to run for reelection, by an appeal to honor or friendship or political necessity. Hardin would dutifully bow to political expedience—for Lincoln's power was considerable among the Whigs—but not if Baker renounced the Pekin Agreement.

Sometime during the winter of Mary's confinement, Edward Baker wrote a letter declining to run for Congress in the next election, thus honoring the Pekin Agreement and his friendship with the Lincolns. Much has been made of that friendship based upon evidence so slender that it pales beside the demonstrable bond that existed between Lincoln and Joshua Speed, Lincoln and Anson Henry, Lincoln and David Davis, or even Lincoln and his best man, James Matheny. Yet Mary Lincoln would bestow upon her husband's former political rival the enduring honor of naming her second son after him—in admiration of Baker's character, in gratitude for his loyalty, and as a reminder to the incumbent to stay off the track. She intended to make Baker an honorary family member.

When Lincoln was elected as the only Whig congressman from Illinois by an unprecedented majority of 1,262 votes on August 3, 1846, no one was happier than his wife. Lincoln wrote to Joshua Speed on October 22, 1846, "Being elected to Congress, though I am very grateful to our friends, for having done it, has not pleased me as much as I expected."

The effort he had made, with his wife's encouragement, since that Valentine's Day in 1843 when he told Alden Hull he wanted to be a congressman, the acrimonious infighting among the Whigs, the attacks of the Democrats (at the eleventh hour he was compelled to answer a charge of being an "open scoffer at Christianity"), had left him disillusioned, if not bitter, about the electoral process. He was learning that the joys of victory in such a battle do not equal the anguish of defeat. Success depends upon a measure of confidence. The candidate expects victory and accepts it pleasurably as his due, while losing comes as an insult. Lincoln often pretended to transcend such emotions, but his wife and his friends knew very well that humble, ambitious Abe Lincoln was only human. His ambition, said Herndon famously, was "a little engine that knew no rest."

The coming of a second child and the guarantee of a term in the U.S. Congress evoked a strong countercurrent in the affections of this middle-aged lawyer/politician. A few days after his thirty-seventh birthday, he put aside his legal work and took to writing poetry. Perhaps it was partly to amuse his wife, who was nearly nine months pregnant in the dead of winter. He could put his hand on her swollen belly and feel the infant rolling and kicking within. He spent a great deal of time at home with her that last week of February before the baby was born, and during the week before and after the delivery. They loved to read poetry to each other. He split wood and hauled water and kept the fires burning, and when she was resting he would return to writing his poems, his own act of parturition.

> *My childhood-home I see again,*
> *And gladden with the view;*
> *And still as mem'ries crowd my brain,*
> *There's sadness in it too.*
>
> *O memory! Thou mid-way world*
> *'Twixt Earth and Paradise,*
> *Where things decayed, and loved ones lost*
> *In dreamy shadows rise.*
>
> *And freed from all that's gross or vile,*
> *Seem hallowed, pure, and bright,*
> *Like scenes in some enchanted isle*
> *All bathed in liquid light.*

As distant mountains please the eye,
    When twilight chases day—
As bugle-tones, that, passing by,
    In distance die away—

As leaving some grand water-fall
    We ling'ring, list its roar,
So memory will hallow all
    We've known, but know no more.

Now twenty years have passed away,
    Since here I bid farewell
To woods, and fields, and scenes of play
    And school-mates loved so well.

Where many were, how few remain
    Of old familiar things!
But seeing these to mind again
    The lost and absent brings.

The friends I left that parting day—
    How changed, as time has sped!
Young childhood grown, strong manhood grey,
    And half of all are dead.

I hear the lone survivors tell
    How nought from death could save,
Till every sound appears a knell
    And every spot a grave.

I range the fields with pensive tread,
    And pace the hollow rooms;
And feel (companions of the dead)
    I'm living in the tombs.

Lincoln's verses, written during the last week of February 1846 and re-
vised and expanded during the spring and autumn of that eventful year, il-

luminate a turning point in his psychic life, and illustrate Wordsworth's definition of poetry as emotion recollected in tranquillity. The poem refers to his return to his childhood home in Indiana sixteen months earlier and the profound emotions he was then too busy to record. Marking the passage of time, old friends, and relations, Lincoln is also paying tribute to the boy and youth that he once was, in a past that appears "hallowed, pure, and bright."

How different he had become, this man of thirty-seven, who sat writing by lamplight while his child and his pregnant wife were asleep in the room above. He had prevailed in a world far from pure, a world full of dangers, strife, and corruption. He owned his own house; he had married a captivating woman of fine breeding; he had a promising career; and soon he would be headed for the U.S. House of Representatives.

THE BABY WAS not yet weaned, but Mary had trimmed her waistline enough so that she could agree to sit for Mr. Shepherd, the daguerreotypist. Lincoln was fascinated with every new invention and discovery—it took little persuasion for the congressman-elect to submit to Shepherd's art.

So on a bright day the tall man and his short wife, dressed in their finest, strolled together up Seventh Street toward Capitol Square. He was dressed in a black frock coat with wide lapels, a black silk waistcoat and white shirt with high wing collar, and a satin stock tied neatly at the throat. Since November, Mary had been working on her dress of pale delain striped with black silk—wing stripes on the bodice, long stripes flaring on the skirts. Over this she wore an open shoulderette of dark lace, clasped with a cameo brooch.

She watched her husband, proud of his outfit and grooming. It was a constant effort to get him to dress like a gentleman, now nagging, then praising his appearance. She observed as he sat, ramrod straight, a man with large, powerful hands and burning eyes under dark brows, his smooth face still youthful, lean but not yet sculpted with troughs and hollows—except for the deep shadows under his intense eyes. The head with its shiny hair carefully side-parted and slicked down was slightly tilted, and the ear that showed was outstanding, outsized as if from a supernatural effort to hear the thoughts of men or spirits. He would smile at her if he could, his wife looking so lovely behind the artist, but smiling was not permitted. Better to relax the smile muscles and look grave or even dour.

As Mary took her turn in the chair, she did not look dour or grave; the corners of her full mouth were upturned naturally, the wide-set blue eyes under the broad brow were bright. As Lincoln watched his "child-wife" pose for Nicholas Shepherd, he saw a pretty woman in her prime, not yet thirty, a woman in love, her plump, well-shaped hands relaxed on the delain of her homemade dress, her auburn hair side-parted, framing the face. Her thick, shoulder-length hair fell in coils, fresh from the curling iron. Mrs. Lincoln would never look more beautiful before the camera.

Nicholas H. Shepherd, fussing with his silver plates, knew that the congressman-elect and his wife were no ordinary customers. Satisfying the Lincolns would bring more clients. He did not know that he had taken the only likeness of Mary Lincoln that would capture her beauty for posterity—a peculiarly fragile, ill-fated beauty that otherwise would flourish almost exclusively in her husband's memory. Lacking this picture, we might never understand her allure. Shepherd did not know that he had taken the first picture of the future president, that eight years would pass before there came another image, sadder and wiser, or that the Lincolns would never again visit a studio to be photographed together, or ever appear in the same photograph. Mary would not allow such a sitting, fearing that the difference in their size would make them appear ridiculous.

Years later, she would say, looking at the companion daguerreotypes, "They are very precious to me, taken when we were young and so desperately in love."

JOURNEYS
AND
DISCOVERIES

THE ROAD TO WASHINGTON

WIVES WITH SMALL CHILDREN did not customarily break up housekeeping to accompany their husbands to Washington, D.C., for the sessions of Congress.

The 850-mile journey from Springfield was difficult and expensive. The salary of $2,000 per year hardly justified uprooting an entire family and transplanting them for the eight-month session of the first year, and the three-month session of the second—with a four-month recess in between. Housing in Washington was costly, and in the affordable boarding-houses, it was far from luxurious. So the decision for the Lincolns to go together was a bold one and not exactly practical. They had to rent out their new house, so there was no turning back. It was an act of faith in their partnership, and of devotion and goodwill on both sides.

Each had high expectations that were distinctly different, if complementary. Lincoln wanted to advance the Whig cause and make a name for himself on the national level as he had in Illinois. There is little indication before he left Springfield that he knew how he would go about this in Washington. He had political principles, but he had no practical agenda.

For her part, in 1847, Mary Lincoln wanted to live in a political and cultural center. For one whose knowledge of the world did not extend beyond the road from Lexington to Springfield, Washington seemed promising. She had heard of a city of stately monuments and brick mansions, green parks and wide boulevards, a center of culture, art, and refinement where she might finally discover like-minded spirits, a society that would appreciate her learning and sophistication. She believed that her manners and good breeding would contribute to the success of her less refined husband.

On their way to Washington, the Lincolns planned to visit Lexington, Kentucky, Mary's hometown. They decided to make this a long visit, so that Lincoln could get to know the Todd family. For Mary it was a chance for her to reaffirm her southern, aristocratic roots; for Lincoln it was an opportunity to study a way of life he had seen only at a distance. Lexington was a very civilized town, with beautiful mansions, fancy carriages, and a level of culture that was then rare in western America. This was the home of Transylvania University, where Anson Henry and Daniel Drake and so many other doctors and scholars had been educated. Many people referred to Lexington as "the Athens of the West."

The importance of *place* to a family is paramount, and the journey from Springfield to Washington via Lexington is symbolic. Lexington was Mary's hometown, her world. She felt more at home there than anywhere else—even Springfield. Washington, their destination, was unknown to both of them; but Mr. Lincoln had been elected to serve in the capital, not his wife.

THE JOUNCING STAGECOACH carried them a hundred miles south to St. Louis, where they stopped the night of October 27, 1847, at Scott's Hotel. There they enjoyed a long-delayed reunion with Joshua Speed and his wife, Fanny, who had made a longer journey west from Louisville. Over dinner Lincoln and Speed had many things to discuss besides old times: the war in Mexico upon which Lincoln must take his stand; the tragic death of Lincoln's friend turned rival, John J. Hardin, at the Battle of Buena Vista seven months earlier. Despite their recent disagreements, Lincoln missed his colleague Hardin, Mary's cousin. He had played a significant part not only in Lincoln's political life, but also in the drama of his courtship.

The next day they boarded a side-wheel steamboat that took them down the Mississippi River to Cairo, where the "Great Muddy" joins the clear stream of the Ohio River. Although there is no record of it, Joshua and Fanny Speed must have accompanied the Lincolns on the weeklong voyage on the Ohio back to Louisville, providing good fellowship and help with the children on their homeward journey. In a letter, Lincoln had cautioned against "allowing a friendship, such as ours, to die by degrees." After that time together on the Ohio River, the men would not see each other for many years—not until Lincoln was elected president.

From the levee on the Kentucky River at Frankfort, an easy forty-mile ride on the Lexington and Ohio Railroad took them to the town of Lexington. The Todd carriage met the train at the depot and drove the Lincolns up Main Street to the family home.

Lincoln took in the high redbrick house with its Federal-style window cornices and brackets under the eaves. It was a long, spacious home with two stories and an attic. Among the family members and slaves who gathered in the wide hall to greet the Lincolns on that chilly day in early November was a very pretty, large-eyed girl soon to turn eleven. This was Emilie Pariet Todd, Mary's half sister, the thirteenth of Robert Todd's sixteen offspring, and she was to play a significant role in the Lincolns' life in years to come. Emilie recalled the homecoming in vivid detail:

> The whole family stood near the front door with welcoming arms and, in true patriarchal style, the colored contingent filled the rear of the hall to shake hands with the long absent one and "make a miration" over the babies. Mary came in first with little Eddie, the baby, in her arms.
>
> To my mind she was lovely: clear, sparkling blue eyes, lovely smooth white skin with a fresh, faint wild-rose color in her cheeks; and glossy light brown hair, which fell in soft, short curls behind each ear.
>
> Mr. Lincoln followed her into the hall with his little son Robert Todd in his arms. He put the little fellow on the floor, and as he arose I remember thinking of Jack and the Beanstalk.
>
> After shaking hands with all the grown-ups, Mr. Lincoln turned, and, lifting me in his arms, said, "So this is little sister." I was always after that called by him "little sister." His voice and smile banished my fear of the giant.

The "giant" would charm the whole family during that restful, memorable three-week visit. He was only nine years younger than his mother-in-law, Elizabeth (Betsy), forty-eight, whose youngest child, Katharine, was only a year older than Bobbie. An older half brother, Samuel, came home from college for the occasion. He delighted in teaching little Bob to call him "Uncle Sam." The other children living at home were Martha, fourteen, seven-year-old Alexander, and Elodie (Jane), who was six. For Mary Lincoln, the return to her Kentucky home meant a spell of comfort and support that she had not known since her first child was born. Negro servants fed and bathed the whole brood of children, and watched over them as they played in the autumn leaves and waded in the brook behind the mansion.

This came as close to a real vacation and "sentimental journey" as this married couple were ever likely to have. They arrived the day before their fifth wedding anniversary, and celebrated it there. Their three weeks in Lexington, in autumnal glory, provided a refreshing bonding experience. Lincoln got to know Mary's father, stepmother, and maternal grandmother, Elizabeth Parker.

As the Lincolns walked side by side along the streets lined with locust trees, she pointed out the sights and scenes of her childhood and early youth: the brick house on Short Street where she was born and lived until she was fourteen, which was now owned by her brother Levi; her grandmother Parker's house a few doors down, an immense Federal-style brick mansion with a three-story central tower and pitched roofs on either side of it, intersecting behind. Through the double-arched windows of the tower, the old lady watched the carriages and drays go by in streets so heavily trafficked that Lexington came to be known as "the city that goes on wheels."

Mary would show him her old school, Ward's Academy on the corner of Second and Market streets, and Mathurin Giron's confectionary shop, with its fancy wrought-iron windows over the green awning that came out over the pavement. It was there in that shop between the saloon and the bookstore that little Mary cultivated her sweet tooth and commenced her lifelong struggle with her waistline. A cousin recalled that "Mary and I could never pass the confectionary shop of Monsieur Giron. Most of our small allowance of pocket money went to swell his coffers."

Lincoln was eager to see the courthouse and Jordan's Row, where the lawyers gathered, schemed, and gossiped. So she showed him "Cheapside," the old hub of public life that surrounded the halls of justice. Day in and day out, slaves were sold in clear view of the courthouse. Saturdays and court days were especially singled out for auctions, where the human merchandise was exhibited on the courthouse steps. Lincoln looked with wonder and dismay upon the three-trunked poplar tree in the courthouse yard where refractory slaves were bound and whipped. Mary knew it had been planted to replace the whipping post of black locust, long rotted to dust, that she remembered from her childhood. On the steps of that civic building on November 15, the second Monday of the Lincolns' stay,

Mary's father himself sold slaves at auction to settle a judgment against him.

Visiting Mary's maternal grandmother, Elizabeth Porter Parker, in her towering house at 501 Short Street was a lesson in family history. Lincoln learned of the old woman's disapproval of Robert Todd's second marriage so soon after her daughter's death; Lincoln began to understand the depth of anger that had strained the family since Mary's early youth, when Grandmother Parker drew the older children toward her and distanced herself from Robert Todd's second family. Mary and her full siblings sought refuge in the warmth of their grandmother's cavernous house during times when their father's home seemed too small for them. Now that Mary was grown, she had made peace with her stepmother (who seems to have lacked no virtue but patience, which seems pardonable in a woman in charge of a dozen children). Coming home again required diplomacy, setting aside time to visit her beloved grandmother while she and her family stayed in the Todd house on West Main Street.

The days quickly passed in sightseeing strolls and carriage rides in the crisp autumn air. After delectable dinners during which candlelight sparkled upon crystal glassware and fine china—dinners prepared and served by black cooks and servants—the gentlemen would repair to the well-stocked library on the east side of the rear parlor. While the maids were bathing the children and putting them to bed, Lincoln read *Niles' Weekly Register,* a periodical of international news and commentary founded by editor and publisher Hezekiah Niles in Baltimore in 1811.

Niles' Weekly Register was known as the finest, most comprehensive nonpartisan periodical in America—the perfect briefing for a freshman congressman. The October and early November editions of the *Register* were full of news about the economy, detailed dispatches from the Mexican war front, accounts of John Frémont's court-martial for insubordination, and the bitter conflict over the Wilmot Proviso, the bill proposing that slavery be banned in the conquered territories. One article stood out. On October 30, 1847, the *Register* printed the remarks of General Waddy Thompson "At the Wilmot Proviso meeting held at Greenville Courthouse, South Carolina." This powerful speech made the important link between President James Polk's aggression against Mexico and the institution of slavery.

General Waddy Thompson was an ex-congressman and former envoy to Mexico. In his speech, Thompson stridently defended the right of a new state to regulate its own policies—long before Stephen Douglas's campaign for "popular sovereignty" and the Kansas-Nebraska Act. "To say to a state that slavery shall not exist within her borders is a usurpation of power," he declared. And he defended the Tenth Amendment of the Constitution, which reserves to the states all powers not delegated to the federal government: "Abolish the Constitution . . . wherever the corrupt interests of venality or ambition may require it, and submit everything to the unrestricted will of a majority, whose interests are not only not identical, but directly antagonistic to those of the minority, which minority we of the south are destined forever to be, and I for one do not shrink from saying that such a government has no charms for me."

This incendiary speech took up many pages of the *Register,* and every word of it was riveting to the young Whig about to take his place in the Hall of Representatives. General Thompson includes the opinion that "the two races cannot exist together as equals. Every effort to raise the African to an equality with the white race has failed." And, "If territory is acquired from Mexico, the issue will—it must come. What then, is the remedy? There is but one—human ingenuity can suggest no other—it is an odious word—men do not like to use it; but if we shrink from the word, much more will we shrink from the thing itself.—That word is not used in the resolutions which have been submitted, but the thing meant is— dissolution. Gentlemen, I ask you, in the event of the assertion of the principle of the Wilmot Proviso by an act of congress, are you ready to dissolve the Union? I am."

So, as of mid-November of 1847, readers of the newspaper could see that the issue of slavery might lead to the secession of the southern states and perhaps civil war. Lincoln read others things in the Todd library: some antislavery poems of Cowper, a biography of Henry Clay. But the current issues of *Niles' Register* made the greatest impression.

THE CLIMAX OF the Lincolns' vacation in Lexington, after their wedding anniversary, came on a dark, rainy Saturday afternoon, November 13. Henry Clay—former senator and perennial presidential candidate—was scheduled to deliver a speech concerning the conduct of the Mexican War. Lincoln called Clay "My beau ideal of a statesman," and Mary had

known and admired him since she was a child. By Friday afternoon the
boardinghouses and taverns were full of reporters and visitors representing almost every state in the Union, but Robert Todd could assure his
company of excellent seats for the event.

The concourse of men and women was so huge that it quickly overran
the courthouse where the speech had been scheduled, so the meeting adjourned to a large brick building on Water Street, the Lower Market-
House. General Leslie Coombs called the meeting to order and moved
that Judge George Robertson be appointed chairman, and Robert S.
Todd vice chairman of the meeting. These men took seats on the platform
that had been hastily erected for the speech. A reporter from Louisville
had set up a little writing table near the dignitaries, and sat there with his
pen, ink bottle, and paper, eagerly waiting to record the words of the legendary statesman.

Amid cheers and applause, Henry Clay, still tall and plumb-line
straight at the age of seventy, made his way through the crowd to the steps
of the platform. Mr. Clay glared at the reporter and frowned. He told the
man with the pen "that he was opposed to any report of his speech being
taken, as he had been so frequently misrepresented; and that he intended
to have it printed under his own supervision, and would furnish copies
then to all." The reporter protested; another pleaded, and so did another,
offering to allow the statesman to revise their notes. In vain the press
corps argued with Henry Clay. He folded his arms, unmoved, his speech
scrolled in his hand. "He declared that if we persisted in reporting," said
the writer from *Niles' Register*, "he would not speak." The journalists
pocketed their pens and took their seats. Clay began:

> The day is dark and gloomy, unsettled and uncertain, like the condition of
> our country, in regard to the unnatural war with Mexico. The public mind
> is agitated and anxious, and is filled with serious apprehensions as to its in-
> definite continuance, and especially as to the consequences which its ter-
> mination may bring forth, menacing the harmony, if not the existence, of
> our Union. . . . I have come here with no purpose to attempt to make a fine
> speech, or any ambitious oratorical display. I have brought with me no
> rhetorical bouquets to throw into this assemblage. In the circle of the year,
> autumn has come, and the season of flowers has passed away. In the
> progress of years, my spring time has gone by, and I too am in the autumn
> of life, and feel the frost of age.

His own son, Henry Clay, Jr., had died valiantly on a Mexican battle-field, and yet the old man was willing to call the motives of his country into question. "How did we unhappily get involved in this war? It was predicted as the consequence of the annexation of Texas to the United States. If we had not Texas, we should have no war."

We would have had no war, Clay argued, except that General Zachary Taylor had been "ordered to transport his cannon, and to plant them, in a warlike attitude, opposite to Matamoras . . . within the very disputed territory." Who ordered this but the secretary of state and the president? And so President Polk, having produced the war, "appealed to Congress. A bill was proposed to raise 50,000 volunteers, and in order to commit all who should vote for it, a preamble was inserted falsely attributing the commencement of the war to the act of Mexico." While Clay would not question the patriotism of those who were constrained to vote for the bill, "I must say that no earthly consideration would have ever tempted or provoked me to vote for a bill, with a palpable falsehood stamped on its face. Almost idolizing truth, as I do, I never, never, could have voted for that bill."

Clay's words resonated in Lincoln's mind long after, and the principles of this oration found their way into the young congressman's own speeches in Washington. Clay defended the Constitution's resolution

> to guard the war-making power against those great abuses, of which in the hands of a monarch it was so susceptible . . . to vest the war-making power in the Congress of the United States. . . . This is no war of defense, but one unnecessary and of offensive aggression. It is Mexico that is defending her fire-sides, her castles and her altars, not we.
>
> I conclude, therefore . . . that Congress has the right either at the beginning or during the prosecution of any war, to decide the objects and purposes for which it was proclaimed, or for which it ought to be continued. . . . *Of all the dangers and misfortunes which could befall this nation, I should regard that of its becoming a warlike and conquering power the most direful and fatal.*

Lincoln was about to become Clay's echo in the Thirtieth Congress. And it was here in his wife's hometown that the young congressman conceived his agenda for Washington.

On November 25, after three weeks of rest, reflection, and enriched family unity, the Lincolns bade farewell and thanks to the Todds of Lexington, and set out eagerly on the next leg of their journey. The overland passage to Washington would take a full week by stagecoach and railroad.

THE RAILWAY TERMINAL in Washington was unimposing, a ramshackle wooden shed north of Pennsylvania Avenue and Second Street. Formerly a boardinghouse, it had been gutted to the roof and opened at either end. Crowds of noisy loiterers, ruffians, pickpockets, ragged beggars, and hackney coach drivers converged upon the trains as they screeched to a halt at the track ends.

On the cold night of Thursday, December 2, 1847, Abraham Lincoln and his weary family arrived at this unpromising terminus, where they had been conveyed from Relay Station in Western Maryland on the clattering coaches of the B&O branch railroad. A hackney driver delivered them and their baggage to the nearby Brown's "Indian Queen" Hotel on Sixth Street and Pennsylvania Avenue, near the noisy Centre Market.

After a much-needed night of sleep, they awoke that Friday morning to the rattling and creaking of drays and two-wheeled carts on their way to market, and the cries of street vendors. The contrast between Lexington in the golden light of autumn and Washington in the December gloom was sobering. Washington was a village sprawled on a swamp, floating a few scattered marble temples. Dickens had called it "a monument raised to a deceased project."

Any dreams they might have cherished of a well-ordered and gracious metropolis were quickly dispelled by the reality of the Federal City in 1847. A quick walk after breakfast, up Pennsylvania Avenue and around Capitol Square toward Mrs. Sprigg's boardinghouse, one of five row houses in a block of First Street called "Carroll Row," would give the Lincolns an exemplary panorama of Washington's grandeur and squalor. Dominating the landscape was the Capitol on the brow of the eastern plateau, ninety feet above the Potomac, surrounded by a park of thirty-five acres. They climbed the seventy-three stone steps in front of the building. Over the buildings beyond Pennsylvania Avenue they could view the river to the south.

They were eager to see the boardinghouse where they would spend the winter, the fourth on the right of a row of dwellings that lay beyond the Capitol, with a view of the east portico and the old blue-painted wooden

dome. In a few days Mrs. Sprigg would have the Lincolns' rooms prepared, in that same house Baker and Hardin had occupied during their
turns in Congress. From the steps leading down to the road in front of the
boardinghouse, to the iron railing around Capitol Park, was less than a
twenty-yard stroll.

A semicircle of trees screened the Capitol building from the city below.
Looking down from the dome one could see the vacant mall, with the
canal zigzagging through it toward the Potomac. From Capitol Hill looking west toward the White House, the Lincolns looked out along the
broad tree-lined Pennsylvania Avenue, on either side of which the city
sprawled like "an ill-contrived, ill-arranged, rambling, scrambling village," according to Marian Gouverneur, a town of forty thousand souls, of
which eight thousand were freed colored persons and two thousand
slaves. Six thousand houses between Georgetown and Mrs. Sprigg's were
arranged upon a numbered and lettered grid. The cobblestones on the
main avenue were so few and far between that carriages avoided driving
over them for fear of loosening their wheels. Most of the houses, with
their chimneys smoking, lay along the streets to the north. In the middle
distance between Seventh and Ninth streets stood the magnificent Patent
Office. And in the far distance at the end of Pennsylvania Avenue they
could see the columns of the Treasury building, still under construction.
They admired the bell towers and spires of the many churches—there
were some thirty-seven then, of eight denominations; there were twice as
many taverns to quench the thirsts of the congressmen, office seekers, and
lobbyists, as well as brothels and gambling dens that catered to men with
strong appetites.

As in a country village or the outskirts of Springfield, the houses stood
far apart, quite democratically, mansions shadowing wood-frame houses,
and behind those the pigsties, cow barns, and goose pens that sometimes
left their tenants to run at large. Cows, geese, chickens, dogs, and pigs
roamed the unpaved streets and alleyways; in fact, they were encouraged
to go scavenging in the interest of hygiene, as there was no adequate sani-
tation or sewage system to dispose of waste or carrion.

The single great promenade of the city was a mile of brick sidewalk on
the north side of Pennsylvania Avenue, starting at the foot of the Capitol
and extending almost to the President's House. So on this particular Friday, after inspecting their new quarters at Mrs. Sprigg's, the Lincolns

could return to Brown's Hotel along the brick promenade without ruining their clothing and footwear.

As THE DAYS grew shorter and colder, nearing the winter solstice and his wife's twenty-ninth birthday on December 13, Lincoln found himself in a situation that was at best challenging and at worst distressing. While he approached the most demanding and promising opportunity of his political career and looked forward to busy days and nights in the gilded, gaslit halls of Congress, his wife was in for a rude awakening. Washington promised a decline in domestic comforts with no immediate compensation in the way of status. She had just come from three weeks in Lexington, where the family had been coddled and catered to by "Mammy Sally" and her team of colored servants. Now in a boardinghouse smaller than the Globe Tavern, and more crowded, she would have to take care of her two little boys (the younger of whom was in poor health), her husband, and herself, without much help at all.

On Saturday night, December 4, Lincoln left her, going off with his fellow Whigs Joshua Giddings, Elisha Embree, John Blanchard, John Dickey, Abraham R. McIlvaine, and Nathan Sargent (all of whom lodged with Mrs. Sprigg) to a Whig caucus. There they nominated Robert C. Winthrop of Boston for Speaker of the House, Robert Horner of New Jersey for doorkeeper, Nathan Sargent of Pennsylvania for sergeant of arms (which linguistic felicity must have amused Lincoln), and so on, until late into the night. Then the company repaired to a saloon to drink brandy and gin, talk about the war, and get to know one another.

That very day many of them had read the words of the great patriot Albert Gallatin, Thomas Jefferson's old friend, now nearly ninety, published in the *Washington Intelligencer:* "The war was unprovoked by the Mexicans, and has been one of iniquitous aggression on our part—it necessarily follows that, according to the dictate of justice, the United States are bound to indemnify them for having invaded their territory, bombarded their towns, and afflicted all the miseries of war on a people who were fighting in defense of their own homes." For Lincoln this sounded like a continuation of Henry Clay's speech in Lexington two weeks before.

It was late when the Whigs returned home, and it could hardly be expected that so many men, in such a state of excitement, could get to their beds in silence. As her husband softly entered the room where she and her children slept—as he removed his boots and laid his clothing upon a chair—the weary Mrs. Lincoln must have wondered if this was a place where there would be any peace for her at all.

The next morning the Lincolns could use the leisure of a Sunday to set up housekeeping and explore Capitol Hill. In those days, the widely spaced houses of the quarter composed a quiet neighborhood of church-going people, many in the service trades that accommodated the transient congressmen, officials, diplomats, and office seekers from all over the world. There were four drugstores, three grocers, two liquor stores, a shop that sold sewing supplies, and, for the boys, a taffy maker.

Lincoln would do his best to get the family settled on that day, because on Monday, December 6, at noon, he would take part in the opening of the Thirtieth U.S. Congress. No one who has not been elected to Congress can imagine the excitement of taking a seat in that company for the first time. Lincoln and his wife had a sense of history and destiny. As she said good-bye to him and wished him luck that Monday morning—as he descended the long flight of twenty steps that separated the arched doorway of the boardinghouse from the swampy road that lay between it and the Capitol—Mary turned back toward their rooms and their two children, wondering exactly what she would do until he returned to tell her about it all.

She had given him the confidence—if ever he lacked it—to take possession of that seat in Congress as if no man had ever had a greater right to it. He would act accordingly, without inhibition or indolence; he would presently act like the spiritual heir of Henry Clay.

Like the Representatives Hall in Springfield, the new Hall of Representatives in the Capitol was semicircular, in the shape of a Greek amphitheater whose coffered cast-steel dome was supported by Corinthian columns. There the similarity ended. In grandeur, richness, and comfort, the new hall (completed by Charles Bulfinch in 1819 to replace the interior burned by the British in 1814) outshone any public space Lincoln had ever seen. The huge columns were of variegated breccia marble from local quarries; their white Corinthian capitals came from Carrara, Italy. The floor was of gleaming white marble set with black marble tesserae in a diamond pattern. As he entered the door from the rotunda, the congressman's eye was drawn upward to the peak of the dome, to the skylight and the brass lantern. Sunlight shone upon the semicircular ranks of mahogany desks, more than two hundred of them, small, trapezoidal, squeezed together, each with a little drawer with two peg knobs, each with a two-board shelf beneath for papers and books. The New York cabinet-maker Thomas Constantine had made the desks and chairs. The arm-chairs were comfortable, with slender wooden armrests, padded seats, and backs covered in crimson damask that matched the drapes behind the Speaker's box.

That morning two hundred congressmen streamed into the high-domed hall, many greeting old friends and rivals, familiar with the place; others, newcomers like Lincoln, graciously accepting introductions, shaking hands all around with Whigs and Democrats he knew by reputa-tion. They took their seats. A few desks were vacant, as tempestuous weather along the southern coast had delayed the steamboat lines.

Lincoln's desk was number 191, in the center of the last row of the Whig section, to the left of the Speaker. It was not the best seat, but Lincoln's hearing and eyesight were fine, and from this spot he could cer-tainly make himself heard. Lincoln too had friends here: fifty-three-year-old Joshua Giddings of Ohio, his thick white hair framing his broad, handsome face, a man with large hands and a powerful neck. The Whigs had once forced Giddings to resign from Congress after he had defended the *Amistad* mutineers. The abolitionist sat in front of Lincoln. Four seats to his right in the row before him sat George Ashmun of Massachusetts, whose supporters had returned him to Washington after he had protested against the war in Mexico. Lincoln took an immediate liking to the forty-four-year-old lawyer and Yale graduate.

Right in front of Lincoln and several rows down was another young man he came to admire, "Mr. [Alexander] Stephens of Georgia, a little slim, pale-faced, consumptive man, with a voice like [Stephen] Logan," as Lincoln described him. Notwithstanding his appearance, his voice, as he spoke against the war, would move Lincoln to tears. Stephens, who would become vice president of the Confederacy, soon became Lincoln's fa-vorite colleague in the House. Next to Alexander Stephens sat thirty-eight-year-old Robert Toombs, also of Georgia, sturdy, ruddy, and courageous, appearing to have absorbed all the health that had drained from his younger compatriot.

It was a motley, contentious assembly, that colorful Thirtieth Con-gress, whose opposition to—or support of—the war and slavery did not neatly divide along regional or party lines. Of course, one might expect that on the Whig side of the room there would be antislavery men like Caleb Blood Smith of Indiana, forty years old, two desks to the left of Robert Toombs (who would become the Confederacy's secretary of state); and behind Smith there was John G. Palfrey, an abolitionist Unitarian minister and a Harvard man. These opposed the war, while some Whigs held their peace because their constituents were fighting and dying in Mexico.

But on the other side of the hall sat a blond, slender veteran of Congress only thirty-three years of age, with a youthful, lilting voice. This was the solid Democrat from Pennsylvania, David Wilmot, who had won national fame by authoring the bill that bore his name, the "Wilmot Proviso," which he had introduced in the final hours of the Twenty-ninth Congress in August of 1846. Lincoln had spent hours reading about this in *Niles' Register* and other papers—a bill that in effect would prohibit slavery in conquered territories. The very threat of it had driven many southern Democrats to oppose expansion into Mexico if they couldn't bring their slaves along with them.

There were men of genius, men of breeding, bullies, and buffoons, some who would change the course of history and others (the vast majority) whose names have been forgotten. But the cynosure of all eyes, especially of the newcomers, was the short old man at desk 203, with the birdlike, aristocratic features and the tight-fitting black frock coat with wide lapels—one might easily imagine the slow-moving gentleman wearing a powdered wig and knee breeches, doing the minuet, a ghost of those revolutionary heroes who had composed the first Congress. His desk, near front and center, had a unique acoustic advantage: For reasons not precisely understood, every word uttered beneath the dome, whether shouted or whispered, could be heard at desk 203.

There sat the venerable John Quincy Adams, eighty, son of the second president of the United States and an ex-president himself, who thought it no compromise of his dignity or anticlimax to his career to serve the state of Massachusetts and his country as a congressman in his old age. He had taken his seat in 1831, and now his presence was an inspiration and example even to those who opposed his views. A longtime opponent of slavery, Adams stubbornly challenged the "Gag Rules" that prohibited antislavery proposals in the House. He would simply pipe up on the subject again and again as if the Gag Rules did not apply to former presidents, until at last in 1844 the rules were repealed. And he hated and

vociferously denounced America's aggression in Mexico, as did Albert
Gallatin and Henry Clay.

For all its grandeur the hall was not impersonally huge. From his seat
at the back of the Hall of Representatives, Lincoln gazed in solemn wonder at the eighty-year-old ex-president, the conscience of the legislature,
the embodiment of eighteenth-century ideals, a link with a nobler era—he
had known the Founding Fathers personally. Beyond the patriarch
Adams stood the Speaker's rostrum; and in a niche above the curtained
colonnade behind the rostrum, a sandstone eagle was carved in the frieze
of the entablature, a symbol of the Republic.

As THEY DINED in the evening, Lincoln was eager to share his impressions with his wife. And she was pleased to hear the news after a day of
minding the children in the drafty rooms of Mrs. Sprigg, in weather that
was already too cold for boys to run free in the park around the Capitol.

The dining room in the front of the house overlooked Capitol Park,
with its semicircle of shade trees now bare of leaves, gray in the twilight
mists of December. The dining room table had to be long to accommodate the "mess," as it was called. There were six to eight rooms for lodging at a boardinghouse this size, but the proprietress would serve any
number of boarders if the food attracted them, legislators or other gentlemen who lived in the neighborhood and wanted meals.

Mary Lincoln, with her feeling for words, could appreciate the term
"mess" for all its military, institutional connotations, as well as its descrip-
tive powers: The evening meal shared by a dozen or more men, amid the
clatter of crockery and flatware and the raucous voices of the diners, was
not a polite or peaceful repast. It was a mess. The scene was a far remove
from what she had grown accustomed to in Springfield, let alone Lexington.

In order to understand Mrs. Lincoln's state of mind during that winter,
one must revisit that table in the front room of Mrs. Sprigg's at around
5:30, the dinner hour. The landlady was a Virginian, but she did not keep
slaves in this predominantly Whig establishment, whose tenants and
boarders included the likes of Joshua Giddings and Theodore Weld,
leading abolitionists. Mrs. Sprigg had eight colored servants—four
women, three men, and one boy. And while some waited upon the table
and others cooked, there would be someone to mind the Lincoln boys

while their parents took their supper. Mr. Weld described the average
fare, excepting the chicken, pork, and game, for he was a vegetarian: "We
have always upon the table Graham bread and corn bread. A pitcher of
milk is always set by my plate and deep soup plate for a bowl so that I can
always have a good diet, *good enough*. . . . Mush we always have . . . apples
always once a day; at dinner turnips, parsnips, spinnage with eggs, al-
monds, figs, raisins and bread; the puddings, pies, cakes, etc."

When her headaches or the demands of the children did not interfere
with the supper hour, Mary Lincoln was often the only woman at the
table. The men took pains not to offend her by their language and table
manners. While most of them were distinguished by political vocation,
few might be considered what the Kentucky belle had been raised to call
a gentleman. There were Abraham McIlvaine, forty-three, a dirt farmer
from Chester County, Pennsylvania, and Dr. George N. Eckert, a country
doctor, forty-five, from the same state. The other member from Pennsylvania was the young and handsome lawyer James Pollock, destined to become governor, who had graduated from Princeton. Giddings despised
Pollock for his ambivalence about slavery, while Pollock called Giddings
an agitator—they were continually arguing. Nearly all of the men had left
behind wives and children; Pollock, thirty-six, had left his Sarah to care
for their six children. Perhaps he, who most resembled a gentleman,
might lend a hand now and then with Bobbie or Eddie.

There was the confirmed bachelor Robert "Bennie" Cranston of
Rhode Island, fifty-six, who called himself a gentleman and put on airs.
Then there was an unpleasant, argumentative ex-sheriff named John
Dickey, fifty-five, also from Pennsylvania, and Patrick Watson Tompkins,
a rare Whig from Mississippi.

In addition to these men who rented the lodging rooms of Mrs.
Sprigg's, there were others who routinely took their meals there. These
included the mercurial entrepreneur and publisher Duff Green, a distant
relative of Mary's from Kentucky, busy promoting his newspaper in
Washington. Every week that winter you could read ads for Green's new
antiabolition paper, *The Times,* in all the other newspapers. Green was
naturally at loggerheads with Joshua Giddings. Nathan Sargent (nick-
named "Oliver Oldschool" for his quaint manners) took meals there, as
did Samuel C. Busey, a nineteen-year-old physician who sat opposite
Abraham Lincoln, "whom I soon learned to know and admire," Busey recalled, "for his simple and unostentatious manners, kindheartedness, and

amusing jokes, anecdotes, and witticisms. When about to tell an anecdote during a meal he would lay down his knife and fork, place his elbows upon the table, rest his face between his hands, and begin with the words 'that reminds me,' and proceed. Everybody prepared for the explosions sure to follow. I recall with vivid pleasure the scene of merriment at the dinner after his first speech in the House of Representatives, occasioned by the descriptions, by himself and others of the Congressional mess, of the uproar in the House during its delivery."

That was the evening of December 22, 1847, a night the oil lamps burned late.

ON HIS WIFE'S twenty-ninth birthday, Lincoln had written to his law partner Herndon, "As you are all so anxious for me to distinguish myself, I have concluded to do so, before long." By then Lincoln knew how he would distinguish himself. He had seen President Polk's "Annual Message" to Congress, an address that was published in the Washington papers where Mary Lincoln could read it when the children were napping. As the *Washington Intelligencer* put it, "a single paragraph includes the whole story":

> The wanton violation of the rights of persons and property of our citizens committed by Mexico, her repeated acts of bad faith through a long series of years, and her disregard of solemn treaties stipulating for indemnity to our injured citizens, not only constituted ample cause of war on our part, but were of such an aggravated character as would have justified us before the whole world in resorting to this extreme remedy. . . and finally, under wholly unjustifiable pretexts, [Mexico] involved the two countries in war, by invading the territory of the State of Texas, striking the first blow, and shedding the blood of our citizens on our own soil.

President Polk wanted more money to bring the war to an end. By now it had been going on for nearly two years, costing the nation $27 million and twenty-seven thousand lives.

So on December 22, Lincoln stood up in the Capitol to challenge Polk, in phrases he had been preparing for a long time. The evening of that day, the darkest of the year, Mary Lincoln joined the mess at dinner, eager to hear how her husband had been received. Candles burned brightly on the table and the sideboard. The legislators sounded like a rowdy chorus, reciting the details of the proceedings in the Hall of Representatives. She listened as her husband set the scene:

At noon the representatives had taken their places. First, the Reverend Ralph Gurley in his clerical collar bade the gentlemen bow their heads, and led them in a prayer; then the clerk read the minutes of the day before, and several members leaped up to correct the record in reference to motions they had made. Thomas Jefferson Henley of Indiana offered a resolution to appoint a Committee on Printing, which was roundly approved. Joshua Giddings wanted to take up a petition he had presented the day before, advancing the cause of abolition, but he was denied. Then there were tedious committee reports. Housemate Jacob Thompson stood up to request, in his southern drawl, that the Speaker, Mr. Winthrop, authorize the clerk, Benjamin French, "to read a little more square," so as he might hear him. This brought scattered laughter, because Mr. French, while reading, had a bad habit of turning his face mostly to the left side of the chair, so that those on the right could hear nothing but the mumbling syllables of his speech. Lincoln was good at imitating this sort of antic, as well as the curious habit of French's assistant clerk—who took up the burden from time to time—"that of seesawing his person whilst reading."

There was laughter all around the table.

All of this comic curtain-raiser led to the very serious drama of Mr. Lincoln's first speech in the U.S. Congress, a bold challenge to the president of the United States. In response to Polk's message of May 11, 1846, that the Mexican government had "at last invaded *our territory* [italics in the original], and shed the blood of our fellow *citizens* on *our own soil*" and his recent Annual Message that repeated the accusation, Mr. Lincoln at last had spoken up for the antiwar congressmen, forcefully and memorably.

The eight questions that came to be known as the "Spot Resolutions" were reported by the *Quincy Whig* the next morning. "Mr. Lincoln offered a series of resolutions, asking the President for certain information in connection with statements made in his several war messages, concerning the spot where American blood had been shed on American soil—whose soil it was when that blood was shed, and various other matters of like import." Yet the newspaper could not convey the mixture of indignation and wonder in the hall at the freshman's audacious attack on the chief of state during wartime. Grave as a biblical prophet, the tall Westerner pointed his long forefinger at the imagined spot, demanding to know: "First: Whether the spot of soil on which the blood of our citizens was shed . . . was or was not within the territories of Spain, at least from the treaty of 1819; Second: Whether that spot is, or is not, within the territory which was wrested from Spain, by the Mexican revolution . . ." and so on.

Mary Lincoln knew Shakespeare's *Macbeth,* one of her husband's favorite plays and one he was known to read aloud to anyone who would listen. "Yet here's a spot," says the guilt-crazed Lady Macbeth, rubbing her hands in vain to remove the red traces of her crime. "Out, damned spot! out, I say! One: two: why then 'tis time to do't. . . . What, will these hands ne'er be clean?" And like the congressmen caught in the dilemma of the continuing war, Macbeth, the regicide, admits:

> *I am in blood*
> *Stepp'd in so far that, should I wade no more,*
> *Returning were as tedious as go o'er . . .*

Anybody who had read *Macbeth* realized that Lincoln's Spot Resolutions meant to imply that the president of the United States had blood on his hands, the blood of Henry Clay, Jr., and John Hardin, tens of thousands of Americans and perhaps twice as many Mexicans.

Mary was proud of his first speech in Congress. It had made an enormous impression. As she left the dining room, the laughter, and this male banter, to climb the stairs and check on the children, a doubt hung in the air. Had he been too bold, too impetuous for the time and place? Would the president respond? Was it possible that some of the guilt he had laid at Polk's door might come back to haunt him?

ABRAHAM LINCOLN WAS one of very few congressmen who brought his wife and children with him to Washington, and it was more of a burden than a comfort. Husband and wife found themselves separated by a barrier greater than any they had known in marriage, more distinct than the iron fence around the Capitol that cast its shadow on the snow in the sunlight. He moved in a world of male privilege, power, and opportunity for growth. She toiled from chair to cradle to bureau to closet in a room with a smoky fireplace, two beds, a chamber pot, and a pile of wood with bugs in it.

The room might have been large enough, with screens separating the beds, if she were not confined there so many hours of the day. The boys were rambunctious, but she dared not let them play outdoors too often in the cold weather; Eddie had a cough, and they feared consumption. Bobbie overran the halls and the parlor, vexing the lodgers. What could she do but defend her sons against their critics? Her defensiveness about the children and other matters pertaining to her status as the only housewife in a mess of "statesmen" led to lasting enmity with two or three of them.

Her social life, such as it was, was a disappointment. On New Year's Day, the congressmen and their wives were invited to a levee at the Executive Mansion. Indeed, it was a long-standing rule of etiquette that they make this call on the president and his wife, "in full dress," at noon.

The excitement of approaching the White House for the first time—passing the bronze statue of Jefferson within the curved carriageway, mounting the north steps and passing under the portico through the Ionic columns and into the huge front hall crowded with people sure of their importance—this thrill for the Lincolns was mixed with insecurity. They were from the West and might be judged rustic until proven otherwise. Also, only a week before, Mr. Lincoln had harshly attacked their host. They now stood in a receiving line in the East Room waiting to shake his hand and exchange pleasantries; perhaps the attractive Mrs. Lincoln, in her silk dress, her hair beguilingly curled, might make such an impression as would distract President Polk momentarily from the business of politics.

Such occasions were a disappointment to a woman as socially ambitious as Mary Lincoln. Of course she would never forget meeting James Madison's widow, Dolley, still the doyenne of Washington society three decades after her husband's presidency. Dolley stood just behind James Polk, who was not an entertaining host by anyone's standards. After the orgies of the Jackson era and necessary austerities of the Van Buren administration, the White House had settled into a genteel, ceremonial dullness. A war was on. There was no music to be heard at White House functions, and no liquor was served. A newcomer might leave the mansion knowing no one she did not know before she arrived.

And in any case, however well Mrs. Lincoln dressed, or spoke, or moved—however gracefully she extended her hand to the president or a senator or ambassador—she could not be taken seriously by Washington society. Many balls, dinners, and receptions were given by Speaker Robert Winthrop, Senator Daniel Webster, and social lions of the old Southern aristocracy of Washington, but the lone Whig from Illinois and his wife were not likely to be invited.

On New Year's Eve the social occasion that made all the newspapers was the reception in honor of General James Shields, the Lincolns' old antagonist, for his valor in the field. The mayor of Washington City presided at a lavish dinner at the Fuller Hotel. Many distinguished members of Congress, including Senator Stephen A. Douglas and several of Mrs. Sprigg's Whig boarders, were invited. The Lincolns were not.

"The idea that there is no rank in our court," said William Haley, a contemporary writer on etiquette, "has long been exploded by actual experience. The position occupied by officials, under the Constitution, gives them necessarily a certain rank, according to the importance and nature of the office, the length of term, and the age, required by law, of the incumbent." The wife of a thirty-eight-year-old first-time congressman found herself low in the pecking order.

As always, Mr. Lincoln had a circle of friends and colleagues, an audience for his witty anecdotes. Sometimes the men went bowling together at an alley near the boardinghouse. But so far as anyone recalls, Mrs. Lincoln did not make a single friend in Washington. Not a letter exists to or from anyone she met in the winter of 1847–48. She had her children and she had Mr. Lincoln, when he was not working or bowling. They would go and listen to the Marine Band play on Saturday nights on the Capitol lawn, weather permitting.

She could go shopping along Pennsylvania Avenue in the small stores where silks and dress goods were "very handsome" and moderately priced. She had charge accounts at the clothiers P. H. Hood and Co. and Walter Harper and Co., which she was forgetful about paying on time, much to Mr. Lincoln's consternation. Below Brown's Hotel, Mr. George Kraft had opened a lavish new confectionary, where Mary could buy candy, ice cream, and jellies for the boys. But she was warned to beware of thieves and street beggars in this city where gangs roamed the streets at night and fights were common.

The newspapers complained of "the want of light in this city . . . we are behind the age . . . it is a blurr [sic], a stigma of reproach on our citizens. . . .

It is now in our power to spread the most brilliant light throughout the city, and why not make some proposition—make a beginning. Mr. Crutch-ett's gas properly placed through our streets, would dispel this horrid gloom that settles down on us at night."

There was light to be found in the theaters at night, and the Lincolns attended plays as often as they could. Soon after they settled at Mrs. Sprigg's, the "Chinese Museum Exhibition" opened at the Odd Fellows Hall at Seventh and D streets. A newspaper account enumerated the "Chinese figures of life size, several hundred Chinese paintings . . . ele-gant carvings in ivory, shell, wood, and stone; models of houses, stores, pagodas . . . specimens of lacquered ware, porcelain vases, lanterns.

"At eight o'clock the Chinese who accompany the collection will as-sume the dresses of the Emperor, civil and military Mandarins of different ranks, Soldiers, Judges . . . Priests of the sects of Buddha and Taou. . . . They will also exhibit the manner of smoking opium." Admittance was 25 cents—half price for children, but Bobbie was too young for such a late-night entertainment.

The busy congressman did find time to take Bobbie for a walk up Sixth Street, beyond City Hall and the palatial Post Office, to the stately marble building that loomed above all in that quarter. The three-story Doric-columned Patent Office covered the city block from F to G streets, and from Sixth to Eighth. The four saloons of the upper floor housed the model room, its glass cases containing the toy-sized models of firearms, plows, steam engines, telescopes, and gadgets of uncertain application— all good for endless conversation between a very tall, chuckling man who never tired of things mechanical and novel, and a little boy beginning to share his father's fascination with such matters. The boy would never for-get it.

MUCH OF LINCOLN'S energy at the beginning of the New Year was taken up with defending his Spot Resolutions against critics in Washington and in Illinois, as Lincoln kept up his pressure on Polk's war policy. John Jamison of Missouri called Lincoln's opposition a "strange position be-fore the American Congress for such a representative from a district that had sent so many men to the war to fight and [as in John Hardin's case] sacrifice their lives." The Democratic convention of Sangamon County singled out Lincoln as "one unfortunate exception who . . . in contempt of the two gallant regiments which they [his constituents] furnished for the war, has lent himself to the schemes of such men as Corwin, Giddings, Hale and others, apologists and defenders of Mexico, and revilers of their own country."

The *Illinois State Register* seized upon the *Macbeth* allusion and cried "Out Damned Spot" in bold type, then went on to refer to the Whig as "spotty Lincoln." It would take him years to live it down. "This 'spotty' gentleman had a severe attack of 'spotted fever' in Washington city not long since, and fears were entertained that the disease would 'strike in,' and carry him off." Experience would make him a more skillful politician, more careful in his tactics, but he would never lose that trait of stubbornness, the determination to march to his own drummer.

The heat of the abolitionist sentiments in Mrs. Sprigg's parlor did not immediately transform his moderate approach to the problem of slavery. Certainly he was more and more disturbed by it. His view of the slave jails and whipping posts of his wife's hometown hardly prepared him for the heavy slave traffic of Washington, a major port and distribution center for the domestic slave trade. A few hundred yards east of Carroll Row stood an auction block and holding pens, and on the mall in front of the Capitol building were larger slave pens. Lincoln later recalled a "view from the windows of the Capitol, a sort of Negro-livery stable, where droves of Negroes were collected, temporarily kept, and finally taken to Southern markets openly maintained." Only seven blocks from the houses of legislature, Robey's Pen, as it was called, was described once by an English writer as "a wretched hovel right against the capitol. . . . It is surrounded by a wooden paling fourteen or fifteen feet in height, with the posts outside to prevent escape, and separated from the building by a space too narrow to permit of a free circulation of air."

In their shopping and strolling along the streets of Washington, the Lincolns might turn away from such an awful spectacle. But no one could avoid the dreary clanking and shuffling sound of the slave coffles, the herding of black people in chains and leg irons through the streets from pen to auction block. The largest dealer in slaves in America was just across the river in Alexandria, the firm of Franklin & Armfield. The fact that there were far more freed blacks than slaves in Washington, and that they had opportunities to get an education and own their own businesses, only highlighted the grim injustices of the "peculiar institution." How many died of cold in Robey's Pen?

The Potomac was frozen over. On a cold night in early January the Lincolns left the children with servants at the boardinghouse. Dressed in their finest, they made their way down from Capitol Hill in the darkness along Pennsylvania Avenue, past slave pens, past the big gaslit hotels—the National, and Brown's Indian Queen—hurrying through the shuttered Centre Market to C Street and Eleventh on their way to Carusi's Saloon.

Carusi's was not a tavern but a ballroom and a performance space that had been used for inaugural celebrations. Tonight the platform and chairs had been arranged to welcome the Ethiopian Serenaders, "Messrs. German, Stanwood, Harrington, Pell, White, and Howard, since their return from Europe, where they had the distinguished honor of appearing before Her Majesty, Queen Victoria" and other nobility, under the skillful direction of Mr. J. A. Dumbolton. The Ethiopian Serenaders, freed blacks, were by all accounts the greatest minstrel show of the Victorian era, beloved for their clowning, banjo playing, singing—and above all their dancing.

The Lincolns paid twenty-five cents apiece for their tickets and sat down together in the crowded hall. The performance began at 7:30. The entertainment that so delighted them, and drew peals of laughter and rounds of applause from people of all ages the world over, was both a celebration of racial difference and an unconscious escape from it. In chorus the freed blacks sang:

> *Ober de ribber we used to float,*
> *While I cast de seine from my little boat,*
> *As far and wide my nets I'd fling*
> *And thus ob my lub, I'd sweetly sing;*
> *Oh! Coralie, sweet Coralie,*
> *How happy I've been since you lub'd me,*
> *Oh! Coralie, sweet Coralie,*
> *Meet me tonight by de cypress tree.*

The minstrels sang to the accompaniment of the flutina, banjo, tambourine, and drums. And they danced as no Americans had ever danced before, the juba dance, a lively combination of jigs and reels and soft-shoe, hand-clapping and knee-slapping, perfected by William Lane, known as "Master Juba." "His limbs seem to be formed of caoutchouc [rubber], slightly diluted with gutta-percha, hence his elasticity and aplomb.... His pedal execution is a thing to wonder at, if his flexibility of muscle did not confound us. He jumps, he capers, he crosses his legs, he stamps his heels, he dances on his knees, on his ankles, he ties his limbs into double knots and untwists them as one might do a skein of silk and all these marvels are done at strict time and appropriate rhythm." Thus wrote an English reviewer in 1846. An Englishman who saw the juba at Vauxhall, a London theater, declared, "The only national dance that we really believe in, as a fact, is that of the Niggers." For the English, the minstrel show was a cruel entertainment, a kind of freak show that made a display of racism, while for most Americans the sweet tunes of Frank Howard and Stephen Foster softened and idealized the brutal realities of slave life on the plantations.

> *Some moonlight night, false Coralie,*
> *My sheeted ghost you'll dimly see,*
> *While from my lips dis mournful song*
> *Shall chill your heart as it floats along:*
> *Oh! Coralie, false Coralie,*
> *I died 'cause you would not love me.*
> *Oh! Coralie, false Coralie,*
> *I'm sleeping under de cypress tree.*

ON FRIDAY, THE fourteenth of January, the Lincolns, and all the other legislators of Mrs. Sprigg's mess, were looking forward to a long weekend after an intense session of debate over the war. Two days before, Lincoln had made a lengthy and impassioned speech in defense of his Spot Resolutions, one that was widely published that week and the next, in which he said of President Polk: "He is deeply conscious of being in the wrong—that he feels the blood of this war, like the blood of Abel, is crying to Heaven against him.... By fixing the public gaze upon the exceeding brightness of military glory—that attractive rainbow, that rises in showers of blood—that serpent's eye, that charms to destroy—he plunged into it, and has swept, *on* and *on.*"

Mary was awed and perhaps fearful of her husband's vehemence. Very recently she had observed that attractive rainbow of military glory as it arched over General James Shields, at the dinner at which she was not welcome; but she was also proud of her husband's courage and the poetry of his long speech.

Waiting upon the table at Mrs. Sprigg's that evening was a black man, who was lawfully wedded to a woman who cooked, and minded the children from time to time, and otherwise made herself useful. The man had worked for Ann Sprigg for several years and "had become well and favorably known to members of this House," according to Joshua Giddings in a resolution he later offered before Congress as testimony to an outrage none of them could ever forget.

In the presence of the entire mess, three men armed with pistols burst in through the front door, and, identifying the black waiter by name, seized him violently and pinioned him. They gagged him with a rag and clapped irons on his wrists and ankles as his wife looked on in horror. While training their pistols on the boarders and the waiter, they dragged the helpless man gazing sorrowfully after his wife down the frozen ruts of First Street toward Robey's slave-holding pen. Within a matter of hours he was "dispatched for the slave market at New Orleans."

The three thugs who had stormed Mrs. Sprigg's and keelhauled her waiter were "engaged in the internal slave trade" and had extraordinary information about the black man's status. As Giddings explained to Congress, the waiter, who had been "under contract to purchase his freedom for the sum of $300, had by great industry paid that sum within about $60." Evidently the time had run out on his contract, and the laws of the District of Columbia sanctioned the return of the unfortunate man to the slave market.

On Monday morning, the seventeenth, Joshua Giddings described the "outrages" as "inhuman" in a formal resolution before the House "that a select committee of five members be appointed to inquire into and report upon the facts aforesaid; also, as to the propriety of repealing such acts of Congress as sustain or authorize the slave trade in this District, or to remove the seat of government to some free State." The motion was tabled by a vote of 94 to 88 (Giddings, Lincoln, Dickey, McIlvaine, and others of the mess falling in behind John Quincy Adams against tabling the motion). Nothing would come of Giddings's antislavery proposal for a long time.

The barbarous incident did not add to the Lincolns' sense of security in a city where they were already on guard against burglars, confidence men, and pickpockets. Samuel Busey observed that Mrs. Lincoln rarely seemed to leave her room except to take meals with her husband. He did not remember seeing the baby at all.

IT WAS A dreary winter with only a few bright spots to illuminate the routine of the housebound mother of two. They celebrated Mr. Lincoln's birthday on a Saturday, February 12; early the next week it was announced that he and Mary's old flame Senator Stephen Douglas had been designated as Illinois managers of the "Birth Night Ball" on the twenty-second, held to raise funds for the construction of the Washington Monument. At last there would be a social occasion at which she might shine, as the wife of a "manager"; attentions would be due to her as they had not been at any White House levee.

But that shining prospect turned to ashes the day before George Washington's birthday, when an unexpected event shook the Capitol to its historic foundations and cast a gloom over the city that would not lift until spring.

Congress was in session. Lincoln had just cast his vote upon a question, and Speaker Winthrop had stood up to put another question to the House, when he heard someone cry out on the left of the chair, "Mr. Adams is dying!" The old man had indeed fallen, slumped over the left arm of his chair. His right arm held on to his desk for support. The member sitting next to him caught him in his arms to keep Adams from falling to the floor. Men rushed from their places to surround the stricken patriot, and they lifted him into an open space in front of the clerk's table.

A remark frequently heard was, "Well, this is just what Mr. Adams could have wished; it is an appropriate ending of his public career: he falls, like a second [William Pitt] Chatham, in the Senate House." Gradually the members dispersed, to discuss the sad event in taverns and hotels. Mr. Adams had suffered strokes before, but now at eighty it seemed unlikely he would survive.

Mr. Lincoln departed by the north doorway under Franzoni's sculpture of Clio, the muse of History, recording events in her book while riding in the winged chariot of Time. The chariot wheel frames the elegant face and hands of Simon Willard's unerring clock; the figure served as an inspiration on most days, and on this day as a memento mori. Lincoln passed through the iron gate and across the park in the chilly mist to tell his wife the news. She would be sewing, preparing a silk dress to wear to the Birth Night Ball, and he would have to explain to her that instead of a ball there would be a funeral.

John Quincy Adams died a little after seven o'clock in the evening of February 23, 1848. For Lincoln, the sudden absence of the old man was a particularly sad turn of events: Out of the 230 representatives that year, Adams was one of a few men of true conviction, a leader who could be counted upon to vote his conscience; the freshman Whig from Illinois often followed his lead. Now Lincoln was appointed to the Committee of Arrangements for the obsequies scheduled for February 26.

On the Saturday of the funeral, soldiers, police, marching bands, the Masons and other fraternal orders, and thousands of spectators began to gather at dawn on the Capitol grounds. The doors of the main building were thrown open to the public, but those of the House of Representatives, where the religious ceremony was to take place, were closely guarded. Clio, the figure of History, was draped in black crepe, except for the arm that held her recording pen. The muse, her head turned to the left, happened to have her marble eyes fixed upon Mr. Adams's vacant seat.

At eleven o'clock, after the religious ceremonies, Lincoln and the rest of Congress, the diplomatic corps, the government leaders, and the clergy left the building by the east portico. He fell in behind the marching soldiers, the band, and the chaplains as the great funeral procession left by the north gate. Behind Lincoln and his committee came the pallbearers and the casket along the western portion of the public grounds on the way to the congressional cemetery, the "City of Silence."

The shops and businesses were closed and hung with mourning drapery. Journalists estimated that more than fifteen thousand men, women, and children had gathered for the great man's funeral.

The ball that Mary had so eagerly anticipated, the party to raise funds for the Washington Monument, was finally held on March 1 in Jackson Hall, on Pennsylvania Avenue not far from the Capitol. A reporter said it was elegant, and that Chef Gautier's supper, served until eleven at night, was excellent, but regretted that it "was not so numerously attended as could have been wished, and as would have been the case but for the postponement and its mournful cause."

. . .

So the Birth Night Ball was disheartening. But as spring approached, Washington was not without other diversions for the young couple. Just a few doors from Jackson Hall, at 4½ Street and Pennsylvania Avenue, Hiram Powers's sensational statue "The Greek Slave" was on exhibit at the Odeon from 9:00 A.M. until 10:00 P.M. The naked Grecian maiden of marble with chained wrists had become the most famous and beloved statue carved by any American in the mid-nineteenth century. The manager of the tour wrote in his 12½-cent pamphlet:

> The ostensible subject is merely a Grecian maiden, made captive by the Turks and exposed at Constantinople, for sale. The cross and locket visible amid the drapery, indicate that she is a Christian, and beloved. But this simple phrase by no means completes the meaning of the statue. It represents a being superior to suffering, and raised above degradation by inward purity and force of character. Thus the Greek Slave is an emblem of the trial to which all humanity is subject, and may be regarded as a type of resignation, uncompromising virtue, or sublime patience.

The sensation that drove hundreds of thousands of people in major cities to pay 25 cents admission to ogle the statue—citizens unaccustomed to nude statuary—was the erotic effect of a maiden on sale as a sexual object. Spectators generally remained silent upon the political implications of the beautiful figure; but it did not escape the notice of the abolitionist press or sensitive observers like the Lincolns, who found themselves increasingly perplexed by the paradox of slavery in the capital. An anonymous reviewer for *The National Era* wrote:

> In the midst of the pleasing emotions excited by this admirable work of art, there came sad thoughts of that wondrous hardness of that nature which can weep at sight of an insensate piece of marble which images a helpless virgin chained in the market-place of brutal lust, and still more brutal cupidity, and yet listens unmoved to the awful story of the American slave! Waste not your sympathies on the senseless marble, but reserve some tears for the helpless humanity which lies quivering beneath the lash of *American Freeman*.

Right across the street from the Odeon stood another haven of culture, a new playhouse. Ever since the Lincolns arrived in Washington, the newspapers had been full of advertisements and commentary about the construction of the Adelphi Theatre in a large brick building on the south side of Pennsylvania Avenue. The managers, Messrs. Brown and Nichols, "spared neither pains nor expense to make their establishment superior to any theatre of its size in the country." At last it had opened in late December, and the managers lived up to their promise, delivering first-rate new dramas, farces, and classics, using their own actors as well as stars from New York and Philadelphia. There was enormous excitement when Brown and Nichols announced that the beautiful actress (and child prodigy) Julia Dean would be appearing in early March, in several plays, including *Lucretia Borgia* and *Romeo and Juliet*.

Mr. Lincoln had been unusually busy that week with his work on the Committee on Post Office and Post Roads, so the only likely date for him to take his wife to the theater to see the Shakespeare was Friday, March 10, the last night Miss Dean would appear as Juliet.

Lincoln had a good deal to tell his wife, in his humorous tone, about the events of that day. Since the patriarch Adams's sudden departure, the House had lost a degree of civility, and tempers seethed and erupted unchecked. Like schoolboys left without proper supervision, the congressmen fell to name-calling, and the House broke out in fistfights. Only this afternoon—in the midst of what appeared to be a placid session—Hugh Haralson of Georgia suddenly leaped for the throat of George Washington Jones of Tennessee, both Democrats and old enough to know how to control their rancor, or at least limit the conflict to standard vituperation, but they swung at each other and had to be pulled apart like growling dogs. When at last the Southerners were persuaded to make peace, shake hands, and apologize to the assembly, the House then had to vote on whether to accept the apology. Lincoln voted with the majority in favor of acceptance. Hearing such stories, Mary Lincoln may have wondered if the U.S. Congress was a healthy social environment for her husband, for whose improvement—social and professional—she held such high hopes.

But now they were on their way to an oasis of civilization, the new Adelphi Theatre. Walking down Pennsylvania Avenue, they could see the façade glowing from a block away—the managers used nothing but the finest sperm oil in their lanterns. Four doors opened under the marquee.

And as the Lincolns entered the brick theater, their eyes were immediately drawn upward to the painted rococo dome, the proscenium arch, and the two private boxes on either side of the stage, all richly designed by Edward Pollock. The parquette (orchestra) seated four hundred in plush burgundy-cushioned chairs; the second tier held three hundred.

They took their seats and waited for the curtain to rise upon that famous prologue:

> Two households, both alike in dignity,
> In fair Verona, where we lay our scene,
> From ancient grudge break to new mutiny,
> Where civil blood makes civil hands unclean.
> From forth the fatal loins of these two foes
> A pair of star-cross'd lovers take their life;
> Whose misadventured piteous overthrows
> Do with their death bury their parents' strife.

Sitting side by side in the semidarkness of the theater, the Lincolns were transported by the timeless tragedy far from Springfield, far from the Capitol and the boardinghouse. Eagerly they awaited the entrance of Miss Julia Dean.

The tall, willowy, graceful figure—the radiant round face with the features of a porcelain doll—had a riveting impact before the actress uttered a word. Not yet eighteen years of age, she had been famous since her 1846 New York debut in Sheridan Knowles's *The Hunchback*. The large eyes were dark, with arched eyebrows, and her gaze was at once soft and soul-searching. Actor Joseph Jefferson recalled, "The gentle eyes are raised, so full of innocence and truth and now she speaks . . . so low, so sweet and yet so audible."

> What's in a name? that which we call a rose
> By any other name would smell as sweet . . .

"It sinks into the hearts of all who listen," Jefferson continued. "They are spellbound by her beauty, and as she gives the lines with warm and honest power a murmur of delight runs through the house."

Having seen so little of Shakespeare on the stage, the couple could laugh and weep with Shakespeare's lovers in innocent sympathy. Holding

hands in the grand theater, they were swept up, with all the other spectators, by Julia Dean's ingenuous performance. Uncritical, they may not
have realized they were seeing the greatest Juliet of their time. The acts of
the tragedy as they rose in hopefulness and fell in terror and pity came
home to them all too well. What lovers do not see some part of themselves
in *Romeo and Juliet?*

> *My bounty is as boundless as the sea,*
> *My love as deep; the more I give to thee,*
> *The more I have, for both are infinite.*

Inside the golden band on Mary's left hand Lincoln had had engraved
the words "Love Is Eternal." So Romeo and Juliet must have felt on the
night that they wed in Friar Laurence's cell, against their parents' wishes.
And even death, in the end, cannot diminish their passion as each lover
longs to follow the other beyond life. Shakespeare's message is plain
enough: The path of true love is never straight and smooth; and life is finally sad. The play's last act, drenched in tears, poses questions to all
lovers, generation after generation: Must true love always end in tragedy?
Are none of us spared? On this question the curtain dropped, and the audience, stunned and weeping, called the company forth for their bows
with deafening applause. The Lincolns added their clapping to the din
before filing out the aisle and the door, and then up Pennsylvania Avenue
as the crowd dispersed around them.

It had been a romantic evening, and a performance that Mary would
refer to many years afterward. Yet the next morning she faced the same
difficulties in the boardinghouse, although she would have Father's help
with the children over the weekend.

During that winter he did what he could to distract and entertain his
wife, and to help her with the children when his schedule permitted it, as
child care was sporadic. But for every concert on the Capitol lawn, for
every minstrel show, for every stage play or hour in the Odeon exhibition
hall, there were long hours when she saw no company but the little boys
in the cramped quarters of the boardinghouse where she tried to keep
them from breaking the furniture. Her husband often worked day and
night, so she rarely saw enough of him. Meanwhile, the other boarders
saw more of Mrs. Lincoln and her loud, unruly children than they liked.

By the end of March, the time she might have taken them out of doors, Mary Lincoln had made several enemies at Mrs. Sprigg's mess.

It is not known exactly when she told her husband she had seen enough of the Federal City and the four walls of their bedroom. Once she got the idea, and began recalling the comforts of her Kentucky home, he did not dissuade her from returning there. Later correspondence indicates that there must have been an outburst on Mary's part, an event that so disturbed the peace at Mrs. Sprigg's that the unhappy wife was urged to leave Washington for a spell. That there was such an event seems a certainty; the details are lost to history.

So not long after their night of Shakespeare, when the shad and herring were arriving at the Centre Market and spring weather was suitable for traveling, Mary Lincoln packed her bags and trunks. Mr. Lincoln took them to the train station in a hackney cab. Another congressman, James A. Black of South Carolina, had dropped dead on April 1, and Mary Lincoln had seen enough of black crepe and funereal pomp in Washington for one term of Congress. Mr. Lincoln would have to attend that funeral on his own. As for her, she was headed for the comforts of her father's house in the Bluegrass State, and she could not tell him exactly when, or if, she would be returning.

In that mood of anxious uncertainty, he kissed her good-bye.

SEPARATION

H E WROTE TO HER on April 9, but that letter and many other pieces of their correspondence that spring and summer have not survived. It is likely that she or some relative entrusted with the precious letters would have burned any that revealed too much about the tensions that had driven Mrs. Lincoln from Washington. Nevertheless, the long letters from this season that have been preserved represent the most complete and intimate conversation between husband and wife that can be found, in their own words.

There are four letters in Lincoln's hand from April 16 through July 2; there is one long letter from Mary dated simply May 1848; and numerous remarks in Lincoln's letters refer to lost notes from his wife.

Dear Mary,   *Washington, April 16, 1848*

In this troublesome world, we are never quite satisfied. When you were here, I thought you hindered me some in attending to business; but now, having nothing but business—no variety—it has grown exceedingly tasteless to me. I hate to sit down in this old room by myself. You know I told you in last Sunday's letter, I was going to make a little speech during the week; but the week has passed away without my getting a chance to do so; and now my interest in the subject has passed away too. Your second and third letters have been received since I wrote before. Dear Eddy thinks father is *"gone tapila."* Has any further discovery been made as to the breaking into your grand-mother's house? If I were she, I would not remain there alone. You mention that your uncle John Parker is likely to be at Lexington. Don't forget to present him my very kindest regards.

I went yesterday to hunt the little plaid stockings, as you wished; but found that McKnight has quit business, and Allen had not a single pair of the description you give, and only one plaid pair of any sort that I thought would fit "Eddy's dear little feet." I have a notion to make another trial to-morrow morning. If I could get them, I have an excellent chance of sending them. Mr. Warrick Tunstall, of St. Louis is here. He is to leave early this week, and to go by Lexington. He says he knows you, and will call to see you; and he voluntarily asked, if I had not some package to send to you.

I wish you to enjoy yourself in every possible way; but is there no danger of wounding the feelings of your good father, by being so openly intimate with the Wickliffe family?

Mrs. Broome has not removed yet; but she thinks of doing so tomorrow. All the house—or rather, all with whom you were on decided good terms—send their love to you. The others say nothing.

Very soon after you went away, I got what I think a very pretty set of shirt-bosom studs—modest little ones, jet, set in gold, only costing 50 cents a piece, or 1.50 for the whole.

Suppose you do not prefix the "Hon" to the address on your letters to me any more. I like the letters very much, but I would rather they should not have that upon them. It is not necessary, as I suppose you have thought, to have them to come free.

And you are entirely free from head-ache? That is good—good—considering it is the first spring you have been free from it since we were acquainted. I am afraid you will get so well, and fat, and young, as to be wanting to marry again. Tell Louisa I want her to watch you a little for me. Get weighed, and write me how much you weigh.

I did not get rid of the impression of that foolish dream about dear Bobby till I got your letter written the same day. What did he and Eddy think of the little letters father sent them? Dont let the blessed fellows forget father.

A day or two ago Mr. Strong, here in Congress, said to me that Matilda would visit here within two or three weeks. Suppose you write her a letter, and enclose it in one of mine; and if she comes I will deliver it to her, and if she does not, I will send it to her.

Most affectionately   A. LINCOLN

This letter is a perfect snapshot of the marriage as of 1848, six years after the wedding. Lincoln's affection for his wife, despite their recent difficulty, is transparent. He misses her. Flattering her by feigning jealousy, and the fear that she might want to marry someone else, he not only writes to her, he has written letters to both of their children. (What a pity those have not survived!) Without her and the children, life had "grown exceedingly tasteless."

Mostly the letter speaks for itself. "Gone tapila" is probably the two-year-old's lisping phrase for "gone to the Capitol." Two of Mary's best friends were daughters of Robert Wickliffe, who had fallen out with Robert Todd over the slavery issue. The "Mr. Strong" mentioned in the final paragraph is Newton D. Strong of Pennsylvania, who married Matilda Edwards, Mary's former roommate, who once complicated the Lincolns' courtship. One does wonder about the "Mrs. Broome" who "has not removed yet," and whether Mary's exile might have involved a quarrel with that mysterious boarder.

In Kentucky, Mary and the children divided their time between her father's brick mansion on Main Street and the tall, airy summerhouse they called "Buena Vista" on the Leestown Pike, eighteen miles from Lexington. The rambling wood-frame house with its shuttered windows stood on a knoll overlooking hemp fields and a brook that ran from a nearby springhouse. Buena Vista was aptly named for the view from its double portico: the garden of roses, lilacs, and day lilies; and all the countryside below was very fine indeed. On the side of the house were an ell and a shaded porch that connected the main house with the stone slave quarters.

From her room in Buena Vista, Mary wrote to her husband on a Saturday night in May after the children had gone to bed.

My dear Husband—

You will think indeed that *old age,* has set *its seal,* upon my humble self, that in few or none of my letters, I can remember the day of the month, I must confess it as one of my peculiarities; I feel wearied & tired enough to know, that this is *Saturday night,* our *babies* are asleep, and as Aunt Maria B[ullock] is coming in for me tomorrow morning, I think the chances will be rather dull that I should answer your last letter tomorrow—I have just received a letter from Frances W[allace], it related in an *especial* manner to THE BOX I had desired her to send, she thinks

with you (as good persons generally agree) that it would cost more than it
would come to, and it might be lost on the road, I rather expect she has
examined the specified articles, and thinks as *Levi* says, they are *hard
bargains*—But it takes so many changes to do children, particularly in
summer, that I thought it might save me a few stitches—I think I will
write her a few lines this evening, directing her not to send them—She
says Willie is just recovering from another spell of sickness, Mary or none
of them were well—Springfield she reports as dull as usual. Uncle
S[amuel Todd] was to leave there on yesterday for Ky—Our little Eddy,
has recovered from his little spell of sickness—Dear boy, I must tell you a
story about him—Bobby in his wanderings to day, came across in a yard,
a little kitten, *your hobby,* he says he asked a man for it, he brought it tri-
umphantly to the house, so soon as Eddy, spied it—his *tenderness,* broke
forth, he made them bring it *water,* fed it with bread himself, with his
own dear hands, he was a delighted little creature over it, in the midst of
his happiness Ma came in, she you must know dislikes the whole cat race,
I thought in a very unfeeling manner, she ordered the servant near, to
throw it out, which of *course,* was done, Ed screaming & protesting
loudly against the proceeding, *she* never appeared to mind his screams,
which were long & loud, I assure you—Tis unusual for her *now a days,* to
do any thing quite so striking, she is very obliging & accommodating, but
if she thought any of us, were on her hands again, I believe she would be
worse than ever—In the next moment she appeared in a good humor, I
know she did not intend to offend me. By the way, she has just sent me up
a glass of ice cream, for which this warm evening, I am duly grateful. The
country is so delightful I am going to spend two or three weeks out there,
it will doubtless benefit the children—Grandma has received a letter from
Uncle James Parker of Miss[ouri] saying he & his family would be up by
the twenty fifth of June, would remain there some little time & go on to
Philadelphia to take their oldest daughter there to school, I believe it
would be a good chance for me to pack up & accompany them—You
know I am so fond of *sightseeing,* & did not get to New York or Boston,
or travel the lake route—But perhaps, dear husband, like the *irresistible
Col Mc,* cannot do without his wife next winter, and must needs take her
with him again—I expect you would cry aloud against it—How much, I
wish instead of writing, *we* were together this evening, I feel very sad
away from you—Ma & myself rode out to Mr. Bell's splendid place this
afternoon, to return a call, the house and grounds are magnificent,

Frances W. would *have died* over their rare exotics—It is growing late, these summer eves are short, I expect my long *scrawls,* for truly such they are, weary you greatly—if you come on, in July or August *I* will take you to the springs—*Patty Webb's* school in S[helbyville] closes the first of July, I expect *Mr. Webb,* will come on for her. I must go down about that time & carry on quite a flirtation, you know *we,* always had a *penchant* that way. ~~With love~~ I must bid you good night—Do not fear the children, have forgotten you, I was only jesting—Even E[ddie's] eyes brighten at the mention of your name—My love to all—

Truly yours,

M L—

When it comes to the question of her returning to Washington, she is coy; he is insistent, not that she return at once, but that she come to him when it suits her and when she can assure him she will behave herself. This is an important theme in their correspondence during that spring and summer. She informs him of her desire to travel with the Parker family and go to him in late June, and next, perversely, she compares him to the uxorious "Col Mc" (Colonel John McClernand, a Democratic congressman from Illinois who needed his wife in Washington and planned to return with Mrs. McClernand in December), saying, "I expect you would cry out against it." That is, Mary thinks he would cry out against her returning, suspects him of being halfhearted about her company, and wants to be wooed. She even threatens a flirtation with her old flame Edwin Webb, but she is only teasing.

"How much, I wish instead of writing, *we* were together this evening, I feel very sad away from you." In these last sentences her longing for him assumes an erotic tone, as she alludes to flirtations past and present, and as in closing she writes "with love I must bid you good night," and tellingly crosses out "with love" as she was *without* it—certainly not because she does not feel the passion, but because she cannot express it in the physical way that has been their nightly ritual.

On May 24 he sent her a bank draft in the amount of $50. She did not acknowledge it in her next letter to him, but he has little "fear but that you got it; because the want of it would have induced you [to] say something in relation to it." He was gone all the second week of June, in Philadelphia and Wilmington at the Whig convention, and then stumping for their

presidential nominee, General Zachary Taylor. Mary had written him a
letter asking if she might eventually return to Washington, a request probably written in late May, so he would have found it waiting when he returned. Below is his response, a letter full of longing and affection, but
also an expression of dark ambivalence. Clearly Mary Lincoln's departure
at the end of March was some kind of exile for an offense or a violation of
domestic order; he requires her word of honor there will be no more
of that.

My dear wife: *Washington, June 12, 1848*
    On my return from Philadelphia, yesterday, where, in my anxiety I had
been led to attend the whig convention I found your last letter. I was so
tired and sleepy, having ridden all night, that I could not answer it till today; and now I have to do so in the H.R. The leading matter in your letter, is your wish to return to this side of the Mountains. Will you be a *good
girl* in all things, if I consent? Then come along, and that as *soon* as possible. Having got the idea in my head, I shall be impatient till I see you. You
will not have money enough to bring you; but I presume your uncle will
supply you, and I will refund him here. By the way you do not mention
whether you have received the fifty dollars I sent you. I do not much fear
but that you got it; because the want of it would have induced you [to]
say something in relation to it. If your uncle is already at Lexington, you
might induce him to start on earlier than the first of July; he could stay in
Kentucky longer on his return, and so make up for lost time. Since I
began this letter, the H.R. has passed a resolution for adjourning on the
17th July, which probably will pass the Senate. I hope this letter will not
be disagreeable to you; which, together with the circumstances under
which I write, I hope will excuse me for not writing a longer one. Come
on just as soon as you can. I want to see you, and our dear—*dear* boys
very much. Every body here wants to see our dear Bobby.
Affectionately   LINCOLN

Between the wife's plea for reinstatement and the husband's condi-
tional (gently scolding) reply—"Will you be a *good girl* in all things, if I
consent?"—it is likely that three weeks passed. On June 25, a Sunday,
each wrote a letter to the other, neither of which survives, but Lincoln's
letter to his wife included a bank draft for $100 to cover travel expenses

from Lexington to Washington. Given Mary Lincoln's temperament, she was not thrilled by his provisory invitation of June 12, but without letting him know of any exact plan, she led him to believe she would be leaving Lexington sooner rather than later.

Then she dug in her heels.

On July 2 he wrote her a long and charming letter whose tone is appealing if not conciliatory. In it he mentions a long speech he had made in the House on June 20 in favor of internal improvements. He would have sent her a copy three days earlier "but I did not . . . thinking you would be on the road here, before it would reach you. I send you one now." She was keeping him in suspense about her plans to return.

The letter is chatty, mentioning common acquaintances and Lincoln's leisure activities.

> Mrs. Richardson is still here; and what is more, has a baby—
> so Richardson says, and he ought to know. [William Richardson was
> a Democratic congressman from Illinois.] I believe Mary Hewett has
> left here and gone to Boston. . . .
>
> The music in the Capitol grounds on Saturdays, or rather, the interest
> in it, is dwindling down to nothing. Yesterday evening the attendance was
> rather thin. Our two girls, whom you remember seeing first at Carusis, at
> the exhibition of the Ethiopian Serenaders, and whose peculiarities were
> the wearing of black fur bonnets, and never being seen in the close com-
> pany of other ladies, were at the music yesterday. One of them was at-
> tended by their brother, and the other had a member of Congress in tow.
> He went home with her; and if I were to guess, I would say, he went away
> a somewhat altered man—most likely in his pockets, and in some other
> particular. The fellow looked conscious of guilt, although I believe he
> was unconscious that every body around knew who it was that had
> caught him.

The black fur bonnets—not to mention the behavior of "our two girls"—mark them as prostitutes. The ease and humor with which the Lincolns discussed such sexual escapades indicate that Abraham and Mary were not at all prudish about such matters. No doubt they enjoyed a similar attitude toward their own sexuality—unlike some other Victorians of their generation. His comic reference to the girl with a member of

Congress in tow who "went away a somewhat altered man—most likely in his pockets, and in some other particular," was calculated to raise a question in a wife's mind. How does the lonely politician spend his nights when his wife is far away? The letter continues:

> I have had no letter from home, since I wrote you before, except short business letters, which have no interest for you.
>
> By the way, you do not intend to do without a girl, because the one you had has left you? Get another as soon as you can to take charge of the dear codgers. Father expected to see you all sooner; but let it pass; stay as long as you please, and come when you please. Kiss and love the dear rascals.
>
> Affectionately   LINCOLN

Always concerned about her comfort, he encouraged her to hire more child care. Only one note of irritation enters the otherwise affectionate letter, as he reminds her that shopkeepers have dunned him for money he did not know she had spent. "Mention in your next letter whether they are right." It was the beginning of a difficult conflict over Mary's handling of accounts that would only grow worse with the years.

One can almost hear the sigh of resignation as he signs off: *Father expected to see you all sooner; but let it pass; stay as long as you please, and come when you please.*

What might have escaped Father's understanding is that July and August were months when sensible mothers with little children fled the dank heat of Washington and the noxious vapors of its canals to avoid typhoid—if they had the means. Eddie was given to colds and the grippe. This was no time to leave the fresh air and clear sunlight of Buena Vista.

MARY LINCOLN WAS always a hardy and enthusiastic traveler, so her husband's plan to make a monthlong campaign tour of his journey to Springfield in mid-September 1848 appealed to her.

The two major themes of Lincoln's career in Congress were his opposition to Mr. Polk's war and his tireless efforts to get a Whig elected president. So after Congress adjourned sine die on August 14, Lincoln threw his energies into the coming presidential election and hopes of electing

General Zachary Taylor ("Old Rough and Ready") on the Whig ticket. After spending a couple of weeks attending Whig rallies and conventions in Maryland, he packed his bags and boarded the train to Baltimore en route to points north. Somewhere along the campaign trail—perhaps Worcester, Massachusetts, where he spoke at City Hall, or perhaps New Bedford, where he addressed a crowd at Liberty Hall—his wife joined him.

Mary and Bobbie were delighted to see him. Little Eddie had been ill and was still not wholly recovered, but Mr. Lincoln had a salutary effect upon them all. And the long campaign tour—eight cities and towns in Massachusetts; Albany, New York City, Buffalo, and Niagara Falls in New York; Milwaukee, and Chicago—gave his wife an opportunity to see him in action, honored and applauded as she had hoped he might be in Washington. She shared in his glory, enjoying the sort of attention that was her due as a congressman's wife.

Commenting upon his speech in Chelsea, Massachusetts, on September 20, the reporter for the Boston *Atlas* wrote, "The Hon. Abraham Lincoln made a speech, which for aptness of illustration, solidity of argument, and genuine eloquence, is hard to beat." Lincoln spoke at a huge mass meeting in Boston two days later, following William Seward on the podium at Tremont Temple. Forty-eight-year-old Seward, former governor of New York, was one of the two most powerful Whigs in the state—the other being the journalist Thurlow Weed— and Lincoln was honored to meet Seward and share the podium with him, unaware of the parts they would play in each other's lives a decade hence.

The Boston *Atlas* again praised Lincoln, who "spoke about an hour, and made a powerful and convincing speech. . . . The audience then gave three hearty cheers for 'old Zack,' three more for Governor Seward, and three more for Mr. Lincoln, and then adjourned; thus ended one of the best meetings ever held in this good Whig city." With much fanfare, they left Boston by train en route to Buffalo, where they would board the steamer *Globe* bound for Chicago. Stopping briefly at Niagara Falls, they beheld the silver cataracts and maze of rainbows, the wonder of nature. The power and glory of the falls seemed a fit symbol for their optimism about life then—its capacity to surprise and change and nourish the body and spirit as it rushed to seek its own level.

Arriving in Chicago on October 5, they registered at the Sherman House Hotel, and the next evening Lincoln was principal speaker at a Whig rally that had been announced that afternoon. Despite the impromptu nature of the event, the crowd quickly overran the courthouse and adjourned to the public square. It was like Niagara, the force of party politics, pursuing a goal, seeking its level. They had come to see Mr. Lincoln defend General Taylor from the charge that he lacked principles, ridicule former president Martin Van Buren and his newly formed Free-Soil party, and argue that the Whigs were more committed to halting the spread of slavery than was the opposition. *The Chicago Journal* called Lincoln's two-hour speech "one of the very best we have heard or read since the opening of the campaign."

The adventure that had begun nearly a year before, the odyssey that had encompassed so many hopes, defeats, excitements, and disappointments, now was sounding a positive note. Mrs. Lincoln was pleased to see that her family warranted notice now, even as it passed through great cities: "Hon. A. Lincoln and Family passed down to Springfield this morning on his way home from Congress," the *Chicago Democrat* announced on October 7.

They were returning home, to all appearances, in triumph.

HAD THEY KNOWN that Washington was not going to suit Mary and the children, they might never have leased out their home in the Illinois capital for a year's term. Their Springfield residence from mid-October until April of 1849 was, again, the Globe Tavern, which—under new management—had been renovated. There were advantages to returning there (the return speaks well of their memory of the Globe), as Mrs. Lincoln needed help. Her husband would be on the road with Anson Henry for the rest of October and early November, campaigning for the Whig ticket. After celebrating General Taylor's victory in the presidential election on November 7, Lincoln stayed with his family only two weeks before setting out for the second session of Congress in Washington. At the Globe Tavern, Mary did not have to worry about cooking meals, hauling water, washing clothes, and keeping the fireplaces stoked. She would not be alone, and she could depend upon the maids at the Globe for a certain amount of help with the children.

As Mrs. Lincoln returned to the Globe in a new role—the wife of a member of Congress and the mother of two boys, five and two—she might have hoped for greater respect than was immediately forthcoming from the neighbors. From Boston to Chicago, she and her husband had been feted, flattered, and cheered as bearers of the Whig banner. In the rest of Illinois, and even in Springfield, Mr. Lincoln and his wife found themselves on the defensive because of his protests against the war. In Jacksonville (the martyr Hardin's hometown), where Lincoln appeared on October 21, a correspondent for the *Illinois Register* wrote, "Lincoln has made nothing by coming to this part of the country to make speeches. He had better have stayed away." And in Petersburg two days later, that paper reported that "Lincoln attempted . . . to make a defense of his course in Congress" when a local spokesman denounced him. "Lincoln beat a retreat to Springfield," swearing that his critic's vituperation was not only unnecessary but "unconstitutional."

As she helped him pack his bags after Thanksgiving and bade him farewell again, she had reason to fear that during his four-month absence she would find herself once more in the position of explaining and defending her husband to her family and the community. So many had sacrificed their husbands and sons for a war that Lincoln opposed with deep conviction.

He would serve faithfully and assiduously during the second session. But from December 7, when he took his seat in the House (three days late), until the inauguration of President Taylor on March 5, 1849, the day after Congress adjourned, Lincoln accomplished little to redeem himself in the eyes of those who had elected him or those in Washington he had offended by speaking out against President Polk. He lingered at the Inaugural Ball until four o'clock in the morning, when he walked home to the boardinghouse bareheaded in the cold dawn. He had lost his hat in the cloakroom.

Lincoln's hat, that famous stovepipe repository of jottings, letters, and receipts—not to mention the headquarters of even more famous thoughts and reflections—has assumed iconic status. Autumn to spring for years it had been vital to the lawyer's attire. His losing the hat at the Inaugural Ball invites comment and begs interpretation, which is probably why the slight detail has survived for more than a century and a half. The congressman had lost his hat, and he had lost his head as well in that mad swirl of Washington politics and brinkmanship. During the next three months he would discover that he had lost the game of politics altogether for the foreseeable future, although he would hang on to hope until there was nothing left of it. The very next day, March 7, he was to try his first case before Chief Justice Taney and the Supreme Court (a complex appeal involving the Illinois statute of limitations), and he would lose that, too, on March 13.

Was there a letter from his wife in Lincoln's hat? It is curious that not a scrap of mail between the Lincolns has survived the long winter of their separation, 1848–49. Either they wrote no letters, or they did not care to preserve them; they lost them in transit, or some descendant entrusted with the correspondence thought better to destroy it as evidence unflattering to one or both of the writers. If the Lexington letters did not exist, we might not wonder. The silence is troubling. What is there to be said about a marriage when husband and wife are five hundred miles apart for a full season? Certainly they missed each other, as they had in the spring, and Lincoln and his sons missed one another. Little Eddie so adored his father (*his eyes brighten at the mention of your name*) that one cannot help but wonder if the child's failing lungs may have been aggravated by his father's absence.

They missed one another, but in that year, April 1848 until April 1849, when they were together as a family no more than seven or eight weeks all told, and most of that time on the New England to Chicago campaign tour, they grew accustomed to being apart. So about the time Lincoln lost his hat at the Inaugural Ball, he was also losing touch with his wife, and she with him. He lingered in Washington for a week before heading for home on March 20, preoccupied with patronage matters, as if he might make his constituents forget their disappointment in him by getting them jobs. He also submitted a patent application for expansible air chambers that buoy steamboats over shoals.

After ten days on the road, he arrived in Springfield on March 31.

DURING THE MONTH of April 1849 they worked together with carpenter John E. Roll to repaint and remodel their house at Eighth and Jackson, preparing to reclaim it from the two bachelors who had lived there for a year. But although Mr. Lincoln had returned to his family, his wife soon discovered that he was not really with them in spirit. He remained preoccupied with political matters in Washington, relatively petty concerns, as if he had not been quite prepared to leave there and so was not altogether at home yet in Springfield.

If you make a bad bargain, hug it the tighter. That perverse adage now seemed to apply to Mr. Lincoln's tenure in Washington. Not much was left of it, but still he was loath to let go.

The Whigs' success in putting Zachary Taylor in the White House, and Lincoln's energetic part in that election, had given him and Edward Baker influence over patronage, the distribution of government jobs to friends and loyal party members. From the day Taylor was inaugurated until late that spring, Lincoln was lobbying and writing letters on behalf of dozens of candidates, making the most of his power while he still had it. Immediately, he recommended Dr. Anson Henry as secretary of the Minnesota Territory (for no friend did Lincoln lobby more tirelessly than for Dr. Henry), and Archibald Williams of Quincy, Illinois, as U.S. district attorney there. All the way home he was stopping to post letters recommending this job seeker and that to be appointed postmaster, clerk, or marshal, and the scribbling for patronage did not cease during the whole month of April.

No patronage matter so greatly consumed Lincoln's attention as the presidential appointment of commissioner of the General Land Office at Washington, a position that had been promised to Illinois. It was a remunerative and important office. The commissioner reported to the secretary of the interior and was directly involved in ordering the survey of lands, offering government land for sale, issuing swamp grants and railroad approvals, and determining boundaries in new territories. Lincoln preferred his lawyer friend Cyrus Edwards, a brother of Ninian's, while Baker supported J.L.D. Morrison, a Mexican War veteran. As of March 27, 1849, they had not agreed on a candidate. Everyone understood that if Lincoln and Baker could not agree and persuade one candidate or the other to withdraw, the influential office, which paid $3,000 a year for four years, might actually go to another state.

Aware of the impending crisis, William B. Warren, of Morgan County, and some other Whigs wrote to Lincoln, urging him to take the position if he could, rather than see it lost to the people of Illinois. This was in early April. By the time he replied on April 7, his own interest in the job was evident: "I must not only be chaste but above suspicion. If the office shall be tendered to me, I must be permitted to say 'Give it to Mr. Edwards, or, if so agreed by them, to Col. Morrison, and I decline it; if not, I accept.' With this understanding, you are at liberty to procure me the offer of the appointment if you can; and I shall feel complimented by your effort, still more by its success." He adds that Baker's influence here is considerable and that Baker stands ready to recommend him in a pinch.

This letter is characteristically Lincolnesque in its oblique expression of his desires, its ill-concealed ambition. A man with famous powers of persuasion and arbitration, nowhere does Lincoln suggest that he plans to broker a deal with Baker or pressure his candidate Edwards to back down. He is content with a stalemate, and the longer it goes on, the more attractive the job looks to him.

When Morrison would not decline, Edwards informed Lincoln of it on April 15. Lincoln's response was cryptic, both noncommittal and vaguely supportive: "What I can do for you, I shall do, but I can do nothing till all negotiation between you and Don [Morrison] is at an end, because of my pledge to Baker. Still they know at the Department I am for you." Then he goes on to confess that his Whig friends have sent a letter to Washington stating that if the precious office can only be saved for Illinois by Lincoln's filling it, he will do so "only on their refusal to give it to you." By now Cyrus Edwards must have been thoroughly confused.

The next letter Edwards received was one from Dr. Anson Henry requesting that Edwards write a letter to President Taylor recommending Mr. Lincoln for the very job for which Lincoln had recommended Edwards. Anyone who still believes Lincoln's pursuit of it was disinterested, and purely owing to the high principle that misplaced patronage would ruin party loyalty, has not paid close attention to the chronology.

All that April and May, while the Lincolns were painting and refurbishing their home to resume a peaceful life in Springfield, Mr. Lincoln was plotting his return to Washington as commissioner of the General Land Office. And he did not even realize just how much he wanted that job until April 25, when he got wind that Justin Butterfield of Chicago had gone for it without consulting him or Baker. It was a surprising development. This was the same dapper lawyer who had flattered Mary Lincoln and the other Springfield ladies as he stood to defend the Mormon prophet six years earlier.

At first Lincoln was annoyed, because Butterfield had supported Henry Clay for president before the Whig nominating convention, and had done little for Zachary Taylor thereafter. Lincoln wrote to a clerk in the General Land Office: "He is my personal friend, and is qualified to do the duties of the office; but of the quite one hundred Illinoisians, equally well qualified, I do not know one with less claims to it." Attacks on the character of other office seekers Lincoln was promoting were beginning to arouse an almost paranoid response from him. Turner R. King, whom Lincoln had proposed for a job in the local land office, had been accused of having a gambling problem. Lincoln wrote to Secretary of the Interior Thomas Ewing on April 26 that he recognized "the principal object of the fault-finders, *to be to stab me.*" The machinations of job seekers and their rivals were beginning to wear him down, as the smell of lead paint filled the house on Eighth Street, and Mary Lincoln lay there coping with her seasonal headaches, which the fumes did nothing to mitigate.

Receiving letters on May 15 from Washington that Butterfield was likely to succeed, Lincoln bitterly complained to the secretary of the navy, William B. Preston, who had once assured him that "no man from Illinois should be appointed to any high office" without Lincoln's being consulted. Again he referred to Butterfield as his friend, before unleashing a tirade that would have better suited an enemy. Digging up the Whig victory of 1840, he called Butterfield one of the "drones" who got his appointment as district attorney without ever having "spent a dollar or lifted a finger in the fight." He was furious that during the recent campaign "when you and I were almost sweating blood to have Gen'l Taylor nominated, this same man was ridiculing the idea, and going for Mr. Clay. . . . Yet, when the election is secured, by other men's labor, and even against his effort, why, he is the first man on hand for the best office that our state lays any claim to. Shall this thing be? Our whigs will throw down their arms, and fight no more, if the fruit of their labor is thus disposed of."

Time would tell. As it turned out, two of the most venerable Whigs, Daniel Webster and Henry Clay, both endorsed Butterfield, and so did many other party members who were not likely to "throw down their arms" if the lawyer from Chicago reaped the fruit of their labor. No one seemed nearly so incensed over Butterfield's candidacy as Lincoln.

In May and June of 1849, Abraham Lincoln became obsessed with the fate of this position, commissioner of the General Land Office—as much for his own genuine desire to have the job as for the sheer injustice of Butterfield's getting it instead. He wrote countless confidential letters to Whigs all over the country, of which this one to Duff Green is typical: "A man by the name of Butterfield will probably be appointed Commissioner of the General Land Office. This ought not to be. That is about the only crumb of patronage which Illinois expects"; or to Hon. Elisha Embree: "It will give offense to the whole whig party here. . . . write General Taylor at once, saying that either *I, or the man I recommend* should, in your opinion, be appointed to that office. . . ." He drew up a form letter and a long list of names, and when his own hand faltered in the letter-writing campaign, he turned it over to his wife. In May and June, Mary wrote the letters.

Why did this "crumb of patronage" matter so much to the ex-congressman that he should pursue it with such feverish energy? Furthermore, why should his wife support him in what appeared to be a quixotic effort, which—if it succeeded—would inconvenience the family? The job paid more than the seat in Congress, yet it hardly paid enough to make them comfortable in Washington. Finally they were all together again, re-decorating their home in Springfield, preparing to begin life anew there. The Lincolns had not been happy together in the capital. Was there any reason to believe they would be content there a year or two from now, with Mr. Lincoln pushing papers in one of the government departments?

The truth is that Mr. Lincoln was clinging to the last filament that might connect him to Washington, where he had gone with such high hopes and where his performance had frustrated the expectations of so many here at home. Senator Stephen Douglas and General James Shields flourished there while he floundered. Now his strained effort to gain the land office post was out of proportion to the value of the position, as he would come to realize. He had begun by telling people that his law practice was more important, and really it was. But in May he was not acting rationally. Perhaps he was ill. According to William Herndon, that spring Lincoln turned down an attractive offer to join the Chicago lawyer Grant Goodrich in a partnership. He declined, saying that he had a tendency toward consumption, and the study required to practice in the big city would kill him. Perhaps he was depressed; he certainly was not behaving "in character."

As for Mary Lincoln's support of his plans in 1849, it is proof of her devotion to him, in spite of her own preferences and interests. For the time being, she was content in Springfield. She wanted him to be president, but she knew the land office was not an obvious stepping-stone to the White House.

The events of that June would have the appearance of a farce if there were not so much underlying desperation and anguish in Lincoln's actions. The "confidential" campaign, of course, did not remain confidential. Butterfield heard that Lincoln planned to journey to Washington to press his suit. So Butterfield came down to Springfield on June 9, packed for Washington. Late that night he scribbled a note to Lincoln asking "whether it would not be better for us both to remain at home; which I am willing to do, if you are—please send me an answer by the bearer." Like a duelist, Butterfield did not go to Lincoln's door in person, but sent his friend Levi Davis to wait upon his rival's reply.

Lincoln and his wife, roused from sleep in a dark house, answered the door and listened to Butterfield's petition. Lincoln, who had purchased a dollar's worth of spermaceti candles only four days earlier, begged pardon, saying he "could not conveniently get a light" to put his response down on paper. But standing there in his nightgown, he told Davis to tell Butterfield "that if he were at liberty to consult his own feelings, he would cheerfully accede to your proposition, and remain at home, but he had so far committed himself to his friends that he could not accede to it." The statement is such a stew of truths, lies, and half-truths that it is obvious why "Honest Abe" did not want to commit it to paper.

Anyway, the race was on, each man saddling up his portfolio of recommendations and endorsements on June 10, a Sunday. The *Illinois State Register* reported: "Lincoln and Butterfield 'went off handsomely,' the former having a slight advantage in the start, though Lincoln had the 'inside track' (in the opinion of his friends); it being a 'steeple chase,' . . . the goal being the federal capital. . . . Bets run high, though the backers of Lincoln give slight odds."

ON JUNE 21, 1849, the mercury read 95 degrees in the shade. It was the hottest day of the year in Washington, so "intolerably hot," said the *Intelligencer,* "the intensity of the heat operates against business of all kinds." Laborers were dying of sunstroke, so it was suggested that the painting at the Capitol and other outdoor work be suspended, "at least during the hottest part of the day."

Lincoln lay partly dressed on the bed of a bleak room he shared for a few days with a man from Lancaster, Ohio, named William Coffey.

Lincoln must have thought he was in hell. The cholera epidemic, which had killed one hundred people in New York the week before, now threatened Washington, notorious for its noxious canals. The smell of "nuisances" permeated every street and dwelling: dead carcasses, offal of fishmongers' and butchers' stalls, the stagnant water of marshes, sewers, and cellars, hog sties and foul privies, the drainage from soap factories and dye works. City workers, their noses stuffed with tobacco, plied the side gutters of the streets spreading lime from large-wheeled carts, hoping to purify the "cholera breeders."

Things had gone terribly wrong. Lincoln arrived in Washington to find the entire city in mourning over the death of President James Polk, who had died, exhausted, on June 15, at only fifty-three years of age. One might have thought the former president had martyred himself three months after leaving the White House for no better purpose than to remind all patriots that Lincoln had attacked him.

The National Whig described the "Tribute of Respect": "The west front of the Capitol is festooned with black and the national flags over the Hall of Representatives and the Senate are half-mast. . . . The President's House and the several public departments and bureaus display the symbols of mourning. The Mayor of Washington has caused a portion of the front of City Hall to be similarly draped." Business was suspended; the schools had a holiday.

Between the obsequies for President Polk and the stultifying heat and stench, it was impossible to talk to any important officials or to get anything done. In fair weather and without a dead president lobbying against him, perhaps the office seeker might have had a fighting chance of gaining his object.

Yet it was clear to Lincoln, as he lay on the bed drenching the bedclothes with his sweat, that all had been decided against him and for Justin Butterfield before they began their race to Washington. The secretary of the interior, Thomas Ewing, favored Butterfield. And while General Taylor had agreed to delay the appointment until Lincoln could present his case, this was more of a gesture to accommodate the Whigs of central Illinois (who preferred Lincoln to the Chicago lawyer) than a serious intention to countermand Secretary Ewing's wishes.

According to a descendant of Ewing's who had interviewed William

Coffey, after learning of Butterfield's appointment, Lincoln stretched out "on the bed which was all too short for him, his big feet sticking over the footboard." He lay there in deep depression for a full hour or more, after which he roused himself and said, "Well, I reckon the people will find some use to put me to yet."

THE SHADOW OF DEATH

H E WOULD RETURN to Springfield a humbler man than when he departed, grateful for the comforts of home, friends, and family, and
eager once again to lose himself in the intricacies of the law.

Lincoln wanted healing and comfort, but soon found himself in the
role of the consoler. Two weeks after his return, in mid-July 1849, Mary's
father was stricken with the cholera that was spreading from the East
Coast cities and the Deep South now to the West. While Lincoln had
been in Washington, hundreds of men, women, and children were dying
in Lexington, including most of the physicians. Robert Todd had moved
his family to the salubrious Buena Vista for the summer while he campaigned against Colonel Oliver Anderson for a senate seat. His speech-
making and hand-shaking in crowd after crowd had worn down his
resistance while mortally exposing him to the disease. After making a
speech at Spencer's Mill, he was taken with a chill and was so weak he
could not rise from his bed. With the last of his energy he drew up his will
and signed it, and at one o'clock in the morning of July 16, he died.

On July 18, the *Lexington Observer & Reporter* announced "the death
of another of our most respected, beloved, useful and distinguished citizens, Robert S. Todd, Esq. . . . No man more truly and faithfully con-
formed to all the requisitions of virtue and benevolence, and no man
occupied a higher position in the society in which he moved. . . . He was
emphatically 'the noblest work of God—an honest man.' "

This news could not have reached Springfield before July 24, although
Mary may have heard a week earlier her father had fallen ill. The death of
her vital fifty-eight-year-old parent, with whom she had recently spent
nearly half a year, was a severe blow to Mary Lincoln. Since the death of
her mother when Mary was seven, her father had become the object of all

his daughter's filial affection, and never had he been more loving and generous to her than he had been since Bobbie was born.

Robert Todd left an enormous vacancy in the world upon his sudden death, as do all men of large energies and accomplishments. Lincoln would do what he could to help fill that void, but he could only do so much to console his wife. The grass and weeds had grown high in his absence, so he bought a scythe and handle at Irwin's store. Lincoln had liked and respected Mary's father greatly, and had his own sorrow to assuage. She watched him in the yard, swinging the scythe in flashing arcs, laying the long grass down in swaths of green and gold.

The rest of that summer Lincoln stayed close to home, preparing the house for winter, reestablishing his law practice with Herndon, and writing a few letters concerning matters of patronage. If politics was not finished with him quite yet, he was decidedly finished with politics so far as he knew. The administration seemed committed to offering him some kind of compensation for his loss to Butterfield, and first they tried appointing him secretary of the Oregon Territory, a job he declined on August 21. A month later the secretary of state offered him the Oregon governorship, and he turned that down too.

Mary Lincoln had a voice in this decision. After supporting her husband unconditionally in his ill-fated pursuit of the land office job, she was not about to be uprooted and shipped west to dwell among miners and Indians. Although the position held a certain remote prestige, and paid $3,000 per year (as much as the General Land Office), it would amount to political exile for a Whig politician to spend four years in a largely Democratic frontier community. Lincoln cited "private reasons" for declining the post, and it was well known that Mary Lincoln, still in mourning, was in no mood to leave home again, not for the wilderness of the Northwest.

Meanwhile the large, fractious family that mourned Robert Todd in Lexington and Springfield had come to further grief over the rich man's will. Todd had left the greater part of his estate—his slaves and houses, his land and his cotton manufacturing business—to his wife, with the balance to be distributed equally among his children. But when the will was read in September, Dr. George Todd, twenty-four, Mary's youngest full brother, stood up to challenge the document. Bitterly resentful of his stepmother, Todd plotted to deprive her of her rightful portion. Kentucky law required that the will bear the signatures of two witnesses, and the paper that Todd had signed with his frail hand bore that of only one. The court rejected the will; thus, observing the Kentucky statutes, the judge ordered that Robert Todd's property be divided equally among all the heirs. The heartless George (whose wife later divorced him on the grounds of cruelty) was to receive the same share as the widow, and Mary Todd would get as much as her stepmother's seven-year-old daughter.

This was an ill turn of events for the widow, who had six children to support. She was now ordered as executor to liquidate the Todd holdings at forced sales and distribute the proceeds in just proportions among all fourteen children. The estate was further complicated by an ongoing lawsuit Robert Todd had initiated against Robert Wickliffe, who had married Mary Todd Russell, a very wealthy Todd cousin. Robert Todd claimed that Wickliffe had confiscated his late wife's property, including slaves, against her will. Because Mary Todd Russell had been, reportedly, the wealthiest woman in Kentucky, and she had left no other heirs, the suit was potentially worth a fortune to the Todd family.

Lincoln promptly filed a "bill of revivor" in the Fayette County Court on October 2 "on behalf of Mr. & Mrs. Abraham Lincoln and the other heirs of Todd" so that the lawsuit would not die with his father-in-law.

The developments in Lexington required tact, business sense, and legal acumen. The Springfield Todds—Mary and her three sisters, Elizabeth Edwards, Frances Wallace, and Ann Marie Smith, and their husbands—trusted Lincoln to represent their interests. There must have been a significant inheritance at stake for each of the daughters, because on October 18, during the busiest session of the circuit court, Lincoln left his law practice in the hands of Billy Herndon and set off for Lexington with Mary and the boys.

Despite the seriousness of Lincoln's mission, the journey had the air of an autumn holiday for the family, as the Lincolns were returning to that gracious family home where they had been happy; and Mr. Lincoln was now welcome as a trusted son, a worthy heir to Robert Todd.

Robert Todd's widow and his favorite daughter were now bonded in their mourning as they had not been while that gentleman lived. Mary and the boys stayed with Elizabeth Todd and her children at Buena Vista. Lincoln rode the train back and forth to Lexington, where he prepared the case of the Todd heirs vs. Wickliffe while lodging with Levi Todd, Mary's brother, in the old home at the corner of Short Street and Mechanics Alley. That case, which left a voluminous record in the files of the Fayette Circuit Court, told the complex tale of a wife cheated of her riches, and her octoroon grandson deprived of his freedom—charges of cruelty and coercion on one side and a defense of the marriage on the other. Lincoln was fascinated to learn that there was Negro blood in his wife's family, with black Todd descendants living in Africa. As the depositions were being transcribed, Lincoln knew the case would be difficult for his side.

Yet Lincoln did his best for the widow and her family in this case and also in the delicate matter of Todd's administration versus the Todd heirs, that is, Dr. George Todd versus the widow and the rest of the family. George eventually persuaded Levi to join him in the action. In George Todd, Lincoln saw the vestiges of the fury that the children of Robert Todd's first wife harbored against the second wife and her brood. George was a short man, florid from whiskey, and he stammered. He began by complaining that Elizabeth had failed to inventory the family silverware in the estate return—keeping it for herself—and went on to list certain slaves and livestock that escaped the probate. Lincoln proved that the silver and livestock were Mrs. Todd's personal property.

The lawsuit was a revealing window on the Todds' family history and dynamic. In George Todd, Lincoln was privileged to observe a sort of "evil twin" in action, one whose grievance was an angrier version of Mary's own complaint about her stepmother. But George had never gotten over it, while Mary, to her credit, had managed to grow beyond the bitter feelings of her childhood, make peace with Elizabeth, and become a generous lifelong friend to several of her half siblings. Lincoln saw this in his wife and could not help but admire it. He himself harbored resentment toward his own father—for reasons now lost to history—that he never quite shed.

Dr. George Todd tried to persuade his Springfield sisters to join him in the lawsuit against Mrs. Todd, but with Lincoln's support and calm advice, they declined; a widow with six minor children and a complex estate to settle needed no more trouble from her family. When time came to leave Lexington, on November 7, 1849, Lincoln was able to assure Mary's stepmother that she could administer her husband's estate without interference. And Mary Lincoln, packing her bags, took pride in the knowledge that her husband had taken charge of the crisis in a way that would have pleased her father.

The Todd mansion on Main Street, the house where they had spent so many happy days on the way to Washington, was sold at auction that year. On January 21, 1850, Mary's beloved maternal grandmother, Elizabeth Porter Parker, died. She had been called as a witness in the Wickliffe suit, to no avail, and it was said that the labor of testifying, and the family feud, had put an insupportable strain on her fading strength.

The Lincolns would never return to Lexington again, and their departure that autumn marks the close of an important chapter in their lives. They had known happiness in Kentucky, in the circle of Robert Todd's family, an idyllic ease and security that they would never recapture.

LESS THAN A month after their return to Springfield, on December 13, Eddie Lincoln, only three months shy of his fourth birthday, fell ill. The chronic nature of his sickness during his life suggests consumption. The boy had always been somewhat frail, so during the weeks approaching Christmas, father and mother did their best to remain optimistic and keep up everyone's spirits. Eddie had been sick before and had always recovered; surely the toys and sweetmeats and Christmas cookies would quicken the child's pulse and bring color to his cheeks. But Christmas came and went, the holiday trimmings came down after New Year's, and Eddie Lincoln's condition went from bad to worse.

They summoned Dr. William Wallace, sister Frances's husband, who arrived with his black bag, smiling assurances. He examined Eddie, wrote a prescription, offered encouragement, and Lincoln hurried to get the medicine so they could dose the child. It did little good; Dr. Wallace came again and wrote another prescription. Hope turned to despair. Father and mother took turns keeping watch over the child as the chills and fever came and went. As he slept they hovered over him to be sure he was breathing.

The tense situation exposed the parents' limits. During that month Mary saw that he could hardly attend to business, and Lincoln learned the full measure of his wife's obsessiveness and anxiety. She developed the bizarre habit, "when engaged in thought, of pulling out one hair at a time from her head." Of course he was worried too; the record indicates that he got very little work done that January apart from supreme court appearances in Springfield January 15–18. No doubt he spent many sleepless nights watching over the dying child and trying to comfort his wife, and

many hours running back and forth to the pharmacies until the last medicine failed. Eddie breathed his last at 6:00 A.M. on February 1. He had
been ill for fifty-two days. Lincoln had counted the days on the calendar.

It was bitterly cold that first weekend in February, with the mercury
plunging to 10 degrees below zero in the early mornings. Lincoln moved
from fireplace to fireplace, piling wood on the fire and stirring the coals
with a poker while the crying of his wife filled the house. He could weep
without inhibition, and sometimes he could not see for his own tears. The
older boy was stunned, and Lincoln tried to explain to Bobbie what he
himself hardly understood. There is no grief worse than this, although
parents of that time were aware that very sick children were nearly as
likely to die as not.

The funeral was held in the Lincolns' parlor the day after Eddie died.
Dr. James Smith, a large portly Scotsman, pastor of the First Presbyterian
Church, read the prayers to the mourners. Then the cortège of carriages
departed for Hutchinson's Cemetery, eight blocks west of the capitol,
where men with pickaxes had broken up the frozen earth to receive
Eddie's little casket. The preacher made ghosts with his breath in the
frozen air.

> Man, that is born of woman, hath but a short time to live, and is full of mis-
> ery. He cometh up, and is cut down like a flower; he fleeth as it were a
> shadow, and never continueth in one stay. In the midst of life we are in
> death: of whom may we seek for succour, but of thee, O Lord, who for our
> sins art justly displeased.

A girl who later married Ninian Edwards's son arrived back at the
house before the Lincolns, and recalled that "Mr. Lincoln came into the
room and picked up a card which lay on the table. It was the last prescription written by the doctor for the child. He [Lincoln] looked at it—then
threw it from him and bursting into tears left the room."

As for Mary Lincoln, the third death of a loved one in half a year—the
death of her own little boy—seems to have transported her, for weeks, beyond any comfort. According to a neighbor "she lay prostrated, stunned,
turning away from food, completely unable to meet this disaster." Bending over his wife as she lay in her bed, Lincoln begged her, "Eat, Mary,
for we must live." And by and by she revived, for she had a great deal to
live for.

. . .

"IN THE MIDST of life we are in death," says the *Book of Common Prayer*, and the Lincolns had learned that hard lesson in eight years of marriage. During the next four years they would strive to build a fortress against death by strengthening their home and family, and making the most of life in Springfield. For a while there would be no more talk of Mr. Lincoln's political career. When rumors reached Springfield that Justin Butterfield had resigned the office in Washington that Lincoln had wanted so badly, the *Illinois Journal* reported: "Abraham Lincoln, who was defeated . . . by, as we think, the withholding of certain papers on his behalf,—will not now from the peculiar state of his private affairs, accept the office, even if it should be offered to him."

In March 1850, when the weather broke, he hired John Roll and Isaac Smith, the plasterers, to whitewash the rooms that had grown gloomy with wood smoke and mourning. Then he engaged the brick contractor Nathaniel Hay to build a wall foundation in front of the house to support the picket fence they wanted in place by summer. This would give their home an aspect of greater permanence and security. A full moon rose in late March, an inspiration for lovers, and it was at that time or in early April that Mary conceived her third child. Easter Sunday, March 31, arrived with its message of hope and regeneration, the story of death in life and life in death. It was more meaningful to the Lincolns than ever before, although they did not know that Mary would soon bear a son who would in some measure console her for the loss of the other.

Willie Lincoln was born on December 21, 1850, near the winter solstice, a week after Mary's thirty-second birthday. And a very joyful Yuletide that was for the family, in contrast to the anxiety and forced gaiety of the year before. They named the boy William Wallace in honor of Mary's brother-in-law, the physician whose attention to the children had meant so much.

She would need the doctor's care again in January, when she suffered what Lincoln called "baby-sickness" in a letter to his stepbrother John D. Johnston on the twelfth of that month. Lincoln had received a letter from Harriet Hanks two days earlier, in which she informed him that his father was dying. Johnston had written twice recently, urging Lincoln to visit his father on his deathbed, and Lincoln had not answered—not because he had forgotten "or been uninterested about them—but because it appeared to me I could write nothing which could do any good. You already know I desire that neither Father or Mother shall be in want of any comfort either in health or sickness while they live; and I feel sure you have not failed to use my name, if necessary, to procure a doctor, or any thing else for Father."

Lincoln's letter to Johnston, in which he conveys his final regards to his father, is one of the most peculiar and revealing that has survived. Lincoln had not visited his parents since May 1849. Thinking his father was dying then, he had dropped everything to make the six-day round-trip journey to Charleston, Illinois—in the midst of the land office imbroglio. The time away might have cost him the job. The new summons to the deathwatch for Thomas Lincoln revived feelings of resentment that are scarcely concealed between the lines of Lincoln's response:

> My business is such that I could hardly leave home now, if it were not, as it is, that my own wife is sick-abed. (It is a case of baby-sickness, and I suppose it is not dangerous.) I sincerely hope Father may yet recover his health; but at all events tell him to remember to call upon, and confide in, our great, and good, and merciful Maker; who will not turn away from him in any extremity. He notes the fall of a sparrow, and numbers the hairs of our heads; and He will not forget the dying man, who puts his trust in Him. Say to him that if we could meet now, it is doubtful whether it would not be more painful than pleasant; but that if it be his lot to go now, he will soon have a joyous [meeting] with many loved ones gone before; and where [the rest] of us, through the help of God, hope ere-long [to join] them.

It was true that Lincoln had a full schedule, with cases in the supreme court the entire week of January 13; his wife was sick abed, and it was bad weather for traveling. Yet he might have gone sooner or later, or at least showed some interest in seeing the dying man once more even if he felt little of it. The flowery Book of Common Prayer platitudes sail recklessly near irony—for a man known in Coles County as an infidel—and his message "that if we could meet now, it is doubtful whether it would not be more painful than pleasant," is transparently angry. Of course it is not pleasant, ordinarily, for a parent and child to say good-bye forever, but pleasure is hardly the point of such business. Lincoln's comment suggests a long-standing quarrel unresolved. In the absence of other evidence it appears that the disagreement was over money. Lincoln had money, his parents had nothing, and each thought that the other owed something. The last meeting, a year earlier, had probably been painful.

Thomas Lincoln died five days later, on January 17, 1851. The fact that his only son did not attend the funeral is insignificant, given the fact that he could not have received the news and made his way to Charleston in time to see his father lowered into the ground. What is meaningful is that none of Lincoln's children ever laid eyes on their paternal grandparents, who were respectable. If Mary or Abraham had desired it, the arrangement could have been made easily enough, and it would have delighted the old folks. But they did not. Under his wife's influence, and perhaps from his own inclination, Lincoln appears to have decided to distance himself and his offspring from his father's family—although a sense of duty would induce him to continue to help them financially.

Sole heir of Thomas Lincoln, Abraham sold eighty acres of his father's farm to his ne'er-do-well stepbrother John D. Johnston for a dollar, on August 12, 1851. Mary Lincoln joined her husband in signing the deed.

LINCOLN'S HARD WORK at his legal practice paid off. His income in the 1850s rapidly increased until he was earning well over $2,000 per year, and with his wife's inheritances from her father and her grandmother, the family had no financial worries. Lincoln was able to retire the old Salem obligation he had wryly come to call "the National Debt." They hired maidservants, who stayed for as long as they got along with the mistress of the house. One left her window open at night the better to entertain gentlemen callers, which was too much for Mrs. Lincoln's nerves, particularly when her husband was on the road for weeks at a time. Some quit because they could not abide Mrs. Lincoln's temper. According to Margaret Ryan, an Irish housemaid who lived with the Lincolns in the 1850s, "Mrs. Lincoln often struck" the servant girls when they crossed her.

In 1852, Lincoln was home from New Year's Day until April 8, three days before Easter, then he went north to Pekin for the spring session of the Tazewell Circuit Court. From that day until the end of the year he was gone more than 150 nights out of 267. Sometimes he was absent for a month or six weeks running, and Mrs. Lincoln was not happy about it. Bobbie, nine years old, had been enrolled at Abel W. Estabrook's Academy, just around the corner on Edwards Street and Seventh. Boys had begun to tease him, calling him "cock-eye," and he needed his father's attention. Willie was taking his first steps and learning to talk, and Lincoln was missing out on much of that joyful growth in the child's life.

For companionship Mary drew close to some neighbors who attended Dr. James Smith's "revival services" at the First Presbyterian Church. They rode back and forth to the meetings together in the Lincolns' rickety carriage. These neighbors were Elizabeth Black and her sister-in-law Mary Remann, both twenty-nine, who lived in a large house a block north of the Lincolns at Eighth Street and Market. The young women were bonded in grief, for Mary Remann had lost her husband in 1849 when he was only thirty-two; Elizabeth Black had lost a baby boy at the end of March 1852, and her husband now was in St. Louis on an extended business trip. Mrs. Lincoln—no stranger to domestic tragedies and loneliness—found that she was able both to encourage these friends and to take solace in their society and in the spiritual fellowship of the church.

On April 13, two days after Easter, the ladies attended a prayer service Dr. Smith conducted, along with three elders of the church. The record of that meeting states that the elders "received on examination Mrs. Elizabeth Black—Mrs. Julia E. Jayne [wife of Julia Jayne Trumbull's younger brother, Dr. William Jayne]—Mrs. Mary Lincoln & Miss Nancy Sperry." Miss Sperry was a Springfield hatmaker.

What this means, exactly, is that these women had convinced the church elders, Henry Van Hoff, Edmund G. Johns, and Joseph Lewis, of their religious "experience" and commitment; and that they were "duly received into the fellowship of the church." According to a letter from Mrs. Black to a Dr. Thomas Logan, when Mr. Lincoln learned of these developments, and Mrs. Lincoln sought his approval, he wrote a cheerful letter from Pekin "stating that he learned with gladness of her desire to associate formally with the congregation at First Church," and "he thought religion was a thing every woman ought to have." He would pay for a pew there shortly thereafter.

Mrs. Black noted in her diary that on April 17, 1852, "I took Mary and Willie to church today and had them baptized by Dr. Smith." Still mourning her child, Mrs. Black was joyful when her husband, William, paid her a surprise visit on May 1. But when he departed after the weekend, she was left "cold and lifeless." She recalled, "Mrs. Lincoln insisted on our coming down in the evening—we did so, and found Dr. Smith there." Mary Lincoln consoled her, and so did the pastor's prayers. On the fifth,

Mrs. Black sat and sewed with Mrs. Lincoln, who seemed to need her company as much as Elizabeth needed hers. Mrs. Lincoln sent not one but two messages inviting Mrs. Black on Thursday, May 6; so she took her children down the street with her "and spent the afternoon with Mrs. Lincoln," who was not feeling her best. Mary was suffering from an ailment called, in those days, "nursing sore mouth," ulcers in her mouth that were believed to be the result of prolonged nursing. It was probably a form of thrush, and had nothing to do with nursing but resulted from a depression of the immune system. Doctors treated it with goldenseal. She continued to breast-feed Willie until he was eighteen months old, to delay ovulation and pregnancy as long as possible.

On May 7, Elizabeth Black "called on Mrs. Lincoln—found her in better spirits." In this decade more and more friends and relatives of Mary Lincoln would remark upon her mood swings; as her cousin Margaret Woodrow had observed, Mrs. Lincoln had "an emotional temperament much like an April day," laughing one moment and crying the next. Age and experience temper passions in most people while magnifying them in others. Mary was of the volatile type; yet as of 1852 her moodiness had not kept her from bonding with neighbors who were grateful for her attention.

On June 10, Mr. Lincoln returned to Springfield for the summer. He bought a bolt of fine muslin for his wife. He bought an expensive new carriage from Obed Lewis on June 22 and paid $260 in cash for it. Mrs. Lincoln would be pleased to ride with her husband in the new carriage on his way to deliver a tribute to the late Henry Clay in Representatives Hall on July 6. "An impressive eulogy," the *Illinois Journal* called it. "During the proceedings business was suspended, stores closed, and everything announced the general sorrow at the great national bereavement."

Orville Browning was back in town that July, staying at the American House, assisting Lincoln in a difficult embezzlement case. His charming stout wife, Eliza, was with him on this visit, and Mrs. Lincoln liked both of them. She invited the Brownings to dine with them on the evening of July 22, when the gentlemen were encouraged to relax in their shirt-sleeves, on "one of the warmest days of the season," as Browning confided to his diary.

Sometime in the middle of that sweltering July the Lincolns took comfort in each other's arms; she then conceived her fourth child, who was born April 4, 1853. Two doctors attended her, as the labor and delivery were particularly difficult. The baby's head was abnormally large, and his passage caused damage to the birth canal from which the mother never fully recovered. Fifteen years later she was still complaining of this "disease of the womanly nature" that had afflicted her "since the birth of my youngest son." In those days physicians did not attempt to repair such injuries, but let nature take its course, which can be cruel. The Lincolns, forty-four and thirty-five that year, would have no more children, and there is cause to believe that Mary's physical condition limited their physical intimacy.

They named the boy Thomas, after Abraham's late father, honoring him in death as they never had in life. Lincoln, amused by the sight of the boy's large head and slight body, called him "the tadpole," and the nickname "Tad" stuck with him for life.

The father of three boys remained in Springfield only six days after the painful birth. He left for Bloomington on April 10 and did not return home from the grueling circuit until two months had passed. The pain and sadness that came in the wake of that traumatic birthing she would have to endure and overcome without him. From one day to the next he had no way of knowing the state of her health—mind or body. No letters from this interval have survived to tell us how either of them felt about it.

AT HOME IN SPRINGFIELD

LATE ON A WEDNESDAY NIGHT, February 7, 1854, while the two older boys slept in the bedroom across the hall and Tad lay in the cradle beside her, Mary Lincoln read her new book. It was a large book, an octavo bound in green cloth.

Mr. Lincoln had brought the novel home that evening for her amusement. He was, as he said, "not much a reader of this sort of literature," a romance novel called *Early Engagements* by one Mary Frazaer, the nom de plume of Sarah Marshall Hayden, the teenage daughter of a lawyer friend of Lincoln's who lived in Shawneetown. A publisher in Cincinnati had just brought out the steamy, cleverly written novel, and Lincoln had agreed to do what he could for the book here in the capital. That morning he had picked up fifty copies at the express office, delivered twenty-three copies to Birchall and Owen's bookshop, twenty-four to another bookstore; he dropped off a copy each at the *Register* and the *Journal* for review, and saved one for his wife.

As Lincoln got into bed beside her that night and the next, he found her "greatly interested in it." It is no wonder. The novel is about a Southern belle, Florence—whose mother died when she was still a child. Away at boarding school she falls in love with a minister who possesses every virtue except ambition. The author comments: "The world delights to honor those only, who, in the heat and fury of battle, most deeply steep their hands in human gore—or the orator whose unrivaled eloquence is expended on topics grateful to its ear." The heroine at last confides to the hero's sister her amazement "that one of your brother's superior talents, should be so devoid of ambition. . . . I cannot but regret, for his sake, and that of humanity in general, his present obscure location."

In all the years Mary had known Abraham Lincoln, he had never appeared "so devoid of ambition" as he did now. William Dean Howells, in his 1860 campaign biography of Lincoln (which Lincoln thoroughly edited for mistakes), said that during this period he was "happy in his home, secure in the affection of his neighbors, with books, competence, and leisure—ambition could not tempt him."

Yet on the night of February 7, 1854, as he joined his wife in bed with a novel whose theme kept her awake—passages of which she would be moved to read aloud to him—Lincoln was beginning to feel the stirrings of his dormant desire for distinction. The events of that year would make his return to the political arena irresistible, and his wife was eager to see it.

THE POLITICAL LANDSCAPE of 1854 was shaken and reshaped by the Kansas-Nebraska Act, engineered by Mary's old beau, the fiercely ambitious Senator Stephen A. Douglas. Douglas's bill, an effort to organize the new territories under the principle of "popular sovereignty," stipulated that Kansas and Nebraska would be admitted to the Union with or without slavery as the citizenry might determine at the time of admission. This, in effect, repealed the Missouri Compromise of 1820, which had preserved the country north of 36 degrees 30 minutes latitude as free soil. "Free-Soilers" and independent Democrats, men like Senator Salmon Chase of Ohio, Charles Sumner of Massachusetts, rich abolitionist Gerrit Smith, and Lincoln's old friend Joshua Giddings, were outraged at this betrayal of their principles. The senators called it "a gross violation of a sacred pledge . . . a criminal betrayal of previous rights" in a tract they drew up in protest. As Lincoln followed the controversy in the newspapers, he declared—after the bill became law in May—"We were thunderstruck and stunned."

Douglas may truly have believed, as he told one journalist, that the repeal of the Missouri Compromise was "a matter of no practical importance" because "the laws of climate, and of production, and of physical geography" would prohibit slavery from flourishing in the territories. But Douglas did not grasp the seriousness of the moral issue that was dividing the country, the fear of a "slave power conspiracy." By the end of the summer, the bill that Douglas had introduced in January had not only split his own party down the middle; it had so unsettled the Whigs (whose conservative wing resisted the general antislavery movement) that the short-lived party fell apart. From its ashes, that autumn, would arise the antislavery party that Horace Greeley would call "Republican," invoking the idealism of James Madison and Thomas Jefferson.

In the editorial columns of the *Illinois Journal,* Simeon Francis persisted in calling the Kansas-Nebraska Act "the Douglas swindle." On July 8, the Lincolns read in the paper that Mary's childhood friend from Lexington, the forty-three-year-old abolitionist Cassius Clay, was coming to Springfield on Monday, July 10, to give a speech in the state house rotunda in the afternoon. She remembered him as a muscular, short-necked man with a handsome, large head and furious eyes.

Clay's political opinions and his incendiary style of speaking were well known, and so was his reputation as a knife fighter. At the last minute, the Illinois Democrats challenged the arrangements for him to speak in the rotunda. These government officials did not want Cassius Clay to use their statehouse as a platform for his abolitionist, anti-Nebraska sentiments; besides, the man was known to incite brawls and riots. In bright midday light, Mary and Abraham Lincoln strolled uptown toward Capitol Square to discover that handbills had been posted on trees, fences, and storefronts, with the following message:

THE ROTUNDA OF THE STATE HOUSE CANNOT BE OCCUPIED
FOR CASSIUS M. CLAY'S LECTURE TODAY.
(Signed) A. STARNES, JOHN MOORE
COMMISSIONERS

More than inhospitable, this was outrageous. Clay would say "he found himself somewhat in the condition of John the Baptist, who came preaching in the wilderness. Even in his own state—a slave state—the common courtesy of friendship had never been withheld from him; no court house or state house door had ever been shut against him. There was a spirit of magnanimity in Kentucky men, that was superior to such meanness as that."

The day was clear and cool, as the temperature, which had been in the nineties, had dropped over the weekend into the low seventies. The crowd that gathered outside the statehouse to hear the charismatic orator at 1:30 was directed by the organizers—Lincoln's friend Orville Browning and Judge Thomas Moffett—to reconvene in a grove five blocks away, southwest of the square.

The little park that provided shade for the audience that summer after-

noon lay just below Ninian Edwards's house on the hill. A makeshift platform was erected, large enough for Mr. Clay, and Mr. Browning and Judge
Moffett, who introduced the speaker. By 2:30, when Clay mounted the
podium, fifteen hundred or more people had assembled, sitting or lying
on the grass, horse blankets, and wagons.

Lincoln, who, with Browning, had called on Clay upon his arrival in
Springfield, sprawled up front on the turf whittling a stick with his jack-
knife. Mary Lincoln sat nearby on the tailgate of a wagon, listening as Clay
spoke for nearly two and a half hours and the shadows lengthened. Once
in a while some bold Democrat would heckle him, but he kept right on
talking. Some called his oration the ravings of "the foulest traitor that ever
meditated the destruction of his country"; others called it "a Great
Heroic Speech." Nobody ever expressed lukewarm feelings about Cassius Clay.

"I stand before you," he intoned, "as the advocate of constitutional liberty. I believe in democracy such as was taught by the men of '76 and '86,
but not in the sham democracy of office holders and office seekers of '54.
I believe in equal rights, and in the universal brotherhood of men. Now. Is
it that the Declaration of Independence was only a rhetorical flourish because, as Mr. [Senator John C.] Calhoun said, 'Men are not born equal,
because they are born children, and not men, because they are unequal in
strength, height, and mental capacity'? No, this is a miserable quibble.
The Declaration of Independence asserted an immortal truth. It declared
a political equality—equality as to personal, civil and religious rights."

As Clay warmed to his subject, Abraham Lincoln listened, from time to
time shaving a curl of white wood from the stick he was shaping with his
knife. Clay's words were whittling at his conscience. Mary Lincoln
watched her husband watching Clay, and over the heads of the rapt
throng, the handsome round face of the speaker himself. "It is a modern
doctrine that slavery was supported by the Constitution. It is contrary to
its letter, spirit, and the history of its formation." Clay denounced the fugitive slave law: "Slavery was simply tolerated by the framers of the Constitution, but now like the porcupine in the fable, it thrusts out its quills and
pronounces itself well satisfied, and if its neighbors don't like it they may
do better somewhere else."

An angry voice demanded: "Would you help a runaway slave?"

"That would depend," Clay drawled, "upon which way he was running." And then came the blessed relief of laughter all around. A terrible tension had been building.

As Clay heated up his rhetoric, approaching the sensitive topic of Kansas and Nebraska, some "government office holder in Springfield," as a journalist described him, called out that the speaker should be "taken down." Clay stared him down and finished his argument. He called Douglas's swindle "the last great wrong, the Nebraska and Kansas outrage."

At the end of his speech, the Lincolns heard Clay raise the frightening specter of disunion. "So long as slavery will remain a local institution . . . I will stand by the Union, with or without slavery. But when I see that the South has mistaken your forbearance for cowardice, and your magnanimity for meanness of spirit . . . and that you are committed with every energy to slavery propagandism, then I am against the Union." He called for an organization of freemen of all political parties to "bury past animosities . . . unite in hurling down the gigantic evil which threatens even your own liberty . . . Slavery must be kept a sectional, and liberty a national institution."

As Cassius Clay spoke, he kept looking toward Lincoln, gratified that the husband of his lifelong friend Mary "gave me a most patient hearing. I shall never forget his long, ungainly form, and his ever sad and homely face." Lincoln would not forget Clay either.

"When Lincoln listened to my animated appeals for universal liberty for more than two hours . . . I sowed good seed in good ground, which in the providence of God produced in time good fruit." Like the speech on the Mexican War that Lincoln had heard Henry Clay deliver in Mary's hometown, now Cassius Clay's speech on the evils of Kansas-Nebraska proved a seed that would bear fruit very soon. Clay's argument and some of its tone would echo throughout speeches Lincoln made, in debating South Carolina senator Calhoun on September 9 at a meeting in the courthouse, and in Bloomington three days later. During the first week of October, when twenty thousand visitors who had come to the state fair swelled Springfield's population, Senator Stephen Douglas chose to address a crowd at the statehouse, defending his Kansas-Nebraska Act. On October 4, Lincoln answered Douglas in a speech that lasted three hours, dissecting Douglas's defenses while the senator piped up now and then to object. One difference between Lincoln and Cassius Clay was that Lincoln never lost his sense of humor.

"It is vain for any advocate of the repeal of the Missouri Compromise to contend that it gives no sanction or encouragement to slavery. If I have a field around which the cattle or the hogs linger and crave to pass the fence, and I go and tear down the fence, will it be supposed that I do not by that act encourage them to enter? *Even the hogs would know better—* Much more *men,* who are a higher order of the animal world."

MARY LINCOLN'S ENTHUSIASM for her husband's return to politics was as great as his, and she may have imagined greater prizes. According to a campaign biography he drafted for *Chicago Tribune* journalist John L. Scripps in 1860, "in the autumn of that year [1854] he took the stump with no broader practical aim or object than to secure, if possible, the re-election of Hon. Richard Yates to Congress. His speeches at once attracted a more marked attention than they had ever before done." Yates was anti-Nebraska, and Lincoln seized the opportunity to make himself heard on the most urgent topic of the time. Mary Lincoln, the entranced reader of *Early Engagements,* the friend of Cassius Clay, was beginning to glimpse a world of possibilities. If her husband lacked ambition at the moment, and had "no broader practical aim" than the reelection of Yates, she would fuel his ambition with her own. Knowing his conscience, his tendency to put his party's goals ahead of his own, she would do everything in her power to see that he made more self-serving choices.

This brings us to a curious incident described by William Jayne, the younger brother of Mary's friend Julia. In the interest of advancing Yates's candidacy and strengthening the Whigs' position in Sangamon County, the Whig leaders wanted Lincoln to run for a seat in the state legislature. The situation proved awkward. As much as he wished to oblige his colleagues, he did not want to appear to have taken a step backward in his career, from a seat in the U.S. Congress to a ladderback chair in the statehouse. Rather than declining, he sent mixed signals. He told a committee of the "Know-Nothing" party he was not in sympathy with their xenophobic platform but that they might vote for him if they pleased; so, for that matter, might the Democrats. More important, "he did not promise to run."

Dr. Jayne, who had been the Lincolns' family doctor for four years, and was a leader of the Know-Nothing party in Springfield, "took the names of Judge [Stephen] Logan & Abrm Lincoln to the Sangamon Journal Office" on September 3, "and had them published as candidates for the H.R. of the Illinois Legislature." Lincoln was out of town, stumping for Yates in Jacksonville.

When Mary Lincoln saw her husband's name in the newspaper as a candidate for the General Assembly, she was vexed. She marched up Sixth Street, making the dust fly, past Capitol Square to the newspaper's office. She told Simeon Francis that Mr. Lincoln was no such candidate, and to withdraw his name. Francis complied, assuming that Mrs. Lincoln knew her husband's wishes and was conveying them in his absence.

Judging from Dr. Jayne's account of the incident, it was not nearly so simple. The next day, "when Lincoln came home I went to see him in order to get him to consent to run. This was at *his* house: he was then the saddest man I Ever Saw—the gloomiest: he walked up and down the floor—almost crying and to all my persuasions to let his name stand in the papers—he said: 'No—I can't—you don't know all—I say you don't begin to know one half and that's enough.' "

The half that we now know about Lincoln's trouble at that moment does not explain why he was "almost crying" as he refused to explain to Dr. Jayne why he could not run for the legislature. Lincoln's loyalty to the Whig cause, Yates's candidacy, Lincoln's anti-Nebraska passion, and his neighbors, all cried out for him to run for the local office. His refusal would be seen as stiff-necked. As it turned out, Lincoln finally acquiesced. According to Jayne's account, "I did . . . go and have his name reinstated and there it stood." It stood because Lincoln let it stand, and he won handily.

So what was the dark emotion that furrowed his brow that day in September and drew him to the verge of tears? It was the fact that he would take that seat in the Assembly against his wife's wishes. In the winter, the legislature would vote for a new man to replace the pro-Nebraska senator James Shields. The Lincolns wanted that Senate seat, and the Illinois constitution prohibited a state legislator from running for the U.S. Congress or Senate. Lincoln might have dryly conveyed the essence of this conflict to his friend Dr. Jayne, or he might have parried Jayne's questions with that forensic humor that was his stock in trade. Lincoln's emotional display so soon after his wife had confronted Simeon Francis and removed his name from the ballot can only be explained by domestic turmoil. His generosity and party loyalty had cost him time, and earnings, and now it was about to cost him a run for the U.S. Senate. Mrs. Lincoln was exasperated, and that was the half, or more than half, that Dr. Jayne would never know.

On September 18, 1854, Mary Lincoln sold eighty acres of land in Curran Township that her father had given her, for $1,200. Lincoln's legal work for the Illinois Central Railroad, a major client, had gone unpaid for a year, and his return to politics meant that they would be needing money.

The forty-five-year-old lawyer permitted himself to be elected to the Illinois General Assembly on November 7, while watching his candidate, Yates, lose his bid for the U.S. Congress. As soon as a solid anti-Nebraska legislature took their seats in Springfield, Lincoln—much relieved—began letter writing and lobbying to replace James Shields in the U.S. Senate. As he wrote to Charles Hoyt of Aurora on November 10: "Some friends here are really for me, for the U.S. Senate; and I should be very grateful if you could make a mark for me among your [Whig party] members. Please write me at all events, giving me the names, post-offices, and *political position* of members round about you. Direct to Springfield."

By January 6, 1855, Lincoln calculated that he had more than twice as many votes for the coveted office as any other man, so his colleagues would understand if he resigned his seat in the Illinois Assembly to go for the U.S. Senate. The sale of Mary's property in Curran Township would provide the family with a margin of financial ease during a demanding season. They could cut the proper figure of a senator-to-be and his wife during the round of Yuletide parties, for which many yards of dress goods were required, as well as a maid. The live-in servant was particularly important for a woman with three children; although Robert, at eleven years of age, was old enough to pick up after himself, he was notoriously undisciplined. Willie, at age four, and the toddler Tad, not yet two, required constant supervision.

Just in time for the holiday festivities, Mary's favorite sister, her half sister Emilie Todd, came from Lexington to visit Elizabeth, Ann, Frances, and Mary. Nineteen-year-old Emilie was very pretty, with wide-set dark eyes and soft, round features. She was also charming. Emilie was welcome everywhere, and while she divided her time among the various households, according to her memoir, "I saw Mary Lincoln every day during my six months visit to Springfield."

Sister Emilie's recollections present the most complete picture of the Lincolns' domestic and social life during the winter of 1854–55. "Springfield was in the midst of a whirl of gayety; parties and balls followed each other in quick succession; and Sister Mary was very gay that winter. I was struck with her exquisite taste in dress. One gown, I remember, was a lovely lavender brocade which she had made herself, and which she wore with a round point lace collar." Emilie recalls that Mrs. Ninian Edwards entertained the Lincolns several times, and so did Ninian's brother Benjamin, a Democrat.

And she remembers a particularly delightful party at the residence of the wealthy banker Nicholas Ridgely, in his mansion on the southwest corner of Fourth and Monroe streets, below the Second Presbyterian Church. "Mary grew restless and anxious, and finally said, 'Mr. Lincoln, we must go home.' " They had left the children with the maid, and there seemed to be no cause for worry, but Mary was concerned, and Emilie heard her sister tell Mr. Lincoln again, "We must go home"; but he was enjoying himself. When he asked if they might stay a bit longer, she told him that if he liked he might stay, but she would get someone else to take her.

"With his unfailing kindness," Emilie recalled, he agreed to take Mrs. Lincoln home, reassuring her that everything would be fine there, and then they could go back and enjoy the rest of the party.

But everything was not all right at Eighth and Jackson. As they walked through the door they smelled smoke. The house was on fire, the maid was asleep, and if Mr. Lincoln had not manned the pump and buckets, his children might have burned. He later remarked proudly that "he was glad he had a wife who could sniff fire a quarter of a mile away."

Although Emilie probably did not lodge with the Lincolns, during that exciting and stressful year when he was running for the U.S. Senate she was a frequent visitor in their home. She recalls long buggy rides in the country during which little Robert "would help us out of the carriage, and we would gather wild flowers and carry home great armfuls." She remembers Mary reading aloud the stories and poems of Sir Walter Scott to the boys, and reviewing books for her husband: "I heard him say he had no need to read a book after Mary gave him a synopsis." With a keen ear Emilie recorded Mary Lincoln's bantering in Negro dialect, mimicking the voice of Mary and Emilie's old nurse Mammy Sally as she told how the jaybirds went to hell every Friday night: "Ole man Satan's done got the latch pulled, caze he keeps track of the time an' when Mr. Jay pecks three times, the do' flies open."

Emilie does not forget Mary's temper, or Lincoln's maddening abstraction. But she has a good understanding of the chemistry between the married couple: "Mr. Lincoln appealed to the eternal feminine in Mary. She mothered her husband as she did her children, and he seemed very dependent on her. She would call him back and make him wrap his throat in a muffler. She watched his health as she did that of her little sons."

She recalls one supper party at Ninian Edwards's house for which Mary put on a new dress she had made, white silk with a brocade of blue flowers. When Lincoln came from work she asked him to change his clothes for the party. Smiling, he replied, "Fine feathers enough on you to make fine birds of both of us," and added, "Those posies on your dress are the color of your eyes." Delighted with his attention, Mary told Emilie that she had "trained" her husband to see color. "I do not think he knew pink from blue when I married him." Lincoln was indeed more observant of form and structure than of hues and tints.

Emilie varies such pleasant memories with evidence of the tensions that challenged the Lincolns' happiness. "One evening Bob and I were playing checkers. Mr. Lincoln was looking thoughtfully into the fire and apparently did not hear what Mary was saying. Finally a silence. Mary put down her piece of embroidery. . . . Your silence is remarkably soothing, Mr. Lincoln, but we are not quite ready for sleep just yet.' "

When Lincoln still failed to respond, she put down her embroidery again, rose, and took his hand. Raising her voice, she declared, "I fear my husband has become stone deaf since he left home at noon." Stirring from his reverie he at last replied, "I believe I have been both deaf and dumb for the last half hour, but now you shall not complain," at which point he told a hilarious anecdote about one of his clients that "broke up the game of checkers and left us all speechless with laughter."

Emilie bears witness to an important transition. The Lincolns had not lost the romantic affection that had drawn them together, but the scaffolding of the marriage had begun to tremble; she could see cracks in the foundation. "Mary often watched for her husband and when it grew time for him to come home she would meet him at the gate and they would walk to the front door swinging hands and joking like two children.

"She had a high temper," Emilie recalls, "and perhaps did not always have it under complete control, but what did it matter? Her little temper was soon over, and her husband loved her none the less, perhaps all the more, for this human frailty, which needed his love and patience to pet and coax the sunny smile to replace the sarcasm and tears—and, oh, how she did love this man!"

Most of the eyewitness accounts of marital discord in the Lincoln household from the Springfield years refer to 1855–60, the period when he was least at home. James Gourley, a shoemaker and deputy sheriff who lived a block east of the Lincolns, recalled that "Lincoln & his wife got along tolerably well, unless Mrs. Lincoln got the devil in her: Lincoln paid no attention—would pick up one of his Children & walked off—would laugh at her—pay no Earthly attention to her when in that wild furious condition. . . . She always Said that if her husband had Staid at home as he ought to, that She could love him better."

The record shows that Mary always had a terrible temper. For about twelve years of the marriage, until she passed the age of thirty-six (after Tad's traumatic birth), she usually managed to control it. Through humor and mutual affection the couple appear to have been able to diffuse Mary's rages and avoid violence. Sometime after that, as Emilie Helm's memoir suggests and later incidents prove, Mrs. Lincoln began to lose control over her actions.

BOTH OF THE Lincolns were under considerable stress that winter as the Senate election approached and their hopes and fears mounted. For two weeks at the end of January 1855, Springfield was snowbound. Strong winds blew the heavy snow along the roads and against the window-panes, piled high drifts that made the houses and barns look Moorish and sunken, and obliterated the railroad bed so trains were marooned both north and south of the city. Snow and wind tore down the telegraph lines. The mails ceased, and on the twenty-first and the twenty-eighth, the churches did not open their doors.

This was the month that the candidates for the Senate were to have brought their campaigns to a climax. Now the worst snowstorm in four-teen years postponed the voting. Communication between towns was im-possible. Lincoln trekked back and forth to the general store to lay up staples. For his wife he bought a new pair of gloves, sewing materials, overshoes, a little shawl, two combs, and cotton flannel. He spent much of the day hauling wood and moving from fireplace to stove stoking the fires and poking the logs, yet between rooms they could still see their breath. In the morning at five o'clock, it was 3 degrees below zero outdoors, and the edge of the blanket would be frozen stiff from their breath. The pump froze, so all water for drinking and washing had to come from melting snow and ice in a pot on the black cookstove. When Robert and William got cabin fever, their father would have to dig a channel out the door so they could go outside all bundled up and make snowmen.

At night the Lincolns pored over the notebooks they had made listing the members of the Illinois legislature and their party affiliations: Democrat, Whig, anti-Nebraska Democrat, etc. In those days the state legislatures elected the U.S. senators. In the Illinois Senate they counted eleven Democrats, nine Whigs, and five anti-Nebraska Democrats. In the House there were thirty Democrats, twenty-eight Whigs, fourteen anti-Nebraska Democrats, a Nebraska Whig, and an abolitionist.

Between now and February 8, when the legislature would vote for the new senator, there would be little opportunity for Lincoln to change anyone's mind, but it was the same for the other candidates, Lyman Trumbull and James Shields. As the Lincolns discussed the election over their coffee, they had reason to feel confident. He had written to a friend, "I understand myself as having 26 committals; and I do not think any other man has ten." Mary, running her finger down the ledger, could see that there were a total of 57 anti-Nebraska legislators—likely to vote for Lincoln—as against 43 pro-Nebraska. The Whig candidate (and he was the favored Whig) stood with a fourteen-vote majority.

Sleigh bells were jingling in the distance; moonlight shone on the silver prairie. Locomotives on the C&M Railroad were out with their snowplows clearing the tracks. On January 24 a train arrived from Alton, and four days later another chugged in from Bloomington, the first to arrive from the north since the snow began. In ten days the Assembly would gather for the election.

By now Mary and Abraham Lincoln had been in and out of politics, losing and winning, long enough to understand that almost anything might happen in a state election. The parties were in confusion over slavery and the Kansas-Nebraska Act, and both Whigs and Democrats felt pressure from the Know-Nothings, who were not welcome in either camp.

On the morning of the election, Lincoln understood that it was primarily a contest of Nebraska versus anti-Nebraska (Free-Soil) forces, not Democrats versus Whigs. Yet the old party loyalties would still influence the outcome. While Mary prepared the midday meal for her children that Thursday, February 8, Lincoln monitored a closed caucus of every anti-Nebraska man in the legislature except for five who failed to show up in time: Norman Judd, Burton Cook, John Palmer, George T. Allen, and Henry S. Baker. The absentees were all Democrats—but there were still enough anti-Nebraska Democrats in the room to assure him his candidacy was strong. The caucus voted unanimously for Lincoln, then dispersed to smoke and chat until three o'clock, when the actual election would take place.

One Whig recalled: "We supposed the absentees would vote with us and we felt confident that we should elect Lincoln on the first ballot." Yet Lincoln—for good reason—was suspicious.

Mary Lincoln climbed the grand wooden staircase under the dome of the capitol, with Emilie Todd beside her, both dressed in their finest. As they went to join Julia Jayne Trumbull, Elizabeth Edwards, and other ladies in the gallery, Mary was as proud and confident of Mr. Lincoln as were those Whigs who had attended the caucus. She knew that her old friend and bridesmaid's husband, forty-one-year-old Lyman Trumbull, was also a candidate, but the odds were decidedly against him.

Also in the gallery overlooking the curved ranks of desks, the gentlemen in frock coats and stovepipe hats, the raised Speaker's platform, sat the wife of Governor Joel Matteson and their daughters. Lincoln might have been governor of Illinois, as Ninian Edwards's father had been, but it was a grander thing to be elected to the U.S. Senate. As she took her seat in the gallery that afternoon, Mary Lincoln had every reason to believe she would soon be the wife of a U.S. senator. At age thirty-six, she was about to learn a lesson in practical politics even more painful than the reproof of March 1843 when Mr. Lincoln had surrendered his congressional nomination to their friend Edward Baker.

The backstage maneuvering had been mysterious, convoluted; even the strategists most responsible for the final outcome could not have predicted it. From all appearances, the Senate seat was Lincoln's. Incumbent senator Shields was damaged goods. Trumbull was well liked and highly respected—in 1852 the bespectacled, scholarly-looking Judge Trumbull had been reelected to the Illinois Supreme Court unanimously; yet, being an anti-Nebraska Democrat, he lacked the support of most of his party, and Lincoln controlled the anti-Nebraska Whigs. Trumbull had campaigned valiantly in the Eighth District despite a severe illness that had left him feeble and so thin that his clothing hung loosely upon him as he sat at his desk, looking up at his wife, Julia. The Whigs, including the Lincolns, were proud of him for speaking out against Douglas and the repeal of the Missouri Compromise; Trumbull was a good man, and no apparent threat to Lincoln so far as Mary knew.

Of the ladies in the balcony, perhaps only the governor's wife, flanked by her pretty daughters, had an inkling of what was about to happen in the crowded hall. As Trumbull's biographer Horace White put it, "The senatorial election had been the topic of chief concern throughout the state for many months, and now the interest was centered in a single room not more than a hundred feet square. The excitement was intense, for everybody knew the event was fraught with consequences of pith and moment, far transcending the fate of any individual." There is a bit of hyperbole, inspired by consequences known to the biographer in 1913; nonetheless, the events were highly dramatic. At least one of the actors, Abraham Lincoln, demonstrated that the consequences far transcended the fate of the individuals.

For a week, Lincoln had been hearing of a plot to steal the Democratic nomination from Lyman Trumbull, who had offended so many of the "regular" pro-Nebraska Democrats. These men, using James Shields as a "stalking horse" on the first ballot, would then cast their votes for the influential Governor Matteson. Because Matteson had taken no position on Nebraska—and was in a position to grant favors—he might retrieve the defecting Democrats, and gather some Whigs too if they lost confidence in Lincoln. Anything might happen in open balloting. Still, Lincoln's chances were excellent. What Mary, and perhaps Lincoln himself, could not fathom was the degree of dissension among the Democrats: how intensely the "regulars" of the party—especially James Shields and Joel Matteson—hated Trumbull.

The joint session was called to order. Senator Ben Graham nominated James Shields (the incumbent, who, tarred with the brush of the Kansas-Nebraska Act, could not win). John Palmer nominated Trumbull.

Representative Stephen T. Logan, acting as Lincoln's "floor manager," nominated Lincoln. The first ballot came as no great surprise to the crowd:

Lincoln   45
Shields   41
Trumbull   5
scattering 8

Lincoln was troubled to discover that Trumbull's five votes came from those same anti-Nebraska Democrats who had failed to show up for the caucus earlier in the day. More troubling was the news that the "scattered" votes included some for Joel Matteson; so it was not an idle rumor that Shields, who could not win, was a front for Matteson. And sooner or later the Democrats—including some anti-Nebraska men—would throw their ballots to the governor.

Now this nightmare became a reality, as by the sixth roll call Lincoln's vote had fallen to 36 and Trumbull's stood at 8, while Shields still fell far short of a majority. So on the seventh call Shields threw his votes to Matteson, who then gathered several anti-Nebraska Democrats into the fold.

On the next call Matteson's count climbed to 46 while Lincoln lost eleven votes and Judge Trumbull doubled his total. Everyone was uneasy.

Lincoln knew he was in trouble. On the tenth ballot Matteson had 47 votes, Trumbull, incredibly, had 35, and Lincoln held only 15. The mystery of his dwindling numbers that afternoon Lincoln himself only partially understood. He later wrote: "The three Senators (Judd, Cook, Palmer) & one of the two [anti-Nebraska] representatives above named 'could never vote for a Whig,' and this incensed some twenty Whigs to 'think' they would never vote for the man of the five," that is, Matteson. This made Trumbull attractive.

In fact, the Illinois Whigs were so confident of their solidarity in the antislavery cause, they became excited by the possibility that Democrat Trumbull, if elected, would give far more support to their free-soil principles in a hostile quarter. This was the strange reasoning that ruled the day, much to Lincoln's dismay and the Democrats' despair. Most Democrats hated the renegade Trumbull, and if they had had their wits about them, they would have been better off voting for the Whig, Lincoln. It was party loyalty twisted beyond recognition by the slavery controversy that ruined

Lincoln's run for the Senate that afternoon. To him it must have seemed like a very bad joke.

In keeping with his principles, Lincoln knew but one recourse. After the tenth ballot, when Matteson held 47 votes, Trumbull 35, and Lincoln 15, he instructed his supporters to vote for Trumbull. There was no other way to defeat Matteson and the pro-Nebraska forces. Trumbull could do nothing for Lincoln. Lincoln's supporters would obey him, while at least three of Trumbull's—being Democrats—would not vote for any Whig.

When the rumpled, tousled Stephen Logan stood up to cast his vote on the eleventh ballot, there were tears running down his face. "He said that the demands of principle were superior to those of personal attachment, and he transferred his vote to Trumbull." To Mary Lincoln's horror, and the exasperation of the Democrats, the remaining fourteen of Lincoln's supporters followed Logan's example. An independent voter switched to Trumbull, and the judge became U.S. senator by a majority of one.

Lincoln gradually accepted the terms of this defeat, but for his wife, it was a different matter. Uncertain of whom to blame—Mr. Lincoln, the villain Matteson, or the "two-faced" Julia Jayne and her ambitious husband—Mary Lincoln never got over it. Angry and disappointed, she descended the stairs into the main hall, avoiding insincere condolences, looking for her husband and some plausible explanation for the debacle.

Joseph Gillespie accompanied Lincoln home in the cold twilight, and recalled, "I never saw him so dejected. He said the fates seemed to be against him, and he thought he would never strive for office again. He could bear defeat inflicted by his enemies with pretty good grace, but it was hard to be wounded in the house of his friends." The victory party that Elizabeth and Ninian Edwards had prepared at their house for the Lincolns would now honor Senator-elect Lyman Trumbull and his wife, Julia. It must have been a difficult moment for Mary Lincoln to enter the house where she had once lived, where she and Julia Jayne had been the best of friends, and where Mr. Lincoln had first come to court her, in the knowledge that the triumph she had anticipated was not to be hers after all.

Someone said to Lincoln that he must be disappointed, whereupon he approached the senator-elect and, extending his hand, replied, "Not *too* disappointed to congratulate my friend Trumbull."

The day after the election, Lincoln wrote to Illinois congressman Elihu

B. Washburne: "The agony is over at last," and "I regret my defeat moderately, but I am not nervous about it." Two weeks later, when he had more perspective, he wrote to William H. Henderson: "I started with 44 votes & T with 5. . . . a less good humored man than I, perhaps would not have consented to it. . . . I could not, however, let the whole political result go to ruin, on a point merely personal to myself."

Mary Lincoln would never speak to Julia Trumbull again—if she could avoid it—although their lives and their husbands' careers were interlocked. According to Julia, as the two women stood outside the Presbyterian church on a Sunday morning a year later, "I took pains to meet Mary but she turned her head the other way and pretended not to see me."

There are many paradoxes in Lincoln's political career, and not the least of these is the fact that his defeats were as advantageous as his victories. If he had gone to Washington as a senator in 1856 for six years, his campaign against Douglas would not have occurred in 1858. The famous Lincoln-Douglas debates that put him in the national spotlight and made him a contender for the presidency in 1860 would have had no occasion.

THE MOST INDUSTRIOUS and lucrative years of Lincoln's law practice were 1855 through mid-1857. Mary may have disapproved of his partner, William Herndon, but she could not argue with success. Those were the years of the famous patent infringement suit that Lincoln won for Cyrus Hall McCormick, inventor of the reaper; this was the time he represented the Illinois Central Railroad against the county of McLean in a tax dispute, for which he eventually received a fee of $5,000, money that he used to finance his later political campaigns.

For hundreds of other lawsuits in Springfield and on the circuit, Lincoln was paid in cash, chickens, or firewood, and gold he spent immediately, so it is impossible to know his exact income. But the Lincolns were comfortable. Mary could afford fine silks and whalebone, linen and lace; she could dress like a lady. She continued to make shirts and trousers for the children, twelve-year-old Bob, five-year-old Willie, and Tad, three, but now she made clothing of finer and more durable goods. The rambunctious boys made the house seem too small; the Lincolns discussed enlarging it to make more room for the family and enable them to entertain more graciously, as their social circle and Mr. Lincoln's career demanded.

So that the boys could have a play area safe from the increasing carriage traffic, the Lincolns extended the brick and picket fence along the south side of the house. He purchased two thousand bricks on June 2, 1855, to build up the foundation wall along Jackson Street; and by summertime he had built a high board fence all the way around to the carriage barn so the boys could play in the backyard without Mary's having to watch them every minute.

Lincoln planted some rosebushes in the front yard, but soon forgot to tend them, so they withered and died in the heat. In July, while the busy lawyer was in Chicago and Rockford working on the McCormick case, his wife bought thirty-four panels of flowery wallpaper and eight pieces of border to redecorate the parlor. But she was impatient for more extensive home improvements.

In the spring of 1856 they would "raise the roof" of the house at Eighth and Jackson, doubling their living space for a cost of $1,300, near the amount they had paid for the cottage in 1844. They engaged the carpenters Daniel Hannon and Thomas Ragsdale, who commenced the sawing and hammering in early April when Lincoln left Springfield to work the Logan circuit, and the artisans were driving the last nails at the end of May when Lincoln returned from Bloomington. The workmen extended the north wall, squaring the foundation and creating a rear parlor behind the front north parlor. They constructed a full second story with eleven-foot ceilings, five bedrooms, and a "trunk room." Now husband and wife had separate adjoining bedrooms above the northwest front parlor. Mr. Lincoln's room looked out on the street, and Mary's was in the middle of the house, above the rear parlor and the fireplace. Across the stair hall from his bedroom was a large guest bedroom above the south sitting room, and across from Mrs. Lincoln's was the boys' bedroom, with maid's quarters and storage room in the rear above the kitchen. There were false fireplaces in each of the front bedrooms; these were manteled niches for wood-burning Franklin stoves that were more efficient and safe than open fireplaces.

The downstairs was also completely reconfigured. The front parlor now opened onto the new rear parlor, making one long space for gracious entertaining. And across from the rear parlor was a small but charming dining room, now separate from the kitchen that was confined to the rear of the house and dominated by an Iron Royal Oak cookstove in the west wall.

In keeping with the original Greek Revival style of the house, delicately curled brackets adorned the cornices under the roof, and recessed pilasters supported the corners. An elegant grillwork balustrade guarded the upper windows of the south porch. These renovations evoked a variety of responses in the neighborhood, reflecting the mixed feelings about the ambitious, frugal wife. In a letter to her daughter, Mrs. John Todd Stuart quipped: "I think they will have room enough before they are done, particularly as Mary seldom ever uses what she has."

The renovation made room for the explosion of activity the growing boys brought on, their friends, toys, cats, and dogs. Lincoln loved animals: horses first, that were his faithful companions and partners on the Eighth Circuit; some of their names, such as "Old Bob" and "Old Buck," have come down to us. He was so fond of cats that his wife referred to them wryly as his "hobby." He liked to get down on the carpet in the parlor and play with the cats and children, petting a tabby and talking to him in a low voice until the animal purred contentedly. Robert used to try to "harness up" the cats to a cart, but they didn't take to it; the boys had better luck with the dog, who would submit to the harness and pull a wagon out to the woods to get sassafras roots for tea.

William Herndon wrote of Lincoln: "He exercized no government of any kind over his household. His children did much as they pleased. Many of their antics he approved, and he restrained them in nothing. He never reproved them or gave them a fatherly frown. He was the most indulgent parent I have ever known." Like many of Herndon's impressions, this one is trustworthy within limits—the limits of Herndon's actual observation. He had seen them throwing inkpots and dancing on the furniture in the law office, but Herndon was never allowed inside Lincoln's home. Numerous anecdotes indicate that there were bounds to the patience of even these very indulgent parents. Lincoln was known to take up a birch switch when the boys got out of hand, though he was more likely to cut the air with it than strike one of his sons. Once when Robert and some friends were trying to teach the dogs to stand on their hind legs, they got the notion of noosing the animals and hoisting them by a rope thrown over a barn rafter. The howling mongrels brought Mr. Lincoln bearing the stave of an ash barrel. He would not tolerate cruelty of any kind, and brandishing the slat of wood, he chastised the boys and freed the poor dogs.

Ardelia Wheelock, who lived across the street, recalled an evening when she was helping Mrs. Lincoln dress for a party to be held at Jesse Dubois's house. Willie and Tad had just come from a taffy pull, and they were pretty nearly covered with molasses. Watching their mother and father dress for the Dubois party, the boys decided they wanted to go too. The Duboises had five children. Mrs. Lincoln said no, they would stay at home with Bob. He was then a teenager, a student at the local "Illinois State University" (a prep school), and old enough to babysit, although he would prefer not to.

The little boys sent up such a cry of protest that Mr. Lincoln came to their defense. "This will never do," he said. "Mary, if you will let the boys go, I will take care of them."

"Why, Father, you know that is no place for boys to be."

But Lincoln said he would take them in the back way, and they could play in the kitchen. He made the youngsters promise to stay in Mrs. Dubois's kitchen; then Ardelia and Robert went to work scrubbing them clean of taffy and getting them into clean clothes. In the hurry Tad's breeches got put on backward. He began squalling that he "couldn't walk good," but Lincoln paid him little mind, only warning him to pipe down and behave himself as he had promised, or be sent home. He led the children down Eighth Street to the Duboises' house, Tad limping a little. Robert and Mother followed after.

Of course the kitchen could not contain Willie and Tad. They burst into the parlor, playing hide-and-seek among the voluminous skirts of the Springfield ladies, who rolled their eyes at this demonstration of the anarchy that the Lincoln family dared to carry into society.

THE MONTH OF May 1856, when the Lincolns raised their roof, was the month that national conflict over the Kansas-Nebraska Act turned to violence.

In the agonizing clash over slavery and the rights of slave owners, Lincoln had more of his wife's sympathy than he had—for instance—of Joshua Speed's, but Mary Lincoln had not yet caught up with her husband in his antislavery sentiments. All three were from Kentucky, a culture based upon slave labor. Speed was a farmer. Mary had been raised, in part, by slaves. Each struggled differently to resolve the moral issue. "I fear to do any thing, lest I do wrong," Lincoln wrote to Owen Lovejoy, an abolitionist minister, on August 11, 1855. But by the spring of 1856 Lincoln's doubts had given way to a passionate resolve. In this election year, Lincoln, who previously had shunned abolitionists and other radicals, decided to try to persuade them to tame their rhetoric. Together with the moderate Whigs and Democrats they might work to elect an anti-Nebraska, Free-Soil candidate for president.

During his busiest time of the spring term of the Vermilion Circuit Court, Lincoln caught a train from Danville seventy miles to Decatur, then another train almost as far north to Bloomington. He had time to make notes in case he should be asked to speak. In Bloomington he joined his friend Judge David Davis for the anti-Nebraska state convention on May 29. As a delegate from Sangamon County, Lincoln served on the nominating committee, and was himself selected to be a presidential elector.

Passions on both sides of the slavery issue had boiled over that week. A proslavery posse had attacked the Free-Soil citadel of Lawrence, Kansas, wrecking the presses of the *Herald of Freedom* and burning the Free State Hotel to the ground. Then the ruffians went on a looting spree. On the nineteenth and twentieth of May the abolitionist Charles Sumner delivered his "Crime Against Kansas" speech in the U.S. Senate, which provoked furious responses from the Southern Democrats. One of them, Senator Andrew Butler, Sumner had censured for his devotion to "the harlot, Slavery." Three days later Butler's nephew, Congressman Preston Smith Brooks, attacked Sumner as he sat alone at his desk in the nearly empty Senate chamber, beating him senseless with a gutta-percha cane.

Against this tempestuous background of events, at the end of the anti-Nebraska convention in Bloomington there were calls for Lincoln to address the delegation. It was a broadly heterogeneous gathering of Free-Soilers who sat on stools and benches or stood shoulder to shoulder against the walls in Major's Hall, upstairs from Humphrey's Cheap Store, calling for Lincoln. There were abolitionists, Whigs, disgruntled anti-Nebraska Democrats, Know-Nothings, unaffiliated citizens united only in their opposition to the extension of slavery; even some "regular" Democrats had come along with friends to see the show.

Lincoln rose to his full height, always an imposing spectacle, and began talking. In those days he had a way of beginning a speech so softly and gently that everyone felt they were listening to private thoughts meant for them alone. By degrees he would ratchet up the volume as well as his argument until the heat of his words began to dissolve the boundaries that separate individuals and to melt the audience into a unit. Neighbors would steal glances at one another, nodding and murmuring, "Yes, that's right!"

This was the legendary "Lost Speech" of which there are many rhapsodic accounts but, unhappily, no text. Although a number of journalists were present, including writers from the *Chicago Tribune* and the *Alton Weekly Courier*, as well as William Herndon, David Davis, John L. Scripps, and many others who meant to record Lincoln's words, he was so electrifying that the writers dropped their pencils.

"It is my opinion," Herndon recalled, "that the Bloomington speech was the grand effort of his life." Before this, Lincoln had approached the slavery question as a matter of policy, evading "the question of the radical and the eternal right. Now he was newly baptized and freshly born . . . enthusiasm unusual to him blazed up; his eyes were aglow with an inspiration; he felt justice. . . . His speech was full of fire and energy and force."

According to Henry Clay Whitney's recollection, Lincoln began by saying, "We are in a trying time. Unless popular opinion makes itself very strongly felt, and a change is made in our present course, *blood will flow on account of Nebraska, and brother's hand will be raised against brother!* . . . We are in a fair way to see this land of boasted freedom converted into a land of slavery in fact. . . . I read once in a law book, 'A slave is a human being who is legally not a *person* but a *thing.*' And if the safeguards to liberty are broken down, as is now attempted, when they have made *things* of all the free Negroes, how long, think you, before they will begin to make *things* of poor white men?"

John L. Scripps confirmed Herndon's description: "Never was an audience more completely electrified by human eloquence. Again and again, during its delivery, they sprang to their feet and upon the benches, and testified by long-continued shouts and the waving of hats, how deeply the speaker had wrought upon their minds and hearts." Lincoln unified them. This was the birth of the modern Republican party, although they did not yet dare to call it that. When the speech was done and the applause was still ringing in the air, Jesse K. Dubois took Henry Whitney by the arm and shouted in his ear: "That is the greatest speech ever made in Illinois, and it puts Lincoln on the track for the Presidency."

Politics, which had always drawn the Lincolns together, now became a source of discord. Lincoln was campaigning vigorously for John Charles Frémont, the Free-Soil candidate, against the Democrat James Buchanan and the xenophobic former president Millard Fillmore. Mary's disagreement is evident from a letter she wrote to Emilie Todd Helm dated November 23, 1856, almost three weeks after the election of James Buchanan. Mary's letter opens with apologies for not writing sooner; she begs indulgence as "a staid matron, & moreover the mother of three noisy boys," then quickly settles down to the theme most on her mind: "Your husband, I believe, like some of the rest of ours, has a great taste for politics & has taken much interest, in the late contest, which has resulted very much as I expected, not hoped—." Emilie's husband, Ben Hardin Helm, was a lawyer with political ambitions, whose father had been governor of Kentucky.

Mary continues, dipping her pen: "Altho' Mr. L[incoln] is, or was a *Fremont* man, you must not include him with so many of those, who belong to *that party*, an *Abolitionist*. In principle he is far from it—All he desires is, that slavery, shall not be extended, let it remain, where it is." As we know from Lincoln's letters of the period, this is not all he desired—the containment of slavery—although that had to be his public policy for a time. Revering the Constitution and its protection of property rights, he could not join the abolitionists, who would have deprived the slave owners of their legal property—human though it was. But he told Speed that the sight of slavery was to him "a continual torment," and had the power of making him miserable. For a year he had been speaking out against it, and he was eager to see this evil sink away of its own ignoble weight.

Mrs. Lincoln saw the matter in a different light. She explained to her sister, "My weak woman's heart was too Southern in feeling, to sympathize with any but Fillmore, I have always been a great admirer of his, he made so good a President & is so just a man & feels the *necessity* of keeping foreigners, within bounds." It did not please Mr. Lincoln that his wife disagreed with him, and he was violently opposed to the Know-Nothings. He told Joshua Speed: "As a nation, we began by declaring that '*all men are created equal.*' We now practically read it 'all men are created equal, *ex-*

cept Negroes.' When the Know-Nothings get control, it will read 'all men are created equal, except Negroes, *and foreigners, and Catholics.* ' " Then, said Lincoln, he would prefer "emigrating to some country where they make no pretense of loving liberty."

His wife expressed a less liberal sentiment: "If some of you Kentuckians had to deal with the 'wild Irish,' as we housekeepers are sometimes called upon to do, the south would certainly elect Mr. Fillmore next time." The intolerant Fillmore would have put a lid on Irish immigration. Not until Mr. Lincoln himself was running for president would Mary again see eye to eye with him on the major political issues of the time, and even then she would continue to challenge him, speaking out when she believed he was in the wrong.

MARY RECALLED THAT the first part of the winter of 1857 "was unusually quiet, owning to so much sickness among children with scarlet fever, in several families some two & three children were swept away—." Scarlet fever was deadly in those days, and an epidemic would have kept a mother with three small boys virtually quarantined in a cold January, worrying that one might sicken and die.

The house must be kept warm. Perhaps it was her mortal fear that caused Mary Lincoln to lose patience with her husband on Wednesday the twenty-eighth of January. Mrs. Lincoln had asked him to make up the fire in the south parlor, the informal sitting room with the rocking horse and the stereoscope, where Lincoln liked to lie on the floor and read. He exhibited the same inattention, negligence, or catatonia that Sister Emilie described. Mary told him once, she told him twice to stoke the fire, but he did not hear. She told him again. At last she declared, "I'll make you hear me this time," and slammed him across his blank face with a length of cordwood. The maidservant Margaret Ryan saw her do it, and did not have such abiding love for her mistress as to keep quiet about it. Lincoln went to the drugstore on January 29 to purchase gelatin, the hardening ingredient for a silken plaster bandage. This incident can be fairly dated January 28, 1857, through Herndon's account, as well as a receipt dated January 29, 1857, showing that Lincoln had himself purchased the gelatin for the court plaster at a drugstore on that day.

The next day dawned bright, clear, and mild. William Herndon met

Lincoln in the clerk's office of the Illinois statehouse and followed him into the law library, curious about the court plaster his friend wore on his formidable nose. That day Lincoln had two cases to argue before the supreme court. "Someone in the courtroom asked Lincoln what was the matter; he made an evasive reply in part to the question."

There are several picturesque anecdotes of Mary Lincoln's physical abuse of her husband during the Springfield years. She chased him out of the house with a broomstick; she threw a bucketful of water on him from the upstairs window one night when he asked to be let in at a late hour. A tale roughly dated 1857 describes Mary chasing her husband outdoors with a kitchen knife until he disarmed her, "quickly hustled her to the back door [and] pushed her in . . . saying 'There, damn it, now Stay in the house and don't disgrace us before the Eyes of the world.' "

Perhaps the most disturbing of these stories is one that Jesse K. Dubois related to Jessie Weik in the 1880s. Dubois, the state auditor, lived a block south of the Lincolns, across Eighth Street near the corner of Edwards. One morning Dubois stopped at Lincoln's office "and found him going home with a piece of meat for breakfast." Lincoln invited Dubois to come along with him, and Mrs. Lincoln met them at the door. Dubois recalled that "Ms. L had some aristocratic company from Kentucky."

"Upon opening the paper of meat she became enraged at the kind Lincoln had bought. She abused Lincoln outrageously and finally she was so mad she struck him in the face. Rubbing the blood off his face," he told Dubois to come away with him. The story is not dated, but since Dubois and his family moved to Springfield after his election as state auditor in 1856, the incident probably occurred sometime during the period under review. Dubois was a man of integrity, a trusted friend of the Lincolns who later assisted David Davis in the administration of Lincoln's estate.

The well-documented incident of the firewood and the court plaster lends credence to the rumors that Mary Lincoln did physically abuse her husband now and again. By 1857 it was an established fact. How often did such things occur? There is no way of knowing. But by most accounts Mary was herself shocked by her violence, which was beyond her control, and was genuinely sorry for it afterward. How did Lincoln respond? Sometimes he laughed at her. We also have Sheriff Gourley's account that Lincoln would pick up one of the boys and walk away from the house until his wife returned to her senses.

Herndon said that Lincoln never spoke of his domestic trials to him or any other of his friends. "It was a great burden to carry, but he bore it sadly enough and without a murmur." Herndon saw Lincoln in the law office, arriving at daybreak instead of his usual hour of nine o'clock; whenever Lincoln arrived that early, Herndon would discover him "lying on the lounge looking skyward, or doubled up in a chair with his feet resting on the sill of a back window. He would not look up on my entering, and only answered my 'Good Morning' with a grunt."

On such occasions, Herndon claims, "I knew exactly that a breeze had sprung up over the domestic sea, and that the waters were troubled. . . . the evidence of his melancholy and distress was so plain, and his silence so significant," that his friend would grow restless, and leave the office for a couple of hours. By then, he said, "the cloud of despondency had passed away"; yet on such days Herndon observed that his partner did not go home for lunch, but ate cheese and crackers from the store below, and he lingered at the office "till late along in the night, when, after all the world had gone to sleep," Lincoln might be spied strolling home along Eighth Street in the darkness, and quietly slipping in through the door of his house. How Herndon knew this is a mystery, unless he was tailing him. Herndon's eyewitness testimony is reliable, but his opinions and secondhand information must always be scrutinized. Because he detested Mary Lincoln, his opinions of her and the marriage are always suspect when they are not favorable.

So she struck her husband from time to time, and she was horrified by her behavior and very sorry; he sulked and brooded and grieved over it if he could not laugh it off. He was perseverant and forgiving. He would stay away awhile, and then go home. It is unlikely that sexual intimacy, that reliable conjugal balm, was an easy remedy for their troubles during the late 1850s, after the damaging birth of Tad. Childbirth was so dangerous in that era that doctors often advised women who had sustained vaginal injury to abstain from intercourse for fear of their lives. They would have to find other ways to be reconciled after their quarrels.

Herndon was in a position to receive confidences from Lincoln's friends, one of whom maintained "the theory that after all, Lincoln's political ascendancy and final elevation to the Presidency were due more to the influence of his wife than to any other person or cause."

"The fact," Milton Hay insisted, "that Mary Todd, by her turbulent nature and unfortunate manner, prevented her husband from becoming a domestic man, operated largely in his favor; for he was thereby kept out in the world of business and politics." Lincoln stayed away on the circuit longer than any of his colleagues, and corresponded with his wife less frequently. In Chicago once, when lawyer Norman Judd's wife inquired after Mrs. Lincoln, Lincoln replied he had not heard from her since he started out on the circuit three weeks earlier. "But Mr. Lincoln, aren't you married?" Mrs. Judd sarcastically inquired. Lincoln tried to explain that "if there was anything the matter Mary would write," but his answer was unsatisfactory to the wife who was accustomed to exchanging letters frequently with her husband when he was absent.

ENDURING MARRIAGES DO not follow a simple trajectory to success or ruin. They proceed in a jagged arc, as husband and wife agree, disagree, compromise, and experience estrangement and reconciliation in the adventure of their life together.

The Lincolns knew how to settle their differences. A week after the conflict over the wood fire, the two of them managed to follow through on long-standing plans to give a party for friends, family, and business associates. It was the biggest party they had ever given, and an opportunity to show off the transformation of their home—the expanded north parlor, the new wallpaper, carpets, and furniture. Mary had sent out nearly five hundred invitations—some in her hand, some in her husband's—to friends in Springfield, Chicago, St. Louis, Jacksonville, and Petersburg, for the open house on Thursday evening, February 5, at 8:00. On February 16, 1857, she wrote proudly to Emilie Todd Helm: "I may perhaps surprise you, when I mention that I am recovering from the slight fatigue of a very large & I really believe a very handsome and agreeable entertainment, at least our friends flatter us by saying so."

That night it had poured rain, and in Jacksonville there was a bridal party for the Springfield bookseller's daughter Cordelia Birchall, who drew many away to see her marry a Mr. Warren in that town thirty miles west. So only three hundred folks—gentlemen in frock coats and muddy boots, ladies in hoops and crinolines—squeezed into the refurbished parlors of the Lincolns' home that night instead of five hundred. In the main parlor "a long table was stretched nearly the whole length of the room, while above the table was a succession of shelves growing narrow upward." Meats, cheeses, and pastries were arranged on the shelves.

Guests helped themselves to the food while the waiters poured coffee. Looking at the food tower out of the corner of his eye, Lincoln asked a fellow, "Do they give you anything to eat here?"

Hopefully Lincoln had been able to remove the bandage from his nose. The Lincolns' response to the marital setback that winter was to throw themselves into the social life of Springfield, the whirl of parties and "grand fetes," as Mary called them. She told Emilie, "Within the past three weeks, there has been a party, almost every night," and adds suggestively, "You will think, we have enlarged *our borders,* since you were here," referring not only to their walls and roof, but to their social circle. On Friday, February the thirteenth, the governor, William H. Bissell, formerly a free-soil Democrat, now a Republican, hosted a ball that the Lincolns attended. There Mary saw many people to whom she had introduced Emilie, "beautifully dressed & dancing away very happily." According to the *Illinois Journal,* Governor Bissell and his wife did "the honors of host and hostess with ease and grace. . . . Throughout the evening, a fine brass and string band discoursed most delicious music, and the dancers kept the cotillions filled until a late hour." Lincoln was not a good dancer, but his wife was, and he would oblige her. Taking her hand in the candlelight of the ballroom, they might find themselves in step again, in the figures of a closing cotillion.

The year had gotten off to a bad start. This would be the last calendar year before Lincoln became a national figure, and the days and nights of a private life are precious. After Lincoln was chosen as the Republican Senate candidate in the spring of 1858, and the debates with Stephen Douglas began that summer, Abraham Lincoln's life was no longer his own. Soon everything the Lincolns said or did was of surpassing interest to their neighbors and the press. Their quarrels were grist for the mill of backyard fence gossip; their privacy was so compromised that neither quarrels nor reconciliations could transpire naturally.

But that year of 1857 that began in a clash and a disappointment ended in harmony. This did not come about in a day, but over the course of many months, during which the record indicates the sensible give-and-take that keeps marriages afloat. A few days after the governor's party, a newsboy came to deliver a copy of a new journal, the Springfield *Republican,* and both of the Lincolns were at home. Lincoln had told the founding editor, John E. Rosette, that he "thought the establishment of the paper unfortu-

nate, but I always expected to throw no obstacle in its way." The reason
for this ambivalence is obvious: The Whig party had only recently col-
lapsed under the weight of the slavery controversy. Some were grieving
over it, while others, like Mary Lincoln, had not quite given up on Whiggery and were not ready to accept the new alternative, a party with so
radical-sounding a name as "Republican."

Mrs. Lincoln took one look at the news carrier and his offending paper,
scowled, and asked her husband, "Now are you going to take another
worthless little paper?"

Mr. Lincoln replied *"evasively"* (as Lincoln recalled in his account of
the conversation): "I have not directed the paper to be left." It was the sort
of hairsplitting subterfuge to which Honest Abe would resort when the
truth was at stake and unspeakable. Of course he had not directed the
paper to be left—the editor had done that. Lincoln had merely agreed "to
patronize it to the extent of taking and paying for one copy." As soon as he
left the house, Mary addressed a letter to the *Republican* saying that they
were rejecting the new journal, which the editor acknowledged with a
peevish notice in the following issue.

Lincoln would not argue with her any further over the *Republican,* a
topic that might aggravate their political differences, any more than he
would wrangle with her over a healthy shade tree she asked a workman to
cut down. He loved the beautiful tree, but it stood in the way of renovation. The plan would have to be altered, said the workman, to save the
tree. "Cut the tree down," said Mrs. Lincoln, but the carpenter did not
want to do it. So he went to Lincoln's office to see what he would have to
say.

"Have you seen Mrs. Lincoln?" her husband inquired testily, having
heard the man's plea. He said he had.

"Then in God's name cut it down clean to the roots," Lincoln
snapped, knowing that neither they nor the tree stood any chance against
his wife's stubborn will.

July of 1857 was the month they took their pleasure trip to Niagara Falls
and New York City. They would be gone nearly two weeks, the longest
time they would ever spend alone together; four months later they would
celebrate their fifteenth wedding anniversary. Mr. Lincoln had been hard
at work on the circuit, away from home most of that spring and summer.
The chronically delinquent Illinois Central Railroad owed him nearly

$5,000; their headquarters was in Manhattan, and he thought he might have better luck collecting if he went there in person. In any case it was a good opportunity to take his wife on a much-needed vacation. Leaving the boys in the care of their Irish housekeeper, the couple departed on the train for Toledo on July 22; from there they would take a steamboat across Lake Erie to Buffalo, where they boarded another train on the Erie and Ontario Railway. That would take them the last twenty-two miles over the limestone tableland with its scattered red ash and cottonwoods, and then forests of rugged white pines and red cedars, to where they could see the mills and rapids and horseshoe falls to the east out the right-hand windows of the coach.

They registered on July 24 at the Cataract House, one of the two finest hotels on the east side of the river, according to the popular *Nelson's Handbook for Tourists*. Tourists had yet to overrun the scenery. The falls were then, perhaps more than now, one of the most enchanting spots on earth, a haven where couples fell in love; or if they had lost the passion that had first drawn them together, they might find it again in the presence of that magnificent flood crowned with rainbows.

The Lincolns began their courtship as romantics—readers of Byron, Thomas Moore, and Walter Scott—familiar with old ballads and sentimental verse, flowers in the hair, and duels for honor. Like all romantics of the Victorian age, they found their reveries and ideals melting in the crucible of the mid-nineteenth century, by the fires of industrialism, the forces of capital, and the withering of agrarian traditions. Yet here, in the roar and spray of Niagara Falls, they might recapture some of the iridescent aura of youth.

Lincoln's poetry had dwelled upon the beauties of nature, and he had a special feeling for this place, which he recorded soon after his first visit to Niagara. It excited his sense of wonder: What was the mysterious power that drew people to it from all over the world? "There is no mystery about the thing itself," he begins. "If the water moving onward in a great river, reaches a point where there is a perpendicular jog, of a hundred feet in descent, in the bottom of a river,—it is plain the water will have a violent and continuous plunge at that point . . . will foam, and roar, and send up a mist, continuously . . . during sunshine, there will be perpetual rain-bows."

Yet this physical dimension of Niagara Falls "is really a very small part of that world's wonder. Its power to excite reflection, and emotion, is its great charm." He then launches into a reflection that would do credit to a team of geologists and physicists—estimating the quantities of water, its speed, and the area of the earth's surface that gathers it. And his conclusion is that the greatest wonder is not the visible falls, but the *invisible* action of the sun lifting up this quantity of water into the heavens so it can rain down again from the clouds.

In a turn of phrase he moves from the metaphysical to the mystical: "But still there is more. It calls up the indefinite past. When Columbus first sought this continent—when Christ suffered on the cross—when Moses led Israel through the Red Sea, nay, even, when Adam first came from the hand of his Maker—then as now, Niagara was roaring here. . . . Contemporary with the whole race of men, and older than the first man, Niagara is as strong, and fresh to-day as ten thousand years ago."

As the Lincolns visited the sites, such thoughts of mortality and immortality animated their conversation. It is inevitable in that place. Coming from the village, you could hear the roar of the falls before you could see them. Walking along the street that ran between the Cataract House and the International Hotel on the cliff, they could see the river at the point where the iron suspension bridge, 360 feet long, wide enough for two carriages to pass, spanned the rapids with its four pairs of elegant arches. Then, standing on the bridge, they could see the river rushing toward its leap. They looked down at the cataract as it thundered in their ears, the mad tumult of the waters hurled foaming in wild breakers down the descent, fretful and impetuous.

Crossing the bridge to the pine-wooded Bath Island, they stopped at the little wooden tollhouse. They paid 25 cents apiece and wrote their names in the ledger, allowing them passage back and forth across the bridge during their three-day visit. From Bath Island they crossed another bridge to Goat Island. For anyone who loved flowers as much as Mary did, this was a Garden of Eden. Goat Island, an area smaller than Kew Gardens in London, had more native varieties of trees and flowers than any other spot on earth. Among the hundreds the Lincolns had never seen were the Virginia creeper, the American hornbeam, red mulberry, wild crabapple, staghorn sumac, purple flowering raspberry, elderberry, and snowberry. Many were in blossom that time of year: several kinds of asters, blue and red, the common yarrow, daisy fleabane, boneset, and tall goldenrod. She could wear them in her hair or in her bosom; she could take bouquets back to the hotel to put in water glasses.

Niagara "is a solemnizing prospect, and we should suppose," says the rhapsodic guide James Campbell, "few could gaze upon it without feeling that they had attained to a higher conception of the awful power and might of the eternal."

ANOTHER KIND OF power and might was to be found in Manhattan, where the New York and Erie Railroad train chugged to a halt at the foot of Duane Street on July 28. The city was uneasily growing to accommodate seven hundred thousand souls, with another three hundred thousand in Brooklyn and the other boroughs. A terrible thunderstorm that night drenched the streets and roofs of New York and damaged the telegraph lines, so the news from abroad was scarce.

A cynical reporter complained that the city was getting dull. "Murders have ceased to stimulate us. We have become hardened to crime and danger. We should not mind being garroted a little for the sake of a new sensation." In fact the Lincolns could hardly pick up a newspaper during that stormy week without reading of a garroting. That very day the *Times* reported, "a Mr. Van Liew was found dead about midnight, Monday in the neighborhood of Mercer and Canal streets. He was returning home with a bottle of porter he had been out to purchase for his sick wife, when he was set upon by garroters." The city was in an uproar over the inefficiency of the police force, and that story dominated the headlines. "Mayor [Fernando] Wood palls upon the taste, and the Epic warfare of our two Polices is now a tale of yesterday. We have almost come to the end of the possibility of injunctions,—unless indeed the Street Commissioner should obtain an injunction on the Broadway people who have the audacity to propose keeping that thoroughfare clean, for an infringement of his Constitutional Right to keep it dirty. We should almost welcome the Cholera or the Yellow Fever as an agreeable fillip to the monotony of our existence."

Such grim satire might have brought a smile to Mr. Lincoln's face as he turned the pages of his newspaper and sipped his coffee in the humid hotel room. The writer had summarized the real news of the day in New York: the threat of cholera; the two polices (the regular understaffed force, and the "special police," local volunteers who went unpaid); rampant crime resulting from overpopulation and inadequate law enforcement; and finally, the "Broadway Association" that was organizing to keep the main thoroughfare clean.

Rain or shine, Mary Lincoln would go shopping on Broadway, from the hotel district above Madison Square, where the famous thoroughfare crossed Fifth Avenue below Delmonico's Restaurant, all the way down to Union Square and beyond to A. T. Stewart's "Marble Palace" with its domed atrium and mahogany cabinets. There she could browse freely among dresses, bonnets, and foundation garments of excellent quality at low markups. Macy's and Brooks Brothers were under construction. At the small boutiques like Lord & Taylor on Grand and Christie streets, clerks would be fussing over the out-of-town shoppers, making them self-conscious.

Muslins, laces, and silken gauze were all in vogue, and so were pointed shoulder capes. There was a gorgeous cape composed of a network of narrow ribbons, with a broad ribbon edge, that was to be worn over an evening dress of sheer barege, and flounces woven in lace patterns. Mary loved floral trimmings, and there were hats with field flowers and lotus leaves, and chenille straws trimmed with red coral and scarlet blossoms displayed on hat stands in the store windows. She saw shawls and dresses she coveted, dresses that were far beyond her means.

Someday, when her husband was president, she would be able to return to New York and buy such beautiful things, and have the proper occasions to wear them. As she and Mr. Lincoln strolled arm in arm along South Street and looked out at the East River, the great-wheeled ferries churning back and forth to Brooklyn, the gulls soaring above, and the many tall ships bound for the seven seas, she teased her husband good-naturedly.

"I saw the large steamers at the New York landing, ready for their European voyages, [and] I felt in my heart, inclined to sigh, that poverty was my portion, how I long to go to Europe," she wrote to Emilie Helm. "I often laugh & tell Mr. L—that I am determined my next Husband *shall be rich.*"

Mr. Lincoln could laugh with her, for he was doing very well professionally, despite his difficulty with the railroad company, his biggest client. On July 29 he had written a note of agreement to pay him $200 in thirty days, plus 10 percent annual interest, and it was countersigned by Mr. James Primm of the Illinois Central. It was all they could pay now;

Lincoln would sue for the rest. The company was on the verge of bank-ruptcy, but he would eventually get his money.

Meanwhile, if there was no abundance of cash for tulle dresses, shawl-shaped mantillas of guipure lace, or evening dresses with lilac flounces, there was enough to dine at Delmonico's, looking out at Madison Square Park where fashionable ladies and gentlemen strolled arm in arm under parasols. There was money for amusements—the theater and musical events they saw listed in the papers. On Friday night at Niblo's Garden on lower Broadway at Prince Street they could see the Italian ballerina Teresa Rolla performing excerpts from the new Adolphe Adam work, *La Bouquetière,* followed by their vaudeville company in a double bill of melodramas: *Delicate Ground* and *The Secret.* At Wallack's Theatre at Broadway and Thirteenth the great musical comedy team, Mr. and Mrs. John Wood, would be singing and clowning in their popular burlesque *Shylock.*

As she watched the rain fall on the cobblestone streets outside the hotel, Mary Lincoln thought of her children. She had never been away from them for much more than a day or two. Lincoln was accustomed to it, so he might try to distract her. But it must have been hard for her dur-ing the last days of July as they approached Bobbie's birthday. He would be fourteen years old on August 1, and they would not be home in time to celebrate with him. Perhaps they might buy him a birthday gift, at J. Ruthven's on John Street where they made whistles and balls and chess-men, or at Jesse Crandall's—in a workshop on Fulton Street, he made sleds and velocipedes.

After the weekend of Bobbie's birthday they would begin the long journey home by rail, arriving on August 4.

"This summer has strangely & rapidly passed away—," she wrote to her sister Emilie, "spent most pleasantly in traveling east," and as the leaves of the maple, the red oak, and the shagbark hickory turned golden and left the trees bare, it must have seemed to the Lincolns that in the absence of stirring events, their life was passing thus, "strangely and rapidly," and, for the most part, pleasantly. Two-thirds of their time as a married couple had gone by when the year of the comet came with its por-tents and disturbances, and then nothing would ever be the same.

He would turn forty-nine in 1858, the year she turned forty; he had begun to refer to himself as "the old man," in the office and around

Statehouse Square. It was a culture that did not mindlessly glorify youth. A man was lucky to have reached the ripe age of forty-nine in an era when life expectancy was not much longer than that, and to have a plump and exuberant wife of forty when so many mothers died in childbirth.

THE
RISING STAR

ANOTHER RUN FOR THE SENATE

ALTHOUGH LINCOLN HAD AVOIDED the political arena for nearly a year, by the spring of 1857 *The Chicago Journal* was calling him the "successor of Stephen A. Douglas in the U.S. Senate." His speech in Bloomington against slavery had branded him as a spokesman for the new Republican party.

However, it was not other people's opinions that inspired Lincoln to come from behind the scenes in the Republican party and move fleetingly to center stage; it was the Supreme Court's outrageous decision in the Dred Scott affair. Scott was the slave of an army surgeon who had lived for a while in the Wisconsin Territory (now Minnesota), where slavery was prohibited by the Missouri Compromise. Returning to Missouri, Scott sued for his freedom on the grounds that he had once lived in a free territory. On March 6, 1857, Chief Justice Roger B. Taney ruled that Congress had no right to prohibit slavery in the territories—that the Missouri Compromise was unconstitutional—so the black man's residence in Wisconsin did not make him a free man, because that place had never really been free soil. Moreover, as a Negro, Scott had no legal rights—he could not sue for his freedom even if he lived in a "free state." To Lincoln's dismay, Dred Scott was returned to his master.

When Stephen Douglas came to Springfield to speak in the statehouse on June 12, Lincoln (and probably Mary) heard Douglas defend the Court's decision in Dred Scott. "The representative hall was a perfect jam," said the *Illinois State Register,* and "a very large number of ladies were present on the occasion. We were pleased to see in attendance, Col. W. H. Herndon, the Hon. A. Lincoln, the Hon. S. M. Cullom and many other prominent men in the Republican party."

Lincoln was eager to respond to Douglas's speech. He felt a responsibility to do it, just as he had felt obliged to unite the scattered opponents of the Kansas-Nebraska Act in Bloomington the previous spring. It was a matter of right and wrong that people surely must understand if someone would simply explain it to them. So on the evening of June 26, Lincoln delivered a passionate speech in the statehouse, answering Douglas and denouncing the Dred Scott decision. After paraphrasing Douglas's "popular sovereignty" argument, that men of any party could choose for themselves whether Kansas should be a free or slave state, Lincoln quipped: "If there should be one real living free state Democrat in Kansas, I suggest it might be well to catch him, and stuff and preserve his skin, as an interesting specimen of that soon to be extinct variety of the genus."

On this occasion, Lincoln boldly confronted an explosive topic that lay beneath the surface of his arguments with Douglas: "the amalgamation of the white and black races." Intermarriage evoked such disgust in the minds of most people that, as Lincoln said, "Judge Douglas evidently is basing his chief hope, upon the chances of being able to appropriate the benefit of this disgust to himself. If he can, by much drumming and repeating, fasten the odium of that idea upon his adversaries, he thinks he can struggle through the storm."

That night in June, Lincoln put aside all caution, putting himself squarely at the bull's-eye of the question: "Now I protest against that counterfeit logic which concludes that, because I do not want a black woman for a *slave* I must necessarily want her for a *wife*. I need not have her for either, I can just leave her alone."

So the Republican party in the West, and Abraham Lincoln as its spokesman in Illinois, had become a force to be reckoned with. This was the only speech he gave that year, but it was printed as a special supplement to the *Illinois Journal* on June 29, and widely reprinted in papers such as the Decatur *Chronicle* and the Clinton *Central Transcript*. Now it was nearly certain that he would be the Republican nominee to face Douglas for the Illinois seat in the U.S. Senate in 1858. The Great Debates between Mary Lincoln's former suitors had practically begun.

ROBERT LINCOLN'S FIFTEENTH birthday, August 1, 1858, fell on a Sunday, and they would try to make up to the boy for having missed the occasion the previous year, when they had been traveling. As the firstborn of the boys, Robert Lincoln typically suffered more of the oedipal complexities of his relationship to his parents than did Willie and Tad. Far more intimate with his mother than his father, at twenty-one he would write: "My father's life was of a kind which gave me but little opportunity to learn the details of his early career. During my childhood & early youth he was almost constantly away from home, attending courts or making political speeches—." Mary Lincoln had told James Gourley that if her husband had stayed home more, she might have loved him better. Robert shared his mother's resentment, and his father's efforts to overcome it were not altogether successful.

During the lawyer-politician's long absences, Robert Lincoln, in his mid- and late teens, had to take his father's part in comforting his mother, in her irrational fears—of tinkers, burglars, and thunder—as well as in her increasingly frequent rages. This is an unhealthy burden to put upon an adolescent, and Robert probably never quite forgave his parents for it. The boy was now enrolled in a prep school, the newly founded and misnamed Illinois State University. There John Hay, a senior at Brown University and soon to become Lincoln's secretary, had studied, and now Clinton Conkling (Mercy Levering's son) joined Robert in classes where they studied mathematics, history, and Latin—none too rigorously, as he later commented: "We did just what pleased us, study consuming only a very small portion of time." His father seized upon the Latin part of Bobbie's curriculum as a way to compensate for his own deficiencies in that lawyerly tongue, while bonding with his standoffish son. Lincoln used to go about his chores—chopping wood, hauling water, doing dishes—while declining Latin nouns, sometimes in chorus with Bobbie, sometimes solo.

While Mary may have worried over the tension between her husband and eldest son, she was pleased with Lincoln's affectionate connection with the younger lads, when he was at home. Their neighbor Ardelia Wheelock recalled "the frequent picture of Mr. Lincoln going down the street, wearing his customary tall hat and gray shawl, leading by the hands both Willie and Tad, who were usually dancing and pulling him along. Always his thoughtful face was bent forward, as if thinking out some deep problem, yet he was responsive to the questions of the children. He often brought Tad home on his shoulders."

During the summer and the autumn of 1858, there could have been no problem more difficult than balancing his consuming political career with the demands of marriage. Mary was determined that he should succeed, while remaining jealous of his time away from her and the children. Again Ardelia Wheelock testifies to Lincoln's thoughtfulness: "It was the invariable habit of Mr. Lincoln to be most considerate of Mrs. Lincoln. In the new and growing city it was sometimes difficult to get and keep a maid. At such times Mr. Lincoln would help freely in the kitchen. On coming from his office he would take off his coat, put on a large blue apron, and do whatever was needed."

And Wheelock gave equal credit to Mary's efforts, reporting that "in the numerous political gatherings at Mr. Lincoln's house, Mrs. Lincoln was a very great help to her husband. A lady of refined tastes, with a large social experience, and with considerable insight, she carried the social end of the campaign admirably." Ardelia Wheelock was referring then to the senatorial campaign of 1858, when Mrs. Lincoln used to ask eighteen-year-old "Delie" to come from her home across the street and help serve coffee, tea, and gingerbread to the partygoers welcoming Mr. Lincoln home after one or another of the Great Debates.

There were to be seven official "joint" debates, one in each congressional district of Illinois—excepting Springfield and Chicago, where the candidates had already carried on virtual debates by speaking publicly on consecutive nights. They agreed to share the stage in Ottawa, Freeport, Jonesboro, Charleston, Galesburg, Quincy, and Alton. Ottawa was scheduled for August 21, and Alton, the last, for October 15. From August 11 until the end of October, Lincoln rarely slept in his own bed, as the momentum of the campaign carried him by train, carriage, and on the shoulders of the crowd to podiums in dozens of towns and villages all over the state.

Mary followed his progress in newspaper accounts that captured the excitement of the debates. In Ottawa the sun was blinding and the heat of August was oppressive, yet ten thousand people filled the town square to hear the candidates. "By wagon, by rail, by canal people poured in . . . men, women and children, old and young, dwellers of the broad prairies, had turned their backs on the plough, and had come to listen to these champions. . . . Military companies were out; martial music sounded, and salutes of artillery thundered in the air. Eager marshals in partisan sashes rode furiously about the streets. Peddlers were crying their wares at the corners, and excited groups of politicians were canvassing and quarreling everywhere," wrote a reporter. Before the contest began, Lincoln said to

Judge Lyle Dickey, "Hold my coat while I stone Stephen." When Lincoln was done speaking, his supporters carried him on their shoulders to Mayor Joseph Glover's house to celebrate.

The carnival atmosphere and lionization of Lincoln and Douglas had a surprising momentum. On August 27, it was unseasonably cold and threatening rain in Freeport, yet fifteen thousand people overran the town of seventy-five hundred to hear Stephen Douglas frame the fatal argument that slavery could be excluded from the territories by inhospitable local legislation. Douglas's "Freeport Doctrine," as it came to be known, arose in response to Lincoln's sharp question: Could any territory prohibit slavery—even if the citizens abhorred it—*before* the formation of the state's constitution? By saying "yes"—that local police regulations could exclude slavery from a territory, despite the Dred Scott decision—Douglas satisfied his Illinois constituents, while infuriating President Buchanan and most of the Democratic party.

Lincoln, at home briefly on the night of August 31 en route to Clinton, could share with his wife a sense of satisfaction. Although his Senate seat hung in the balance, the debate at Freeport was getting such extensive press coverage nationwide that Douglas's controversial Freeport Doctrine would cripple him as a presidential candidate in 1860. Meanwhile, Mary's husband was becoming a figure of national importance. She had long believed they would live in the White House, and now it appeared that one of the major obstacles to that goal, the perennial presidential hopeful Stephen Douglas, had alienated the southern Democrats. He was becoming, as Lincoln had prophesied, "a *dead* lion *for this work* . . . at least a caged and *toothless* one."

As for Lincoln, the candidate was growing—in strength of personality—to fit the role of a national celebrity. Attorney Joseph Gillespie, who introduced Lincoln when he spoke in Edwardsville in September, noted his effect on the crowd: "They were perfectly enraptured. The bare sight of the man threw them into ecstasies." Yet as of September 13, Gillespie said, Lincoln seemed unaware he had any reputation outside of Illinois. As the two men were riding the coach to Greenville, Lincoln told him that he had only one personal complaint about Douglas, which was that he "arrogated to himself a superiority on account of having a national reputation. . . . I would not do that if we occupied each other's places." But in fact Lincoln had known nationwide fame since he had delivered the "House Divided" speech on June 17, 1858. The speech, with its widely quoted sentences—"A house divided against itself cannot stand. I believe that this government cannot endure, permanently, half *slave* and half *free*"—was so unforgettable and threatening that many believed it would cost him more votes than it gained.

Whatever else a politician may become, he must begin as a performer. Like any performer, the politician may feign humility all he pleases; yet he thrives upon attention. All the applause and fanfare, the cheering and serenades at his hotel windows, were not lost upon the vanity of the prairie lawyer. If a pretty girl like Rosa Haggard came to him at the hotel where he was staying, wanting his autograph in her album, he would return the warmth of her gesture in kind.

To Rosa—   *September 28, 1858*

> *You are young, and I am older;*
> *You are hopeful, I am not—*
> *Enjoy life, ere it grow colder—*
> *Pluck the roses ere they rot.*
>
> *Teach your beau to heed the lay—*
> *That sunshine soon is lost in shade—*
> *That* now's *as good as any day—*
> *To take thee Rosa, ere she fade.*

The verses, with their romantic echoes of Burns and the Cavalier poets, are as flirtatious as they are paternal. There would have been no explaining them to his wife, who was developing a jealous streak that would eventually become infamous. News spread in the town of Winchester, where Lincoln addressed an outdoor meeting west of town on the twenty-eighth, and at the courthouse the next night, that the candidate was writing poetry for young ladies. So another came to him all a-blush on September 30 with *her* album in hand.

To Linnie—   *September 30, 1858*

> *A sweet plaintive song did I hear,*
> *And I fancied that she was the singer—*

> *May emotions as pure, as that song set a-stir*
> *Be the worst that the future shall bring her.*

Winchester Sep. 30—1858 A. LINCOLN

After the joint debate at Galesburg on October 7, a procession escorted Lincoln to the home of Mayor Henry R. Sanderson, and a Miss Anna Hurd presented Lincoln with a banner. The custom there was to give distinguished visitors a ritual bath—the mayor acting as the "Master of the Bath"—and so Mr. Lincoln was ceremoniously stripped and scrubbed. This may have seemed like excessive exposure. Mrs. Lincoln made up her mind to accompany her husband to the seventh and final debate, far down in Alton.

MARY LINCOLN HAD not laid eyes upon her husband in three weeks. He had returned home from speaking in Urbana the weekend of September 25, and she remembered the crowds outside their house on Saturday night, cheering under a full moon, as the Republican Clay Club welcomed him home with a serenade.

Now on October 15 she boarded a special train (a half-price excursion fare) from Springfield with several hundred other hometown citizens to hear Mr. Lincoln and Mr. Douglas in their final joint debate. On the train with her was Robert Lincoln, dressed in a uniform with stripes and braids and brass buttons, to march with the "Springfield Cadets" stepping to the beat of "Merritt's Cadet Band" for the glory of the Republican cause.

Mrs. Lincoln followed the reports of the Lincoln-Douglas debates in the columns of several newspapers, where journalists had made much of the contrast between the candidates' appearance and conduct during the tournament. Forty-five-year-old Douglas traveled in a luxurious private railroad car, wood-paneled and brass-fitted, trimmed with banners and bunting; attached to it was a flatcar bearing a shiny brass cannon. Two men in uniforms attended the weapon, and when the Douglas entourage drew near its destination, the cannon would herald the arrival of "the Little Giant"—all five feet four inches of him—with a boom and a powder flash. Lincoln rode in a common coach, and sometimes arrived in a Conestoga wagon, escorted by a few friends on horseback and on foot. On the platform Lincoln wore a weather-beaten, wrinkled black frock coat with sleeves too short and trousers that showed his ankles, while Douglas stood in a blue serge suit with silver buttons and a shirt of brilliant white linen—the picture of the prosperous statesman.

The contrast between Douglas's pride and what a *Chicago Times* reporter called Lincoln's "air of a perfect 'Uriah Heep' pleading his humility" gained emphasis from the presence of Mr. Douglas's wife and the absence of Mr. Lincoln's. Adele Cutts Douglas, twenty-three, was widely considered to be the most beautiful American woman to be seen outside of a professional theater company. Her profile had the limpid perfection of a Vermeer portrait, but she stood out in a crowd for other reasons, being several inches taller than her husband and maintaining a regal bearing, moving slowly and gracefully. Her breeding was impressive: Her father was President James Madison's nephew. Dolley Madison's grandniece, Adele had grown up in the house of the president's widow when Dolley's salon was the center of Washington high society. The young woman was also well educated, having attended a rigorous Catholic school in Georgetown.

Adele's presence sent a mixed message to the public: While her beauty and dignity enhanced her husband's image, her constant attendance reminded folks that Douglas, unlike Lincoln, was a man given to intemperance and occasional debauchery. He loved his liquor. Douglas wanted watching, needed a wife to look after him. She was not his first wife, as the Lincolns knew. Adele had rescued Stephen from the consuming grief that followed the loss of his first wife, Martha, who had died in January 1853 after complications of childbirth. For nearly two years Douglas had drifted, traveling in Europe and Russia, failing to drink enough whiskey to kill him or the memory of his beloved Martha. He returned to America in 1856 to face James Buchanan in a harrowing race for the presidential nomination, which Douglas narrowly lost. He met Adele in the summer of that year. Many people said she had saved the widower from ruin—taking over the management of his household and raising his two sons, Robert and Stephen, as if they had been her own.

Riding toward Alton on the special half-priced train from Springfield, Mary Lincoln counted among her concerns the inevitable comparisons that would be made between the candidates' wives. There was the famous Adele Cutts Douglas, now the doyenne of Washington society, hostess of a newly decorated mansion where grand balls and housewarming parties attracted thousands of visitors in a day; and here was Mary Lincoln, the self-styled "staid matron, & morever the mother of three noisy boys." Twenty years earlier she could have had Douglas herself, if she had wanted him.

Two of the three noisy boys she had left across the street in Springfield in the care of the Solomon Wheelocks and their teenage daughter Ardelia. Mary and her son Robert would be on hand to witness the pageant and performance at Alton on the Mississippi River, the final debate. For some people, this meeting might be regarded as anticlimactic. By now the press corps had so thoroughly covered the candidates, their positions, and their personalities that they could no longer expect to generate the same enthusiasm, or to gather crowds equal to Freeport's or Charleston's. The men were nearly exhausted, especially Douglas.

Thousands came up the river by steamboat from St. Louis, while others made the pilgrimage to Alton by wagon, on horseback, or in buggies. Alton was so far south, its Madison County constituents were mostly Democrats, so the banners Mary saw in the depot, and the cries she heard in the street as she made her way to the hotel, were overwhelmingly for "Stephen A. Douglas, the people's choice" and "popular sovereignty," with only scattered voices piping up for "Old Abe" and "free territories and free men." Rowdy visitors talking politics packed the taverns, and peddlers sold flags, sweetmeats, and beef jerky on the streets.

Mary met her husband at the Franklin House on State Street, a block north of Broadway. He had come from Quincy on the steamboat *City of Louisiana,* 115 miles down the Mississippi, in the company of Stephen Douglas—the only time the debaters traveled to a site together—arriving at five o'clock in the morning. First they stopped at the Alton House, Douglas's hotel near City Hall, and then Lincoln's supporters escorted him to the Franklin House. After the "pompous entry" of Douglas, "heralded by the firing of guns and strains of martial music," Lincoln's quiet reception, "without parade or fuss," was anticlimactic.

After three weeks apart, the Lincolns' reunion was bittersweet. In this Democratic stronghold, husband and wife shared a sense of resignation, not of all their aspirations, but of the high hopes that had led Abraham Lincoln to challenge Stephen Douglas in the first place. Lincoln had done his best; he had done far better than most people thought he would. But in their hearts the couple knew that whatever he had done, it was not likely to win him this seat in the U.S. Senate.

Mrs. Lincoln, struggling with a headache, was certainly weary after the long train ride, and discouraged by the pro-Douglas demonstrations and enthusiasm she saw all around her. Her husband had traveled nearly 4,500 miles and made more than sixty speeches during the campaign. This afternoon in Alton, with his back to the great cliffs and facing the Mississippi River, he would make his last speech of the debates, and one of his most powerful. But, first, he would see to it that the Franklin House had properly prepared for his family.

When he had done all he could to make Mary comfortable in their hotel room, Lincoln went downstairs to the lobby to take his ease in the morning light and gather his thoughts. He was sitting there when, looking up, his eyes met the dark-lidded, bemused gaze of Gustave Koerner. The white-haired German American lawyer and judge had been an anti-Nebraska Democrat who turned Republican in 1856. He was president of the Illinois State Convention, which had nominated Lincoln. The judge had followed the debates in the newspapers, but like Mary, he had never attended one himself. For five years he had been one of Douglas's harshest critics, arguing that he had "sold out his political principles for Southern support for the Presidency in 1854"; now he was an enthusiastic Lincoln supporter.

After greeting the judge heartily, Lincoln said, "Let us go up and see Mary." Koerner had not seen her since she was Miss Todd, years before at a party in Lexington, Kentucky. The best room in the second best hotel in Alton, Illinois, could not have been very spacious or luxurious in 1858. But the three travelers made themselves comfortable there in the cozy disarray of baggage half-unpacked and hats and clothing strewn on the bed and bedposts and chairs.

"Now, tell Mary what you think of our chances!" said Lincoln. "She is rather dispirited."

Koerner boasted that the Republicans would carry the state and dominate the legislature. "St. Clair [County] is perfectly safe," he said. Then he tried to assure Mrs. Lincoln that "the outlook in Madison [County] was good." But she could look out the window and hear the crowds shouting for Douglas and see for herself that Madison County was dubious. Mr. Koerner was a gentleman but perhaps too much of an optimist. The St. Louis morning papers had reported "that more than a thousand Douglas men had chartered a boat to attend the Alton meeting," and these were Free-Soilers whom Lincoln had failed to convince that Douglas was a dead lion for their cause.

"I found Lincoln a little despondent," Koerner recalled.

After lunch, they made their way through the traffic toward City Hall, a new brick building not far from the railroad station and the boat landing. By City Hall, workmen had erected a wooden platform on the broad public square that was jammed with people, horses and buggies, brass bands and squadrons of cadets, including Robert Lincoln. The crowd—one of the smallest to watch the debates—numbered a little more than five thousand.

The panoramic setting against the bluffs of Alton in mid-October was magnificent, with the trees turning red and gold. The speakers faced a gentle slope that reminded one reporter of a Greek amphitheater. To the southwest, they could see the sunlit stream of the Mississippi River, and Bloody Island, where sixteen years earlier Lincoln had gone to duel with James Shields. On the platform, seats for about twenty-five people were reserved for leaders of the two parties. Below were chairs and benches for dignitaries and their wives, and beyond this inner circle the crowd stood, or sat, or sprawled, on the natural terrace that rose uphill to the east, and to the south swept down to the river.

Governor Cyrus Edwards, Colonel F. S. Rutherford, editor George T. Brown of the *Alton Courier,* and John Pearson, the local bookseller, were some of the Republicans who escorted Lincoln and Koerner to the stage. Koerner had not seen Douglas since 1856. Politely shaking the senator's hand, he was shocked by his appearance. "His face was bronzed . . . but it was also bloated, and his looks were haggard, and his voice almost extinct. In conversation he merely whispered." Mary Lincoln had not seen her old suitor in almost two years, and was sorry to find Douglas in such bad condition. Next to him, her husband looked the picture of health.

This was the first time Mary Lincoln witnessed the new chemistry between Lincoln and the public. It was a stunning development. While remaining essentially the same man she had married, he had grown, like other great men, to accommodate the hopes, dreams, and even the fears of his contemporaries. Emilie Todd Helm recalled how her sister Mary commented, "Mr. Douglas is a very little, *little* giant by the side of my tall Kentuckian, and intellectually my husband towers above Douglas just as he does physically." When the debates began at two o'clock in the afternoon, the difference in stature between the men was as dramatic as the contrast between the stately Adele Cutts Douglas and the short, plump housewife from Springfield.

At this last debate, Stephen Douglas was given the opening and the conclusion. Koerner observed that "in addressing his audience he made himself understood only by an immense strain, and then only to a very small circle immediately near him." The arguments were well rehearsed, and Mary Lincoln had read them in the newspapers; therefore much of the suspense had drained from the spectacle. Yet she and her son still felt the excitement of the conflict, and the dramatic contrast between the candidates' opinions and appearances: the short, florid Douglas with his carefully groomed mane, and the tall, rumpled country lawyer with his windblown thatch of black hair.

Perhaps the thing that most struck Mary Lincoln was the difference in the tones of voice of the two orators. Anyone could hear it, even a spectator who did not know a word of English: the great solemn dignity of Douglas, his refinement and assurance; Lincoln's charming humility, his sense of humor that was not afraid to make jokes at his own expense, his lilting voice that mounted arguments so irrefutable that they seemed almost to come not from a single mind but from a source of truths. His early speeches had sometimes been overwrought. Now his language was direct and passionate.

As usual, Douglas began by defending popular sovereignty and chiding Lincoln for his House Divided speech, "a slander upon the immortal framers of our constitution," saying it was an invitation for the northern states to make war upon the South. Douglas accused Lincoln of being evasive as he refused to answer the question as to "whether he would vote for the admission of any more slave States in the event the people wanted them." A foot shorter than Lincoln, Douglas stood on his tiptoes, his back arched, and spoke as from a great height—as if he were the distinguished professor and Lincoln some lazy and recalcitrant pupil.

And Lincoln allowed him that role, played to it, meanwhile enlisting the sympathy of the audience. Who is not delighted to see pomposity deflated, its bubble pricked; who is not amused when the clever student or class clown outwits the tyrannical schoolmaster? When Douglas was speaking, his followers applauded and cheered for his forceful arguments while the Republicans held their peace; but when Lincoln stepped up and replied to Douglas, Mary Lincoln saw how her husband's sense of humor drew the audience together. This is a gift only partly owing to language. Much of it consists in the performer's attitude, his understanding of the humor inherent in any situation, no matter how serious. It flickered across Lincoln's mobile features before he spoke.

"Ladies and gentlemen:—I have been somewhat complimented by a large portion of Judge Douglas's speech—I mean that portion which he devotes to the controversy between himself and the present Administration. [Cheers and laughter]. . . . At Quincy, day before yesterday, he was a little more severe upon the Administration than I had heard him upon any former occasion, and I took pains to compliment him for it. I then told him to 'Give it to them with all the power he had'; and as some of them were present I told him I would be very much obliged if they would *give it to him* in about the same way. [Uproarious laughter and cheers.]"

This was reliably effective country rhetoric, aligning himself with Douglas against Buchanan—over Kansas—for just long enough to put the crowd at ease, and then teasing Douglas about his fickleness. Lincoln observed, "He reads something from Mr. Buchanan, from which he undertakes to involve him in an inconsistency; and he gets something of a cheer for having done so. I would only remind the Judge that while he is very valiantly fighting for the Nebraska bill and the repeal of the Missouri Compromise, it has been but a little while since he was the *valiant advocate of* the Missouri Compromise. [Cheers.] I want to know if Buchanan has not as much right to be inconsistent as Douglas has? [Loud applause and laughter; 'Good, good!' 'Hurrah for Lincoln!'] Has Douglas the *exclusive right*, in this country, of being *on all sides of all questions?*"

Looking around her, Mary Lincoln could see that almost everybody was laughing or smiling. They were now prepared to listen to whatever Lincoln had to say. Douglas wished to place Lincoln in an abolitionist role, but he would not play it. Douglas wanted to demonstrate that Lincoln would interfere with slavery in the states where it had long been established, but Lincoln denied it. Yet he insisted that when the Declaration of Independence said that all men were created equal, the founders had never meant to *exclude* the Negro. The first man to say that the Negro was not included was Chief Justice Taney in the Dred Scott case; and the second was "our friend Stephen A. Douglas. [Cheers and laughter.]"

Lincoln repeated the main arguments of his House Divided speech, defending them against the judge's attacks. Koerner observed that while Lincoln was sunburned, he looked as fresh, cool, and collected as at the beginning of the campaign. He delivered his propositions clearly, "and his whole speech was weighted with noble and deep thoughts." His words reached far beyond the moment.

"Has any thing ever threatened the existence of this Union save and except this very institution of Slavery?" Lincoln asked. "That is the real issue. That is the issue that will continue in this country when these poor tongues of Judge Douglas and myself shall be silent. It is the eternal struggle between these two principles—right and wrong—throughout the world. . . . The one is the common right of humanity and the other the divine right of kings."

Lincoln's words made such an impression on the multitude that after Douglas made his closing remarks there was only a scattering of applause. The people wanted to be on their way before the daylight failed.

By the time the debate was over and the crowd had gone away over the seven hills of Alton and by the steamboats on the river, it was nearly time for supper. Lyman Trumbull—whose wife, Julia, had become estranged from Mary after Trumbull defeated Lincoln in the senatorial contest of 1855—led the Lincolns and their supporters to dinner at their hotel. Mary still had not forgiven Julia, so being thrown together once more with the Trumbulls, leading Democrats of Alton, was not to Mrs. Lincoln's liking. Judge Trumbull sat at the head of the table, with Mr. and Mrs. Lincoln to his right. Opposite them sat Robert R. Hitt, the shorthand reporter for the *Chicago Tribune,* and his brother John Hitt, a farmer. To Mrs. Lincoln's right was twenty-four-year-old Horace White, a reporter for the *Tribune* who also accompanied Mr. Lincoln as a representative of the state central committee.

Lincoln conversed with Trumbull, who was excited by the events of the day. Lincoln asked, "Do you think we've made any impression on these people?" Trumbull replied that Madison County folks were not generally very demonstrative at their public meetings, but it appeared to him that Lincoln had made a favorable impression. Mrs. Lincoln ate her supper, engaging in conversation with young Horace White and Robert Hitt, the gentlemen from the *Tribune.* She found them charming. She asked if they would like to accompany Mr. Lincoln and herself on the train up to Springfield the next morning, a Saturday, and rest there with them the next week before returning to Chicago.

"Thanks for your courtesy, Mrs. Lincoln," said the suave Mr. Hitt, "but I will never call at your house until you live in the White House." Then Mary Lincoln laughed, saying, "there is not much prospect of such a residence very soon." She was making light of her disappointment. On that day the woman who had so firmly believed her husband would be president was plagued by doubts in this stronghold of the Democrats. The evening was dispiriting, after all these months of rallies and parades and ballyhoo, the long columns in newspapers from coast to coast. All that time he had been away from her and the boys, and forfeiting income from his law practice. What had it all come to? She could see that Mr. Lincoln had improved his skills as a speaker and performer—that was in itself a benefit.

Leonard Swett had been correct: The first ten lines of the House Divided speech had spoiled Lincoln's run for the Senate. On the bitter, rainy day in early November 1858 when the votes were counted, what Mary and her husband could not see, is that this loss of the Senate seat to Douglas foreshadowed a more important victory.

THE PLEASURES OF 1859

THIS WAS THE YEAR Darwin rocked Christendom with the publication of *The Origin of Species* in England. War erupted between France and Austria, and northern Italy was torn apart by nationalist uprisings. Daniel Emmett's song "Dixie" was performed for the first time in a Broadway theater. The gold rush in the Colorado Rockies drew a hundred thousand prospectors to the Kansas Territory, hell-bent on getting rich quick. A good slave in Kansas cost more than $1,500.

A new American flag, twenty by thirty feet, fluttered in the cold wind on a pole on the dome of the Illinois statehouse. There was a martial cast to things. Decker's Band played for a crowd of dancers at the cadets' ball. The concert hall was decked out in flags and bunting, and at the far end was a bivouac of white tents and an armed militia.

The Lincolns had only three blocks to stroll west to the governor's mansion on Jackson Street. Five hundred people flocked there to the open house given by the Republican governor William Bissell and his wife, wishing them a happy new year. The capital was still young and a bit wild. Judge Josiah Francis fined Richard Bailey $6 and damages for being drunk and disorderly, having fallen through the show window of James Rayburn's clothing store.

Eighteen fifty-nine was the last year that the Lincolns could be said to enjoy, or at least experience, any semblance of a normal private life. Their privacy had eroded in the carnival atmosphere of the 1858 Lincoln-Douglas debates, but Lincoln withdrew from the spotlight during 1859, resuming the law practice he had left almost entirely in Billy Herndon's hands during the debates. Until late summer of that year he rarely addressed the public. When he did, upon the invitation of Bloomington's Young Men's Association, or at Cook's Hall in Springfield, it was with the whimsical, Whitmanesque entertainment called "Discoveries and Inventions," a celebration of man's ingenuity—from the wheel to the steam engine—and of the power of language, rather than any of the themes he had debated with Douglas. For a while Lincoln appeared to have retired from politics—although the appearance was deceptive. He wrote to his friend Dr. Anson Henry: "I am glad I made the late race. It gave me a hearing on the great and durable question of the age . . . and though I now sink out of view, and shall be forgotten, I believe I have made some marks which will tell for the cause of civil liberty long after I am gone. . . . Mary joins me in sending our best wishes to Mrs. Henry and others of your family."

Indeed she had joined him once more: They would spend more time together in 1859 than they had since their vacation to New York and Canada in the summer of 1857, and more than they ever would again. One of the paradoxes of this marriage lay in the contradiction between their mutual ambition and their need to be alone together. He was drawn to the larger world of politics, while she wanted him to herself; yet she must share him with the world if he was to advance to high office with her at his side. Now for a little while and for the last time she would have no competition for his attention save the law practice that paid their bills. In early January they would bundle up and go to hear Mrs. J. M. Mozart sing songs and ballads at Cook's Hall on the east side of the square; then late that month there came the banquet celebrating the hundreth anniversary of the birth of Robert Burns, their favorite poet.

When the legislature convened and the courts were in session on February 2, Democrats and Republicans alike trudged through the mud and fog to a large evening party at the Lincolns' well-lighted house at Eighth and Jackson. Lincoln may have been on the sidelines politically speaking, but still they entertained friends and supporters who continued to believe in his future.

When he departed for Chicago in late February, she missed him so much that on the twenty-eighth she scribbled an anxious note to his friend Ozias Mather Hatch: "Mr. Hatch, If you are going up to Chicago today, & should meet Mr. L. there, will you say to him, that our *dear little Taddie,* is quite sick. The Dr. thinks it might prove a *slight* attack of *lung* fever. I am feeling troubled & it would be a comfort to have him, *at home.* He [Tad] passed a bad night, I do not like his symptoms, and will be glad, if he hurries home." She enlisted Hatch as an advocate rather than a mere messenger, and addressed the letter to him rather than her husband. She liked and trusted Hatch—who looked like a biblical prophet, with his shaggy beard and grim mouth and blazing eyes. Illinois secretary of state for two years, a highly opinioned nativist who remained friends with Lincoln despite their political differences, Hatch could be counted upon to present Mrs. Lincoln's case firmly and bring her man home to his family.

In the midst of a lawsuit, *Haines and Haines* v. *Talcott et al.* on March 2, Lincoln managed to curtail the litigation, and hurried home to Springfield the next day.

ONE OF MARY'S best friends, Hannah Shearer, once lived directly across the street with her husband, the physician John Henry Shearer. They had lived there for a year with their two little boys, until shortly after Lincoln lost the election of 1858. The doctor was consumptive and had to move to a healthier climate, a mountain town called Wellsboro in Pennsylvania.

Mary missed Hannah, and Lincoln missed the doctor, to whom he had once given a daguerreotype of himself, hollow-eyed and gaunt, which Mary criticized as "coarse." Her letters to Hannah Shearer provide intimate glimpses of the Lincolns' marriage during 1859. On Easter Sunday, April 24, Mary Lincoln writes that she does not feel well, but will try to attend the christening of "Julia Baker's renowned 'baby' [Julia Baker being Ninian and Elizabeth Edwards's daughter];" she recalls that a few evenings since, Mr. Hatch came to tea with Mr. & Mrs. Jesse Dubois. Lincoln once said that Dubois had "the elegant manners of a Frenchman, from which nation he had his descent." Soon these couples would be preoccupied with Lincoln's bid for the presidency, but that evening in the Lincolns' parlor, sipping from the blue and white china teacups, they lightheartedly discussed the pleasure trip they would all make to Council Bluffs, Iowa, in mid-May. There was land out there that Norman Judd, a lawyer for the Rock Island Railroad, meant Lincoln to accept as collateral on money owed him. They would all go out to Iowa to see what the land was worth.

Spring was upon them. Having compared her Easter bonnet to the headwear of the other ladies, Mary went to Smith's store on Adams Street on Tuesday and spent $5 on a silk hat.

The pleasure trip to Iowa they were planning was postponed, "owing to some business, Mr. L— found he had to attend to in Chicago," she wrote to Hannah Shearer in June. The "business" Mrs. Lincoln declined to specify was the tip of the iceburg of his ambition, moving with glacial but steady persistence. The *Chicago Press and Tribune* of June 1, 1859, notes in fine print, in the "Personals" column, that "the Hon. Abraham Lincoln, of Springfield, and Hon. B. Gratz Brown, of St. Louis, were in this city yesterday." Brown, a Democrat turned Republican, was the radical Free-Soil congressman from Missouri, often mentioned in the Great Debates for his failed effort to emancipate the slaves in his home state.

On Tuesday, May 31, Lincoln had taken a room in the grand Tremont House, a three-hundred-room brick hotel six stories high on the busy corner of Lake and Dearborn. He was one of five lawyers representing some Mennonite farmers in *Farni and Farni* v. *Tesson,* a complicated debt action in the U.S. Circuit Court. The weather was mild, a relief from the violent thunderstorms and tornadoes that had ripped through Illinois since Thursday the week before. The thermometer in the window of Reed's Apothecary on Lake Street stood at 61 degrees most of the day.

Also staying at the Tremont was Lincoln's political ally William Kellogg, the moderate congressman from Illinois's fourth district. Kellogg and Brown represented opposite poles of the Republican world of opinion regarding slavery. As Lincoln would need the support of both factions to run for president, he was in Chicago as much for covert politicking as for his law practice. The Farni case would go to the Supreme Court, but Lincoln would give it up long before. Now it was important because the Mennonites were part of the German American community whose support he needed. Just yesterday he had quietly purchased the *Illinois Staats-Anzeiger,* a German newspaper, and turned it over to Theodore Canisius to manage.

The stone courthouse stood in the middle of the square bounded by Randolph and Washington streets to the north and south and Clark Street to the west. A block north Lincoln walked with his satchel of papers, and another block west on Lake Avenue to get back to his hotel. He passed the elegant, Moorish façade of A. H. Miller the jeweler, on the corner of Randolph and Clark, admiring the smooth new Nicholson pavement underfoot. At 93 Clark Street stood Buck's Apothecary: in the back was a splendid marble soda fountain where he and little Willie could sit on stools and eat ice cream and drink cold water.

Willie and his mother had arrived in Chicago a few days after Lincoln. Mary and her eight-year-old child were glad to get out of central Illinois, where hurricanes and tornadoes had wreaked havoc—especially in Jacksonville, not thirty miles from Springfield. Houses were blown to pieces; thousands of hogs, horses, and cows were killed. A horse was found "with a rail run through him lengthwise, so that both ends were visible." Eight people were killed in Jacksonville and twenty wounded. Mrs. Route was blown out of a window "and carried a distance of over a hundred yards, and when found, scarcely a particle of clothing had remained on her body." People were buried alive in their houses. A little boy was swept up by the wind for some distance; when found in a tree, with only his arm broken, he exclaimed: "Pa, when I was up there ever so high, I saw a great big wagon fly over my head."

Mary Lincoln, pathetically fearful of lightning and thunder, and her son Willie gratefully joined Mr. Lincoln in splendid rooms at the Tremont, on or about Saturday, June 4. In a letter to his friend Henry Remann, Willie mentions that they attended not one but two theaters on Saturday night. One performance was certainly the Chinese Jugglers, "the greatest Wonder of the age! . . . in full and rich Oriental Costumes," in Metropolitan Hall. He begins his note to Henry, "This town is a very beautiful place," and ends with, "The weather is very very fine here in this town," which must have been soothing to his mother's nerves. This was the time of year her headaches pursued her like tornadoes. Lincoln and his son shared one room, while Mary slept in the other.

In the afternoon, they would stroll a block west on Lake Street to Lincoln's favorite restaurant, Tom Andrews's "Head Quarters," to dine; then it was no more than a block north to South Water Street, where they could show Willie the river and the boats.

"You know, I enjoy city life," Mrs. Lincoln wrote to Mrs. Shearer. Mary loved Chicago. The city had burgeoned from a swampy town to a bustling trade center in the 1850s, as the population doubled from 70,000 to 140,000. The streets in the peninsular area bounded by the Chicago River and Lake Michigan had been raised three feet on layers of pine, sand, and gravel, then paved with stone. Engineers had dredged and widened the river, and all along its banks the carpenters had built loading piers for the busy warehouses and factories.

The main approach to Chicago by railroad was unique, the scenery breathtaking. The train from Springfield through McLean left the prairie behind at Joliet and dipped into a marshland south of Chicago; to the east of the marsh was a palisade of trees. Gradually through forest clearings the passenger could glimpse the inland sea, Michigan, the Queen of

Lakes, as vast and blue as the June sky. Farmhouses gave way to stone mansions along North Street—some twenty-seven hundred new houses had been built in 1855. Then the train left the land behind as it chugged onto a narrow causeway running north and south parallel to Michigan Avenue. One could look out the left side of the coach and see wooden houses and piers and a forest of masts over a blockwide strip of water. The grain elevators towered at the edge of the city and the church spires within. Then at last one could see the sheds and tin roofs of the Illinois Central Railroad depot.

The Lincolns usually took this route because he had a "chalked hat," or free rail pass, after 1854 as a result of having done so much legal work for the Illinois Central. The depot stood only three blocks from the Tremont Hotel, along Lake Street, no more than a five-minute carriage ride in the usual traffic of omnibuses, drays, buggies, and pedestrians. The carriage pulled up to a splendid Corinthian entrance, two stories high, with double-deep columns on each side. The Tremont covered the city block, within walking distance of a half-dozen theaters and the finest retailers of jewelry, furniture, women's apparel, boots, and hats to be found west of Cincinnati. The neighborhood must have whetted Mrs. Lincoln's appetite for style whether or not she had money to appease it; soon enough she would.

After a few days of shopping and sightseeing they returned to Springfield on June 9, a bright and cool spring day, in time to prepare for a small party they were hosting that evening for Orville Browning and others.

ON JUNE 26, 1859, Mary Lincoln wrote to Mrs. Shearer, "For the last two weeks, we have had a continual round of *strawberry* parties, this last week I have spent five evenings out. . . . This last week, we gave a strawberry company of about seventy." In those days of simple pleasures, the ripe red berry was cause enough for celebration, a symbol of springtime and balmy weather before the scorching afternoons and restless nights of summer. The Lincolns were much in demand in Springfield society as party guests, and would do their turn as host and hostess; by most accounts they were gracious, warm, and witty hosts, enjoying themselves as they entertained.

They were as happy together then as they would ever be, yet there was an empty space near the center of Mary's emotional life that she freely reveals to Mrs. Shearer: "I shall never cease to long for your dear presence, a cloud always hangs over me, when I think of you." Here is a woman with three children, a faithful husband, and her choice of friends among many women who admired her despite her occasional harshness and pride—yet she is inconsolably forlorn. "What I would not give, for a few hours conversation, with you this evening. I hope you may never feel as lonely as I sometimes do, surrounded by much that renders life desirable."

Granted, Mary Lincoln, at the age of forty, had a penchant for self-dramatization and even self-pity; but this last sentence in her June letter to Hannah Shearer nevertheless is an essential brushstroke of autobiography. *I hope you may never feel as lonely as I sometimes do, surrounded by much that renders life desirable.*

Let us pause for a moment in the middle of 1859 to consider Mary Lincoln's surroundings. On this Sunday afternoon she is probably writing her letter at the secretary desk that folds out of a niche in tall bookcases with glass-fronted doors, on the interior wall of the rear parlor. To her left in the east corner stand two side tables with long spool-turned legs in the Elizabethan style, on either side of a late Empire sofa with an ornate walnut serpentine back and tufted upholstery in black horsehair. Each of the side tables supports a cradled globe—one of the world, and one of the heavens—serving Lincoln's scientific curiosity and imparting a symbolic force in this house whose owners hovered between earth and the immortal stars, in a precarious suspension.

Within reach of the sofa was a round mahogany center table with a pedestal base. Books and papers were stacked there, a pitcher for water, and drinking glasses. The furniture of the parlors, front and back, each anchored by a fireplace, was selected by Mrs. Lincoln with loving care from stores and cabinetmakers in Chicago and Springfield. The Brussels carpet was a mauve trefoil figure on a field of red, and the wallpaper bore a pale blue design. Looking to her right, down the length of the room toward the front parlor, she could proudly admire the red floor-length curtains she had sewn for the street windows, the golden valances surmounting them, and the elegance of the tall pier mirror that stood between the windows—the looking glass that served her as she prepared to attend ever more important functions, to receive increasingly distinguished guests. It was a fine mirror, big as a window, with a rococo openwork crest and curved legs and frame in the late Empire style. The whole room had that feeling, that blend of sensibilities—the richness and high spirit of Victorian design resting on the strong, heavy lines of the Empire—English fancy and French formality. The rocking chair before the front fireplace had a carved floral motif on the crest rail. The side chairs, in one of which she sat, musing, at her desk, were all of mahogany in the late Empire style, with a plain curved crest rail and an hourglass-shaped splat.

Surrounded by much that renders life desirable, including the girandole on the mantelpiece behind her, a three-branched candlestick with hanging prisms of crystal that scattered rainbows around the room; next to them, the pair of French porcelain pitchers, and many other fragile treasures arranged on the five shelves of the scrolled whatnot in the corner behind her: small blown glass decanters; ceramic vases; seashells (including a pearly conical trochus, conches, whelks, and periwinkles) that she loved to arrange with fresh flowers; a statuette of Parian ware. She had acquired these things over the years, mostly since 1856, when the house had been enlarged and they were no longer troubled by debt. Each curio, table, or glass vessel seemed the most important of its kind, until she possessed it and would begin to dream of another. None could have been displayed as they were now until the boys had been taught to restrict their rougher play to the outdoors or the sitting room on the far side of the stair hall.

The sitting room was the size of the front parlor, but brighter. Tall windows on either side of the fireplace admitted the southern light and showed views of cornfields in the middle distance. Daylight played upon the prisms that hung from a five-branched candelabrum on the mantel. The curtains were light green and the carpet pale blue and green with pink medallions. A center table of walnut, with cabriole legs and scroll feet, stood before the fireplace. There the children played, and Mary would sew, and sometimes Mr. Lincoln would read a book if he were not sprawled on the carpet, his back supported by an overturned side chair, its canted rear legs poking out over his tousled hair.

Beneath each window was a simple side chair: S-curved back with a single horizontal slat, crest rail with decorative carving in the center, and seat of striped linen. Between the front windows stood a sewing table with two drawers on a pedestal stand. Above this hung a tall rectangular mirror in a gilt frame that reflected—when the room was unoccupied—one of the few pictures in the house: a hunting horse in a wooden frame, hung with a visible wire and golden tassels.

Lately they had purchased a stereoscope, the new invention of Dr.

Oliver Wendell Holmes, whose poetry and "breakfast-table sketches" the Lincolns admired. The rectangular slides, each with two photographs taken side by side, lay strewn upon the felt cover of the table. Viewed through the binoculars of Holmes's device, the slides produced an uncanny illusion of depth, so that the Lincolns could envision themselves on the Champs-Élysées of Paris, or overlooking the Thames from London Bridge, or viewing their beloved Niagara Falls from Table Rock.

It was in this cheerful room, when the boys were outdoors playing or upstairs in bed, that Lincoln would read aloud to Mary over the center table as she sewed a shirt or mended a stocking—passages of a speech or a newspaper column, or lines of his favorite poem by Oliver Wendell Holmes, "The Last Leaf," a rather melancholy, sentimental ode to have been written by a medical scientist and inventor:

> *The mossy marbles rest*
> *On the lips that he has pressed*
> *In their bloom:*
> *And the names he loved to hear*
> *Have been carved for many a year*
> *On the tomb.*

Like Lincoln, Dr. Holmes was a visionary, who gazed deeply into the mystery of life by the device of double vision, but who at times failed to see what was right in front of him.

WHAT ELSE DID MARY have? In the little dining room to her left, behind the stair hall, six fancy chairs with stenciled crest rails surrounded a drop-leaf walnut table. A sideboard against the wall beside the kitchen door was stacked with printed Staffordshire plates and china teacups, plates of plain white ironstone, and others of earthenware. She had six pressed glass goblets, a set of coin silver flatware from Chicago, and a pressed glass cake stand.

The kitchen was dominated by a modern wood-burning cast-iron cookstove that stood on a zinc heat shield to protect the wide-planked floor. A tall kitchen cupboard stood in the corner next to the stove, and a dry sink next to the outside door. There was room too for a worktable and a small rush-seated chair under the stairs. A ladder-back rocking chair sat a few steps from the stove, and near it a stoneware butter churn. She had all the pots, pans, and utensils of earthenware, tinware, ironware, and woodenware any household could want, and an Irish servant named Mary who knew how to wield them and who had been "a very faithful servant" and "as submissive as possible," since winter. Mr. Lincoln was paying the Irish girl 75 cents per week "on the side" to remain faithful and not to fuss with the mistress; Mrs. Lincoln was none the wiser. So she retained the maid for cooking, cleaning, and child care until February 1860, when they parted ways.

She had fine dresses and bonnets—although she longed for better—and seamstresses to fashion what she could not. The biographer Jean Baker has observed that Mary's shopping in the spring of 1859 was becoming compulsive: In the month of April hardly a day passed without a trip to Smith's to buy yards of silk, ribbons, threads, tablecloths, pins, shoes, and buttons. In the barn out back she had a cow that Mr. Lincoln kept for milk and cream and butter. They kept dogs and cats. They had a horse named Bob who frightened her so that she dared not ride into the country to visit Mrs. Parrish, Hannah Shearer's sister. They owned a serviceable carriage. They had ten cords of seasoned firewood in the shed near the barn ready to fuel the stoves in winter. Sometimes they had bedbugs, but so did everyone, and they had Dead Shot powder, sold at Corneau & Diller's, to kill them.

Mary Lincoln had a fine house—not a brick mansion, but as fine a wood-frame house as any of that size—and land around it, three children who had survived infancy (one on his way to college), high social standing in the provincial capital, and good health despite her headaches and chronic female troubles. She had some good friends and a few enemies that she had come by honestly and vigorously and that she valued more than many of her relatives.

She possessed all these things and more that we cannot describe, for we have not begun the inventory of the comfortable bedrooms upstairs at Eighth and Jackson where the Lincolns spent their peaceful nights. Nor can we ransack their drawers and closets, or their jewel boxes. We do know that Mr. Lincoln liked to give his wife jewelry when he could afford it.

Mary Lincoln was indeed surrounded by much that renders life desirable, including the Presbyterian church at Third and Washington where she offered prayers of thanksgiving on Sundays. They purchased a pew in the seventh row for $50. She had all of these things. Yet she was so lonely that her fondest wish for her friend was that Hannah might never be as lonely as she was. She was lonely because she did not have *him*, Abraham Lincoln, her husband. Perhaps she had never possessed him as she wished; perhaps no one, and nothing, could take him in. He was beginning to seem—to many people—larger than life. He had certainly outshone every politician in the West with the possible exception of Stephen Douglas, whose star was waning.

During the seventeen years they had been married, Mr. Lincoln had been absent almost half the time. When he was home he was kind and considerate—that is, when he was present in mind and spirit. He doted upon the boys, and since they idealized their father in his absence, he took pains not to disappoint them when he returned. He played on the floor with Willie, making delicate boats out of wood scraps; he practiced Latin declensions with Robert; he carried Tad on his shoulders to market. He took all of the boys and their friends to the circus. Any mother would be grateful for this paternal devotion, which has a lasting impact on children.

As for Mother, too often she got the husk of his presence in the evening, immobile and silent in a chair, staring into space, thinking or dreaming. If lightning struck, literally, or a suspicious-looking tinker came banging a copper pot at the door, he could be a great comfort, stroking and petting her until she had quit screaming or shuddering. He called her his puss, his child bride then, and who knows how much of her hysteria was owing to her desire to get his full attention, an emotional deficit on her part, an emptiness that may have existed before she ever met him but which he was not quite able to fund, given his own dread of intimacy. They played at that game for most of their lives: child-bride and father-husband, a game that cannot continue without the child's resentment and rebellion on the wife's side, and on the husband's part the longing for womanly courage and wisdom. One has only to sample the affectionate letters between Mr. and Mrs. Orville Browning, or Mr. and Mrs. David Davis, to see the dynamics of conjugal love between emotional equals, without patronization or adolescent rebellion in husband or wife. Marriages thrive upon an emotional balance.

It would have been a pleasure for them to forget their differences in the warmth of the marriage bed, steeped in the solvent of erotic love; but time and the wounds of childbirth had diminished that reliable solution. They were left with the prosaic truth of each other: a middle-aged woman and man in two chairs, bound by their children, their home and possessions, their memories, social conventions, and their burning ambition. They were still drawn together by the mysterious lure of the future.

TRAVELING TOGETHER

A LL THAT SUMMER and autumn the Lincolns found opportunities to travel together, and they planned their journeys carefully. They enjoyed each other's company whenever arrangements could be made to leave the children at home.

She wrote to Hannah Shearer on August 28: "I anticipated a quiet summer at home. Within a week after [July 14] we started unexpectedly on an excursion, travelled eleven hundred miles, with a party of eighteen. Many of the party, were your acquaintances, Mr. & Mrs. Dubois, Mr. & Mrs. Tom Campbell [Mary's first cousin], Mr. Hatch *of course,* and some few others, I believe you know." The others included Mr. and Mrs. William Butler (the boardinghouse keepers), Mr. and Mrs. Stephen Logan, and Lieutenant Governor John Moore. And the practical purpose for this working vacation was to inspect the properties of the Illinois Central Railroad; an annual tax assessment was in dispute. A special coach and locomotive was put at the party's disposal at Springfield, and in the withering heat of midsummer the merry party traveled from Dunleith to Cairo via Chicago and back again. They stayed in luxurious suites at the Tremont Hotel.

"*Words* cannot express what a merry time we had, the gayest pleasure party, I have ever seen. Mr. Lincoln says I may go up to the White Mountains, Niagara & take New York & Philadelphia in our route. Will go on, in time to bring *Bob* home next summer, if *one dare* anticipate, so far in advance." She was aware of how capricious fate might be, how much can happen in a year.

Robert had left "for college, in Boston, a few days since, and it almost appears, as if light & mirth, had departed with him." Yet her husband cheered her with their plans and dreams of travel to eastern cities. In the meantime he would have the pleasure of her company, and her moral support, as he journeyed to Ohio and Indiana in September to address Republicans, Independents, and curious Democrats upon the questions of slavery and states' rights—the issues that would shape the country's destiny and his own. He had received letters of invitation from Peter Zinn of Cincinnati and William T. Bascom of Columbus to stump for Republican candidates in the fall elections. The same day, September 6, he stopped at Corneau Diller's drugstore on the east side of the square and bought his wife a vial of perfume. On Wednesday the fourteenth she went to C. M. Smith's store to buy Mr. Lincoln a new silken necktie, black stock, and for Willie a cap and a couple of pairs of socks.

She had not traveled with her husband to hear a political speech since the last of the Great Debates, in Alton. This was a more relaxed journey. Lincoln would be following Douglas in Ohio, where the Little Giant had spoken at Columbus on September 7 and in Cincinnati on the thirteenth. The Republican committees far and wide were clamoring for Lincoln's speeches to support candidates in the autumn elections, but there was no immediate office at stake for him, so Mrs. Lincoln could enjoy the oratory and the performances without worrying over whether he lost or won.

The train trip to Columbus would take most of the day and night of Thursday, September 15. The Lincolns sat together in the stiff, high-backed seats of the railroad coach, listening to the clicking of the wheels on the track, watching the great central plain of Indiana roll by them, the wheat and corn crops tall and green, promising a rich harvest. They enjoyed their leisure in silence and conversation, a time when they had few worries and counted many blessings. Lincoln was on an errand he might enjoy for the benefit he would do his fellow Republicans running for office. The moon was full that night, and it shone on the orchards and grain fields of central Ohio and lighted their way to the Old Neil House, the famous hostelry on High Street, a broad, treeless avenue that faced the magnificent capitol building. The colossal six-story hotel stood on a corner, wrapped around with a Doric colonnade, with striped awnings over the sidewalks. Andrew Jackson had slept there. So had William Henry Harrison, Henry Clay, and Charles Dickens.

After breakfast the next morning they drove out to the county fair to enjoy the shows of livestock, baking and quilting competitions, and the musicians, dancers, and jugglers that made the rounds of those rustic gatherings. The Lincolns would attend as much to be seen as to see, in order to drum up an audience for his speeches. Even in Ohio his reputation preceded him, and folks gathered to shake his hand. Sometime before lunch they went to a daguerreotype studio so Lincoln could have his picture taken; as usual, Mrs. Lincoln declined to be photographed.

At two o'clock in the afternoon, Mary Lincoln took a seat on the east terrace of the statehouse and listened while George M. Parsons, chairman of the Republican County Committee, introduced her husband. Lincoln then began with characteristic modesty, explaining that he had never before addressed an audience in Ohio and begging them not to expect too much of him: "I hope, therefore, that you will commence with very moderate expectations; and perhaps if you will give me your attention, I shall be able to interest you to a moderate degree."

More people would have attended if the acrobats, blooded horses, and prize bulls at the Franklin County fair had not distracted them. But this was the nature of politics in 1859—it was a spectator sport, competing with prizefights and horse races for attention. Lincoln was simply continuing his crowd-pleasing debate with Douglas long distance. Douglas was down the road in Wooster, attacking the attorney general and Buchanan's whole administration. Without the Little Giant's bombastic presence, the spectacle in Columbus lacked color, so only a few hundred people heard Lincoln's familiar arguments attacking popular sovereignty and clarifying the true intentions of the Founding Fathers to cast off slavery.

Mary sat near the reporter for the *Cincinnati Daily Commercial,* who described the view of the speaker on that fair afternoon: "Abram Lincoln is a dark complexioned man, of a very tall figure, and so exceedingly 'well preserved' that he would not be taken for more than thirty-eight, though he is rising of fifty years of age. His countenance should be called a very good one; his features are strongly marked. . . . We don't know his lineage, but he is evidently of the Kentucky 'race' of men, and a fine type of that race."

This particular Friday afternoon, she was taken not so much by Mr. Lincoln's appearance in the fresh silk tie she had bought him as by a distinct difference in his tone and style of delivery of the well-known arguments. In the absence of Douglas himself playing against him, Lincoln could be more sportive, bolder, even sarcastic. He took mischievous pleasure in mocking Douglas's rhetoric, mimicking "the giant's" drawling, histrionic pronunciation of the "gur-reat pur-inciple of popular sover-eignty." Often he made his audience laugh. "He [Douglas] has a good deal of trouble with his popular sovereignty. His explanations explanatory of explanations explained are interminable," Lincoln wryly declared, draw-ing out the tongue twister musically, popping and crackling his conso-nants. Lincoln spoke for more than two hours, so it is not possible to capture the full flavor or the subtlety of his arguments. But one image fixed itself in the minds of all who heard him.

Lincoln cautioned that Douglas's ideas and the Dred Scott decision had brought about an insidious and dangerous change—"the gradual and steady debauching of public opinion." Five years earlier, no man would have put in print the idea that "the Negro had no share in the Declaration of National Independence . . . and when 'all men' were spoken of Negroes were not included." But as of last year, "there was not a Douglas popular sovereign in Illinois who did not say it."

"A very significant change it is, being no less than changing the Negro, in your estimation, from the rank of a man to a brute. They are taking him down, and placing him, when spoken of, among reptiles and crocodiles, as Judge Douglas himself expresses it." (In Memphis, Douglas had told the crowd "that he was for the negro against the crocodile, but for the white man against the negro.") And this phrase, which he had heard Doug-las repeat many times in Illinois, Lincoln interpreted thus: "As the negro ought to treat the crocodile as a beast, so the white man ought to treat the negro as a beast."

Around five o'clock that afternoon, Lincoln concluded his speech with a burst of rhetorical fireworks: "In a pre-eminent degree these popular sovereigns are at this work; blowing out the moral lights around us; teach-ing that the negro is no longer a man but a brute; that the Declaration has nothing to do with him; that he ranks with the crocodile and the reptile; that man, with body and soul, is a matter of dollars and cents."

As Lincoln bowed, acknowledging the cheers and applause, bidding his friends adieu, his wife accepted the congratulations and good wishes of the ladies and gentlemen who surrounded her. She waited while her husband was presented to all the ladies. Then the Lincolns left to dine at the hotel, and had a little rest afterward. That night at City Hall, he would give a shorter version of his speech for the Young Men's Republican Club.

The next morning, it was only a three-hour journey by rail west to Dayton where they would change trains, catching the Hamilton and Dayton Railroad south to Cincinnati. Reflecting upon their reception in Columbus, the Lincolns saw no grounds for elation or disappointment. The turnout had been small but appreciative, notwithstanding the comments of a Democratic journalist who said that the Republican club "must have been mortified by the very meagre audience." The Douglas opposition was always on the attack. He judged that "Mr. Lincoln is not a great man—very very far from it," and was amused that he had gone off to have his picture taken. "We think that Mr. Lincoln will never be invited here again, and that was perhaps his opinion" when he had his likeness preserved "as a remembrance for his Columbus friends."

Lincoln had friends and foes in Columbus, and there were many more people there who cared little about him one way or the other. He and his wife were treated fairly. But there was no way the reception in Columbus could have prepared them for Cincinnati. Maybe the effect of his barnstorming tour was cumulative, as it was widely covered by the *Cincinnati Daily Commercial* newspaper. During his layover in Dayton, Lincoln addressed a crowd that gathered to hear him at the courthouse. The morning papers had announced his coming, so he could hardly refuse. At one o'clock he mounted a wooden crate at the corner of the building and spoke there for nearly two hours. Mary was not present; she was resting at the Philips House Hotel nearby. After the peal of applause, he shook hands and signed autographs. Little Annie Harries handed him her Bible to sign, and he wrote in it, "Live by the words within these covers and you will be forever happy." Lincoln followed his friend Samuel Craighead, a prominent Dayton lawyer, around the corner to Edgar's grocery on Main Street, where a staircase led to Cridland's daguerreotype gallery. There the men sat for their portraits while a young painter, Charles Nickum, from Edmunson's studio across the hall, was called upon to sketch Lincoln. The young artist had to work fast so that the Lincolns would not miss their four o'clock train to Cincinnati.

"Keep on," said Lincoln encouragingly. "You may make a good one, but never a pretty one."

They made the train in time, and it stopped briefly in the town of Hamilton, twenty-five miles north of Cincinnati. There a crowd had gathered at the depot to see Mr. and Mrs. Lincoln. When the train jerked to a halt in the station at 5:30, Lincoln was standing on the back platform of the caboose with his escort, Congressman John A. Gurley of Cincinnati.

Gurley was not much taller than Mary Lincoln, and the sight of the colossal and the diminutive politicians standing side by side was comical. Mary heard her husband use a joke that he often applied to her: "My friends," he announced, chuckling and pointing a long finger at himself, "this is the long of it. And this," he said, tenderly laying his hand on Gurley's pate, "this is the short of it."

Lincoln stepped down from the train and mounted a makeshift platform the citizens had set up for him near the station. The day was still balmy and clear; the sun was low in the west. He delivered a brief critique of the popular sovereignty doctrine, including these closing remarks: "This beautiful and far-famed Miami Valley is the garden spot of the world. My friends, your sons may desire to locate in the west; you don't want them to settle in a territory like Kansas, with the curse of slavery hanging over it. They desire the blessings of freedom, so dearly purchased by our Revolutionary forefathers."

A few more jabs at Douglas and the "border ruffians of Missouri," and Lincoln bowed for the applause. He swung back onto the train to rejoin his wife, to enjoy some cold water and an hour of rest before the jamboree that awaited them in Cincinnati.

CINCINNATI, WITH ITS bustling waterfront on the Ohio River opposite the Licking River, was a port of entry, a cultural and manufacturing center, and a commercial hub in the vast four-state area of Ohio, Kentucky, Illinois, and Indiana. They called it the "Queen City" of the West for its beautiful architecture, parks, and gardens, and its shops and theaters. Famous actresses and singers came to perform there at Pike's opera house. With a population of two hundred thousand in 1859, Cincinnati was the world's largest meatpacking center—one could not escape the odor of the slaughterhouses and soap factories—but men and women came here to buy clothing, perfume, and lotions. The city was famous for soap making, printing ink and paper, and also for the manufacture of men's and boys' clothing, shoes, sheet copper and tin, and lager beer.

The Queen City was also ahead of its time as an abolitionist center—the home of Salmon Chase, and of James G. Birney, whose antislavery weekly *The Philanthropist* had provoked riots in the 1830s. Cincinnati also had a large German American population, strongly supportive of Lincoln and the Republican party. For these reasons, as well as a more efficient Republican organization in the southwest corner of Ohio, the Lincolns could expect a warm reception.

In two prominent, separate columns, the newspaper proclaimed that Mr. Lincoln was arriving that evening, "and will be received with becoming pomp and circumstance. His political friends propose, we believe, to make his reception equal to that given the Little Giant. . . . As we are in the way of lionizing the politicians of Illinois, we see no reason why Mr. Lincoln should not have as big a turn out as Douglas. He is a very able man, and a droll one, full of facts and a sort of odd wit that takes the crowds immensely. He speaks tonight at Fifth Street market place, and will be well worth hearing."

As the train rolled into Union Depot at Third Street, more than a dozen members of the Republican committee were on hand to welcome Mr. and Mrs. Lincoln and John Gurley. As they stepped down onto the platform, they saw "a large concourse of persons who had assembled to greet the Champion of Freedom." Soon they could hear the welcoming cannon fire. The committee escorted the Lincolns to the Burnet House, the city's brand-new inn, an enormous H-shaped building whose six-story central section was surmounted by a copper dome and cupola where the Stars and Stripes flew from a staff. The hotel was the most luxurious in the West. The Lincolns went up the wide marble steps and passed through the columns of the high portico; then the doors were closed to the cheering crowd behind them.

After freshening up, they took tea in the salon with the Republican leaders, including Benjamin Eggleston, Peter Zinn (who had first invited Lincoln to Ohio), and thirty-seven-year-old Rutherford B. Hayes, then city solicitor of Cincinnati. Lincoln "shook many hands and took his tea in very great haste." There was not much time, as he was scheduled to speak at eight o'clock.

An open carriage delivered the Lincolns a few blocks north to Market Square, and a mounted escort made way for them through the swelling crowd. Several brass bands played patriotic tunes and fanfares. As the shadows of twilight gathered, the German brigade of the Tenth Ward and other uniformed men marching in formation lit the way with torches. Mary had never witnessed anything quite like this enthusiasm for her husband—the sheer magnitude of it. They were cheering for her, too.

Now the view of Market Square from Fifth Street—as the sky turned to deep blue over Cincinnati and the stars of Pegasus appeared overhead—

was spectacular, hectic. Rockets and torches cast irregular lights upon an American flag that flew on a high pole, higher than the mainmast of a ship, higher than the tallest five-story buildings that bounded the square. Four thousand men, women, and children, not to mention their dogs, horses, and buggies, had gathered around the flagpole in front of the long, low, tin-roofed market, the men in their shirtsleeves and galluses, the ladies in pale ruffled summer dresses and straw bonnets. Somewhere they had set up a ceremonial cannon, which boomed as steadily as it could without melting, and "without regard to economy of powder, for after every discharge there was a shrill jingle of falling glass." Perhaps the town glaziers owned the cannon.

Until the Republican procession pressed through the throng, the people appeared to be watching the tall façade of the Hanging Rock Stove Foundry with its arched windows. But two doors to the right of that building was a smaller store with a gabled roof and an iron balcony on the second story. This was E. & D. Kinsey's jewelry store; the Kinseys lived above. Lincoln would speak from the balcony above the striped awning. A new gas streetlamp stood just to the right of Kinsey's shop, and with the gaslight and the processional torches, everyone would get a good view of Mr. Lincoln. The *Enquirer* reporter described him as "a tall, dark-visaged, angular, awkward, positive-looking sort of individual, with character written in his face and energy expressed in his every movement."

Now turning from his wife, taking her encouragement with him, he alighted from the carriage and bounded upstairs to the balcony. It was Benjamin Eggleston's privilege to introduce the speaker, an "astounding honor" he called it, of presenting this luminary to "two acres and a half of people, the distinguished statesman and expounder of the Constitution, 'no other than the Hon. Abram Lincoln of Illinois' from whom they expected to hear, on the rights of man, and 'particularly freedom.' "

Lincoln stepped forth and took a bow. He waited for the crowd's applause and huzzahs to die down. Then he began, with an extravagant compliment to his "fellow citizens of Ohio," saying he had never spoken in "so great a city as this," prompting the reporter from the *Commercial* to mutter, "What will they say to that in Chicago, where you have spoken so many times? Don't you know that that is the 'great city'?" But the throng received the flattery in good spirits, and the people were pleased to discover that "there would be no difficulty in hearing Mr. Lincoln, as he spoke with singular clearness of enunciation and deliberation, duly punctuating every sentence as he uttered it." Enjoying the sound of his voice, they settled in for his long speech, "shifting legs, taking as easy attitudes as could be contrived on the boulders [paving stones], and listened expectantly."

As accustomed as Mary Lincoln was to hearing her husband speak, this particular oration, so near the banks of the Ohio under the rising moon, was uniquely moving and memorable. In two days she had heard him give three speeches. This was the fourth, and none of them except the first had he had any time to "try out" on her. So this speech struck her with the same immediacy and novelty as it did the thousands of strangers. Sometime between the hour he agreed to speak in Ohio and this moment when he stood in Market Square, he had decided to turn his old debate with Douglas into a fresh drama. Using the hilly city of Cincinnati as a backdrop, the stars over the river as a proscenium arch, and the slave state of Kentucky beyond as a "dress circle" audience, Lincoln—who had been a surveyor—cleverly used the geography of America to stage a political play. He stood at center stage, at the lower boundary of free soil. Across the river lay Kentucky, where he and Mary were both born and raised, and where so many of their friends and relatives still lived.

"It has occurred to me here to-night, that if I ever do shoot over the line at the people on the other side of the line into a Slave State, and purpose to do so, keeping my skin safe, that I have now about the best chance I shall ever have."

The crowd laughed at that, and gave the speaker a big hand.

"I should not wonder that there are some Kentuckians about this audience; we are close to Kentucky; and whether that be so or not, we are on elevated ground, and by speaking distinctly, I should not wonder if some of the Kentuckians would hear me on the other side of the river. [Laughter.]

"I say then, in the first place, to the Kentuckians, that I am what they call, as I understand it, a 'Black Republican.' [Applause and laughter.] I think slavery is wrong, morally, and politically. I desire that it should be no further spread in these United States, and I should not object if it should gradually terminate in the whole Union. [Applause.] . . . I understand you differ radically with me . . . you believe slavery is a good thing; that slavery is right, that it ought to be extended and perpetuated in this Union." He put it bluntly. He was leading up to the audacious insistence that the Kentuckians nominate Stephen Douglas for the presidency next year. As he went on in this vein, the booming cannon underscored his challenge ("to the great injury of sundry panes of glass in the vicinity"). And no one, least of all Mary Lincoln, whose headaches made her hypersensitive to such racket, could ignore the portent of the cannon fire, the sense that the war of words must lead to a war of armies. Nor could Mrs. Lincoln deny the fact that her husband, in nominating the Democrat Douglas for the presidency as he stood on that "elevated ground," was casting himself in the opposing role as the obvious Republican candidate. That was how it looked to the audience. And in a matter of weeks, on November 6, it would be an Ohio newspaper, the *Sandusky Register,* that would first announce Lincoln's candidacy.

She heard him forcefully present the case he had made the day before, concerning the debauching influences of Douglas's popular sovereignty. The "change in public sentiment has already degraded the black man in the estimation of Douglas and his followers from the condition of a man of some sort, and assigned him to the condition of a brute. Now, you Kentuckians ought to give Douglas credit for this. That is the largest possible stride that can be made in regard to the perpetuation of your thing slavery."

At that moment a man shouted to Lincoln: "Speak to Ohio men, and not to Kentuckians!" The disgruntled heckler was more likely a moderate Republican than an offended Democrat. After all, Lincoln had been invited here to give support and momentum to local candidates for the "opposition" (Republicans as well as the American party) with hopes "that he may not give a too strictly partisan cast to his address," as Rutherford Hayes had urged in a letter. And yet Lincoln showed little concern for the candidates for governor. His speech was thoroughly and unapologetically partisan; he was speaking from principle as the leader of his party at the crossroads, and his quick response to the man who demanded that he speak to Ohio men and not Kentuckians was, "I beg permission to speak as I please."

After all, he was running for president.

THE NEXT DAY, a Sunday, they would spend with William M. Dickson, a prominent Cincinnati lawyer, and his wife, Annie M. (Parker) Dickson,

Mary's cousin. They would have one more night in the luxurious Burnet House before departing for Indianapolis, where he would speak once more, at the Masonic Hall, before returning home.

It is surprising to learn that in 1859 a politician and his wife, stumping on behalf of colleagues, donated not only precious time away from work and home; they were also expected to pay their own expenses. Calling for his bill upon leaving the hotel, Lincoln was assured it had been settled. It had not. Rather it was "passed about from one distinguished Republican to another" until the bookkeeper wearied of trying to find out who was responsible. Days after returning to Springfield, the Lincolns received a bill of particulars from the Burnet House: $52 for the weekend—half a week's income—when they had stayed but twenty-four hours. And the invoice included bottles of brandy, wine, and whiskey, and a box of cigars. Mr. and Mrs. Lincoln did not smoke cigars, and he did not drink spirits, so he questioned the charges. He received the reply that these refreshments were "for the local Republican committee as well as the entertainment of Mr. & Mrs. Lincoln." Piqued about the bill, Lincoln continued to protest until at last he heard "that there were Republicans who were unwilling that he should be imposed upon in such a matter, and who gladly paid it."

Soon after their return from that delightful tour, which Mary described to Mrs. Shearer as including "beautiful portions of Ohio," and their "charming visit to Cincinnati," Lincoln left home to go to Wisconsin. He would not return for ten days. The Wisconsin Agricultural Society had invited him to give the keynote address at their annual fair in Milwaukee, an occasion he used to reflect not only upon the art of farming, crops, and soil, but on the high principles of free labor and universal education. The same night, September 30, he made a political speech at the Newhall House, a talk that he reprised the next afternoon in Beloit, and the night after in Janesville, Wisconsin. Why, Lincoln demanded, did slavery exist on one side of the Ohio River and not on the other? Why in Kentucky and not in Ohio? There was little difference in the soil or climate, and the people on one side of the line loved liberty as well as on the other.

Meanwhile Mary felt lonely. The day he was in Janesville she complained to Mrs. Shearer that she missed Bob so much "that I do not feel settled down, as much as I used to." The weather had been beautiful in Springfield, so in the daylight she could enjoy walks with the boys, watching the leaves of the red oaks, silver maples, and hickory trees turn yellow, red, and gold, gathering sky-blue asters in the fallow fields. Nights were lonely. In Mr. Lincoln's absence she entertained their friend, the bachelor Ozias Hatch.

On October 4, Lincoln traveled from Janesville to Chicago, where he spent one night before resuming work in the DeWitt Circuit Court in Clinton. He would have only a Sunday at home on the ninth before returning to Clinton again for the week. There in the courthouse and the Barnett Hotel, among the lawyers and traveling salesmen, all the talk was of the election. His efforts on the stump in Ohio had succeeded. Republican candidates were triumphant all over the North and the West, and when Lincoln returned on Saturday, the day after the election, he hardly had time to embrace his wife and children before they heard the clashing and tootling of a brass band outside their windows, come to serenade the "Giant Killer."

"Several hundred Republicans, headed by a band of music, formed in procession and proceeded to his residence," wrote the reporter for the *Illinois State Journal.* Dr. William Jayne (Julia's brother) paid him a tribute. They persuaded the weary lawyer to come out and follow the procession by lamplight and torchlight to the statehouse, where the crowd could fully express their appreciation for their hero. Lincoln delivered a spontaneous address, declaring, "The recent glorious victories achieved by the Republicans in Ohio and other states is clearly indicative that the good old doctrines of the fathers of the Republic would yet again prevail."

She had not seen her husband all week, and now that he was home, the neighbors had carried him away on their shoulders. In the pile of letters that had arrived in his absence was a telegram of singular importance. It was an invitation from one James A. Briggs, an influential New York Republican, inviting him to speak at Henry Ward Beecher's church in Brooklyn. This would take him farther from her than any journey she could readily imagine.

On October 18 the Lincolns picked up the *Illinois State Journal* to read the opinion that Abraham Lincoln's "name was now inscribed high upon the role of distinguished men spoken of in connection with the Presidency." At first the chatter connected Lincoln with the second spot on the ticket; after his journey to New York, the idea of his being vice president would fade.

When Robert returned from Exeter in mid-October for a two-week visit, it was a comfort to Mrs. Lincoln. Her husband would be away from home much of the time during that bitterly cold November and December, making speeches in Missouri and Kansas. She would not be going with him. She traveled to St. Louis to visit cousins there for a week, and there she saw Julia Dean again on the stage, recalling the time that she and Mr. Lincoln had seen the great actress in Washington.

She wrote to Mrs. Shearer late on a Sunday evening. The boys were still awake and making a rumpus. Her pen was vexing her, spattering ink and running dry. "Tomorrow I must rise early, as it is *receiving* day. . . . How I wish you were with us. The weather is intensely cold, and our winter has been rather quiet. . . . Willie's [ninth] birthday came off on the 21st of Dec and as I had long promised him a *celebration,* it duly came off. Some 50 or 60 boys & girls attended the gala"—for which the proud mother had taken the time to write all of the invitations by hand.

During the days before Christmas 1859, the snow had fallen steadily, "as if it meant to furnish good sleighing until after New Years. It pleased those who like and can afford to ride after fast horses and jingling bells. . . ." Good news came on December 23: the Republicans had decided that their national convention would be held in Chicago. This favored the Illinois candidate, Abraham Lincoln. On Christmas Eve the *Journal* printed Clement Moore's "A Visit from St. Nicholas" on its front page so parents would not forget to read it to their children that night by the fireside, as the snow fell.

There would never be another quiet winter for this family, or a Yuletide so peaceful and carefree.

THE NOMINATION

THE MOMENTOUS INVITATION for Lincoln to speak in New York arrived at a time when neither he nor his wife, nor any astute Illinois Republican, could deny he was a presidential candidate. He had protested long enough that "I do not think myself fit for the Presidency," in various letters, one written on April 16, 1859, to an editor in Rock Island who wished to propose his name, another to an admiring Republican lawyer in Columbus on July 27, using the same stock phrase. But when William E. Frazer of Pennsylvania, a supporter of Senator Simon Cameron for president, wrote to Lincoln on October 24 asking for his public commitment to Cameron, Lincoln tipped his hand. In responding, he said that before a Republican national convention had nominated a candidate, he would be committed to no one, "having enlisted for the permanent success of the Republican cause. . . . I shall labor faithfully in the ranks, unless, as I think not probable, the judgment of the party shall assign me a different position."

Compared to men like Salmon Chase and William Seward, both of whom had been governors, Lincoln *was* apparently unqualified, having had no executive experience whatsoever—he did not even manage his law office or his house on Eighth Street. But these troubled years—the passage historians call "the gathering storm"—demanded superior and perhaps unconventional leadership. Lincoln had great confidence in himself, and these were not ordinary times. He, and not Chase or Seward, had been summoned to address the most important issues of the day—the Kansas-Nebraska Act, Dred Scott, the Fugitive Slave Act, and, most recently, the violence and execution of John Brown. Lincoln had inspired the people, because of uniqueness of character, rare gifts of communication, and a vision that happened to belong to a country lawyer without an executive résumé. No one understood this better than Mary Lincoln, who never wavered in her belief that her husband would be president. She must be given credit for his receptiveness to the lofty calling, which began echoing incredibly from west to east and back again with increasing clarity, until Lincoln finally answered it.

Norman Judd, head of the Illinois central committee, favored Lincoln's candidacy by persuading the Republican National Committee to hold its party convention in Chicago. And when Jesse W. Fell requested information that newspapers might use, on December 20, 1859, Lincoln complied, sending the now-famous "little sketch" that begins, "I was born February 12, 1809, in Hardin County, Kentucky," apologizes for his lack of book learning, admitting, "When I came of age I did not know much. Still somehow, I could read, write and cipher to the Rule of Three," and ends with the droll self-portrait: "I am, in height, six feet, four inches, nearly; lean in flesh, weighing, on an average, one hundred and eighty pounds; dark complexion, with coarse black hair, and gray eyes—no other marks or brands recollected." He does not mention that he is married, or that he has three sons.

THAT WINTER LINCOLN was swamped with requests to lecture. One invitation that he could not refuse was the offer to address an audience at Henry Ward Beecher's church in Brooklyn, in a series called the Plymouth Lecture Course, a lyceum for young gentlemen. It would have appealed to both of the Lincolns: as an opportunity for the candidate to extend his reputation and his support to the eastern seaboard; as a chance to visit Robert Lincoln at Exeter; and as a rare opportunity to earn money while broadening his political prospects.

James A. Briggs had offered him a $200 honorarium, a handsome fee in 1859. In subsequent negotiations Lincoln was able to get another $150 in travel expenses and, perhaps most important, a postponement of the date until late February. "Abe Lincoln . . . must come," wrote another member of the lyceum committee. "We want to hear a speech from him, such a one as he delivered in Cincinnati would be perfectly satisfactory." Lincoln wanted time to prepare a more sophisticated speech than had pleased his wife and the crowd in Ohio. He also wanted the press coverage of the New York speech—which newspapers would reprint widely if Lincoln hit his mark—and the late February date would come closer to the Republican nominating convention in the spring of 1860.

Haste and apologies, absentmindedness, and missed deadlines characterize Lincoln's correspondence in early February. He was preoccupied with his New York speech, a ninety-minute tour de force whose goal was no less than a historical proof that the majority of the signers of the Constitution had formally voted to regulate slavery in the territories. He had been spending hours in the statehouse library—at the long green baize-covered table between the Corinthian columns—researching volumes of congressional proceedings and taking notes. As he had done in the past, Lincoln probably "tried out" the important speech on his wife. It was uncharacteristic, Herndon says, "devoid of all rhetorical imagery, with a marked suppression of the pyrotechnics of stump oratory. It was constructed with a view to accuracy of statement, simplicity of language, and unity of thought . . . logical, temperate in tone," so as to suit the critical New York audience. Lincoln would not have left Springfield before hearing his wife's opinion of so important a speech any more than he would have left without her approval of his wardrobe and grooming. A hundred-dollar check was written to the tailors Woods and Henckle for a new suit; he got new boots, and a haircut, all subject to Mrs. Lincoln's review. He appeared in Mathew Brady's studio on February 27, looking more handsome and presidential than ever before.

Like many politicians, Lincoln was unsettled by inflated expectations of him, by excessive praise that would disturb the equilibrium of any man's vanity and humility. On January 30, 1860, the Lincolns read in the local paper that "Abraham Lincoln has arrived at that period of life when man's mental and physical powers are in the prime. God gave him a mind of unusual strength, and time and labor and study have made him one of the great men of the land. The purity of his patriotism, his incorruptible integrity and his ability to sustain himself and the country in any position in which he may be placed, no one who knows him can for a moment doubt." It is one thing for a man's wife to have such thoughts, and quite a different matter for her to read them in the local newspapers, then in a hundred papers written by strangers.

Mary Lincoln delighted in city life, and had such fond memories of the days they had spent together in Manhattan during the summer of 1857, it must have been hard for her to bid him farewell on February 23. He was bound on a great adventure, a speaking tour that would make him famous not only in New York, but also in Providence, Concord, Manchester, Dover, Exeter, Hartford, New Haven, Woonsocket, Norwich, and Bridgeport.

Arriving in New York the night of the twenty-fifth, Lincoln discovered that his speech had been moved from the church in Brooklyn to the Cooper Union auditorium in Manhattan, the largest in the city. At the lectern there on Monday evening, February 27, Lincoln addressed the most sophisticated and influential audience of his career to date. He rose to the occasion. "No man," said eyewitness journalist Noah Brooks, "ever before made such an impression on his first appeal to a New York audience." One of the men called to the stage afterward to comment on the speech, sponsor James Briggs, forthrightly added Lincoln's name to Seward's and Chase's as one of three possible standard-bearers "in the canvass for President." Horace Greeley paid tribute—he was about to throw the mighty support of his newspapers behind Lincoln.

By March 1, when Lincoln spoke to a huge gathering at Smyth Hall in Manchester, sponsors were introducing him as the next president. Yet the single surviving scrap of correspondence to his wife sounds far from triumphant, or even cheerful. After visiting Robert and speaking at Exeter on Sunday, March 4—which should have been a day of rest—he wrote to Mary, "I have been unable to escape this toil. If I had foreseen it, I think I would not have come east at all. The speech at New York, being within my calculation before I started, went off passably well and gave me no trouble whatever. The difficulty was to make nine others, before reading audiences who had already seen all my ideas in print."

Far beyond having gone "passably well," the New York performance had been a spectacular success, and as of Sunday his toil had been steady but not onerous. That is all that survives of a longer letter once in the possession of Robert Lincoln, now lost; the fragment endures because Robert quoted from it in a letter he wrote to a scholar in 1908. As with so much of his parents' correspondence, Robert chose to deprive historians of this full letter, as being perhaps too revealing. The passage has the apologetic tone of a man who has been gone from home longer than he expected.

HE RETURNED TO Springfield on the Great Western Railroad of Illinois on March 14, "in excellent health and in his usual spirits." Spring was in the air on that eve of the Ides of March, and so was persistent discussion of Lincoln's strengths as a presidential candidate. At the station his neighbor Milton Hay welcomed him on behalf of the Springfield Republican Club: "No inconsiderable portion of your fellow citizens in various portions of the county have expressed their preference for you as the candidate of the Republican party for the next Presidency. . . . There are those around you sir who have watched with manly interest and pride your upward march from obscurity to distinction." And Hay might have added, one who had watched with *womanly* interest and unrivaled pride. "We feel well-assured that we shall look in vain amongst all the high names of the Republic for the man combining in himself, in his record, and in his history more of those elements which fit the man for the time, the occasion and the place than yourself."

After three weeks apart, the Lincolns were eager to discuss his progress toward that longed-for goal. He returned to his law office, trying to make up for lost time and fees, and hardly a day passed that entire spring without some new endorsement for Lincoln appearing in the local paper, reports from Republican county committees all over Illinois, and newspapers from the *Xenia* (Ohio) *News* and the *Cincinnati Gazette* to the *Baltimore Turnzeitung* and the *Fort Wayne* (Indiana) *Times*.

He was home only eight days before an important court case, *Johnston v. Jones and Marsh,* drew him away to Chicago and the U.S. District Court. During the two weeks he was there, a dozen friends—from Illinois, Ohio, Indiana, and Iowa—were lobbying to secure Lincoln's nomination. These included Norman Judd, Leonard Swett, and David Davis, his informal campaign manager. On March 24, Lincoln wrote to Samuel Galloway, "My name is new in the field; and I suppose I am not the *first* choice of a very great many. Our policy, then, is to give no offense to others—leave them in a mood to come to us, if they shall be compelled to give up their first love."

When Lyman Trumbull wrote in April, asking Lincoln for a frank statement of his feelings about the field of candidates, including himself, he responded with the now famous Lincolnesque understatement: "The taste *is* in my mouth a little." This was April 29, 1860, a point in time when all of his associates, including Trumbull, of course, knew very well that the flavor of the presidential nomination had intoxicated Lincoln to a degree that, as he confided to his old friend, "this, no doubt, disqualifies me, to some extent to form correct opinions."

Ten days later, the Illinois Republican convention in Decatur treated Lincoln to a hero's welcome. They had erected a flimsy pavilion on State Street, a hundred feet by seventy, and three thousand people were crowded in and around it when their favorite arrived, making a late, dramatic entrance. When they invited him to take a seat on the platform, they had to lift him hand to hand over the heads of the crowd, who meanwhile were cheering and applauding with all their might. Then somehow they made a path for old John Hanks, Lincoln's Macon County cousin, who marched up the path with fence rails and a sign that proclaimed:

ABRAHAM LINCOLN

THE RAIL CANDIDATE FOR PRESIDENT

IN 1860

And the crowd, screaming, cheering, throwing hats and papers into the air, blew part of the roof off the temporary convention center.

Mary Lincoln was probably not present that night he was christened "the rail-splitter," or the next day when John Palmer offered the resolution that instructed the delegates from Illinois "to use all honorable means to secure his [Lincoln's] nomination by the Chicago Convention, and to vote as a unit for him." Although the road from Springfield to Decatur was only thirty miles, political conventions were generally too rowdy for candidates' wives and daughters. She was certainly with him in spirit in those hours of triumph, and if she had been left behind once again, she would soon hear the details of that momentous occasion in his own words.

Only a week later, more than ten thousand gathered for the Republican convention in the Chicago "Wigwam" (a huge temporary wooden shack), but in those days a candidate as prominent as Lincoln stayed away. So would New York senator William Seward, the front-runner. Fifty-eight years old, the abolitionist Seward had twice been governor of New York. Dapper and witty, this veteran politician knew he would never have a better chance at the presidency than in this year. His moral convictions as well as his shrewd political instincts had made him a leader in the formation of the Republican party.

While Lincoln and his wife were aware of the forces arrayed against him, particularly Seward's constituents, they had much cause for hope. On the eve of the convention, a delegate from Winchester, Nathan M.

Knapp, sent a telegram saying, "Things are working; keep a good nerve—be not surprised at any result—but I tell you that your chances are not the worst. . . . Be not too expectant, but rely upon our discretion. Again I say brace your nerves for any result." Mary's nerves, never too steady, were certainly tested by such tidings, with the stakes so high. As a sliver of moon rose in the night sky just after supper, it offered its promising light for them to wish upon. Sleep would not come easily to the Lincoln household on the night of May 17.

Lincoln rose early and went to his law office. But it was not a day that he could get much work done, so he joined editor E. L. Baker and Charles Zane, and some other young lawyers—Christopher Brown and Pascal Enos—to play ball in the lot next to the office of the *Illinois State Journal* between Carmody's liquor store and a clothing shop. They played the "Game of Fives," a handball game, slapping the ball against the high solid wall of the Logan building. Lean and quick, at fifty years of age he could still outplay most of the youngsters. As the sun climbed and the shadows shortened in the alley, Lincoln played to channel his nervous energy and his excitement over the deliberations heating up the Wigwam two hundred miles away. There his fate was being decided. His wife, putting up early fruit for preserves and baking pies, was in the same state of distraction. The men playing ball with Abraham Lincoln could hardly refrain from raising the question, in earnest or in jest. For it was possible that this gangly, sweating athlete in shirtsleeves and galluses, swatting the handball or joking over a failed return, would soon be nominated as their candidate for president of the United States.

Many were working for him in Chicago: Judd, Swett, Governor Richard Yates, Gustave Koerner (whose German-language newspaper Lincoln secretly owned), and the portly Judge David Davis, his old friend from the circuit. "Make no contracts that will bind me," Lincoln had charged them, to their dismay. How could they bargain for him if they had nothing to trade? Simon Cameron of Pennsylvania wanted a cabinet post as the price of delivering up the votes of his state on the second ballot. What were Lincoln's friends to do? Pushed to the wall, in the heat of battle, the perspiring judge received a telegram from Lincoln: "I authorize no bargains and will be bound by none," and Davis snarled at this cohorts, "Lincoln ain't here, and don't know what we have to meet." They would do what had to be done.

Chris Brown noticed that Lincoln was "nervous, fidgety—intensely excited." He broke up the game to tell vulgar stories: Ethan Allen went to England, and "the English took great pleasure in teasing him, and trying to make fun of the Americans and General Washington in particular, and one day they got a picture of General Washington, and hung it up in the Back House [the privy] where Mr. Allen could see it . . . and they finally asked Mr. A if he saw that picture of his friend in the Back House?" Ethan Allen said no he hadn't, "but said he thought it was a very appropriate place for an Englishman to keep it. Why, they asked?" And Mr. Allen said, "Because there is nothing that will make an Englishman shit so quick as the sight of General Washington."

Restless, around 10:00 A.M., Lincoln said, "Let's go to the telegraph office," which was just around the corner on Washington Street, north of the square. During the next hour and a half, his ear cocked for the clatter of keys, he passed back and forth from the telegraph office to Baker's newsroom on the second floor of the *Illinois State Journal* building, leading a growing company of lawyers and other friends, and watched all around by the humming populace of Springfield, which grew giddy with rumors and predictions. News of the first and second ballots rattled over the wires while Lincoln was near the key—it looked promising. The second ballot showed him gaining upon Seward as a result of the change in the Pennsylvania vote.

Lincoln had perched for a while in the crowded newspaper office when the messenger, Clinton Conkling, burst into the room. He held the telegram that stated the results of the third ballot: Lincoln had the votes necessary, and "nomination made unanimous amid intense enthusiasm."

Baker led the throng in *Three cheers for the next president!*

Young Charles Zane heard Lincoln say, "I knew it would come to this when I saw the second ballot."

Outside, the crowd gathering at the corner of Washington and Sixth streets echoed the cheering in the news office. "He received all with apparent coolness," Zane recalled; "from the expressions playing upon his countenance however a close observer could detect strong emotions within." Where was his wife? Who was keeping her company while Lincoln stood at the center of a party of adoring friends? "After spending a few moments in receiving their cordial congratulations looking in the direction of his home he said, 'Well gentlemen there is a little woman at our house who is probably more interested in this dispatch than I am; if you will excuse me I will take the dispatch up and let her see it.' "

He walked south on Sixth Street across Washington. In front of the Marine Bank building, a cashier, Robert Irwin, hurried out to the sidewalk to shake his hand. Everywhere Lincoln moved, the people moved around him, respectfully making way, or excitedly holding out a hand for him to shake, or touching him on the shoulder.

The Lincolns had precious little time alone for embracing or celebration. The news preceded Mr. Lincoln, racing down the streets ahead of him so that his words were scarcely necessary. Within minutes after the decisive message came over the wire, the bells in the church towers began to toll, and soon after that the first thunder of the hundred-cannon salute shook the windowpanes. She might have met him at the door with her own cry of congratulations. Mother and Father must explain to the little boys why the city was in an uproar, and why their house was about to be overrun with friends and strangers. She must grind the beans for pots of coffee. Republicans would be calling on the Lincolns all that afternoon, "for the purpose of congratulating him upon his nomination," hallooing and cheering and banging at the door.

At eight o'clock that night they went to meet the citizens assembling at the statehouse to celebrate the triumph. John Conkling, who had attended the convention and had been chosen as an elector for Sangamon County, delivered a speech. So did George R. Weber, an editor at the paper. "Every allusion to Mr. Lincoln was followed by deafening cheers," the *Journal* reported. A singer only known now as Mr. Reese sang "a capital song" of victory, and at nine o'clock the meeting adjourned.

The immense parade, following the drums and brass of the Young America Silver Band, started toward Mr. Lincoln's residence by torchlight beneath the sliver of moon and the stars of Gemini, singing and cheering in the cool night air. When the people got to the picket fence at Eighth and Jackson they began calling Lincoln's name. He soon appeared in his front doorway, "a signal for renewed applause." And when the cheering died down he began a speech only a few minutes long while his wife stood behind him, ever mindful of the effect such tumult would have on a six-year-old up past his bedtime. Someone in the crowd shouted, "We will give you a larger house on the fourth of next March," which evoked laughter and cries of assent. And Lincoln replied that he would "invite as many as could find room."

"Deafening cheers greeted the invitation, and in less than a minute Mr. Lincoln's house was invaded by as many as could 'squeeze in!' " the reporter observed. The Lincolns received the people cordially, and he shook hands with as many as he could as they filled the two parlors and the dining room and spilled over into the kitchen and out onto the back porch. They stayed for hours, talking and laughing, and now and then sending up another cheer for "the next president." Many were "so well pleased with the day's work that they could not make up their minds to go home until after midnight."

The reporter took special notice that the last of the crowd to leave were a number of ladies who "called upon Mr. Lincoln and wished him success in the coming campaign."

THE MORNING AFTER that invasion of revelers there was a great deal to be done to put the house back in order, because that evening, they would be receiving distinguished company at the most momentous gathering they had ever held in their home. The Committee of the Republican National Convention was coming to offer him the ceremonial, formal notification of his nomination. It was the weekend, so the children were out of school, and the nominee for president would not be expected at the law office. The family would have much of Saturday to themselves, to reflect upon the events of the day before. Children need attention at a time like this, for they are antennae of psychic change. They have questions and concerns that are best addressed during the activities that anchor a household—sweeping a carpet, dusting the picture frames. *"Is Pa going to be president? Are we going to move away and leave our dogs and friends and horses?"* The parents would have to find a way to answer such questions honestly without causing anxiety.

The train bearing the committee members arrived at 7:00 P.M. The Lincolns, at home a few blocks from the Great Western Railroad depot, could hear the brass and drum sounds of the Young America Silver and the German Saxe Horn bands welcoming the dignitaries as they stepped off the special train from Chicago, accompanying them as they marched to the Chenery House to dine. One could hear the cannons firing salutes, and the skyrockets going up in the twilight. Bonfires blazed at the streetcorners.

A little after eight o'clock the deputation came down Eighth Street, led by the convention president, the Honorable George Ashmun of Massachusetts. The group included the governor of New York, Edwin D. Morgan; the governor of Massachusetts, George S. Boutwell; Senator James Simmons of Rhode Island; Seward's friend, the New York orator William Evarts; Ohio poet William Davis Gallagher; Norman Judd; the Honorable Amos Tuck of New Hampshire; Francis P. Blair, the great abolitionist and Republican party founder, with his two sons, Frank and Montgomery, of Maryland; and the Honorable David K. Cartter of Ohio, who called out the last four votes that clinched Lincoln's nomination. There were others, including half a dozen editors—Charles Carleton Coffin of the *Boston Journal* and the Honorable Henry J. Raymond of *The New York Times* among them.

Never in the town's history had such an illustrious and well-tailored party of gentlemen been seen walking the streets of Springfield with their top hats and walking sticks. When they arrived at Lincoln's house, Willie and Tad were perched on the gateposts to welcome them.

"Are you Mr. Lincoln's son?" asked William Evarts.

"Yes, sir," said Willie.

"Then let's shake hands," said Evarts. They all began shaking Willie's hand, while Tad watched before singing out, "I'm a Lincoln too!" And then amid much laughter they began wringing Tad's hand.

The gentlemen entered the house and assembled in the north parlor, where they found Lincoln standing near the fireplace, dressed "with perfect neatness, almost elegance," in his new frock coat, black bow tie, and vest. He wore an expression of extreme gravity and some discomfort, bowing as the committee pressed into the room. The reporter from the *Boston Journal* observed "an evident constraint and embarrassment. He stood erect, in a stiff and unnatural position, with downcast eyes. There was a diffidence like that of an ungainly schoolboy standing alone before a critical audience."

He stood at one end of the parlor—between the fireplace and the bookshelves, in front of the couch and the globes of heaven and earth—while his visitors clustered at the other. George Ashmun stated the committee's business, "a most pleasant duty," to notify him of the convention's decision. Lincoln listened, his expression earnest almost to a point of sternness, and when Ashmun had finished, everyone allowed for a dignified pause. Lincoln at last responded, "I tender to you . . . my profoundest thanks for the high honor done me. . . . Deeply, and even painfully sensible of the great responsibility which is inseparable from this high honor—." According to Coffin, "It was a sympathetic voice, with an indescribable charm in the tones. There was no study of inflection of cadence for effect.... The lines upon his face, the large ears, sunken cheeks, enormous nose, shaggy hair, the deep-set eyes, which sparkled with humor, and which seemed to be looking far away." In the room beyond, his wife waited. In that space where he was now acknowledging the "great responsibility," the Lincolns had been discussing the matter for a decade or more.

Having accepted the nomination and dispensed with the formalities, Lincoln relaxed, and "a smile, like the sun shining through the rift of a passing cloud sweeping over the landscape, illuminated his face," the Bostonian wrote, swept away by the candidate's charm. Lincoln declared he would "not longer defer the pleasure of taking you, and each of you, by the hand." He did so heartily, and when he came to tall Bill Kelly of Pennsylvania, Lincoln asked the judge his height. "Six feet three; what is yours, Mr. Lincoln?" Lincoln admitted he was six feet four.

"Then Pennsylvania bows to Illinois. My dear man, for years my heart has been aching for a President that I could *look up to,* and I've found him at last in the land where we thought there were none but *little* giants." The reference to Stephen Douglas was not lost upon them.

With pride and restless attention Mrs. Lincoln listened to the formalities, then the banter and laughter, from the far room. By some bylaw of etiquette, the candidate's wife was left out of the ceremony, but must wait to receive the company in another space.

"Mrs. Lincoln will be pleased to see you gentlemen," said Lincoln at last. "You will find her in the other room. You must be thirsty after your long ride. You will find a pitcher of water in the library [the east end of the parlor]." Then the gentlemen slowly filed through the stair hall into the south parlor to shake Mrs. Lincoln's hand. She would be delighted—during the days to come—to read the flattering notices about her and her home in the national papers, descriptions of "an elegant two-story dwelling fronting west, of pleasing exterior, with a neat and roomy appearance," and "this amiable and accomplished lady . . . she adorns a drawing-room, presides over a table, does the honors on an occasion like the present, or will do the honors at the White House with appropriate grace. . . . She is one of three sisters known for their beauty and accomplishments. . . . Mrs. Lincoln is now apparently about 35 years of age [she was forty-two]; is a very handsome woman, with a vivacious and graceful manner; is an interesting and often sparkling talker."

That day a reporter for the *Baltimore Evening Patriot* heard there was a story to go along with Mr. Lincoln's offer of ice water to the thirsty delegates. The neighbors, knowing that the Lincolns kept no wine or spirits in the house, sent bottles of brandy, wine, and whiskey around to Eighth and Jackson so that the visitors might be offered refreshments befitting their status and the occasion. As much as Lincoln appreciated this kindness, "he could not consent to violate a long established rule of conduct." And so he returned the bottles of liquor, resolving "to treat his guests with plentiful drafts of delicious and pure ice water." Gustave Koerner, a friend who had been a member of the platform committee in Chicago, recalled arriving at the house early to find "a long table set on one side, on which stood many glasses, a decanter or two of brandy and under the table a champagne basket. Cakes and sandwiches were just being placed on the table by a colored man. Mrs. Lincoln entered the room and asked Koerner & Lincoln what they thought of the nice spread she had laid out. 'We told her at once that this would hardly do.' The meeting was to be a solemn business, and several of the men were temperance people. She remonstrated in her very lively manner, but we insisted on dispensing with this hospitality, which we appreciated ourselves, but which might be misconstrued. I finally told the black man bluntly to take the things out into the back room, which he did," said Koerner. And he added that Mrs. Lincoln continued to argue with him.

Lincoln had been out of the room for the last of the discussion, but when he returned, hearing what the fuss was about, he softly said, "Perhaps, Mary, these gentlemen are right." Over the years this anecdote gave rise to the myth that the Lincolns had argued bitterly over the liquor and that their conflict contributed to Lincoln's discomfort that evening. But there is no evidence that they ever disagreed about the ice water.

AS WAS THEN customary, Lincoln did not travel to campaign personally. For the next five months, he did not leave Springfield. Governor John Wood offered him the use of his two executive offices in the statehouse, roomier and more suitable for the Republican candidate than a law office. There Lincoln could be found from morning until evening most days, receiving visitors from all over the country, writing letters that said almost nothing that could be used against him in the campaign and nothing that would commit him to future policy or personnel decisions. Patiently he posed for painters and sculptors. Overnight he had become a celebrity, a change he accepted good-naturedly, knowing that the electorate would naturally want to know everything they could learn about the man who would be president. Strangers asked for his autograph; they wrote to pose odd questions about his past or his ancestry or to remind him of an old acquaintance. The rooms soon filled with "presents of a symbolic nature"—curios and charms, ax-helves, railroad ties, log chains, wedges, a chair of state made up of thirty-four different kinds of wood representing the states of the Union. Knox College sent him an honorary LL.D. degree, which caused Orville Browning to wisecrack that from now on he would have to "consider yourself a 'scholar,' as well as a 'gentleman,' and deport yourself accordingly."

On a bright morning, Browning called upon Lincoln in his suite of offices in the Old State Capitol and conversed with him while the painter Thomas Hicks worked at an easel in the corner. Statuettes of Lincoln carved by L. W. Volk "as natural as life" were already on sale at Chatterton's jewelry store. Artist and sitter begged Mr. Browning to return in the afternoon, as the painter found Mr. Lincoln more attractive in conversation with his friend. "Lincoln bears his honors meekly," Browning observed. He mentions that "as soon as other company had retired," Lincoln got to telling funny stories, as he used to do, for a couple of hours.

There is no mention, on this day, June 12, or on June 13, which Browning whiled away with Lincoln in a similar manner, that the twelfth was the day Mary's sister Ann Todd Smith lost her ten-year-old son to typhoid fever. Ann was married to the merchant Clark Moulton Smith, and they lived in a fine house four blocks west on Fifth Street, behind the governor's mansion. On June 13, Mary wrote to Norman Judd's wife, Adeline, that the child had been ill for weeks. "I trust never to witness *such suffering ever* again. He is to be buried this afternoon." That was the afternoon Hicks completed Lincoln's portrait. There are six hours in an afternoon, in all weather, and perhaps Lincoln found time between sittings to attend the church and the cemetery—but there is no mention of it. "The family are almost inconsolable, & for the last week, I have spent the greater portion of my time, with them," Mary wrote to Adeline.

During that week when Lincoln was being feted and cheered at rallies and torchlight processions, trying fitfully to practice law, and entertaining journalists, politicians, and portrait artists, his wife was in the house of grief, without his support. She wrote, "I am quite *unnerved* just now, and we have so much company, that I could scarcely leave home." She mentions Robert's absence, "almost *a year,* a *long year,* & at times I feel *wild* to see him." If she felt like going anywhere, she would go to see him at school. Mrs. Judd invited Mary to accompany her to Minnehaha Falls near Minneapolis, and she replied, "I would be very happy to accompany you, if I could gain courage, feeling much depressed, from recent occurrences, I know well, that nothing would benefit me more, than such an excursion."

A LONG-TAILED COMET appeared every clear evening in the northwest, and if they stood in the dust of Eighth Street they could see it over the capitol dome, a mysterious portent.

To their horror, two weeks later ten-year-old Willie came down with "a hard and tedious spell of scarlet fever, and he is not yet beyond all danger," Lincoln wrote to Anson Henry on July 4, a day that usually was devoted to patriotic rallies, fireworks, and speech-making. But this holiday Lincoln was indisposed. "I have a head-ache and sore *throat* upon me now, inducing me to suspect that I have an inferior type of the same thing," he wrote to Dr. Henry. The weather had been oppressive, the thermometer rising into the high nineties every day.

Scarlet fever was a fearsome disease that often killed children, and if they survived, it sometimes compromised the child's immune system, which proved, ultimately, to be Willie's case. A letter from Lincoln dated June 26 indicates that he was at Mary's side as she nursed Willie through that illness—symptoms of high fever, chills, and vomiting, the characteristic red and inflamed tongue, the red skin eruptions. The Lincolns must have been terrified that seven-year-old Tad would catch it. But he did not, and by July 16, the family was strong enough so that Lincoln could return to work. (The twelve days from July 4 to 16, 1860, are conspicuously undocumented, lacking outgoing correspondence save a single letter, and no record of visitors or other business activity.) On the evening of the sixteenth, some traveling opera singers treated the Lincolns to a serenade.

A New York journalist who went to interview Lincoln on a hot Sunday, July 17, knocked at his door. The young black servant William Johnston let him in, showed him a seat in the parlor, and carried his note of introduction upstairs to Mr. Lincoln. Mrs. Lincoln was nowhere to be seen, but to the journalist her influence was evident. "The house was neatly without being extravagantly furnished. An air of quiet refinement pervaded the place. You would have known instantly that she who presided over that modest household was a true type of American lady." He noted the fresh flowers on the table, the hunting prints and nature scenes framed upon the walls. "The adornments were few, but chastely appropriate: everything was in its place, and ministered to the general effect. The hand of the domestic artist was everywhere visible." The thought that sprang to the writer's mind was "what a pleasant home Abe Lincoln has."

The visit that the journalist had planned for ten minutes went on for two hours; afterward he interviewed the neighbors, who agreed Lincoln was the "best of husbands, kindest of parents, the most irreproachable of citizens." The Lincolns were getting very favorable press—at least from the journalists who came to call on them—and they had good reason to be optimistic about the coming election.

In that intimate letter to Dr. Henry dated July 4, Lincoln wrote, "We know not what a day may bring forth, but today it looks as if the Chicago ticket will be elected. I think the chances are more than equal that we could have beaten the Democracy united. Divided as it is, its chance appears indeed very slim." Disagreement over protecting slavery had split the Democratic party, with Douglas the choice of the moderates, and John C. Breckinridge of Kentucky becoming the nominee of the southern "Secessionists." A month later Lincoln wrote confidently to Simeon Francis, "It really appears now, as if the success of the Republican ticket is inevitable."

Independence Day was scarcely celebrated in Springfield that year because of the terrible heat, the illness in Mr. Lincoln's family, and a general surfeit of parades, brass bands, and fireworks since the nomination. It is a wonder the whole town had not gone deaf. But at Portsmouth, Massachusetts, Robert Lincoln was proud to be invited to read the Declaration of Independence aloud in the town square, and the honor was reported in the Springfield papers. A few days later, thirty-three-year-old Frank Fuller, a friend of Robert's who also had spoken at the Portsmouth celebration, had political business in Cleveland and decided to extend his journey to Springfield so he could meet Robert's illustrious father. Robert's letters had mentioned Fuller, a dentist who also dabbled in politics; it was Fuller who had invited the young Lincoln to read the Declaration in Portsmouth.

Frank Fuller encountered Lincoln on the street and fell in step with him as he was on his way to the statehouse office. Artist C. A. Barry was working on a crayon portrait of the presidential nominee, and from nine until noon Fuller conversed with Lincoln as he posed for his portrait. Then the two men walked to Eighth and Jackson, where Robert's friend "was warmly received by Mrs. Lincoln." He showed them a copy of the poster for the Independence Day festival in which Robert had played his part, spreading the paper on the floor after lunch. "The boys climbed all over me and I interested them in my repeating watch," which also fascinated Lincoln, who had never seen one. With the press of a spring, the watch pinged the hours and minutes.

The visitor from New England had a special gift for Mrs. Lincoln. Knowing that she loved poetry, he had brought along a collection of the poems of Albert Laighton, a slender little book bound in orange cloth published in Boston by Brown, Taggard & Chase, and in Portsmouth by Joseph Hiller Foster. The poet was a friend of Fuller's, and Fuller had persuaded the Cornhill bookstore of Brown, Taggard & Chase to publish the unknown author.

Mrs. Lincoln, thrilled with the gift, asked Mr. Fuller if he would read some lines aloud. This was the Lincolns' custom with poetry. So the visitor began to read the sensual and elegiac poems full of flowers, ghosts, and angels:

Flowers

They are the autographs of angels, penned
In Nature's green-leaved book, in blended tints,
Borrowed from rainbows and the sunset skies . . .

One poem, titled "In Memoriam," about the death of a beautiful woman, appears to have made a deep impression, with its powerful concluding lines:

O, moaning wind! O, falling leaf!
Ye shall not fill my soul with grief
For her whose feet so early trod
The starry steeps that lead to God!

Whose heart shall never bear again
Life's weight of weariness and pain.
Tenderly and joyfully
Thrill the chords of memory!

Was it Lincoln's late mother, or his sister Sarah, or his intimate friend Ann Rutledge that this poem brought to mind? The phrase "chords of memory" would become immortalized eight months later when William Seward's criticism of a draft of Lincoln's first inaugural address evoked the words "the mystic chords of memory, stretching from every battle-field . . . will yet swell the chorus of the Union, when again touched, as surely they will be, by the better angels of our nature." Lincoln perfected the unforgettable phrase.

"I am positive," Fuller recalled, "that the book went to the White House with the family, for I saw it there and read some selections from it to please Mrs. Lincoln." The young man must have made quite an impression upon the president, who appointed him interim governor of Utah in 1861.

THE SPRINGFIELD REPUBLICANS held a rally on July 24 in the heat of the day, and afterward the principal speaker, Carl Schurz, went home with the Lincolns. He wrote to his wife of the warm hospitality he had received, and said of Lincoln's wife, "His lady had decked herself out very prettily and already knows how to wave a fan. She chats quite nicely and will be able to adapt herself to the White House without difficulty." He remarked upon the charming simplicity of the Lincoln children, and was amused that Tad insisted on going barefoot.

Masses of dark clouds rolled out of the west on the evening of August 3, and when the rain finally came in the twilight, it fell in torrents. The wind tore the roofs off buildings, uprooted trees and shrubbery, and scattered the grain. The sound of the thunder was like artillery, and it threw Mrs. Lincoln into a panic. She would stand in the middle of the parlor trembling until her husband, knowing her terror, hurried home to reassure her. The storm demolished Withey's carriage factory, a three-story brick building containing fifty carriages and buggies that were crushed under the tumbling masonry. On West Washington Street, a lightning bolt struck Crowder's stable, which caught fire and burned to the ground; the chimney of Corneau & Diller's drugstore, where the Lincolns shopped, fell through the roof; a number of homes were damaged. The Lincolns were thankful their house was spared and no one in town was seriously hurt.

News of the hurricane appeared in the *Journal* of August 8, the day of the largest Republican demonstration that ever occurred in Springfield. The banner headline read: WE ARE COMING and CLEAR THE TRACK, each phrase uncoiling in a ribbon from an elephant's trunk. THE PRAIRIE'S ON FIRE / FOR LINCOLN. People came from all over Illinois, Indiana, Wisconsin, and Missouri; a crowd estimated in the hundreds of thousands overran a town whose population was not more than ten thousand. There were not enough beds in Springfield to accommodate the pilgrims, who slept in spare rooms, buggies, and barns, and curled up in blankets in backyards, vacant lots, and muddy streets.

That morning the "Wide Awakes"—one of the Republican marching and support clubs founded during the 1856 campaigns—were erecting five platforms for the speakers at the fairgrounds west of town. A throng gathered on Eighth Street, lining up at Lincoln's gate and filing to the door to shake his hand. The crush was frightening, as one lady recalled: "Those waiting to shake hands with Mr. Lincoln stood in a line blocks long waiting their turn. One man pushed his way to the front and said, 'I came all the way from Chicago to shake hands with the next president and I'm not going away without doing so.'

"Mr. Lincoln pressed forward, gave him his outstretched hand and said, as he did so, 'God bless you.' "

It was not idle speculation that the prairie lawyer would be president. That day the *Journal* observed "that the New York *Herald,* the New York *Times,* the New York *World,* and the New York *Tribune,* the four leading dailies of that city all concur in the opinion which the sign of the times unmistakably confirm, that Mr. Lincoln, unless some unforeseen contingency occurs, will be the next President of the United States." Then they offered numerical proof, citing the many states that Frémont had carried in 1856, and arguing that the Republicans would win in all of them again. Two days earlier, Cassius Clay had asked if Lincoln had started writing his inaugural address. He probably had.

At last Lincoln agreed to follow the crowd to the fairgrounds, much to his family's relief, for the visitors had made a swamp of the turf and destroyed the shrubberies. "Lincoln's arrival on the grounds occasioned a stampede for his carriage, whence he was lifted and carried above the crowd to one of the stands" (*Peoria Daily Transcript,* August 13, 1860). The mob pressing in upon Mr. Lincoln and jumping onto the platform caused it to splinter and break down. When they led him to another platform, the same thing happened.

So he decided to deliver his brief remarks to the multitude from the seat of his carriage. "This assemblage having been drawn together at the place of my residence, it appeared to be the wish of those constituting this vast assembly to see me; and it is certainly my wish to see all of you." His desire could not have been equal to theirs. Even as he spoke, some prankster was unhitching his horses to detain him. Lincoln expressed surprise that "my appearance among you would create the tumult which I now witness.... I am gratified, because it is a tribute such as can be paid to no man as a man." He wished to deflect the crowd's adoration to the principles and ideals he represented, but it was too late. He begged them to turn their attention to his friends who would be speaking, "and that you will kindly let me be silent," a request that was lost in the deafening applause.

"Finally, to release him from the mob, a man on horseback pushed through, got him on and took him back to a hotel in the city," said one eyewitness. "The enthusiasm was beyond all bounds," wrote the reporter from the *Cincinnati Gazette.* They had never seen "such a tribute of personality and admiration . . . paid to any human being." Well, perhaps one man had seen such a thing: Lincoln's friend Joseph Gillespie, who had seen Lincoln mobbed in Highland in the autumn of 1858, where "the bare sight of the man threw them into ecstasies. I have got the first inkling of the amazing popularity of Mr. Lincoln.... I could perceive that there was some magnetic influence at work that was perfectly inexplicable, which brought him and the masses into a mysterious correspondence with each other."

During the previous year and a half, Gillespie had watched this "mysterious correspondence" between the candidate and the crowd increase until now, "at Springfield I witnessed a manifestation of regard for Mr. Lincoln such as I did not suppose was possible." The first sign Gillespie had of Lincoln's presence upon the fairgrounds was that "the crowd I was in was surging along resistlessly as an avalanche towards the centre of the grounds. Every man in that vast concourse seemed to be frantic & shouting at the top of his voice: There he is, Hurrah for Lincoln and the like and rushing to get sight of and to shake hands with him. Lincoln's life would not have been worth a [illegible] if the crowd could have reached him for they were rushing towards him from all directions and would soon have overwhelmed him." Anyone could see the danger at a glance; some levelheaded fellows formed a cordon around the carriage. Only by heroic effort were they able to keep the people from crushing their idol before the horseman rescued him, "and quiet was soon restored."

Given this "friendly" demonstration, Lincoln's friend could scarcely imagine "the *fury* of a mob when its exhibitions of *regard* were so terrible."

When the candidate escaped, riding double horseback into town, he could not risk going home to his wife with thousands of admirers in pursuit of him; he was forced to take refuge in a hotel.

Meanwhile Mrs. Lincoln waited for her husband in the house at Eighth and Jackson, past the hour when she might have expected him. Word came to her that Mr. Lincoln would be delayed, and hopefully she received some sort of explanation. She could see her husband being swept into a maelstrom where men's love could scarcely be distinguished from their rage.

"MARY, WE ARE ELECTED"

DURING THE WEEKS before Election Day it was all but certain that Abraham Lincoln would be the next president of the troubled United States. Spoken or unspoken of, the nearness of triumph produced a mounting turbulence in the Lincolns' house and hometown.

Perhaps Mary speaks for both of them in a letter to her friend Hannah Shearer, October 20, 1860: "Your kind letter was received a week or two since & if every moment of my time was not occupied, should have answered it sooner." This is no exaggeration. The Lincolns had agreed to make the house as accessible as possible to the Republican hordes, and Mary Lincoln was very generous to the dignitaries who visited Springfield and expected to dine with the family at home or stay in the guest room for the night. In addition to taking care of her sons and making sure that her husband did not forget to eat, Mrs. Lincoln was in a continual state of siege by parades of Wide Awakes and other Republican fanatics. They seemed incapable of completing any demonstration in Springfield without passing by the house at Eighth and Jackson, knocking to be admitted, then overrunning the parlors, if not the entire house upstairs and down. "This summer, we have had immense crowds of strangers visiting us."

In weeks to come there would be a constant flow of houseguests wanting to shake the hand of the next president, although Mr. Lincoln declined to acknowledge the prize that seemed inevitable to so many people; in politics anything might happen to prove a man a fool for saying too much. Nonetheless, he must mind his image. In addition to the demands of keeping the house and carpets and draperies in presentable condition, Mary faced—with excellent humor—the responsibility of helping Mr. Lincoln make decisions regarding his clothing and appearance.

Dozens of painters and sculptors came to capture his likeness, with more and less success. Mrs. Lincoln politely passed judgment on these, in one case writing a letter to a Philadelphia artist complimenting him on a painted miniature that Lincoln himself agreed was "without fault." On October 19, when Mr. Lincoln received a letter from eleven-year-old Grace Bedell suggesting that he would be more electable if he grew whiskers, he must have consulted with Mary about that drastic change in his appearance.

"You used to be worried," she wrote to Mrs. Shearer, "that I took politics so coolly, you would not do so, were you to see me now." When she had time to think, her concerns were intense. "Fortunately, the time is rapidly drawing to a close, a little more than two weeks, will decide the contest. I scarcely know, how I would bear up, under defeat. I trust that we will not have the trial."

She was correct—*that* particular trial they would not have to face. The November sun rose in a cloudless sky. Lincoln entertained callers in the governor's rooms at the statehouse until sundown, and then he went to the telegraph office to hear the returns tapping over the wires. Well before midnight the news from New York and Pennsylvania confirmed the Republican victory. He received the news coolly, but with pleasure. All around him Springfield was in pandemonium. Men were shouting from corners and housetops, women were waving and cheering from windows and doorways; at the statehouse, folks threw their hats into the air. Some lay down on the floor and rolled over and over, knowing no better way to express their ecstasy.

Toward midnight Lincoln went to join his wife, saying, "Mary, Mary! *We are elected!*" And side by side they attended a victory supper of coffee and sandwiches at Watson's confectionary. It was a glorious night for the couple, a night of joy, relief, and that curious condition of unreality when the object of longing is possessed—the dream has come true yet still seems dreamlike. It was a long night, but at least they could leave Watson's, hand in hand, when they wanted, and go to bed without having to kick the guests out of the house.

THE DREAM, THE longed-for prize, was finally a reality, but with it came a measure of dread. The Lincolns were well aware of secession threats; the likelihood of challenges to the Union took up many of Lincoln's waking thoughts. But Mary did not anticipate that her husband would be hung in effigy at Pensacola, Florida, two days after the election, or that two weeks later he would be burned in effigy at Aiken, Georgia. Within a month, a wealthy and influential gentleman of New Orleans would pull out his wallet at the St. Charles Hotel and announce to the Democrats, "Here are $5,000 which I will subscribe to a fund to procure the assassination of Lincoln and [vice president–elect] Hamlin. Who'll swell the pile?" According to the Springfield newspaper it took no more than ten minutes to collect "more than $40,000 for this infamous purpose." Henry Villard of the *New York Tribune* reported, "The appearance of Mr. Lincoln has somewhat changed to the worse within the last week. . . . he looks more pale and careworn than heretofore is evident to the daily observer."

Mercy Conkling, who had visited Mary on November 6, found her on that day "in fine spirits," generously inviting her old friend to visit the White House soon with her family. But another acquaintance wrote a month later that Lincoln might pray for deliverance from his friends, "for I certainly believe they could not have acted more cruelly towards him, than to have him made President." Prophetically, the writer adds: "It will kill him and set his wife beside herself, I verily believe."

On November 20, reporter Villard had observed that after Lincoln was "nearly tortured to death" by well-wishers and office seekers at the statehouse, "the people gave him no rest after dark; even at his private residence, at half-past six, he was once more crowded upon in his parlor, and had to undergo another agony of presentations." On a school night, if Mary Lincoln and her sons were to have any peace and quiet, they would be driven upstairs to the bedrooms, for "the whole lower story of the building was filled all the evening with well-dressed ladies and gentlemen," who struggled to keep their composure during "the constant influx of an ill-mannered populace. Mrs. Lincoln had to endure as many importunities," almost, as her husband. More than once she heard strangers asking one another, as they glanced at her, "Is that the old woman?"

She was looking forward to leaving town the next morning. Quietly they had arranged a trip to Chicago to meet Mr. and Mrs. Hannibal Hamlin, the vice president–elect, and his second wife, Ellen. Lincoln remembered the dark-eyed, jet-haired Maine congressman from their days in the House of Representatives. But they had not seen each other since their nomination.

This was to be the first official visit of the president-elect and his wife, and Lincoln wanted to make it a festive occasion. On the nineteenth he wrote to Joshua Speed inviting him and Fanny to meet them in Chicago. "Mary thinks of going with me; and therefore I suggest that Mrs. S. accompany you." The former chargé d'affaires of Paris, Donn Piatt, now a journalist and Lincoln booster, was visiting Springfield with his wife, Louise, the beautiful and witty author of the famous "Belle Smith" letters to the Washington papers. Lincoln invited them to come, along with Lyman Trumbull (at the moment Lincoln's most intimate political adviser) and Trumbull's wife, Julia Jayne—who remained on awkward terms with Mrs. Lincoln.

A small gathering gave them a hearty send-off from the Springfield station at eleven o'clock. The party traveled on a regular train, in no special luxury. Henry Villard remarked that the conductor paid the distinguished passengers so little consideration as to allow "ironed convicts, one a murderer, to enter the car and take seats between the families of Mr. Lincoln and of Senator Trumbull."

Piatt, the former French minister with the long beard and elegant manners, could not conceal his amusement at Mary Lincoln's conversation, character, and political opinions. A week earlier he had dined at the Lincolns' table, and he described the supper as "an old-fashioned mess of indigestion, composed mainly of cakes, pies, and chickens, the last evidently killed in the morning to be eaten, as best they might, that evening." Piatt was shocked to see how Tad and Willie climbed up in Lincoln's lap during the meal, patting his cheeks, and pulling his nose, without being reprimanded or dismissed. When the conversation turned to the slave question, Piatt found Mrs. Lincoln's candor jarring. "This good lady injected remarks into the conversation with more force than logic," and Lincoln took them, "with about the same good-natured indifference with which he regarded the troublesome boys." Her talk of the incoming administration struck Piatt as "very womanly, but somewhat ludicrous." She said, "The country will find how we regard that abolitionist sneak Seward"—an inflammatory remark which Lincoln brushed aside, "very much as he did the hand of one of his boys when that hand invaded his capacious mouth."

The journey to Chicago took nine hours, with stops at Lincoln, Bloomington, and Lexington. In each town the president-elect paused to make a little speech to the crowd in the station. By the time they reached the big city, Mr. Lincoln was excused from making a speech because of the lateness of the hour. Hannibal and Ellen Hamlin had arrived much earlier in the day, so they were prepared to greet the Springfield party when they showed up in time for supper. Ellen, described as "plain but witty and warm-hearted," was married to Hamlin in 1856 after her older half sister Sarah, Hamlin's first wife, died of tuberculosis. Ellen, in her early twenties, was already a veteran of three seasons in the nation's capital as a senator's wife.

The Chicago summit was an experiment, a rehearsal for great state occasions soon to come. Lincoln arranged it, and he did so with calculation. He wanted his wife with him, and the protocol required it; he needed Trumbull to advise him concerning the organization of the new government; and inviting Piatt and the wives would create a divided party, so the men could go about their business—discussing cabinet appointments and patronage—while the women went sightseeing and entertained one another.

The first full day, a Thursday, was entirely given over to sightseeing and socializing. The next day, Friday, November 23, was set aside for the general reception of the public. From 10:00 A.M. until noon, thousands of people passed through the main parlor of the Tremont House. According to the reporter from the *Chicago Tribune,* the weather was the worst of the season, very cold and snowy, "yet the people were not at home." They had come in droves to see the president-elect.

"A constant stream of visitors poured in at the Lake Street entrance of the Tremont House." For more than two hours the line filed through the middle parlor of the Dearborn Street front. Mr. Lincoln in his dark suit shook hands and spoke with each person as he or she passed; to his right stood Mrs. Lincoln, and next to her the swarthy, handsome Hannibal Hamlin. At five that evening Lincoln dined privately with Trumbull and Hamlin, and the ladies were left to their own devices. Likewise on Saturday, when the gentlemen retired to the home of Judge Ebenezer Peck to discuss cabinet organization, the wives dined separately.

Sunday the Lincolns devoted to church services, in the morning attending St. James Church with Congressman Isaac Arnold, and after lunch visiting the Mission Sabbath School, where the president-elect made a little speech to the children. Monday morning, the Lincolns and their party left Chicago at 9:30, returning to Springfield at 6:30 in a cold rain that discouraged ovations and speeches at their homecoming.

There are no accounts of how the ladies dressed or exactly what impression they made upon the journalists who followed in their footsteps. We do not know how they got along. But of the four women who graced the Chicago meeting in those chilly days in November, the greatest pressure was upon the wife of the future president, to shine, to excel, to take a leadership role in everything from fashion to conversation. And it was not a company calculated to reassure the Springfield matron. To begin with, Julia Jayne's presence was as galling to her as ever. Young Ellen Hamlin had a wealth of social experience in Washington, and Louise Piatt had lived with her husband in Paris, where she wrote her popular letters to the *Ladies' Home Journal* as "Belle Smith Abroad." These cosmopolitan women had a great deal to show and tell Mrs. Lincoln about what Washington society would expect of the president's wife. If her plain dresses and hairstyle had gone unnoticed, it would not happen again.

When great changes of fortune come upon us, we register them in a variety of ways. Lincoln, who had seemed immune to change, was growing a stubble of beard. He wished to cling to his image, ever the homespun country lawyer, plain-speaking, rumpled, down-at-the-heels. Despite his new hats, suits, and boots—many of them gifts from merchants—he still sometimes looked rustic. As tokens and presents of clothing from admirers arrived from all over the world, the president-elect beheld them with amusement. A milliner from Brooklyn sent a very elegant top hat. "Mr. Lincoln took the hat . . . put it on his head and walked up to a looking glass. Glancing from the reflection to Mrs. Lincoln, he said, with his peculiar twinkle of the eye, 'Well, wife, there is one thing likely to come out of this scrape, anyhow. We are going to have some *new clothes*!'"

Mrs. Lincoln returned from Chicago with a keen sense of responsibility to transform herself, from bonnet to boots, from couture to conversation, in order to fulfill her role as mistress of the White House.

WHEN HE WAS not occupied with visitors to the statehouse office, when he was not wrangling and negotiating with differing Republicans over the structure of the new cabinet, Lincoln whiled away a few hours now and then playing chess. A reporter observed him at the chessboard sometime during the week of Thanksgiving. "Mr. Lincoln, like the rest of Anglo-American mankind, feasted on roast turkey, and having special cause to thank his Maker, attended Divine Service." The holiday gave him extra leisure. The *New York Times* reporter looked to the president's chess game for clues to his character, and began by recording the great delight Lincoln took "in the ordinary, as well as of the political chess board." He noted that Lincoln "plays a very fair game, but not a first rate one. He has a habit of whistling and singing all the time," his favorite tune being, at the moment, "I Wish I Was in Dixie's Land," the brand-new song Daniel Emmett had composed the year before for Bryant's Minstrel Show. Let it never be denied that Lincoln loved to sing as well as he could. The reporter also noticed what Mary Lincoln knew too well: "While playing chess, Mr. Lincoln seems to be continually thinking of something else." His chess partners all agreed that Lincoln "plays as if it were but a mechanical pastime to occupy his hands while his mind is busy with some other subject."

Beyond these eccentricities, the New York reporter found the president-elect's chess game in keeping with his character: "The exhibition of temper under all circumstances—the stubborn defense in hopeless resistance—the spirited attack with the weaker force, and all the incidents of mimic warfare contribute to develop the strong points of a man's disposition. Nor does Mr. Lincoln suffer by judgment under this rule. He plays what chess players call a 'safe game.' Rarely attacking, he is content to let his opponent attack while he concentrates all his energies in the defense," patiently waiting for his opponent to make a mistake. "Self-reliant in adversity, magnanimous in success, and undaunted by defeat, he is the model of a chess general."

In the game of chess that is life, Lincoln's mate employed a different style of play from her husband. She was plagued by irrational fears and insecurities but these did not prevent her from acting and speaking boldly, sometimes recklessly. As a "chess general" she would be inclined to attack, to take the game to the enemy. There was little she could do for the president-elect now in Springfield but listen as he worried over the future administration—the pressures brought to bear by cabinet hopefuls William Seward and Simon Cameron—and expressed his alarm over the secession of South Carolina from the Union five days before Christmas. She would see to it that he had clean linen and ate enough to keep body and soul together.

She had an independent agenda, a preemptive plan she believed would assure Mr. Lincoln's success in Washington. An administration was most likely to succeed if Washington society—diplomats, journalists, wives of generals and senators—all looked to the White House and the president's wife for leadership in style and manners, and for congeniality. She must do everything in her power to please the dowagers, belles, and dignitaries of Washington, that their families might be better disposed to support the president's policies. By the quick calculus of an innate materialism, very different from Lincoln's values, Mary Lincoln concluded that the president's wife required—in order to assume her responsibility—the best clothing money could buy; and her residence in Washington must have only the finest décor.

The new year brought to Springfield the illustrious and powerful Senator-elect Salmon Chase, upon Lincoln's invitation. Rumors abounded that Lincoln would name this ex-governor of Ohio his secretary of the treasury. At the same time, the Honorable Amos Tuck of New Hampshire (a favorite of Mary Lincoln, and on the short list of cabinet hopefuls Lincoln and Hamlin agreed upon) at last accepted Mrs. Lincoln's long-standing invitation to come and stay at Eighth and Jackson. On Sunday it was her honor to accompany these gentlemen to the morning service at Dr. Brown's Presbyterian church. Chase was a devout Christian. The scene in church made a lasting impression upon a visiting lawyer who wrote to his wife that Chase "is a splendid-looking man. Lincoln looks older than when we saw him last—looks care worn but firm & Jackson like—His wife is not quite so impressive as I expected to see her. She was dressed richly but plainly, looks like a good motherly kind of woman."

While the visitor's comment was not meant for Mrs. Lincoln—this was not the impression she wanted to make. Three days later, accompanied by Robert's mentor from Exeter days, Amos Tuck, and her brother-in-law Clark Moulton Smith, Mary Lincoln boarded the eastbound train to New York. Her sister Ann's husband, Clark, a short, dapper merchant equally familiar with groceries and dry goods, would lead her through the perplexity of shops. Her close friend Mercy Levering Conkling explained Mrs. Lincoln's mission to her son Clinton as follows: "Mrs. L. has gone East to get an outfit for the *White House,* which her friends here think quite unnecessary in the present state of political affairs." That very day the merchant ship *Star of the West,* loaded with men and supplies for Fort Sumter, was fired upon in Charleston Harbor. Many people believed "that the Rubicon is now crossed," that these were the first shots of the war. Mississippi seceded on the ninth, Florida on the tenth, and Alabama on Friday the eleventh of January, as Mrs. Lincoln's train was making its way from Albany to Manhattan.

Lame duck president James Buchanan, hoping to serve out his term in peace, did not respond militarily to the assault on the *Star of the West*. But when Southern leaders insisted that Federal troops withdraw from Fort Sumter, he flatly refused. After so many southern states seceded, U.S. Fort Sumter became a symbol of "foreign authority"; the decision whether to give it up or reinforce it would be the first great challenge of Lincoln's administration.

If Mrs. Lincoln's best friends frowned upon her shopping excursion, Mr. Lincoln did not look much more favorably upon it. She was establishing a reputation as a loose cannon, first for the frankness of her political opinions, and now for her freedom of movement in public, where every gesture of the president-elect's wife was subject to hard scrutiny. More than one journalist noted her presumption. We already have Piatt's opinion. Herman Kreisman, hearing of Mrs. Lincoln's New York visit, wrote to newsman Charles Ray in Chicago, "Mrs. Lincoln's journey is considered very much out of place, the idea of the President's wife kiting about the country and holding levees at which she indulges in a multitude of silly speeches is looked upon as very shocking." Kreisman was in Washington on January 16, when he wrote this to Ray, so his comment may be a more reliable reflection of opinion there than of Mrs. Lincoln's actual behavior in New York.

Little is known of her doings, although a great deal has been written of the shopping trip since 1932, when Dr. W. A. Evans published his astute psychological study *Mrs. Abraham Lincoln: A Study of Her Personality*. Dr. Evans argues that "in January 1861 there occurred the first act of Mrs. Lincoln indicating that she might not be mentally 'right.' " Taking advantage of her financial credit as the president's wife, under her brother-in-law's guidance, she shopped at the finest stores, including A. T. Stewart's, the "Marble Palace" on Broadway. She purchased not only the finest jewelry and dresses for herself, but also articles for the White House, such as lace curtains. Newspapers of the period confirm this fact, including *The Cleveland Herald* of January 10, that Mrs. Lincoln was bound for "a few days stay to make purchases for the White House." This must have struck readers as odd and overweening, as Mrs. Lincoln had yet to see the condition of the Executive Mansion, which was still occupied by President James Buchanan and his niece, Harriet Lane. The reporter for the *Herald* also mentions that the president of the railroad and his superintendent had issued Mrs. Lincoln "the courtesies of the road" and a special car from Cleveland to New York. This was flattering.

Traveling without her husband, Mary Lincoln soon discovered the privileges and perks that accrued to her new status. Now she would be treated with all the fawning attention that the world showers upon celebrities and other people of influence. In those first heady months of indulgence she found it very gratifying. One Springfield minister quipped that Mrs. Lincoln was so inflated with self-importance "that she ought to be sent to the cooper's and well secured against bursting by iron hoops." The *Ladies' Home Journal* would soon be calling her the "Illinois Queen."

Despite Clark Smith's advice, or perhaps because of it (the man who advertised himself as the purveyor of "The Best Ladies' Goods in Illinois" surely had his own agenda in New York), Mrs. Lincoln "recorded her first evidence of poor judgment in money matters," wrote Dr. Evans. "The peculiar direction and bent of this error were later to become a quality of her insanity." She took advantage of an unlimited line of credit, and overspent; her purchases of silks, jewelry, and lace were lavish and inappropriate, as if driven by what is now recognized as clinical mania.

She arrived on Saturday, January 12, occupied a suite at the Astor House, and enjoyed herself immensely, shopping and sightseeing. Robert came down from Harvard to join her. On the nineteenth, Commodore Silas Stringham led Mrs. Lincoln and her friends on a tour of the Navy Yard, where they inspected the ship *North Carolina* and other vessels and battlements. This was just the sort of quasi "state visit" with military overtones that the president-elect would have avoided, knowing the South was up in arms, but his wife was a free agent and innocently eager to go where important people invited her. "Mrs. Lincoln was received everywhere with the greatest courtesy," said the reporter for *The New York Times*. On Tuesday the twenty-second, the night Lincoln expected her home, she attended the Academy of Music, where she occupied a private box and "she was the observed of all observers." During the course of the evening, "a large number of ladies and gentlemen entered the box and were presented to Mrs. Lincoln by Hon. Edwards Fisk."

The stay in New York was a long one—nearly two weeks—at least three days longer than the Lincolns had agreed upon. Father and the boys missed her. Henry Villard, of the *New York Herald,* was then covering the president-elect's activities with microscopic intensity and rare sensitivity. Villard wrote that since his wife's departure Lincoln had been keeping house alone, and "in the management of kitchen and in other domestic concerns he is sadly destitute of both talent and experience," and so his wife was not likely to be pleased with the state of the household upon her return. Villard describes the forlorn husband bundled up in his overcoat, top hat, and shawl, trekking up Tenth Street in the snow to the railroad depot "for three successive nights in his anxiety to receive them" (Robert and Mary).

The nights of the twenty-second, twenty-third, and twenty-fourth, Lincoln stood watching the train pull into the station, waiting for the coaches to unload the last of the passengers, searching in vain for the faces of his wife, son, and brother-in-law; then, turning back, he shouldered through the cold again to the disheveled and incomplete household. He had expected her on Tuesday the twenty-second. Had they so far misunderstood each other? Why did she not send him a telegram?

At last she arrived in Springfield on January 25, attended by porters bearing parcels. "Mrs. Lincoln returned in good health and spirits; whether she got a good scolding from Abraham for unexpectedly prolonging her absence, I am unable to say," wrote Villard. "I know she found it rather difficult to part with the winter gayeties of New York."

DURING THOSE LAST three weeks in their hometown there was a great deal to be done. On February 6, the family held what journalists variously called "the first levee given by the President elect" and "the farewell soiree," from seven until midnight. The mood mingled elements of festive beginnings and melancholy farewells at "the most brilliant affair of the kind witnessed here in many years." Mr. Lincoln stood near the entrance of the north parlor to receive guests as they entered, then passed them along to his wife who stood nearby at the center of the room, the cynosure of all eyes, impeccably dressed and coiffed. Villard remarked that her "splendid toilette gave satisfactory evidence of extensive purchases" in New York. She wore a dress of antique moiré silk with a French collar and a full train. A string of pearls adorned her neck, and "her head dress was a simple and delicate vine arranged with much taste." Mrs. Lincoln would

Mary Lincoln, 1846, Springfield,
Illinois, by N. H. Shepherd

Abraham Lincoln, 1846, Springfield,
Illinois, by N. H. Shepherd

The Lincolns' home in Springfield

Lincoln, 1857,
by Alexander Hesler

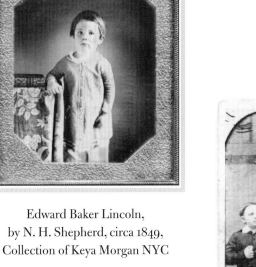

Edward Baker Lincoln,
by N. H. Shepherd, circa 1849,
Collection of Keya Morgan NYC

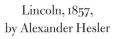

MRS. LINCOLN & SONS.

Entered according to Act of Congress in the year 1861, by E. Anthony in the
Clerk's office of the District Court of the U.S. for the So. District of New York.

Willie, Mary, and Tad Lincoln,
by Preston Butler, 1860,
Collection of Keya Morgan NYC

The White House during the Civil War

Two images of Mary Lincoln, 1861,
by Mathew Brady

Willie Lincoln, 1862

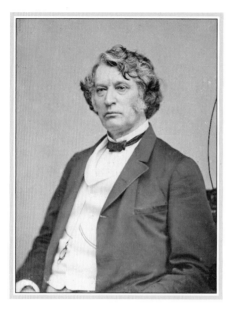

Charles Sumner, circa 1863,
by Mathew Brady

William H. Seward, circa 1865,
by Mathew Brady

Edwin Stanton, circa 1863

Mrs. Lincoln in mourning for Willie,
by Mathew Brady, 1863,
Author's Collection

Lincoln and Tad, February 1864, by Mathew Brady

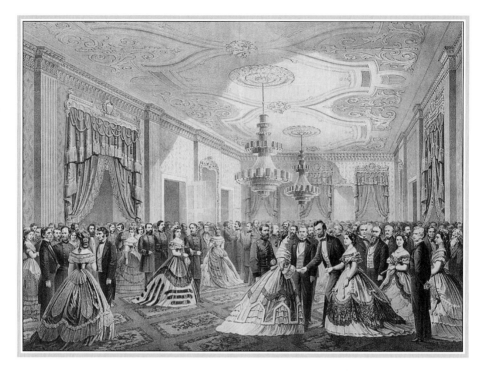

White House reception, 1865

Lincoln, February 1865,
by Alexander Gardner

Robert Lincoln, circa 1868

be pleased to read the Missouri reporter's comment that "she is a lady of fine figure and accomplished address and is well calculated to grace and do honor at the White House." That was her aim.

Overwhelming numbers of friends and well-wishers pressed into the modest dwelling. They squeezed into every available space on both the first and second floors and occupied every chair and couch. Conversation was nearly impossible in the din.

The morning after, the Lincolns could assess the damage with nostalgia and some sense of relief. There was no need to put the house in order, because they would not be living here for another four years. A former railroad executive, Lucian Tilton, had rented the house for $350 a year. They sold some of their furniture and put the rest in storage. Mary was seen in the back alley fueling a fire with decades of old documents and letters; the survival of significant letters is owing to passersby who begged for handfuls of paper for souvenirs. The boys, like any children who are about to leave the home where they grew up, were full of questions and anxieties, requiring reassurance that both parents took pains to provide. What could they take to Washington and what must be left behind? The rocking horse? The sled, the stereopticon, the favorite blanket or pillow? Would they ever see their playmates again? What about old Bob, the horse, and the stubby-tailed, rough-coated mongrel dog, Fido, who liked to chase his tail? Tad begged to be allowed to take care of Fido. "It would be better," said Mr. Lincoln, "for Fido not to come to Washington. A train filled to capacity and lurching and speeding across the country at 30 mph would be no place for a dog." The dog would find a good home with their neighbor, John Roll.

Packing up the last of the boxes and luggage they would be taking to Washington, the Lincolns bade farewell to the house at Eighth and Jackson. They took up residence for the next few days at the newly renovated, gaslit Chenery House hotel across the street from Lincoln's law office on West Washington Street.

On a rainy morning, February 11, 1861, Abraham Lincoln prepared to leave Springfield. With him were his son Robert and Robert's school friend George Latham; Lincoln's young secretaries John Nicolay and John Hay; his brother-in-law, Dr. William S. Wallace; politicians Norman Judd, David Davis, Orville Browning, Ozias Hatch, and Jesse Dubois; twenty-three-year-old Elmer Ellsworth, a diminutive militiaman and law student Lincoln had befriended; and the colossal pistol-packing Ward

Hill Lamon, a former law associate now serving as Lincoln's bodyguard. In addition, there were some reporters, railroad officials, and military personnel.

Mrs. Lincoln did not board the private car at the Great Western Railroad depot that morning; she was probably not in the crowd of a thousand or more that gathered around the brick building to hear his famous farewell speech and who waved hats and hankies under their umbrellas as the *L. M. Wiley* pulled out of the station. History has strangely lost track of Mrs. Lincoln on that sentimental occasion. It is possible that she had unfinished business in Springfield, and even more likely that there were unresolved security questions; according to Villard, Lincoln "opposed their going with him." The fact that she and the boys joined him the very next morning in Indianapolis discredits rumors that they had quarreled.

Inside the humid brick railroad station, Lincoln stood in a crowd of friends and neighbors, shaking hands. They made way for him and his party as they boarded the train. He had not planned to deliver a speech. As he stood on the rear platform and faced these people he had known for so many years, Lincoln felt an emotion well up in him that words could hardly hope to express. He raised his hand, bidding them be silent.

"Friends—No one, not in my situation, can appreciate my feeling of sadness at this parting." If his wife had been at his side, the sadness would have been slightly different; her absence was more than symbolic—they were bidding farewell to a chapter of their life together, after nineteen years of marriage.

"To this place, and the kindness of these people, I owe everything." He had not forgotten John Stuart's lending him law books; how William Butler and his wife, Elizabeth, had given him room and board when he could not pay for it; how Butler had even sold Lincoln's horse for him and helped pay off his New Salem debts. He remembered the kindness of Anson Henry and the other doctors who had nursed him through his illness in the winter of 1840–41. He remembered the generosity and open-mindedness of Simeon Francis and his wife, Eliza, who had abetted him in his courtship of Molly Todd. Francis, who had believed in him from the first, had put the power of his newspaper at Lincoln's disposal. The local Whigs had campaigned for him. He recalled his bibulous, loquacious law partner, Billy Herndon, whose indiscretions had cost him an invitation to Washington, and whose wounded pride now distanced him from the crowd that stood on the cinder and gravel track in the rain. The day before, Lincoln had told his devoted law partner to keep both names on the shingle—when he was done being president he would return to Springfield and they would practice law again as if nothing unusual had happened.

He could not forget the neighbors: Widow Sprigg with her seven children, whose daughter took care of Willie, and of Tad, who used to hide under the bed when his father came for him, thundering in mock fury: "Where is that *bad* boy?" William Florville, the black barber, had driven him to the station that morning, "Billie the Barber" who had cut Lincoln's hair with more and less success for twenty years in his swivel chair in a mirrored room on East Adams. Then there was James Gourley, whose yard backed up to Lincoln's. The two families shared a milk cow, and the kind gentleman often came to soothe Mrs. Lincoln's delicate nerves when Lincoln was gone and lightning flickered in the distance.

In that proud, tearful gathering of a thousand souls there were more memories of the Lincolns, so that as he spoke his last words to them and met those admiring, adoring eyes, hardly a man or woman could not flash back to some vivid scene. Just about everyone knew the story of Lincoln the babysitter, who stayed with the children while his wife went to church. One day he was pulling Tad in a wagon with one hand while reading a book with the other. The baby fell out of the wagon. While Tad cried and squalled on the ground, Lincoln went on pulling the wagon, oblivious, until his wife came running, scooped up the baby, and gave her husband a tongue-lashing that still could be heard years later.

Many more of them had seen the tall, gaunt figure on a winter morning, bound for market, wrapped in a gray woolen shawl, a basket on his arm, and Tad and Willie dancing around him, swinging from his free arm, asking him a dozen questions he was too distracted to answer. The Reverend Noyes Miner remembered how the Lincolns put their carriage at his disposal whenever he needed it. Then there was Mary Remann, the widow who comforted Mary Lincoln when little Eddie died. Mrs. Lincoln could not bring herself to open the child's chest of drawers until the moment she saw poor Mary Remann mending old clothes for her boy Henry— whereupon she threw open the haunted bureau and gave Mrs. Remann all of Eddie's things for Henry to wear.

Fewer people knew the intimate story of the Lincolns and the Dallmans' newborn. Charles and Harriet Dallman lived in a brick bungalow around the corner from the Lincolns. Their second child was born about the same date as Tad, in the spring of '53, but the Dallman baby was dying because Harriet Dallman was too ill to nurse him. When Mrs. Lincoln got word of the problem, she sent Mr. Lincoln to the house. He entered softly so as not to disturb the ailing mother, gathered up the infant from the cradle with his big hands, and carried him over to Mary. She put the baby to her breast to nurse until he was satisfied. Then Lincoln would return the baby to his own home; often he would sit next to the cradle, rocking it with his toe until the child was sound asleep.

There was a whole generation of boys, some older than Robert, some younger than Tad, who recalled the sometimes droll, other times rollicking giant of Springfield, who walked with long strides, flat-footed, and seemed to have endless patience with children and their curiosities and questions and pranks. He liked to take them to the circus when it was in town. They would lie in wait for him, see him coming from work, and climb on him as if he were a long-limbed, perambulating tree. He swung them on his strong arms. He knew everyone's name: the Sprigg boys, Al Arnold, Cook Irwin, Billy Baker, Mort Uhler, Al Kamp, China Conners, Ed McClernand, Henry Remann, and Fred Dubois. Dubois recalled how they tied a string from an elm to a fence just the height of Lincoln's stovepipe hat. The boys hid around the corner of the wall and waited for Lincoln's hat to hit the string. When he came along, unsuspecting, his hands folded behind his back, deep in reverie, the string knocked his hat off, startling him, and he looked for the boys after their laughter. Charging at once, they climbed upon him. Carrying as many as he could, he made his way to Webster's grocery at Monroe and Ninth, where he treated the rascals to nuts and cakes. He seemed never to be too busy for them. "None of us can ever recall a cross or petulant word which he uttered," said Fred Dubois.

So many memories, and impressions, rumors, and legends milled in that crowd under the canopy of umbrellas around the caboose. Someone recalled Mary Lincoln chasing her husband around the yard with a broom, or a knife. Some said it never happened. Someone said she once tossed a bucketful of water on his head when he came home late one night. Many had heard that when her rages and railing at him got out of hand, he would laugh, and put one of the boys on his shoulder, and go for a walk on the railroad tracks until she "cooled down." The rainy air was full of ghosts and portents. And as Lincoln's sad eyes met the gaze of this or that neighbor, friend, or townsman, his words spoke not only for him and his family but for the entire collective spirit of Springfield, an American town no different from twenty others except, perhaps, for the unique gifts he had brought to it.

"Here I have lived a quarter of a century, and have passed from a young to an old man. Here my children have been born, and one is buried. I now leave, not knowing when, or whether ever, I may return, with a task before me greater than that which rested upon Washington. Without the assistance of that Divine Being, who ever attended him, I cannot succeed. With that assistance I cannot fail. Trusting in Him, who can go with me, and remain with you and be every where for good, let us confidently hope that all will yet be well. To his care commending you, as I hope in your prayers you will commend me, I bid you an affectionate farewell."

JOURNEY THROUGH OVATIONS

Decatur! Danville, State Line, Lafayette, Thorntown, Lebanon!
With Mr. Lincoln's private train pausing at every village whistle-stop and switchback from Illinois to Indiana so he could address the cheering crowds, his wife and the little boys had no difficulty in catching up with him the next morning at the Bates House hotel in Indianapolis. That Friday he was fifty-two years of age, "Old Abe," one of the youngest men ever to be elected president.

Lincoln and his advisers had plotted the meandering 1,904-mile tour over eighteen railroad lines with overnight stops in Indianapolis, Cincinnati, Columbus, Pittsburgh, Cleveland, Albany, New York City, Philadelphia, Harrisburg, and Baltimore with the intention of showcasing the president-elect and his young family. Since Lincoln was relatively unknown to the public, and the first Westerner to be elected president, there was more than the usual curiosity about this rustic "rail-splitter" who made such a peculiar impression in the journal engravings and cartoons. During nearly two weeks on the trains, Mrs. and Mrs. Lincoln strove generously to satisfy that curiosity, under difficult conditions. More than seventy speeches were recorded during the twelve-day journey. No one anticipated such throngs along the route, such fanfare, such an outpouring of emotion. Crowd control was usually impossible, the cheers and cannon salutes were deafening, and for a large part of the trip Lincoln had a head cold. He spoke until he was hoarse.

A thirty-four-gun salute announced his arrival at the Indianapolis depot. There the governor welcomed the party as they descended from the train under the pressure of a crowd estimated at twenty thousand. Governor Oliver Morton escorted them to a carriage pulled by four white horses, leading a procession of soldiers, firemen, brass bands, both houses of the legislature, and the municipal authorities to the Bates House, where a mere five rooms had been reserved for the presidential party. They would have to sleep three and four to a room.

From the first day on the road, journalist Villard observed a distressing mix of adulation and frenzy. "Since the moment of his arrival here he has hardly had a minute to rest. No precautions having been taken to protect him from insolent and rough curiosity, he was almost overwhelmed by merciless throngs before he reached his hotel." There he found "the stairways blocked up by an immovable humanity, and he only got in by wedging himself through in a determined manner." At seven o'clock a reception was opened in the main parlor. Three thousand men and women filed past "their Presidential victim" and his son, both of whom expressed to Villard their annoyance at the numerous incivilities—folks gawking and pointing and exclaiming "There's Old Abe" and "See yonder the Prince of Rails" (Bob's new nickname).

Mrs. Lincoln's arrival the next morning, on her husband's birthday, February 12, must have been a relief to him. The weather was splendid. Army general-in-chief Winfield Scott believed that Mrs. Lincoln's influence would actually ensure the safety of the party and enforce upon the festivities a greater decorum. Those who wished Lincoln harm as an individual might honor the sanctity of his young family.

Their journey together got off to a rousing start, what reporter Villard called a "journey through ovations." Other newsmen and travelers picked up the phrase. Cincinnati, which had pleasant associations for Mrs. Lincoln, put on a splendid show for the presidential party: military parades and bands, the welcome of the mayor and civil dignitaries. But none of these things were so inspiring as "the spontaneous turnout of at least a hundred thousand people, comprising all classes, from the rich merchant and manufacturer down to the humblest day laborer to do honor to the man that will be called upon to save the Union by upholding the Federal Constitution and laws."

Arriving at the Burnet House in Cincinnati, Lincoln stood on the balcony and overlooked the throng. "My friends, I am entirely overwhelmed by the magnitude of the reception which has been given, I will not say to me, but to the President elect of the United States of America." Lincoln had wisely asked that the reception committees in every city be bipartisan, and he always insisted that the crowd's size and enthusiasm were not for him, personally, but for the office, the free institutions, and the Union

that he represented. Two years earlier, Mary Lincoln had heard her husband speak in this city, addressing the Kentuckians across the Ohio River,
assuring them that they were friends and that Ohio would respect Kentucky's laws, despite their differences over slavery. Mary thought then that
he might be president—she heard it whispered all around her—and he
had been elected. Now, on his way to the White House she heard him address their native state again: "We mean to treat you . . . as Washington,
Jefferson and Madison treated you. We mean to leave you alone, and in no
way to interfere with your institution."

After dinner there was an immense reception for the president and his
party, as there would be in every major city where they stopped. Late at
night Lincoln returned to the hotel suite, where he learned that Tad
would not go to sleep until his father had tucked him in. The boy had gotten used to this bedtime kiss during the many recent months that Lincoln
had been in Springfield. Now in the midnight of unfathomable tumult
and change, Tad needed—as they all would—the comforting rituals of
home.

THE TRIP FROM Cincinnati to Columbus, under sunny skies, was a
happy interlude for the family, who traveled in relative peace and quiet in
the last car of the three-car train. The president-elect, despite suffering
from a cold and being somewhat stiff in the limbs from his hand-shaking
marathon of the night before, "was in the best of humor all day," according to Henry Villard, "and chatted and laughed continually. Mrs. Lincoln . . . conversed with the ladies and gentlemen around her in the most
lively manner." Bob, despite having imbibed a great deal of Catawba wine
with the Republican youths of Cincinnati, "contributed much to the general good feeling by his gay, colloquial ways." Round-faced, with a shadow
of mustache, Robert had become a handsome young man, and his time
away at school had brought him out of his shell; he was still shy, but socia-
ble. New England schooling had polished his manners without diminishing his Western charm.

Crowds hailed the train at Milford, Loveland, Miamiville, Morrow,
Corwin, Xenia, and London, and at each stop Mr. Lincoln would step out
onto the platform, say a few words of greeting, acknowledge the applause,
and retire. There was a complex emotion in the air, building every hour,

until the turnout seemed out of proportion to the event. In Columbus, a
city of twenty thousand, more than fifty thousand people had come to
welcome Mr. Lincoln. No American politician had ever seen anything like
it. He told the audience that their enthusiasm was not a tribute to him, but
a manifestation of "good-will towards the government, and affection for
the Union."

David Davis, Lincoln's campaign manager, gives an insider's view of
the tour in a letter to his wife from Buffalo, February 17, "scenes of excitement that I never witnessed before. . . . a trip of this kind is killing—One
can never get to bed until 12 oclk & have to get up to prepare for the day
at ½ past 5. . . . The whole trip from Indianapolis to this city has been an
ovation such as has never before been witnessed in this country. It is simply astonishing—The people seem wild with excitement everywhere—&
turn out in large masses everywhere. . . . I don't think that it is Lincoln's
person or character that calls out the enthusiasm—It must be, that the
present state of the country calls forth such an enthusiasm as has never
been witnessed."

Judge Davis recounted that on Tuesday morning, February 12, twelve
thousand people surrounded the Bates House hotel, and only with great
difficulty could the presidential party reach the carriages and make their
way to the depot. "At Cincinnati, the whole population were in the
streets—It would have been impossible to have reached the carriages except through a line of soldiers—we were two hours and a half marching to
the hotel—amid waving of handkerchiefs from the balconies and windows and housetops all along the route—and the streets were so lined
with people that it was difficult to reach the hotel—& to let the carriages
pass. This was repeated at Columbus, & all the way between Columbus
& [illegible]."

At Pittsburgh they arrived in the pouring rain, which Lincoln welcomed because he thought it would limit the size of the crowds. But rain
made little difference to the tide of citizens. The police cordon broke
down, and it was an enormous effort for the family to reach their carriage.
Then, according to John Nicolay, "it looked for a while as if we would
never get the carriage out of the crowd that was pushing and yelling
around us." The muddy streets around the Monongahela House were
thronged with people who blocked access to the hotel and jammed the
lobby.

By now the reporter observed "a shade of melancholy over the Presidential party," which various participants, especially the banjo-picking Colonel Lamon, tried to brighten by singing ballads and telling stories. He looked like Wild Bill Hickok, with his drooping mustache, ruffled shirts, and holstered guns. Lamon's massive presence was reassuring as it became clear that the crowd's "enthusiasm"—which David Davis, John Nicolay, and others described repeatedly—had a sinister side to it. At Rochester, a man cried out, "What will you do with the secessionists, then?" Lincoln replied, "My friend, that is a matter which I have under very grave consideration." The gatherings were vaguely menacing, and the smell of gunpowder was in the air, literally and figuratively. At lunch at Sourbeck's hotel in Alliance, Ohio, on February 15, a cannon salute disrupted the meal, shattering a windowpane over the table and sprinkling shards on Mrs. Lincoln.

The train rolled into Cleveland in a snowstorm. Rather than battle the concourse and weather at the end of the line, the railroad officials thought it best for the Lincolns to get off at the Euclid Street station, two miles from the city center. Still, the light artillery signaled their debarkation with a thirty-four-gun salute. The president-elect took his seat in an elegant barouche drawn by four white horses while Mrs. Lincoln and the children were whisked away in a closed carriage to their hotel. They arrived at the Weddell House in time to dress for a levee given in Lincoln's honor that evening. The ladies of Cleveland held a separate party for the president-elect's wife, whose nerves, hopefully, had recovered sufficiently for her to enjoy the honor.

The press was kind to Mrs. Lincoln, flattering her manners, dress, and person although they saw little of her. She now shunned the limelight as a matter of policy, or temperament—it is difficult to know. Politicians' wives were expected to be gracious, but demure. At a whistlestop in Ashtabula on February 16 Lincoln was greeting the people in his hoarse voice when someone called for Mrs. Lincoln. Her husband explained that "he could hardly hope to induce her to appear, as he had always found it very difficult to make her do what she did not want to."

That weekend the glorious march of triumph became a nightmare. As the train made its way through an unruly crowd of ten thousand in Buffalo at the Exchange Street Depot, the engineer, and Lincoln's bodyguard Lamon, could see trouble coming. Only a few soldiers and policemen had been detailed to escort the president-elect and his party, and the dense horde, high-spirited at 4:30 on a Saturday afternoon, refused to make way for the guards. Former president Millard Fillmore—silver-haired, strikingly handsome—and a deputation of other dignitaries stood on the platform waiting to greet the president-elect. But no sooner had Lincoln stepped down from the coach and taken Fillmore's hand than "the crowd made a rush," Villard noted, "and overpowering the guard pressed upon him [Lincoln] and his party with a perfect furor. A scene of the wildest confusion ensued. To and fro the ruffians swayed and cries of distress were heard on all sides. The pressure was so great that it is really a wonder that many were not crushed and trampled to death." Only the brave efforts of the men accompanying the president-elect and his family enabled them to escape the Exchange Street Depot: the strong arms of Colonel Edward V. Sumner, the bull-necked Ward Hill Lamon, Elmer Ellsworth, lithe Nicolay and Hay, and the valiant Major David Hunter, who dislocated his shoulder in the mêlée. An eyewitness recalled that the party had to literally "struggle with might and main for their lives," and one can only imagine Mary Lincoln's terror—her mounting concern for herself and her children. By the time they reached the carriages, most were taken, and some of the presidential party had to get to the American Hotel on foot. Arriving there, they found thousands of people blockading the hotel doors, and so "had to undergo another tremendous squeeze to get in."

Somehow they maintained their poise. Lincoln addressed the multitude from the hotel balcony as usual, avoiding policy statements until he could "get all the light I can, so that when I speak authoritatively I may be as near right as possible . . . allow me to say that *you*, as a portion of the great American people," he concluded—after the day's violence—"need only to maintain your composure." At 7:30 there was a public reception, and later two choral serenades.

The next morning Mrs. Lincoln kept to her room while her husband attended the First Unitarian Church service with former president Fillmore. After prayers they returned to the hotel to get Mary so she could join them for lunch at the old gentleman's gracious home on Niagara Square. Lincoln welcomed his wife's company. Although Fillmore, sixty-one, was a former Whig, and self-educated, he had little else in common with Lincoln, and had not supported him in the election. It was a magnanimous gesture on his part to welcome the Republican to Buffalo. A nativist, and one who had taken a conservative stand on the slavery issue, Fillmore would not be an easy man for Lincoln to get on with, and the presence of Fillmore's young wife, Caroline McIntosh, and Mary Lincoln in the luncheon party would be a distraction from politics. Relieved of their social obligations, the Lincolns returned to the hotel to find Willie and Tad playing leapfrog with the proprietor's son. Removing his hat and coat, the president-elect joined the game, demonstrating that he could still leap.

When time came for supper, the family dined in private. In five days the "journey through ovations" had lost much of its luster and fascination and was beginning to resemble hard work. They would have to be up before daybreak to board a 6:00 A.M. train for Utica and Albany. As the publicity mounted and the crowds increased, they sensed that the hardest days lay ahead.

Albany was a disaster. Governor Edwin Morgan ordered Company B of the Twenty-fifth New York regiment to the station to guard the Lincolns. But the soldiers arrived late. When the train, trimmed with American flags, slowed to a screeching halt at the Broadway railroad crossing, the mob surged in upon it. Men and boys climbed over and under the coaches, while the bodyguards on the train kicked at them and threw them back. Mayor George Hornell Thatcher was so roughly treated he could hardly reach the platform. When he asked Mr. Lincoln if he would please wait inside for the military guard, Lincoln agreed that would be a good idea. It was a long wait, while the ruffians fought hand to hand with the policemen. "All was confusion, hurry, disorder, mud, riot and discomfort. At last the soldiers arrived . . . muskets soon cleared a way for the carriages."

How did father and mother explain this scene to Robert, Willie, and Tad? Three blocks before their hotel on Broadway they passed Stanwix Hall playhouse, where John Wilkes Booth would perform that evening as Duke Pescara in *The Apostate*. It is said that the actor cursed the presidential party as they passed. Although Lincoln by now was pale and wan, his voice a whisper, he made a speech at the capitol steps; he addressed a joint meeting of the legislature within: "While I hold myself without mock modesty, the humblest of all individuals that have ever been elevated to the presidency, I have a more difficult task to perform than any one of them. . . . when the time comes I shall speak as well as I am able for the good of the present and future of this country. . . . In the mean time, if we have patience; if we restrain ourselves; if we allow ourselves not to run off in a passion, I still have confidence that the Almighty, the Maker of the Universe will . . . bring us through this." After the threatening turbulence of their welcome at the Broadway depot, Mrs. Lincoln had cause to wonder if the Almighty would bring her family safely to Washington, D.C.

A squabble between the legislature and the governor concerning the honors of entertaining the president-elect produced what the *New York Herald* condemned as "a miserable botch, characterized by snobbery throughout" the visit. After supper at the governor's mansion, the president-elect stood for a 9:00 P.M. levee in the banquet room of his hotel, the Delavan House, while the ladies held a reception for Mrs. Lincoln in a separate room. As there was no private entrance to the hotel, the police force could not make a path through the drunken mob in the lobby for the ladies to reach the parlor where Mrs. Lincoln patiently waited, and that part of the celebration was "worse than a failure."

After a restless night, the Lincolns and their party left Albany, on Tuesday morning, February 19, worn out, having been "leveed and receptioned by remorseless ladies and gentlemen." According to the *Herald* reporter, Mr. and Mrs. Lincoln were too angry to sleep. They expressed deep gratitude for having been delivered from the hubbub and confusion, and vowed never to return. Lincoln was so exhausted and sick that he took no pleasure in conversation, but his wife bravely took up the burden, as friends called upon them. "Mrs. Lincoln chit-chatted with her friends, and seemed all life and enjoyment. . . . the Lincolns are common sense, homelike folks unused to the glitter and flutter of society."

His hair uncombed, forehead furrowed, clothing rumpled and in disarray, Lincoln sat in the rear of the saloon car, brooding. In Montgomery, Alabama, Jefferson Davis had just been inaugurated president of the Confederacy.

The New York political organizer Thurlow Weed, an ally of William Seward, had come to Albany in advance of Lincoln's visit to Manhattan. Weed was aptly named, being tall and gangly like Lincoln, with long arms and legs, and able to thrive in challenging environments. Incredibly, he had served in the War of 1812, and forty years later was instrumental in building a bridge between the old Whig party and the new Republicans. Weed had a long nose and a prominent cleft chin, and aggressive expressions to match his opinions. He had founded the *Albany Evening Journal,* and now at age sixty-four he was at the height of his powers as a political operative. He had wanted Seward to be president, but now bowed to Lincoln. Weed's presence here offered assurance that Lincoln's reception in New York City would be more comfortable than his experience in Albany.

They were not disappointed. The reception in New York City compensated for the trials and discomforts of the week past. Mary saw to it that Mr. Lincoln was well groomed and attired for Manhattan. After leaving Utica she ordered William Johnson, their black servant, to bring Mr. Lincoln's new coat and hat out of the boxes he seemed to have forgotten. A journalist from the *Times* noticed that during the entire trip Mr. Lincoln had worn a "shockingly bad hat" and a thin, threadbare overcoat. Now in his fresh stovepipe hat and his new coat of black broadcloth, Lincoln looked "fifty percent improved," said the newsman, and "the country may congratulate itself that its President-elect is a man who does not reject, even in important matters, the advice and counsel of his wife."

Despite the presence of a powerful Democratic anti-Lincoln contingent in the great city, the welcoming of the president-elect went smoothly, from their arrival at Thirtieth Street Station at three o'clock on the nineteenth until their departure via the Cortlandt Street Ferry, hailed by artillery fire and a cheering throng, early in the morning of the twenty-first. Mayor Fernando Wood, boss Thurlow Weed, and the superintendent of police had taken every precaution to see that Gotham received the Lincolns more graciously than had Albany. Narrow-eyed, square-jawed Wood was a racist and a staunch defender of slavery in the South, but he was also a shrewd politician who knew better than to alienate the man bound for the White House. Wood had seen to it that thirteen hundred of New York's finest had been detailed "to keep the enthusiasm of crowds within the bounds of good manners." In shiny new belts and yellow calf gloves, one hundred and fifty policemen met the party at the train station, where thirty-five carriages stood in line outside. Mary Lincoln kissed her husband and once again smoothed his unruly hair before they left the station for the carriages.

The procession of eleven barouches, following a squadron of mounted policemen, made its way downtown in a stately fashion. Flags were flying from almost every window and lamppost, and the streets were lined with people waving and cheering. "Mr. Lincoln bowed and smiled constantly, and seemed vastly delighted with the spectacle." They passed under banners proclaiming "Welcome Lincoln" and the now-famous words from his Cooper Union Speech, "Right Makes Might," as well as "Welcome Abraham Lincoln, We Beg For Compromise."

As they rode down Broadway the Lincolns could remember their last visit to New York together, in that idyllic summer of 1857, after their trip to Niagara Falls. Standing on the docks, Mary had dreamed aloud of traveling to Europe, and joked with her husband about someday marrying a rich man. Now he was one of the most powerful men in the world. They would stay at the Astor House, their familiar New York hotel at Broadway and Barclay Street, in a suite of rooms, second floor front. The crowd, which Lincoln addressed briefly from the portico, was estimated at a quarter of a million.

The next day was mostly taken up with Mr. Lincoln's formal reception at City Hall, where Mayor Wood in his welcoming speech entreated Lincoln "for a restoration of friendly relations between the states . . . by peaceful and conciliatory measures." Lincoln responded with ambiguous gestures of reassurance: "There is nothing that can ever bring me willingly to consent to the destruction of this Union . . . unless it were to be that thing for which the Union itself was made." He used the figure of the ship of state, saying "so long as the ship can be saved *with the cargo*, it should never be abandoned," meaning by *the cargo* both the prosperity and the *liberties* of the people—in other words, he was making no promises about conciliatory measures. He must find other ways to charm the politicians of New York City.

When he had finished speaking, the members of the state government and the city council were introduced to him. Then Mayor Wood invited Lincoln to please himself about shaking hands with the members of the crowd that pressed around City Hall—the police would open and close the reception at his bidding. "I can stand it a little while," he replied, amiably, "and the tide continued to pour in," said the *Times* reporter. "It was amusing to see the bewildered look of the injected visitors suddenly emerging as from the compressions of a pop gun to the comfortable quarters between lines of police. Some looked wildly about . . . some stopped to pin up sundered garments, smooth their wrinkled attire." The correspondent for the Baltimore *Sun* noted that Lincoln's "style of shaking hands and chatting with people is prepossessing, frank, genial, unassuming, and in a word—Western." Women were appallingly aggressive, a development that irritated Mrs. Lincoln. The *Chicago Tribune* remarked, "In the heat of the excitement a female made her appearance, and was dragged through the doorway, with hoops and bonnet materially damaged. When introduced to Mr. Lincoln, she told him she was from Illinois, and though she had experienced a rough voyage, she would go through a tighter squeeze to see him."

In the afternoon, Mrs. Lincoln took the children to Barnum's museum across the street; in the evening, the Lincolns attended the opera, Verdi's *Un Ballo in Maschera,* where Mrs. Lincoln stayed only long enough to take a bow with her husband. A glittering diamond brooch clasped her lace collar. She waved a small ivory fan, acknowledging the applause. She had to hurry away to attend a levee in her honor in the ladies' parlor of the Astor House. Wearing a black chenille and gold head covering and a high-necked, pale gown, she took her place at the south end of the parlor between the socialite Mrs. James Watson Webb on her right, and her sister Elizabeth, Mrs. Ninian Edwards, Jr., on her left. Elizabeth had caught up with the party in New York, and she was a great support to her sister during the rest of the journey. Mrs. Lincoln would be pleased to be seen as the *Times* reporter regarded her, "plainly dressed in a light colored silk." As Mrs. Webb introduced hundreds of ladies and gentlemen to Mrs. Lincoln and her sister, they were "received by Mrs. Lincoln with an ease and grace, and at the same time with a cordiality, which augur well for the social qualities of the future mistress of the National Mansion." Among those who paid respects to the first lady were Colonel James Watson Webb, Mr. and Mrs. Hannibal Hamlin, Henry Raymond (editor of the *Times*), Horace Greeley (editor of the *Tribune*), and Simeon Draper, chairman of the New York Republican party.

In this city so sharply divided between Democrats and Republicans, the Lincolns made a favorable impression. One gentleman staying at the hotel, George Shepard of Detroit, described Mrs. Lincoln as "a plump, amiable, modest, pleasant, round-faced agreeable woman with no silly airs." Her husband received a good deal of ribbing about wearing black gloves to the opera instead of white; except for that gaffe, the Springfield couple were well reviewed by the critics of fashion and manners. Furthermore, during their two days in Manhattan, which Mr. Lincoln would never see again, they both had a good time.

. . .

THE DELIGHTS OF New York City became a remote memory during the last two days of the journey. As the train moved south, every mile and whistle-stop plunged the presidential party into greater danger. At 4:00 P.M. they arrived in Philadelphia, where a hundred thousand people saw their carriage deliver them to the new Continental Hotel at Ninth and Chestnut streets. The Continental—which the *Times* reporter called "the finest hotel in the world"—was woefully unprepared. "Such a conflict of rude vulgarity and impertinent curiosity, as I have never seen," said the journalist. "The people were wild. Forgetting that some show of respect was due the proprietor and the guests of the house, the populace, eager, impulsive, thoughtless and rough, crowded into the hotel . . . the proceedings were disgraceful to the authorities of the city, insulting to Mr. Lincoln." The president-elect delivered his inaudible speech: "As your worthy Mayor has said, there is great anxiety amongst the citizens of the United States at this time. . . . the crisis, the panic, the anxiety of the country at this time is artificial." And when he had bidden the citizens good night, he withdrew from the balcony to dine with his wife privately.

Over supper, if they could hear themselves over the thunder of the crowd, fireworks, and brass bands, they would consider the Philadelphia schedule. Tonight at 8:30 was the public reception in the ballroom. Tomorrow, Friday the twenty-second, was Washington's birthday. Lincoln had agreed to make a speech at Independence Hall and raise a new flag of thirty-four stars at seven o'clock in the morning. The picturesque ceremony, meant to occur as the first rays of sunlight shone upon the church spires and chimneys, was to be the climax of Lincoln's visit to the city of brotherly love, and so the flag-raising had been much heralded by the press.

Mr. Lincoln had little rest that night. Near ten o'clock, he and his wife were standing beneath the chandelier in the grand parlor, shaking hands and chatting with the innumerable and tireless guests, when Norman Judd drew him out of the receiving line. He must come along at once to Judd's room. What could be so urgent that he would leave his wife alone with this mob? In bewilderment and suspense, Mrs. Lincoln went on smiling and bowing and shaking hands while Mr. Lincoln went upstairs.

In addition to being one of Lincoln's inner circle, Judd was an attorney for the railroads. So he was among the first to hear that there was trouble down the line. He opened the door to the suite where a short man with sloping shoulders, a short black beard, and deep-set eyes rose to shake Lincoln's hand. Allen Pinkerton, a Chicago detective who worked for the Wilmington and Baltimore Railroad, explained to Lincoln that he had just come from Baltimore—a city with profound Southern sympathies— where he had been investigating "suspicious persons" who might wish the president-elect harm. In Lincoln's words, "Pinkerton informed me that a plan had been laid for my assassination, the exact time when I expected to go through Baltimore being publicly known. . . . He urged me to go right through with him to Washington that night. I didn't like that. I had made arrangements to visit Harrisburg, and go from there to Baltimore, and I resolved to do so. I could not believe there was a plot to murder me." He told Judd and Pinkerton he would think it over.

As Lincoln left Judd's room, perplexed and incredulous, and sidled through the crowded hall, William Seward's son, Frederick, stood in his way. He asked if he might have a word with him in private. Then, in Seward's room, according to Lincoln, "he told me he had been sent, at the instance of his father and General Scott, to inform me that *their* detective in Baltimore had discovered a plot there to assassinate me. They knew nothing of Pinkerton's movements. I now believed such a plot to be in existence."

He did not tell his wife about the plot that night before bed, as he did not wish to trouble her sleep. It is unlikely she rose with him in the darkness to ride in the carriage to Independence Hall and watch him raise the new flag at dawn. It is improbable that she heard him praise "that sentiment in the Declaration of Independence which gave liberty" or pose the question, "Now my friends, can this country be saved upon that basis? If it can, I will consider myself one of the happiest men in the world if I can help to save it." If she had been standing within earshot, Mr. Lincoln would not have made the chilling pronouncement that he did: "If it can't be saved upon that principle, it will be truly awful. But if this country cannot be saved without giving up that principle . . . I would rather be assassinated on this spot than to surrender it." No president had ever been assassinated.

Joseph Howard of the *Times,* traveling with the family in their private car to Harrisburg that morning, was amused by the study in contrasts between the exhausted husband and his well-rested, vivacious wife. Lincoln "availed himself of the time granted by the printed time-table to take a good hour's sleep. . . . he does not sleep with his mouth open, nor does he snore." Mrs. Lincoln "was very wide awake," conversing with the wife of a Springfield friend, "and had they been the centre of attraction at a Saratoga ball-room, they could not have been more entirely complaisant, more brilliant or self-possessed." The journalist takes this opportunity to provide his readers with a full-length portrait of Mrs. Lincoln. He must begin by correcting his scribbling colleagues "with hatchets to sharpen": Mrs. Lincoln has not the features of Juno, the form of Venus, or Minerva's wisdom; but neither does she chew tobacco, dress outlandishly, or curse, nor does she ever, in public or private, "kick up shindies."

He estimates that Mrs. Lincoln is a middle-aged lady of perhaps thirty-eight or forty. "On the top of her head . . . the hair *does* grow, and very lux-uriantly too, of a dark brown color, and elastic fibre. Her head is large and well-developed, presenting the organs of firmness and language in a highly developed and well-matured condition. Her forehead is broad; her eye clear and intelligent, and rather blue than gray; her nose is—well, not to put too fine a point on it—is not Grecian; her mouth is large, well-shaped, and capable of great expression, while her chin rounds gracefully," confirming his "opinion that she is a *decided*—not obstinate—woman. Her form inclines to stoutness, but is well-fashioned and comely, while her hands and feet are really beautiful. . . . Her carriage is good, her manners are pleasant, her greetings are affable, and, without doubt, her intentions are correct."

Reporter Howard congratulates Mrs. Lincoln on being versed in the knowledge of "housewifery and substantial living" rather than skilled in politics and accustomed to the excitements of Washington society. She goes to her "unaccustomed position . . . taking with her, her sound sub-stratum of common sense, her natural tact, that great aider of us all." She would need all of that common sense and determination to endure the pressures, humiliation, and terror of the next six hours as the train neared Harrisburg, not to mention the harrowing passage through Baltimore the next morning.

At a brief stop at Leaman Place, Pennsylvania, before Lancaster, Lin-coln told the gathering he was too unwell to say much to them. He re-peated his tried and true formula, saying he had merely come out to see them and let them see him, "in which he had the best of the bargain." As usual, there were cries for Mrs. Lincoln to appear, which she usually declined to do. This time she broke with custom, and as she joined him he put his arm around her shoulders and told the old joke: He had decided to give the crowd "the long and short of it!"

At Vine and Second Street Depot in Harrisburg, all was confusion. "There was no order; no discipline, but grab the first carriage" to the hotel, the Jones House, where the *Times* reporter described a riot, "the crowd outside of the hotel immense." The horse guards protecting Lincoln as he addressed the throng broke ranks. "Dragoons flourished swords, and their horses plunged most violently; militia men plunged bayonets, and their victims yelled most wildly." The horses trampled innocent people. "The soldiery, who were to keep the line open, forgot their duty before a large number at the party had got in, carelessly punched people with their bayonets, hurt several bystanders seriously." Howard noted that evening that "Mrs. Lincoln being physically prostrated by hard labor, did not give the anticipated reception," but went to bed early.

There was a darker reason Mrs. Lincoln retired early in Harrisburg— disturbing news. After addressing the legislature at the statehouse, Lincoln had returned by military escort to the Jones House parlor where, at three o'clock, Norman Judd had assembled a conference of Judge David Davis, Colonel Edwin Sumner, Ward Hill Lamon, Captain John Pope, Major David Hunter, Governor Andrew Curtin, and legislator A. K. McClure. The Baltimore assassination plot came as a surprise to everyone but Lincoln and Judd. Some worried that a covert circumvention of Baltimore would be denounced as cowardly, but at last this scruple was put aside in the greater concern for Lincoln's safety. Judge Davis gravely put the question to Lincoln, who replied that after thinking it over since the night before, he was disposed to carry out Judd's plan of going secretly on a separate train.

Lincoln was less concerned about personal safety and ridicule than he was about leaving his wife and children at this point in the journey. According to Pinkerton's account, "Mr. Lincoln had remarked that none should be acquainted with his secret but Mrs. Lincoln. This he said he could not avoid, as otherwise she would be very much excited at his absence." She was very much excited by her husband's solemn presence as he explained the plan for him to go immediately in a special train to Washington while she and the children continued the scheduled trip via Balti-

more. She was horrified to hear of the assassination plot and the plan that
he travel without her. According to A. K. McClure's view, Mary Lincoln
was so upset, "she narrowly escaped attracting attention to the movements which required the utmost secrecy." It would take all of Lincoln's
powers of persuasion to get her to cooperate. Under duress she bargained
with the men: She would go along with the plan, and hold her peace, if
her old friend Ward Hill Lamon would guard her husband and never
leave his side until he rejoined her. She trusted Lamon as a fearless fighter
who would lay down his life for Lincoln, and she agreed to go on alone
only if he would accompany her husband. But she was not happy about it,
and her fury over the decision and its consequences was, we shall see,
thoroughly justified.

This was a pivotal moment in the progress of the marriage, a wicked
fork in the road. She was now powerless to influence a decision that concerned the safety of her husband and children; the presidency had become more important than the family. She and her sons were going to risk
Baltimore while the president-elect was escaping to Washington. No one
was to know this but a dozen men and one terrified woman who suddenly
found herself—as her husband's surrogate and decoy—aboard a train tar-
geted by assassins. By all but the most sentimental measures, his life was
now more valuable than his family's. If history has lost sight of this fact,
the wife and husband would not soon forget it.

LATE THAT NIGHT, guarded by Lamon and Pinkerton, Lincoln boarded
the special train from Philadelphia to Washington via Baltimore. They
quietly passed through Baltimore at 4:00 A.M. on February 23, arriving in
Washington at 6:00 A.M. The story of Lincoln's skulking into Washington, disguised in an old overcoat and a soft wool cap pulled low over his
forehead, has often been told. The caricature of Lincoln disguised in a
Scots plaid tam and kilts is even more widely known; it will suffice to say
here that he arrived safely, and immediately telegraphed Mrs. Lincoln in
Harrisburg. His secret journey from Harrisburg to the capital was an easy
ride.

What is scarcely known is the fate of Mrs. Lincoln and the presidential
party as they kept the publicized schedule. The train pulled out of Harrisburg at 9:00 A.M., and about the same time, a dispatch from that city to the

Baltimore newspapers "announced, rather vaguely" that Mr. Lincoln had already arrived in Washington via an express train. Almost no one believed it. "Nine out of every ten believed it a ruse to prevent a large gathering at the Calvert Station where he was expected to arrive," said the Baltimore *Sun*. A second telegram confirming that the president-elect had reached Washington was likewise dismissed as a hoax. About eleven o'clock, people began to gather at the corner of South and Baltimore streets, until the crowd extended from Holiday to Calvert, ready to rush the points where Mr. Lincoln was likely to debark at the Calvert Station. Toward noon, the throng would swell to fifteen thousand, while thousands more surrounded the Bolton Depot, where for a while it was rumored the train might make its appearance.

Aboard the train, the party tried to stay calm as they considered the dangers of approaching the hostile city. According to the Baltimore *Sun*, one of the assassins' plots "was, if possible, to throw the cars from the road at some point where they would rush down a steep embankment and destroy in a moment the lives of all on board." From the coach windows, Mrs. Lincoln could see the extreme precautions that had been taken against explosions or derailment: Flagmen stood within sight of one another all the way from Harrisburg to Baltimore. Each sentinel held a white and a red flag. The red flag raised meant that the track was all clear, and the white was to be used if there was danger. In addition, an armed pilot engine ran a hundred yards ahead of the presidential express, to shoot assailants.

A crowd becomes a mob not simply because of its numbers, but by the animus of its worst elements. There may not have been dedicated assassins among the tens of thousands of spectators who thronged the avenues leading to the Calvert Station, and stood on the hills of Franklin and Courtland streets overlooking the depot, but there were many who were spoiling for trouble. The early dispatches announcing that Mr. Lincoln had arrived in Washington had convinced almost no one. Baltimore's mayor, George William Brown, had waited patiently at the depot with the chief of police, Marshall Kane, and four hundred policemen. But when officers of the Northern Central Railroad informed the mayor and the police that Lincoln had bypassed their city, they were offended. They left the scene and ordered the policemen to report to the police station—leaving all but a skeleton crew of constables and detectives to guard the train. The dwindling of the police force excited the mob.

"Never before were there assembled in this city such a bamboozled and confounded crowd." The reporter for the *Chicago Tribune* mentioned the number of billy clubs and other weapons that had been purchased in the local markets by "well known rowdies," and he concluded that had Mr. Lincoln appeared, "the general impression is that there would have been serious trouble . . . the very worst characters in Baltimore were there congregated, to restrain whom, under existing circumstances, would have been impossible. . . . All things considered, there were chances and indications of real danger."

The roar and tumble of the mob caused the engineer to slow the locomotive at Charles Street, a block before entering the station. He hoped to allow the party to dismount safely there, but it was hopeless. The people rushed the cars, pressing their faces to the windows, smudging the glass, grimacing, shouting "Here's Old Abe!" and "Look out for him! Here he is!" According to one reporter, "as soon as the train stopped, the crowd leaped upon the platforms and mounted to the tops of the cars like so many monkeys, until, like a hive of bees, they swarmed upon them, shouting, hallooing, and making all manner of noises." So, with a jerk, the train moved forward again.

The special train, soot-black and trimmed with wilted flags, steamed and rumbled into the Calvert Street Station at one o'clock. Cold rain and harsh wind blew from the northwest. Conductor George Rawlings stood on the train platform, waving his arms, shouting at the rushing, yelling assembly that Mr. Lincoln was not on board but "Mrs. Lincoln, her family and suite only, who would be pleased to pass unmolested to the carriages in waiting to convey them."

The mob could not hear the conductor. They would not have believed him anyway, and what ensued was a riot the mayor and police chief had chosen to let happen. Hoodlums, jerking the windows of the train coaches ajar, thrusting their heads inside, shouted "Here he is" and "There he goes," "Come out, Old Abe," and "We'll give you hell, you bloody black Republicans." The pressure of the people from all sides was so great that many bystanders were pushed from the platform and fell back into the sea of bodies. The *Sun* reporter saw the throngs "swayed hither and thither with a force perfectly irresistible, and persons were knocked from the platforms and trampled on, and others had their clothing torn."

New York Times reporter Joseph Howard, on the train with Mrs. Lincoln, her children, and her entourage, recalled that their worst fears were realized when "some rude fellows entered the private compartment in which Mrs. Lincoln was sitting . . . but were promptly turned out by Mr. Hay, who locked the door." At last a few police detectives broke through the crush and joined forces with Colonel Sumner, Major Hunter, Colonel Ellsworth, and others to escort the president's family and friends and the reporters. They ran a gauntlet of abuse, "an exhibition of rude vulgarity and disregard of personal comfort that I have never seen equaled," wrote Howard. "Without thinking of the consequences to us, the crowd rolled in upon us like vast tidal waves, and bore us with irresistible force against the side of the car. To go either way was a physical impossibility. If we had been in the crowd, we could have moved with or through them; but as it was, we were compelled to stand still, and sustain, as well as we were able, the terrible rush of an excited, rude and thoughtless populace. Oaths, obscenity, disgusting epithets and unpleasant gesticulations, were the order of the day. . . .

"After half an hour of this sort of thing, Mrs. Lincoln and her son[s] were taken to a carriage," which delivered them to the home of John S. Gittings, director of the B&O Railroad. The reporter for the *Chicago Tribune* concluded, "Mr. Lincoln would certainly have been in great danger, and it is unanimously believed that he acted wisely in going to Washington as he did."

Mary Lincoln's thoughts on this subject and her feelings about the events described above are nowhere recorded. An editorial in the Baltimore *Sun* on Sunday, February 25, challenges the accounts of *The New York Times* and the *Herald* that Mrs. Lincoln urged her husband to bypass Baltimore without her—calling them ludicrous. "We have information, on the other hand, that Mrs. Lincoln warmly opposed the project, and to disprove the whole story determined in fulfilling the programme to Baltimore in her own person, and did so. If this be true, *she* ought to be the President elect."

The editorial writer, expressing the feelings of most Baltimoreans, if not Mrs. Lincoln's, sharpens the edge of his sarcasm: "At all events it is true that while Mrs. Lincoln went by another route, he [Mr. Lincoln] affectionately left Mrs. Lincoln to come by that on which the cars were to be thrown off the track at some point between Harrisburg and Baltimore, when a horde of ruffians was to 'rush down a steep embankment and destroy in a moment the lives of all on board.' " The editorial was quoting the information of its own investigative reporters. "And the route was followed by Mrs. Lincoln, when no one knew that Mr. Lincoln was not on board; and she arrived safely in Baltimore and passed on to Washington. So there is some pluck in the White House, if it is under a bodice."

THE
WHITE HOUSE

DEBUTS

HEN MARY LINCOLN ARRIVED in Washington in the late afternoon of February 23, 1861, she saw that her husband was not at the station to meet her. William Seward and Illinois congressman Elihu Washburne awaited Mrs. Lincoln and the boys on the platform. The handsome young Washburne was familiar to Mary, a man who had worked hard to get Mr. Lincoln elected. Senator Seward she knew only by reputation, as Lincoln's rival for the nomination; she distrusted him, and was unprepared for the impression he made upon strangers—especially those he wished to charm.

Seward was not tall, but his compact figure held the confidence of one who is accustomed to being looked up to. While he had never been a beauty, in his youth he had been attractive enough to take exception to his enormous nose and his jug-handle ears. Now in his late fifties, he had won his fight with vanity, but still tried to hide those ears under the sideburns of his tousled white hair, and would prefer to be seen in profile, as the ears were comical while the nose was reliably noble-looking. He affected high white collars to set off his strong jawline. His eyes were wide-set, fine, and dark, with bushy eyebrows. Now he introduced himself to Mrs. Lincoln, his eyes twinkling with good humor. It was difficult not to like Mr. Seward, but Mary would try her best.

So it was diplomatic for Mr. Washburne of Illinois to come along with Mr. Seward to escort Mrs. Lincoln's family to the Willard Hotel. The crafty New Yorker had made himself indispensable to Mr. Lincoln; now it was important that Seward come to terms with Mrs. Lincoln, and the company of the loyal Washburne would be reassuring.

. . .

MR. LINCOLN HAD just finished meetings at the hotel with the elderly General Winfield Scott, army chief of staff, and postmaster general– designate Montgomery Blair. As Mrs. Lincoln entered the lobby with her sons, her husband was entertaining Stephen Douglas and a delegation of politicians from Illinois. It might have comforted Mrs. Lincoln to see the familiar faces, had she been less weary and in need of getting the children settled in their rooms.

That night there would not be much time for a heart-to-heart talk about the Baltimore fiasco. After a few words, Lincoln hurried from the Willard to a private dinner at William Seward's at seven o'clock. Return- ing from Seward's toward nine, the president-elect found the main recep- tion room at the hotel so thronged with friends and well-wishers that he plunged into it, shaking hands, forgetting to take off his hat. At nine o'clock he received the delegates to a peace conference that had been meeting for a week, trying to compromise with the secessionists. Ohio senator-elect Salmon Chase and Lucius Chittendon of Vermont made in- troductions. After this, Lincoln held a reception for congressmen and generals who were still crowding the Willard's anterooms, waiting to shake hands, or whisper into the president-elect's ear. Finally, at ten o'clock, he received President Buchanan's cabinet members. He could not have retired much before midnight.

Lincoln joined his wife and children for breakfast on Sunday morning the twenty-fourth, a clear, cold, windy day. Soon he was off to church with Seward, and after the service he spent two hours at Seward's home on Vermont Avenue, across from the White House. Mrs. Lincoln needed time to rest, unpack, and set up whatever housekeeping could be man- aged in a hotel for herself, three boys, and her harried husband. Yet it does seem curious that he would leave them on a Sunday, right after breakfast, to attend an Episcopal service at St. John's—he who rarely went to church—and that he did not return to his displaced family until the midafternoon.

His wife and children would have been grateful for his attention, and he had been in Seward's company almost constantly. The cigar-smoking Seward, with his taste for brandy, and the abstemious Lincoln made an odd couple. Since December, Lincoln had been trying to persuade this brilliant politician to accept the position of secretary of state; now, with the inauguration nearly upon them, Lincoln was still negotiating with Seward over the structure of the cabinet and his place in it, and the two could not agree on a policy toward the seceding states. Seward preferred a cabinet and a policy that would appease the South, and Lincoln would not abide it. Not until days after the inauguration would Seward become secretary of state.

From Monday on, during the week of February 25, the Lincolns' duties in their separate spheres of influence kept them apart. Eager to please the public, Lincoln announced, "let all come that could; he was glad to see and welcome all; he was public property now, and would, so far as possible, ignore personal ease." Perhaps the Union needed this sacrifice; perhaps it did not. But once a statesman has declared that he is public property, the public will duly possess him, heedless of his personal ease.

Society was skeptical of the Lincolns' ability to meet expectations, but they did their best, from the moment of their separate arrivals at the Willard Hotel, where they would stay until the inauguration on March 4. The marriage had depended for many years upon a rhythm of necessary separation following periods of domestic intimacy. Husband and wife—each with different strengths—needed each other for support; the family required the balance between them. Now the steadiness of that rhythm was gone forever, replaced by the frustration that came of constant proximity in a world where intimacy was almost impossible. It is significant that now that Lincoln could not leave home, soon his wife would travel often, and for weeks at a time.

Lincoln's schedule that Monday included a crowded but distinguished morning reception, visits to the House of Representatives and the Senate at midday, and then calling upon the Supreme Court justices in the afternoon. Meanwhile Mrs. Lincoln was attending several receptions in her honor that Mrs. Stephen Douglas had arranged. The diplomatic corps and most members of the opposition paid their respects. The evening culminated in separate receptions given by Mr. and Mrs. Lincoln in two parlors of the Willard. "The rooms were crowded, and everyone was delighted with the ease, dignity and eminent good nature with which Mrs. Lincoln sustained the infliction," wrote *The New York Times*. A lady sat down at the piano and played "The Star-Spangled Banner," and the party joined in on the chorus. A man who had had too much to drink stormed out of the room complaining that the singing was "improper and an insult in these times."

This became the pattern. Lincoln met from early morning until midnight with senators, prospective cabinet members, generals, and Supreme Court justices, negotiated over the formation of the administration, and listened to urgent pleas for compromise by such luminaries as Kentucky senator John Crittenden and his old friend and adversary, Stephen Douglas. Mrs. Lincoln held receptions, two or more a day, in the afternoon and late evening. The weather was springlike, the moon was full, and people walked in the dusty streets without lanterns, coming from and going to the Willard. On March 1, Mrs. Lincoln went to call upon Miss Harriet Lane at the White House. Miss Lane, the thirty-year-old niece of President Buchanan, had been hostess and "Democratic Queen" of the White House during the four years of her bachelor uncle's term. She could not have been more gracious, having invited Mrs. Lincoln weeks earlier "to accept the hospitalities of the White House immediately on her arrival here, in order that she may have an opportunity of inspecting the apartments before she takes possession, and to familiarize herself with the internal management of the Presidential mansion."

Harriet Lane had flaxen-blond hair, wide-set eyes of violet blue, and a tall, shapely figure, and she moved with regal grace. Orphaned in her teens, she was adopted by Buchanan, who saw to it that she was given the finest education. She graduated from the Georgetown Visitation Convent in 1848, while her uncle was secretary of state. Ever tactful and vivacious, Miss Lane "filled the White House with gaiety and flowers" and worked tirelessly to diffuse tensions at her parties during the "gathering storm" of the late 1850s. A popular and widely admired hostess, she would be a hard act to follow.

The White House that had been good enough for Buchanan looked seedy to Mrs. Lincoln. She could not conceal her disdain for the peeling wallpaper, threadbare carpets, outmoded chandeliers, and the "deplorably shabby condition as to furniture (which looked as if it had been brought in by the first President)," according to Mrs. Lincoln's cousin, Elizabeth Grimsley. Downstairs, passing the imposing columned entrance of the North Portico and the enormous vestibule, Mrs. Lincoln could see that some effort had been made to maintain the elegance of the East Room, where she had met the Polks and Dolley

Madison in 1849, and the Blue and Red rooms. But it was a faded, threadbare grandeur.

The upstairs rooms, particularly the family and guest rooms, were a
fright, fit for bats and ghosts. Where two decent beds might have sufficed
for President Buchanan and his niece, the Lincolns would need a dozen
for their present ménage; and the seven bedrooms had fallen prey to dust,
rust, mice, a leaking roof, and other forces of nature that corrupt ancient
bedding and wooden furniture. It would all have to be thrown out or done
over, and Mary Lincoln saw instantly the means by which she could prove
herself worthy of her role.

DURING THE TWO days before the inauguration, Lincoln withdrew to
polish his address and make final decisions about the cabinet. At last the
Lincolns would have some time to converse, and he could share his
speech with her. Lincoln and Seward had put their heads together over it,
and Seward had made valuable suggestions, particularly concerning the
concluding sentences. He had suggested the poetic trope of the bonds of
affection among brethren that will not be broken and had gone so far as to
produce the phrase "mystic chords," yet something essential was lacking.
The Lincolns had brought the little ocher-covered book of Albert
Laighton's poems from Springfield. Steeped in the Maine poet's work for
eight months, they could recall the final lines of "In Memoriam":

> *O, moaning wind! O, falling leaf!*
> *Ye shall not fill my soul with grief*
> *For her whose feet so early trod*
> *The starry steeps that lead to God!*
> *Whose heart shall never bear again*
> *Life's weight of weariness and pain.*
> *Tenderly and joyfully*
> *Thrill the chords of memory!*

Now the final paragraph of the inaugural address required only the influence of Laighton's verse to achieve its poetic apotheosis: "The mystic
chords of memory, stretching from every battlefield, and patriot grave, to
every living heart and hearthstone, all over this broad land, will yet swell

the chorus of the Union, when again touched, as surely they will be, by the better angels of our nature."

What time the Lincolns had that weekend to discuss the speech had to be carved out of a schedule that was joyful, if hectic, for all. On Saturday, March 2, a party of eighteen friends and family arrived at the Willard, having traveled to Washington from Springfield on the train. These included Mrs. Ninian Edwards (Elizabeth Todd); Mrs. Lincoln's cousin, thirty-six-year-old Elizabeth Todd Grimsley; Mrs. Charles Kellogg (Margaret Todd) and her husband; Edward L. Baker (editor of the *Illinois State Journal*) and his wife, who was Ninian and Elizabeth's daughter Julia; Miss Elizabeth Edwards, also a daughter of Ninian and Elizabeth; and Mrs. Clement B. White (Martha Todd).

All the family members were the Lincolns' guests at the hotel until after the inauguration, and then several would stay at the White House. Mrs. Lincoln saw to it that everyone was comfortable. The little clan would be a support to her as she navigated the unfamiliar rapids of Washington society and protocol. Saturday night she held a reception for ladies at Willard's, which the crème of Washington society avoided. According to Mrs. Howard Taft, who did show up that evening, "The Lincolns were not welcome in the capital."

Inauguration Day, March 4, dawned chilly and overcast. Neither of the Lincolns had slept soundly. She paced by the window much of the night watching strangers come and go; he rose at dawn to study his speech. More than thirty thousand people were gathering for the swearing in of the new president, but the crowd was orderly. Hearing dozens of reported threats of assassination, General Scott had seen to it there was adequate deterrence: All along Pennsylvania Avenue, green-coated sharpshooters stood guard on housetops, while troops blocked off the side streets. Nearer the Capitol, the general had stationed two batteries of light artillery to the north and south.

The morning had been gloomy, but now the slanting light of late winter was breaking through the clouds to shine on the inaugural parade. Tight security measures, as well as protocol, required that the Lincolns make their way to the Capitol separately. At the stroke of noon, portly James Buchanan arrived at the Willard to escort his successor to the ceremony. A band played "Hail to the Chief" when the men exited the hotel. As Lincoln and Buchanan rode along in an open barouche with Maryland senator James A. Pearce—a Democrat—and Lincoln's old friend, Senator

Edward D. Baker, the bystanders could scarcely see them for their mounted guard of one hundred marshals in costumes of orange, pink, and blue.

While Lincoln was preoccupied with the state of the Union and the speech that was scrolled in his hand, his wife's attention would be divided between thoughts of him and of the impression she would make in the gallery of the Senate. Such hours reveal the dynamics of a marriage. Although man and wife are gazing in the same direction, he falls within her line of sight, while she is invisible to him.

Escorted by Senators James Dixon of Connecticut and John P. Hale of New Hampshire, Mary Lincoln rode in a carriage with her sons and sisters, and took her place in the diplomatic gallery of the Senate chamber. Looking down, she saw her husband and James Buchanan seated up front, below the secretary's desk, with the Supreme Court justices. They watched Mary's tall, handsome cousin from Kentucky, Vice President John C. Breckinridge, deliver the oath of office to his successor, Hannibal Hamlin, who in turn swore in Breckinridge as senator from Kentucky. Within six months, young Breckinridge would be a brigadier general in the Confederate army.

Outside, the sky was brightening, and the sun shone upon the sea of bobbing black top hats. The audience enjoyed the fine martial music of the bands, and "the antics of a lunatic, who climbed a tall tree in front of the capitol and made a long political speech, claiming to be the rightful President." Festivity concealed profound anxiety. At a quarter to one, the crowd saw the stout Senator John P. Hale emerge from the central door of the Capitol with Judge David Davis, Mrs. Lincoln, her sons, and her sisters. They took their seats upon the platform, and soon came the fat clerk of the Supreme Court carrying the Bible, leading old Justice Roger Taney by the hand.

Lincoln and Buchanan emerged into the sunlight, and the crowd cheered them. Then the parade of dignitaries filled the stands— diplomats, congressmen, judges, and military officers of high rank. When all were seated, Senator Baker introduced Lincoln with a simple sentence: "Fellow citizens, Abraham Lincoln, President of the United States, will now proceed to deliver his inaugural address."

As Lincoln rose, "calm, collected and serene in manner, and put on his spectacles," Mrs. Grimsley, seated with Mrs. Lincoln, observed how much of Springfield had made its way to the center of the tableau. Here was Mr. Lincoln, behind him his wife and her sisters and sons; here was Edward Baker, after whom Lincoln had named his late son; here was Stephen Douglas, who stepped forward to take Lincoln's hat, saying if he could not be president, he could at least be the president's hat-bearer.

Mr. Lincoln spoke for thirty-five minutes; "his cheerfulness was marked, and his clear, firm tones of voice . . . penetrated the extremeties of the hushed and attentive crowd, who covered acres of ground." His dedication to international law, the Constitution, and the Union brought hearty and prolonged cheers from the audience; and he stirred the greatest response with his final appeal: "*You* have no oath registered in Heaven to destroy the government, while *I* shall have the most solemn one to 'preserve, protect, and defend' it." Many rounds of applause and cheering stopped the speech for a while, and after Lincoln closed with his poetic phrases, invoking "the better angels of our nature," men lifted their hats and women waved handkerchiefs, clapping and cheering for a long time.

The parade of the presidential party to the White House, escorted by cavalry clattering around their carriages and citizens swarming and cheering, provided a raucous transition from ceremony to an elusive privacy. For ten days no rain had fallen, so boots and carriage wheels and horses' hooves kicked up a grainy cloud of dust on Pennsylvania Avenue, making it difficult to breathe or see. When the procession arrived at the curving driveway before the Executive Mansion and the military gave their parting salute, then the family at last could begin to relax. "The gate closed upon Mr. Lincoln and his suite, and he was safely and comfortably installed in his new home," observed the *Tribune* reporter. But the gate did not lock.

Under Harriet Lane's supervision, the cook, butlers, and waiters of the White House served an elegant dinner for seventeen of the Lincolns and their relatives. "Needless to say," Mrs. Grimsley recalled, "after the excitement and fatigue of the day, it was most thoroughly appreciated." She hastened to add that physical fatigue was the least part of it. The riflemen on the rooftops, the barrels of light artillery, the crowds in pursuit, and the booming cannon had kept the whole party from Springfield in fear for their lives.

Mr. Lincoln could not eat his meal without interruption. Nearly a thousand people appeared outside the door, "the delegation from New York," and they would not be quiet until he rose and went to the portico to greet them. He made a two-minute speech, which seemed to satisfy them, and then he returned to the table. After the company had eaten, Mrs. Grimsley recalled, "We scattered to our various rooms for a short rest before preparing for the Inaugural Ball." Now the president and his wife might have an hour or two of privacy upstairs in which to review the events of the day—if the little boys did not take all their attention at bedtime with their questions and demands.

The Marine Band was tuning up; the ball was soon in progress in the "white muslin Palace of Aladdin," a temporary wood-frame and canvas pavilion behind City Hall, a ten-block carriage ride east on D Street. The president and his wife arrived at a quarter to eleven. Entering the grand makeshift "palace," all aglow with high-hanging lanterns, Senator Henry B. Anthony and Vice President Hamlin walked on either side of the president, who was pulling self-consciously at his white kid gloves. Senator Douglas escorted Mrs. Lincoln, who was dressed in blue silk and wearing a necklace and bracelets of gold and pearls. "Tonight," wrote one reporter, she is "more charmingly *distinguée* than ever. She seems to feel that her station is as high as that of any of the Queens of earth, and yet she does not, with all her dignity, mingle any sign of hauteur." As the band struck up "Hail Columbia," Mr. Lincoln and Washington's mayor, arm in arm, led a grand march across the pavilion, and Mrs. Lincoln followed with Stephen Douglas. Then the president stood with Mrs. Hamlin at the upper end of the room, at the head of the receiving line, while Mary stood lower down.

By 11:30, when aides informed him it was time to enter the supper room, it was evident that Lincoln was already exhausted. In the room set aside for eating and drinking, local chef Gautier had raised an astonishing vista of his famous pyramids of meats and cakes—and in only an hour it would be time for the dancing of the ceremonial quadrille. At 12:30, Mrs. Lincoln and her partner Douglas led the dance. Behind them came Vice President Hamlin and Mary's niece, the pretty Miss Elizabeth Edwards, "acknowledged to be the belle of the evening" by the Baltimore *Sun* reporter. Mr. Lincoln danced reluctantly, if at all. By two o'clock the president was gone, leaving his wife to oversee the dancing and socializing until four o'clock in the morning.

The president had too much on his mind to enjoy the inaugural ball. He later recalled, "The first thing that was handed to me ... when I came from the inauguration was the letter from Major Robert Anderson [of Fort

Sumter] saying that their provisions would be exhausted before an expedition could be sent to their relief." Lincoln's response could determine whether or not there would be war.

He had left his wife behind, dancing in the "white muslin Palace of Aladdin," and now found himself in a stark, unforgiving reality.

As JOSEPH HOWARD remarked in a dispatch to *The New York Times* dated March 10: "There are duties, connected with the Presidential office. . . . social necessities which must be met, and on the fulfillment of which depends in no small degree the harmony of our relations with the rest of mankind." These duties the president and his wife had every intention of fulfilling.

Mrs. Lincoln took her role as "mistress of the White House" as seriously as her husband took his role as president. While Lincoln arranged for the confirmation of his cabinet members, among whom Seward was at first the most recalcitrant and overbearing, Mrs. Lincoln prepared for the public receptions. She interviewed half a dozen dressmakers, finally choosing a forty-three-year-old ex-slave named Elizabeth Keckley. Tall and dignified, the attractive seamstress had bought her freedom only six years earlier and started her own business in Washington, where her clients included the wife of Senator Jefferson Davis. Mrs. Lincoln's choice of the dressmaker of Varina Davis—whose taste was faultless—was politically shrewd. In Washington, she would be dressing to please a Southern audience. Mrs. Keckley went to work immediately on Mrs. Lincoln's dress, then on that of her cousin, Mrs. Grimsley.

In the afternoon of March 7, the cabinet and the diplomatic corps had a sampling of the Lincolns' hospitality as the foreign ministers and ambassadors—many in their colorful native dress—paid their official visits to the White House. During the hour-long levee, "President Lincoln was constantly engaged in animated conversation" with the dignitaries, as was his wife, who was formally presented just after the cabinet members. The minister from Portugal made a speech in French, which Mrs. Lincoln understood without the translation that had been provided for the president.

On March 8, after supper, the bedrooms upstairs bustled with the activities of five ladies and one gentleman, attended by various maids and valets, getting dressed for the first public levee, which was to commence at eight o'clock. The ladies had conferred, seeing to it that their dresses were varied in color and appropriate to the occasion. Miss Edwards's embroidered Paris muslin, and the little diamond cross she wore around her neck, were becoming to a very young lady. Tall Mrs. Grimsley, in a headdress of white roses, wearing blue watered silk, her long train studded with turquoises and pearls, was yet not overpowering. Mrs. Baker shone in a low-necked lemon-colored dress with short sleeves and a long train, a point lace cape, and a headdress of red verbenas with gold sprays. Mrs. Kellogg and Mrs. Edwards, Mary's sisters, were subdued, Margaret in a pearl-colored brocade, with white and red camellias in her hair, Elizabeth in a brown satin brocade.

Mrs. Lincoln was in a state of agitation that accelerated into panic as the hour neared 7:30 and her new mulatto modiste had yet to arrive with the dress she had ordered. It was a crimson watered silk adorned with pearls, a point lace cape, and trimmings—an intricate piece of work—and as the hour drew near she became convinced that the garment would never arrive. Losing her temper altogether, she declared that she was not going downstairs to the reception at all, ever, "for the reason that she had nothing to wear." In vain her sisters pleaded with her: There was still time, there were other dresses.

Just then the busy seamstress hurried up the stairs with the dress on her arm, and Mrs. Lincoln's dismay turned to fury. "Mrs. Keckley, you have disappointed me—deceived me. Why do you bring my dress at this late hour?"

Mrs. Keckley explained that she had just finished it, and thought she would be on time.

"But you are not on time, Mrs. Keckley; you have bitterly disappointed me. I have no time now to dress, and what is more, I will not dress, and go downstairs." The dressmaker apologized. She begged Mrs. Lincoln to allow her to dress her, promising to have her ready in a few minutes. The angry woman refused. "No," she continued, "I won't be dressed. I will stay in my room. Mr. Lincoln can go down with the other ladies."

It took all of the pleading and cajoling of the dressmaker and the five ladies to get Mrs. Lincoln to arise and allow herself to be outfitted. When she saw the magnificent dress on her, perfectly constructed and fitted, she began to soften. As Mrs. Keckley was arranging the headdress of white and red camellias and pearls, Mr. Lincoln entered with Willie and Tad. He came to her, in his plain black suit, the frock coat with the wide "turnover collar." She saw that his black hair was slicked down, shiny, and parted in the middle in a fashion that he did not fancy but seemed to think suitable for this evening. He threw himself on the sofa, quoting poetry all the while to divert her, while pulling on his white gloves, which he hated.

"You seem to be in a poetical mood to-night," said Mrs. Lincoln, amused in spite of herself. "Yes, Mother, these are poetical times," he replied. He told her how charming she looked in her new dress, what a success Mrs. Keckley had made. Then he complimented the other ladies.

The roar of the crowd below, several thousand friends and strangers jamming the North Portico and backed up to Lafayette Square, had been building for hours. The time had come to go downstairs. Mrs. Lincoln had one more spell of distress, refusing to descend when she could not find her handkerchief. Tad had run off with it and put the precious accessory out of sight. "The handkerchief found, all became serene. Mrs. Lincoln took the President's arm, and with smiling face led the train below. I was surprised at her grace and composure," Mrs. Keckley recalled.

If Mrs. Lincoln had stage fright and took it out on her seamstress, if Mr. Lincoln affected to part his hair in the middle, it is no wonder. All of America that could squeeze into the vestibule and parlors of the White House to ogle, size up, and otherwise judge the president and his wife were going to amazing trouble to do so, from cabinet members and Supreme Court justices to matrons of Washington society, from generals and diplomats to the rank-and-file citizens who had come from far away to say they had been there. It was the first and perhaps the most heavily attended social event of the Lincolns' tenure in Washington; it was also "the last public function in Lincoln's administration in which representatives of both North and South mingled freely." Their premiere levee was a success beyond any expectations.

Near the door of the East Room the president stood, towering over the visitors, his head bowing, his arm working like a sawyer's, shaking hands. He shook twenty-five hands per minute, smiling all the while and exchanging greetings. (Someone counting said it would amount to three thousand handshakes by eleven o'clock.) Mrs. Lincoln stood to her husband's right, John Nicolay just behind her, with John Blake, commissioner of public buildings, assisting in making introductions to the lady who "stood near her husband with dignity and ease. Self possession, under such circumstances one would not naturally expect, but it was there." Joseph Howard of *The New York Times* described Mrs. Lincoln's "naturally pleasing manner, an open heart, and a working brain. Her dress will commend itself to all who admire simple elegance." To the president's left stood the hulking Ward Hill Lamon in his lacy shirt, his drooping mustache, his long hair curling over his collar, a pistol tucked in his waistband.

"Mrs. Lincoln is eminently qualified for her position," the journalist continued. Howard judged that there had never been such a levee, and that it could not have been more perfect. "Mr. & Mrs. Lincoln sustained the fatigue of the day with remarkable ease . . . we congratulate alike them and our country that the first reception given . . . was so eminently popular, successful, and complete in all essential particulars." This auspicious beginning, which had favorably impressed so many, sent a clear message to Washington society that she was as capable as Mrs. Polk or Miss Lane of sustaining "the responsible place which she has been called to fill."

John Nicolay, who had been put in charge of White House protocol upon the family's arrival in Washington—much to Mrs. Lincoln's invidious displeasure—wrote proudly to his fiancée, Therena Bates, that "the event was voted by all the 'oldest inhabitants' to have been the most successful ever known there." Nicolay was a hard man to please, but even he had to admit they were off to a good start. A serious journalist of twenty-eight when Lincoln tapped him to be his personal secretary, Nicolay, unlike the boyish, handsome John Hay, looked older than his years. A native of Bavaria, he had a gaunt, goatish face, a little widow's peak of hair on his broad, high forehead, and large ears that he covered with the hair left on the sides of his head. His White House responsibilities had made him still more serious, even stern, so that he was often called the Cerberus of Lincoln's office, the fierce doorkeeper with the awful power of denying people access to the president.

Now, consulting manuals of protocol and the secretary of state, Nicolay was busy helping to direct the change in administrations. In those days the changing of tenants in the Executive Mansion was informal, to say the least. The ceremony and practical transition consisted of little more than Miss Lane's welcome dinner, and one family departing and a new one taking their place, with polite words in passing. Buchanan, for instance, advised Lincoln that one of the water wells was more salubrious than another. He also made the memorable comment that if Lincoln was as happy entering the White House as Buchanan was upon leaving it, "you are the happiest man in this country." Edward McManus, the doorkeeper,

Thomas Burns, his assistant, Thomas Stackpole, the steward, and a cook and a few maids stayed on to offer continuity.

The ritualized protocol that John Nicolay learned on the job did not apply to daily domestic life in the White House. That was left for the new family to improvise, and never was this more of a challenge than it was in 1861, on the threshold of civil war. Washington stood literally in the line of fire between North and South, and death and danger would become familiar to this family.

No president with small children had ever lived in the White House, so there was neither precedent nor provision for such a household. The Lincolns were surprised to discover that not only were they living in a fishbowl, but most of their house was a public concourse, like a hotel lobby or a government bureau, where anyone could and did enter, loiter, and wander about. A percentage of the visitors—all of whom came on "important" business to see the president—did not respect the boundaries between the public spaces and private quarters. McManus opened the door at nine o'clock in the morning, and political beggars who had crowded the portico tumbled into the vestibule. They quickly filled the downstairs waiting rooms and lined up, pushing and jostling to ascend the stairway to another waiting room adjacent to Lincoln's office. Their voices could be heard all over the house. It was the custom of the democracy that the public must be admitted, but the crisis of the times made that custom a barbarous anachronism.

During the first month, Mrs. Grimsley observed, "the house was full of office seekers; halls, corridors, offices, and even private apartments were invaded; and this throng continued and increased for weeks, intercepting the President on his way to his meals." At night some hid, and in the morning the president would step over their sleeping forms in the corridor on the way to his office. According to John Hay, the president "was extremely unmethodical; it was a four-years struggle on Nicolay's part and mine to get him to adopt some systematic rules. . . . Anything that kept the people themselves away from him he disapproved." All such efforts on Mrs. Lincoln's part, and the secretaries', met with resistance.

So the young family found the turmoil in their new home almost incessant, and the Lincolns persuaded the sturdy, matronly Mrs. Grimsley to stay on until they found their bearings. It would be six months before that kind lady returned to her husband and teenage son in Springfield. After so much change and stress, it is hardly surprising that both of the young

Lincoln boys came down with the measles during the third week of
March. Mrs. Grimsley's recollection of this development, and a letter
newly come to light from a Dr. Inos Blake to his friend Harriet Lane
(March 21, 1861), give a revealing picture of Mr. and Mrs. Lincoln at this
time. According to Mrs. Grimsley, the boys did not like their new nurse,
Frederica. And Mrs. Lincoln, Grimsley wrote, was "over-anxious," and
"withal not a skillful nurse" and "totally unfitted for caring for them." By
degrees she, Mrs. Lincoln's cousin, was "inveigled into the nursery,"
where Tad and Willie affectionately referred to the middle-aged woman as
"Grandmother."

Here is Dr. Blake's account of the scene as of March 21, the date of his
letter to Harriet Lane: "Mrs. Lincoln's two little boys have been sick with
the measles. After setting up with them all night until daylight and on retiring to take some rest, she directed her mulatto servant man to ring
Frederica's bell and to say to her when she answers it, that she wishes her
to remain with the children until she returned to them. On receiving the
message Frederica went to Mrs. L's bedside and asked her if she had directed the yellow fellow to ring for her."

Mrs. Lincoln said that she had.

"I do not choose to be disturbed so soon," replied the nurse.

Whereupon Mrs. Lincoln "promptly dismissed her for her imperti-
nence, much to the joy of all the domestics."

This does not sound like a mother whose anxiety has rendered her incapable of caring for her sick children. This is clearly a woman in command of the situation. Mrs. Grimsley's portrait of the president, and his
conduct during the children's illness, has a greater ring of truth, which
perhaps does not suffer from similar distortions of memory. She spoke of
the "depth, tenderness and purity of Mr. Lincoln's nature, his gentleness
and patience." Busy as he was, he would press through the oncoming
crowd in the corridor to the room where the children lay, and kind words
"flowed from his lips constantly to these sick children, the anxious
mother, and all others." After tea and a bite to eat, he would read to them
until a messenger summoned him back to work.

Mr. Lincoln's "workshop," as he called his office, lay in the southeast
corner of the second floor, on the far side of the oval library, which served
as the family's living room. The Lincolns' bedrooms were on the southwest side—hers adjoining the library, his beyond hers. The children's
rooms lay across the corridor, above the private dining room. The only

change the president would make in the structure of the interior was to create a hallway at the rear of the house connecting his office with the family rooms, so he could pass back and forth without being noticed.

AFTER THREE WEEKS the Lincolns had become aware that such easy access to their quarters invited not only a loss of privacy, but imminent danger. Threats of assassination came regularly; Mrs. Grimsley recalls one evening when the whole family fell ill after eating Maryland shad, and they suspected someone had stolen into the kitchen and poisoned their fish. The second White House levee of the season was scheduled for Saturday the twenty-second. That morning someone crept into the stables and tried to poison one of Mrs. Lincoln's long-tailed black carriage horses with flour of sulfur.

At that evening's levee, while controversy swirled over the reinforcement of Fort Sumter and Fort Pickens, Professor Francis Scala of the Marine Band dedicated a march to Mrs. Lincoln. Despite the fine work of the musicians and florists, the occasion was anticlimactic and poorly attended. The Lincolns were experiencing the beginning of Southern society's avoidance of the White House. The rest of the weekend of March 23, the Lincolns conducted no business and received no visitors; it was time to take some control over their lives. "The intense pressure," Nicolay wrote that Sunday, "does not seem to abate as yet but I think it cannot last." The president was working twelve hours a day on average, and his secretaries could not keep up with him. They were trying to get him to limit his office hours—ten in the morning until three in the afternoon.

The following week the Senate adjourned for Easter in a flurry, and the president argued with his secretary of state over relief of the southern forts. On March 28, the Lincolns held their first state dinner for the cabinet members, the vice president, and their wives—the first occasion at the White House that truly bridged the political and the domestic worlds. Among the guests was the correspondent for the London *Times,* William Howard Russell, who appreciated the richness of the scene, as he viewed it through the spectacles that he raised, now and again, from the gold chain around his neck. The observant journalist arrived early, with William Seward.

First of all the Englishman was fascinated with Mrs. Lincoln, whom he considered quite ordinary looking, "her manners and appearance homely, stiffened, however, by the consciousness that her position requires her to be something more than plain Mrs. Lincoln, the wife of the Illinois lawyer." He was amused by her constant use of the word "sir" in every sentence, a quaint provincialism, and how "she handled a fan with much energy, displaying a round, well-proportioned arm"; he admired her vivid, gorgeous dress, and her simple jewelry. "Mrs. Lincoln struck me as being desirous of making herself agreeable; and I own I was agreeably disappointed, as the Secessionist ladies at Washington had been amusing themselves by anecdotes which could scarcely have been founded on fact." Some said she chewed tobacco.

That day Lincoln had learned from General Scott that sources in the South had informed him that the abandonment of Fort Sumter now would be insufficient to retain the loyalty of the states that wavered in their allegiance to the Union. If the Republic wished to retain the eight states that hung in the balance, Fort Pickens would have to be given up as well. Seward, in arguing not to reinforce the embattled forts, was at loggerheads with Montgomery Blair and Salmon Chase, among others. Lincoln would have to share General Scott's distressing news with the cabinet before the end of the evening.

The president and his wife received their guests in the graceful ellipse of the Blue Room, whose tall windows overlooked the South Lawn and the Potomac River. It had been a beautiful spring day, and the full moon shone on the water. All the chairs and settees were richly upholstered in blue and silver damask, and their woodwork was splendidly gilded, as were the cornices of the windows and doors. Over the marble mantel, broad mirrors, ornately framed, reflected the glittering chandeliers. The frescoed ceiling was cerulean blue, the walls were draped with hangings of blue and gold. The guests moved upon a carpet of blue and white as one by one and two by two they entered from the bright main hall, and Seward and Nicolay took care of the introductions.

As the company waited for General Scott, dinner was put on hold; at last, word came that Scott had taken ill and would not join them. The Marine Band, at Nicolay's order, played a march, and the company repaired to the state dining room. Taking their seats around the long table were the handsome Postmaster General Blair in his old-fashioned high collar, and his wife, Minna, mainstays of Washington society; Secretary of the Treasury Salmon Chase and his twenty-one-year-old daughter, the beautiful titian-haired Kate; William and his wife Frances Seward, frail now but still striking, with her dark intense eyes; old Attorney General Edward Bates with his long white beard, and his kind wife, Julia. There was Caleb Blood Smith, the archconservative secretary of the interior, and Simon Cameron, the shifty, thin-lipped secretary of war. Hannibal Hamlin and his wife, Ellen, took their seats. Then came the austere, extravagantly whiskered, toupé-wearing Gideon Welles, secretary of the navy, and his pleasant wife, Mary, Mrs. Lincoln's favorite, a plain woman with high, long cheekbones and a pointed chin.

It was a formidable, feisty company of twenty-eight that Mr. and Mrs. Lincoln engaged from opposite sides of the table. Russell recalled "a Babel of small talk" that ceased only when the president launched into one of his yarns. Russell was charmed by the manner in which the Westerner used storytelling as a conversational ploy; "where men bred in courts . . . or versed in diplomacy, would use some subterfuge, or would make a polite speech, or give a shrug of the shoulders as the means of getting out of an embarrassing position," Lincoln would tell a story and make everyone laugh.

William Howard Russell reserved his most lavish praise for the secretary of the treasury and his captivating daughter, Kate Chase. Salmon Chase, bald and broad-shouldered, appeared to the Englishman to be the most impressive and intelligent man in the room, "tall, of good presence, with a well-formed head, fine forehead, and a face indicating energy and power." The drooping lid of his right eye, which seemed sinister at first, flawed his features; otherwise he was the perfect picture of a statesman. Russell found Kate "very attractive, agreeable, and sprightly," conversing "easily, with a low melodious voice." Clearly entranced, an admirer noted "her head tilted slightly upward, a faint, almost disdainful smile upon her face, as if she were a titled English lady posing in a formal garden for Gainsborough or Reynolds." Conscious of her power, Kate was the belle of the evening, and of every occasion she attended. Salmon Chase, widowed for fifteen years, now relied upon his daughter to serve as hostess in his new home in Washington, a role she embraced with skill and enthusiasm. Her father would never abandon his ambition to be president, and Kate planned to cultivate a social oasis that would be fair competition for the White House. She promptly showed herself to be Mrs. Lincoln's chief social rival. It was probably on this occasion—one of Kate's few visits to the Executive Mansion—that the two women had the following exchange:

"I shall be glad to see you any time, Miss Chase," said Mary Lincoln.

"Mrs. Lincoln, I shall be glad to have *you* call on *me* at any time." Kate's response appears as such a gaffe—given the custom that the president's wife did not call upon others—that perhaps the young woman really meant well. But Kate's answer has long been construed as a challenge to the president's wife to keep up with her. Miss Chase would become the first leader of *new* Washington society—Western, Northern, and liberal—to challenge Mrs. Lincoln's ascendancy. People soon realized that the younger woman with celebrated charm and magnetism was not only avoiding Mrs. Lincoln's receptions—she was scheduling her own entertainments to conflict with them.

The absence of General Scott—the seventy-five-year-old onetime hero of the Mexican War, the symbol of military intelligence that all dreaded but must hear—haunted the table. He was said to be upstairs in a guest room, too sick to come down. Not until the dinner plates were cleared away did the president call the cabinet to order in the Red Room, while the women adjourned to an adjoining parlor.

Only then did Lincoln put aside his mask of levity and humor. As the gentlemen stood or lounged with their drinks, the president informed them of General Scott's news and advice: The forts in South Carolina as well as Florida must be abandoned if the eight remaining slaveholding states were to be retained. There was "a very oppressive silence," according to Montgomery Blair, before Blair himself began to denounce Scott for playing "politician and not General." The fault line in the cabinet was exposed. There were those, such as Blair, Chase, and Welles, who believed that the president had fallen too much under Seward's influence: It was the secretary of state's policy to placate the rebels and delay in supporting Fort Sumter. And there were others, such as Caleb Smith, who supported Seward and Scott. A more heated debate might have taken place then and there had it not been for the late hour, the calming influence of the meal and pleasant conversations that had gone before, and consideration for the ladies, who were eager to join the gentlemen.

The next day, Good Friday, the cabinet members would come to an agreement to reinforce the southern forts. But for the evening of the state dinner, Mrs. Lincoln had done her part to set the stage for harmonious diplomacy in that contentious company of men.

• • •

THE DAY BEFORE Easter, March 30, Mr. and Mrs. Lincoln announced
their new schedules: His visiting hours would be from 10:00 A.M. to 3:00
P.M. every day but Sunday; Mrs. Lincoln would be "at home" from 2:00
until 4:00 P.M. each Saturday for a public reception. Three days later, the
president delighted his secretaries by curtailing his visiting hours even
further, closing the doors at 1:00 P.M. That was the plan, but it was difficult to hold Lincoln to it. After lunch he liked to open the doors for what
he called "the Beggar's Opera," the line of people so desperate to see him
they ignored his posted hours, hoping he might relent. He referred to
these sessions as his "public opinion baths."

From New Year's Day until the beginning of Lent it was the White
House custom to hold evening levees open to the public every week, usually on a Tuesday, Friday, or Saturday. Because Lincoln assumed office
during Lent, they were at liberty to hold as many or as few levees as they
pleased. There was one more scheduled, for April 5, which was canceled
"because of public business," according to one reporter. But since that
evening was less busy than most, and a White House visitor found Lincoln "ill at ease, and not self-possessed," the decision to close the doors
was probably personal rather than official. Attendance at the previous
levee had been discouraging, so for the time being the public would have
to be content with Mrs. Lincoln's afternoon parties. The family needed
more time to themselves.

Even under the relentless pressure of their first days in the Executive
Mansion, the Lincolns had not lost sight of the boys, Tad, who would be
eight in a few weeks, and ten-year-old Willie. They would not be ignored.
They were vivacious, and irrepressible—not that anyone in authority was
likely to try to repress them. Nothing united the Lincolns so much as their
love for their children, and in the White House their philosophy was, Let
the children have a good time. They raced upstairs and down from attic to
cellar of the old mansion, taking possession of every closet, nook, and
cranny, as only curious children can do. The boys were similar looking,
although Willie had a longer, brighter face, the aspect of a cherub, and
light-colored hair, while Tad had more of the dark imp about him. John
Hay said that "William was, with all his boyish frolic, a child of great
promise, capable of close application and study." He could draw up a railway timetable, precisely conducting an imaginary train from Chicago to

New York. He played the piano in the Red Room every day but Sunday. Some say that he had a religious disposition and wanted to be a minister. Tad lisped, and did not learn to read until he was a teenager. John Hay recalled him as merry and kindly, "lawless and full of odd fancies and inventions, the chartered libertine of the Executive Mansion." It was Tad's idea to bombard the president's office with a toy cannon during a cabinet meeting.

It did not take the boys long to discover the White House bell system, the chief works of which were housed in the attic. Tad located the central pinion or "yoke" of the mechanism and yanked away at it gleefully, ringing every bell in the house from the president's office and secretaries' rooms to the doorman's and the scullions'. All ran to the president's office to answer the alarm, fearing an invasion or some other disaster. When the assembled staff had been reassured there was no danger, they saw the humor in it, knowing what pranksters had bewitched the bells. A porter put an end to the boys' mischief, and they were barred from the garret for a while.

Mrs. Lincoln soon found playmates for her sons. At one of her first receptions she met Mrs. Horatio Nelson Taft, wife of the chief of the Patent Office, who told Mrs. Lincoln that she had two boys nearly Willie's and Tad's ages: Bud Taft, twelve, and Halsey (Holly) Taft, eight years old. "Send them around tomorrow please, Mrs. Taft," said Mrs. Lincoln. "Willie and Tad are so lonely and everything is so strange to them here in Washington." Mrs. Taft also had a pretty, dark-haired daughter named Julia, sixteen, who agreed to accompany the boys on their first visit to the White House, "on a bright windy day in March, 1861."

The boys got along so well that Mrs. Lincoln asked them to come every day and bring Julia. For nearly a year they played together, spending nights at the White House or at the Tafts'. A memoir Julia Taft Bayne published sixty years later is a precious source of information about the Lincolns' domestic life. She remembers that Mrs. Lincoln was pleasant and kind, a woman in whom she could confide and who confided in her. She recalls Mr. Lincoln as an affectionate man who liked to kiss her cheek, muss her curls, and call her pet names. Between the lines she makes it clear that her elders had drafted her as a babysitter, unpaid and unacknowledged. She ended up spending much of her seventeenth year supervising four lively boys on weekdays, then giving them Sunday school lessons, and at times their shenanigans tried her patience. "In those days children did not question the plans made for them by their elders," Julia writes, about herself. In particular, Julia Taft did not question plans made by the president's wife when her own father, chief of the Patent Office, was about to lose his job. Horatio Taft would need Mrs. Lincoln's support in order to be reassigned in the federal bureaucracy.

"I wish I had a little girl like you, Julia," Mrs. Lincoln said time and again. But if she had had such a daughter, the girl would not have been working for her as Julia did. It is Julia who provides us with the disturbing anecdote of Mrs. Lincoln and the bonnet ribbons.

Julia's mother, Mary Taft, owned a straw bonnet fashioned by William, the renowned milliner on Pennsylvania Avenue. The delicate straw was trimmed with exquisite purple ribbon embroidered with black arabesques, and that same ribbon was used to fasten the bonnet with a bow under the chin. The afternoon after the bonnet was delivered, a Wednesday, Mrs. Taft wore it to a Marine Band concert on the White House lawn. Julia accompanied her mother to the event, admiring the "elegant raiment" of many of the ladies, who dressed in their finest clothes for these White House entertainments.

When the concert was over, the Tafts strolled to the south elevation, where the president and his wife were sitting, to exchange greetings. Julia noticed that Mrs. Lincoln was staring fixedly at her mother's bonnet. Presently Mary Lincoln drew Mary Taft aside so she might have a word with her in confidence—Julia fancied it had something to do with the hat—and she was puzzled to see a look of amazement on her mother's face.

Not until they got home did Julia learn by eavesdropping on her parents' conversation that Mrs. Lincoln had asked Mrs. Taft to give her the purple ribbon that adorned her hat. It seems that William had trimmed a bonnet for Mrs. Lincoln with the same precious band, but the designer ran out of it before he had cut the lengths for the chin bow. This was an outrageous request, but Mrs. Lincoln would not take no for an answer. "I really did like this bonnet," Mrs. Taft told her husband. "I'll have to let her have it and it's provoking." Only the hatmaker himself, William, could think of a solution: He promised to restore Mrs. Taft's bonnet with an equally fetching violet ribbon embroidered with white figures.

"I suppose," Julia wrote, "as first lady of the land, she felt that she had a right to have what she wanted in the matter of dress." But of course that right did not extend to the snatching of ribbons off her friend's bonnet, or pressing Julia Taft into service as a governess. "It was an outstanding characteristic of Mary Todd Lincoln," Julia concluded, "that she wanted what she wanted when she wanted it and no substitute."

MRS. LINCOLN'S EFFORTS to regain control over her life met with little success. "The process of disintegration went on rapidly," Elizabeth Grimsley recalled, "and in a few weeks there was a thorough change socially." There was more truth in cousin Lizzie's observation than she could have known then, and very bitter truth it was.

After Confederate cannons bombarded Fort Sumter on April 12, it rained torrents upon the occasion of Mrs. Lincoln's reception the next day, Saturday afternoon, as if the weather were commentary. The Russian minister and his wife and the Swedish, Spanish, and other representatives of foreign courts paid their respects. Commissioner Blake performed the introductions, and the president appeared briefly at the dreary gathering, but it was the beginning of the end of Mrs. Lincoln's salon as a meeting ground for all. "The Maryland and Virginia families who had always held sway, and dominated Washington society," avoided the White House. Furthermore, many Republicans preferred the hospitality of Kate Chase, and of the intellectual Fanny Campbell Eames, wife of a prosperous attorney, whose house on the northwest corner of Fourteenth and H streets was a magnet for the most fascinating men in the city—including Nicolay and Hay. Many visitors considered Mrs. Eames's to be the most attractive salon Washington had known since the demise of Dolley Madison.

As the president called up seventy-five thousand militia men, and Virginia passed an ordinance of secession, Washington prepared for war. Mrs. Lincoln and her children saw their home turned into a barracks on April 18 as Senator James Lane and Major David Hunter led sixty Kansas guardsmen to bivouac in the East Room. The same night, John Hay awakened the president to inform him of a plot to kidnap and kill him. "He quietly grinned," Hay recalled, and returned to bed. Lincoln had decided he was not going to live in fear, and refused for the rest of his life to take seriously the nagging threats of assassination that wore upon his wife like the merciless drip of a water torture. The next day Hay wrote in his diary that he "had to do some decorous lying to calm the fears of Mrs. Lincoln in regard to the assassination suspicion."

As the Sixth Massachusetts Infantry, responding to Lincoln's call for troops, marched through Baltimore on April 19, a mob attacked them, killing four soldiers and nine civilians. There was growing panic in Washington. Until the arrival of the Seventh New York Regiment a week later, the president was worried that the capital would be invaded because—as Nicolay put it—the three thousand members of the District Militia defending the city could not be trusted. "We were not only surrounded by the enemy, but in the midst of traitors." Under these pressures the process of disintegration that Mrs. Grimsley narrowly observed was not only social, but personal to the Lincolns.

On the day of her first state dinner, Mary Lincoln had written to Hannah Shearer that, while the lack of leisure was hard on her nerves, "I am beginning to feel so perfectly at home, and enjoy everything so much." On a clear, warm afternoon, Saturday, April 27, the band of the Seventh New York Regiment serenaded the president and his family on the South Lawn. The band of brass horns, drums, and fifes played "soul-stirring national airs," as the president, Nicolay and Hay, Simon Cameron, Mrs. Lincoln, Mrs. Grimsley, Julia Taft, and the children came out on the portico to listen. The boys, who had spent the day at the Tafts' house, had returned to hear the concert. Tad and Willie each had a Union badge attached to his jacket, and "seemed to enjoy the music vastly," according to a local reporter.

But that same day Julia's father recorded in his diary that "troops from the North are pouring in fast now. There is now here about eighteen thousand men under arms. All the Public Buildings are swarming like Beehives with soldiers, in fact the City is like a great camp, and not half are here yet." Soon the War of Rebellion would dominate all conversation, the children's games would have no other theme, and the thunder of cannon and the awful impact of gunfire would put an end to Mrs. Lincoln's enjoyment of her new home.

Suddenly that spring there came a new rift between the president and his wife: a gulf of state secrets. He had knowledge of mobilizations and troop movements of interest to everyone, but which he could not share with his wife. Mrs. Grimsley remarked upon this in a letter to her cousin on May 8, speculating on rumors that troops entering Baltimore were "to march from four points into the city. Take possession peaceably if they can," and establish a military depot. "How true it is I cannot say, as Mr. Lincoln will not tell us."

That morning Edward Baker joined them for breakfast. Their old friend, now a senator from Oregon, found his patriotism so rekindled that he wanted Lincoln to appoint him major general of the volunteers. Balding, and showing a double chin above his winged collar, the veteran campaigner looked older than his fifty years. He liked his liquor and a hand of cards, but now Baker wanted more than anything to vacate his Senate seat and go to war. Mrs. Grimsley could not abide him—she found the senator bombastic and patronizing—but Mary continued to admire and love him for his enduring loyalty, as a man she could trust and confide in. There were persistent rumors in the parlors and newspapers that General Scott and the president wanted Mary to return to Springfield for her own safety as well as the children's. While Mr. Lincoln would not comment upon Scott's opinions, he assured his wife that *he* did not wish her to leave. As for Mrs. Lincoln, she would not hear of it.

Social affairs gave way to military receptions. The next evening, May 9, the Lincolns hosted a levee in the East Room for the cabinet and their families, and all the commissioned officers of the army and navy that had thus far arrived in the city. They showed up in parade dress, a thousand or more crowding the cavernous room. And while the Marine Band played, Commissioner John Blake and Ward Hill Lamon—newly appointed marshal of the City of Washington—performed the ceremonies of introduction.

If the gentlemen had their secrets, so did the ladies. In the cold light of day, Mary Lincoln marched into the East Room. Looking around disdainfully at the ripped and threadbare curtains and battered carpet of a ballroom that had been ravaged by the boots and rifles of the Kansas guardsmen who had lived there for a week, Mrs. Lincoln resolved to reclaim and restore her home. She would make the house and her wardrobe fit competition for the salons of Kate Chase and Fanny Eames.

She and Elizabeth Grimsley would leave the next morning for the great northern cities to purchase the necessary materials.

HOUSEKEEPING

M RS. LINCOLN HAD A STRATEGY for turning the White House into a showplace—a center of calm civilization in the midst of pandemonium. On May 10, 1861, she and Elizabeth Grimsley left Washington by steamboat, bound for New York, leading a party that included Colonel Robert Anderson, now known as the "hero of Sumter" for his valiant command there, and Mr. William S. Wood. In New York they would visit the "Park Barracks."

Mr. Wood, sometimes called Mrs. Lincoln's "business manager," was that same suave "organizer of pleasure excursions" who had overseen the journey from Springfield to Washington. During that difficult passage, he and Mrs. Lincoln became such close friends that she asked Ward Hill Lamon to persuade the president to appoint Mr. Wood interim commissioner of public buildings—against Lincoln's better judgment. It was a serious and demanding office, and Wood had no government experience. Mrs. Lincoln liked the idea that Wood would go along with her plans for the White House; the man who owed his job to Mrs. Lincoln was not likely to cross her.

Upon Mrs. Lincoln's arrival at New York's Astor House in time for supper, the *New York Times* reporter said she had "come North mainly to visit her son Robert, who is at college." But Mrs. Lincoln had other things on her mind, and the president would quickly hear of her doings. Obsessed with the commissionership of public buildings, Mrs. Lincoln was in touch that day with confidants in Washington, who informed her that someone other than Mr. Wood—one George H. Plant—would receive the appointment. Worried that this post so crucial to her success might fall into the hands of some antagonist, she wrote again to Ward Lamon, attacking Plant's intelligence, manners, and morals. She begged her old friend Lamon "to speak to Mr. L. on the subject," confident that Lamon would not let her down.

The first week Mrs. Lincoln was in New York she spent $7,991 that can be accounted for. (Multiply that figure by fifteen to approximate today's dollar value.) On Monday she bought a carriage for $900. On Thursday she went to Haughwout's Importers and Decorators at Broadway and Broome Street, where she ordered "one fine porcelain Dining Service of One Hundred and Ninety pieces decorated royal purple and double gilt, with Arms of the United States on each piece." She liked the Solferino*-and-gold Haviland china so much that she ordered a second set for herself, with the initials M.L. in place of the seal. Each set cost $1,195, but the government paid for both. The salesman encouraged her to spend—extending infinite credit, flattering the lady on her good taste—and the more Mrs. Lincoln acquired, the more she wanted. In the same store, she purchased a dessert service for $837 and a breakfast and tea service for another $759. Eventually she would have the old gold flatware of the White House replated at a cost of $1,783. But not this week, when she would also be buying some personal items including two black point lace shawls for $650 apiece, and a camel's hair cashmere shawl for $1,000, both from A. T. Stewart's fabulous "Marble Palace" on Broadway, Mrs. Lincoln's favorite retailer.

After a weekend in Boston visiting Robert, Mrs. Lincoln returned to New York with renewed enthusiasm. Mrs. Grimsley and Mr. Wood could hardly keep up with the president's wife, and later events prove that the interim commissioner was powerless to restrain her. In two days she spent $1,164.98: on "fancy matting" at Humphrey & Co., $96.00, and the balance on rugs—crimson Wilton carpeting for the Red Room, green for the president's office, and more—mostly at Stewart's. Time was running out. They had been gone now for eleven days and the most important business had yet to be done, in Philadelphia.

Public appearances, mostly visiting battleships and forts in the northern cities, had diverted Mrs. Lincoln from her main purpose—interior decoration. Now it was May 22 and she had to hurry home. On the way, her train had an important stop to make. William H. Carryl and Brother, "Importers and Dealers in Curtain Materials and Trimmings of Every De-

---

*Solferino, a reddish purple somewhere between violet and magenta, was a new designer color that was introduced in France in 1859 and quickly became intensely fashionable.

scription," the preeminent purveyors of curtains, drapes, valances, and wallpaper, was in Philadelphia. Next door to the Continental Hotel, the Carryls had an elegant little three-story shop, sandwiched between the hotel and a mansion on Chestnut Street. Inside the store was a kaleidoscope of swatches, a rainbow of samples of goods from all over the world. Mrs. Lincoln spent $7,500 there before returning to Washington on May 23.

WHILE MRS. LINCOLN was shopping, her boys were enjoying themselves at home. Two weeks earlier she had requested that Mrs. Taft's children keep Tad and Willie company while she was out of town, and Mrs. Taft had "consented with some misgivings." The boys went back and forth from the White House to the Taft home over on Ninth Street. According to Julia Taft, Willie and Tad took their meals every day with the Tafts the first week; the second week, everybody dined at the White House. So the four boys had one another, and they also enjoyed the company of the dashing young militia commander, Colonel Elmer Ellsworth.

The picture of the White House family would not be complete without the colorful figure of Elmer Ellsworth, twenty-three, a surrogate older brother to the boys. "A great pet in the family," Mrs. Grimsley called him, and they had treated him like a son since he began studying law in Lincoln's office the year before. He had a room at Willard's, but he stayed most nights in Robert's bedroom in the Executive Mansion, where he caught the measles from Tad and Willie. It was embarrassing for this hero to catch a childhood illness, but, standing only five feet in height, he was not much taller than Willie, and had it not been for Ellsworth's neat mustache and uniform, he might have been taken for one of the boys as he romped with them on the lawn.

Notwithstanding his cleverness and dignity, Colonel Ellsworth, with his curly black hair and hazel eyes, looked like a doll, a toy soldier. In 1861, dolls were made in his image, dressed in the colorful Zouave uniform he had made famous. Zouaves were soldiers who modeled themselves on the Algerian infantry, with their exotic uniforms. Tad had a Zouave doll he called "Jack," innocent of the irony that he had played war games with the original. Ellsworth achieved early fame as a drillmaster who founded militia regiments in the years preceding the war. He got them up in the baggy red Zouave breeches, gold-braided blue jackets, and tasseled fezzes, and wherever the men performed their complex drills they drew crowds. Their charismatic leader also cultivated the "beau-ideal of a soldier" by a temperance that equaled Lincoln's and a zealous patriotism that prohibited him from accepting pay for serving his country. A romantic figure, the little colonel romanticized the art of war at a time when it was still possible—and perhaps necessary—to do so.

Everybody loved Ellsworth. Lincoln took him into his law practice in Springfield, although Ellsworth preferred swordplay to law, and sent him to stump for him during the presidential campaign. On the journey to Washington, he protected and entertained the children. The day after Lincoln was elected, the first letter he wrote was to the secretary of war, Simon Cameron, requesting that Ellsworth be appointed chief clerk of the War Department. But even before this, Lincoln had asked Cameron to make the young soldier chief of U.S. militia, with offices, staff, and pay equal to that of a cavalry major. Cameron held off.

As he waited for his post, the gallant Ellsworth was not idle. In mid-April he went to New York, where he organized a crack regiment from a ragtag crew of firefighters. He brought them back to Washington about the time Mrs. Lincoln left for the north to go shopping. The eleven hundred soldiers bivouacked in the vacant Capitol, in the south wing. There they held mock sessions of Congress, dissolving the Union and uniting it again. Ellsworth called them his monkeys, these fellows who swung from the edges of the unfinished dome, brushed sentinels aside, and paced the parapets with their shouldered rifles. On May 7 there was a Zouave militia swearing-in ceremony that Lincoln and Tad attended. During the following weeks the boys watched Elmer and his infantry drilling at their camp and imitated the soldiers in their games, blurring the line between war and play.

While Mrs. Lincoln was heading home on the train with visions of Haviland china and crimson carpets, the president and General Scott were planning to invade Alexandria. On May 23, Virginia voted for secession, and soon the town across the Potomac would aim cannons at them if something was not done. Soon after Mrs. Lincoln arrived, the president escorted her to a parade and flag exercises of the Seventh New York Regiment at Camp Cameron. On the same day, Julia Taft, her brothers, and the Lincoln children watched Ellsworth and his men perform a gymnastic drill. As she and the boys took their leave, Ellsworth "stood at the corner waving his cap and calling 'Come again'; he looked very bright and handsome," Julia recalled.

That was the last they would ever see of Ellsworth alive. He and his men were ordered to cross the Potomac at 2:00 A.M. and seize the lightly guarded city. Hardly a shot was fired as the Virginia detachment hastily retreated in the morning fog. Giddy with enthusiasm over his first military engagement, Ellsworth led his Zouaves on a charge to the center of town, where they spied, to their disgust, a Confederate flag flying defiantly atop a hotel, the Marshall House. Colonel Ellsworth marched in, bolted up the stairs, and pulled down the flag. As he came down with the offending banner over his arm, the hotel proprietor, Mr. James Jackson, stopped him with a double-barreled shotgun, blasting a hole in his breast that drove a gold medal into the fatal wound. The medal was inscribed with the words *Non Solum Nobis, sed Pro Patria* (Not for us, but for our country). Another Zouave promptly shot and killed the rebel tavernkeeper.

Now the Union had its first martyr, and the Lincoln White House its first funeral. To a reporter who wanted comment, the president replied: "I cannot talk. Ellsworth is dead and it has unnerved me." Neither of the Lincolns could control their emotions before or during the young colonel's funeral; both sobbed at the mention of his name.

In the dilapidated East Room of the White House, the Reverend Dr. Smith Pyne, rector of St. John's Episcopal Church, intoned the solemn words of the burial service over the rosewood coffin with the glass top that displayed the soldier: *In the midst of life we are in death.* When nine days later Stephen Douglas, forty-eight, died of typhoid in Chicago— exhausted from weeks of campaigning in support of the Union cause— Lincoln ordered that the Executive Mansion and other government buildings be draped in mourning for thirty days.

Lincoln wrote a long and thoughtful letter to Colonel Ellsworth's parents, in which he spoke for himself and his wife, saying, "In the untimely loss of your noble son, our affliction here, is scarcely less than your own." The bloodstained flag Ellsworth had died to pull down was presented to Mrs. Lincoln, but she could not keep it out of Tad's hands. The boy would steal the flag out of her chest of drawers and play with it— sometimes waving the rebel "Stars and Bars" in public, where it caused much bewilderment and outrage.

The war had come home to them. General Winfield Scott, called "Old Fuss and Feathers" for his blustery manner and feathered cockade, advised the president to proceed with caution to gain control of the Mississippi, blockade the South and starve it, and *above all* avoid battle in Virginia. But all the North cried—in the name of Elmer Ellsworth—"On to Richmond!" and Lincoln had read somewhere that wars were not won by men of caution. Against Scott's advice, Lincoln sent thirty thousand raw troops to advance on Manassas Junction in Virginia, where General Pierre Beauregard's rebel army threatened the capital.

From the heights of Centreville—less than twenty-five miles from Washington—congressmen, bureaucrats, and reporters in linen dusters watched and waited for the battle. They carried pearl-handled revolvers and silver flasks of whiskey. Ladies in crinolines and bonnets, bearing picnic baskets and parasols, sipped cool wine and gazed through opera glasses over the green fields and undulating forests enclosed in blue and purple hills. The crowd watched and cheered as the battle lines surged together and back and forth in the roar of cannon. Puffs of smoke burst over the treetops and bayonets flashed in the sunlight.

It was a bright, hot Sunday in July. The Lincolns went to church, where prayer had never been more difficult. What could a Christian pray for other than such a miracle as that the battle would be lost and won before any soldier was injured? Hardly a man on the battlefield knew what he was doing or why he was there. The three-month Federal volunteers, in carnival dress—blue and scarlet shirts and outlandish Turkish breeches, some in turbans, others in the checked flannels of Michigan lumberjacks, others in homespun gray—marched into a nightmare battle of mistakes. Men died by the hundreds in the meadows, in the woods, on the banks of Bull Run.

As the Confederate soldiers pursued the Federal troops, orderly retreat turned to bedlam. The departing civilian spectators found themselves in a jam of buggies among caissons, artillery, and ambulances. The screams and moans of the wounded and dying rose from the plateau of Manassas while bodies littered the ground in weird positions, as if they had been thrown from a dray.

Lincoln sat in the telegraph office of the War Department, a small square room upstairs in a humble building seventy yards west of the White House, where he was to spend much of the next four years. He re-

clined in a desk chair, his coat off, his feet propped on an iron safe. Studying dispatches and war maps with cabinet members in the afternoon, he
was satisfied with the results of the battle, which appeared to be a Union
victory. He ordered that the new carriage be brought around for his afternoon ride.

Mrs. Lincoln had instituted the ritual of the afternoon carriage ride
during the spring when it became clear that the president needed a daily
respite and fresh air if he was not to work himself to death. And as the out-
ing gave the two of them some time alone together, she would not permit
even a nearby battle to interfere with it. According to Mrs. Grimsley, there
was considerable excitement in the White House—children and staff
included—but no anxiety just yet. Almost everyone was confident that
General Irvin McDowell and his Union army would rout the Confederate
army at Manassas, press on to Richmond, and put an end to the rebellion.

They were in for a terrible surprise. Returning from his carriage ride
with Mrs. Lincoln at 6:30, passing through the columns of the portico, the
president learned from William Seward and secretaries Nicolay and Hay
that "the battle is lost. The telegraph says that McDowell is in full retreat,
and calls on General Scott to save the Capitol."

That night they did not sleep. Reclining on the couch in his office, Lincoln listened to congressmen and senators, some nearly in a state of
shock, giving eyewitness accounts of the defeat. Five thousand men were
dead, dying, and writhing in pain beside the stream of Bull Run, and this
was only the beginning. Julia Taft's father wrote in his diary, "The
Ellsworth Zouaves are all cut to pieces, only about 250 left out of 1100."
Rumors flew about that General Beauregard's army would chase the flee-
ing Federal soldiers into the streets of Washington. At two o'clock in the
morning General Scott arrived at the White House, insisting that Mrs.
Lincoln, Mrs. Grimsley, and the children should leave immediately and
go north until the city should be secured.

Mary Lincoln asked her husband. "Will you go with us?"

"I will not leave at this juncture." Those were the exact words of the
president's reply, according to Mrs. Grimsley; and just as promptly, Mrs.
Lincoln declared, "Then I will not leave *you* at this juncture." Now the
gruff general realized Mrs. Lincoln's determination, and he would pressure her no more on the subject. Instead he asked if Mrs. Grimsley would
take the boys and leave town, but this request also met with a stern refusal.

• • •

MRS. LINCOLN DID leave Washington, along with Mrs. Grimsley, Robert, Willie, Tad, and John Hay, in mid-August. But then it was not out of military necessity, but to escape the heat and pestilential atmosphere of Washington in summer. Departing on the fourteenth, they would spend three weeks in the resorts of Long Branch, New Jersey, and Niagara Falls.

On the way to Long Branch, Mrs. Lincoln stopped in New York to acquire more furnishings for the White House and clothes for herself and her family. Again en route from Long Branch to Niagara, she spent several more days in Manhattan, according to the *New York Herald*. Taking rooms at the Metropolitan Hotel, she was "busily engaged in shopping and completing her purchases of numerous articles which will be required by herself and her family during the fall." By now Mrs. Lincoln's shopping was attracting attention, and Mrs. Grimsley recalled "we could not step in or out of a carriage without one of that fraternity [of reporters] being at our elbow. . . . Mrs. Lincoln could not anticipate the storm of censure which fell upon her."

Everything about Mrs. Lincoln's shopping interested the journalists, from the price tags to her personal style. They were charmed by Mrs. Lincoln's insistence upon carrying her own parcels—which then became a fashion—and vicious in criticizing her excesses. One wrote, "She has evidently no comprehension that Jeff Davis will make good his threat to occupy the White House . . . for she is expending thousands and thousands for articles of luxurious taste in the household way that it would be very preposterous for her to use out in her rural home in Illinois."

The reality of the situation, which Mrs. Lincoln seems to have understood only dimly, is that the congressional appropriation to refurbish the White House was $20,000. Anything she bought for herself and her family had to be paid out of the presidential salary of $2,083 per month. Mrs. Lincoln was not an accountant, but quickly she learned that the official budget was an insult to her aspiration to make herself and the White House splendid. For the time being, Mr. William Wood was her accountant. Knowing he would not cross her, she lobbied vigorously to keep him in place until her work was done. On July 29, just days before she left for New York and Long Branch, she sent a bouquet of flowers to Senator Orville Browning, Lincoln's confidant, with a note saying, "You will al-

ways find a true friend in me if you would give your influence and support to Mr. Wood when his name comes up as commissioner of public
buildings."

Mrs. Lincoln's efforts on Wood's behalf are surprising. A month earlier
Lincoln had received an anonymous letter warning him of "the scandal of
your wife and Wood. If he continues as commissioner, he will stab you in
your most vital part." John Nicolay and Schuyler Colfax later recalled the
"war" the Lincolns had over Wood, and how for days thereafter they were
too angry to speak to each other. While her husband was consumed by urgent political and military business, Mrs. Lincoln was becoming en-
meshed in the world of Washington influence peddling and intrigue,
flattery and treachery. It is a world that no one can truly comprehend, because the rules of the game played there have never been agreed upon.
She thought that William Wood had become indispensable to her, although he was both dishonest and dull-witted. She would turn against
him in early September.

Marriages endure and sometimes thrive upon agreeable illusions. In
the Lincolns' case, no idea could be more absurd than that Mary Lincoln
was a better judge of character than her husband was—that he was too
naïve and trusting to look out for his own interests. Yet she believed this,
and he appears to have let her believe it as long as the story gave her pleasure and caused him no harm. She wrote that he was "almost a monomaniac on the subject of honesty," and told Elizabeth Keckley, "He is so
sincere and straightforward himself, that he is shocked by the duplicity of
others." On another occasion she said, "He is too honest to take proper
care of his own interests, so I feel it to be my duty . . ."

Once, when Mrs. Lincoln was begging her husband to "inquire a little
into the motives of Salmon Chase," Lincoln replied, "Mother, you are too
suspicious. I give you credit for sagacity, but you are disposed to magnify
trifles." Then, as he proceeded to defend Chase, Mrs. Lincoln said he was
blind to the truth, but that if he lived long enough, he would discover that
she had "read the man correctly." This caricature of Innocent Abe and
Shrewd Mary is nearly opposite to the truth. Lincoln's insight into the
souls of men, Chase included, is now solidly established. Without it he
could not have managed that complex, refractory array of cabinet members, senators, and generals who together saved the Union.

In 1861 Lincoln had risen to a position where his strengths of character
came to the fore and flourished, while his wife, deprived of his attention

and guidance, succumbed to her weaknesses. Acquisitive, she now had unlimited means to acquire; vulnerable to flattery, she was now set upon by a host of professional sycophants, affable serpents; hungry for social influence, she now occupied a high seat of power where the social fabric intertwined with the political. And she did not have the restraint to keep from exercising her influence in the sphere of government.

Removed from the familiar environment of Springfield, Mary Lincoln was disoriented, destabilized. Like a lost child in some cautionary tale, she was immediately set upon by scoundrels who corrupted her. In addition to William S. Wood, these jackals included John Watt, the White House gardener, and a shady former diplomat called Chevalier Henry Wikoff, once an agent for both France and England, now a gadfly and undercover reporter for New York newspapers.

The first snake in the garden, and probably the most poisonous, was Watt the gardener, a thirty-seven-year-old Scot who had served as groundskeeper since Millard Fillmore's time. Mrs. Lincoln loved flowers, and Watt kept the conservatory blooming luxuriantly in all seasons. As soon as Mrs. Lincoln entered the mansion, Watt began showering her with roses and lavender, along with praise to match the posies. Presently he drew her aside in the hothouse to whisper the ancient secrets of leading the life of a queen on a countess's budget. Watt "suggested to Mrs. Lincoln the making of false bills so as to get pay for private expenses out of the public treasury," according to Orville Browning, and then "aided her in doing so." She did not have the moral compass to judge this as being good or wicked. It simply seemed the way things were done in this place, the way they had always been done; the gardener and his accomplices would see to it that Mrs. Lincoln would have the money she needed when she needed it—in exchange for certain . . . considerations.

No one had to persuade her that she needed more money. Every new day reminded her of it, as did the merchants and carping society ladies. As she ordered the contractor John Alexander to begin work on the White House in June—laying carpets, refinishing floors, hanging wallpaper and curtains, replacing moldings and cornices, adding some mirrors and regilding others—she quickly exhausted the $20,000 government allowance. On July 3, she purchased $1,500 worth of Dorflinger cut glass ware from Zimandy's in Washington, engraved with the United States seal.

Ten days before Mrs. Lincoln and the children left for Long Branch, the Lincolns were obliged to host a formal dinner for Prince Napoleon Joseph Bonaparte (cousin of Emperor Napoleon III), his entourage, and forty guests. The president was so busy that day with a cabinet meeting, General George McClellan's vexing memoranda, and approving an act providing for warships, he neglected to greet the prince with due ceremony. So Princess Clothilde declined the dinner invitation, "preferring for the present to avoid the profanation of vulgar eyes," in Nicolay's words. Because Prince Napoleon was planning to visit the Confederacy as well, this dinner was crucial, and there was not enough money in the budget to make the proper impression.

Watt came to the rescue. In those days, as now, influential people were given ample time to pay their bills. Watt drew up a requisition for the dinner that totaled $900 and submitted it to Caleb B. Smith, secretary of the Department of the Interior, on Mrs. Lincoln's behalf. Smith rejected it. Thinking the tab exorbitant, he asked William Seward's opinion; Seward and his wife had entertained the Bonapartes, using the same caterers, and the bill came to $300. Undaunted by Smith's veto, Watt went ahead and contracted with the caterers, florists, and wine merchants to serve the prince and his retinue in high style. They would want for nothing.

The prince, with his royal red sash across his breast, appeared in the Blue Room at 7:00, as the Marine Band struck up the Marseillaise. Mrs. Lincoln, dressed in a white silk and grenadine gown, took his arm as they entered the dining room; Mrs. Grimsley, in a salmon tulle dress, entered with the president. Then came the cabinet members, diplomats including British minister Lord Lyons and French ambassador Henri Mercier, and the generals—General Scott, portly and infirm, leaning upon short George McClellan. Although Mrs. Lincoln and Mrs. Grimsley were the only women at the dinner, it was a resounding success.

The outcome owed as much to Watt's magical conjuring of the food and drink as to Chevalier Wikoff's advice about French courtesies, which, on August 3, 1861, stood Mrs. Lincoln in good stead. The prince at last acknowledged the "elegant hospitality" and admitted that "Paris is not all the world." A reporter for the *New York Herald*—probably the obsequious Wikoff himself—commented, "The President's lady received and entertained the most polished diplomats and the most fastidious courtiers in Europe with an ease and elegance which made republican simplicity seem almost regal."

Such a triumph, the president must understand, does not come without a price. Sooner or later the reckoning must arrive. John Watt continued to labor over the bill until it became a masterwork of double-entry bookkeeping. If he could not get Mrs. Lincoln's $900 sooner by charging the secretary of the interior for food, wine, and flowers, he would get it later by billing the treasury for pots, plants, manure, and even the labor of coachmen, chefs, draymen, and horses that had rendered small services, or none, at the Executive Mansion. (The press called this fraud "the Manure Fund.") The gardener need not trouble Mrs. Lincoln with the details. It was no wonder that John Watt had escaped punishment while altering payrolls during the Pierce administration. The Scot knew the system.

MRS. LINCOLN AND her children returned to the White House on September 5, 1861, to the smell of paint, the racket of hammers, and a cloud of plaster dust. The painters, drapers, and cornice molders had been at work during her absence, and the house would be in chaos until the renovation was finished in October. Money for the work was running out, and so was the president's patience.

He had been concerned with military appointments and preparations, riding all over the Washington area reviewing troops and fortifications. Mr. Lincoln was thin and weak, having struggled with an intermittent summer fever. Now he had another worry: The bills for his wife's expenditures in the spring and summer were piling up, and they were exorbitant. For months the president had considered appointing a permanent commissioner to replace the shifty William Wood. On August 10, Benjamin French, former commissioner of public buildings under Franklin Pierce, had visited the Lincolns at the White House. Although Mrs. Lincoln did not receive him warmly, French went home convinced that the president was about to tap him to replace William Wood. Cost overruns moved Caleb Smith to order that all painting be suspended on August 22, until further notice. By the end of September he would advise there were no funds left to pay for the imported wallpaper Mrs. Lincoln had ordered, regardless of what Wood had approved.

Gossip about Mrs. Lincoln's dealings with William S. Wood had begun to annoy the president. And while Mary Lincoln was in Long Branch, a congressional committee investigating government contracts had taken testimony from an engraver and merchant, Samuel A. Hopkins, that Wood had discouraged him from seeking one government contract because Wood had an interest in a competitor. Later, when Hopkins wanted to sell the government some cannons, Wood said, "Well, I can help you in that matter. Say nothing about the price. . . . If the government wants them, they can as well afford to pay more as less."

In short, the man Mrs. Lincoln had been promoting and defending was a crook. On September 6, the president dismissed Wood, replacing him with Benjamin French. On September 8, a cloudy, mild Sunday, the Lincolns went for a carriage ride, across Long Bridge, past Fort Jackson, and northwest along the river toward Arlington. That morning he had pleased Mary by pardoning a soldier that McClellan had ordered shot for sleeping on guard duty, telling the general, "It was by request of the Lady President." Now as they rode toward Virginia, watching the ducks on the water and the sails on the horizon, they had grave matters to consider. Mary must know of William Wood's dishonest conduct and distance herself from him immediately. The president's wife must be above suspicion and reproach; she must keep honorable company; and under no circumstances should the two of them be seen again disagreeing about the fitness of a public official or military officer.

That same day, Mrs. Lincoln wrote to the secretary of the interior, Caleb Smith, who was suspicious of John Watt. She staunchly defended the gardener's honesty and accounting practices, while mounting a violent attack against her former friend William Wood. It seems there was no honor among these thieves, and Wood—furious at his demotion and wishing to take Watt down with him—had accused Watt of colluding with Mrs. Lincoln to cheat the treasury. Simon Cameron was about to send the gardener to war as a foot soldier, but the next week Mrs. Lincoln wangled him an appointment to the cavalry whereby he was "attached to the White House."

She seems to have had no idea what a tangled web she was weaving. And her husband was too busy with affairs of state to monitor her purchases, conversations, political maneuvering, or correspondence. She was not only indebted to Watt for his infamous Manure Fund, she was much obliged to the unscrupulous Chevalier Wikoff and a dozen vendors and henchmen. So much work was left to be done, with diminishing resources. On September 28, Mrs. Lincoln received word from Commissioner French advising "that no funds are available to pay for the papering of the President's House." This was after Wood had given *his* permission to purchase $3,549 worth of French wallpaper from Carryl and Brother.

For several days Mrs. Lincoln had been sick with chills. She had taken to her bed, where she felt safe. On Sunday the twenty-ninth she was feeling weak, but she sat up and wrote a long letter to cousin Lizzie. She had sorely missed Mrs. Grimsley since her departure in August. Mr. Lincoln had warned his wife that if her chills and fever did not subside in a few days he wanted her to go north until cold weather came. Now it was beautiful fall weather, a cool, clear day, and she lay in the "stately guest room" across from the oval library where her husband read books and newspapers and played with the boys.

"Where so much is demanded of me," she wrote to Mrs. Grimsley, piteously, "I cannot afford to be delicate. . . . If at the close of this week, I am still sick, I expect I will go up to Boston, take quarters at the *Revere House* for two or three weeks—& return here in November. I trust however, I may not be under the necessity, yet I am feeling *very far* from well— September and early in October—are always considered unhealthy months here—my racked frame certainly bears evidence to the fact."

Of all Mrs. Lincoln's letters, this is among the most revealing of her character at a specific point in time—unconsciously revealing, as if she were thinking aloud with no fear of what impression her thoughts might have on anyone else. Commenting on a recent letter from her sister Elizabeth, she launches into a critique of family members in which she succeeds, ironically, in projecting her own flaws upon others. She calls Elizabeth's letter "very *characteristic*—said if *rents* and means permitted, she would like to make us a visit I believe for a season—I am weary of *intrigue*," she complains of her sister's angling, which was hardly in the same league as her own intrigues with John Watt. She grants that Elizabeth "can be very agreeable" when not singing the praises of her children—as if Mary Lincoln never stole a conversation by praising her own. "Such personages" she says, loftily—referring to her sister—"always speak for themselves."

Mary writes that she regrets Elizabeth's "little *weaknesses,* after all, since the *election* she is the only one of my sisters who has appeared to be pleased with our advancement." Mrs. Lincoln is angry with her sister Frances for showing insufficient gratitude. Lincoln appointed her husband a paymaster of volunteers; and while Frances has spoken to Elizabeth of Mr. Lincoln's kindness, "She little knows, what a hard battle, *I* had for it—and how near, he came getting *nothing.*"

Mrs. Lincoln reserves the brunt of her fury for "poor unfortunate Ann" Marie Todd Smith, wife of the ambitious merchant Clark Smith who had guided Mrs. Lincoln through the clothing racks of Broadway. The devoted mother of five children—including a boy named Lincoln, and another who had died recently at age ten—Ann inspires a tirade of more than two hundred words. Describing her younger sister's personality, she uses such phrases as "a miserable disposition & so false a tongue," "a woman whom no one respects," a woman of "malice" and one whose "*wrath,* generally rises, with good people, in proportion to her vindictiveness." Mrs. Lincoln only pauses to catch her breath midway and claim, "*She* is so seldom in my thoughts I have so much more, that is attractive, both in bodily presence, & my mind's eye, to interest me."

The day wore on. Mrs. Donn Piatt would be arriving below stairs in an hour, so the Lady President must bring her letter to a close.

"I must mount my white Cachemere & receive her," she grandly concludes, referring to a shawl as costly as a carriage.

BY THE TIME Colonel Edward Baker returned from the Battle of Ball's Bluff in a pine coffin on October 22, the paperhangers and upholsterers had the White House so torn up it was unfit to receive the remains of their old friend. As much as they wanted to have the funeral service in the East Room, it was out of the question, with gas piping still lying about, uncrated furniture stacked in the halls, and the suffocating smell of paint and varnish.

So what should have been the second funeral in the Lincoln White House had to be held in the home of another of Baker's friends, Colonel James W. Webb, on October 24. The Lincolns, not yet accustomed to the sudden death of friends and relations or the rituals of martial mourning, grieved openly. The president "walked up and down his room for hours lamenting the loss of his friend. Mrs. Lincoln's sorrow was equally poignant," W. H. Russell recalled.

The day before the battle across the river, Baker had come to visit. They sat on the green lawn in a brilliant swirl of autumn foliage, Willie tossing and kicking the leaves merrily before him. The colonel at last got to his feet, shook hands with Lincoln, and lifted Willie up to kiss him good-bye. Mrs. Lincoln handed Edward Baker a bouquet of autumn flowers, and he said, "Those flowers and my memory will wither together." And on that same day, October 21, James Upperman, one of the White House gatekeepers, wrote to the secretary of the interior to report "sundry petit, but flagrant frauds on the public treasury," results of "deliberate collusion" in the Executive Mansion. Upperman's timing was unfortunate, as the Lincolns would have to face two personal disasters in the same week.

Colonel Baker was at the head of the dash on Leesburg, a town of strategic importance near the upper Potomac. The embalming proved devilishly difficult because Baker's body had been torn to pieces by the passage of at least eight bullets. The heavy bronze casket lay in the back room of Webb's house at Fourteenth and H streets, from which it would be carried to the congressional burying ground on October 25. Sensitive, precocious Willie Lincoln wrote an elegy for his fallen hero, and it was published in the *National Republican*:

> *There was no patriot like Baker,*
> *So noble and so true;*
> *He fell as a soldier on the field,*
> *His face to the sky of blue.*

Mrs. Lincoln wore a lilac silk dress to the viewing, with matching gloves and bonnet. This evoked so much ridicule and outrage in society that her associates sent a delegate to scold her in case she was unaware of her impropriety.

Mary's friends understood that her clothing was not the worst of it. Her lavish spending, tampering with White House payrolls, and influence peddling were no longer a secret. From the day of Lincoln's election, his wife had been lobbying to get positions for friends and family and to keep "enemies" like Chase and Seward out of office. Her general correspondence is heavy with letters begging for and acknowledging her favors. "We have for the first time in the history of presidents, a president's wife who seems to be ambitious of having a finger in the government pie. . . . She has ere this made and unmade the political fortunes of men," a reporter commented on October 15, 1861, in the *Albany Atlas & Argus*. "The American people are so unused to these things, that it is not easy for them to like it."

The American people did not like it, and Mrs. Lincoln's scheme for making the White House a fashionable social mecca at all costs—financial and moral—was backfiring. Word of the accounting irregularities and the Manure Fund began to spread noxiously. By mid-October the president was aware that something was awry among the domestic staff, but he chose to look the other way, telling Benjamin French, "I am getting along so well with all here that I greatly dislike to make a break amongst them, unless there is something very definite and certain, impelling to it." Unfortunately the embezzlement rumors mingled with suspicions of sedition—spies in the White House. Watt and Stackpole, the steward, both were known to have rebel sympathies, and soon Mrs. Lincoln would be tarred with that brush as well.

Two days after Baker's funeral, John Watt went to Caleb Smith's home in the evening to relay a request from Mrs. Lincoln. "Mrs. L. seems to be greatly distressed & very anxious that such explanations [of the Manure Fund fraud] should be made to the Prest. as will settle the matter," Smith wrote to Seward on the twenty-seventh. French, the new commissioner, had gone to discuss the scandal with the grieving president, who "declined to go into an examination of the matter but said he would determine in a few days what he would do."

By November, the distance between the president and his wife had grown so abysmal that she confided more in John Watt and Chevalier Wikoff than in her husband. Without a circle of reliable women friends, she had attracted a following of male admirers. These included the estimable Senator Charles Sumner, whose friendship with both of the Lincolns gave him extraordinary access to the president's office; poet and editor Nathaniel P. Willis; English historian John Lothrop Motley; and later the notorious congressman and general Daniel Sickles. Sickles had murdered his wife's lover in a jealous rage in 1859, and was the first man ever to be acquitted on the grounds of temporary insanity. He joined the army after completing his term in Congress, and would lose his leg at Gettysburg and win the Congressional Medal of Honor.

Lincoln did not discourage his wife's social life, but he did not have time to keep up with it. He would drop in upon Mrs. Lincoln's receptions and more private evenings with her gentlemen friends, and have a word or two with them. He was always welcome, but he did not linger. There was more important business upstairs, day and night, with John Hay, General

McClellan, Secretary Seward, and a parade of generals and congressmen who had little respect for the hour.

On November 10, Mrs. Lincoln took the train to New York with John Watt to make more purchases for the White House, but how she intended to pay for the items, or the journey, is unknown. John Hay wrote that day to Nicolay: "Hell is to pay about Watt's affairs. I think the Tycoon [President Lincoln] begins to suspect him. I wish he could be struck with lightning." Mrs. Lincoln and her gardener returned on November 13. On the sixteenth the president wrote to Adjutant General Lorenzo Thomas that "Watt who, I believe, has been detailed to do service about the White House, is not needed for that purpose, and you assign him to his proper place in Regiment."

The president was under intense pressure that week because of the *Trent* affair, which disrupted diplomatic relations with England. Union naval officers had detained two Confederate diplomats bound for London and Paris on a British mail steamer, the *Trent*—a neutral vessel. The action was unauthorized and technically illegal, causing outrage in England and talk of war. It would be weeks before the matter was resolved and the Confederate prisoners set free. That same week when Lincoln was arguing with cabinet members over the *Trent* affair, he was also patching together a State of the Union message, so he did not press Lorenzo Thomas any further concerning Watt, the crooked gardener.

PERHAPS MARY LINCOLN dreamed that all would be forgiven once people noticed the brilliant improvements she had made in the Executive Mansion.

The visitors to her first morning reception of the season, on Saturday, December 7, from one o'clock until three, were impressed. Congressmen, senators, ambassadors, and their families approached the North Portico on that unseasonably warm day and saw the sun shining on the freshly painted Ionic columns. Passing under the projecting screen of columns, they ascended the steps under the gleaming freestone balustrade.

The floor of the great vestibule had been covered wall to wall with a protective canvas floorcloth that had been painted to represent a geometric pattern of tiles. The East Room was now magnificent; the old crimson drapes and valances had been restored and new ones hung, with heavy gold braids and tassels, fine lace curtains beneath overcurtains of red silk and brocade; the newly polished chandeliers glittered; chairs and settees had been refinished and upholstered in satin brocatelle. The walls were covered with a velvet-textured Parisian paper in a pattern of garnet, gold, and crimson. Mrs. Lincoln received special praise for her choice of the Wilton weave cut-pile carpet, which one journalist described thus: "Its ground was of pale green, and in effect looked as if the ocean, in gleaming and transparent waves, were tossing roses at your feet." Overhead the flowers and cupids of the frescoed ceiling shone vividly in the glory of their fresh colors.

In the Blue Room, Benjamin French did the honors of introducing the visitors to the president and Mrs. Lincoln. Despite the pleasant compliments about the refurbishing of the president's house, French could feel a palpable tension in the air. The president stayed at the reception only a little while. The company heard earthshaking cannon fire across the river, where the Army of the Potomac was now said to number two hundred thousand men under the command of thirty-six-year-old General-in-Chief George McClellan. The gunners were running artillery drills at the forts. It was costing a fortune to arm, clothe, feed, and train the soldiers for McClellan's grandiose plans to invade Virginia by land and sea. The expense of interior decoration during wartime would not meet with approval everywhere.

Commissioner French gazed upon the décor admiringly. Bowing and smiling, he presented the visitors, a duty he no longer relished. Long-faced, with bushy side whiskers, Benjamin French had until recently been heartbroken over the death of his first wife from breast cancer. He was sixty-one, and notwithstanding his passion to serve his country, French had longed for death until he began to court the woman who would become his second wife. He observed the marriage between Mr. and Mrs. Lincoln with curiosity. A generous soul, French liked both of them at first; but his familiarity with Mrs. Lincoln over time bred a combination of admiration and contempt. He admired her stamina as she withstood the rigors of entertaining in the White House, whatever the state of her health. But he had grown exasperated with her haughtiness, her bad temper, and what he concluded was a kind of madness: the compulsion to spend money on things she did not need. Mr. French was in a position to know more about this than anyone else.

A week later, on Friday, December 13, her birthday, Mrs. Lincoln was in a panic when she sent for Commissioner French. It was evening, and French had company, so he could not go to her immediately, but he sent word he would be at the White House at nine o'clock the next morning. He awoke with a raging headache, but remembering his promise, he got out of bed, dressed, and made his way through the fog to the White House to see what was the matter with Mrs. Lincoln. In four hours the guests would be arriving for her weekly "morning" reception, and she was in a pitiful state. She and Mr. Lincoln had quarreled. She had asked him to approve the bills she had run up exceeding the $20,000 congressional appropriation, and he had refused. He said he would pay the bills himself, but she had not yet informed him that the contractor's bill alone exceeded the budget by $6,700.

What was she to do? She had tried so hard to do her duty as mistress of the White House without troubling Mr. Lincoln. The unflappable Mr. French, his skull in the vise of a headache that made him see double, listened to the lady pour out her heart to him. "She was in much tribulation," the gentleman recalled. She wept. Mr. Lincoln had gone to work; he was probably upstairs in his office doing deskwork on a morning without visitors. "Mrs. L. wanted me to see him & endeavor to persuade him to give his approval to the bills; but not to let him know that I had seen her!"

Benjamin French had been happily married to his first wife, Elizabeth, for thirty-five years. They built a fine house at 37 East Capitol Street, just behind the Capitol, where they raised two sons. He had recently taken a second wife, Mary Ellen, and once again was as happy as a man can be who understands the adventure of matrimony. French was wise enough to know that there are few things more damaging to a marriage than lies and deceit. The Lincolns' marriage was in serious trouble when it had come to such a pass that husband and wife could not communicate about finances, even for the redecorating of a house, which should be a joyful thing. It was a bad sign that they must have an emissary—also complicitly deceitful—to make peace between them.

Wanting to console Mrs. Lincoln, the commissioner agreed to talk to the president. As he climbed the newly carpeted stairs with their brass rods, surrounded by splendor, French understood the system well enough to know that if the president approved the additional bills, then Congress would make a "deficiency appropriation." He could explain this to Lincoln in hopes he would be relieved to get the business behind him, like the unpleasant matter of Watt and the manure. What French had not reckoned upon was Lincoln's temper. Few people ever saw it, but when he lost his temper he was a terror to behold.

After a pleasant exchange of greetings, Lincoln's usual "How do you do?" and "What can I do for you?" the commissioner stated his business. He went over the budget and acquisitions and the specific numbers, and as he presented his case for approving the overrun, Lincoln's countenance darkened.

"He was inexorable," French recalled. What Lincoln had to say that morning narrowly avoids an indictment of his wife: "It would stink in the land to have it said that an appropriation of $20,000 for furnishing the house had been overrun by the President when the poor freezing soldiers could not have blankets. I swear I will never approve the bills for *flub dubs for this damned old house.* It was furnished well enough when we came— better than any house *we* have ever lived in. Rather than put my name to such a bill I would pay it out of my own pocket!" When he had calmed down he apologized. "If I had not been overwhelmed with other business I would not have had any of the appropriation expended, but what could I do? I could not attend to everything."

Benjamin French, with the finesse that would assure his place in the administration, quietly attended to the White House accounting problems. Long familiar with the byzantine interactions of Congress and the White House, he understood how two deficiency bills would cover the shortfall in Mrs. Lincoln's budget. But there was a rift like a crack in a china plate growing between Mr. and Mrs. Lincoln, and it appeared to Mr. French it might never be mended.

DARKNESS DESCENDING

N EW YEAR'S DAY, 1862, dawned bright and mild. The several thousand people who were preparing to attend the White House levee
could go without their overcoats.

Mrs. Lincoln was regally attired in a black silk brocade with purple
clusters in it and a velvet headdress. Willie and Tad, scrubbed, dressed,
and brushed, stood at her side; so did Mr. Lincoln and Mr. Nicolay in formal coats, as the diplomatic corps "in all their stars and crosses and gold
lace appeared and were presented to the President," Nicolay recalled. Mr.
French was pleased to see the British minister. "Lord Lyons was received
with peculiar distinction & seemed to be particularly pleased to be present." Given the dilemma over the *Trent* affair, this was a relief to all. At
11:25 came the Supreme Court justices, and five minutes later the generals
and admirals in their uniforms.

At noon the gates opened to the public. The crowd that pressed upon
the North Portico and filled Lafayette Square was clamorous, jostling, unruly. The police directed people to line up under the colonnade and enter
in an orderly fashion, no more at one time than could fit abreast through
the vestibule door. They made way for Senator Orville Browning when he
arrived at one o'clock, an impressive man with a strong chin, high forehead, and intense eyes, dressed impeccably in a long double-breasted
black coat that flared at the hem. In June of 1861, he had replaced the late
Stephen Douglas in the Senate. Browning was Lincoln's closest friend in
Washington; they had known each other for twenty-five years. He saw the
president almost daily, and these very busy statesmen managed to find
hours to discuss political, military, and personal matters. Browning sometimes dined with the Lincolns, and often accompanied them to church.

He missed his wife, Eliza, who remained in Quincy, Illinois, and wrote to her often—long, affectionate letters full of news and endearments.

That day there was as much good news as bad, and the mob trafficked in rumors. The unseasonably warm weather was considered unhealthy, breeding smallpox, cholera, and typhus. General McClellan was ill, probably with typhoid. His enemies here wanted him out of the picture—he was ineffectual—and if typhoid fever would do the job, there were many who would not regret it. The presence of the smiling Lord Lyons was a good omen. It seemed unlikely that England would join forces with the Confederacy. The rumors of Mrs. Lincoln's collusion to defraud the treasury now seemed unfair in the light of her gracious presence, as she stood smiling for hours at the president's side, in the East Room she had made so grand. Yet there were darker rumors whispered in the corridor and the cloakroom: that Mrs. Lincoln had secessionist sympathies, that it was the president's wife herself who had "leaked" the State of the Union message to the press so it got published days before its proper delivery on December 3, to the embarrassment of the administration.

Browning stayed with the Lincolns at the packed reception, watching the smiling president in his black suit shaking hands and murmuring greetings. He had a quaint way of shaking hands in a rocking motion as if he were sawing wood—it had the effect of pulling the guests along past him so they could not linger. Browning lingered until the reception was over, after three o'clock.

He walked up Pennsylvania Avenue in the balmy air, and then strolled around the Capitol, in view of the unfinished dome, to his room in the boardinghouse. Taking off his coat, he sat down to write in his diary: "I thank God for his mercies of the past year. . . . And I invoke his blessing upon me and mine through the year upon which I am just entering. . . . Give me grace to do His will, faithfully to perform all the duties which devolve upon, and to shun all the sins, and the temptations to sin which beset me, and to enable me to live a better, and more useful life in the future than I have ever done in the past." Browning was no stranger to sin, and as the war dragged on, the president's friend would find himself beset by temptations greater than Mrs. Lincoln's.

The crowd at the New Year's levee had been immense, teeming with citizens of every station of life. For the first time in his fifty-six years, Orville Browning's pocket had been picked. The lucky thief had gotten Browning's purse, "which contained I think $50 to $100 in gold—I do not know exactly how much." There were pickpockets in the White House, rogues and vandals who would snip swatches of Mrs. Lincoln's new brocade curtains or slice strips of the sea-green carpet for souvenirs. There were other kinds of thieves and chiselers who would steal state secrets, ambush reputations, or buy and sell souls if they could.

Out of the shadows came Chevalier Henry Wikoff, like a villain in a melodrama, with thick dark side whiskers instead of a mustache, thinning hair combed down over his forehead, and dandy attire and poses. He had the ingratiating face and wringing hands of Uriah Heep. Here was a man so completely lacking a moral compass that he himself could not have explained his motives except as a yearning for adventure. Independently wealthy, the young traveler from Philadelphia had charmed Queen Isabella of Spain, who knighted him. He had so impressed Lord Palmerston that the old prime minister employed Wikoff as a British spy in France. That is when he endeared himself to the Bonapartes as a double agent; soon thereafter the police threw him into prison in Genoa, after he tried to abduct an American lady he was courting there. He lay in the dungeon for a year and a half. Wikoff was convinced that the British, embittered by his duplicity, had trumped up charges against him in Italy.

By the time the chevalier wormed his way into Mary Lincoln's confidence, he was fluent in four languages, a master of style, flattery, and intrigue, working as an undercover journalist for the *New York Herald*. Some said a cabal in New York had hired him to provide information useful to them as leverage to gain influence—or even for blackmail. Others believed he was a Confederate spy. He did not really need the money, he just loved to rub shoulders with the rich and powerful and had a disposition to make mischief. Fascinated by the chevalier's knowledge of books, manners, and gossip about the rich and famous, during the winter of 1861–62, Mrs. Lincoln gave this chameleon the run of the White House, where he was seen visiting at all hours. He was often the first to arrive at receptions and the last to leave.

John Hay despised him, calling the chevalier a "vile creature" and "a monstrosity abhorred by men and women." Henry Villard "heard him compliment her [Mrs. Lincoln] upon her looks and dress in so fulsome a way that she ought to have blushed and banished the impertinent fellow.... She accepted Wikoff as a majordomo in general ... a guide in matters of social etiquette, domestic arrangements, and personal requirements, including her toilette, and as always welcome company for visitors in her salon and on her drives." Reporters took note that the chevalier had taken Lincoln's seat in the barouche.

Was she trying, consciously or unwittingly, to get her husband to notice her? If so, the effort was as frustrating as when she had had to rouse Mr. Lincoln from his torpor with a stick of firewood. At least in those days they inhabited the same rooms when he was home. Nowadays he moved in a different dimension, from his bedroom to his office, on the beaten path back and forth to the War Department, subject to forces and emotions she only vaguely understood. Mrs. Lincoln rarely set foot in his office, and she never saw the inside of the War Department, where he spent many hours of the day and night.

At some levees she stood by Mr. Lincoln in the receiving line, "while my smiling guests pull me in pieces," as she confided to young William Stoddard, her secretary. After the huge New Year's levee there were similar receptions scheduled for every Tuesday evening from 8:30 to 10:30 until February 4. That day she meant to break with custom, canceling the public levee in favor of a private party to which she issued six hundred invitations. The entertainment would take place on February 5. It was a bold plan, likely to arouse controversy, and Lincoln submitted to it only after a spirited argument.

"Mother, I am afraid your plan will not work."

"But it *will* work, if you will only determine that it *shall* work."

"It is breaking in on the regular custom." The custom entailed a series of costly state dinners that made Mrs. Lincoln uneasy because she did not have control over the guest list, the seating, or the conversation. Her new plan was to substitute three large "private" evening receptions for the many state dinners.

"The idea is economical, you must admit," she said.

"Yes, Mother, but we must think of something besides economy," the president replied, as if his wife thought of little else. She quickly assured him she *did* think of something else.

"Public receptions are more democratic than stupid state dinners—are more in keeping with the spirit of the institutions of our country, as you would say if called upon to make a stump speech. There are a great many strangers in the city, foreigners and others, whom we can entertain at our receptions, but whom we cannot invite to our dinners." Chevalier Wikoff could be numbered among these, and his circle of sinister friends. Lately

Mrs. Lincoln had been employing Wikoff to issue the invitations to her parties. According to Elizabeth Keckley, who was working at the White House that day, January 8, fitting a dress on the president's wife, this conversation took place in Mrs. Lincoln's bedroom. It was a cold but pleasant day after a successful levee the night before.

The children were playing with the Taft boys at General McClellan's house, a mansion at Fifteenth and H streets just across Lafayette Square. The young general, having recovered his strength, was out riding as the ground thawed. His wife, "Nell" McClellan, had a new baby, and was fond of children; she welcomed the four boys, who had the run of the house. During the holidays and much of January, the boys were together every day. The previous evening, the Tafts had gone with Willie and Tad to the levee.

Now, across the park with its light covering of snow, the boys were busy playing hide-and-seek and war games in the halls of the McClellan mansion. Mr. and Mrs. Lincoln could consider the question of receptions versus state dinners without the children interrupting. The president resisted his wife's idea, knowing it would invite criticism. He was under constant pressure even from his own party—the more radical, abolitionist wing—who found fault with his military and moral leadership, and recently had begun to censure his wife for her extravagances. Traditionally all White House receptions had been open to the public; the only functions with a restricted guest list were the state dinners. Nicolay, supervisor of protocol, quickly perceived the danger, remarking, "Half the city is jubilant at being invited, while the other half is furious at being left out in the cold."

The president let his wife have her way. She had almost always had the last word when it came to social and domestic arrangements, and now that they lived in the White House, she still expected to dominate her sphere. The invitations went out in late January, and they indeed had the poisonous effect that Lincoln feared. Rumors that there would be dancing, champagne, gourmandizing, and merrymaking in the White House while soldiers were freezing on the battlefield made the Lincolns' party a perfect occasion to divide public opinion. Some saw this as a celebration of the new social vitality of the capital; others saw it as an affront to the high-minded radicals, who could not possibly attend the entertainment. Lincoln's relentless critic, the radical senator from Ohio, Benjamin Wade, led the chorus of abolitionists and others who refused to attend. "Are the President and Mrs. Lincoln aware that there is a civil war? If they are not, Mr. and Mrs. Wade are, and for that reason decline to participate in feasting and dancing."

Senator Wade, one of the Committee on the Conduct of the War, was busy flushing out spies and secessionists in Washington. "Arrests are made of secessionists almost every day," Taft wrote in his diary, "and many more might be made with propriety." While Mary Lincoln set the table for the party her enemies insisted on calling a "ball," the House Judiciary Committee was planning to investigate her "gallant" Chevalier Wikoff for sedition in connection with the pilfering and premature publication of the State of the Union message. And the president's wife would soon be accused of treason.

THE WEATHER THAT had gotten colder in January gave way to rain and mud in the middle of the month, and "a good deal of alarm in the City on account of the Small Pox . . . cases of it in almost every Street in the city," according to Horatio Taft. There was also bilious fever, malaria when the mud bred mosquitoes, and the typoid that had sidelined George McClellan; all of these plagues worried the Tafts whenever Julia got a cold, and she got them often.

On a warm Saturday, Willie and Tad joined the Taft boys for dinner at their house. While they were playing there, Mrs. Lincoln sent a courier: "The Madam says you *must* come with her boys," meaning that all of the boys were expected. It was her second summons; the first had been ignored. This time the boys did as they were told—off they went to the White House to play there and have dinner again whether they were hungry or not.

The first thing they wanted to do was run up the stairs to the rooftop. The boys had been having a grand time recently on top of the White House with its views of the Treasury building and the gothic Smithsonian castle and the ever-changing river. Up there in the warm air off the swamp they had built a fort where they could play war games. As Mr. Taft heard later, "The roof is copper, flat & with a high stone balustrade all 'round. They have built a cabin there which they call the *'Ship of State' or rather* the Quarter deck. They have a Spy Glass and report all strange sails on the river and objects on the Virginia Shore. They say that Mr. Lincoln is

Commodore." Ten-year-old Willie was the imaginative one, the story-teller who led the others in their adventures. The thirsty boys would pause now and then to drink cups of water the servants sent up from the White House taps, newly fitted with pipes that drew water from the Potomac. From time to time Mr. Lincoln would climb up and join them, to give military advice and lend a dimension of reality to their fictive world, and he would return to his office refreshed. That particular day, he relieved the secretary of war, the unreliable Simon Cameron, of his duty; he would soon replace him with that formidable rock of virtue and tireless application, Edwin Stanton.

Toward the end of January came a thaw, and the streets were ankle-deep in mud. "There is a great deal of sickness in the City," wrote Horatio Taft, "but we hear less about the Small pox than we did a month ago." He and his family had been vaccinated repeatedly. There were other mysterious, deadly diseases for which there were no vaccinations and only vague terms. On January 29, Willie and Tad walked through the rain to go and play with the Tafts. Twelve-year-old Bud, Willie's special friend, had a bad cough and was too sick to go outside. Holly, after finishing his lessons, went to the White House to play with the Lincolns on the "Ship of State," atop the mansion.

That was the last time Willie Lincoln ever played with the Taft boys. It rained the next day and the next, and over the weekend the rain turned to wet snow. Bud got well, but sometime that week Willie Lincoln fell ill. According to Elizabeth Keckley, who helped nurse him, the boy first caught cold, and then in the first days of February the cold graduated to chills and fever. The child would burn with fever and get the sweats, drenching his bed so it had to be changed; later in the night he would shake with the chills. The Lincolns called in Dr. Robert Stone, who was then considered the finest physician in Washington. Mrs. Lincoln was so distressed that she wanted to cancel the party for Wednesday the fifth, but the president advised her against it since the invitations had already gone out and the doctor's view was optimistic. A few days before the event, Dr. Stone "pronounced Willie better, and said there was every reason for an early recovery." The doctor himself encouraged the Lincolns "to go on with the reception. Willie, he insisted, was in no immediate danger." Closing his black bag and bowing, the physician left the mansion. They were all greatly relieved. Robert Lincoln was home from Harvard for a few days, and his presence was a comfort as well.

Willie Lincoln lay in the "Prince of Wales" bedroom with its dark purple wall hangings and golden tassels—so named for the future Edward
VII, Victoria's son, who had stayed there in 1860, when he was nineteen.
A new bed of rosewood, its headboard ornately carved in the French
style, dominated the enormous bedroom, which opened across the hall
from the president's. Above the bed, inches from the ceiling, hung a
gilded coronet that bore the American shield—the eagle with arrows in
one talon, olive branches in the other—and from the coronet hung purple
satin drapes trimmed with yellow fringes, gathered and drawn with
golden braids. The bedspread was also a pattern of purple and gold,
darker than the lilac wallpaper. The yellow trimmings, gold tassels, and
fringes did not relieve the gloominess of the regal décor, but instead reminded visitors that darkness and death come even to princes. Two high
windows looked out on the north lawn, and a fireplace glowed to Willie's
right on the east wall. A sofa stood between the windows, a tall walnut
wardrobe across from the fireplace. There was plenty of room for side
chairs, a bureau, and a large marble-top table.

There Willie had his toy soldiers, his picture books, and his lap games
when he was strong enough to play. His parents read to him when he was
too weak to entertain himself. Mrs. Keckley saw him curled up in a chair
holding a pencil and paper, drawing or scribbling verses. "He was the sort
of child people imagine their children will be, before they have any,"
wrote the late biographer Ruth Painter Randall. Mr. Taft, who saw so
much of the child, noticed he "had more judgment and foresight than
any boy of his age," and Taft's daughter Julia said Willie "was the most
lovable boy I ever knew, bright, sensible, sweet-tempered and gentle-
mannered." Laura Searling, the deaf journalist who wrote perceptively
about the Lincolns, was always charmed by Willie's appearance. "Willie
had a gray and very baggy suit of clothes, and his style was altogether different from that of the curled darlings of the fashionable mothers; but
there was a glow of intelligence and feeling on his face which made him
peculiarly interesting and caused strangers to speak of him as a fine little
fellow."

He missed his new pony, which he had been riding around the park
and the parade grounds; he missed his brother Tad, who had his own
sore throat and fever. Although Tad was not as sick as Willie, it was best
to keep the boys apart until both were cured. When the fever and chills

subsided, Willie was content with his books, gazing out the window at the sentries, or tracing the birds and grape clusters on the headboard with his fingers.

The day of the reception, February 5, the child took a turn for the worse, and Dr. Stone was summoned again. Mrs. Keckley stood by, to encourage Mrs. Lincoln and get her dressed. The worried mother sat by Willie's bedside "a long while, holding his feverish hand in her own, and watching his labored breathing. The doctor claimed there was no cause for alarm." Mrs. Lincoln kissed her boy and smoothed his hair, then she and her dressmaker went across the hall to get ready for the party. She sat before the mirror in a dressing gown, frowning while Mrs. Keckley began to brush and pin her hair. Mrs. Lincoln had planned the party carefully. She had ordered the wine from Clement Heerdt & Company in New York. Maillard of New York would cater the affair—he had been in Washington since Monday supervising the team of chefs, bakers, and waiters; she had ordered rare flowers from Bucat's in Philadelphia, and others from a greenhouse in New York. Yesterday she had conferred with Francis Scala over the program of "operatic gems" his thirty-two musicians would play. The music must be tasteful, so as not to support the false rumor that Mrs. Lincoln wanted a ball in wartime. She had never intended that there would be dancing.

On Saturday they had received word of the death of Queen Victoria's husband, Prince Albert. So Mrs. Lincoln would dress in half-mourning out of respect for the queen, since the White House was expecting Lord Lyons, the British minister, to attend the reception. Mrs. Keckley had designed a low-cut satin dress with deep flounces of black lace looped with ribbons of black and white. Mrs. Lincoln wore a neckline corsage of crape myrtle bound with black lace. The seamstress pinned it on, then crowned her with a wreath of white and purple flowers. She wore no jewelry but a string of pearls. Her bosom and her arms were bare—this was the style then in evening gowns, which sported long trains a lady had to manage carefully in a crowd.

Mrs. Lincoln's low-cut dress invited a good deal of comment that evening, beginning with her husband's. He was standing with his back to the fireplace, looking solemnly at the figures in the carpet, when suddenly he heard the rustling of crinolines. He looked up at her and, smiling, remarked, "Whew! Our cat has a long tail to-night." She probably did not know that Lincoln's irreverent secretaries had started calling her "the hellcat" behind her back.

"Mother, it is my opinion, if some of that tail was nearer the head, it would be in better style." Mrs. Keckley observed that her mistress "turned away with a look of offended dignity." She asked to be summoned if she was needed in the sickroom, then took Mr. Lincoln's arm, and the two of them went downstairs to meet their guests.

The weather had been bright and clear that day for the first time in weeks, although it was still cold. The moon in its first quarter rose at eight and shone brightly on the freshly painted pillars of the White House. At nine o'clock the guests began to arrive in carriages. They showed their cards to the doormen, hung their wraps in the vestibule, and streamed into the corridor and the parlors. They noticed how the brass chandeliers had been garlanded with fresh flowers; they saw enormous flower arrangements in blue-and-white porcelain vases on every table. A huge Japanese punch bowl was brimming with ten gallons of a champagne, arrack, and rum concoction.

Many people criticized the Lincolns' party before and after, but that night was an unqualified success. The band began with the "President's March" and ended with "Mrs. Lincoln's Polka," both composed for the occasion; and between the presidential march and polka, the musicians performed instrumentals from *Maniello, I Poliuto, Il Trovatore, La Traviata,* and other opera favorites. Nicolay, Seward, and the Lincolns measured the success of these affairs in terms of attendance, by the number and importance of the guests. Reporters judged them as works of art, for the music, costumes, and culinary expertise.

Who attended? Most of the cabinet members and their wives: Seward, Stanton, Welles, Smith, and Chase; a hundred or more congressmen and senators; high-ranking army and navy officers and their wives, including General James Shields, the dashing General McClellan and his pretty wife, Ellen, and General John Frémont and his wife, Jessie. Perhaps most gratifying to the secretary of state and the Lincolns was the colorful panoply of the diplomatic corps. The Union wanted evidence of international support, and it showed up in dazzling abundance—Henri Mercier of France, Lord Lyons of England, Baron Stoeckl of Russia, Garcia y Tassara of Spain, Chevalier Joseph Bertinatti of Italy—all decked out in their ribbons, sashes, and medals. Diplomats and French princes repaired to the Blue Room, where they conversed with Mrs. Lincoln, and even more with General Irvin McDowell, who was educated in France. The Prussian prince Felix Salm-Salm, whose name delighted John Hay, was there to boast of his service as a cavalry officer on the staff of General Louis Blenker's German brigade. On this night there was no receiving line—everyone introduced himself.

Even Miss Kate Chase, the daughter of the secretary of the treasury, honored the company with her presence. She wore a beige silk gown that perfectly set off her copper-colored hair, and attracted so much attention that people whispered that she held her own court even at White House functions. Robert Lincoln was there also, to admire Miss Chase and partake of the champagne punch.

At eleven o'clock the guardians of protocol shepherded the principal players to lead a promenade around the East Room as the band played a march, so as to get the company in formation to move down the corridor toward the state dining room in the southwest corner of the mansion. The president and his wife led the company to the door of the dining room—which was found to be locked. While the steward scrambled for the key, someone in the hungry throng yelled, "I am in favor of a forward movement," and quickly another wag added, "An advance to the front is only retarded by the imbecility of commanders," two comments upon the Union generals' inertia—which even General McClellan heard without offense, in the spirit of jollity.

When the steward at last opened the door, the guests squeezed in. They were "struck with admiration" by the scene, a "coup d'oeil of dazzling splendor." The room was forty feet long by thirty feet wide, and so bright with color it seemed to be full before anyone entered. Eyes were drawn to the exotic blossoms radiating from the five-foot-high vase on the long center table, and flowers on either side in smaller vases. The presentation of the supper was a marvel: The guests forked delicacies from a model frigate in full sail and a Chinese pagoda, made of hardened sugar; little cupids held a war helmet whose plumes were of spun sugar; more cupids supported a candelabrum whose soft light shone upon a champagne fountain of several terraced bowls shouldered by water nymphs carved from nougat. On one side table stood beehives filled with charlotte russe, and on another a sugar replica of Fort Pickens on which were piled slices of carved meat.

They dined on tender pheasant, fat partridge, venison steaks, and Virginia hams; they battened upon canvasback ducks and fresh turkeys, and thousands of tidewater oysters shucked an hour since and iced, slurped raw, scalloped in butter and crackermeal, or stewed in milk. There were more cheeses and casseroles than anyone could later remember. They indulged their craving for sweets with Maillard's famous confections: chocolate mousse, cakes and pastries of every shape and flavor, and glacé à l'orange. They washed it all down with glasses of fine claret and sauternes.

The party, which went on until 2:00 A.M., cost about $1,000, which the president paid out of his own pocket. Nicolay, not given to enthusiasm, called it "altogether a very respectable if not brilliant success," and singled out the ladies' dresses and the food for special praise. The voluptuary Senator Browning went ahead and called it brilliant, and stayed until the end. The reporter for the *Sunday Morning Chronicle* waxed poetical, confessing, "No language can describe that shifting mosaic beauty and gay colors, as uniforms and foreign stars—gems, laces, and illusion—like all the rainbows since the flood, were blended in confusion."

Confusion surely reigned in Mary Lincoln's heart as she excused herself time and again from that dazzling scene to climb the stairs and enter the dim room where Willie lay in a fever. She must check upon his breathing. Dr. Stone had said there was no cause for alarm. But as night wore on and morning came, there was no denying the child was getting worse.

AS THE PRESIDENT had feared, many of the papers outside of Washington criticized the "ball" as showing the Lincolns' frivolity and extravagance during wartime. And the doctors monitoring Willie's symptoms—high fever, chills, and digestive troubles—informed the newsmen that the boy had the bilious fever. It was not so alarming a word as "typhoid," the disease that Willie really had contracted.

Lincoln spent most of the week attending Willie when he was awake, and consoling Mary when the child was sleeping. They sat in the oval library across the hall from the Prince of Wales bedroom. Lincoln read Emerson's *Representative Men*. Senator Charles Sumner had recently introduced him to the great writer, and now perhaps the president might take some consolation in Emerson's philosophy. On February 10, *The*

Washington Star reported that Willie was "much better today, but Tad is thought to have contracted the same illness." The cruelty of the "bilious remittent fever," as the phrase suggests, is that it comes and goes over a period of days, allowing hope that gives way to despair as the symptoms worsen.

That day—a bright, cold morning when the mercury stood at 20 degrees—Mary Lincoln's Chevalier Wikoff was subpoenaed to testify before the House Judiciary Committee. They were investigating sedition in general, and espionage in the White House in particular. Wikoff's connection with the *New York Herald* was indisputable, and the *Herald*'s premature publication of the president's annual message was a minor scandal. It was a victimless crime, since nothing in the publication amounted to a fatal breach of security. But it demonstrated that there was a potentially dangerous security leak in the White House, and the signs were pointing toward Mrs. Lincoln's parlor door.

Chevalier Wikoff, for the moment chivalrous, confessed that he had telegraphed the message to the *Herald* containing excerpts of the president's address. And he refused to divulge his sources. For this contempt, they bound him over to guards at the Old Capitol Prison, a filthy, rat-infested former boardinghouse behind the Capitol, on Maryland Avenue, fitted with cells and locks. He could stay there until he found his tongue, or until they decided to let him out. Another one of Mary Lincoln's circle, the mercurial, hot-tempered Daniel Sickles, was engaged as Wikoff's attorney, but his representations on the chevalier's behalf were so furious that Sickles himself was nearly jailed for contempt.

The chevalier was familiar with prisons. There he reflected, and brooded, and schemed, charming the guards and inmates, who included the infamous Rose O'Neal Greenhow, a secessionist spy (with whom Wikoff had done business), and Mrs. Augusta Heath Morris, accused of smuggling government letters south. Rose Greenhow was a clever and vicious enemy of Mrs. Lincoln, who gossiped darkly about the president's wife from the day she arrived in Washington. Wikoff had a way with ladies, even in jail. He was able to charm these inmates with promises of pardon and leniency if they would let it be known that they would write to the commissioners, or at least get the word out through the grapevine, that Mrs. Lincoln herself had taken the president's manuscript for long enough so that Wikoff could copy it.

This was brilliant work on the part of Henry Wikoff and a cabal that included Daniel Sickles, the lady spies, and the editors of the *New York Herald*. The chairman of the Judiciary Committee, John Hickman of Pennsylvania, was a radical Republican who, like Benjamin Wade, detested Lincoln's position on slavery. While Lincoln opposed slavery, he honored the Constitution's protection of property rights; and as president, he was not prepared to lose the "border states" by joining the abolitionists.

While the *Herald* protested that Wikoff was not their White House source—and disowned him—the newspaper condemned Hickman's "kitchen committee" and his "infamous attempt to break up the domestic relations of the President and sow misery in his family." One of their editorials was titled THE SATANIC ELEMENT OF THE ABOLITIONISTS ASSAILING THE PRESIDENT THROUGH HIS FAMILY, and it protested, "They invade the sacred privacy of his home, and seek to infuse poison into his domestic relations by scandalous insinuations." Of course it was Chevalier Wikoff who had worked all of these diabolical wonders, but the public was not aware of that. The rumors about Mrs. Lincoln had yet to be proven, and he was in a fine position to lay them to rest for certain considerations— like being let out of the cold cell in the Old Capitol Prison. He knew the Lincolns were under extreme duress, as disease had infused a deadlier poison into their household. They would want no more trouble there than they already had with two sick children.

Willie Lincoln was wasting away. Typhoid works slowly and cruelly over a period of weeks, depriving the victim of digestive function, perforating the bowels, causing hemorrhaging and peritonitis. Willie experienced "mental wandering and delirium." Paregoric may ease the racking abdominal pain; delirium may take the child into a haven of sweet dreams, or it may deliver him into a labyrinth of nightmares. Mary Lincoln sat by his side almost constantly, as the president paced back and forth from the sickroom to his office.

The president used to say that he felt like an innkeeper asked to provide rooms in one wing of his hotel while putting out a raging fire in the other. Now as he hurried from the Prince of Wales room, where Mary kept watch over the feeble child, to his office to discuss matters of sedition with William Seward and Ben Wade, he was emotionally overwhelmed. Rumors of his wife's spying for the rebels had grown too noisy for endurance. A deal was in the offing whereby the disgraced gardener John Watt would be given up as a sacrifice for the wily chevalier.

Lincoln could not risk the possibility that a subpoena might come for his wife to testify before Hickman's committee. She would balk; they would have to drag her from the house. He realized this on his birthday, February 12. The next day, on a cold morning, the president set out alone, on foot, up Pennsylvania Avenue to the Capitol; the mud had hardened in ruts too treacherous to travel on horseback. He did not bother with Hickman's committee on the south side of the building, but strode under the dome to the left to find the room where the Senate Committee on the Conduct of the War had just convened.

The guard at the door admitted the president, but was too tongue-tied to announce him. This was unprecedented. A senator later told the postmaster general: "There at the foot of the table, standing solitary, his hat in his hand, his tall form towering above the committee members, Abraham Lincoln stood. Had he come by some incantation, thus appearing of a sudden before us unannounced, we could not have been more astounded. The pathos written upon his face, the almost unhuman sadness in his eyes . . . and above all an indescribable sense of complete isolation—the sad solitude which is inherent in all true grandeur of character and intellect—all this revealed Lincoln to me."

No one had any idea what to say, so they sat still and silent. The committee had not summoned him, and they did not know he was aware they were about to "investigate the reports, which, if true, fastened treason upon his family in the White House." When the president at last broke the silence, he spoke in the most sorrowful tone: "I, Abraham Lincoln, President of the United States, appear of my own volition before this committee of the Senate to say that I, of my own knowledge, know that it is untrue that any of my family hold treasonable communication with the enemy."

Again a heavy silence descended upon the room as Lincoln looked into the eyes of the men around the table. Then he turned and was gone, "as silently and solitary as he came." So without any formal discussion, the committees in the Senate and the House, Ben Wade and John Hickman, "dropped all consideration of the rumors that the wife of the President was betraying the Union. . . . We were so greatly affected that the committee adjourned for the day."

The next day Henry Wikoff testified that it was John Watt, the disreputable gardener, who had filched the speech from Lincoln's study for long enough so that the journalist could copy passages. Watt was cashiered, while the chevalier got off scot-free.

Cruelly isolated, Lincoln had no adequate outlet for the fury and humiliation his wife had caused him. Orville Browning had gone to Pittsburgh on the thirteenth to meet his wife and daughter, and would not return until the twenty-first. Fortunately, he was bringing them to Washington soon. Browning was the one friend in whom he could confide his concerns about Mrs. Lincoln. Although she did not have to endure the feeding frenzy the journalists would have enjoyed had she been subpoenaed, the public at large would always suspect her of disloyalty to the Union, so great is the power of rumor in the rough-and-tumble world of politics. She had several brothers in Confederate uniforms.

Three days later, on February 17, a newspaper pronounced Willie Lincoln to be "past all hope of recovery." In his anguish, Lincoln turned to Johann Wolfgang von Goethe, checking out several volumes of the German poet's work from the Library of Congress. Perhaps there were words in *Faust* that would be instructive to the Lincolns, who might have believed at times like these that they had made a pact with the devil.

YET WHEN THE worst blow fell, they were ill prepared for it.

After heart-lifting remissions on Valentine's Day and February 19, Willie Lincoln's lungs filled with fluid. He died at five o'clock in the afternoon of February 20, 1862, mercifully carried off by pneumonia. A century and a half has passed, and yet it still seems intrusive to dwell upon that horrible scene—the shock, the querulous disbelief, the savage cries of sorrow. A few muted voices have come down to us, voices of those who were inside the White House and recollected the catastrophe.

Nicolay was dozing on the couch of his office at five o'clock when the president roused him. Lincoln had just come from the bedside of his dead son. "Well, Nicolay, my boy is gone—he is actually gone!" Bursting into tears, Lincoln turned away and passed into his own office.

They summoned Mrs. Keckley. "I assisted in washing him and dressing him, and then laid him on the bed, when Mr. Lincoln came in. I never saw a man so bowed down with grief." Lifting the cloth from Willie's gaunt face, Lincoln is supposed to have murmured that the boy was too good for this earth, and how hard, hard it was to have him die. "Great sobs choked his utterance. He buried his head in his hands, and his tall frame was convulsed with emotion. . . . His grief unnerved him."

Senator Browning arrived at about this time, bringing some bills from the Senate. Nicolay told him Willie had just died, whereupon Browning hurried to see to Mrs. Lincoln. While the president's outburst allowed for depiction, his wife's did not. The witnesses remain silent about it, except for Mrs. Keckley, who made a halting and purple attempt that does not bear repeating except for the phrases, "Mrs. Lincoln's grief was inconsolable. The pale face of her dead boy threw her into convulsions. . . . paroxysms of grief. . . ." Seeing the woman prostrated and convulsed, Browning immediately sent a courier for his wife, Eliza. The Brownings had known the Lincolns since before they were married, and Mrs. Browning, now fifty-five, was an earthy, wise woman who would know how to handle this situation if anyone could. With Tad's mother completely disabled, one of the greatest immediate concerns was the younger child, who was not quite as sick as Willie had been. Listening to the screaming, thrashing, and sobbing in the adjoining room, Tad was frightened to hear that Death had come for his older brother—like the hooded reaper in a picture book—and now Death might be coming to take him, too. The president was lying down with Tad in his bed, and it is hard to say who was consoling whom. For the moment, according to Mrs. Keckley, the disaster had "made him [Lincoln] a weak, passive child."

From that evening until two days after the funeral, Eliza Browning did not leave the White House. Sometimes her daughter Emma came to help. They and Mrs. Keckley attended Mrs. Lincoln, who was confined to her room. Henceforth the seamstress would also serve as a maidservant. The doctors Robert Stone and Neal Hall—who had been practicing their art upon her sons—would now be called to provide opiates and elixirs that would subdue the mother. Nicolay, who managed ceremonial affairs, asked Lincoln if he should "charge Browning with the direction of the funeral." And Lincoln told him by all means to consult with Browning. They wired Robert to come from Harvard, and asked Mary's sister Elizabeth Edwards to come from Springfield.

Every afternoon, when he was finished with his work at the Senate, Browning hurried to the White House, where he sat by Tad's bedside reading or talking to the child, or watching him sleep, until two o'clock in the morning. Sometimes Browning was alone, and sometimes Eliza sat by his side.

Having made arrangements with the morticians Brown and Alexander, Browning dutifully attended the embalming on February 21, in the presence of the family doctors and Isaac Newton, Lincoln's commissioner of agriculture. Frank T. Sands was the chief undertaker. Perhaps it was he who suggested the precaution of covering the breast of the corpse with the green and white blossoms of the mignonette (*Reseda odorata*), known for its overpoweringly sweet fragrance. Little Willie, pathetically wasted, was dressed in one of his old brown suits, white socks, and low-cut shoes, like an ill-used marionette. A reporter, clearly at a loss for words, brightly commented, "The embalmment was a complete success, and gave great satisfaction to all present."

Willie's remains were placed in a little metallic casket of faux rosewood and lay on a table in the Green Room, the parlor adjacent to the East Room where the funeral was held on February 24. The day before, Browning had informed Benjamin French of the Lincolns' desire that French should take charge of the funeral arrangements at the White House, and the cortège to the temporary interment in Oak Hill Cemetery in Georgetown. Just after breakfast on the twenty-fourth, French went to the White House, driving through a heavy fog. After checking on the furniture in the East Room—the semicircle of chairs, the lectern, the mirrors dressed in black crepe—he gazed briefly upon Willie's body in the Green Room, took a deep breath, and mounted the stairs to see the president. The office was vacant, so French picked up a book and read for a half hour. Julia Bates, wife of the attorney general, had been called in to spell the Brownings while they dressed for the funeral. Tad was still unwell; not the least of his problems was that his mother was unavailable. His father spent every moment with him that he could.

When Lincoln finally entered his office from the rear corridor, he "appeared quite calm and composed. He talked about his family and about the war," French recalled. "The servant came in and told him 'Tad' desired to see him. He left immediately for his son's room." The president returned presently, and then Seward joined them. Soon after that, French was excused to attend to funeral details. He thought it remarkable that there was no sign of the president's wife. "I did not see Mrs. Lincoln at all."

When at last she came down the stairs, supported by her husband and

Robert Lincoln, they went directly to the Green Room and shut the door, having requested "that there should be no spectator of their last sad moments in that house with their dead child and brother." That was at noon. During the half hour the family was closeted with the dead boy, lightning cleaved the dark sky outside, thunder as terrible as artillery fire made the crockery shudder, and violent winds charged in from the northwest, bringing such a tempest as the city had not seen in years. French recalled, "The terrible storm without seemed almost in unison with the storm of grief within." When the three mourners emerged from the Green Room, the men helped the poor mother up the stairs to her bed. That was the last Commissioner French would see of Mrs. Lincoln for a long time.

The gale blew the roofs off tall houses, shattered glass windows, leveled fields of military tents, turned muddy streets into canals and canals into rapids. Gusts of wind destroyed several churches and many shacks, uprooted trees, blew out the skylights of the Library of Congress; waves inundated the Long Bridge over the Potomac to Alexandria. A hundred mourners, drenched and chilly, sat in a semicircle in the East Room: the cabinet members, all the Illinois congressmen, the vice president and his wife, General McClellan, who sat beside Edwin Stanton, and many other friends and government officials including Senator Lyman Trumbull and the Brownings of Illinois.

Mr. Lincoln and his son Robert entered the room at two o'clock and took their seats. Mrs. Lincoln remained in her bedroom while the Reverend Dr. Phineas Densmore Gurley, of the New York Avenue Presbyterian Church, delivered the funeral oration. He spoke no more than half an hour, decorously eulogizing "the beloved youth . . . a child of bright intelligence and of peculiar promise." The Reverend Dr. Gurley offered comfort to the grieving president on behalf of the nation, "while to the unprecedented weight of civil care which presses upon him is added the burden of this great domestic sorrow; and the prayer of the Nation ascends to Heaven on his behalf, and on behalf of his weeping family, that God's grace may be sufficient for them."

The enormous room, with its three colossal chandeliers, made the circle of mourners look small. Some knew the telltale odor of mignonette, sickly sweet, a heavier scent than honeysuckle. After the black-garbed preacher recounted Willie's virtues—his inquisitive, conscientious mind, his affectionate disposition, his gentle words and manners—he felt impelled to comment upon the absent mother and her condition: "It is easy to see how a child, thus endowed, would, in the course of eleven years, entwine himself round the hearts of those who knew him best; nor can we wonder that the grief of his affectionate mother today is like that of Rachel weeping for her children, and refusing to be comforted because they were not."

Lincoln could not comfort his wife in her affliction, and she could not console him or Tad. A death in the family—which sometimes bonds the mourners in their sorrow—in the Lincolns' case only drove them further apart.

Blame and Guilt are the furies that haunt houses where death takes children like Willie Lincoln; and in this case there was more than enough blame to go around. There was the cursed, polluted water of the Potomac that Mary Lincoln had ordered to be piped into the White House early in 1861, at a cost of $4,420; there was the fetid marsh behind the White House along the Tiber Branch that had become a compost of dead animals and human waste unloaded in sewerage drays from the overcrowded city. Rush and Reynolds Barracks stood on the White House grounds, three hundred yards from the South Portico, an army hospital stricken with two epidemics of typhoid that winter. There was General McClellan and his typhoid fever, and his house across the square where the boys had been allowed to play as they roamed all over the neighborhood north and south, and consorted with the neighboring soldiers, and defied their nurse's orders to keep out of the marsh. They played on the roof in all kinds of weather, and no one could keep them from drinking the cold tap water.

There was the father who was too busy waging war to supervise his boys' adventures and hygiene. There was the mother who was too obsessed with rugs and wallpaper, lace shawls and silken gowns, and planning lavish soirees to spend time with her children. There was their ignorance of the invisible enemy, the diseases that hung in the heavy air of Washington, to which western children had no immunity. The Taft boys, Bud and Holly, had not died of typhoid! She would never allow them in the house again.

Mrs. Lincoln seems to have borne most of the guilt. Bad news travels fast among one's enemies, and they were soon blaming Mrs. Lincoln for reveling while her child lay dying. "Mary Lincoln believed her son's death a judgment for her party," her preeminent biographer concluded. If her critics were hard on her, calling her a "Delilah," condemning her "frivolity, hilarity and gluttony" in the papers, she was even harder on herself. She withdrew into a cave of sorrow, penitence, and intermittent madness more punishing than her enemies could devise. As miserable as she was, at least in that posture of mortification she could escape the censure of her friends and family. No one would dare reproach the bereaved mother—in her condition—with talk of lavish expenditures, corruption, and sedition.

The strict etiquette for mourning in Victorian times required twelve months of first degree mourning for a spouse, parent, or child. Lincoln's duty to the army and navy enforced a discipline upon him that helped him get through the stages of grief without his wife's support. For several weeks after the funeral, the president secluded himself in the Prince of Wales room for an hour on Thursdays, the day of the boy's death, when he could give way to his sorrow. Then he would emerge with his eyes red from weeping, wipe his eyes with a handkerchief, and go back to work. Something had to be done about the idle McClellan—the cabinet and Congress wanted him relieved of command. As for Mrs. Lincoln, subdued with laudanum, she did not get out of bed for weeks. Her husband would sit beside her where she lay lost in the distant maze of her grief, denial, and guilt. At night he lay down with Tad in his bed. The child was recovering now, and responding to his father's words of sympathy.

The best the busy president might do for his wife was to find relatives and nurses who would attend her. She "confines herself to her room, feeling very sad and at times, gives way to violent grief," her sister Elizabeth wrote. When witnesses describe "violent grief" and "paroxysms," they are tactfully avoiding more graphic descriptions of behavior dangerous to the mourner, or others, that required sedation or restraints. Elizabeth stayed for months, but despite Mr. Lincoln's pleas that she remain, she found the situation desperately depressing and finally unendurable. "My presence here, has tended very much to soothe, the excessive grief that natures, such as your Aunt's experience," she wrote to her daughter Julia, "and moreover to aid in nursing the little sick Tad." Elizabeth observes that Tad suffers from the loss of his brother, but will allow no mention of it, and that "his mother has been but little with him, being utterly unable to control her feelings."

One week after Willie's funeral, Thomas Stackpole, the doorkeeper, informed Senator Browning of Mrs. Lincoln's collusion with gardener Watt to defraud the treasury, and that she had stolen the president's speech "of Defrees, Superintendent of Government Printing, and she gave it to Wykoff in the Library, where he read it, gave it back to Defrees." (Stackpole wanted Watt fired so that he could take over the graft.) Browning felt the responsibility to tell the president this; and because of his "distressingly loving" (Mrs. Lincoln's phrase) interference, and Lincoln's subsequent banishing of Watt and Wikoff, Mrs. Lincoln remained angry with Orville Browning for some time. This mortifying sideshow was no incentive for Mrs. Lincoln to rise from her sickbed. As stunned as she was by grief, she knew of the disgrace.

Later that month, Elizabeth wrote, "The Wikoff case, has added very much to her unhappiness and to Mr. L's also." Then on April 7, the news came that their brother Samuel Todd, twenty-two, had been killed at the Battle of Shiloh. The Reverend Noyes W. Miner, a Springfield friend, visited that week to see what he might do for the Lincolns. Mrs. Lincoln told the minister that on the Sunday night of the battle she had watched her husband pace the floor all night, never lying down for a moment. When Miner tried to console Mary upon the news of her brother's death, he found her response defensive and unnatural: "Mr. Miner, I have two brothers who were at that battle at Shiloh. And I hope they are either dead or taken prisoners. You seem surprised. . . . But they would kill my husband if they could, and would destroy our Government, and I repeat it, *I hope they are either dead, etc.*" The comment illustrates the disconnection between Mrs. Lincoln's thoughts and feelings at the time. She could not have meant what she was saying—yet she did not wish to betray any hint of sympathy with the rebels.

Although Lincoln begged Elizabeth not to go home just yet, by early April she was so depressed she told Julia, "My very brain feels palsied." In a few weeks she was gone. Lincoln's efforts to get another relative to replace her were unsuccessful. Meanwhile he wrote to General Irvin McDowell's wife asking her please to pay Mrs. Lincoln a visit, and he also persuaded Mary Jane Welles, the wife of Gideon Welles, to come and help with Tad and Mrs. Lincoln. Mary Jane had lost five children herself, and was comforted by the belief that they awaited her in heaven. At last Mr. Lincoln asked the superintendent of nurses, Dorothea Dix, to recommend a good woman to come and take care of his wife and son. And so Rebecca Pomroy, a kind matron of deep religious convictions, packed her bag and left the hospital on ten minutes' notice and went to stay at the White House. She had lost her husband and two sons in the war, and knew the workings of grief.

When Mrs. Pomroy arrived on a beautiful day in spring, she found the house dark and the president sitting beside the bed where his wife lay in a slough of despair so deep that no one could reach her.

1863: A NEW YEAR

AT THE CROWDED LEVEE on New Year's Day, the president's wife dutifully stood in the ellipse of the Blue Room receiving the public. She was dressed in heavy black silk trimmed with ruffles of black satin at the sleeves and front of a shoulder cape clasped with a jet brooch. Her hair was pulled back plainly with a velvet headband, and she wore bracelets and earrings of jet. Her features had softened, but her mouth, forcing a half-smile, was a meager, prim line.

In that sumptuous parlor with its broad mirrors and life-size portrait of George Washington, she stood next to Benjamin French while he introduced her to the line of jostling visitors. They were eager to see the First Lady, who had not appeared at a public function in nearly a year. She had angered many by canceling the Marine Band concerts on the White House lawn, until Gideon Welles explained to the president that it was not fair for Mrs. Lincoln to impose her sorrow upon others when the people already had so much of their own. So the concerts resumed, but in Lafayette Square.

The crowd flowed from the Blue Room to the East Room, where the president was receiving, passing through the Green Room where Willie had lain in his casket. Mrs. Lincoln would not set foot in the Green Room after her child's death, nor would she ever again enter the bedroom where he died. All things that reminded her of him—his toys and books, his little friends Bud and Holly Taft, even his brother Tad—she sent away, or in Tad's case avoided, for a while. Now Tad was at his father's side with the secretaries Hay and Nicolay, and Marshal Ward Hill Lamon, who was making the introductions.

"Oh, Mr. French," sighed Mrs. Lincoln, "how much we have passed through since last we stood here." Two of her brothers, in Confederate gray, had been killed in battle. As thousands of soldiers died at Shiloh, Seven Pines, and Second Bull Run, and in the awful massacre of Union forces recently at Fredericksburg, Virginia—where the rebels had halted the Federal advance—rumors of Mrs. Lincoln's secessionist sympathies persisted. In her mourning dress and heavy black veil, she visited the military hospitals with Ann Stephens, the popular novelist, passing out fruit, flowers, and bottles of wine to the wounded soldiers and helping them write letters home. She was chastened and contrite, walking through the aisles of the crowded wards, and sights and odors that some found sickening she bore with composure. She explained to Mrs. Stephens that these visits to cheer the soldiers were also a comfort to her.

Mr. Lincoln had removed General McClellan from supreme command, replacing him with General Ambrose Burnside, who had blundered so tragically at Frederickburg before Christmas. More than twelve thousand Federal troops were killed and wounded on the terraces of Fredericksburg, and maimed survivors lay in the hospitals all over Washington.

BY THE SUMMER of 1862 she had been strong enough to travel with Tad and Robert. In mid-July they had spent a relaxed week in New York, and in the autumn she and Tad made a more ambitious journey to New York en route to Boston to visit Robert at Harvard. This time in Manhattan they stayed at the Metropolitan Hotel. There, on a crisp evening in late October, at ten o'clock, "the friends of the President holding official Federal positions in this city, together with the United States naval officers . . . tendered Mrs. Lincoln the compliment of a serenade." Still dressed in mourning, she did not speak, but asked Colonel Andrew Hamilton to convey her sentiments from the balcony: "I am instructed by the honored consort of the President of the United States, to whom this tribute of respect is paid, to tender you her thanks in the name of herself and her husband, for whom she feels a part of this honor is intended. The honors of office are ever accompanied by cares and responsibilities, commensurate with the dignity of official position."

Anti-Lincoln sentiment was sweeping New York. She would do what she could do for him in Manhattan—visiting the Navy Yard on October 29 in the company of Brigadier General Robert Anderson, the hero of Fort Sumter. Four days later she wrote to her husband.

My Dear Husband,

I have waited in vain to hear from you, yet as you are not *given* to letter writing, will be charitable enough to impute your silence, to the right cause.

What would the *wrong* cause have been? Anger? Apathy? The "right" cause would have been overwhelming business, but this was not a particularly demanding week for the president. He was taking his ease at their summer retreat, the Soldiers' Home, in the evening. He was enjoying the company of his new friend Captain David Derickson of Company K, the detail of Pennsylvania volunteers who guarded the president as he moved from the White House to that gingerbread Victorian cottage three miles north. Mary continues:

Strangers come up from W[ashington]—& tell me you are well—which satisfies me very much—your name is on every lip and many prayers and good wishes are hourly sent up, for your welfare—and McClellan & his slowness are as vehemently discussed. . . .

Dear Little Taddie is well & enjoying himself very much. . . . A day or two since, I had one of my severe attacks, if it had not been for Lizzie Keckley, I do not know what I should have done—Some of *these periods,* will launch me away—

These were the headaches that accompanied her depression, and they came now more frequently and with more violence. She tells him how kind and attentive all "the distinguished in the land" have treated her, and how they would worship him if he would replace McClellan; and then she asks for a check for $100 to pay for Taddie's new suits, fur wrappings for the carriage, and a small loan to Mrs. Keckley.

"I must send you, Taddy's tooth," which he had been wiggling for days, and finally pulled.

"One line," she pleads in closing, "to say that we are occasionally remembered, will be gratefully received—by yours very truly, M.L."

She and Tad were gone again from October 20 until November 27, six weeks during which no letters or telegrams from Lincoln to his wife have survived. He was in good spirits, as time healed the wound of Willie's passing. The autumn weather was perfect. He spent a good deal of time with John Hay, and even more time with the short, stout Captain Derickson, who rode with him back and forth from the White House to the Soldiers' Home. Major Thomas Chamberlin, a drillmaster who visited the summer home in October, was in a position to observe the president's leisure hours there. As he recalled, David Derickson, and Henry Crotzer, an officer of Company D, often dined with the president while his wife was up north; James B. Mix, a cavalry officer, breakfasted with the president before they rode out for the day. The president enjoyed this camaraderie, seemingly unaware or uncaring that fraternizing with captains and dragoon lieutenants was not conventional behavior for the commander in chief. This would provoke envy and comical gossip. Outrageous rumors reached Major Chamberlin, that "Captain Derickson . . . advanced so far in the President's confidence and esteem that, in Mrs. Lincoln's absence, he frequently spent the night at his cottage, sleeping in the same bed with him, and—it is said—making use of His Excellency's night-shirts!" By mid-November the rumor of Derickson's special relationship with the president had reached the ears of Mrs. Gustavus Fox, wife of the assistant secretary of the navy, and a good friend of the Lincolns. She noted in her diary that she had heard "there is a Bucktail Soldier here devoted to the President, drives with him & when Mrs. L. is not home, sleeps with him. What stuff!"

What stuff, indeed. These rumors seem more sensational now than they did in 1862 when it meant little more for men to share a bed than that they had only one bed, or they were cold, or they fell asleep while they were talking. There was not then the forgone conclusion that male bedmates were lovers, which has caused so much ink to be spilled in our own time. Whether the captain did or did not sleep in the president's bed, or wore his nightshirt, it is clear that the men had become close friends. When another military unit arrived to relieve Company K, Lincoln wrote a letter to the effect that as long as any guard had to be employed, "none would be more satisfactory to me than Capt. D. and his company."

During Mrs. Lincoln's long absences the president got lonely, and since female companionship was out of the question, the company of men would have to suffice.

SHE HAD RETURNED from New York prepared for the holiday season, but she limited entertainments to small dinner parties for close friends and members of the White House staff. So the New Year's levee was an important step forward for her. Fatigued by the unending line, Mrs. Lincoln excused herself after a little more than an hour and went upstairs to her rooms. She had proven to herself and the public that she could once again do her duty as hostess, and now she would rest. It was the first of many levees, receptions, and parties that she would hold in 1863.

That morning she had sent a message to Orville Browning inviting him to come with her and the president on a carriage ride when the levee was over. Since Willie's death there had been an awkwardness between her and Browning. Of course he and Liza had been very helpful during that awful time; but with such familiarity comes a sense of obligation, which the president's wife preferred not to extend to a gentleman of Browning's importunate nature. Then there was all of the unpleasantness about Wikoff and Watt, and the senator's unwelcome opinions about her association with these characters. And now Browning was at odds with the president over the Emancipation Proclamation, which declared that the slaves were free in the Confederacy; Lincoln had signed it that day, just before the open house. Browning feared that racist Union soldiers would lay down their arms in protest.

Nevertheless, old friends are the best, and they must make every effort to keep Browning. He meant well. He arrived promptly at 2:30, against the tide of the crowd leaving the White House to find that the president was behind closed doors in conference with General Burnside, who was lamenting his staff's lack of confidence in him: "It is my belief that I ought to retire to private life." Busy with Burnside, and then with General Henry Halleck, Lincoln begged to be excused from the carriage ride. The Battle of Stone's River was raging in Tennessee, the news had been distressing, and the president wanted to stay in the telegraph office of the War Department, where he could hear the dispatches.

So on that mild, clear afternoon in January, the coachman drove Browning and Mrs. Lincoln past the colonnade of the Treasury building and out E Street to a house across from the Post Office on Eighth, with its Corinthian columns of solid white marble. At the house facing the great portico they stopped to pick up Mrs. Major John Montgomery Wright of Chicago, one of Mary's friends, and then headed north on Ninth Street, the breeze on their faces, and out the toll road to the Soldiers' Home. The roads were dry and firm.

Mrs. Lincoln talked excitedly. On New Year's Eve she had gone to a séance in Georgetown with old Isaac Newton, the secretary of agriculture, who was on familiar terms with all the creditable spirit mediums in the city. They had driven together to the home of Cranston Laurie, chief clerk of the Post Office. There in the dark parlor a trance medium "made wonderful revelations to her about her little son Willy," Browning noted, and also "things on the earth." The medium informed the circle of spiritualists that "the cabinet were all the enemies of the President, working for themselves, and that they would have to be dismissed, and others called to his aid before he had success." It did not take a spirit medium to convince Browning there was some truth in the prophecy. At the moment he thought the cabinet members were all mad or secretly plotting against Lincoln, to have allowed him to issue the Emancipation Proclamation.

Browning and the two ladies drove out to the Soldiers' Home and back, rolling along in the southeast diagonal of New Jersey Avenue past the train station and around the Capitol to Mrs. Carter's boardinghouse, where the senator lived. There he bade them good evening, and Mrs. Lincoln and her friend drove on together, conversing about things not meant for the senator's ears. He thought spiritualism was rubbish. In those days it was a hobbyhorse for the wealthy and idle, a pseudoscientific curiosity, and a conduit for repressed sexuality. Sometimes the practice brought comfort to those in mourning. From the 1850s, when Margaret and Kate Fox, sisters from Rochester, became known for their rappings and spirit messages, séances had become a craze in America. Mediums gathered people from all walks of life to sit in darkened parlors and hold hands. The air was erotically charged. They called upon spirits to knock at the door of life and bring news that there was an invisible world beyond the grave, where the dead dwelt.

Celebrated mediums like the Fox sisters and twenty-one-year-old Henrietta Colburn of Hartford, Connecticut, and Washington, D.C., (a friend of Joshua Speed's) got wonderful results. Scientists challenged or defended the authenticity of the "manifestations" the spirit mediums produced: horns and banjos that were played by invisible hands, levitating furniture, bells ringing. The Fox sisters had been in Washington not long since, and Mrs. Franklin Pierce, the former president's wife, mourning the death of a son killed in a train wreck in 1853, went to the mediums to hear news of him. One of the Foxes' patrons was the fantastically whiskered Horace Greeley, who hosted séances in his New York mansion. Mrs. Lincoln's foppish friend Nathaniel P. Willis, the poet, was one of the circle; so were the writers William Cullen Bryant and James Fenimore Cooper and the historian George Bancroft. Now and then a high-priced medium would be exposed and disgraced for taking advantage of vulnerable mourners. But then another would come along, prettier, cleverer, younger, more sincere-seeming, reviving hope in sad people who yearned to converse with their dead. In 1863, it was not considered crazy to attend séances, or even to accept the advice of mediums—although it is well known that people who are unbalanced can become unhinged by dabbling in the occult sciences. If one had a great need, or just an open mind, she was welcome to the circle. Spirit mediums were not effectively debunked until Houdini's famous campaign against them fifty years later.

The secretary of the navy, Gideon Welles, and his wife, Mary Jane, had consulted mediums when their children died. It was widely known that Queen Victoria, Mary's idol, kept in touch with her late husband Albert via the gardener-medium John Brown; and the Empress Eugénie fell under the influence of the clairvoyant Madame Blavatsky, who made little messages from the dead flutter down from the ceiling. According to the journalist Noah Brooks, who came to Washington in November 1862 and became part of the Lincolns' inner circle, Mrs. Keckley led poor Mrs. Lincoln to the spiritualists. The black seamstress had received some solace from mediums when her own son died in the war, and she hoped they might console her mistress.

About the same time Brooks arrived from San Diego, Henrietta (Nettie) Colburn came to Washington from a successful speaking tour in New England. Her powers as a trance medium and lecturer had made her famous. Traveling with Parthenia R. Hannum ("Parnie")—who assisted her as her "control" spirit—Colburn had come to the capital to help her wounded brother, who was in a military hospital, and the spiritualist community embraced her. A letter of introduction to Thomas Gales Foster, an eminent speaker on spiritualism, made the ladies welcome to stay at his house on Twelfth and D streets, near the White House. Foster was eager to introduce the pretty medium, with her oval face, dark brown sausage curls, and piercing eyes, to Mr. and Mrs. Cranston Laurie and their daughter, Belle Miller. Mr. Laurie was chief clerk at the Post Office, and his house at 21 First Street in Georgetown was a haven for séances. Belle

Miller was an autokinetic medium, who specialized in levitating pianos. It was a spectacular specialty that she would not employ for worldly gain, but piously restricted to darkened parlors.

Mrs. Lincoln and her friend Isaac Newton had gone together to Georgetown to welcome the New Year with a séance at the Lauries'. The president was putting the finishing touches on the Emancipation Proclamation, and so he begged to be excused. His wife had gone primarily to see Belle Miller in action moving heavy furniture by remote control; but soon after Mary arrived, someone suggested that they fetch Nettie Colburn and Parnie Hannum. Mrs. Lincoln sent her coach for them. She had heard that Nettie, via her control, Parnie, could communicate with the dead. Mrs. Lincoln was not disappointed. The young woman fell into a deep trance and brought word from Willie, as well as advice on worldly matters, as Orville Browning reported in his diary.

"This young lady must not leave Washington," Mrs. Lincoln said after Nettie Colburn came out of her trance. And weeks later, when Miss Colburn tried to leave town, explaining that she must make her living traveling as a public speaker, Mrs. Lincoln persuaded Isaac Newton to get jobs for the mediums in the Department of Agriculture. He did, of course, and for months Nettie and Parnie earned a dollar a day packing seeds for a few hours, leaving their evenings free to practice the occult arts.

Later Mrs. Lincoln wrote to George Harrington, assistant secretary of the treasury, wanting to get higher-paying jobs for Colburn and Hannum in the Treasury Clipping Department. This was one of several letters she addressed to Harrington for the purpose of procuring offices for friends, or friends of friends. In March of 1862, Charles Sumner told Charles Francis Adams that the president's wife was constantly meddling with patronage affairs at the beginning of the administration. As her health and spirits improved, she resumed the dangerous dual pastimes of influence peddling and shopping. During the January thaw, Horatio Taft often saw her on the Avenue, "the President's carriage with its tall driver & footman ... standing in front of some Merchants door while Mrs. L. sits in her seat and examines the rich goods which the obsequious Clerk brings out to her." This was a distraction and an obsession. No merchant would deny her credit, and soon she would be in debt again.

Mrs. Lincoln's influence peddling was another kind of obsession, and fatally allied to her mounting debt. The dismissal of Watt and Wikoff did not stop the corruption. Thomas Stackpole, who earned only $50 a month, was always on the lookout for an extra dollar; he made an arrangement with John Hammock, who ran a restaurant on Pennsylvania Avenue and Fourteenth Street near Willard's. Here is how it worked: If one of the restaurant's customers needed a trading or travel permit, he told Hammock. Hammock went to Stackpole to get a price. When they had struck a bargain, the cash flowed through Hammock to Stackpole, who "had the ear of Mrs. Lincoln." Stackpole probably had Mrs. Lincoln's ear not because of any great gifts of conversation, but because he had an envelope full of cash.

News like this travels quickly. Soon the superintendent of Old Capitol Prison heard of it. "The bargain and sale of trading permits, official favors and Government secrets, chargeable to Stackpole's influence with Mrs. Lincoln, was so extensive," Superintendent William P. Wood recalled, "that I deemed it my duty to inform Secretary Stanton of the fact." Stanton told Lincoln, who sent for Wood in order to get the "details of the nefarious practice." During a long interview in the course of which the superintendent explained the connivance and Mrs. Lincoln's part in it, he found that the president was deeply moved. With all his patience and dignity, Lincoln could not conceal his distress.

"There are few men who are entirely sane," Lincoln observed. "And more women are tainted with insanity and victims to insane delusions than it would be prudent to admit. The caprices of Mrs. Lincoln, I am satisfied, are the result of partial insanity." He asked Wood if he had ever given any thought to the subject, as a man who daily worked with criminals, and Wood, no doubt uncomfortable with the conversation, tersely replied, "Only in a casual way, Mr. President."

The president had his own eccentricities regarding finances, which for the most part went unnoticed, but would have been troublesome to a wife as concerned about money as Mrs. Lincoln was. Few issues in a marriage are as likely to disturb the peace as a disagreement over money, or lack of communication about it. He was not forthcoming with the details of his investments, the management of his salary, or his financial planning. If he had been, his wife would have been furious with him. Mr. Lincoln's salary was $25,000 per year, paid in monthly warrants of approximately $2,083. As Harry Pratt, the preeminent authority on Lincoln's finances, has written, "With problems of the war occupying his every waking minute, he had no time for personal affairs." Lincoln had no idea what to do with the money he was making, or if he did, he acted as if he did not. To begin with, he neglected to deposit the warrants (which are government checks), allowing them to accumulate in his desk drawer until the spirit moved him to walk to the Riggs Bank, endorse them, and hand them over in a dusty pile. According to Pratt, the records show that at one time he possessed seven warrants, and on another occasion he had eleven, in his desk. Altogether he lost some $2,000 in interest as a result of neglecting to invest the monthly earnings promptly.

At one point, in 1863, he became so perplexed over his purchase of government securities that he decided to turn the matter over to Salmon Chase. The distracted president put on his hat and coat and began filling his pockets with his holdings: demand notes, bonds, Treasury notes, certificates of deposit, a bag of gold worth $883, salary warrants, and greenbacks. When he was loaded up, he started for the Treasury. Maunsell B. Field, who was an assistant secretary of the treasury, saw him walk into Salmon Chase's office without knocking, his rusty stovepipe hat tipped back on his head, his gray shawl wrapped around his shoulders. Wide-eyed, Chase watched the president empty his pockets onto the desk. The two men did not converse for more than five minutes. Lincoln asked Chase to convert the jumble of properties into government bonds, then went back to work. Salmon Chase turned the assets over to George Harrington for investment.

When Mrs. Lincoln tells us, as she so often does in her letters, that her husband was not expressive about the most important things, we must include among these things the subject of money. All he ever told her while they were in the White House about their financial future is that he would not have enough to retire; he would have to return to his law practice in Springfield. Things unspoken between husband and wife are sometimes sensed, and suffered, more intensely than matters easily expressed. While Mrs. Lincoln may not have known exactly how her husband was neglecting their assets, she might very well have sensed it, as he was neglecting her in so many other ways.

MRS. LINCOLN'S PRIVATE secretary, the twenty-eight-year-old William O. Stoddard, was mystified at first by the lady's changing moods. One day he found her kindly, generous, thoughtful, and hopeful; and on another day she could "appear so unreasonable, so irritable, so despondent, so even niggardly, and so prone to see the dark, the wrong side of men and women and events." He confides, "It is easier to understand it all and to deal with it after a few words from an eminent medical practitioner." Then Stoddard trails off, leaving us with the cryptic statement that all physicians and most middle-aged people will understand better than he did, when he was not yet thirty, Mrs. Lincoln's irrational fear of poverty, and her outlandish financial schemes. The panic would come and go in a week's time, and then "no unhappiness of disposition could be discovered." Stoddard was writing his recollection in the 1880s, and whether he is referring to the vagaries of menopause or to what physicians then called hypochondria or hysteria is uncertain.

In any case, Lincoln feared for his wife's sanity. According to Mrs. Keckley, during one of Mrs. Lincoln's "paroxysms of grief the President kindly bent over her, took her by the arm, and gently led her to the window. With a stately, solemn gesture, he pointed to the lunatic asylum.

" 'Mother, do you see that large white building on the hill yonder? Try and control your grief, or it will drive you mad, and we may have to send you there.' " There was no lunatic asylum in view of the White House; perhaps the incident occurred at the Soldiers' Home. In any case, this anecdote has entered the record as emblematic of Lincoln's concern about his wife's mental health at the time.

Mrs. Lincoln's interest in spiritualism was a relatively harmless pastime. By the standards of the day, it was more likely to be ridiculed than condemned—although clergymen cautioned it was the devil's work. While notably superstitious, Lincoln was not a spiritualist, but he is supposed to have attended two séances, one of them conducted by Miss Colburn in the Red Room of the White House on April 23. Gideon Welles and Edwin Stanton were part of the circle, and it is said that the spirits that night were idle until Lincoln left the company to go upstairs, whereupon one spook pulled Welles's whiskers and another pinched Stanton's ear.

Lincoln was not a believer, but he did not discourage his wife from attending the séances, for it did comfort her when a medium was successful in evoking Willie's ghost. Still, the president did not want to see her duped. A short, dapper Englishman, "Lord" Charles J. Colchester, appeared on the scene in the summer of 1863. His title, like his profession, was dubious, but he won Mrs. Lincoln's confidence, and soon the medium began conducting wonderful séances at the Soldiers' Home. According to the journalist Noah Brooks—the most reliable witness to these events—"By playing on her motherly sorrows . . . in a darkened room, he pretended to produce messages from the dead boy by means of scratches on the wainscoting and taps on the walls and furniture." Lincoln was concerned enough about Colchester's influence to consult with Dr. Joseph Henry, an eminent scientist and secretary of the Smithsonian Institution. The scientist invited Colchester to demonstrate his powers in one of the rooms of the Smithsonian. Henry reported to the president that the "medium" was a fake—the sounds he produced were coming from his own body; but Henry could not prove this without thoroughly examining him, and the trickster refused to disrobe.

Noah Brooks, who had become a close friend to both of the Lincolns, was likewise worried about Colchester's manipulation of the vulnerable Mrs. Lincoln. When she invited Brooks to attend a séance in the White House, the journalist declined, but before the medium's White House appearance, Brooks arranged to attend "a Colchester sitting" in another house, without Mrs. Lincoln. He paid his dollar and joined the circle. After the lights went out, "the silence was broken by the thumping of a drum, the twanging of a banjo, and the ringing of the bells." Brooks leaped up shouting "Strike a light" and grabbed the hand that was beating the drum with a bell—Colchester's hand—at which point the charlatan struck Brooks on the forehead with the spiritual drum.

Realizing his days as a trance medium in the capital were numbered, Charles Colchester approached the president's wife and requested a travel pass to go to New York. In wartime, no one left the city without the War Department's permission. Two days after Brooks received his head wound at the séance, the president summoned him to the White House "on a matter of the most distressing importance." Mrs. Lincoln met Brooks in the parlor with a letter in hand from Colchester threatening her, saying that if she did not get him the travel pass, "he might have some unpleasant things to say to her." So Brooks suggested that Mrs. Lincoln invite Lord Colchester to visit her the next day, and he, Brooks, would come at the same hour.

In a White House drawing room the next morning the two men were introduced—much to the medium's embarrassment—and Mrs. Lincoln excused herself, leaving them alone. Brooks lifted the hair from his forehead to show Colchester the very real cut he had received at the séance, which was probably more evidence than the charlatan needed that he was in big trouble. The journalist called him a swindler and a humbug, and told him to leave the city at once. "If you are in Washington to-morrow afternoon at this time, you will be in the old Capitol prison." Leaving town had been the medium's intention since the day before, and soon he was gone, with or without his travel pass. He vanished from the Lincolns' lives, and from history.

Colchester's banishment, occurring in the summer of 1863, marked the beginning of the end of Mrs. Lincoln's séances at home, but it was not the end of her commerce with spirits. She continued to consult with mediums in Boston, New York, and Philadelphia until a few years before she died. Nettie Colburn never lost her credentials as a trance medium. An intriguing letter from Joshua Speed to Abraham Lincoln dated October 26, 1863, recommends "My very good friend Mrs. Cosby [Anna Mills Cosby, daughter of a prominent Washington architect] and Miss Netty Colburn her friend." Speed advises it will "sure be some relief from the tedious round of office seekers to see two such agreeable ladies—They are both mediums & believers in the spirits—and are I am quite sure very choice spirits themselves." This letter is intriguing for several reasons. It hints of a past discussion of ghosts between Speed and Lincoln, and Speed's assumption that his friend would not condemn the mediums out of hand. The letter—probably solicited by Colburn and Cosby—gives no indication that Speed knew that Mrs. Lincoln had already encountered Nettie Colburn. It further complicates the testimony about the Lincolns' involvement with spiritualists, which is sketchy, emerging as it does from sensationalist journalism and from Nettie Colburn Maynard's 1917 book *Was Abraham Lincoln a Spiritualist?* Maynard's recollection is so inconsistent with established facts and dates that it serves us only as background.

What is certain, and what Speed's letter confirms, is that the Lincolns were moving in different circles. Spiritualism did not draw them together. Most evidence shows that as Lincoln, in mourning, read the Bible for comfort, Mary retreated into the spirit world and the society of spiritualists such as John Pierpont, a clerk in the Treasury Department, and Thomas Gales Foster, a clerk in the War Department who was also a popular speaker on the topic of ghosts, and of course the Cranston Lauries, and their daughter, Belle Miller, who lifted pianos. Lincoln was grateful that the scandals of the White House accounting fraud and the theft of his annual message were fading. If folks wanted to gossip about Mrs. Lincoln's consorting with spirit mediums, this would be a welcome distraction from their calling her a spy.

DR. ANSON HENRY, Lincoln's intimate friend from Springfield days, arrived in Washington on February 15, 1863. It is noteworthy that Dr. Henry was open-minded about the adventures of the spiritualists; time and again he encouraged Mrs. Lincoln to take what comfort she could in their philosophy.

The president had appointed Dr. Henry surveyor general of the Washington Territory in 1861. Now Henry had come far "around the Horn" to persuade the president to fund better roads and military posts in the Territory, and of course he had also come to spend time with the Lincolns. The president was so busy that Henry waited in the line for two days with senators and congressmen without getting an audience. Lincoln was consumed with worry over his generals' plan to attack Charleston, and advising General William Rosecrans to copy a successful Confederate tactic: using small mounted raiding parties to disrupt enemy supply lines and communications.

On February 17, Dr. Henry finally sent his cards in to Robert Lincoln, who was home from college, and to Mrs. Lincoln. "Ten minutes after, I was shown into Robert's room, who appeared very glad to see me. He said his mother was in bed, not being very well, but would like to see me this evening any time after 8 o'cl." The weekend had drained Mrs. Lincoln. On Valentine's Day they had received the famous midgets, Charles S. Stratton and his bride, Lavinia Warren—also known as Mr. and Mrs. Tom Thumb—and the Saturday reception that evening had been exceptionally crowded because of the publicity surrounding the miniature newlyweds. That day, Mrs. Gustavus Fox had found Mrs. Lincoln "in high spirits," but after another White House dinner, for General Benjamin Butler, on Sunday, she took to her bed.

The evening before sending his cards in to Robert and Mrs. Lincoln, Dr. Henry had passed the time with Julia Jayne Trumbull, Senator Lyman Trumbull's wife. The doctor greatly desired to effect a reconciliation between the women, who had been estranged since the senatorial election of 1855. Now he felt an obligation to the families to try once more to bring them together. He discussed the matter with Julia, who, he said, "received me most kindly, and is a most lovely woman." As Henry wrote to his wife, Julia gave him the impression that Mary's "distinguished position has turned her head a little . . . Julia and her don't visit—"

That night he retired to his hotel doubting whether Mrs. Lincoln would receive him at all. But the next evening he found himself in her presence, and knew that she was delighted to see him; she opened her grieving heart to her old friend. Dr. Henry had brought her and Mr. Lincoln together after they had broken off their engagement in 1840, and she would always consider him their "best and dearest friend." She told him all her troubles, "and especially about the breach between herself and her own family friends in Springfield." Without hearing their side of the story, the doctor concluded, "I think Mary is right, & that they were the aggressors," but he meant to take it up with the Edwards family in Springfield. There were two main causes of conflict: First, there was the family's expectation that the Lincolns would provide lucrative offices to all family members who applied; second, there was Mrs. Lincoln's arrogant, defensive bearing. Whatever the president did for Mary's relatives they considered insufficient. Ninian Edwards—near bankruptcy—accepted a position in the Army Commissary Department; Dr. William Wallace was appointed local paymaster of volunteers. But jealousy is a corrosive compound, and Mrs. Lincoln had neither the grace nor the inclination to diffuse it among her relations. Her open hostility to her sister Ann, seething in her letter of September 29, 1861, aggravated a family tension that called for tact. Mary Lincoln did not create the problem, but she did not have the temperament to solve it. Her husband tried as hard as he could. Soon he would take a bold political risk in welcoming Mary's half sister Emilie, a Confederate widow, into the White House, securing an amnesty and travel passes for her, among other privileges.

There was nothing Anson Henry could do about Mrs. Lincoln's family problems, but he did try to open the door between Mary and Julia. "Mary and Julia have both made me their confidant, telling me their grievances, and both think the other *all* to blame. I am trying to make peace between them. It is as I told you," he wrote his wife, "Mr. Trumbull was jealous of Col. Baker's influence with Mr. Lincoln, and this was the cause of open family rupture." Of course this is Mrs. Lincoln's side of the story. He does not mention that Mrs. Lincoln had never forgiven the Trumbulls for "stealing" the senatorial election of 1855, and how her grudge persisted after Lincoln and Trumbull had resumed their necessary alliance. The men had never been intimate friends, but Mary and Julia had. To his regret, Dr. Henry failed to reconcile them.

Henry's business agenda in Washington was more successful, owing to the president's loyalty and devotion. Congressmen waited for weeks to see Mr. Lincoln alone, while Dr. Henry soon found himself at the president's dinner table, "no one having the right to claim the freedom allowed an old and confidential friend. I have a warrant for claiming this in the fact that he has told me things, which he says he has never yet named to anybody else." Dr. Henry remembered the terrible winter of 1840–41, Lincoln's suicidal "hypochondria," the blue mass pills that were a specific for syphilis, and how the young Lincoln had "thereby got an impression that Dr. Henry is necessary to my existence." The smiling doctor looked much the same at sixty years of age as he had at forty, excepting a few more pounds of flesh, and more silver in the fringe of whiskers around his chin. With his physician's eye he noted Lincoln's sunken cheeks above the black beard that he had seen only in photographs, and observed that his hands trembled and his gait was peculiar, shuffling. The White House had not been kind to the prairie lawyer. Lincoln had stopped taking the blue mass pills. Perhaps he no longer needed them—perhaps he had never needed them—but he certainly looked as if he needed attention.

The doctor came to dinner on February 21, the day after the first anniversary of Willie's death. The president had been in very low spirits, reading the German novelist Jean Paul Richter, now remembered for his terrible pronouncement, "God is dead, the sky is empty. . . . Weep, children, you have no more father." Benjamin French had seen Lincoln on Monday morning the eighteenth and noted, "He certainly is growing feeble. He wrote a note while I was present, and his hand trembled as I never saw it before, and he looked worn and haggard." French said Lincoln would be "glad when he could get some rest. He replied that it was a pretty hard life for him." Dr. Henry's company now was a pleasure, and Lincoln wanted to keep him in Washington for as long as possible.

On the morning of March 5, the president and the doctor had breakfast together in the small private dining room with a view of the north lawn and the park. The winter sun rising over the city was low in the clear sky, the day dry and cold. After decades of dosing himself with elemental mercury in the form of blue mass pills, Lincoln had stopped two years earlier because he said they made him feel "cross." Dr. Henry was the picture of health; he and Eliza had five children, and Lincoln wanted news of them.

The old friends chatted for a half hour before Lincoln led Henry upstairs to his office, where the doctor took note of the maps pinned to the north wall above the settee and armchairs, across from the hearth where the wood fire snapped and danced, across from the long table where the cabinet met. "He took great interest in what I had to say of their [Oregon and Washington's] importance & the rapid settlement of the country," Henry recalled. The president became so absorbed and animated in conversation that Anson Henry had to remind him it was past ten o'clock. Lincoln promptly pulled the bell cord that hung over his desk near the east window where the light was pouring in. The men took their leave with a promise to see each other the next day. Then the doctor pushed his way against the tide of visitors who were clamoring for a few minutes of the president's time.

Outside, Dr. Henry found his colleagues, a delegation from Oregon and California who were lobbying to get Stephen J. Feld of California a seat on the Supreme Court. Without Henry's privileged access, they could not have succeeded. After waiting until the president had stopped receiving visitors, Henry "told them to sign a recommendation for the judge, and their program for Territorial offices," and said he would get the papers into the president's hands. The next morning, over breakfast, Lincoln told Henry he would meet the Western delegation at three o'clock. The president was as good as his word, and at the appointed time, he agreed to most of their requests.

"A very sharp piece of diplomacy," the doctor wrote proudly to his wife. It all had begun with Mary Lincoln. She was concerned, as others were, about the president's mood and knew that Anson Henry would cheer him.

A popular reception had taken place on the evening of March 3, "exceedingly crowded," according to Benjamin French. He marveled at Mrs. Lincoln's grace "as I stood at the side of 'The Queen' of all this show—she herself habited as it became her in rich black satin and jewels of the richest kind. The President too, 'honest old Abraham,' looked better than I ever saw him before at a reception." But it was all a show. Just before the doors opened, Lincoln had whispered to Mr. French that rebels had captured the Union ironclad gunboat the *Indianola*. Earlier that day, Assistant Secretary of the Navy Gustavus Fox had spent an hour with Lincoln and found him depressed, and Admiral John Dahlgren found him "nervous and uneasy."

When Dr. Henry announced that he would soon be going home, now that he had accomplished his goals in the capital, Lincoln would not hear of it. He drolly "ordered" his friend to take a room at the White House across from his office and stay with the family at least until spring, when that long sea voyage would be more pleasant. Tad's birthday was coming up, on April 4, Easter weekend. Mrs. Lincoln had the idea that it would lift their spirits, and inspire the Army of the Potomac, if they would all sail down to Aquia Creek Landing and review General Joseph Hooker's troops. And of course they wanted Dr. Henry to come along with them.

ON A BLUSTERY Saturday afternoon, Tad Lincoln and his mother and father boarded the presidential steamer *Carrie Martin* bound for Virginia. Their party included Dr. Henry, his friend from Oregon, Captain Medorem Crawford, Noah Brooks of Sacramento, and Attorney General Edward Bates, also a close friend of the doctor's.

Soon after the ship left the Navy Yard it began to snow. According to Noah Brooks, "so thick was the weather, and so difficult the navigation, that we were forced to anchor for the night in a little cove in the Potomac opposite Indian Head, where we remained until the following morning." Mrs. Lincoln, Tad, Bates, and Crawford went to bed, and Lincoln, Brooks, and Anson Henry stayed up talking as the snowflakes fell in the light of the ship's lanterns outside the cabin. They sat "telling stories and discussing matters, political and military, in the most free and easy way," Brooks recalled.

Their five-day visit to Virginia had a festive, holiday air, despite the cold, the austere accommodations, and the underlying gravity of the military display. Hooker's aides had fitted out three of the finest hospital tents for the presidential party. The Lincolns and their guests reviewed the showy "honor guard," the Philadelphia Lancers, six corps of infantry, a cavalry corps of fifteen thousand, and an artillery force manning three hundred cannon. The president, in his stovepipe hat and black coat, sat his horse adeptly, by the side of the handsome, copper-haired General Hooker. Tad, escorted by an orderly, spurred his pony here and there, "his gray cloak flying in the gusty wind like the plume of Henry of Navarre," wrote Brooks. "It was a grand sight . . . banners waving, music crashing, and horses prancing as the vast column came winding like a huge serpent over the hills past the reviewing party, and then stretching far away out of sight." According to Anson Henry, there were 150,000 soldiers gathered at Falmouth, prepared to die for the Union.

There were somber hours as the president and Mrs. Lincoln visited the hospital tents, where there were so many gruesome reminders of the struggle going on beyond the colorful pageantry. The Lincolns passed down the rows of cots "speaking to every man, shaking hands with many of them, asking a question or two here and there, and leaving a kind word." Brooks noticed that some of the men shed tears of gratitude as they looked upon Lincoln's "sympathetic countenance, touching his hand, and hearing his gentle voice." At her friend General Sickles's headquarters, Mrs. Lincoln patiently endured the vulgarities of the German princess Salm-Salm, whose husband Felix was a colonel in the regiment; greeting the commander in chief, she boldly planted a kiss upon his lips.

By midweek the sky had cleared and the weather grew warm. The war news from Charleston was discouraging. The Federal fleet of nine ironclads under Flag Officer Samuel Du Pont that had attacked Sumter had been battered and repulsed by torpedoes, and five ships had been disabled. Yet the spirit of the troops in Virginia and the huge size and readiness of the Army of the Potomac gave the president hope for the future. Mr. and Mrs. Lincoln were touched to see that there was friendly communication between the Union soldiers here and the Confederate pickets on the far side of the Rappahannock River, which had coursed through so many scenes of battle. The young men would send messages, photos, and jokes back and forth in pouches—as if they had no intention of killing one another. One photo that came through the lines from the rebels was of a Confederate officer, endorsed with the phrase, "A rebellious rebel." Mary Lincoln—always fascinated by language, and curious, if not suspicious—told her husband that the caption meant that the officer must be a rebel against rebels, that is, a rebel with Union sympathies. Mr. Lincoln, amused by her interpretation, begged to differ, explaining to his wife that the gentleman who sent the photo to General William Averill—who had been his classmate—"wanted everybody to know that he was not only a rebel, but a rebel of rebels, 'a double-dyed-in-the-wool sort of rebel.'" And so they bantered, playfully, at the front.

The entire party had a fine time at headquarters, reviewing the troops during Easter week, despite Mr. Lincoln's growing concern over the youthful General Hooker's vaunting assurance. "That is the most depressing thing about Hooker," said Lincoln wryly to Noah Brooks. "It seems to me that he is overconfident." One evening as they were taking their ease after a long day of reviewing, Brooks commented to Lincoln that as the weather had grown brighter, it appeared that he had grown "more cheerful and even jocular." And the president replied, "It is a great relief to get away from Washington and politicians. But nothing touches the tired spot."

THE WAR COMES HOME

ON MAY 6, 1863, less than three weeks after the Lincolns' pleasant visit to the army headquarters in Virginia, the war grew terrible beyond anyone's imagining.

Dr. Anson Henry was still a guest in the White House, with no apparent business apart from providing the president with moral support. Mrs. Lincoln was still managing her grief with the help of the spirit mediums, and her behavior was so erratic that at one point Lincoln wrote a letter to Charles Sumner—one of her best friends—apologizing for her. At two o'clock that May afternoon, Lincoln asked Noah Brooks if he would wait with Dr. Henry in his room across from the oval library. Lincoln was going over to the telegraph office, and he wanted his friends to be waiting for him in case there was important news. They could not go with him to the War Department—the cipher room was off-limits to all but military personnel.

An hour later, Lincoln returned with a telegram in his hand and shut the door. Brooks later wrote that he would "never forget that picture of despair. . . . His face, usually sallow, was ashen," precisely the color of the "French gray" wallpaper of Dr. Henry's bedroom. Lincoln asked Brooks to read the telegram. The message was that the night before, Hooker had retreated, moving his beaten army back across the Rappahannock. Thirty thousand men had fallen at Chancellorsville, two-thirds of them Federal soldiers.

"Never, as long as I knew him," said Brooks, "did he seem to be so broken, so dispirited, and so ghostlike. Clasping his hands behind his back, he walked up and down the room, saying, 'My God! My God! What will the country say! What will the country say!' " The people would be crushed, because only a week earlier General Hooker had issued "A Congratulatory Order," declaring, "The enemy must either ingloriously fly or come out from behind his defenses and give us battle on our own ground, where certain destruction awaits him." Federal troops in Northern Virginia outnumbered Confederate soldiers 130,000 to 60,000, and most Washingtonians believed victory was at hand. But Hooker *had* been over-confident.

Dr. Henry held himself together until Lincoln rushed out of the room, and then began to weep. He feared for the president's sanity, as did Secretary Edwin Stanton, who was afraid that Lincoln might commit suicide. As they heard the sounds of a carriage pulling up to the White House porte cochere, Brooks and Henry moved to the window. They watched Lincoln climb into the carriage with General Halleck, bound for the wharf, where they would board a steamer to Falmouth, Virginia. They must see firsthand what had happened to the Army of the Potomac.

Where was the president's wife? Spring was the time of year that Mrs. Lincoln suffered the worst of her debilitating headaches. Apart from the séance she hosted on April 23, she had done no entertaining for three weeks. Noah Brooks, who was fond of Mrs. Lincoln, and mentions her often in his writing, does not recall her presence on that sad afternoon in 1863.

HOOKER'S FAILURE GAVE Robert E. Lee's Army of Northern Virginia precious time to reorganize. On June 8, as Generals Lee and James Longstreet reached Culpeper, Virginia—the first post on their route to invade the North—Lincoln was taking his wife and youngest son to the railroad depot. They jolted along Pennsylvania Avenue in the carriage with rubber again grown thin on the wheels; he had vowed to get new treads but had not gotten around to it, so the ride was bumpy. At the station, he kissed Mary and Tad good-bye and put them on a three o'clock train to Philadelphia. They would stay at the Continental Hotel, and she planned to spend time with friends and do some shopping. There was some concern that the Confederates might attempt a raid on Washington, which was not the cause of Mary's leaving the city, but the danger might delay her return.

She wrote to him daily, but her telegrams have not survived. The first night she was gone, his sleep was troubled. He wrote to her: "Think you better put Tad's pistol away. I had an ugly dream about him." On June 11 he wrote again: "Your three despatches received. I am very well, and am glad to know that you and Tad are so." On June 15, he was proud to report to her that he had gotten new tires for the carriage, although he had no time to go for a drive. He was obsessed with battle tactics, frequently communicating by wire with Hooker and toiling in meetings with Halleck, Welles, and Stanton. In response to her inquiry as to his state of body and mind, the best he could answer was "tolerably well." The enemy had gotten as far as Winchester, and Union troops escaping toward Harper's Ferry sustained terrible losses: four thousand soldiers dead, wounded, and captured; also artillery, hundreds of horses, and loaded wagons lost. General Longstreet was leading his men north from Culpeper, Virginia, sixty miles from Washington, and Hooker reported "it is not in my power to prevent" an invasion.

On June 16, the rebels crossed the Potomac, yet Lincoln did not try to discourage his wife and son from coming home. That day he wrote her this vague message: "It is a matter of choice with yourself whether you come home. There is no reason why you should not, that did not exist when you went away. As bearing on the question of your coming home, I do not think the raid into Pennsylvania amounts to anything at all." So little correspondence has survived between husband and wife that one is tempted to make much of a pittance. It is irresistible because Lincoln chose his words so carefully. Clearly she had asked whether she should come home; plainly he told her the war should not keep her away. So his first two sentences are telling. He would not order her to come home—it was not his way to order her about, any more than it was her habit to submit. The second, cryptic sentence addresses a great chasm between them. Simply translated, it means that since she left, nothing has changed; and if she wanted to be apart from him before, it will be no different now. The tone is distant and cool, not at all welcoming.

Surely she understood his letters better than anyone else can. Her response was to return to him the next day, June 17, 1863. She and Tad arrived at the depot on North Capitol Street, and the heat and stench of the city assailed them. The family spent the next week preparing to leave the White House for the cooler atmosphere of the Soldiers' Home. While Mrs. Lincoln set up housekeeping there, the president was absorbed with military affairs, particularly the appointment of General George Gordon Meade to replace General Hooker as the Confederate army moved through Maryland into Pennsylvania. The Confederate advance north was frightening because the Federal command had no idea where they might attack.

Mrs. Lincoln and Tad settled in to the bright, gabled summer home. The daily half hour's ride over the three miles from Pennsylvania Avenue provided a welcome relief from the pressures of the presidency. In the Executive Mansion, "Mrs. President" was oppressed by protocol, guards, and too many servants for the staff to be unobtrusive or obedient. Intimacy between husband and wife was nearly impossible there; at the Soldiers' Home they were able to recapture some of the rituals and habits of the Springfield days. They read aloud to each other; they received intimate friends in casual dress. Charles Derickson, ordered to deliver a message to the president late one night, found Lincoln in bed with his wife. In that Gothic Revival "cottage" on the hill, Mary Lincoln once again felt she fulfilled her role as mistress of the house. At least there was an illusion of peace.

A hundred and twenty miles north, on July 1, Federal and Confederate troops converged on Gettysburg. By the time General Lee arrived in the midafternoon of that fateful day, the Confederates held the town. The president had no news of the fighting until later. On July 2, Lincoln rose early to take his coffee and biscuits at the Soldiers' Home before riding into the city. He went directly to the telegraph office in the War Department, and at midmorning was sitting at the table there reading distressing telegrams from General Meade. The first day of the crucial battle had been a disaster, with heavy casualties on both sides—and victory had gone to the South.

After her husband had gone to work on this particular Thursday morning, Mrs. Lincoln was in no hurry to leave the cottage. She ordered the driver to bring the carriage around at ten. They rode out the west-curving Rock Creek Church Road without incident, covering a half-mile in about five minutes. There the road forked and they took the left turn south, while the Church Road went on to Mount Pleasant Hospital. Mrs. Lincoln felt a shock to the carriage. The front seat jarred loose from its bolts, and the driver, as if pushed by an invisible hand, flew into the air and off to the side of the road, tumbling to a stop while the carriage ran on. The reins dangled in the rods, the horses spooked and broke into a wild gallop, and Mrs. Lincoln, panicked, leaped from the carriage, hit the ground, and rolled. She was probably knocked unconscious; the most serious of her bruises and scrapes was the wound a reporter described as "on the back of the head—the blood flowed freely." It is not known whether the coachman went for help, or someone on the turnpike saw the runaway horses and traced them to the injured lady. But according to the same reporter, surgeons from the nearby hospital "were instantly upon the spot, and administered promptly to her injuries." She appeared well enough to continue on to the White House instead of going to the nearby hospital—she insisted she was. So the surgeons hailed a passing carriage and helped her to her seat, and Mrs. Lincoln, "now quite recovered from her fright," arrived at the mansion at about the time the president usually took his lunch.

Sometimes at noon he was so overwhelmed with visitors that he would forget to come down to eat his biscuit and apple and drink his glass of water, and Mrs. Lincoln would send him a tray of food. On this day, when she arrived at the White House, bruised, bleeding, and limping, with a bandage wrapped around her head, he was in the telegraph offices reviewing the gruesome dispatches from Gettysburg. He hurried from the War Department to see what was the matter. His frazzled wife must have appeared to him like a twisted reflection from the distant torrent of the battle.

Because she would not allow him to consider her own cuts and bruises as serious at such a time, or because he was so preoccupied with the maimed and dying soldiers at Gettysburg, Lincoln could not face the possibility that Mary was in danger. And she would rather not worry him. He wired Robert: "Don't be uneasy. Your mother very slightly hurt by her fall." But Lincoln soon summoned nurse Rebecca Pomroy. According to her recollection, the wound on the back of Mrs. Lincoln's head soon became infected and began to suppurate. The physicians had to lance the wound and drain it over a period of three weeks, during which Mrs. Lincoln required the nurse's attention around the clock. She who had always suffered from headaches was now stricken in her vulnerable cranium during weeks when her husband was at his wit's end over the exasperating conduct of his generals.

During those terrible days of July 1863, Lincoln wore a path between his office and the cipher room of the War Department. In the evenings he visited his wife, who lay recuperating in her bed at the Soldiers' Home. His correspondence during this period contains an unusual number of misspellings, suggesting that he was writing in haste or having difficulty concentrating. The Battle of Gettysburg ended in unprecedented carnage, with more than forty thousand dead and wounded and the near-entrapment of Lee's troops between the Federal armies and the flooding of the Potomac. Meade's weary generals let Lee escape, and thus—in the president's opinion—they had lost their best chance to end the rebellion. The news of Lee's escape came July 14, before the noon cabinet meeting, and Lincoln's vexation was extreme. Secretary of the Navy Gideon Welles found the president prostrated with depression, lying on a sofa in the War Department, "dejected and discouraged."

Three days earlier, Lincoln had written asking his son Robert, who was then in New York, to "come to Washington." When Robert failed to respond his father wrote again, irritably, on July 14, "Why do I hear no more of you?" The laconic young man was already en route to Washington. Arriving at his father's office in the late afternoon of that same day, July 14—about the time the president usually left the White House for the Soldiers' Home—he "found him in much distress, his head leaning on the desk in front of him." And when he lifted his head there were tears in his eyes. He was weeping because General Lee's troops had escaped south across the Potomac to Williamsport despite Lincoln's repeated commands that Meade pursue the Confederate army with all his force. "If I had gone up there," he told Robert, "I could have whipped them myself."

A few weeks shy of his twentieth birthday, Robert arrived to find one parent prostrated with sadness and the other with a head wound. He approached his mother's sickbed with that mixture of devotion and trepidation of the child who has too often done a parent's duty. Mary Lincoln had always drawn strength from Robert's presence, from the days when Mr. Lincoln was away from home on the Eighth Circuit for months at a time. Now Bob sat with her and told her about New York, and she tried to reassure him that she would be all right. Then John Hay—five years his senior, and like an older brother to Robert—whisked him away on a tour of Washington's night life, the concert saloons and taverns, where they saw "some very queer dancing and singing at one place" and some excellent singing at another. The night of July 17, Hay reported to Nicolay, on vacation in the Rockies, "Bob [Lincoln] & I had a fearful orgie here last night on whiskey and cheese. The house is gradually going to the bad since you left." Neither Bob Lincoln nor John Hay was a habitual drunk. It seems to have taken the young men a good deal of "medicine" that week to endure the problems in the White House and the Soldiers' Home.

The heat and humidity in Washington were terrible, even at the Soldiers' Home. Robert Lincoln had his usual calming effect upon his mother; by July 18, he had persuaded Mrs. Lincoln and Tad to accompany him on a vacation to the White Mountains. A week later Mrs. Lincoln was well enough to travel, although she was still disoriented from her head wound. Robert and others observed that her mental stability—which had scarcely recovered from the trauma of Willie's death—seemed permanently impaired by the carriage accident.

Robert and his mother and brother traveled via New York and Boston and took the steamboat across Lake Winnipesaukee to Center Harbor, where they rested for the night before taking a private carriage up the White Mountains to Tip Top House on Mount Washington. They remained there at that cool and peaceful retreat until September while Mrs. Lincoln convalesced.

ALTHOUGH MR. LINCOLN did not acknowledge it, there was a widespread suspicion that the runaway vehicle was the work of a saboteur and that Mrs. Lincoln was the victim of an attack meant for the president. Someone had loosened the bolts on the driver's seat. Lincoln protested that the carriage had not been properly serviced, but he might have felt a pang of guilt that the disaster had befallen his wife instead of himself. She would remember this lesson that assassination threats are not always idle. Horrible things can happen. Later, Robert Lincoln, encountering his aunt Emilie Todd Helm at Fort Monroe, confided to her: "I think mother has never quite recovered from the effects of her fall. . . . It is really astonishing what a brave front she manages to keep when we know she is suffering. . . . She just straightens herself up a little more and says, 'It is better to laugh than to be sighing.' Tad would go all to pieces if she reversed the words of that opera, and so would my father."

After Gettysburg, and before the disastrous defeat of Federal forces at Chickamauga in northwest Georgia that September, there was some calm in the White House. John Hay wrote that Washington was "as dismal now as a defaced tombstone. Everybody is gone." But on August 7 he noted that the Tycoon—his nickname for the president—"is in fine whack. I have rarely seen him more serene & busy. He is managing this war, the draft, foreign relations, and planning a reconstruction of the Union, all at once." He was relieved to see his wife and sons removed to a healthier climate, but he missed them. From July 28 until September 24 he wrote nine letters that have survived, and they are affectionate as well as revealing in their choice of subjects. On August 8 he writes, "My dear wife. All is well as usual, and no particular trouble any way." He alludes to an ongoing dialogue about their finances: "I put the money in the treasury at five per cent, with the previlege [*sic*] of withdrawing it any time upon thirty days notice. I suppose you are glad to learn this."

She would certainly be glad to hear that at last he was paying attention to their finances, and she hoped he might continue to do so whether or not he told her. He asks her to "tell dear Tad" that his pet goat is lost and that he is in distress about it. "The day you left Nanny was found resting herself, and chewing her little cud, on the middle of Tad's bed. But now she's gone!" Goats will be goats, and perhaps Nanny had been chewing the draperies. After a report on the hot weather, Mr. Lincoln writes a long paragraph concerning the recent election in Kentucky.

Money, politics, and a tender expression of sympathy for Tad's pet—all these subjects appear above the salutation "Affectionately, A. Lincoln" when his family had been gone for eleven days. Other letters that August and early September report on military developments. By September 20, he is pleased to tell her that there is no sickness in Washington, and the next day he writes, "The air is so clear and cool, and apparently healthy, that I would be glad for you to come."

That Sunday the Battle of Chickamauga was raging in the Georgia woods, and soon Lincoln learned of the near rout of Federal troops there and heavy losses on both sides. On Wednesday the twenty-third he received the sad news of the death of his brother-in-law, Confederate Brigadier General Ben Hardin Helm. Judge David Davis found Lincoln in his office at about four o'clock, and recalled that he had rarely seen his old friend more grief-stricken. Sister Emilie's husband was only thirty-two years of age. Lincoln had offered him a commission as an army paymaster for the Union, but he had turned it down.

"Davis," said he, "I feel as David of old did when he was told of the death of Absalom." King David's son Absalom had plotted to overthrow his father's kingdom. How could Lincoln break the news to his wife? She had totally misunderstood his last telegram, somehow getting the impression he thought it was sickly here and not fit for her return. He wrote her back urgently insisting "it was never healthier, and I really wish to see you," demanding that she answer immediately. Mary replied she had a terrible cold, and was "anxious to return home as you may suppose." But she would not leave that day, or that week, so he would have to inform her through the impersonal telegraph service of the War Department, to which no message could be entrusted but those fit to be seen by strangers.

So he wrote his wife a long dispatch on Thursday the twenty-fourth summing up the Battle of Chickamauga as a setback for the Union—as the Confederates had gained ground, a great deal of artillery and many prisoners. Almost parenthetically he mentions that "your brother-in-law Helm" was one of six Confederate officers killed. The president did not want telegraph operators to know that he was brokenhearted over the death of a rebel general.

Mary and Tad returned home on the twenty-eighth of September, and it appears that the month of October, their last month of the year at the Soldiers' Home, was a tranquil and happy time for the family. The leaves of the oaks, maples, and beeches were turning and would soon be a riot of color. Lincoln was confident that if Generals Rosecrans and Burnside could hold their ground in East Tennessee, then they "had the enemy by the throat." The crisp mountain air had benefited Mary, and she was enjoying as much health as she ever would. A friend, Francis S. Corkran of Baltimore, invited Mrs. Lincoln to go grape picking. Lincoln wrote on her behalf—as he sometimes did when she was indisposed—"Mrs. L. is now at home & would be pleased to see you any time. If the grape time has not passed away, she would be pleased to join in the enterprise you mentioned."

On October 3, the president issued his cheerful Proclamation of Thanksgiving, which formalized Thanksgiving as a fixed Union feast day to be celebrated the last Thursday of November. It opens with the words, "The year that is drawing towards its close, has been filled with the blessings of fruitful fields and healthful skies." An eloquent expression, it seems as much personal as stately, the reflections of a man who has weighed the bounties and misfortunes in the balance of an eventful year— the year of Gettysburg, Chickamauga, Mrs. Lincoln's carriage accident, and the death of Ben Hardin Helm.

What might they do for Mary's sister, the widow Emilie Helm?

The Lincolns had been in touch with the Todd family in Lexington, and on October 15, the president telegraphed a pass allowing the grieving woman to go home to Kentucky. By early December, Lincoln's pass got Emilie and her daughter Katherine as far as Fortress Monroe, Virginia. There the Federal officers demanded that Emilie Helm swear an oath of allegiance to the United States before proceeding to Kentucky. "Distressed, heartbroken as she was and fearing she might be sent back South, alone and almost penniless, she firmly refused to take the oath," her daughter recalled. Uncertain of how to proceed against the lady, one of the officers told her, "We will have to telegraph the President of your decision."

This was a moment of truth for the Lincoln-Todd family, a crisis in which family loyalty had to be weighed against political expediency. In December of that divisive year 1863, Lincoln was under withering criticism, not only by the Democrats but by the progressive wing of his own party, which wanted Salmon Chase to replace him. Yet upon hearing of Mrs. Helm's refusal to swear allegiance to the Union, the president immediately replied, "Send her to me." He turned a deaf ear to the unkillable rumors that Mrs. Lincoln—whose half brother Alexander had recently died in rebel gray near Baton Rouge, and whose son Tad had been seen waving Ellsworth's Confederate flag from a White House window—was a secessionist, a spy. Let people say what they would, the Confederate widow could stay with the Lincolns in Washington for as long as she pleased.

Emilie Todd Helm's arrival in Washington under military guard, on or about December 9, did cause a stir. The most beautiful of the Todd women, with her large, wide-set eyes and her raven-black hair parted in the middle and swept back in a shiny chignon, the twenty-seven-year-old widow was not the sort to go unnoticed in any circumstances. Emilie and Katherine Helm must have reminded the soldiers of the flowerlike, infamous spy Rose O'Neal Greenhow, and her little daughter, photographed the year before in the Old Capitol Prison.

Mary Lincoln had left Washington alone on December 3 to spend a week in New York. Upon arriving she had wired her husband complaining of exhaustion and a severe headache, hoping to hear he was doing well. Two days later she wired again, "Do let me know immediately how Taddie and yourself are." Neither Mr. Lincoln nor Tad had been well since mid-November, so it seems peculiar that "Mother" would have left them. On November 18, the day before Lincoln was to give his Gettysburg address, Tad was too ill to eat his breakfast, and Mrs. Lincoln was beside herself, remembering Willie. She did not go with her husband to Pennsylvania, and friends noted that he was despondent. He returned from Gettysburg with varioloid, a kind of smallpox; ever since then he had been too ill to leave the White House, and sometimes too weak to leave his bed. The newspapers reported on November 28 that Tad was recovering from scarlet fever. While the president was wiring assurances to his wife at the Metropolitan Hotel, "All going well," and "All doing well," on December 5 and 6, he was still confined to his room with smallpox.

Sister Emilie and her daughter arrived in Washington about the same time Mrs. Lincoln returned from her New York shopping trip, December 8, 1863. Mrs. Helm's visit to Washington is mostly known from the recollections she left in her diary: "Mr. Lincoln and my sister met me with the warmest affection, we were all too grief-stricken at first for speech. I have lost my husband, they have lost their fine little son Willie and Mary and I have lost three brothers in the Confederate service. . . . Sister and I dined intimately, alone." The president and Tad were convalescing, and Washington was undergoing an epidemic of smallpox. Lincoln confided to Orville Browning, "Mrs. Helm was in the house, but he did not wish it known."

Emilie Helm's diary from that cold, dreary week in the White House focuses upon the dynamic between Mary and Abraham Lincoln, particularly his concerns about his wife's mental health. Emilie describes Mary's efforts to conceal her sorrow and anxiety from her husband. "Sister is doing everything to distract my mind and her own from our terrible grief . . . we can't get away from it, try as we will to be cheerful and accept fate. Sister always has a cheerful word and a smile for Mr. Lincoln, who seems thin and care-worn." A disturbing incident occurred one morning when Emilie came upon her sister "sitting in a drooping, despondent attitude," holding a newspaper she had been reading. The papers dropped to the floor as Mary held out her arms crying, "Kiss me, Emilie, and tell me you love me! I seem to be the scape-goat for both North and South!"

"Then suddenly as if she had thrown off a dark cloak and stood revealed in a gay costume," Emilie recalled, "she held her head up and smiled." Amazed by the transformation, Emilie then realized that Mr. Lincoln had entered the room. He too had observed his wife's forced gaiety, and supported it with the light comment: "I hope you two are planning some mischief!" But the president was deeply concerned. Later that day he spoke to Emilie privately, begging her to stay with them in the summer: "I feel worried about Mary, her nerves have gone to pieces; she cannot hide from me that the strain she has been under has been too much for her mental as well as her physical health."

Lincoln asked Emilie what she thought. Equally worried, Emilie replied, "She seems very nervous and excitable and once or twice when I have come into the room suddenly the frightened look in her eyes has appalled me." And then she told him she believed that if anything should happen to him or to the children Mary could not survive it. Once again Lincoln asked Emilie to stay as long as she could.

In another diary entry, Mrs. Helm tells of the night Mary Lincoln knocked on her door as she was preparing for bed, asking if she might come in. Emilie was staying in the darkly draped, ghost-ridden Prince of Wales guest room where Willie had died. She noticed that her older sister had a strange luster in her eyes and seemed abnormally excited. "She was smiling though her eyes were full of tears." Mary told Emilie that there was comfort to be had after the passing of loved ones. When Willie died, at first she thought she could never recover from her sorrow; only her husband inspired her to smile again and be cheerful for his sake.

Now, with her eyes brimming with tears, she confided that "if Willie did not come to comfort me I would still be drowned in tears . . . he lives, Emilie!" The thrill in the haunted woman's voice was unforgettable. "He comes to me every night, and stands at the foot of my bed with the same sweet adorable smile he has always had; he does not always come alone; little Eddie is sometimes with him and twice he has come with our brother Alec and is with him most of the time. You cannot dream of the comfort this gives me."

Mary went on like this for some time, in her nightgown, her hair down, and Emilie noted that her "eyes were wide and shining and I had a feeling of awe as if I were in the presence of the supernatural. It *is* unnatural and abnormal, it frightens me." Even confirmed spiritualists of the time considered the raising of spirits to be a group activity that required strict "controls" and an experienced medium. At forty-five years of age, Mrs. Lincoln had begun to experience the delusions and hallucinations of what now would be diagnosed as clinical psychosis, and the signs were heartbreaking for those who loved her.

EMILIE HELM ALSO recollects the unwanted attention of Mrs. Lincoln's friend and admirer, the self-styled hero of Gettysburg, General Daniel Sickles. A former congressman from New York, Sickles had lost a leg in the battle, and spent the rest of his life denigrating General Meade's part in it. Sickles was also an infamous womanizer, best known perhaps for the 1859 murder of Philip Barton Key for having an affair with his wife, which drew attention to the murderer's own philandering. He gunned down Philip Key—son of Francis Scott Key, author of "The Star-Spangled Banner"—in Lafayette Square, right across from the White House. Edwin Stanton would serve, successfully, as his defense lawyer.

Sickles shared Mrs. Lincoln's passion for mediums and séances, and was the sort of romantic flatterer she found irresistible. Emilie recalls that the dapper general visited the White House twice that week, swinging in on his crutches, and she comments, "He seems on very intimate terms here." Although she did not wish to be seen, General Sickles greatly desired to see Mrs. Helm. Arriving one evening with Senator Ira Harris, Sickles had Mrs. Lincoln summon the pretty widow on the slender pretext that Harris wanted news of his friend General John Breckinridge, about whom Emilie knew nearly nothing. It appears that the real reason the men wanted Mrs. Helm to join them was to flirt with her, and when she showed no enthusiasm for the game, they decided to taunt and torment her instead. She was equal to the challenge. When Harris boasted, "We have whipped the rebels at Chattanooga and I hear, madam, that the scoundrels ran like scared rabbits," the doe-eyed rebel retorted, "It was the example, Senator Harris, that you set them at Bull Run and Manassas."

Sickles was so offended by Emilie's retort that he stumped upstairs, insisting that he see the president. Mr. Lincoln was keeping to his bed, still recovering from the variola. John Stuart, his old law partner, sat by his side, chatting, and it is to Stuart that we owe the anecdote. At first Lincoln was amused by the general's red-faced, furious account of the conversation with Mrs. Helm. Lincoln explained, chuckling, "The child has a tongue like the rest of the Todds." Hearing this, Sickles lost what was left of his patience, and, slapping the table, blurted, "You should not have that rebel in your house"—a thought that had occurred already to Emilie herself, if not to the president. For all his humor, Lincoln felt that the general had violated a sacred boundary.

"Excuse me, General Sickles," the president interrupted, "my wife and I are in the habit of choosing our own guests. We do not need from our friends either advice or assistance in the matter. Besides . . . the little 'rebel' came because I ordered her to come, it was not of her own volition."

Naturally, sister Emilie and her child did not stay very long in the White House. Almost twenty years younger than her unbalanced half sister, the widow was in no condition to prop up Mrs. Lincoln. No matter how much the president pleaded with her, she had to leave. She stayed until Mary's birthday, on Sunday, December 13. That evening the Shakespearean actor James Hackett visited the president; according to John Hay, Lincoln and Hackett spent hours in conversation over the finer points of Falstaff's character and the plays in which he figures. General James Wadsworth and the leering Daniel Sickles were also guests that night. But as Hay describes the occasion, Mrs. Lincoln and Mrs. Helm were not part of that company, and Hay paid his respects to the ladies in another room of the mansion.

Emilie Helm and her daughter left soon thereafter, so as to arrive in Lexington before Christmas, and Mr. Lincoln consoled his wife by taking her to see Mr. Hackett in *Henry IV* at Ford's Theatre, then to hear the famous poet and novelist Bayard Taylor lecture on Russian culture at Willard's Hall.

FIRE AND ICE

FIRE AND ICE

THE LINCOLNS' DESIRE for four more years in the White House shaped the year 1864, as their original ambition for the presidency had ruled their lives in 1860. But everything had changed. Neither of them had ever suffered so much as they had during the last three years, nor had the country. If there had been fleeting moments of glory and pleasure for the president and his wife, those moments were overshadowed by the trauma and grief they had known.

The year began with the now familiar, scarcely contained riot of the New Year's open house. First came the morning parade of brightly costumed diplomats and their wives, then the military brass led by General Halleck—five hundred officers with their swords and medals—paid their respects. Then the doors of the vestibule were pushed open to the public hordes that milled and chattered in a great concourse that backed up all the way to Vermont Avenue. It was a brilliant day, and the wind blew in from the west. Secretary Nicolay said he had never seen a greater crowd. An impatient lady threw open a window from the portico to the vestibule and climbed in; a number of men and children followed her until the police shut down the "leak."

Orville Browning, approaching the portico with Senators Solomon Foot and James Doolittle, measured the crowd and shuddered. "Such a mob around the door we did not try to enter." Inside, as protocol directed—Lincoln in the East Room, Mrs. Lincoln in the Blue Room—the president and his wife did their duty of greeting the visitors, smiling and shaking hands. Mrs. Lincoln arrived late, at 11:30, and excused herself an hour later. Although her escort, Benjamin French, said she "did her part of the reception with her usual ease and urbanity," he seemed surprised when she went upstairs. Assuming that his duty ended with hers, he left the house. He was later embarrassed to discover that she had only gone away for a few minutes, and then had returned to please the crowd. This goes to show how chaotic these occasions were. William Stoddard had to stand in for Commissioner French in making the introductions.

Two days later Mrs. Lincoln left for a five-day shopping excursion to Philadelphia to replenish her wardrobe. During the next twelve weeks, the Lincolns hosted nineteen formal entertainments in the White House—levees, morning receptions, soirées, and state dinners—knowing that Mr. Lincoln's second term hung in the balance. No president had served two terms since Andrew Jackson, and Lincoln would need every advantage, including those that came from social success in a town where rivals such as Salmon Chase were eager to show him up. At one poorly attended evening reception on January 14, Benjamin French noted that while "Abraham was in his usual trim & usual good nature," Mrs. Lincoln was dejected. French may not have known the extent to which the president's wife was compensating for an emotional handicap. She was more capable of pulling herself together for state functions than she had been during the year of Willie's death, but she was neither stable nor healthy, and it still required considerable effort for her to meet the public.

One of Mary Lincoln's strategies for coping with the emotional stress that came with her social position was the cultivation of enemies. Lincoln refused to squander his energy that way; but for some people the division of the world into friends and foes simplifies life, reducing the overrun field to a smoother meadow with the scythe of a vigorous animosity. Just as Mrs. Lincoln hated her sister Ann, her bridesmaid Julia Jayne Trumbull, William Herndon, and her former ally William Wood, she now hated Salmon Chase—secretary of the treasury—and his beautiful daughter, Kate.

Chase longed to be president. Soon after arriving in Washington, his twenty-one-year-old daughter established a salon in their town house that continually diverted high society from entertainments at the Executive Mansion. In November, Lincoln had displeased his wife by attending Kate's wedding to the textile heir Senator William Sprague of Rhode Island. Mary intended to have nothing to do with Kate Chase Sprague, or her tall, presidential-looking father, who had already hired an expensive campaign biographer, traded Treasury favors with the Kansas-Pacific Railway for campaign financing, and solicited Republican endorsements. Mrs. Lincoln could not have known that on January 18, Chase had written to a major supporter in Ohio: "At the instance of many who think that the public interest would be promoted by my election in the chief magistry, a committee, composed of prominent Senators and Representatives and citizens, has been organized here for taking measures to promote that object." This letter formalized his scheme to run for president.

Mary Lincoln could not have known about that letter, but with the instinct of a natural enemy she vowed, that morning, that the Chases should never again set foot in her house. She had already warned her husband that Salmon Chase pretended to be his friend only "because it is in his interest to be so. He is anything for Chase. If he thought he could make anything by it, he would betray you to-morrow."

"I fear you are prejudiced against the man, Mother. I know that you do him an injustice."

"Mr. Lincoln, you are either blind or will not see." As sometimes happened, she mistook his deliberate priorities for naïveté. His conversations with John Hay, recorded in Hay's diary, prove that Lincoln knew exactly what Chase was up to—his criticism of Lincoln's conduct of the war, Chase's "secret" solicitation of funds and courting of backers for his nomination. Lincoln simply did not care. He needed Chase in his cabinet, and believed that the country could do worse than have Chase in the White House. Finally, he never really believed that Chase, in and of himself, would cost him a second term.

Lincoln's wife had other opinions and worries. Lincoln is supposed to have said she cared more about his reelection than he did, although he did not know exactly why. The fact is that those shopping trips to New York and Philadelphia had resulted in secret debts that could not be kept secret or discreetly paid off if Mrs. Lincoln was no longer Mrs. President. She spoke to Mrs. Keckley candidly about this. The dressmaker was trying to assure her that "Mr. Lincoln is certain to be re-elected" because "he represents a principle," and she was perplexed by Mrs. Lincoln's anxiety on the subject—by her observing woefully, "If he should be defeated, I do not know what would become of us all," and "there is more at stake in this election than he dreams of." When Mrs. Keckley asked what she meant, Mrs. Lincoln explained, "I have contracted large debts, of which he knows nothing, and which he will be unable to pay if he is defeated." This was not really true. Lincoln had more than enough money to pay off the debts, but evidently he was as reticent about his net worth as she was about her unpaid bills.

Mrs. Lincoln confessed that her debts were chiefly in store bills, about $27,000 worth, most of it to A. T. Stewart's Broadway department store. She said that her husband had no idea of what it cost for her to cut an acceptable figure in society, or how much people expected of her, being an outsider, "having grown up in the West. . . . To keep up appearances, I must have money—more than Mr. Lincoln can spare for me. He is too honest to make a penny outside of his salary." And so she dug herself deeper in debt, and traded favors with New York politicians and editors who interceded with the merchants.

When Mrs. Keckley asked her if her husband knew anything about this problem, she got this tormented response: "God no! And I would not have him suspect. If he knew that his wife was involved to the extent that she is, the knowledge would drive him mad. He is so sincere and straightforward himself, that he is shocked by the duplicity of others." She said she valued their happiness too much to tell him the truth (a tactic that was, of course, the opposite of what would have made him happy) and that this was what troubled her so much. "If he is re-elected, I can keep him in ignorance of my affairs; but if he is defeated, then the bills will be sent in, and he will know all." Then, Mrs. Keckley recalled, "something like a hysterical sob escaped her."

Such thoughts were on her mind on January 18, four days after Kate Chase had lured half of her guests away from an evening reception in the Blue Room, and the very day Salmon Chase had written to Ohio declaring he was available to run for president. John Nicolay was going over the guest list for the cabinet dinner, a state dinner to be held at 7:00 on Thursday evening the twenty-first. Mrs. Lincoln read over the list of invited cabinet members and Supreme Court justices and their wives and daughters. She crossed the Chases off the list, as well as Kate's husband, William Sprague, senator from Rhode Island. Shocked as he was by this offense to civility, Nicolay held his tongue. He knew Mrs. Lincoln well enough not to try to reason with her. She had always resented his position as social manager, and he did his best to defer to her whenever he could. Chase, however, was secretary of the treasury. It would be an affront not only to him but to the rest of the cabinet to exclude him from the dinner; and Kate Chase had accompanied her father to every state function since he was appointed—it would be unseemly to shut her out, or her new husband, who was a powerful legislator in his own right.

Mrs. Lincoln was not thinking about manners and protocol. She hated the Chases and thought they were traitors plotting to cheat her husband out of four more years in the White House. Then, she believed, he would receive her invoices from A. T. Stewart, and he would go mad, and they would never be happy again. So she crossed the Chases off the guest list.

Nicolay, on his way to his office beyond the president's to address the dinner invitations, put his head in at the door to Lincoln's room to beg a moment of his time. The secretary pointed to the guest list, and the snub. Quickly sizing up the situation, Lincoln approached his wife, requesting that the secretary of the treasury and his family be reinstated. Nicolay wrote, "After a short conference with the powers at the other end of the hall [Mr. Lincoln] came back and ordered Rhode Island [William and Kate Sprague] and Ohio [Secretary Chase] to be included in the list. Whereat there soon arose such a rampage as the house hasn't seen in a year, and I am again taboo." Nicolay was not exaggerating. By now Mrs. Lincoln's tantrums were familiar to him and John Hay, and between them they referred to her as "the hellcat" and "Her Satanic Majesty." In this same letter to Hay, who was on a mission to Hilton Head, South Carolina, delivering military orders, Nicolay remarks that Mrs. Lincoln's personal secretary, William Stoddard, "fairly cowered at the violence of the storm, and I think for the first time begins to appreciate the awful sublimities of nature."

Stoddard later published his own impressions of Mrs. Lincoln, describing her as "absolute mistress of all that part of the White House," from the first floor vestibule to "the upper floor west of the folding doors across the hall at the head of the stair"—in other words, all but the domain of the president and his aides. This was true enough when she was well. But Stoddard, who liked Mrs. Lincoln, alludes to an illness that rendered her incapable of managing her affairs. He observes that she was willing to accept advice and yield to reason, but only "provided the arguments come from a recognized friend, for her personal antipathies are quick and strong, and at times they find hasty and resentful forms of expression." Stoddard—as we have heard—was perplexed by Mrs. Lincoln's mood changes, and he was given to such veiled observations as "Probably all physicians and most middle-aged people will understand better than could a youthful secretary the causes of a sudden horror of a poverty to come, for example, which, during a few hours of extreme depression, proposed to sell the very manure in the Executive stables." One of her doctors, Thomas W. Dresser, son of the minister who had married the

Lincolns, said, "While the whole world was finding fault with her temper and disposition, it was clear to me that the trouble was really a cerebral disease."

She was so furious at Nicolay that she tried to get him barred from the dinner and to dismiss him from his duties in arranging social affairs. She wanted Stoddard to take over. But Nicolay stood his ground against Stoddard, insisting that if he could not do the job he was paid for, then no one else could—Mrs. Lincoln might do it herself if she liked. She "announced her determination to run the machine without my help," he recalled. But then she went to pieces the afternoon of the event, saying "she had backed down, requested my presence and assistance—apologizing, and explaining that the affair had worried her so she hadn't slept in a night or two. I think she has felt happier since she cast out that devil of stubbornness."

Mr. Lincoln was caught in the middle of this imbroglio. Knowing that his wife's position was indefensible, he was compelled to take Nicolay's side against her, and bore the brunt of her rancor.

"THE DINNER WAS got through with creditably," John Nicolay recalled. This was the best that could be said of the dozen entertainments that followed during the late winter. The public levees were mobbed, overrun with tourists; and many of the more intimate afternoon receptions in Mrs. Lincoln's parlor were poorly attended. The crème of society preferred the company to be found at the Chases' or Mrs. Eames's; they flocked to the entertainments of former New York mayor Fernando Wood, now a Democratic congressman from New York and a staunch advocate of compromise and peace with the rebels. If society pursued political strength, these were not auspicious signs for the Lincolns.

Robert Lincoln and his friend Neil Dennison were visiting during much of January and early February, and their company brightened the gloomy White House. February is a dreary month in Washington, and with Robert's return to Harvard, the president and his wife appear to have entered a tunnel of illness and depression. Mr. Lincoln paid regular visits to his friend Owen Lovejoy, the abolitionist congressman from Illinois, around the corner on Fifteenth Street. Lovejoy was sick, with some undetermined, intermittent fever that confined him to his room for days at a time. He would gain strength and go to work for a while, only to relapse and return to his bed. For Lincoln this must have seemed a metaphor for the prolonged fever of the war, where the army gave him hope one day, only to take it away the next. "This war is eating my life out," he told Lovejoy on February 6, 1864. "I have a strong impression that I shall not live to see the end." That day, a Saturday, Mrs. Lincoln held one of her regular afternoon receptions in the Blue Room. *The Washington Star* reported that it was well attended, but this did not appear to lift the president's spirits much, or for very long, as Orville Browning discovered when he went to see him late in the evening.

Browning was no longer a senator, having served out the term he was appointed to fill upon Stephen Douglas's death. At present, he was a Washington lawyer and lobbyist, and he was opposed to the Emancipation Proclamation. Although he and the president were still friends, and Browning profited from the connection, by 1864 the men had moved so far apart ideologically, there was doubt whether Browning would support him in the coming election.

When Orville Browning knocked on Lincoln's door that night, Lincoln welcomed him gladly, as a friend. The president was in no mood for business. Unfortunately for Browning, but luckily for posterity, Browning had come on an errand whose nature so offended the weary president that he could not conceal his anger. Lincoln, so famous for his composure, his resilient good humor, and his equanimity, abandoned these defenses and raged at Browning as one might only rage at a friend he had known for twenty-five years. In his diary, Browning preserved this rare picture of Lincoln. After taking a seat near the president by the fire in his office, and exchanging greetings, Browning told him he had come on behalf of a Mrs. Fitz, a widow loyal to the Union, who owned a cotton plantation in Mississippi. The Federal troops had swept in, freed all forty-seven of her slaves, and seized ten thousand bushels of corn. Mrs. Fitz had fled to St. Louis, where she now was subsisting, a pauper.

He had come to convey a proposal from the widow: She would ask no compensation for her slaves. But she did want the government to lend her enough Negroes "out of those accumulated upon its hands" (and they had only to look out the windows to see their fires burning in the camps near the Tiber Branch) so she could revive her farm next season, and raise a crop of cotton. Out of the profit, she would pay the Negroes the same wages the government would if it employed them.

Well? What did the president think of that? Browning thought the proposition was "reasonable and just, and worthy at least of being considered."

At this point in his diary, Browning falters. Did Lincoln leap out of his seat, run his long fingers through his hair, and stride away across the room to put distance between himself and the visitor before unleashing his fury upon him? The diarist discreetly states, "He became very much excited, and did not discuss the proposition at all." Did Mr. Lincoln swear oaths, or accuse Browning himself of dereliction and presumption? Evidently. Browning was stunned by the president's demonstration of feeling, and seems to be protecting both of their images as he records the dialogue.

"I would rather take a rope," Lincoln swore, "and *hang* myself than do it." If he did not discuss Mrs. Fitz's proposition, as Browning attested, he surely made it clear how he felt about it. "There are a great many poor women who never had any property at all who are suffering as much as Mrs. Fitz," Lincoln cried. "Her condition is a necessary consequence of the rebellion . . . the Government can't make good the losses occasioned by rebels."

To Browning it seemed that Lincoln's anger had transported him beyond logic. The advocate persisted, reminding his friend the president "that she was loyal, and that her property had been taken from her by her own government, and was now being used by it." And thus Browning was edging dangerously toward the heart of their quarrel over the Emancipation Proclamation. Browning seems to have been blind to the fact that it was his own attitude toward the Negroes, and Lincoln's proclamation, that had caused the president's outburst, rather than the isolated case of Mrs. Fitz.

"I think," said Browning stubbornly, "it is a case eminently proper for some sort of remuneration . . . her demand is reasonable . . . certainly entitled to respectful consideration."

"She had lost no property!" Lincoln replied. "Her slaves were free when they were taken"—by virtue of the Proclamation—and so she is "entitled to no compensation." But Browning would not be silenced. He pointed out that some of her slaves "had been taken in 1862, before his proclamation," and getting no response, continued, "Yes, a portion of her slaves at least, were taken in 1862, before your proclamation, and put upon our gun boats—"

That was the last straw—Lincoln was having no more of this. He howled at Browning, "I would rather *throw up* than do what you ask. I *won't* do anything about it."

"I left him," Browning concluded, "in no very good humor." Although he tried once or twice, Browning did not see his old friend again for almost two months. When they did meet again, on April 3, Lincoln lectured him at length about his reasons for issuing the Emancipation Proclamation, as if the lobbyist had been a student in need of remedial tutoring.

Orville Browning's encounter with Lincoln on February 6 is, as noted, a gift to posterity, for his jottings that night offer a rare portrait of the logical, patient man at the end of his rope emotionally. Mary Lincoln was not the only Lincoln capable of a show of temper. There are plenty of witnesses who recall Mrs. Lincoln losing her temper with her husband, but no one remembers Lincoln as being anything other than indulgent and soothing and kind to his wife at her worst moments—as if she were not his emotional equal. He suffered his exasperations inwardly, sublimating those feelings until they could find a safe outlet, such as his blasting of Orville Browning on that winter evening in 1864.

February was a cruel month for this family. Lincoln's birthday, which should have been a joyous occasion, fell between the anniversaries of the children's deaths: Eddie's on February 1 and Willie's on the twentieth. The Lincolns continued to go to the theater—a pleasant diversion that brought husband and wife together for a few hours out of the political and social pressure of the White House. On the evening of February 8 they attended the Washington Theatre, at Eleventh and C streets, a seedy quarter, to see Laura Keene in *The Sea of Ice,* a stirring melodrama by the French playwright Adolphe Philippe Dennery.

If they wanted escape from their worries on a cold night during the war, they had come to the wrong play. Dennery's piece, famous for its spectacular stage effects, concerns mutiny aboard a passenger ship bound for America along a wintry northern route. A villain possessing a treasure map and "mad for gold" has corrupted the crew, persuading them to lower the good captain and his family overboard in a skiff so the mutineers can go in search of the treasure. The tragic fate of Captain Ragul de Lascours, his wife, Louise, and their daughter Marie eerily resembles that of the Lincolns. Just as Mary Lincoln had abandoned Tad in the months after Willie's death, so Louise de Lascours has left one of her children, "confided her to the care of others—and for three years . . . and I fear that heaven will punish me as a bad mother." In the first minutes of the play she speaks these lines, which must have brought tears to Mary Lincoln's eyes: "Our children! they should be with us, always and for ever. A lifetime is not enough to love them—to admire them—to listen to their laugh, and to enjoy their sweet caresses; even sleep seems a theft from the parents' joy."

The captain is a paragon, "an honest man and a good father," his wife says, and "when I look on your calm fearless face, hear your persuasive voice, my foolish fears vanish; and when your hand presses mine, I believe in future days of happiness." Mrs. Lincoln liked to hold her husband's hand in the theater, and press it at such moments. She had much in common with the captain's wife, played by Laura Keene, the dark-eyed beauty with the long oval face. Louise whispered to her husband, "Raoul, can you rely on the fidelity of your crew?" "Why do you ask?" he responds. "Because," she explains, "I fancy that at times there is something sinister in their looks."

When he dismisses her fears as childish, she protests. "No! I am not deceived. They hate me; yesterday the carpenter passed me without saluting," and the helmsman sneered at her. The captain tries to reassure her, but she is right—mutiny is afoot. Lust for gold drives men to desperate acts. They will lower the captain, his family, and a loyal crewmember over the side, and the Lascours will spend their last days freezing to death on a dwindling ice floe. Louise's fine speech would echo in Mary Lincoln's own comments about her husband, years later: "You have been the most tender husband, the best of fathers, and the most generous friend—there is not a blot upon your life—and common failings have never sullied your pure and noble nature; I have striven to become worthy of you, but if I have failed, pardon me, and let your loving look rest on me as a blessing.... I feel that we shall meet in another world, where our children shall be angels."

Contemporary theatergoers say that there was not a dry eye in the house during the final moments of Act II, as Laura Keene knelt to pray in her melodious voice, on the ice floe, which by some trick of nineteenth-century stagecraft appeared to be vanishing into the sea. We go to the theater to laugh, cry, or be frightened out of our wits. We go with those we love in order to sit in the dark and share an affecting vision. If the dreamlike experience has something in common with our real lives, then the sharing continues as we leave the theater, sometimes late into the night. *The Sea of Ice,* subtitled *The Prayer of the Wrecked,* gave the Lincolns an uncommon opportunity for intimate communion.

TWO NIGHTS LATER it was fire rather than ice that brought the family together.

"Put crepe on your hat," Nicolay wrote to John Hay. "Tonight at about 8:30, while Cooper was gone to his supper, the stables took fire and burned down. The carriages and coupe alone were saved—everything else went—six horses, including the President's, ours, and Tad's two ponies. . . . Tad was in bitter tears at the loss of his ponies, and his heaviest grief was that one of them had belonged to Willie." Cooper, a driver and one of the stable hands, believed that it was arson; that morning Mrs. Lincoln had fired her coachman, and he was the chief suspect.

Mrs. Lincoln had been indisposed that day. Having invited Elizabeth Blair Lee and her uncle Ben Gratz of Lexington for a visit at midday, she sent them away, asking them to return in the evening. As they were leaving the grounds that night, Lee recalls that she was "stopped by the cry of fire." The brick building that housed the White House livery stood to the east of the mansion toward the Treasury building, on the far side of a boxwood hedge. From his window Lincoln saw the flames. He ran out, leaped over the hedge, and opened the stable doors in an effort to save the horses, but the heat and smoke drove him back. The firefighters arrived promptly, but because of the barn's highly combustible contents, the wood and hay, the men could do little more than stand by and contain the blaze.

The family stood in the East Room and watched the stables burn—all of them weeping. The next day Lincoln would speak to Commissioner French about having the stables restored, but nothing could be done for the poor horses. The most Lincoln could say to his distraught son to console him is that they had "gone where the good horses go." It was little comfort that the dismissed coachman, Patterson McGee, was arrested the next day.

The mercury plunged, and the Potomac froze solid so one could skate to Virginia. By midmonth the natives would be calling it the coldest winter of the decade. The city was plagued with typhoid, smallpox, and "bilious fever." The president's fifty-fifth birthday passed uneventfully, without notice in the press. The next day, the thirteenth, he was so shaky he could hardly make it to Mrs. Lincoln's afternoon reception, and it was hoped he was not stricken with the illness that was killing his friend Owen Lovejoy. He scribbled a note to Salmon Chase to postpone a meeting, explaining, "I am unwell, even now, and shall be worse this afternoon." He took to his bed on Sunday, and was sick much of the week, although he managed an appearance at his wife's Blue Room reception on the twentieth. General George Meade, who attended the same affair, was also under the weather. Mrs. Lincoln, worried about her husband, wrote to General Sickles, "To night, I will try & persuade him, to take some medicine & rest a little on the morrow."

Lincoln appears to have taken his wife's advice, for the next day, Sunday the twenty-first, there is no correspondence in his hand or any record of business. She would have preferred that he keep to his room another day, but Monday morning found him back in his office, feeble, but attending to affairs, mostly of a political nature. That day he received his party's endorsement for the presidency by an overwhelming majority. But he still had to manage the legal and political challenges of the infamous "Pomeroy Circular," a letter released under the postal privilege of Kansas senator Samuel C. Pomeroy opposing Lincoln and urging that Salmon Chase be nominated to replace him. What Mary Lincoln had warned her husband against seemed to be coming to pass: an arguably treasonable attack upon a sitting president that was meant to ruin his candidacy for a second term. The anti-Lincoln pamphlet claimed that his reelection was "practically impossible," and would damage "the cause of human liberty and the dignity and honor of the nation."

That day Lincoln drafted a letter to a concerned congressman to clarify his position. It was the president's wish that the government not object to any newspaper's "preference for the *nomination* of any candidate," but that the government not offer its patronage to anyone who would oppose the *election* of any candidate "fairly nominated by the regular Union National Convention." This was a dignified and confident response. Nicolay, who had read the vicious circular on Wednesday, wrote to John Hay that "the treasury rats are busy night and day and becoming more and more unscrupulous and malicious. . . . Corruption, intrigue and malice are doing their worst, but I do not think it is in the cards to beat the Tycoon [Lincoln]."

Despite his extreme fatigue on February 21, the president allowed himself to be cajoled by an old Illinois friend, Brigadier General Richard J. Oglesby, to attend a Sanitary Fair Commission benefit at the Patent Office the next evening. These Sanitary Fairs, which the Christian Commission and city volunteers sponsored, were highly effective in raising funds for the military hospitals. The Lincolns were heartily devoted to the hospitals, and sometimes went together to visit wounded soldiers on holidays. Although the president told the committee "he was all tired out; he ought not to go; he needed rest," at last he gave in to their entreaties, knowing that his absence might be damaging to him in an election year. Lincoln agreed to go to the fair on the condition that he would not be called upon to address the crowd. He knew when he was too exhausted to make speeches in public.

The hour arrived. General Oglesby, all smiles, met the president, Mrs. Lincoln, and Robert Lincoln at the White House and drove with them in the restored carriage, across F Street to the Doric marble palace on Seventh Street that housed the Patent Office and the Department of the Interior. They entered the fair rooms at 7:30 to find a crowd that exceeded all expectations—more than three thousand had come to attend an auction, honor the wounded soldiers, and see the president and his wife. They sat on the platform behind the principal speakers. Byron Sunderland, pastor of the First Presbyterian Church, began the exercises with an ardent invocation. The main speaker, Lucius E. Chittendon, registrar of the treasury, having lost the notes for his address, was anxious. But relying on his memory and his natural eloquence, the Vermont lawyer and public servant spoke movingly of the sacrifice their young men had made for liberty and the Union, and of the grace of charity. Then Benjamin French read a poem he had written for the occasion. When he was done, and the crowd applauded, they began calling for the president to say something.

The more Mr. Lincoln declined, the louder they called upon him. At last he "stepped forward, and said that he appeared before the audience to apologize for not speaking rather than to speak." And that was pretty much all he did. For about four minutes he made lame jokes about how the committee had perpetrated a fraud upon him by promising he wouldn't have to speak; how he was unprepared, and how great a burden it was that every word he said ended up in print. So he could not speak now, really, for "if he made any mistake it might do both him and the nation harm." There was nervous laughter and applause. "It is very difficult to say sensible things," said the gaunt author of the Gettysburg Address. His wife listened—astonished, mortified, fuming. She was relieved when he sat down.

They stayed for a while to congratulate the other speakers and the fair organizers and to shake hands with the many people who stood in line to greet the president. The night was cold, and the coachman had taken the horses around the corner to a stable to keep them warm. As the party stood on the portico steps awaiting the carriage, Richard Oglesby became aware of an explosive charge mounting in Mrs. Lincoln and wondered what could be the cause of it. He did not have to wait long to find out. Her outburst, when it came, arose from humiliation that had boiled up into desperate resentment. Mrs. Lincoln was painfully sensitive to any behavior that might diminish their chances of a second term in the White House.

"That was the worst speech I ever listened to in my life," she declared. "How any man could get up and deliver such remarks to an audience is more than I can understand. I wanted the earth to sink and let me go through." Not a word more was spoken. Oglesby and the Lincolns got into the carriage and returned to the White House in an icy silence.

The Lincolns might have been relieved when Salmon Chase— embarrassed by charges of disloyalty and corruption—withdrew his candidacy on March 5. But the perennial candidate John Charles Frémont— the Republicans' 1856 standard-bearer—had a host of supporters among the radicals. And significantly, Lincoln himself had no confidence that his administration would be reelected. The military draft, the interminable war, the mounting numbers of dead and wounded, and the divisions within his party all appeared to him as fatal obstacles to his chances. He and Mrs. Lincoln returned to the Sanitary Fair—where he had embarrassed her—on its last day, March 18, 1864. And perhaps he redeemed himself in her eyes with a speech that concluded with a hymn of praise to the American woman: "If all that has been said by orators and poets since the creation of the world in praise of women were applied to the women of America, it would not do them justice for their conduct during this war. I will close by saying God bless the women of America!" That must have pleased her. Women had not yet the right to vote, but they could influence the outcome of an election, as many had proven.

• • •

THE THEATER CONTINUED to serve them as a source of energy, a bonding passion. During the late winter of that year, America's foremost Shakespearean actor, Edwin Booth, was performing many plays in repertory at Grover's Theatre, at Pennsylvania Avenue and E Street, a ten-minute walk away. There they saw *Richard III, Julius Caesar, The Merchant of Venice, Hamlet, Richelieu,* and *The Fool's Revenge;* and the Lincolns were so enthusiastic about Booth's performances, they returned to their box to see him play in *Richard III* again on his last night of the run, on March 10, 1864.

Good Friday and Easter came at the end of March, and the Lincolns were briefly relieved of the pressure of entertaining. The worst snowstorm of the year came during Holy Week, and a reception was scheduled for Wednesday, March 23. It was "very handsome, though not large," French recalled. "Mrs. Lincoln was as amiable as possible," considering the poor attendance, and "Abraham was full of fun and story as I ever saw him." Frustrated at the dwindling attendance, Mary chided her friend Charles Sumner for not coming. The next day, embarrassed, she apologized: "I pray you, accept this little peace offering, for your table, a few fresh flowers." She was aware that Sumner did not usually attend receptions, "which of course, in this house cannot be dispensed with," but thought he might make an exception for her.

The president himself postponed the next regular reception on April 5, so that he could escort his wife to the opera, Friedrich von Flotow's *Martha* at Grover's Theatre. News had come from Brooklyn that Owen Lovejoy had died there—the man Lincoln said had been his best friend in Congress. Three days later they went with Secretary of State Seward and his wife and daughter to Ford's Theatre to see the great Edwin Forrest in *King Lear,* that dark and Job-like tragedy. On the ninth, Mrs. Lincoln held the last of her formal afternoon receptions, and her husband, who usually made only a brief appearance at these gatherings, stayed a long while at this one, acknowledging his appreciation of her efforts during this demanding season.

Mary wrote to Charles Sumner saying how much they would all miss Owen Lovejoy, quoting Shakespeare: "An all wise power, directs these dispensations, yet it appears to our weak & oftentimes erring judgments,

'*He* should have died *hereafter.*' " The president would echo her fatalism in a Baltimore speech two weeks later, commenting upon the unexpected duration of the war: "So true it is that man proposes, and God disposes." They were studying in the same school, where a practical fatalism was their daily lesson.

The social and political efforts of that winter exhausted them, and two days after the last afternoon reception, she fell ill. Lincoln had planned to take her along with him on a voyage down the Chesapeake to visit General Butler and the troops at Fort Monroe, Virginia, but he wired Butler on April 11 to say that Mrs. Lincoln was so unwell they would not make it. On April 16, the president himself was so sick, he closed his doors to visitors. And the Lincolns had planned to go together to the Baltimore Sanitary Fair on the eighteenth. That happened to be the day before the last night levee of the season, and they would have to muster every ounce of energy to rise to the occasion.

The last public reception of spring 1864 was a success in sheer numbers, if not in the quality of the company. The *Philadelphia Dispatch* reported that "the crowd was so great around the portals of the White House that several ladies fainted." The journalist noted that the East Room was "adorned with the beauty, grace and fashion of the metropolis," as well as brave military officers who would soon be headed for "glory or the grave." The British minister was on hand, as well as some younger ambassadors and attachés, flirting with "heiresses who are here with their Congressional papas." This sort of scene might have thrilled Mrs. Lincoln three years earlier, before she had seen dozens of such pandemoniums. Now it was all she could do to get through the evening with a fixed smile and a gracious word or two for those who approached her.

"Mrs. Lincoln was splendidly arrayed in rich white silk, trimmed with white ribbon and black lace; and the President shook hands with fearful rapidity," said the Philadelphia reporter. She must be gracious; she must be poised. She must maintain her wardrobe at the height of fashion whatever the cost. This concern was inseparable from her anxiety over her debts to the New York merchants, which in turn was linked to her fear that Mr. Lincoln might not be reelected. Her irrational strategy for holding off the merchants who threatened to sue her was to beg their forbearance while ordering more expensive goods. They obliged her—believing the president's wife must be called to account sooner or later—and the more money she owed, with interest, the better for them in the final reck-oning.

On April 16, contemplating a trip to Manhattan as soon as the lights went out on the final levee of the season, she wrote to her foremost credi-tor, A. T. Stewart, to thank him for his "patience and soliciting as an espe-cial favor to me, having been a punctual customer & always hoping to be so, a delay of the Settlement of my account with you, until the 1st of June—when I promise, that without fail, *then,* the whole account shall be settled. I deeply regret, that I am so unusually situated & trust hereafter, to settle as I purchase." She was in fact *uniquely* situated, being the Lady President, and begging favors of a merchant to whom she owed so much money that she could only extend her credit line by increasing her debt. He had flattered her on her good taste. Now she coveted a rare and costly item. "I desire to order, a black India Camel's hair shawl, yet in sufficient time, will see you, to give directions." Perhaps Mr. Stewart would under-stand once more that she deserved the best even if she could not afford it.

On the evening of April 27, she and Tad boarded the night train for New York. More than four months had passed since she had been to Man-hattan, and now she approached the island with two conflicting impulses: one, to square her accounts with various merchants whose ill will would be dangerous before an election; the other, to lose herself in the kaleido-scopic glow of the clothing shops, which acted upon her like an addictive drug. Since March she had been negotiating—directly, and through inter-mediaries such as her housekeeper, Mary Ann Cuthbert—to pay or con-solidate her debts. Now she was returning to the city with renewed lines of credit.

Yet, arriving at the Metropolitan Hotel, no sooner was she settled in her suite than she wired the president asking for money. "We reached here in safety. Hope you are well. Please send me by mail to-day a check for $50 directed to me. . . . Tad says are the goats well?" Since the horses had burned up in the barn fire, the boy worried about his pets. Lincoln answered, "The [bank] draft will go to you. Tell Tad the goats and father are very well—especially the goats." He was grateful for the effort she had made since New Year's to sustain the social following that favored his can-didacy. Whatever relief from care, politics, and war she might find on Broadway, she deserved it, as well as the $50.

Unfortunately the newspapers, such as the *New York Herald,* were quick to find fault with Mrs. Lincoln's junkets. Reporters followed her at a respectful distance on April 29 and 30, rushing to press with the news that "from the early hours . . . until late in the evening, Mrs. Lincoln ransacked the treasures of the Broadway dry goods stores. The evenings were spent in company of a few private friends." Powerful figures in New York politics, Abram Wakeman, postmaster, and *Tribune* editor Simeon Draper, soon to be collector of the Port of New York, welcomed her. They had close ties to "bosses" Thurlow Weed and James Gordon Bennett, editor of the *Herald.* Wakeman and Draper—in return for favors from Mrs. Lincoln—would help her to control gossip by negotiating with merchants and reporters, and in some cases by paying bills in return for Mrs. Lincoln's IOU.

Mrs. Keckley recalled Mrs. Lincoln's expressed concern "that the politicians would get hold of the particulars of her debts, and use them in the Presidential campaign against her husband; and when this thought occurred to her, she was almost crazy with anxiety and fear." To her it seemed obvious that when hundreds of politicians were "getting immensely rich off the patronage of my husband . . . it is but fair that they should help me out of my embarrassment."

"I will make a demand of them, and when I tell them the facts they cannot refuse to advance whatever money I require." It was not Mrs. Keckley's place to explain to her mistress that one evil does not justify another, or that public officials "owe" nothing to the head of state aside from doing their duty. Mrs. Lincoln did make demands. And some politicos, like Wakeman, and Oliver "Pet" Halsted, Jr., a munitions lobbyist, did her bidding. But it was too little too late, as Mrs. Lincoln's later correspondence with Wakeman proves. Her extravagance and chronic debt had passed from rumor to news to legend, from which no reputation can be rescued. As she reported to Wakeman in October, despite all their efforts at damage control, the New York *Sunday Mercury* was quoting a vainglorious New York merchant who was proud to say he had *forgiven* one of Mrs. Lincoln's debts.

Such secrecy as Mrs. Lincoln practiced does incalculable damage to a marriage, as much as an extramarital affair or a concealed gambling problem. Far too many subjects were taboo: She could not tell him of her debts; he could not talk to her about troop movements. Mrs. Lincoln reflected, "I consider myself fortunate, if at eleven o'clock, I once more find myself, in my pleasant room & very especially, if my tired & weary Husband, is *there,* resting in the lounge to receive me—to chat over the occurrences of the day." At least they could talk about Tad and his unruly goats. They could discuss Tad's theater, which James Haliday, the house carpenter, had hammered up for him in the darkened corridor across from the library, and the embarrassing scene the child had made there the day before they left for New York.

Tad had just turned eleven. He had not yet learned to read, and suffered from a speech impediment. His frustrations made him subject to tantrums and sudden dejections, like his mother. She had been too ill to comfort him after Willie's death; then on the anniversary of that tragedy came the burning of the barn with Tad's ponies in it. Lincoln did his best to console and distract the boy, allowing him the run of the office even during business hours. John Hay recalled how often he saw Tad playing on the floor beside his father's desk until late at night when sleep overtook him. Then Lincoln would lift the child into his arms and carry him off to the president's own bedroom, where Tad slept.

So when Tad asked for a little theater, the request was no sooner made than granted. In the center corridor upstairs, the front window was covered and a stage erected with a velvet curtain, footlights, and props in the darkened space. The manager of the nearby theater, Mr. Leonard Grover himself, provided much of the scenery and costumes. A wicket fence in front of the stage marked the audience space, which was filled with chairs, cushions, and old settees. For his cast, Tad could draw upon playmates, housemaids, and some of the guards detailed to the White House. At showtime he could be sure that the audience would include his parents, as well as any soldiers and staff who were not in the play.

Just as Grover's Theatre had become a refuge for the president and his wife—an escape from the terrible war dispatches and the maddening political intrigues—so Tad's playhouse, a dim hallway in the middle of the Executive Mansion, became a sanctuary, a retreat from the grim reality of Washington that had consumed the idyll of childhood in Springfield. Here he could direct and act out his fantasies, with happy endings if he pleased, or revenge upon his enemies if the play took a tragic turn. In any case, he was supremely in control.

The day before Tad and his mother were to leave for New York, a team of photographers came from Brady's studio to take pictures of the president's office. According to Francis B. Carpenter, who was planning a painting of the president and his cabinet, these photos were "stereoscopic studies" the painter needed for his work, so the artist was on hand to supervise the photographers. When they asked for a dark room to develop the negatives, Carpenter showed them Tad's theater just down the central hall and to the right. Quite innocently, and without disturbing the props or the seats, they set up their chemicals and trays in the darkened space.

A few minutes later the "operator" who had been preparing the chemical baths returned to Lincoln's office, perplexed. Master Tad had locked him out of the room, the developing equipment was within, and Tad was in a rage, "refusing all admission." As the embarrassed operator was in the midst of his account, the boy himself burst into the office, crying, and flew directly at Carpenter. "He laid all the blame upon me—said that I had no right to use his room, and that the men should not go in even to get their things."

Too much had been taken from Tad Lincoln. Mr. Francis Carpenter had been haunting the house since February, when the barn had burned; he had spent many late hours in conversation with the president while Tad played nearby. The painter wanted more than a likeness of Mr. Lincoln—he wanted to capture the soul of the great man. In that moment of confrontation over the evil-smelling chemicals and explosive cameras, Tad hated the painter for what he had done and for what he might do.

Lincoln had not stirred from the chair where he was posing, but at last he said calmly: "Tad, go and unlock the door." Tad left the office, muttering to himself on the way down the hall to his mother's room, where he hoped for more support than he was getting at the business end of the house. Carpenter followed him a few steps down the corridor, "but no coaxing would pacify him," so the painter turned back. Seeing Carpenter in the doorway, vexed, Lincoln asked, "Has not the boy opened that door?" The artist explained that Tad was furious and unyielding. Lincoln got up, his mouth set firmly, and strode out of the room looking to Carpenter like "one bent on punishment, and disappeared in the domestic apartments."

Mrs. Lincoln was busy packing for New York, and the heat of Tad's tantrum was more than she could manage without Mr. Lincoln's help. As in the case of Mary's fits, the best approach was an attitude of cool equanimity, which came naturally to Father. Finding Tad "violently excited," he appealed to the child's affection for him.

"Tad, do you know you are making your father a great deal of trouble?"

Not only was Father the president, but Tad adored him and was mortified at the thought of troubling him. So he burst into tears, and gave up the latchkey.

As Mrs. Lincoln wrote to Mercy Conkling, she considered herself fortunate if Tad had gone to sleep before her weary husband, and Mr. Lincoln was there in her room next to the library, resting on the lounge in his nightshirt. They might discuss the events of the day. They talked of General Ulysses S. Grant, whom Lincoln had put in supreme command of the armies of the United States with the rank of lieutenant general, which had been bestowed upon no other officers save Winfield Scott and George Washington. Like Caesar, Grant appeared in the capital trailing glory. His triumphs at Vicksburg, Mississippi, and Chattanooga, Tennessee, had made the short, cigar-chewing general a celebrity fit to challenge Lincoln for the presidency. Perhaps this was the reason Mrs. Lincoln disliked him, although Grant had no political aspirations, just then.

She overcame her aversion and entertained the general and his wife, Julia, graciously at the Executive Mansion. There for the first time Mr. Lincoln found himself completely upstaged by the conquering hero, who was so beset by the company, he was asked to stand upon a settee in the parlor so as not to be crushed or hidden. Mrs. Lincoln went so far as to invite General Grant and his wife to a private dinner, and then a banquet; but although he was in town, he begged to be excused, saying he was needed in the field. Grant had no interest in society—even in the company of the president and his wife. The fact that he slipped away after they made such an effort to honor him may have affected Mary's opinion of the general's qualifications.

"He is a butcher, and is not fit to be at the head of an army," she said.

Lincoln replied that Grant had been very successful in the field.

"Yes," his wife continued, "he generally manages to claim a victory, but such a victory! He loses two men to the enemy's one. He has no management, no regard for life. If the war should continue four years longer, and he should remain in power, he would depopulate the North. I could fight an army as well myself."

"Well, Mother, supposing that we give you command of the army. No doubt you would do much better than any general that has been tried."

They must change the subject. It would be pleasant to consider the renovation of the Soldiers' Home. In May, Mrs. Lincoln had engaged the upholsterer John Alexander to renovate their retreat in time to move in on

July 4. She was picking out wallpaper, and paintings, and lace curtains for the bedroom. And Congress had approved the budget.

THE PRESIDENT'S IRONIC response to his wife's critique of Grant's warfare suggests an underlying sympathy. The general's progress that spring suffered two tragic battles—the Battle of the Wilderness, west of Chancellorsville, in May, and Cold Harbor, a crossroads a few miles northeast of Richmond, in early June. More than thirty thousand men had been killed or wounded, and Grant himself regretted attacking the Cold Harbor breastworks, which were nearly invulnerable. The best that could be said of the outcome is that it further weakened Lee's already inferior forces.

For nearly two years Mrs. Lincoln had been visiting the hospitals, sometimes with her husband; she also raised funds for the care of the wounded soldiers. She was admired for her calm demeanor and a strong stomach as she passed through the grisly wards, looking into the eyes of the sick and wounded young men, distributing gifts, reading to the soldiers, and writing letters for some who had lost the use of their hands. Now she found her own energy diminished. She wrote to Mary Jane Welles on May 27 that she could not accompany her that day to visit the soldiers because of her "bilious attacks & . . . how much inclined to *nausea* they leave you." Yet as soon as she was able, on May 29, she would go with her husband to visit survivors of the Battle of the Wilderness, now recovering or dying at Campbell Hospital.

Lincoln had no official appointments that Sunday. Francis Carpenter said that the president had hardly slept during the recent battles, and that his face "was the saddest face I ever knew," with black rings under the eyes. The painter said there were days when he could hardly look at Lincoln without weeping. Yet the president would put aside his sorrow this morning, accompany his wife to the hospital, and try to cheer up the soldiers.

It was a brilliant spring day. The carriage took them out Vermont Avenue, the familiar route to the Soldiers' Home. Campbell Hospital lay along the route beyond the contraband camps, where Rhode Island Avenue turned north toward the Seventh Street Turnpike. Sunday was a good day to hear the gospel choir of the freed blacks at the camp on Seventh Street. The Lincolns had visited the camp several times that year. "Mrs. Lincoln contributed money and sent gifts to the older people," one of the singers remembered, and Mr. Lincoln liked to hear the preaching and the music.

First they would visit the wounded soldiers. A large basket of flowers bound in fragrant bouquets rode with them on the leather seat. The roses were in bloom. On the "flats" at the edge of the city hundreds of acres had been deforested to feed the furnaces and campfires of the overpopulated capital; so they could see, in the middle distance, the long, low ward pavilions, and the gambrel roof of the wood-frame house that served as headquarters for the surgeons. Beyond the wards were the farms and woodlands on gentle hills that rose to the National Cemetery and the Soldiers' Home.

As their carriage turned east onto the semicircular driveway to Campbell Hospital and stopped near the flagpole where the Stars and Stripes fluttered in the spring breeze, guards and strolling invalids saluted the president and his lady, who bade them stand at ease. Such visits were often unannounced, so news of the president's arrival passed excitedly through the wards. Inside the plain board sheds the invalids lay on iron bedsteads ranged against the whitewashed walls. The men lay with their heads to the wall, watching in awe as the commander in chief made his way up the middle aisle at their feet, his wife beside him. He was shaking hands, praising the soldiers for their bravery, their sacrifice to the Union. The Lincolns had learned the necessary discipline of looking directly into a soldier's eyes and focusing there. One must not look at the body. The diary of Dr. Darius Orton, a surgeon on duty that day, shows that no effort was made to spare Mr. Lincoln and his wife the sight of the most painful cases. The doctor refers to Private George L. Chase of Massachusetts, who had suffered a gunshot wound in his knee at the Battle of the Wilderness. The operation to repair the wound was successful, and all signs pointed to full recovery. Then suddenly erysipelas inflamed the joint, and the leg had to be amputated.

The youth was just coming out of the darkness of anesthesia when Dr. Orton brought him from the operating room to his bed. The pain and the awful reality were dawning upon Private Chase just as the president and his wife entered the long ward. Mrs. Lincoln went to the boy's bedside and took his hand. When the surgeon told him who the lady was, Chase cried out—incapable of concealing his pain but struggling to muster his dignity—"How do you do, Mrs. Lincoln—Oh! I am so glad to see you." She smoothed the hair back from his forehead and touched his arm, indulging him as she would one of her own sick children. He was not much older than Robert Lincoln. She gave him one of the little bouquets of flowers. The president then leaned over and pressed the boy's hand. They told Private Chase good-bye and moved on to the next cot, bonded in their compassion, knowing that wounded and dying soldiers lay in hospital beds and on hillsides from here to the horizon, and they could comfort only these few, and for only a little while. Private Chase would be dead of sepsis within three weeks.

After the gloom of the wards, it was a relief to be back in the bright, clear air of May, free for an hour or two to ride where they pleased, along the Seventh Street Turnpike, as far as the Soldiers' Home, or farther, to Fort Stevens. A half-mile from Campbell Hospital lay Camp Baker, a former barracks that now was home to thousands of runaways and freed blacks. These were originally called "contrabands" by General Butler, who refused to return Negro runaways, as prohibited war matériel. On Sundays the contrabands welcomed visitors, white and black, who came to hear the inspired preaching and gospel singing. According to the Lincolns' cook at the Soldiers' Home, "Aunt" Mary Dines—who had a fine soprano voice and led the choir at Camp Baker—Lincoln "was very fond of the hymns of the slaves and loved to hear them and even knew most of them by heart."

The bugle proclaimed the arrival of the president and his wife as they got down from the carriage. "And while some sat on a little platform on the right, which the colored men had just finished decorating with flags, President Lincoln came over to where the old folks were sitting and stood and watched everybody."

An old slave they called Uncle Ben opened the meeting with a prayer, and then called upon all the saints to bless the president and Mrs. Lincoln. When the blessing was done everyone stood up and sang "My Country 'Tis of Thee," and Lincoln took off his stovepipe hat and sang too. Aunt Mary recalled that he had a good voice. At last she stood before the congregation and commenced the performance of the gospel singing. She sang "Nobody Knows What Trouble I See" while keeping her eyes fixed on the president. She sang the first verse a cappella, then the whole choir joined in "and really sang as they never did before." Between hymns came a brief pause, then Aunt Mary Dines called out for "Every Time I Feel the Spirit," and the choir leader "saw President Lincoln wiping the tears off his face with his bare hands."

ONE MORE ELECTION

NOW THAT THE SOCIAL SEASON was past, and fewer than five months remained before the election, there was little more the Lincolns could do together to strengthen his position as a candidate. It was not yet the custom for nominees to give campaign speeches. So a great deal depended upon the war's progress and the people's despair over it in both parties.

The Republicans, convening in Baltimore as the "National Union Party," unanimously nominated Lincoln for president on June 8, 1864. The delegates also replaced Vice President Hannibal Hamlin with Andrew Johnson, a former Democratic senator from Tennessee who had remained loyal to the Union. That night, Lincoln attended Grover's Theatre alone, without fanfare. This was no time to celebrate. His wife was still plagued by her headaches and self-conscious over the relentless criticism of her in the parlors and the newspapers. This would grow worse as the election approached, so she would carefully choose when to be seen with him and when not. The previous night she had gone alone to the opera while he awaited the news from the Baltimore convention. Tonight she would remain at home with Tad while Lincoln relaxed at the theater.

On June 16, she and Tad accompanied Mr. Lincoln to Philadelphia, where the U.S. Sanitary Commission was staging its Great Central Fair to raise money for the hospitals. No one could question her sincerity with regard to this cause; here she could reliably do credit to her husband. They rode up on a special train early that morning, arriving at the Continental Hotel in time for lunch. At 4:55 she sat near the podium and watched in pride as he faced the crowd in the assembly hall on the Logan Square fairgrounds.

First they raised a glass to toast the president, welcoming him warmly. Once again she admired how quickly he could switch from a humorous tone, which drew the people to him, to a deep seriousness once he had gotten their attention. "I suppose," he began wryly, "that this toast was intended to open the way for me to say something." Everyone laughed, and then waited. His demeanor turned from gay to grave. "War, at the best, is terrible, and this war of ours, in its magnitude and in its duration, is one of the most terrible. It has deranged business . . . destroyed property, and ruined homes; it has produced a national debt and taxation unprecedented, at least in this country. It has carried mourning to almost every home, until it can almost be said that the 'heavens are hung in black.' " This was surely true of the Lincolns' home.

Lincoln then addressed the question foremost in everyone's mind: "When is the war to end?" Quoting Grant's favorite comment, "I am going through on this line if it takes all summer," Lincoln drank in the applause and cheering, and then said—as the sentiment was so worthy—"I say we are going through on this line if it takes three years more," which brought more applause, mingling with solemn thoughts. "I have never been in the habit of making predictions in regard to the war, but I am almost tempted to make one." All around, he heard cries of *Do it! Do it!* And so Mrs. Lincoln heard him make the fateful prophecy: "If I were to hazard it, it is this: That Grant is this evening, with General Meade and General Hancock of Pennsylvania, and the brave officers and soldiers with him, in a position from whence he will never be dislodged until Richmond is taken." The pronouncement drew loud cheers.

The next morning Lincoln and Tad said good-bye to Mary and left on an eight o'clock train for Washington. They would not be seeing her again for three weeks. Mrs. Lincoln was bound for New York en route to Saratoga. Her husband wired her at the Fifth Avenue Hotel on June 19 to let her know that he and Tad had arrived home safely and all was well. Not much is known about her business in Manhattan. She never went there without shopping, so it is likely that she visited the shops on Broadway; later correspondence suggests that she met with friends like Abram Wakeman, still negotiating with creditors who wished to sue her. She did not stay long or attract much attention, but soon headed for Saratoga and a much-needed vacation. Robert would join her there. She would need rest for the long hot summer to come.

While Mrs. Lincoln took the waters of Saratoga, the president concentrated on his role as commander in chief. He may have believed that Grant's success and the Union's were inevitable, but it was painfully clear that victory would not come soon enough, and the electorate was becoming more impatient every day. He was as frustrated as anyone, and suffering from a stomach ailment that troubled him for the rest of the month.

With some pleasure he telegraphed his wife on June 29 to say that the servants were moving trunks and baggage out to the Soldiers' Home. Once again they would enjoy the cooler, cleaner air north of the White House. But far more than heat and miasma troubled the president's sleep and digestion while his wife was away. Since the Philadelphia fair, the president had known that Grant's army was crossing the James River to attack Confederate supply lines at Petersburg, a town thirty miles south of Richmond. It was a brilliant "back-door" tactic, which surprised General Lee at first. But Grant's assaults on Petersburg had floundered from the moment Lee and his army arrived there on the eighteenth. They were bold and resourceful. In a matter of days Grant lost eleven thousand men. Still outnumbering the rebels 110,000 to 50,000, Grant and Meade captured two railroads to the city as well as the main highways. The siege of Petersburg began. Meanwhile Robert E. Lee had sent General Jubal Early to stop the Federals' ravaging of the Shenandoah Valley, which had reached Lynchburg, Lee's link to the western theater of war.

The day Lincoln accepted his party's nomination, June 27, Sherman's Federal troops attacked General Joseph Johnston's well-entrenched army at the Battle of Kennesaw Mountain in Georgia. This resulted in a tragic defeat for the Federals, with two thousand casualties. For the Confederates it was one more defensive victory that would prolong the war. Meanwhile Jubal Early had General David Hunter and his Union forces on the run back down the Shenandoah Valley. On July 2, Mary Lincoln and her son Robert returned to the White House. The family scarcely had time to greet one another before General Franz Sigel telegraphed news from Harper's Ferry that Jubal Early's Confederate troops were on their way into Maryland. Then the telegraph lines to Harper's Ferry went dead— the work of a saboteur.

Robert E. Lee ordered General Early to drive Hunter and the Federals out of the Shenandoah Valley and then attack Washington. Lee had written to Jefferson Davis that it was forceful policy "to draw the attention of the enemy to his own territory," and the general had made a spectacular— and tragic—demonstration of this at Gettysburg the previous summer.

Word that rebel soldiers were fording the Potomac thirty miles above the capital came from deckhands unloading cargo from the C&O Canal in Georgetown. The news caused confusion and alarm. Secretary Gideon Welles observed that the president himself had been "a good deal incredulous about a very large army" of Confederates descending on Washington from the upper Potomac, but now he was worried.

Mrs. Lincoln turned her thoughts to housekeeping in preparation for the family's annual relocation to the Soldiers' Home. This had been a hot, dry summer. The dust from the unpaved roads was suffocating. They would throw open the windows to the strong light of July, strip the furniture of dustcloths, thrash the carpets. Although she had more help with such tasks now than she had enjoyed in Springfield, she was never a woman to entrust the details of housecleaning entirely to servants. They moved on Independence Day, a dozen loads of furniture passing from house to house. And this year the cottage had undergone a three-thousand-dollar renovation, which included reupholstering the furniture and newly wallpapering most of the fourteen rooms. New paintings and lace curtains hung in the bedrooms, and summer matting made of coconut husks covered the floors. It was a joyful task, this seasonal move from the mansion in the swamp to the airy gabled "cottage" on the hill, where she and her husband could have more privacy and control over their lives.

Just six days after the family moved into the Soldiers' Home, Secretary of War Stanton told them to move out, fearing for their lives. Jubal Early had swept down from western Maryland, having extorted $20,000 from the frightened citizens of Hagerstown under threat of burning their village. Now the rebels were heading for the capital via Frederick, Maryland, only forty-three miles northwest of Washington. General Grant had sent General James Ricketts and a Federal division to help General Lew Wallace and his Baltimore troops halt the Confederates at the Monocacy River near Frederick. But at the end of a day's fighting, a third of Wallace's greenhorns were lost—twelve hundred missing in action—while the invaders had only seven hundred casualties. Wallace had slowed Early's momentum, but the rebels ransomed Frederick for $200,000 and pressed on toward the capital, stopping in Silver Spring to burn down Postmaster General Montgomery Blair's house and loot the home of Mrs. Lincoln's friend Elizabeth Blair Lee.

As of Saturday, July 9, the Lincolns did not know that Wallace had failed to stop Early's troops, fourteen thousand strong, at Frederick. Like the rest of Washington's citizenry, they had grown accustomed to threats of military invasion and were not disposed to panic. But by Sunday, Lincoln knew the danger. Responding to telegrams from Baltimore begging for more troops to defend the port city, Lincoln gravely responded that every soldier was deployed to "the best protection of all. By latest account the enemy is moving on Washington. They can not fly to either place. Let us be vigilant but keep cool. I hope neither Baltimore or Washington will be sacked." To the president, the sacking of either city was a distinct possibility. He had written a cipher telegram to General Grant at two o'clock that afternoon: "Gen. Halleck says we have absolutely no force here fit to go to the field." Lincoln asked Grant to leave behind the forces he needed to hold Petersburg, then come with the rest "and make a vigorous effort to destroy the enemy's force in this vicinity." It was a request, not an order— and Grant stayed put.

That night after supper, Lincoln explained to his wife and son why Edwin Stanton wanted them all to return to the White House. The Soldiers' Home stood within a semicircle of forts that guarded the city to the north, and two miles from Fort Stevens, the enemy's immediate target. The danger was real. In a state of considerable dismay and anxiety the Lincolns packed up and rode back to the White House before midnight.

Jubal Early's defeat of Wallace, and the rebels' crossing of the Monocacy, was duly assessed in the War Department and the White House before the public knew the seriousness of these developments. Civilians were confident that fortifications and artillery north of Washington were more than equal to the raiding parties of a few thousand marauders. Lincoln, Halleck, and Quartermaster General Meigs knew better. The Washington garrison was chiefly composed of inexperienced "100-day men" from Ohio and invalid soldiers who hobbled from their beds at Campbell Hospital and Armory Square to man the cannons as needed. Now as Jubal Early's men came down from Silver Spring in the parching heat and eye-stinging dust of July, Halleck telegraphed the surrounding forts for soldiers; more convalescents were called from their cots, and nearsighted clerks and elderly copyists were being summoned to arms. That Sunday, July 10, as church bells rang over the city, men were reporting to General Meigs to receive firearms and marching orders.

Time was of the essence. Fortunately, the Confederate infantry was so weary from the toil and heat of the long march and days of fighting that on

July 11 they slackened their pace. If they could have marched double-time that Monday, they might have seized the capital. But Lincoln had time enough to order out ten companies of Washington militiamen. For the first time, he even ordered his own bodyguard to man the defenses.

The Confederates marched down the Seventh Street Road. They could see their goal in the distance, the shining dome of the newly finished Capitol. Shortly after noon that day, Ohio general Alexander McCook looked down from the parapet of Fort Stevens and spied the cloud of dust stirred by the Confederate army. Within two hours, the sound of artillery and gunfire could be heard all around the city. Jubal Early was ordering reconaissances to probe the defenses of Forts Reno, Kenney, and Simmons, and a picket line to test the strength of Fort Stevens.

THE LINCOLNS WENT to bed on Sunday night in an atmosphere of confusion and fear. According to John Hay, a courier "had stampeded the servants by leaving a message . . . suggesting that Mr. Lincoln should have a gunboat in readiness to leave in the morning as the enemy was in force within five miles."

The next morning they awoke to the sound of cannon fire, which accompanied their breakfast. At nine o'clock the president rode out to inspect the forts and outworks. According to Francis Carpenter, Mrs. Lincoln was with her husband at Fort Stevens in the early afternoon.

The adventures of Mr. and Mrs. Lincoln on July 11 and 12 tell us much about their feelings for each other, and about their individual needs, during the last full year of their married life. The fact is well documented that on both Monday and Tuesday of that week, Lincoln stood on the parapet at Fort Stevens, conspicuously exposed, in the line of fire; and also that he gave orders to soldiers. His wife was on hand to witness this bravado, or quixotic folly, as some considered it.

But the passage of time has drained the story of its vital essence. The last-minute arrival of Major General Horatio Wright's VI Corps by ship from City Point, south of Richmond—thousands of Grant's finest troops—foiled the Confederate invasion. The attack on Washington became a footnote in the history of the war, regarded as no more than a "period of excitement" and remembered most of all for the picturesque sight of the president in his stovepipe hat standing on the parapet of the fort, making a seven-foot-high target for the sharpshooters spread out beyond. It became a historical curiosity and literary conversation piece, as the last occasion that a U.S. president has ever come under enemy fire or commanded troops in the field.

Like some other incidents in Lincoln's life, notably the clandestine arrival in Washington in 1861, the story of Fort Stevens has suffered from raconteurs who delight in the comic and the picturesque. There is irony in the fact that an attack came in the north when all the Union troops had gone south. The image of Lincoln in his stovepipe on the parapet, a spyglass in his hand, watching the battle while the generals begged him to come down, is amusing. And again, the picture of gentlemen in linen dusters, toting silver hip flasks, and bonneted ladies with picnic baskets— so reminiscent of the spectators of the First Bull Run—strolling out to watch the skirmishing, seems charming to the historian who knows there were few casualties on either side.

But this was not July of 1861, or the First Battle of Manassas. Three years of hideous war had passed, and neither the Lincolns nor the fashionable citizens of Washington were inclined to dress up and go under parasols to the forts to watch men shoot live ammunition at one another. Many of the Lincolns' friends and relatives—Elmer Ellsworth, Edward Baker, Sam Todd, Alex Todd, and sister Emilie's husband, Ben Hardin Helm—had been killed in the war. During the past few months the Lincolns had attended wounded and dying soldiers in the hospitals, a sickening reminder of the harsh realities of combat. The presence of Edwin Stanton, Gideon Welles, and William Seward, all of whom had garrison passes on the second day, July 12, has framed the legend that these officials and a couple of congressmen and their ladies had gone off to Fort Stevens on a lark. The truth is that Fort Stevens was a terrifying site on July 11, and no place for light entertainment on the twelfth.

Sometime in the late morning of July 11, the Lincolns made a conjugal agreement to visit Fort Stevens and show their support to the raw troops at the point of attack. Let us first consider Lincoln's state of mind as he awoke that morning to the sound of artillery. The presence of a rebel battalion at the gates of the capital was a keen embarrassment to the Union and to this president at a time when he could ill afford it. That day the U.S. dollar had fallen to thirty-nine cents on the exchange, its lowest value during the entire war, and the plunge reflected a worldwide lack of confidence in his administration. Horace Greeley was begging Lincoln to join him in negotiating a peace with Confederate leaders at a conference in Canada. Most distressing to the president were the recent attacks upon him within his own party. At last he had accepted the resignation of Salmon Chase, after challenging his appointment of an incompetent radical as assistant U.S. treasurer in New York City. Chase was accustomed to resigning in protest, but he was stunned when Lincoln actually accepted. So was the liberal wing of the party, which became outraged over the sudden change in the cabinet.

Less than a week after replacing Chase, on July 4, Lincoln incurred even greater wrath from Congress by refusing to sign the Wade-Davis bill for Reconstruction. Drafted by Maryland congressman Henry Winter Davis and Ohio senator "Bluff" Ben Wade, the plan was more punitive than what Lincoln had in mind for the South, in terms of the restoration of state governments and the payment of war debts.

So Lincoln pocket-vetoed the Wade-Davis bill, provoking a tide of anti-Lincoln sentiment in Congress. "I am inconsolable," said Charles Sumner, a friend of both the Lincolns. Mary Lincoln's letters to the influential senator that year show how hard she worked to play her part in consoling him, in keeping the Boston Brahmin from turning against them in the campaign. The dapper, courtly Sumner continued to visit the Lincolns while keeping up a spirited argument over the Wade-Davis bill, and Reconstruction, and the constitutional rights of Congress to pass laws concerning slavery. His deep respect for Lincoln and his affection for Mary caused Sumner to remain one of a loyal opposition to the president, whose support was critical for his reelection.

Other legislators, like Wade and Davis, and the hotheaded Senator Zachariah Chandler from Michigan, railed against Lincoln, and conspired to attack him in a printed circular. On Monday morning, July 11, the keen-eyed John Hay observed, "the President concluded to desert his tormentors today & travel around the defenses." At that moment only the Third Division of the VI Corps—who had marched down from Monocacy—and green troops, garrisoned Fort Stevens. The rest of the veterans of Grant's VI Corps, several thousand soldiers who would assure the safety of the capital, were still sailing from City Point—far south on the James River—and debarking at the Washington wharves; from hour to hour the Lincolns did not know the Corps' position or the Confederates' plan of attack.

We think of President Lincoln as a man of prudence and supreme rationality. While this is generally true, Lincoln also had a reckless side to him. It had inspired him to leap from that window where the Illinois legislature was meeting, to avoid a quorum; it moved him to tell off-color jokes to dour senators who begged him to be serious, and to ride out to the Soldiers' Home alone, without his guard, so no one could find him, and then make light of the fact that someone in the bushes shot his hat off. Everything about Lincoln's actions on July 11 and 12—all that is credibly documented—indicates that he was in just such a state of mind on those days. No one would have understood his mood as well as his wife of twenty-two years.

The president of the United States' visit to Fort Stevens at midday of July 11, 1864, and his subsequent conduct there that afternoon, was not prudent, or rational, or carefully considered. The military dangers were manifest. According to Gideon Welles's diary, General Halleck and "the dunder heads at the War office" were "in a perfect maze, bewildered," without any knowledge of Early's army and no practical plan of defense. Painter Francis Carpenter, who was in the White House at the time, said he "always believed the city might have been captured had the enemy followed up his advantage. The defenses were weak, and there were comparatively but few troops in the city or vicinity. . . . The almost defenseless condition of the city was the occasion of much censure."

In just these circumstances the chief executive of the nation, the moral figurehead of the Union, told his wife he was riding out to Fort Stevens, in the direction of the shooting. According to Hay and others, Lincoln was in very high spirits, excited that he was finally going to see action in this war that he had helped to orchestrate at a distance. Perhaps he felt it was time that he showed the troops his life was no more valuable to him than was the life of any soldier. Also, he was exasperated at the manner in which his colleagues on Capitol Hill were treating him, and perhaps eager to express his contempt for the more civilian and clerical aspects of the Washington establishment. There is something desperate about Lincoln's behavior that day that betrays anger as well as courage.

What did his wife think? She knew his temperament, the long brooding that sometimes gave way to an almost boyish excitement and enthusiasm—over a stage play, a machine gun to be tested in the park, or a new pony for Tad. Now he was eager to see the battle. While we have no record of her feelings or of the conversation that passed between them before they rode off together, it seems likely that she did not approve. At that moment, Jubal Early's invasion was imminent, and Fort Stevens was the most dangerous spot in the area. Robert Lincoln was in the White House, and he did not ride out to the fort that day or the next. The idea of her husband or her sons putting themselves in harm's way was appalling to her. But she went.

Did he ask her to go with him? Again, we have no record of the question, or of the answer. But common sense and normative family custom insist that Lincoln would not have asked the mother of his children to accompany him on such an errand. No other woman was going to Fort Stevens. So how did she end up with him, "unattended except by their coachman," riding out Vermont Avenue in the blinding sunlight of midday, headed for the sound of cannons beyond the Soldiers' Home? There is only one answer left to the practical imagination: Lincoln told her he was going, and his wife decided that if he was bound and determined to do such a thing, then she would insist on going along to keep an eye on him.

The record is full of examples of Abraham Lincoln's courage—if that is what we should call his disregard for his personal safety. He resisted having a bodyguard until the final years of his presidency, and continued to play hide-and-seek with the military details that attended him at the Soldiers' Home and the White House. This presented logistical nightmares to District Marshal Ward Hill Lamon and the other security officials who monitored the assassination threats and possibilities. So Lincoln's boldness in visiting the troops comes as no surprise. Mary Lincoln's presence on that day, at the age of forty-six, tells us a great deal about her bravery, after so much has been said about her nervousness and tendency to panic. Courage is only as great as the fear it vanquishes. Those who have not heard the piercing blast of nearby cannon, or the whistling of bullets ricocheting on rock walls, cannot imagine how it jars the nerves. Fort Stevens on this afternoon was no place for cowards. And if Mary Lincoln went up there with fear in her heart, it was not so great as her love for her husband.

The president had sent his personal cavalry guard into battle. So now he and his wife arrived at the barracks without protection. According to a surgeon, "the carriage stopped at the door of the hospital, and the President and his affable lady entered into familiar conversation with surgeons in charge, praising the deeds of the Old Sixth Corps, complimenting the appearance of the veterans." About an hour later, General

Horatio Wright, coming out of command quarters, met the president and "thoughtlessly invited him to see the fight in which we were about to engage, without for a moment supposing he would accept."

At that moment the fight was under way; the crack of rifles and the smell of gunpowder were in the air. In front of the fort, Confederate skirmishers were attacking pickets of the raw Ohio recruits within a couple of hundred yards of the walls. Lieutenant Colonel John N. Frazee ordered the gunners to bombard the advancing Confederates with thirty-pound Parrott guns. As accustomed to ceremonial cannon fire as the Lincolns were, the thunder of these fully loaded cannons must have shaken them.

Perhaps his attendance had become a matter of chivalry, harking back to a time when, some said, he had fought a duel to defend her honor. She kept to the rear, praying he would soon come to his senses and they might drive home. But the president was fascinated. He was probably unaware, gazing out on the scorched earth and fallen timber of the battlefield, that Confederate sharpshooters had taken up positions in the high windows of the houses within striking distance of the fort. Invisible to the Federal gunners, the rebel marksmen would do some of the deadliest work of the day. Private David T. Bull, who wrote the first eyewitness account of the events, three days later, recalled that in midafternoon the Confederates had "massed a heavy force in front of the Fort, thinking that our force would not shell them thru fear of killing our own men." Many were "gathered around a house in front of the Fort," and a sharpshooter on top of the house was aiming at the men on the parapets.

"Old Abe and his wife was in the fort at the time and Old Abe and his doctor was standing up on the parapets and the sharp shooter that I speak of shot the doctor through the left thigh, and Old Abe ordered our men to fall back." According to Private Bull, when the men were out of danger, "the cannon in the Fort opened on them [the Confederates] and fired the house, shelled them till they was in full retreat," at which point the VI Army Corps finished the job, routing them. Bull's is the earliest and most reliable account, conveying the real violence and danger of the moment.

The wounded doctor was not actually Lincoln's physician, but surgeon C.C.V.A. Crawford, a Pennsylvania volunteer. The doctor and several other eyewitnesses wrote accounts later that emphasize the president's stubbornness in standing on top of the ramparts despite everyone's insistence that he get down. "He still maintained his ground,"

General Wright recalled, "till I told him I should have to remove him forcibly." Eventually Lincoln compromised by sitting behind the wall instead of standing upon it. Yet "he would persist in standing up from time to time, thus exposing nearly one-half of his tall form."

At last the Lincolns left the fort, before the greater part of Horatio Wright's troops marched in to reinforce it. The main offensive move of the VI Corps occurred at five o'clock in the afternoon of July 11, and by that time the president and his wife were safe at home in the White House. Lincoln hurried over to the telegraph office to regale the operators with his story, while Mrs. Lincoln retired to the West Wing to embrace her sons and calm her nerves. The newspapers took little note of their visit to Fort Stevens. It gained them nothing politically.

By the next morning, some ten thousand men of the VI Corps had come to the defense of Washington, and Jubal Early had all but given up on his attack. The Confederate sharpshooters held their positions, pouring bullets into the forts, while a few hundred weary rebels fought a rear-guard action to cover Early's retreat toward the Potomac. The president and his wife once again rode out to Fort Stevens in the afternoon, as did his archrival, Senator "Zack" Chandler; Secretary of State Seward and his son Frederick, assistant secretary of state; and Gideon Welles, who arrived at the fort a few minutes after a man was shot and "found the President, who was sitting in the shade, with his back against the parapet towards the enemy." Legend has it that the president kept popping up like a jack-in-the-box to survey the field, and a number of luminaries including Oliver Wendell Holmes, Jr., claimed the distinction of calling to him, "Get down, you fool!" The threat of invasion had subsided, and now only Mary Lincoln and a few soldiers really understood the danger they had been in the day before—a shock fit to trouble anyone's sleep.

No wonder Mrs. Lincoln was plagued with headaches the week after Jubal Early's raid on Washington, and Lincoln could not sleep. According to historian Benjamin P. Thomas, "Men friendly to the Union cause remember July and August 1864 as the darkest days of the war. . . . Confusion reigned in politics. Peace appeared to be a distant dream." That dream was very distant in mid-July. When Secretary of War Stanton made a rare visit to the Soldiers' Home, Mary Lincoln twitted him about the invasion. She told him if she had had a few ladies in her company up at Fort

Stevens, they would never have allowed the rebels to escape. Stanton, glaring at Mrs. Lincoln through his spectacles, had no response ready for her.

Although friends and enemies alike begged Lincoln not to do it, on July 19 he called for another half-million men to be drafted in September. This was so unpopular it provoked a movement among Republicans to force Lincoln to withdraw as their candidate. Salmon Chase and Benjamin Butler were in favor of such an action, naturally. Charles Sumner kept his distance, preferring the more dignified course of persuading the candidate to step aside voluntarily.

"An intense headache, caused by driving out, in the heat of the day, deprived me of the pleasure of seeing yourself & niece," Mary Lincoln wrote to General George D. Ramsay, referring to July 19, the day after Lincoln ordered the odious draft. Ulysses S. Grant was stalled at Petersburg, north of the James River, and his need of manpower was more than a political problem—the loss of life was a dire moral concern. That month his soldiers were digging a tunnel under the siege lines at Petersburg in a devious effort to accomplish underground what seemed, on the face of the earth, impossible.

The Lincolns enjoyed a quiet hour with Gideon and Mary Welles at the Soldiers' Home the evening of July 26. But concern over the Union army command was not far from their minds. Two days later the president wired Grant requesting a meeting at Fortress Monroe—where the James flows into the Chesapeake—on the thirtieth. Citing the pressure of circumstances, Grant begged that he might be excused until a later date. July 30, 1864, was the day that Federal demolition experts detonated "probably the most terrific explosion ever known in this country." The mine erupted under three hundred Confederate soldiers, horses, and matériel, scattering them to the four points of the compass so that it rained body parts, pistols, Bibles, and horseshoes for half a minute, and opened a grave 170 feet long by 80 feet wide by 30 feet deep into which fifteen thousand Union soldiers marched to be trapped, locked in a pathetic, futile battle. The furious rebels mowed down the Federal troops who charged into the crater. Four thousand Union soldiers died and fifteen hundred Confederates. Grant was roundly accused of ineptitude, callous indifference to life, and drunkenness. The sound of the explosion reverberated north and south, confirming Mary Lincoln's conception of Grant as the butcher of Ohio who had no notion of managing his men.

Lincoln may have known of Grant's plans, for on the eve of the catastrophe he confirmed that he would meet with the general the day after the detonation, at 10:00 A.M. on Sunday the thirty-first. When at last the worried president left Washington on the night of July 30 to sail down the Potomac on the USS *Baltimore,* his wife was at his side, prepared to support him as he tried to make sense of the conduct of his generals Grant and Burnside.

THERE WAS LITTLE military news to bolster Lincoln's position until Sherman advanced on Atlanta in late summer. The circulation of the "Wade-Davis Manifesto" in early August caused Lincoln to wonder if his enemies in the Congress meant to oppose his election outright. He doubted that his administration would survive, and Mrs. Lincoln was terribly anxious about their future if he should lose. The heat and reeking air of the city were again unhealthful. Soon after Lincoln learned of the public attack on him by Wade and Davis, on August 6, Mrs. Lincoln and Tad left for Vermont.

She would not return until late September. In his wife's absence during those scorching days of August, Lincoln gave in to feelings of sadness and near despair. In a secret memorandum he wrote, on August 23, 1864, "This morning, as for some days past, it seems exceedingly probable that this administration will not be reelected. Then it will be my duty so to cooperate with the President elect as to save the Union between the election and the inauguration." He asked his cabinet members to endorse the sealed envelope, which he then filed away for safekeeping; he wanted them to know, when they read it after the election, how deeply he was committed to the Union, whether or not he served a second term—and regardless of who replaced him. Editor Alexander McClure, visiting Lincoln at this time, observed, "His face, always sad in repose, was then saddened until it became a picture of despair," as Lincoln found "not even a silver lining to the political cloud that hung over him."

It was some consolation to him that his wife was enjoying her long vacation in the Green Mountains of Vermont, and that she would return refreshed and strengthened for the challenges that would face them in the autumn. He needed her support and cooperation, and by now he knew that he would have little of either if she was not in good health. Despite her headaches, she had been a help to him during the month of July, ever since her homecoming from the resort of Saratoga Springs. And so he looked forward to her return before the election.

Just as Lincoln had watched the ungainly engines of the Republican opposition—the Chase-for-President committee, the farcical spectacle of the Cleveland convention for John Frémont, the abhorrent Wade-Davis Manifesto—start up and backfire, each in its way inspiring support for the embattled president, now he looked on as the Democrats imploded. On August 29, meeting in Chicago, the Democrats chose General George McClellan as their standard-bearer. "Little Mac" was the soldier's soldier, the general's general—his reluctance to take the field notwithstanding. He had organized the raw, ragtag Federal companies into an army, and trained them. The idea that Major General George McClellan would be running on a peace platform was so absurd that he himself did not believe in it. In the final draft of the letter accepting his nomination, McClellan agreed (with Lincoln) that the only way to preserve the Union was a relentless prosecution of the war.

"I don't believe that God has forsaken us yet," Lincoln told Noah Brooks.

The president also understood that voters use the campaign as a forum for protest and a fulcrum for future leverage. Men bound to vote for Lincoln and Andrew Johnson in November chastised the president, his cabinet, his generals, and his wife all summer and long into the autumn. For Mary Lincoln this was particularly painful, as some newspapers planted articles reviving every scandal and rumor about her that had surfaced since 1860. On October 23, she wrote to Abram Wakeman complaining of the "vile fabrications" of the press that she feared would not cease "until they find Mr. L. reelected."

Perhaps the cruelest attack appeared in the *Illinois State Register* the week before the election. On October 30, 1864, the Democratic paper in the Lincolns' hometown published "All About the Domestic Economy of the White House," a scathing recital of the First Lady's acquisitions, renovations, and personal extravagances, her Brussels carpets and Inverness tapestries, her fabulous point lace and $1,000 shawls. They called her a "coarse, vain, unamiable woman," completely without taste, dignity, or discretion, one who allowed scoundrels like Chevalier Wikoff to become fixtures and protocol advisers in the White House. "She introduced sensationalism into the White House economy; courted low company in her innocence of what was superior, and forgetting that her husband's rank made her head of her sex, desired more tangible token that this was so." There was too much truth in this commentary for it not to wound Mary. The writer even mentions Mrs. Lincoln's rival Kate Chase, remarking that the president's wife stooped to compete with the younger socialite in the richness of her parties, apparently unaware that the president's establishment can have no "rivals."

When the hatchet man had exhausted the more conventional grounds for indicting the president's wife, he descended to the most personal insults, complaining that she inflicted upon the public the sight of her "seven times a day on Pennsylvania Avenue," a "sallow, fleshy, uninteresting woman in white laces, & wearing a band of white flowers about her forehead, like some overgrown Ophelia." The attack concluded with the unkindest cut of all: that Mary Lincoln's costly "ball" of February 5, 1862, was an unpardonable offense to a nation traumatized by Civil War. She had "shamed the country," the *Register* declared. Not content with that, the moralist implies that little Willie's death was the judgment of an angry God on the sins of this frivolous adventuress: "Only the death of her little boy could bring this vain and foolish woman to her senses; for a time she scandalized the nation no longer."

During October and early November she kept a low profile, avoiding public appearances—at funerals, at the theater—anywhere a reporter might notice her. Newsmen did not even mention her appearing at the window with her husband and Tad when the torchlight procession of the Lincoln and Johnson Club came marching to serenade them time and again. She kept to her rooms, praying that they would not lose the White House. "I don't know how I would bear up under defeat," she once told Hannah Shearer. She told another friend, "I could have gone down on my knees to ask votes for him and again and again he said: 'Mary, I am afraid you will be punished for this overweening anxiety. If I am to be re-elected it will be all right; if not, you must bear the disappointment.' "

Her anxiety was excessive. Many doubters had underestimated the Republican grassroots organization; others did not understand how deeply the president had inspired soldiers who would vote for him instead of General McClellan. Men risking their lives for the Union loved Lincoln and would vote for him in overwhelming numbers—despising the Democrats who talked of peace. He would win the election handily. He would win because of his wife's support, faith, and prayers, and in spite of her infamous debts, extravagances, bad company, and indiscretions. In

August, Admiral David Farragut's warships seized Mobile Bay from Confederate control. Atlanta surrendered to Sherman on September 1, and three weeks later General Philip Sheridan drove Jubal Early's army from the Shenandoah Valley. At last, to please the radicals, Lincoln discharged the hated conservative Postmaster General Blair from the cabinet. By October, the Republicans who had been badgering him all year—Wade and Davis, Greeley and Weed, Chase and Sumner—returned to the fold, hailing Lincoln as the only hope of the nation. On the stump for Lincoln in Ohio, Salmon Chase explained, "This seems to me the only path of patriotic duty."

THE EVENING OF Election Day was warm and rainy. At about seven o'clock John Hay accompanied the president to the telegraph office. "We splashed through the grounds to the side door of the War Department where a soaked and smoking sentry was standing in his own vapor with his huddled up frame covered with a rubber cloak. Inside a half-dozen idle orderlies; upstairs the clerks of the telegraph." There were Stanton, Welles, Assistant Navy Secretary Gustavus Fox, Assistant Secretary of War Charles Dana, and the cipher operators under Major Thomas Eckert's supervision, all gathered to hear the election returns. A dispatch announced Lincoln's ten-thousand-vote majority in Philadelphia. Another claimed a fifteen-thousand-vote lead in Baltimore. Charles Sumner wired that Lincoln led by five thousand in Boston. Lincoln sent the good news to his wife via messenger, telling the men, "She is more anxious than I."

That is the last we hear of Mary Lincoln on that long, rainy night in November, when Lincoln waited and celebrated with the gentlemen in the telegraph office until midnight. Major Eckert then came in bearing the victory feast—hot coffee and a baking pan of fried oysters. Lincoln did the honors of shoveling out portions to one and all. He talked at length about how bitter the contest had become, and how ironic it was that he, a peaceable, amiable fellow, almost always found himself in elections marked by rancor. He read aloud from the humorist Petroleum Vesuvius Nasby. He did not visit his wife. At two in the morning he and John Hay were still there when a messenger came to get them, explaining that a crowd of citizens wanting to congratulate and serenade the president were disappointed to find his rooms dark.

Soon the crowd of "loyal Pennsylvanians" found their way to the War

Department. "The President answered from the window with rather unusual dignity," Hay recalled, and then "we came home." By then it was
nearly three o'clock in the morning. The Lincolns, as far as anyone
knows, had not spent a minute together during the whole night.

LINCOLN HAD PROMISED Anson Henry, who was far away in the Washington Territory, that he would wire him as soon as the outcome of the
election was certain. Noah Brooks, who had become part of the White
House family, wrote out Lincoln's reelection tidings to Dr. Henry. Then
Brooks signed the telegram, so the president would not have to "blow his
own horn," as he put it. The next day, November 11, Brooks recalled that
Lincoln sent a second message to the doctor, "in order to give his friend a
clear and exact idea of what had happened"—for instance, that Delaware
had gone for McClellan.

Brooks's precision on these points lends credence to a story so poetic
that it sometimes is mistaken for legend. This vignette occurs elsewhere,
independently, in the comments of Ward Hill Lamon, John Hay, and others, but Noah Brooks's account, written in Lincoln's own words as the
journalist took them down on November 11, "on the day mentioned"—the
day Lincoln wired news of his victory to Anson Henry in Washington—is
the most immediate and reliable. It also has the virtue of bringing Mrs.
Lincoln back into the picture, after her vanishing on Election Day.

In the privacy of a guest bedroom, the president told Brooks the story,
urgently, as if it burdened him. Just after his election in 1860, after a day of
frenzied activity, applause, and fanfare, "I was well tired out, and went
home to rest, throwing myself down on a lounge in my chamber. Opposite
where I lay was a bureau with a swinging glass upon it." To demonstrate
the exact arrangement of things to Brooks, Lincoln sprang out of his chair
and moved a bureau a few degrees on its axis. "Looking in that glass," he
went on, "I saw myself reflected nearly at full length; but my face, I noticed, had *two* separate and distinct images, the tip of the nose of one
being about three inches from the tip of the other.

"I was a little bothered, perhaps startled, and got up and looked in the
glass, but the illusion vanished. On lying down again, I saw it a second
time, plainer, if possible, than before; and then I noticed that one of the
faces was a little paler—say five shades—than the other. I got up, and
the thing melted away, and I went off." Lincoln told Brooks that in all the

excitement of the day he nearly forgot about it, "but not quite, for the thing would once in a while come up, and give me a little pang as if something uncomfortable had happened." He and his wife were both superstitious—maybe no more than other Western folk of their generation, who relied upon divining rods to dig wells, planted potatoes only in the dark, and would not cross paths with a black cat. They were alert to dreams, comets, and portents that might be clues to the future. That night Lincoln told his wife about the doubled image. And "a few days afterward I made the experiment again." He chuckled nervously as he told Brooks, "Sure enough! The thing came again." He tried hard to show the phenomenon to Mary, who was troubled by it, "but I never succeeded in bringing the ghost back after that," try as he might.

The joy of that month after the first election was streaked with terrors. Hardly a day passed without some rumor or newspaper report that Lincoln would be assassinated before the inauguration. Mary worried over the mysterious ghost in the mirror. "She thought it was a 'sign' that I was to be elected to a second term of office," he told Brooks, "and that the paleness of one of the faces was an omen that I should not see life through the last term." Now that he had been reelected, Lincoln would naturally be haunted by a prophecy that was half fulfilled.

Brooks was intrigued by the "very remarkable story." An intimate friend of Mrs. Lincoln, he went to her as soon as he could, sat down with her, and repeated the outline of the anecdote. He asked if she recalled the details. She did indeed, and it must have given her pause, so soon after the victory of the second election, to be reminded of the portent following the first. Brooks had touched a nerve. "She expressed surprise that Mr. Lincoln was willing to say anything about it, as he had up to that time refrained from mentioning the incident to anybody."

Mrs. Lincoln obliged the journalist by confirming her belief that the double image was a warning; he did her the courtesy never to mention it again to her or to her husband. The old portent was troubling in light of Mr. Lincoln's recent decline in health. Mrs. Keckley recalls Mrs. Lincoln lamenting soon after the election, "Now that we have won the position, I almost wish it were otherwise. Poor Mr. Lincoln is looking so brokenhearted, so completely worn out, I fear he will not get through the next four years."

GHOSTS IN THE MIRROR

Two blinding events, the fall of Richmond and the assassination of the president, have so overwhelmed the memory of 1865 that they blot out the details of other occurrences. As for the Lincolns' marriage, it can only be glimpsed through interstices and telling silences. They were not getting along.

Mary Lincoln reemerges, a solitary, sad, and fretful figure, in her letters of late November 1864. The strain of the election year and the suspense of the final weeks of the campaign had drained her of all but the dregs of a tearful contentment, a relief that there was still hope. "The *world* has lost so much of its charm," she wrote to Hannah Shearer on November 20. "My position, requires my presence, where my heart is *so far* from being." This note has its emotional counterpoint in Lincoln's passive, low-key acceptance speech to the serenaders on the night of the election: "If I know my heart, my gratitude is free from any taint of personal triumph." Being the president, or the president's wife, was no promise of happiness, or even stability. "I have sometimes feared that the *deep waters* through which we have passed would overwhelm me," she confessed.

For weeks before the election she had kept out of the spotlight, out of the newspapers. She had not dared to influence policy or appointments. Now that the White House was to be hers for four more years, she was under no constraint. A week after the election, she became obsessed over a rumor that Major General Nathaniel P. Banks, a conservative who had been empowered to reorganize a free-state government in Louisiana, had come to lobby for a cabinet post—secretary of war. Forty-nine-year-old Banks, former governor of Massachusetts, called "the bobbin boy" for his hardscrabble beginnings in a cotton mill, seems an unlikely target for Mrs. Lincoln's vengeance. A narrow-shouldered, sad-eyed man, Banks had little going for him in 1864. After leading an ill-fated campaign on Louisiana's Red River in the spring, Banks was under military censure. He went to Washington to get Louisiana readmitted to the Union, where he was blocked by radicals who wanted guarantees of Negro suffrage.

Of all the mediocre generals and office seekers lingering in Washington that November, one of the least likely threats to Edwin Stanton's cabinet position was Nathaniel P. Banks. Yet somehow Mrs. Lincoln got the notion that this Yankee had become a pawn of the president's conservative enemies who were plotting to install Banks at the head of the War Department, where he could do their bidding. On Sunday, November 20, she wrote to Senator Sumner in a panic. It was a long letter begging him, "Will you not exercise your great influence, with your friends who have a *right,* to demand some thing at the hands of a Government they have rescued, from tyranny? I feel assured *now,* whilst this subject, is agitated, your voice & your pen, will not be silent. Gen Banks, is considered a *weak failure,* overrated, and a speculator & associate of secession with Gen Butler." She regrets that Sumner might "consider it unbecoming" for her to make such a request, but "the whole country is anxious about this." What could she possibly mean by it, when no one in the country seems to have been so anxious about Banks as she was? Maybe she thought the election results were too good to be true, the castle was built on sand, and now anyone, even a nobody like Banks, could wrest defeat from the jaws of victory. "I fear the appointment or the promise of it *might* be made, ere Congress meets, *you* can do much, in this case." And in closing, she assures him that their communication is private.

On Tuesday the twenty-second she scribbled a brief note to the lobbyist Oliver S. Halsted (he had paid some of her bills, and she wanted to reimburse him), telling him to come quickly and use his influence, for Banks "is indefatigable, and *may* be appointed immediately—Heaven forbid! . . . there should be no delay in this matter—."

The simple truth is that General Banks was in town on a leave of absence that Lincoln himself had extended on November 14, for the sole purpose of persuading Congress to recognize the newly constituted state of Louisiana. Mrs. Lincoln was living under the same roof—if not sleeping in the same bed—with the man who knew more about Nathaniel Banks's business in Washington than any other, and the only man with the power to include Banks in the cabinet, had he desired it. Lincoln had not the slightest inclination to replace Edwin Stanton as secretary of war—

certainly not with the negligible and recently disgraced General Banks. Edward Bates, weary of office, was soon to resign his post as attorney general. But Banks was not suitable for that role either. If General Banks troubled Mary Lincoln, all she would have had to do that week was ask her husband about him, and he would have been happy to put her mind to rest. It might have amused him.

She did not consult her husband that weekend. Instead, she wrote the hysterical letter to their mutual friend Charles Sumner, and then the note to the notorious lobbyist and rich political opportunist Oliver "Pet" Halsted, Jr., pleading for him to intercede in the imaginary case of the bobbin boy and the cabinet. If word of this got back to the president, it must have embarrassed him. This was just the kind of meddling in affairs of state that had sullied Mary's reputation in the beginning. The knowledge that his wife had gone to other men first with a problem that should have remained at home must have been vexing. It was as if they lived and worked not at opposite ends of the same house, but on opposite sides of the city.

Mrs. Lincoln did not get around to approaching her husband on the subject until Thursday. That day the president had shut his doors to the public. He was preparing his lengthy annual report to Congress on the state of the Union, on every aspect of government from foreign affairs to finances, pensions, and military affairs. If his wife wanted to discuss the structure of the cabinet with him, this was as good a time as any.

Much to her relief, her husband told her that he did not want to bring Banks into the cabinet. On the contrary, Mr. Lincoln was about to send General Banks back to New Orleans. Furthermore—as she later informed Mr. Sumner—although she had heard that William Seward and Thurlow Weed had been urging Banks's appointment, "Mr. L. now says, neither of these gentlemen have ever mentioned the subject to him, he has had no idea of it himself, & that Gen Banks, is to return to his command in New Orleans immediately." Her letter to Sumner is an abject apology for trespassing upon his valuable time, "for having written you so candid & as it *now* appears, so unnecessary a letter, as I did, a few days since. I regretted writing you, immediately after the note was sent, the great excitement the rumor created was the cause of my doing so." As a friend of both Mr. and Mrs. Lincoln, Sumner would have informed Lincoln of his wife's distress, and the president—learning of the imposition upon Sumner—would have expected Mary to apologize.

If she was prey to such rumors, and considered it her duty to protect him, what subject concerning his management of the government or the military could Lincoln afford to discuss with his wife? She knew and dreaded his silences. She would fill the silences and the time alone as best she could with woman's work. She read to Tad and played with him. In the Yuletide season there was shopping to do. Right out the front gate she could walk to Fifteenth Street, and there on the north side of New York Avenue stood the tiny toy shop of Joseph Stuntz. It was merely a two-story house, two windows wide above. On the first floor a showcase gave a view into the tunnel-like store, crammed full of toys, dolls and dollhouses, toy soldiers, trains, wagons, and wooden guns, all handmade by Mr. Stuntz. From the side door in the alley where the public entered, one could smell molasses—the taffy Mrs. Stuntz brewed in the kitchen.

Triumph in the election meant that Mrs. Lincoln could resume shopping. More than a pastime, this activity had become nearly a vocation essential to her peace of mind. She had always justified her costly wardrobe as a prop to her husband's administration; "the people scrutinize every article that I wear with critical curiosity," she told her seamstress, and it was true they were quick to find fault with her as a "provincial." Now she had another rationalization: Salmon Chase had suggested that the treasury needed the revenue that came from expensive imports, so in effect wearing Italian lace and French silk was a demonstration of patriotism. According to Mrs. Keckley, the acquisition and stockpiling of rich clothing and accessories (three hundred pairs of kid gloves, for example) also served a more remote, irrational purpose: With her increasing obsession over money, Mary saw the wardrobe as a hoard of forced savings. If she ever found herself in want, she might sell a shawl.

In the second week of December, Horatio Taft saw Mrs. Lincoln's carriage parked in front of a clothing shop. In his diary, Taft archly notes that Mrs. Lincoln does not condescend to enter the shop herself. "She *might* get jostled and gazed at and that too would be doing just as the common people do." Rather, she sends her footman into the store to fetch the sales clerk, who goes out to the carriage with the goods draped over his arm to show Mrs. Lincoln, who "thumbs the goods and asks a great many questions."

Five days later, December 19, a rainy, muddy day, Mary Virginia Stuart of Springfield—wife of Congressman John Stuart of Illinois, Mrs. Lincoln's cousin—was going from store to store looking for a printer to engrave her greeting cards. She entered a shop, and "who should I meet there but Mary Lincoln, true to her love of shopping; she met me very cordially, asked my opinion about some ladies writing desk that she had been examining, but said unfortunately it was sold, which she regretted." Mrs. Lincoln offered Mary Virginia a ride home, but the lady declined, feeling she was too muddy to be seen in the president's carriage. And then too, she "did not care about too readily accepting kindness which was from the mere force of circumstances," a rather chilly comment to be coming from the wife of Mary's own cousin and Lincoln's first law partner. The women had known each other for twenty-five years. But the Mary Lincoln she saw in the White House was unlike the woman she had known in Springfield.

The next day Mrs. Lincoln left for New York. She could buy things there that were not available in the shops on Pennsylvania Avenue. In Manhattan she purchased the dress she would wear to the inaugural ball, at a cost of $2,000. Missing her on a bitter winter day in Washington, four days before Christmas, her husband thought of her comfort and wired her at the Continental Hotel: "Do not come on the night train. It is too cold. Come in the morning." As long as Mrs. Lincoln was busy Christmas shopping, he was not so concerned about her interfering with patronage matters, which was tempting during this season, right after an election.

Influence peddling, whether practiced by old friends like Orville Browning or by the president's wife, presented thorny ethical problems not only to Lincoln but also to the secretary of war. Just before Christmas, Mrs. Lincoln got caught in the lights of Stanton's righteousness. The dispute defined the relationship between Mrs. Lincoln and the gruff secretary. Unlike Charles Sumner, who enjoyed her company, Stanton disliked Mrs. Lincoln and had no patience with her. His wife, Ellen, refused to call upon Mrs. Lincoln.

In December, an idler named Robert E. Parker, a relative of Mrs. Lincoln, called upon Mr. Stanton requesting a position as a commissary to the army. He showed the secretary a card from the president's wife endorsing his petition. "There is no place for you," Stanton said, "and if there were, the fact that you bring me such a card would prevent my giving it to you." The next day Parker returned, all smiles, with a more formal letter from Mrs. Lincoln stating "if you can grant his petition, which I send enclosed, you will bestow a personal favor upon me." Fuming, Stanton once again showed Parker the door. When he had collected himself, the secretary of war put on his coat and hat and stepped away from his high, slant-topped desk at the War Department, a place he rarely left. Lincoln himself came to Stanton. Now he made his way across the frozen ground to the White House to send up his card to Mrs. Lincoln. Asthmatic, Stanton wheezed as he walked in the cold air.

Mary Lincoln was surprised, wondering to what honor she owed this visit from the secretary of war. It was not his habit to sit, even while working at his desk, so he would refuse the seat offered to him when she came down to the parlor. She was taken aback to discover his purpose: He wanted to know what she meant by writing the letter endorsing her cousin's petition. She replied, confidently, that she believed that being the president's wife, she had the right to ask for so small a favor. The stocky statesman with the immense beard, his brown eyes ablaze behind his square gold-rimmed spectacles, spoke with exquisite politeness.

"Madam, we are in the midst of a great war for national existence. Our success depends upon the people. My first duty is to the people of the United States; my next duty is to protect your husband's honor, and your own. If I should make such appointments, I should strike at the very root of all confidence of the people in the government, in your husband, and you and me." Startled, contrite, she told the secretary of war he was correct and that she would never ask him for anything again. She bade him good day. He took his leave, putting his hat on his head, and returned to his work. But on behalf of her cousin, Mrs. Lincoln promptly approached other officials, notably James A. Hardie, assistant adjutant general of the Army of the Potomac, who was in a position to offer Parker a position as a provisioner in a convalescent camp.

This was the same week, December 16, that John Nicolay complained, "About three days of the week have been taken up with a row with my particular feminine friend here [Mrs. Lincoln] but I have got through it without any serious damage." If Mrs. Lincoln found herself tongue-tied in the presence of Edwin Stanton, she felt no such inhibition in her dialogues with young Nicolay or Hay, both of whom she wished would be gone in the coming year.

THE SOCIAL OBLIGATIONS of the New Year were as intense and demanding as ever: regular open house levees, and more intimate afternoon receptions in the Blue Room. The crowds at the New Year's levee and the first White House reception on January 14, 1865, were larger and more boisterous than ever. There were afternoon receptions on Saturdays during the months of January and February, and these were well attended. The Lincolns had succeeded at the polls and the war had turned in favor of the Union, so the White House was now considered the proper place for all of society to gather.

A married couple's social life is an important piece of the puzzle of their history. An ordinary couple may attend a dinner or a ball as a diversion from the routine of work and domesticity, a chance to interact with each other and friends outside the home. Not the president and his wife. When in Washington, they are hosts but never guests. (President Grant broke the rule several years later, but it has generally been observed before and since.) They are called upon but do not make social calls. They may go to weddings and funerals, but the Lincolns avoided attending such functions together. At levees they often stood in different rooms, and the president came late to the afternoon receptions, hurrying downstairs from his office to greet people for three-quarters of an hour. Sometimes he was too busy to attend at all.

For months on end during the White House years, the social record is nearly all we have of the marriage. That they entertained at all during the months before the second inauguration is significant; that they entertained with good cheer and stamina is admirable. Lincoln was no longer running for president. Mrs. Lincoln was under no pressure to flatter hostile senators and their wives, or the dowagers and figureheads of the Washington establishment who had shunned her in 1861. Benjamin French notes on January 22 that despite the rain and cold, Mrs. Lincoln's afternoon reception was well attended. "Some of the most fashionable ladies in Washington were there & it was peculiarly honored by the Military, Secy of War Stanton, Gen Phil. Sheridan, Gen. Burnside, Gen. Butler," and dozens of other officers, as well as many congressmen and their ladies. "The President appeared well and in excellent spirits, and Mrs. Lincoln never appeared better. She was dressed in admirable taste— A rich black satin gown high in the neck, with a very rich white lace shawl thrown gracefully over it. Pearl and diamond jewelry—a very graceful lace headdress falling back to her shoulders . . . her *toute ensemble* never made a more favorable impression upon me than yesterday, and she greeted every guest with such cheerful good will and kindness as to do infinite credit to her position and her heart."

From event to event the Lincolns decided together to go forward with the entertainment or forgo it, regardless of custom. Despite French's comment above, the president was not well. The photographs that Alexander Gardner took of him between February and April show a startling change in his features. Hollow-eyed, sunken-cheeked, his forehead deeply furrowed, the fifty-six-year-old president looks seventy—although he managed a faint smile. He had lost thirty-five pounds and had a nagging chill in his hands and feet. The main problem seemed to be his digestion, but his circulation was not good either. He liked to remove his shoes and sit close to the fire with his feet near the fender, watching the steam rise from his socks.

Every morning, he joined his wife and Tad for breakfast in the private dining room downstairs on the northwest corner of the house that the sunshine had not yet touched. He would eat his boiled egg and drink his coffee. She could not tempt him with ham, grits, or pastry, though he did delight in bacon. The flatware shone dully on the length of white tablecloth between them. She fretted over some china she had ordered from Philadelphia that had not arrived yet—the dinner party for which it was required was only a week away. She was not well either, but her distress was more mental than physical. The election ought to have put her mind at ease, but she seemed more anxious than ever.

For a year, she and Lincoln had been arguing about Robert's military service. In December 1864 one of the western newspapers, the *Indianapolis Sentinel,* reminded the public that the president's son Robert Lincoln, twenty-one, had yet to serve in the armed forces. This was not the first notice of Robert's avoidance of the draft, nor would it be the last. According to Elizabeth Keckley, "he was very anxious to quit school and enter the army, but the move was sternly opposed by his mother." Mrs. Lincoln protested that they were still mourning the death of their son Willie, "and his loss is as much as I can bear, without being called upon to make another sacrifice." Only a week earlier, Lincoln had written the famous condolence letter to Lydia Bixby, "the mother of five sons who have died gloriously on the field of battle." Now, in January of 1865, he gently explained to Mary that some mothers had given up all their sons, "and our son is not more dear to us than the sons of other people are to their mothers."

Still she objected. She could not bear to see Robert exposed to danger, "his services are not required in the field, and the sacrifice would be a needless one." Lincoln remained firm, insisting that "the services of every man who loves his country are required in this war." And according to Mrs. Keckley's recollection, he took the unaccustomed measure of reprimanding his wife, saying she "should take a liberal instead of a selfish view of the question." This may not have been the end of the argument, but it is the last word of it Mrs. Keckley remembers. On January 19, 1865, Lincoln wrote to General Grant, asking him if he would please read and answer his letter "as though I was not President, but only a friend." Explaining that his son wanted to see something of the war before it ended, Lincoln admitted he did not wish to put him in the ranks (in harm's way), nor did he want to give him a commission to which others were better entitled. He desired that Robert "go into your Military family with some nominal rank." And he promised that he would pay for it so as not to put the public to any expense.

And so Lincoln solved the problem of his son's military service while putting his wife's mind at ease, without risking a backlash of public opinion. Grant was delighted to have Robert "in the manner you propose," and replied two days later that the matter was settled. On February 11, 1864, after the Battle of Hatcher's Run, Virginia, Robert Lincoln entered Grant's service as an aide-de-camp with the rank of captain.

DURING BREAKFAST THE president and his wife had a half hour to discuss such matters as the management of the household and the schedule of entertainments. After Lincoln climbed the stairs to his office, and the old doorman Edward McManus opened the floodgates to the crowd that gathered outside, she often would not see him again until late at night.

It was Edward McManus who occasioned the quarrel between them that escalated into what Mrs. Lincoln called a "scene" on January 30. That morning, unfortunately, they were not alone with their argument. Mary's friend Abram Wakeman, postmaster of New York, was visiting the White House and witnessed the harsh words between the president and his wife. She had abruptly dismissed McManus from his duties as doorkeeper, which he had faithfully discharged for thirty-five years, as "great a favorite through so many administrations," said William Stoddard, and "as well liked by his seventh President [Lincoln] as he was by even General Taylor." Lincoln loved the old leprechaun figure of the Irishman, the first man Lincoln met in the White House who made him laugh. Stoddard said that there was no end of quiet fun in him, intelligence, and loyalty, but somehow he had crossed Mrs. Lincoln. Some say that he was too late in delivering some documents for her; others say that he had betrayed her trust, or that—as the last servant left from the corrupt staff of Stackpole and Watt—he still had the power to embarrass or blackmail her. At any rate, she fired him without notice, and there was little the president could do about it but complain. He did so that morning after breakfast, in front of Abram Wakeman, who was there on business concerning the Port of New York.

All three were embarrassed. Mrs. Lincoln wrote to Wakeman later in the day, inviting him to dinner the next evening at six. The early dinner hour, she explained, was because the president had invited her to the theater to see Edwin Forrest in *Spartacus*. This letter is revealing of her intimacy with Wakeman, already noted, and of the increasing turbulence in the marriage. She informs Wakeman that she has taken his advice and tried to soothe her husband, because she knows "how deeply grieved, the P[resident] feels over any coolness of mine." Elizabeth Keckley once commented, "He loved the mother of his children very tenderly. He asked nothing but affection from her, but did not always receive it. When in one of her wayward, impulsive moods, she was apt to say and do things that wounded him deeply." She knew this, and now she would try to make amends.

"We have had a little laugh together, most fortunately for both my Husband and myself, who [would] have broken our hearts, had it been otherwise." She still maintained her sense of humor, and he had not lost his. Laughter continued to be a balm for them in times of strife when all else failed. They would have broken their hearts, "had it been otherwise, notwithstanding our opposite natures, our lives have been eminently peaceful." So she asks Wakeman's indulgence, and his understanding. "The communication made you this morning, will I am sure, always be sacredly guarded by you—As *scenes* are novelties with us, I felt strangely disposed to tell you." She thanks heaven that the storm has passed, and vows: "I shall ever *even in jest,* take especial pains not to provoke discussions, lest *forbidden subjects,* might be introduced—." That is, of course, a program as likely to create estrangement in a marriage as harmony.

Scenes were not in fact a "novelty" with the Lincolns, and they were becoming more frequent. During the next two weeks Mrs. Lincoln continued to rail against "the serpent" McManus in letters to Abram Wakeman that are peculiarly intimate. The disgraced doorkeeper had gone to New York spreading rumors of his ill treatment by Mrs. Lincoln, and of corruption in the White House. His complaints had reached the ears of Thurlow Weed, a powerful envoy and lobbyist allied not only with Wakeman but with publisher James Gordon Bennett and to William H. Seward. On February 18, she wrote, "I am more shocked than ever, that any one can be so *low*, as to place confidence in a discarded menial's assertions, the game of espionage, has been going on, to a greater extent than we have imagined—if the 'Heavens fall,' E[dward] shall never be restored."

Why was she so threatened by the "discarded menial's assertions" if they were unfounded? Evidently the fracas over the doorkeeper had not been settled, for she begs Wakeman to visit the president and reassure him that Mr. Weed and others were paying no attention to McManus's wagging tongue. "It will gratify Mr. L if you pay your respects to him to day. I believe, if possible I shall love and venerate my blessed Husband more than ever." Why should she confide such a vow to the postmaster of New York? It is a curious letter, full of nonsequiturs and outbursts. The overriding impression is that—as in the case of Nathaniel Banks—Mrs. Lincoln has created a melodrama in which she is the lady in distress. She hopes that her husband will rescue her, but he is preoccupied, or does not see the danger. So she rushes to another man who will give her his attention and who may intercede on her behalf. The election had been won, and the war was nearly over. She had grown so accustomed to real turmoil and catastrophe, steeling herself against adversity—now she was moved to create trouble where none could be found.

In that same letter of February 18, she urged Wakeman to attend her reception that Saturday, six days after Mr. Lincoln's fifty-sixth birthday. This afternoon reception was successful. Yet Lincoln surprised the community by announcing on Monday morning—the anniversary of Willie's death—that there would be no more White House receptions "for the present." The Lincolns were probably in no mood for entertaining. That week Mrs. Lincoln informed her son Robert that she was ill. So was the president. Orville Browning went to visit him the night of February 23, on business, and wrote, "The President looked badly and felt badly— apparently more depressed than I have seen him since he became President."

And yet when Saturday afternoon rolled around, the Lincolns were back at their posts, greeting guests at another reception in the Blue Room. One of the guests, the French diplomat Charles Adolphe de Pineton, the Marquis de Chambrun, a friend of Sumner's, said of the president, "He dominates everyone present and maintains his exalted position without the slightest effort." The Frenchman had not noticed the great effort that concealed the effort on the president's part, or the fact that he did not dominate his wife.

EAGER TO SEE the Lincolns again before Inauguration Day, Dr. Anson Henry set out from the Washington Territory in midwinter. After a long voyage from San Francisco, across the Isthmus of Panama, then up the Atlantic coast to New York on the steamship *North Star,* he arrived in the capital in early February. This time he had come to lobby for a cabinet position, which Mrs. Lincoln assured him was more than possible. "Mr. Lincoln won't refuse anything you ask him, for I *know.*"

On February 8, the doctor accompanied the president's wife to the Capitol to hear the counting of the electoral votes. The president was too busy to attend this joyous occasion. Mrs. Lincoln arrived late and took her seat in the crowded gallery with the diplomatic corps. She and Dr. Henry listened as the votes were counted, beaming as the vice president announced that Abraham Lincoln was elected president of the United States for four years from the fourth of March, 1865, and "the immense audience broke into loud applause, which was not less emphatic on the floor of the House than in the galleries," according to *The New York Times.* She would tell Mr. Lincoln all about it.

Dr. Henry stayed for the inauguration, and for a month afterward, keeping the president company, but Mrs. Lincoln was wrong about the doctor's chances for a job in the administration. Informed that there was no possibility for a cabinet post, Dr. Henry would have settled for the position of commissioner of Indian affairs, or of envoy to the Hawaiian Islands. Lincoln seemed "played out," full of excuses, unable to accommodate even an old friend like Dr. Henry. But Mr. and Mrs. Lincoln wanted Henry to hear the second inaugural address and attend the inaugural ball the weekend of March 4.

On March 4, 1865, the order of the day was carefully choreographed and scripted. The president and his wife were engrossed in matters and details of protocol and conduct, everything from dress and grooming to the final preparation of the manuscript for the inaugural address. Each was required to play a role as custom demanded. Visitors mobbed the city, come to celebrate the anticipated victory of the Union and Mr. Lincoln's stalwart leadership. "Carpet-bagged and blanket-strapped strangers were bolting in every direction, in a dazed hap-hazard sort of way," wrote one Washington journalist.

The Lincolns moved at the center of an extravaganza that whirled and thundered around them like a storm. The rain had turned the streets into rivers of mud. Four years earlier on Inauguration Day the weather had been dry and whirlwinds of dust swept down the Avenue. And there had been the unfinished dome of the Capitol with the workmen's crane hovering over it, looking like the cranium of a patient undergoing some primitive brain surgery. Now the dome was complete, gleaming white, and the bronze Lady Liberty surmounted it, keeping her vigil.

A reporter from *The Washington Star* observed that "four years ago the preparations were of a far more warlike character. The city was filled with rebels who proclaimed their sentiments boldly in the streets, and hinted violence to the Executive. National airs were hissed down in public places . . . cheers for Jeff Davis were of common occurrence." Federal guards had been prepared for violence. "Sharpshooters were posted at convenient spots along the avenue and on the roofs of buildings, and at the market house [midway between the White House and the Capitol] a small force of infantry was posted. . . . Gen Scott, with Magruder and Fry's batteries, were at the corner of Delaware Avenue and B Street, ready for action, the gunners and drivers remaining at their posts throughout the ceremonies." Although the day passed off quietly, the terrible anxiety of the first inauguration made an impression on those present "that probably will never be erased."

A terrible anxiety had beset the Lincolns four years earlier. And yet both of them had been full of hope, and pride, and excitement about their new position in the world. The suffering they had endured since then had chastened them; their greatest hope now was not for glory, but for peace—peace in the land and in their home. Since leaving Springfield they had seen so much strife and sorrow, and so little of each other.

She could scarcely see him on the platform before he delivered his second inaugural address. Outside the Capitol, the wooden planks of the platform were slick with rain, and a chilly breeze blew. She took a seat high above the round white table where the president stood for his speech. The Lincolns shared the view as the bands played "Hail to the Chief": "A sea of faces below and a sea of mud beyond. . . . In the Capitol all the windows were filled with ladies, and the steps and esplanade at the north wing presented the same dense crowd that the central steps did, while on the unfinished parts of the south wing, on all the scaffolding, hundreds of soldiers had clambered up and decorated all that part with army blue."

His hair and beard were cropped close, making him look younger. Just on the other side of the table sat the new Chief Justice, Salmon Chase—Lincoln's erstwhile rival for the presidency—whom Lincoln had named to the high court following the death of Chief Justice Taney the previous October. Chase would administer the oath after the inaugural speech. At one o'clock Lincoln stood and unrolled his manuscript, moving toward the white table that hardly reached the hem of his black coat. As he stepped forward there was some faint applause. "And at the same time the sun burst through the clouds, and though pretty well to the south, lighted up the whole east face very brilliantly," a reporter observed. Lincoln later told Noah Brooks that the sunbeam had made his heart jump.

The people may have expected a speech of triumph and thanksgiving. What they got was a plea for charity. There was little response to be heard, either on the platform or in the crowd that stood in the mud as Lincoln delivered his magnanimous speech in a strong, clear voice: "With malice toward none; with charity for all; with firmness in the right, as God gives us to see the right, let us strive on to finish the work we are in; to bind up the nation's wounds; to care for him who shall have borne the battle, and for his widow, and his orphan—to do all which may achieve and cherish a just, and a lasting peace, among ourselves, and with all nations." It took those final words to summon the crowd's applause.

That day Salmon Chase took the time to address a note to Mrs. Lincoln and send it to the White House along with the Bible the president had kissed during the inauguration. "The page touched by his lips is marked," Chase wrote. "I hope the Sacred Book will be to you an acceptable souvenir of a memorable day; and I most earnestly pray Him, by whose Inspiration it was given, that the beautiful SunShine which just at the time the oath was taken dispersed the clouds that had previously darkened the sky may prove an auspicious one of the dispersion of the clouds of war and the restoration of the clear sunlight of prosperous peace under the wise & just administration of him who took it." Lincoln endorsed the package and they read the letter, savoring the generous sentiments of Salmon Chase.

CITY POINT

THE PRESIDENT WAS ILL. He was able to stand for Mrs. Lincoln's final afternoon reception in the Blue Room on March 11, but he was obviously worn out. The demands of the inauguration, the pressure of political appointments, news of continuing bloodshed as the war ground to its conclusion—all these forces had taken their toll. The excitement of the inaugural festivities had kept him moving, but by March 13, the *New York Herald* noted, "Mr. Lincoln is reported quite sick today, and has denied himself to all visitors." The next morning, he surprised the cabinet by asking them to come to him in his private quarters because he was too weak to leave his bed.

Lincoln was strong enough by March 15 to return to his office and attend to the most urgent business. Knowing how much her husband loved the opera, Mrs. Lincoln arranged for them to go to Grover's Theatre, only a few blocks away, to hear Mozart's *The Magic Flute*. That night they shared their box with Mrs. Lincoln's new friend Clara Harris, the clever twenty-year-old daughter of Senator Ira Harris, and Colonel James Grant Wilson.

In his diary, Wilson recalled the cozy theater box and the president's good humor. Noticing a female singer's large, flat feet, Lincoln remarked, "The beetles wouldn't have much of a chance there." Mrs. Lincoln wished to leave before the end of the last act of the opera, but the president said, "Oh, no, I want to see it out. It's best when you undertake a job, to finish it." He told the story of a preacher who, in the progress of his sermon, declared that no perfect man but Jesus had ever lived—and in the next breath said there was no record of a perfect woman anywhere to be found. Hearing this, an indignant woman arose in the congregation and said, "*I* know a perfect woman, and for the last six years." The minister asked who that might be. "My husband's first wife," the lady replied.

The next day, a break in the dreary weather inspired the president to take a short carriage ride with Tad. But Lincoln was still so weak he had to lean on the coachman's arm while getting in and out of the seat.

Mrs. Lincoln could rely upon the theater to lift his spirits when the weather was too rainy or cold for carriage rides. At the time of the spring equinox, Washington's weather was fickle—frost one day, a soft balmy breeze the next. She planned a theater party for a cold Saturday night, to hear Grau's opera troupe at Grover's. "Mr. Sumner accompanied us," she wrote to Abram Wakeman. "We had a very gay little time. . . . tomorrow eve [March 21] we all go again to hear 'Robin Adair,' sung in 'La Dame Blanche' by [Theodore] Habelmann. This is always the pleasant time to me in W. Springtime. . . . Mr. L—— most probably, goes down to the front (entre nous) this week & wishes me to accompany him—I gladly seize on any change, that will benefit him."

The trip to Grant's headquarters at City Point, Virginia, was as much Mrs. Lincoln's idea as the president's. She wanted to visit Robert at his post as Grant's aide-de-camp, and this was as good an excuse as any to remove her poor husband from the routine that was undermining his health. General Grant wired him the morning of March 20, inviting him to come to City Point and suggesting that the change of scene would do him good. Lincoln received the telegram at 3:20 in an afternoon filled with business regarding political appointments, but he promptly consulted his wife about the trip. The four-hundred-mile voyage by bay and river would take more than thirty hours, but she was enthusiastic about making a merry party of it for the whole family. Only two hours later the president replied to Grant that they "had already thought of going immediately after the next rain. Will go sooner if any reason for it. Mrs. L. and a few others will probably accompany me. Will notify you of exact time, once it shall be fixed upon."

The day fixed upon was March 23, the hour 1:00 P.M. That morning, Mary wrote to Charles Sumner, "The President & myself are about leaving for 'City Point' and I cannot but devoutly hope, that change of air & rest may have a beneficial effect on my good husband's health." She noted that they would be returning on Wednesday, March 29, inviting the senator to join them in their "large private box" at Ford's Theatre, where Verdi's *Ernani* would be performed that evening. But they would not return in time to hear *Ernani.* They were gone longer than they planned—eighteen days, most of the time that was left of their life together.

Strange visitors troubled Mr. and Mrs. Lincoln as they were preparing to leave. A young woman in a state of extreme agitation accosted the gatekeeper, Louis Burgdorf, just after Lincoln had gone into a cabinet meeting. She had three children with her: a baby on her arm, a child she led by the hand, and another trailing behind. "She demanded to see the President," wrote a Baltimore journalist who witnessed the scene, "and on being told that the Cabinet was in session and that she could not see him, she set the children on the floor in the East Room." In that grand and once elegant room that Mrs. Lincoln had furnished—now ravaged from a hundred entertainments, vandals, and the muddy boots of thousands of tourists and soldiers—the little children ran or crawled about, and the wild-eyed woman turned her back on them. She cried that her husband had been killed in battle, and so "she had brought her children to the President and intended to leave them with him."

There was a notable twisted logic to the proposal. "She was ascertained to be a poor deranged creature, whose afflictions had overbalanced her mind." The kindly, long-suffering doorkeeper, who during wartime had dealt with so many varieties of human misery, had no idea what to do with a female lunatic and her three children. So he called for Mrs. Lincoln. Surely she would understand. Being summoned, she left her bedroom where she and her maid were packing for the voyage. Perhaps Tad could play with the children while Mrs. Lincoln calmed the distressed mother.

"By directions of Mrs. Lincoln," said the Baltimore reporter, the woman "was properly cared for."

MR. LINCOLN COULD scarcely take care of himself, although somehow he managed to carry out his duties, the affairs of state. Mrs. Lincoln alternately worried, coddled, and chastised him; in defense he withdrew, which angered her and caused her to pursue him, going to extreme lengths to get his attention. Both were in a state of nervous exhaustion and subject to erratic behavior.

According to Benjamin French, it was about this time that Mrs. Lincoln yielded to an impulse that commingles clairvoyance, terror, and magical thinking: "The most unaccountable thing she ever did was to purchase about a thousand dollars worth of mourning goods the month before Mr. Lincoln died. What do you suppose possessed her to do it?" What possessed her to do it was the fear that he would die—he had been very ill—and the primitive and not uncommon superstition that if we are thoroughly prepared for a calamity, then it cannot happen. Both of the Lincolns believed in portents, and recalled the double image in the bedroom mirror, with its dire warnings. Mrs. Lincoln was morbidly obsessed with her husband's mortality, and her fear heightened her general anxiety, insecurity, and jealousy.

Just as concerned about the president's well-being, but in a different way, was Edwin M. Stanton. The humorless, religious, and brilliant attorney had given up a $50,000-a-year law practice in Washington to replace the corrupt Simon Cameron in 1862. Stanton had served in the cabinet with exemplary shrewdness and stamina. He had begun with a low opinion of the president, calling him "the original gorilla," and repeatedly referring to his "imbecilities."

From his high seat in the War Department, the short-legged secretary of war had a way of looking down on friends and enemies alike, as from a great moral height. Yet the figure he cut was as strange as Lincoln's. His frock coats never quite covered the rear of his long torso; his beard, which flowed from his lower lip and side whiskers past his breastbone, grew black at the edges and white in the middle. By testing Lincoln in military matters, Stanton had seen—as few other men had—the worldly strength and wisdom of the president. He had measured Lincoln as a statesman, with a statesman's eye, and recognized the greatness in him. Stanton had finally come to regard the president not only with respect but also with affection. It was hard to imagine the success of the Union without him.

Stanton was averse to the president's journey to Virginia, because Mrs. Lincoln's insistence on making a party of it compromised Lincoln's security. At first, thinking that he would be traveling alone, the navy had arranged for him to go on an armed blockade runner, a gunboat with four engines that could outrun anything else afloat. But lacking proper toilet facilities, the gunboat was unsuitable for ladies. So instead, Assistant Secretary of the Navy Gustavus Fox and Secretary Gideon Welles reluctantly put at the president's disposal the *River Queen,* a side-wheel passenger boat with an unarmed civilian crew.

Like Stanton, Fox and Welles were aware of the assassination plots that threatened the president every day. The rebels, facing ruin, were desperate and furious. Lieutenant Commander John S. Barnes, the stalwart naval officer who commanded the USS *Bat*—assigned to run with the *River Queen* to guard her—wrote that the president "was in constant danger of assault or abduction. This danger was very seriously impressed upon me both by Mr. Fox and Mr. Welles. Mr. Fox particularly felt that the President was incurring great risk in making the journey and living on board an unarmed, fragile river-boat, so easily assailed."

So Secretary Stanton, on a blustery afternoon in March too windy for kites, was urging his coachman to drive faster to the Sixth Street wharf, hoping to overtake the presidential party that sailed at one o'clock. The group on board included Mr. and Mrs. Lincoln, Tad, bodyguard William H. Crook, Mrs. Keckley, and Captain Charles B. Penrose, whom Mrs. Lincoln called "my officer." With a sense of impending doom, Stanton felt the wind of a rising storm in his long beard and saw the whitecaps on the Potomac as the *River Queen* pulled away from the dock—too late for him to call them back. Frustrated, he ordered his coachman to drive to the Navy Yard, thinking he might get a swift runner to intercept the president's side-wheeler a few miles out. But by the time he arrived at the dock the wind was approaching gale force, and catching the president was impossible.

Perhaps Stanton thought he could put off this ill-conceived voyage using the weather report as an excuse rather than the latest information concerning assassination plots and the news from the front. The Lincolns were not sailing off to a clambake or a military pageant—City Point was the port of entry to a bloody battle. Confederate General John B. Gordon was planning an attack on the Federal troops at nearby Fort Stedman, and Stanton was concerned that the Confederate cavalry, pressing on to the James River, by chance might seize not only General Grant, but also the president.

Lincoln's lack of interest in his personal safety was notorious, and maddening to those charged with protecting him. His stock response to alarms was to say that if a man wished to lay down his life to kill the president, no one could stop him; and furthermore, Lincoln refused to admit that any man would try. His impetuous behavior at Fort Stevens on July 12, 1864, is evidence enough of his fearlessness, folly, or fatalism, call it what you will; such action on the part of a man upon whom so many people depended is not so pure a thing as courage. By the spring of 1865, Abraham Lincoln was so weary and unhappy much of the time that it was a matter of small concern to him whether he lived or died.

He let others worry about it. The war was ending, and Lincoln wanted to witness the last act of the drama firsthand. Hour to hour the troop movements were shifting as tactics changed. Grant, on March 20, had good-naturedly invited the commander in chief to visit him "for a few days," unaware that the party would include Mrs. Lincoln, Tad, and their entourage for an open-ended residence at the perilous front. They were recalling their delightful excursion to Falmouth in April 1863, when Noah Brooks, Dr. Henry, Tad, and Attorney General Bates had accompanied them to review General Hooker's troops—the martial pageantry, the festive air of that week in the spring. Nearly a year later, much had changed. According to Grant, these final weeks of the war were "the most anxious" of all. As the noose tightened on Robert E. Lee, Grant feared the rebels would make a desperate break southward by way of Danville, Virginia, on the North Carolina border, prolonging the war. Both Grant and Stanton had second thoughts about the president's voyage to City Point in the days between Grant's invitation and Lincoln's embarkation.

With a gale mounting on the Chesapeake, it was a rough crossing on the bay to the James River. Crook, the bodyguard, was seasick. He was sharing a cabin with Tad, and recalled that the restless Mrs. Lincoln awakened him just before dawn, saying, "It is I, Crook. It is growing colder, and I came in to see if my little boy has covers enough on him." The president was unwell, but he blamed his gastric troubles on the drinking water. He asked that fresh water be procured when the ship anchored for the night at Fortress Monroe.

As the *River Queen* steamed toward City Point in the late evening of March 24, all those on deck could see the lights aboard the gunboats, transports, and colliers anchored off the high banks of the James River, and more lights in the cluster of warehouses and railroad sheds on the bluff above the wharves. When the ship docked at 9:00 P.M., Grant descended from his headquarters up the hill and went aboard. He wanted to welcome the Lincolns and prepare them to adapt their plans to recent developments. Intelligence was spotty, but Grant knew that the Confederates under the command of General Gordon were likely to attack Fort Stedman, only a few miles to the southwest. The mobilization of troops did not favor a dress review for the president and his family.

The next morning, the president and Mrs. Lincoln, Tad, Captain Penrose, and Lieutenant Commander Barnes of the *Bat* ate breakfast in the heated dining room on the lower deck of the *River Queen*. It was a chilly day, and mist rose from the river. Mr. Lincoln had little appetite for the eggs and sausage, but he was in good humor. He had taken a liking to Barnes, who was doing double duty as a bodyguard. A fine-looking young officer in Union blue joined them—Captain Robert Lincoln, Grant's aide-de-camp—and they were proud and delighted to see him. When they had exchanged embraces and greetings, Robert explained that he had come with word from General Grant. There had been a fight at the front that morning—the defense of Fort Stedman—and the action was still going on. Union troops had succeeded in repelling the attack on their lines, but the ceremonial review would have to be rescheduled.

Mr. Lincoln called for a pen and paper and wrote Stanton a telegram for Robert to deliver to the operator. In this note he makes light of one of the last terrible battles of the war: "Robert just now tells me there was a little rumpus up the line this morning, ending about where it began." Neither he nor his son yet knew how many men had been killed that day.

Apart from Jubal Early's attack on Fort Stevens, and Lincoln's visits to military hospitals, the commander in chief had no firsthand knowledge of war. While more experienced military men expressed anxiety over the president's security, "he never exhibited the slightest concern for his personal safety," according to Barnes. In addition, many witnesses recall his boyish enthusiasm when visiting field headquarters and military installations. The phrase "he seemed as happy as a schoolboy," which Barnes uses in describing the president's mood when reviewing the fleet, occurs in other accounts of Lincoln's approach to the battlefield. Knowing the president's recklessness, Stanton wired him first thing on March 25, a word of caution: "I hope you will remember Gen. Harrison's advice to his men at Tippecanoe, that they 'can see as well a little further off.' "

Far from heeding Stanton's advice, "Mr. Lincoln expressed a great desire to visit the scene of the action," to get as close to the gunfire as they would let him. After breakfast he walked up the hill with some officers to visit Grant's headquarters, a two-story farmhouse with a wide porch below and three dormer windows above, surrounded by a cluster of temporary log houses. It was there Lincoln learned that the battle at the front had been very serious and was still going on. "General Grant was rather opposed to such a trip for the President," but Lincoln insisted. So a locomotive was stoked up to convey Mr. and Mrs. Lincoln, Mrs. Grant, Lieutenant Commander Barnes, and Grant's secretary, Colonel Adam Badeau, to Fort Stedman.

As the open train car lurched and bounced on the railway that had been hastily built from the river terminus to Meade's headquarters in the field, no one was prepared for what they saw. The rebels had attacked the Federal lines at Petersburg at dawn, captured and briefly held Fort Stedman, and driven the Union army back over the railroad embankment, where the train jerked to a halt. Barnes wrote: "The ground immediately about us was still strewn with dead and wounded men, Federal and Confederate. The whole army was under arms and moving to the left, where the fight was still going on."

At that point Lincoln left his wife to proceed on horseback with General Meade and Lieutenant Barnes to a hill from which he could get a better view of the battle. They rode through the field where the fighting had been most intense and saw hundreds of men strewn about, dead and mutilated, burial parties at work, surgeons and nurses carrying water and tending to the wounded. "We passed by two thousand rebel prisoners, herded together. . . . Mr. Lincoln remarked upon their sad condition" and said they were probably "glad to be at rest."

Meanwhile, Mrs. Lincoln, displeased to be separated from her husband in this macabre landscape, had mounted a "field ambulance," a half-open carriage with two facing seats within and the driver's seat above. Beside her sat Julia Dent Grant, a lady with dark hair swept up in a bun, a soft chin, and bright little eyes, while Colonel Badeau faced them, with his back to the horses. They were bound for Meade's headquarters to the rear of the main action, in relative safety. By way of conversation, Badeau mentioned that all the officers' wives had been ordered to the rear—"a sure sign that active operations were in contemplation." Mrs. Grant, a seasoned army wife known for her self-possession, looked out upon the field of corpses unmoved by Badeau's chatter, which did nothing to reassure Mrs. Lincoln of her husband's safety. Nonchalantly Badeau remarked that no lady remained at the front but General Charles Griffin's wife, who had a special permit from the president.

Mrs. Lincoln snapped to attention, scowling. "What do you mean by that, sir?" she demanded. Mrs. Griffin, a friend of Mrs. Grant, was a well-known and attractive woman in the capital. "Do you mean to say that she saw the President alone?" Badeau had meant nothing of the kind. "Do you know that I never allow the President to see any woman alone?" Badeau saw that she was jealous, and he would have done anything to pacify her. Smiling, he tried "to palliate my remark, but she was fairly boiling over with rage."

"That's a very equivocal smile, sir," she cried. "Let me out of this carriage at once. I will ask the President if he saw that woman alone." Twice she asked to get down. The second time that he hesitated to obey her, she stood up, reached past the astonished colonel, and pinned the driver to his seat. It took the coaxing of Julia Grant to persuade the furious woman to let go of the driver so he might rein in the horses and they could all get out together.

Fortunately, General Meade was in sight when the carriage slowed to a halt, and he promptly extended his hand to pay his respects to the president's wife. They went off together for a few minutes, Mrs. Lincoln talking excitedly, Meade softly responding, their voices high and low. When they returned, Badeau saw that Meade, an adroit diplomat, had somehow appeased Mrs. Lincoln. Glaring at Badeau she said, "General Meade is a gentleman, sir. He says it was not the President who gave Mrs. Griffin the permit, but the Secretary of War." It was a clever solution to put the blame on Stanton, who had already fallen from Mrs. Lincoln's good graces.

ON THE BATTLEFIELD, Lincoln was very observant but silent, as if overwhelmed by the evidence of his senses. Barnes noted that he "listened to explanations in a cool, collected manner, betraying no excitement, but his whole face showing sympathetic feeling for the suffering around him." At last he saw a flag of truce flying between the opposing lines, and orderlies coming to bear away the Confederate wounded and bury the dead where they had fallen. "Mr. Lincoln looked worn and haggard. He remarked that he had seen enough of the horrors of war, that he hoped this was the beginning of the end, and that there would be no more bloodshed or ruin of homes."

Lieutenant Barnes told him of a half hour he had spent carrying water to wounded men. He had come upon a red-haired boy, not full grown, in Confederate butternut, moaning, "Mother! Mother!" When Barnes asked where he was hurt, the boy turned his head, showing a bloody gash "where a bullet had plowed a ghastly furrow," and with that effort he breathed his last. Hearing this story, Lincoln broke down and wept, repeating some expression about "robbing the cradle and the grave."

At three o'clock that afternoon, the weary remnant of the V Corps lined up for the promised military review. Mr. Lincoln mounted one of Grant's horses as the drums beat and the colors were raised and lowered for "present arms" and the dusty, aching soldiers who could still march passed by the president.

Nearly four thousand of Lee's men had been captured, killed, or wounded, as against fourteen hundred casualties on the Federal side. The train returning to headquarters rolled slowly through the battlefield, bound for the river. "Mr. Lincoln, overcome by excitement and events of the day, desired to rest on the *Queen* with his family, and, declining the invitation to take supper at General Grant's headquarters, saw no one again that evening." Mrs. Lincoln was in no mood for society either. In camp that evening, Julia Grant drew Adam Badeau aside and told him that Mrs. Lincoln's behavior that afternoon "was so distressing and mortifying that neither of us must ever mention it." At least he must be silent about the matter, while she would have to discuss it with General Grant.

The next morning, Lieutenant Barnes found Mr. Lincoln in his stateroom, recovering from the day before. Reports from the front were reassuring, and he "expressed the greatest confidence that the war was drawing to an end." The president read Barnes some telegrams from Stanton, "expressing some anxiety as to his exposing himself, and drawing contrasts between the duty of a 'general' and a 'president.' " While Stanton admitted that Lincoln's presence was encouraging to the army ("if you are on the ground there will be no pause"), the secretary of war worried about Lincoln's impetuous curiosity. Stanton advised Lincoln to "consider whether you ought to expose the nation to the consequences of any disaster to yourself in the pursuit of a treacherous and dangerous enemy like the rebel army. If it was a question concerning yourself only I should not presume to say a word. Commanding Generals are in the line of their duty in running such risks. But is the political head of a nation in the same condition[?]" By now Grant was sharing that concern with Stanton and Mrs. Lincoln. Knowing the history as we do, we must remember that the Lincolns, Grant, and Stanton did not know what was going to happen from one day to the next. On March 26, 1865, Robert E. Lee and his army were dangerous and unpredictable, and there is little the

Confederates would have relished more than capturing or killing Mr. Lincoln.

When the president arrived at Grant's headquarters after breakfast, the camp was abuzz with news of the arrival of General Philip Henry Sheridan, who had led his men on a march from Winchester in northern Virginia. The short cavalry officer was already a legend, and a hero to his soldiers and the public alike after his victories over Lee near Richmond and Jubal Early in the Shenandoah Valley. Now he had brought his troops down to City Point to join Grant in the Appomattox campaign.

Lincoln found General Grant in conference with Sheridan, General Edward O. C. Ord (commander of the Army of the James), Admiral David Dixon Porter, Major John A. Rawlins (a young Illinoisan who was army chief of staff), Colonel Adam Badeau, and others. They were discussing strategy for the endgame of the war. But after the violence of the previous day's combat, and Sheridan's two-hundred-mile march, the army needed a day of rest, a Sunday as peaceful as the enemy would allow. Since "the President had seen 'a fight instead of a review' the day before," Barnes recalled, the Lincolns must spend the day on a pleasure trip. First they would watch the cavalry ford the James River at Harrison's Landing, then from the deck of the *River Queen* they would review navy ships on the way to Malvern Hill on the left bank of the river. There they would review General Ord's division in parade dress.

After loading the horses and carriage that would transport the ladies on the field, the *River Queen* cast off at eleven o'clock, steaming up the James River with the distinguished party: the Lincolns, the Grants, Adam Badeau, Generals Sheridan and Porter, and Lieutenant Commander Barnes. Porter and Sheridan both remember that the president at first seemed in poor spirits; perhaps his wife had warned him against consorting with the ladies. In any case, by the time they reached the place where Sheridan's ten thousand horsemen were crossing the pontoon bridge in a thundering column, Lincoln was delighted with the scene. When the soldiers saw the president, they cheered him, and he waved his hat to them in greeting.

Soon the *River Queen* sailed through the flotilla of battleships that Admiral Porter had arranged in a double line for the president's review, all decorated with American flags and navy ensigns, their crews on deck standing at attention. "Mr. Lincoln as he passed each vessel waved his high hat as if saluting old friends in his native town." When they reached

Porter's flagship, USS *Malvern,* the *River Queen* pulled alongside. The navy cooks had prepared a sumptuous lunch. Surprised at this feast, the president joked about the difference between army and navy life. No one with the possible exception of Adam Badeau could have sensed that a voyage that had begun so brightly was destined to run aground on the shoals of Mrs. Lincoln's increasingly disordered mind. She was worried and ill, still haunted by the grisly scenes of the previous day, and she did not want to let her husband out of her sight. She would do almost anything to get his attention and keep him beside her.

After lunch, they reembarked on the *Queen* and sailed to nearby Aitken's Landing, where officers from General Ord's division stood waiting on the dock with horses for the gentlemen. The plan was similar to that of the day before: Lincoln, Grant, and Barnes would ride ahead with General Ord and his officers to the parade ground four miles away, while the carriage with Mrs. Lincoln and Mrs. Grant—accompanied by Admiral Porter and Colonel Badeau—would follow at a distance. This time Badeau insisted upon reinforcement: "After my experience, I did not wish to be the only officer in the carriage." Barnes recalled that "there was some delay in starting, owing, it was said, to the unreadiness of the ladies." The cause of that delay was soon apparent—Mrs. Lincoln was upset that once more she had to be separated from her husband. Why could he not ride in the carriage with her? And why was General Ord's wife on horseback up front with the gentlemen?

The answer to the first question was familiar: army protocol. The military men, escorting their commander in chief, rode ruggedly ahead on horseback, discussing business that did not concern women, while the ladies brought up the rear, in the dubious comfort of a jouncing field ambulance, and farther from the enemy. As for the exception made for Mary Ord, the wife of the commanding officer "was not subject to the order for return," according to Colonel Badeau. From their carriage, Mrs. Lincoln and Mrs. Grant watched Mrs. Ord ride off with Barnes to join the generals and the president. Barnes describes Mrs. Ord as "a remarkably handsome woman," and an excellent rider. She may have cut a fine figure high on her spirited bay horse, but her photographs capture a plain woman with a hooked nose, droopy eyes, and dark hair who at a distance might have been mistaken for the president's wife—which could have added to Mrs. Lincoln's discontent.

By the time the president reached the parade ground, the army division had been waiting on the field, at parade rest, for several hours. Having missed their midday meal, the soldiers were hungry. Yet everyone waited for the women in their carriage, who were nowhere in sight. In his account, Barnes, who was with Lincoln and the Ords, reported being mystified by the disappearance of the vehicle, supposing that "Badeau had either missed the route or was entangled in the maze of rough approaches to the pontoon."

But Badeau recounts what happened. Mrs. Lincoln had taken up the theme she had so reluctantly abandoned the day before, this time with even more emotion. As the vision and significance of Mrs. Ord riding a bay horse up front with the gentlemen sank in and took hold, Mary Todd Lincoln worked herself into a frenzy.

"What does the woman mean by riding by the side of the President? and ahead of me?" She looked wildly about, and her companions did not know how to answer her. "Does she suppose that *he* wants *her* by the side of *him*?" Colonel Badeau was afraid there would be a repeat of yesterday's performance or something worse. "She was in a frenzy of excitement," he recalled, "and language and action both became more extravagant every moment." Mrs. Grant's efforts to pacify Mrs. Lincoln only met with defensiveness and rage. "We feared she [Mrs. Lincoln] might jump out of the vehicle and shout to the cavalcade."

She turned on Julia Grant. "I suppose you think *you'll* get to the White House yourself, don't you?"

The lady impassively replied, "Oh, I'm quite satisfied with my present position—far greater than I ever expected to attain," whereupon Mrs. Lincoln smiled wickedly, exclaiming, "Oh! You had better take it if you can get it. 'Tis very nice," and we can hear the music of irony in those last three words. She went on to attack the motives, character, and person of Mary Ord, a friend of Mrs. Grant, who wanted to defend the blameless lady, even against the accusations of a lunatic. All of this confusion and threat of violence caused the carriage to be halted more than once.

At last a young major rode up on his horse to see what was the matter. Knowing nothing of the trouble, but seeing signs of ill humor, he ventured to relieve the tension with a joke for Mrs. Lincoln. "The President's horse is very gallant, Mrs. Lincoln. He insists on riding by the side of Mrs. Ord." The unsuspecting officer had "added fuel to the flame," according to Badeau, and from now on Mrs. Lincoln's temper would rage beyond anyone's control until it had spent itself. "What do you mean by that, sir?"

she cried, in such a savage manner that no one on earth but herself could answer the meaningless question, and the major quickly turned his horse and rode away, "to get out of the way of the storm."

President Lincoln was protesting against any further delay in the parade and review. Generals Grant and Ord led the president to the right, to the front of the line where the bands were playing, the flags dipping in obeisance, and the soldiers standing stiffly at "present arms." Lincoln wore a long-tailed frock coat, unbuttoned, a low-cut black vest with a rumpled white shirt, and a loose necktie. His black trousers had worked up in the long stirrups, so now they showed a hand's breadth of his white socks.

Riding apart, Mrs. Ord asked Lieutenant Barnes if she should join the cavalcade, and a staff officer told them that was fine—they should come along and accompany the reviewing column. When they were halfway down the line of soldiers, Mrs. Ord saw the carriage approaching and said, "There come Mrs. Lincoln and Mrs. Grant. I think I had better join them." Barnes and Mary Ord reined out of the cavalcade, galloped across the field, and met the carriage. "Our reception was not cordial," Barnes later wrote, adding that the particulars "need not be gone into." He admits that "some unpleasantness had occurred," that "Porter and Badeau looked unhappy," and Mrs. Grant, clearly embarrassed, was speechless.

Badeau is more forthcoming. When Mrs. Ord greeted the ladies in the carriage, "Mrs. Lincoln positively insulted her, called her vile names in the presence of a crowd of officers, and asked what she meant by following up the President." Mary Ord, mortified, burst into tears. She wanted to know what she might have done to give offense, and tried in vain to explain herself, but "Mrs. Lincoln refused to be appeased, and stormed until she was tired." She may have acted like that at age thirty in the province of Springfield without much consequence, but now she was the president's wife, and her tantrum had drawn a distinguished audience with a tenacious memory.

"Mrs. Grant still tried to stand by her friend, and everybody was shocked and horrified." Lieutenant Barnes recalled that "it was a painful situation from which the only escape was to retire." Mrs. Lincoln had lost all control over herself. That evening, when the party had returned to City Point, the schedule called for the president and his wife to host a dinner aboard the *River Queen* for General and Mrs. Grant and his staff. After the events of that day—which by now Lincoln must have known from two perspectives—this dinner aboard the steamer promised to be an awkward affair.

Nevertheless the group gathered for their meal, hoping that a calm evening might restore some measure of civility. It was not to be. Grant's secretary Adam Badeau was present at the table, and to his dismay he saw that Mrs. Lincoln's fury was still burning brightly. "Before us all Mrs. Lincoln berated General Ord to the President, and urged that he should be removed. He was unfit for his place, she said, to say nothing of his wife." Julia Grant had already spoken up for Mary Ord. "General Grant sat next and defended his officer bravely," Badeau recalled.

So that second day at City Point had been as long, and nearly as stressful, as the first. Everyone was tired. Young Barnes went to bed early. At eleven o'clock an orderly awakened him with a message from the president: Mr. Lincoln would like to see him at once. Barnes put on his clothes and boots and hurried up the gangplank to the *River Queen,* where he found Mr. and Mrs. Lincoln waiting for him in the upper saloon. "The President seemed weary and greatly distressed, with an expression of sadness that seemed the accentuation of the shadow of melancholy which at times so marked his features." Mrs. Lincoln was incensed.

Barnes felt he had been called as a witness in the midst of an interrogation, a discussion that had been going on for some time. Mr. Lincoln spoke very little. The officer gathered from Mrs. Lincoln's exposition that she had objected to the presence of ladies at the parade, particularly Mrs. Ord, who had led the troops to believe that she was the president's wife. Mrs. Lincoln accused her husband of distinguishing Mrs. Ord with too much attention, while the president gently denied the accusation, saying "he had hardly remarked the presence of the lady."

"But Mrs. Lincoln was hardly to be pacified," Barnes remembered, "and appealed to me to support her views. Of course I could not umpire such a question, and could only state why Mrs. Ord and myself found ourselves in the reviewing column, and how immediately we withdrew from it upon the appearance of . . . Mrs. Lincoln and Mrs. Grant." Barnes was in an impossible situation. Asking permission to retire, he withdrew, "the President bidding me good night sadly and gently."

The next morning Barnes "reported as usual to the President," who welcomed him in the small stateroom that had been converted to an office. Lincoln read aloud some telegrams from Stanton and news from the front while Tad climbed on him and clung to him, and Lincoln kissed and caressed the boy. Tad was not very pleased with this trip. His mother was ill much of the time, and so he was in Crook's care. While his parents surveyed the battlefields, he played by the river.

Barnes asked after Mrs. Lincoln, "hoping that she had recovered from the fatigue of the previous day." The president's answer reveals a depth of understanding and compassion for the frail woman that other witnesses to her tirades did not share. He knew that it was not jealousy alone that had disturbed his wife. Lincoln explained "that she was not at all well, and expressed the fear that the excitements of the surroundings were too great for her, or for any woman." He did not apologize for his wife or try to defend her behavior. He succinctly put his finger on the crux of the problem so that Barnes, at least, could begin to comprehend it.

That morning Robert Lincoln invited John Barnes to accompany the family on a cruise to the Point of Rocks, a few miles west on the Appomattox River. Barnes had misgivings, but the president insisted. Mrs. Grant was aboard and so was Captain Penrose as the *River Queen* took off from the wharf and started up the James. Barnes spent the first few minutes with Mr. Lincoln in his office, where the president tried to put him at his ease; then in the forward cabin Barnes found Julia Grant relaxing, spoke to her, and inquired about Mrs. Lincoln. Julia pointed toward the pilot-house, where Mary Lincoln could be seen standing alone at the rail on the windy deck. Mrs. Grant suggested that Mrs. Lincoln might appreciate the offer of a chair, so Barnes pushed one out the door toward Mrs. Lincoln, bidding her good morning.

She refused the seat, and turned her back on him. Barnes "returned to Mrs. Grant, who had witnessed the failure." Very soon Mrs. Lincoln came to the cabin window and beckoned to Mrs. Grant, who went to join her. The hapless young man watched the windblown ladies in their animated conversation. Mrs. Grant returned to tell him that Mrs. Lincoln objected to his presence on the ship, and wanted him to know it. She had not forgiven him for his lack of cooperation the night before or for his presence during a family quarrel. "This made things rather uncomfortable for a pleasure party," he surmised. So when they docked at the Point of Rocks, the romantic site overlooking the river where Pocahontas had saved Captain John Smith's life, Barnes decided not to go ashore. For a while he stayed aboard with Mrs. Grant, watching as "Mr. & Mrs. Lincoln wandered arm in arm in the woods." Hopefully in that quiet place he could cheer up his wife. After consulting with Mrs. Grant, Barnes asked the captain to put him ashore on the other side of the river, where the quarter-master got him a horse to ride back to City Point.

Among several witnesses to Mrs. Lincoln's trouble, Barnes is most trustworthy because he harbors no bitterness toward the afflicted woman, and actually appears to have absorbed some of Lincoln's compassion. "She was at no time well; the mental strain upon her was great, betrayed by extreme nervousness approaching hysteria, causing misapprehensions, extreme sensitiveness as to slights, or want of politeness or consideration. I had the greatest sympathy for her, and for Mr. Lincoln, who I am sure felt deep anxiety for her." Lieutenant Barnes would always remember Lincoln's kindness toward his wife, "the most affectionate solicitude, so marked, so gentle and unaffected that no one could see them together without being impressed by it."

As Elizabeth Blair Lee commented three weeks later: "No woman ever had a more indulgent kind husband. Some have thought she had not his affections but tis evident to me she had no doubt about it and that is a point about which women are not often deceived after a long married life like theirs."

And so the Lincolns walked arm in arm in that enchanting forest by the Appomattox River, their sons nearby, putting trouble behind them, looking forward to living in peace.

RAIN FELL STEADILY and heavily during the last days of March, delaying Grant's plan of action and dampening everyone's spirits. Mrs. Lincoln had not been well or happy since she arrived at City Point, and now that General Grant had gone off to the front, moving his headquarters west of Petersburg to Dabney's Mill, the president—left behind with the navy—was depressed, too. William Seward found him in that mood when he arrived on March 30 for a two-day visit. Lincoln had been gone from Washington for a week, during which the war had progressed, and now Stanton wanted him to stay, arguing that "your presence will have great influence in inducing exertions that will bring Richmond." Meanwhile, affairs of state required Lincoln's attention and his signature, so the secretary of state had come down the river from Washington with his letters and documents.

Conjugal discord and bad dreams troubled Lincoln's sleep. He dreamed that he awoke to the sound of sobbing and went downstairs to the East Room, where he saw soldiers and a crowd surrounding a corpse upon a catafalque. "Who is dead in the White House?" he asked a soldier. "The President," was the reply. "He was killed by an assassin!" The crescendo of sobbing in the crowded room of the dream awakened him.

Then he dreamed that the White House was on fire, which purportedly served as the excuse for Mrs. Lincoln to return to Washington on the steamer with Mr. Seward on Saturday, April 1. There was no other reason for her to leave her husband and Tad. While the superstitious couple could do nothing to address the awful portents of the assassination dream, perhaps Mary might rescue the White House. Furthermore, she was sick almost to death of City Point—the rain, the generals' wives, the war that always seemed on the verge of ending but went on and on. Certainly her agitated state of mind was a factor in her leaving her family. It is significant that she left Tad in his father's care and that the child seemed satisfied with the arrangement. Tad would be twelve years old on April 4, and Mrs. Lincoln had always enjoyed celebrating the children's birthdays with presents and parties, but this year Tad would pass his birthday without her.

Arriving in Washington, she wired her husband that all was well, adding, "Miss Taddie & yourself very much—*perhaps* may return with a little party on Wednesday." Two days later she would tell Abram Wakeman that she had "left Mr. L with a promise that I would return on Wednesday with a choice little party of friends," a statement contradicting the tentative "perhaps" of her wire to her husband. In the meantime, the only business she conducted was to certify the engagement of two policemen, John F. Parker and Joseph Sheldon, who had been detailed for guard duty at the White House.

The night she arrived, this telegram came from Mr. Lincoln: "At 4:30 P.M. to-day General Grant telegraphs that he has Petersburg completely enveloped from river below to river above." It was the eve of the fall of Richmond. On April 3, Stanton came to inform the president's wife that the capital of the Confederacy had been taken, and she wrote excitedly to Charles Sumner, "The Sec of War, has just left & says that Richmond was evacuated last night & is ours! This is almost too much happiness, to be realized!"

The next day was Tad's birthday, a warm day with a few scattered clouds, and father and son celebrated by sailing on the flagship USS

Malvern to visit the conquered city. As they walked into Richmond under the guard of twelve armed sailors, Admiral Porter and Captain Penrose on one side of the president, Tad and Crook on the other, the smoke of burning buildings filled the air. Even with the guard, the president's stroll through Richmond with his boy was ill advised, for any man with a rifle might have ended Lincoln's life with a well-aimed shot from a distant window.

Lincoln could see the still-undamaged pillars of the capitol building gleaming high above Richmond, while most of the business section of the city lay in ruins. A crowd of former slaves quickly gathered to cheer the Emancipator as the party walked two miles up the steep hill that led to Jefferson Davis's house. The president of the Confederacy had left his home only forty-eight hours earlier. Wearily, President Lincoln entered Davis's little office and sat down in his large leather-covered chair. He lowered his heavy, dark eyelids, raised his chin, and looked around him at the walls covered with military prints and photographs of Confederate ironclads, and at the light that streamed in a window. "He was pale and haggard," Barnes recalled, "and seemed utterly worn out with fatigue and the excitement of the past hour." The lieutenant considered this a supreme moment; it was certainly an occasion when he and others might have expected the eloquent president to say something memorable.

"I wonder if I could get a drink of water," said Mr. Lincoln, to no one in particular. Eventually he roused himself and suggested that they all go look at the house. No one at the time noticed the piece of coal on Jefferson Davis's desk, a camouflaged bomb designed to blow up a ship's boiler, powerful enough to have killed everyone in the room.

BACK IN WASHINGTON, Mary Lincoln was disappointed that her husband had gone to Richmond without her. She was writing a long letter to Abram Wakeman, beseeching, "Pray for me, lest any evil spirits, come near me." Wakeman had warned her that her enemy Thurlow Weed was en route to City Point. The former publisher, political operative, and diplomat had alienated Mrs. Lincoln by slights both real and perceived; he had revived gossip about her corrupt dealings in the White House, and he knew far too much about her debts and influence peddling in New York and Washington for Mrs. Lincoln to tolerate his presence. She thanked Wakeman, but said it was too late to change her plans. She had invited six friends to accompany her to Virginia on Wednesday to witness and celebrate the fall of Richmond.

Meanwhile the revelry had begun, and the city of Washington would be drunk for a week. "I am expecting quite a number of friends, this evening—the buildings & city are to be illuminated. Lights will glare from windows from whence rebellious hearts, have been wont to gaze—from—such is life!" In closing she adds that her husband's health is greatly improved, "And after three days of exposure to rebel shots my darling boy [Tad] is well and happy."

Now she wanted to return to her husband and be with him in the hour of triumph. He had wired her on April 2, "Tad and I are both well, and will be glad to see you and your party here at the time you name." Her party included Senator Charles Sumner, his friend the Marquis de Chambrun—grandson of Lafayette—Secretary of the Interior James Harlan, his wife, their daughter Mary (Robert's sweetheart), and Mrs. Lincoln's maid, Elizabeth Keckley.

As she set out on April 5, Mrs. Lincoln was looking forward to a carefree excursion with her friends and family. Although the sky was overcast, the weather was mild. Mrs. Keckley was excited about visiting Petersburg, where she had grown up, and later recalled the pleasure of the voyage, how "the banks of the river were beautiful, and fragrant with the first sweet blossoms of spring." Mary Harlan looked forward to seeing Robert Lincoln, and the inquisitive marquis was eager for conversation with the president, in whom he had discovered a peculiar sort of American genius. But Mrs. Lincoln complained that the SS *Monohassett* was less comfortable than the *River Queen*. She and her party found themselves in cramped quarters. And when they docked at Fortress Monroe, en route that night, ominous news awaited them.

The secretary of state had been hurt badly in a carriage accident. His team of horses had spooked at a stop on Vermont Avenue, reared, and bolted, throwing the sixty-year-old Seward from the runaway vehicle into the mud. Subdued by morphine, he now lay in his bed at home with a broken jaw and a smashed shoulder, wearing a steel collar to stabilize him.

Seward had wired Lincoln that very morning to say the president's personal sanction was required "to several matters here which are important and urgent in conducting the Government," to which Lincoln replied, "There is no probability of my remaining here more than two days longer." He was used up, as one would be at the end of a long and perilous journey. Excitement had kept him mobile and alert, but victory found him near exhaustion and eager to go home. The terrible news about Seward made it all the more important that he return to his office. Even his wife assumed that he would leave, as she told Edwin Stanton.

Mrs. Lincoln was distressed. Her frantic telegrams to her husband beginning at 4:00 A.M. on April 6, as well as one to Stanton, express grave concern that Lincoln remain at City Point until her arrival at noon. "We have several friends on board & would prefer seeing you & returning on your boat, we are not comfortable here." In all of her telegrams she pleads that Lincoln stay and meet them, or if he must return first, that he take some other vessel: "We are most uncomfortable on this & would like your boat—I know you would agree with me." She offers not a word of consolation, concern, or regret over Seward's misfortune.

Lincoln did not leave immediately. Mrs. Lincoln was on her way with a boatload of friends who expected to be entertained in the fallen cities of Petersburg and Richmond. "Will you dine with us, in Jeff Davis' deserted banquet hall?" she asked a friend. They desired to ride the rails over the battlefields that had lately been cleared of corpses; so the president stayed in Virginia, putting aside his own weariness, the warnings that his life was in danger, and his anguish over his secretary of state. He wished to please Mrs. Lincoln. On April 6, he received her and her party aboard the *River Queen,* in the same stateroom where he had met with a delegation from the Confederacy at a last-ditch peace conference at Hampton Roads in February. He showed them where each delegate had stood— Confederates Alexander Stephens, Robert Hunter, and John Campbell on one side, and Lincoln and Seward on the other. The president was reticent about the proceedings, which had ended in a stalemate, but he read aloud some triumphant dispatches from General Grant; he pulled out a map and pointed to the places where the rebels were sure to lay down their arms. Surrounded, they were nearing the town of Appomattox.

Lincoln excused himself from accompanying his wife to Richmond. He had only narrowly escaped with his life when he toured the city two days earlier, and assassins had laid plans to kill him if he set foot in the city again. He asked if he might remain at City Point while the party sailed to Richmond on April 7, so he could keep in touch with General Grant. That was the day he got the joyful report from General Sheridan that he had routed Lee's army at Sayler's Creek. Lincoln wired Grant: "General

Sheridan says that 'If the thing is pressed I think that Lee will surrender.' Let the *thing* be pressed."

The president did agree to go along with his wife and her party on the train to Petersburg the next day. The engine on the rough track could hardly make its way through the rubble. "Everything bespoke desolation," wrote Chambrun. "All the houses were closed, the shops abandoned or pillaged; crowds of darkies were in the streets greeting and cheering loudly the author of their independence." The party spent most of that afternoon in the military hospitals, visiting and comforting the sick and wounded. Chambrun recalled that "the greater number of wounds were located in the abdominal regions, and were therefore of a serious character and caused much suffering." So the victory tour took a grave turn as President Lincoln spent five hours among the wounded, moving "from one bed to another, saying a friendly word to each man, or at least giving him a handshake."

As they returned to the *River Queen* in the twilight, Mrs. Keckley recalled the president saying to his wife, "Mother, I have shaken so many hands today that my arms ache tonight. I almost wish that I could go to bed now." But the party was not over. All the lamps aboard were lighted. A band played a farewell serenade, and there was a reception for officers. The president requested the "Marseillaise" for the marquis, and "Dixie" for all, now that "it belongs to us." Lieutenant Commander Barnes recalled the conspicuous absence of the president's wife: "Mrs. Lincoln was indisposed and I did not meet her. It was clear that her illness gave the President grave concern."

Barnes was more concerned with Mr. Lincoln's well-being, having just received strict orders from Admiral Porter, who had "talked over the precautions to be taken during the trip, and for him exhibited great uneasiness and solicitude for the President's safe conduct." There was the threat of "infernal machines" such as the coal bomb in Jefferson Davis's office; one of those tossed into a ship's furnace could blow the *River Queen* to sticks and staves. The lieutenant assigned two special officers in charge of "a guard of sailors, with minute instructions for guarding the President's person day and night." Every crew member had to be interrogated, their papers examined and approved. Only then could the president's riverboat return to Washington.

NO WORD OF FAREWELL

THE NEWS OF THE FALL of Richmond electrified Washington on
April 4, 1865, and Mrs. Lincoln had been there to witness the fireworks, marching bands, and volcanic revelry that would not end until ten
days later. On the evening of April 9, Palm Sunday, the *River Queen*
steamed up the Potomac, just ahead of the news of General Lee's surrender at Appomattox Court House. The streets of the Federal City were already swarming with people singing songs of victory and shouting
slogans. Some wanted to hang Jeff Davis and General Lee. The taverns
were aglow with lanterns and gaslights, and the tipsy patrons spilled out
the swinging doors onto the curbs, clinking their glasses.

The carriage that met the presidential party at the dock took the Lincolns, Senator Sumner, and the Marquis de Chambrun past the raucous
crowds on Pennsylvania Avenue. Later the marquis recalled that Mrs.
Lincoln, who had been silent as the carriage rolled through the quieter
streets near the wharves, grew anxious as they approached the lights and
clamor of the Centre Market. "That city is filled with our enemies," she
said. Chambrun recalled that the president raised his arm in a gesture
showing his impatience with such talk. "Enemies!" Lincoln exclaimed.
"We must never speak of that." *We must not be enemies. Though passion
may have strained, it must not break our bonds of affection.*

One of the Lincolns' greatest disagreements in the end, although he
declined to discuss it, was over her belief that the city and the world were
full of enemies. During the few remaining days of his life, Lincoln would
strive to convince the people of the North and South that they were not
enemies but friends. The power of a visionary consists in his ability to
imagine perfection in himself and then in the real world beyond his

thoughts. In this enterprise the president was tireless and heroic, and his determination left no quarter for fear.

His wife's appalling behavior at the front, which Lincoln kept explaining was the result of her illness, was prompted by the demon of terror, fear of their enemies, the dread that someone would harm her, her husband, or their children. That month she told Mrs. Keckley, "No one knows what it is to live in constant dread of some fearful tragedy. The President has been warned so often, that I tremble for him on every public occasion. I have a presentiment that he will meet with a sudden and violent end." Of course her behavior at City Point was inexcusable—but it was not by any means incomprehensible as a perverse displacement of fear. Her fear was warranted, and his lack of it was peculiar.

Plots against the president's life were countless and real, especially during the last desperate weeks of the war. There is abundant testimony that Ward Hill Lamon, Edwin Stanton, William Crook, and various military personnel so badgered Mr. and Mrs. Lincoln with dire warnings that he ignored all of them, while she lived in a strait of unrelieved anxiety. Her hiring of the two guards on April 3 was a sensible response to an imminent danger. Lincoln was as annoyed by her dwelling upon it as she was by his heedlessness.

General Edward H. Ripley, who commanded the Federal troops during the occupation of Richmond, wrote one of the most chilling accounts of the danger that pursued the Lincolns in those days. General Ripley was uneasy about the president's journey to Richmond and "his insistence upon visiting all interesting points," and tried to make Lincoln consent to a large military escort. "He would not allow it, and strolled through the city like a private citizen, followed by crowds of people, white and black. It was a very dangerous thing to do." Ripley surrounded the president with a detail of heavily armed plainclothes detectives and never told him. The day Lincoln toured Richmond, Ripley met with a Confederate double agent, "an enlisted man in Raine's torpedo bureau [probably George Washington Rains, a Confederate munitions specialist]." This was part of the rebel secret service, expert in blowing up river steamers and ammunitions magazines, hotels and bridges, and distributing clothing infested with smallpox virus. Now that the rebel cause was hopeless, the spy now known only as "Snyder" wanted to do everything in his power to avert bloodshed.

Snyder was horrified to see Lincoln and his child walking unprotected through streets teeming with bitter, defeated Southerners, "and it would be but human nature for some one to take the opportunity to revenge the lost cause on the person of the man who represented the triumphant cause of the Union." Agent Snyder's message was this: The torpedo bureau had just dispatched a party of shock troops on a secret mission to kidnap or assassinate the president. He wanted "to put Mr. Lincoln on his guard . . . just at this moment he believed him to be in great danger of violence and he should take the greater care of himself." This was the plain truth, which Lincoln ignored while his wife, Stanton, Lamon, Lieutenant Commander Barnes, and General Ripley tried to get him to face it. He had mortal enemies. Only the most stubborn idealism—a prop for his generous plans for Reconstruction—would cause a sane man in his position to deny there were people who wanted to kill him.

Ripley took Snyder's statement under oath. The president agreed to receive the general aboard the *Malvern* at nine o'clock the morning of April 5. In the admiral's cabin, Ripley sat down at the table across from Lincoln. "Little Tad . . . a small and very restless boy, amused himself by running up and down the length of the sofa behind his father and jumping over his back in passing." As General Ripley unburdened himself of this troubling news, he saw how Lincoln's head drooped upon his hands, his elbows resting on the table. Lincoln had heard a hundred variations on this story during the past four years, and the best he could do was to listen politely as the well-meaning informant presented his case: the presentiment of doom, and the familiar plea for safeguards and protections.

Lincoln lifted his hand in a subtle gesture of denial, as a man would brush away a fly. Thanking the general, Lincoln told him, "It is impossible for me to adopt and follow your suggestions. I must go on as I have begun in the course *marked out for me,* for I cannot bring myself to believe that any human being lives who would do me harm." And so the interview ended, as did all such conversations with Mr. Lincoln. He would die as he lived, in that false and charitable belief.

Leaving the president, Ripley noticed that Lincoln was so weary, gaunt, and pale that he more closely resembled a ghost than he did the successful head of a proud nation in its moment of triumph. His sad eyes suffused the cabin with a melancholy aura. The general would inform the naval officers of the impending threat. Like other would-be guardians of the great man, Ripley had the rest of his life to wonder what a difference he might have made had he been able to persuade Lincoln "to let his friends protect him until the first rage of the enemy over defeat had expended itself." Eventually the rebels might have seen that Lincoln and Grant were the best friends they had in the North.

The point that Ripley makes so forcefully in his memoir is that the president was in more danger during the month of April 1865 than he had ever been in before. The pickets were down. Talk of assassination, more prevalent than ever, had a firmer basis in fact, and if Lincoln did not acknowledge this, his wife did. With a feral instinct for disaster—or a greater sense of reality—she suffered terribly in the crosswinds of the daily rumors and warnings. The menace was enough to drive one mad.

THAT WEEK THE streets of Washington were filled with such merrymaking and so much such joy in the hearts of the citizens, one could put aside one's worries for a while. On a rainy Monday morning, April 10, the Lincolns were awakened by the thunder of cannons at dawn, a five-hundred-gun salute that broke windows around Lafayette Square and summoned the people to celebrate Lee's surrender the day before at Appomattox. Of all the happy people in Washington, perhaps no one was happier than the glaziers and the barkeeps.

The president had heard the news after returning from City Point the night before, and after visiting the injured secretary of state. Seward was immobile and spoke with so much difficulty that the president had to lie down next to him on the bed so they might converse. Reassured that his friend would survive, Lincoln rode on to the War Department, where he received confirmation of Lee's surrender. His escape routes were cut off; what was left of his army was starving. Before bedtime Lincoln told his wife the good news. The next morning she found her bedroom full of roses, lilies, and lavender. She wrote to Sumner, "Mr. L. told me the news, last night at ten o'clock, that Lee & his Army were in our hands." Her note accompanied a bouquet she had delivered to Sumner and the marquis at noon. "If possible this is a happier day, than last Monday [the fall of Richmond], the crowds around the house have been immense, in the midst of bands playing, they break forth into singing."

Despite the deep mud, the streets were mobbed with people singing and cheering, waving flags and saluting one another and the public buildings all around them. There came soldiers, shopkeepers, drovers, day laborers, mechanics, government clerks, and their families, as all the departments, and many businesses and shops, declared a holiday. In the corridor of the Treasury building a crowd sang the "Old Hundredth" hymn, which brought tears to many. *Praise God from whom all blessings flow.* A procession that began at the Navy Yard with six boat howitzers in tow gathered strength and numbers as it rolled up Virginia Avenue and passed the Capitol; by the time the guns ascended Pennsylvania Avenue the concourse was immense, filling the square, the carriageway, and the north portico of the White House with citizens wildly cheering. People who were not shouting were singing along with the brass bands. All were waiting for the president to appear and make a speech. At last Tad Lincoln popped up in the high middle window where the president often spoke, waving a rebel flag, which brought a round of cheers from the uncritical spectators. It was probably the Zouave Colonel Ellsworth's flag. Months ago the same emblem had brought suspicions of sedition upon Mrs. Lincoln, but now it was hailed as a badge of triumph.

According to Noah Brooks, who stood in the White House in the late afternoon watching, by the time the president appeared at his window, the demonstration outside was frightening in its frantic enthusiasm. It seemed that men and women were at their wit's end, desperate to express their feelings. "They fairly yelled with delight, threw up their hats again and again, or threw up one another's hats, and screamed like mad." From inside the mansion "the surface of that crowd looked like an agitated sea of hats, faces, and arms."

Mrs. Lincoln knew that her husband was exhausted. He had kept his appointments that morning—a few minutes with Browning, a session with photographer Alexander Gardner, a cabinet meeting. But as she told Sumner, "Friday's pilgrimage through the hospitals [Petersburg, April 8], although a labor of love, to him, fatigued him very much." Eventually, they knew, he would have to greet the crowd or risk a riot, or at best a bonfire vigil that would keep the family awake all night. So at last in the dusk of that cloudy day the president came to the north window, and after a climax of cheering, the people grew quiet. "The President," according to Brooks, "briefly congratulated the people on the occasion which called out such unrestrained enthusiasm, and said that, as arrangements were being made for a more formal celebration, he would defer his remarks until that occasion." Lincoln called for the band to play "Dixie," adding that the attorney general had ruled that it was now our lawful property. When "Dixie" was done, he called for "Yankee Doodle." He proposed three cheers for General Grant and his men, then three more cheers for our gallant navy. When all that applause had subsided, the president smiled, waved, and returned to his family, and the crowd at last dispersed.

Tad wanted some flags and a navy sword. His father scribbled notes to Stanton and Welles, asking if the boy could have the souvenirs.

THE FORMAL CELEBRATION was scheduled for the next evening, April 11, but the only thing formal about it was the president's speech.

In that week of cloudy skies the government would provide by night what the day denied—illumination fitting the people's festive mood. The week before, after the fall of Richmond, Benjamin French had practiced lighting up the public buildings. In the days before arc lamps and spotlights, this illumination was a more subtle and romantic effect than the patriotic displays of today. French began with his own house, turning on all the gaslights, lighting the lanterns outdoors, and setting candles and astral oil lamps in each window. This was a signal for every householder in the neighborhood to do the same, and as if by contagion the whole city was soon ablaze with light.

French ordered an enormous cloth transparency to be stretched upon a frame 160 feet long that hung upon the columns of the west portico of the Capitol. Lit by powerful gas jets, the cloth was painted with the verses of the 118th Psalm: "This is the Lord's doing; it is marvelous in our eyes." The illumination was so bold and bright that the people could read it from far away down Pennsylvania Avenue. A huge sign bearing the single word UNION glowed in front of the Patent Office, while the Post Office displayed a gaslit courier bearing the mail and the words "Behold, I bring you tidings of great joy." Thirty-five hundred candles were used to light the windows of the Post Office, and six thousand to light the Patent Office. The Treasury building with its many illuminated windows was especially brilliant, and across the front columns hung a gigantic transparency of a $50 bond. The fall of the South meant profits for the North. Shopkeepers ran out of lanterns, flags, and fireworks and ordered boxcars of supplies from New York and Philadelphia. When no more flags could be found in the shops, the chairman of Washington's Board of Aldermen sent to Alexandria to get the proper banners and bunting to festoon his house on H Street.

While the president wrote his speech that day, his wife tried to per-

suade Charles Sumner to join them that evening for the speech and a carriage ride to view the illuminations.

> My dear Mr. Sumner:
>   Presuming it would be agreeable for the Marquis, in visiting our
> Country, to witness *every* novelty that presents itself at this eventful time,
> I have invited him to call informally this evening, about 8½ o'clock, as
> doubtless, a vast assemblage, will be gathered in front of *this* building,
> with music & anticipations of a little speech from the President. It would
> be very pleasant, both for the Marquis & ourselves, if you would accom-
> pany him.

The "little speech from the President" to which his wife refers was no
mere entertainment. The address that he had been writing in stolen hours
over the last two days was both a prayer of thanksgiving and a policy statement regarding Reconstruction. Much of it is a response to a memorandum that Salmon Chase had sent him that very morning. Beginning with
Louisiana, Chase believed that no state should be recognized as loyal to
the Union until it had granted the black man his right to vote; in this
Chase stood shoulder to shoulder with Sumner and the liberal wing of
the Republican party. Lincoln, as a "strict constructionist" of the Constitution and an efficient statesman, was primarily concerned with bringing
Louisiana and the other Southern states "into proper practical relation
with the Union" quickly. "Will it be wiser to take it as it is, and help to improve it; or to reject, and disperse it?" He compared the new, flawed government of Louisiana to an unhatched egg: "We shall sooner have the
fowl by hatching the egg than by smashing it."

Mrs. Lincoln's last beneficial act as a political partner was her tireless
courtship of the liberal senator from Massachusetts. Playfully flirtatious
but chaste, there was nothing insincere about Mary Lincoln's pursuit of
Charles Sumner. They truly enjoyed spending time together. Nevertheless, the president needed Sumner's support; at the very least he wanted
Sumner not to oppose him. For a year or more—at least since their disagreement over the Wade-Davis bill—tensions between the two men had
been mounting over emancipation and Reconstruction. Sumner had regarded Lincoln's bid for reelection with ambivalence; as a radical Republican, he might have worked with others to replace Lincoln. His devotion
to Mrs. Lincoln was a factor in Sumner's campaigning for Mr. Lincoln in

the autumn, and now her constant attentions to the rather vain bachelor kept him in the presidential "family" when he might have joined Salmon Chase in his battle with Lincoln over Reconstruction.

She promised to review her French the next day, to make herself better company to the Francophile senator and his companion, and she wanted them to join the president on the balcony tonight. "I am very anxious to have a good view, for once of the illumination, the effect will be grand, I am sure, and in consequence of having the safest coachman in the Country," she boasts, thinking of Seward's accident or the ubiquitous assassins, "propose that the Marquis & yourself, accompanied by some other lady of course, besides myself, drive around quietly, for about half an hour this eve." The pairing off does not include Mr. Lincoln. "It does not appear to me," she concludes coquettishly, "that this *womanly* curiosity will be undignified or indiscreet, qu'en pensez vous?"

What Mr. Sumner thought of the invitation is not exactly known, although he was accustomed to this sort of banter from Mrs. Lincoln and probably would have been charmed. Yet he was not charmed enough to accept the proposal. As he explained to his colleague Salmon Chase, the president's balcony was no place for a liberal senator to be seen that night. Suspecting that Lincoln might make some controversial statement concerning Reconstruction, he declined "to put myself in the position of opposing him at his own balcony or assenting by silence."

It was a misty evening, and the image of the illuminated Capitol dome floated magically in a reflection upon the hazy sky above it. Mr. Lincoln stood at one White House window above the cheering crowd while Mrs. Lincoln watched from the window adjacent. Her new friend Clara Harris stood by her.

"We meet this evening, not in sorrow, but in gladness of heart," the president announced to the crowd of thousands thronging the square and streets before the Executive Mansion, their torches and lanterns lighting joyful faces and twinkling miles into the distance. Fireworks streaked in sparkling arcs upon the horizon. Mr. Lincoln offered thanksgiving to the Almighty, and praise to Grant and his men. As he moved on to the questions of Reconstruction, he distanced himself from the people, who had come only to celebrate the victory. Now they tried to listen respectfully to a lecture on the challenges that lay ahead, the tricky business of bringing the Southern states "into proper practical relation with the Union," and how to grant the elective franchise to the freed blacks. Behind him, partly concealed by a curtain, Noah Brooks held a lamp so Lincoln could see the curling pages of his speech, densely covered with his scrawl. Below his knees Tad scrambled on the floor, grabbing at pages as they fluttered from his father's fingers, begging for another and another, until the crowd broke into its final rounds of applause and the child proudly held the finished speech in his ink-smudged hands.

THE ARRIVAL OF General Grant on April 13 was the occasion for more celebration. He had come strictly on business—to see Secretary Stanton at the War Department and request an end to military recruiting and purchases. But as soon as the news got out that he and Mrs. Grant had arrived at Willard's Hotel, a crowd gathered below their windows and soon surrounded the building. The manager had to summon a detail of police to escort the general from the hotel and make way for him through the cheering hordes to the War Department. Stanton agreed with the general that no more soldiers need be drafted and the purchases of war matériel could be discontinued. This news, further confirmation that the war was ending, traveled fast. The city fathers prepared to light up the buildings even more brightly than before.

Apart from meeting with Grant and Stanton at midday, and with Secretary Welles in the afternoon, Lincoln conducted little business. The president had been frail since Richmond. He decided to refresh his spirits with a ride on horseback in the spring air, with an escort of dragoons, up the familiar Seventh Street Turnpike and Rock Creek Church Road to the Soldiers' Home. The dogwood trees were blooming white, the willows budding in a haze of green. A gentleman on horseback named Maunsell B. Field, whom Lincoln recognized as a Treasury official, was on his way north when the president overtook him. They fell in together, and Field later recalled how they conversed casually on various topics of the day. But what struck Field most was the darkness of the president's mood. On that beautiful and auspicious afternoon in spring, Lincoln seemed weary and sad.

Mrs. Lincoln was worried about him. It seemed a pity that with everyone around them rejoicing, in a holiday mood, she and her husband were isolated in the shadow of his melancholy. Why did they not go out in a carriage after dark to view the illuminations together? *The Washington Star* described the view from City Hall: "Far as the vision extended were brilliant lights, the rows of illuminated windows at a distance blending into one and presenting an unbroken wall of flame.... High above all towered the Capitol, glowing as if on fire.... Away to the right a halo hung over the roofs, rockets flashed to and fro in fiery lines, and the banners waved above the tumultuous throng."

She thought that General Grant's company might please Mr. Lincoln, so she wrote a note saying, "Mr. Lincoln is indisposed with quite a severe headache, yet he would be very much pleased to see you at the house, this evening about 8 o'clock & I want you to drive around with us to see the illumination." The hurried invitation would not have suited Mr. Lincoln, for the request rudely neglected to include Mrs. Grant. After the terrible scenes at City Point—which deeply grieved the president—this note would not help to mend fences. Grant declined the invitation to the White House—which, under the circumstances, was tantamount to an executive command. Instead, the general and his wife attended a reception at the home of Edwin and Ellen Stanton.

As far as we know, the Lincolns dined alone that night, in anticipation of Robert's arrival from Appomattox. By all accounts Lincoln appears to have benefited from a quiet evening and a good night's rest. After breakfasting with Robert at 8:00 A.M., the president launched into a hectic schedule, the busiest day since his return from City Point on April 9. He had at least seventeen appointments before and after a cabinet meeting that lasted from 11:00 A.M. until 2:00 P.M. After that meeting, the president extricated himself so he could join his wife downstairs in the family dining room. This private time must have been arranged the night before when they were alone, as was their plan to organize a theater party for this evening. They needed to spend more time together. On this busy day Lincoln took a full hour to lunch with his wife before meeting with the vice president at three o'clock, and then several congressmen and the secretary of the treasury, among others. After five o'clock, he left the office once again, to go for a ride with Mrs. Lincoln in the open carriage. She asked him if he wanted anyone to accompany them, and he replied, "No—I prefer to ride by ourselves today."

It was a gray day with a mild breeze that stirred the innumerable flags that flew atop houses and public buildings on either side of the street. The coachman, Francis Burns, was ordered to drive the Lincolns across G Street to New Jersey Avenue and past the Capitol to the Navy Yard. The president wanted to see the battered warships. Later Mary Lincoln recalled, "I never saw him so supremely cheerful—his manner was even playful." He was so happy it startled her, and, laughing, she told him so.

"And well may I feel so, Mary, I consider *this day,* the war, has come to a close." This is what she remembered, in her words. At last they could consider the possibilities of life in the White House during peacetime. She let him talk, for it was not often that he told her his feelings. "We must both, be more cheerful in the future—between the war & loss of our darling Willie—we have both, been very miserable." She later recalled that every word he uttered was "deeply engraven" on her heart; but her memory was imperfect. In the same letter, she told Francis Bicknell Carpenter that Mr. Lincoln was cheerful the last three weeks of his life, and this was not the case. Nevertheless, she was not the only witness who remarked upon Lincoln's buoyant spirits that day. The cabinet heard him tell his recurrent dream of finding himself afloat in an indescribable vessel, moving rapidly toward a vague shore. He had had the agreeable dream last night, and it always preceded a Union victory. This time, he was delighted to say that it meant that the news from General Sherman, still toiling against the Confederate army in North Carolina, would be very good.

He enjoyed the carriage ride, the views of the Potomac as they approached the Navy Yard, the salutes of the navy officers and sailors who welcomed them to the pier, the crowd that spontaneously gathered to cheer the president. The breeze blew softly as the Lincolns walked the iron decks. The warships had sustained damage in the Battle of Fort Fischer, where sixty men had gone down in the torpedoed ship *Patapsco.* The war had not come to a close. Men were still skirmishing and killing one another in North Carolina, Alabama, and Georgia. That very day a Union vessel near Mobile was blown to pieces by a torpedo.

They had heard enough talk of war. "Let us both try to be happy," he told her. On the carriage ride home they must have discussed the plans for the evening. Organizing the theater party had been somewhat frustrating, for reasons that he did not completely comprehend. This morning, Mary had contacted the management at Ford's Theatre to reserve their box, and she had said the Grants would be joining them. But her plans were not turning out as she had hoped. People seemed reluctant to go along.

Mary Lincoln had envisioned a theater party consisting of the president and herself, the conquering hero Ulysses S. Grant and his wife, Julia, and Secretary of War Edwin Stanton and his wife, Ellen. But Mrs. Lincoln seems to have forgotten that Mr. Stanton objected to Lincoln's appearing in public at this time, particularly at the theater; and Mrs. Stanton now so despised Mrs. Lincoln that she emphatically informed Adam Badeau, "I do not go to the White House; I do not visit Mrs. Lincoln." Ellen Stanton had called upon Julia Grant that day to inquire if the Grants had accepted the Lincolns' invitation. When Julia said that she and the general had begged to be excused so they might take the six o'clock train to Philadelphia, as they were eager to return to their children, Ellen Stanton replied, "I will not sit without you in the box with Mrs. Lincoln."

With only a few hours remaining before the curtain went up on *Our American Cousin,* the president of the United States and his wife had found no one to go with them to the theater. Robert was weary from his travels, Noah Brooks had a bad cold, and the Catholic Marquis de Chambrun would not be tempted to attend the theater on Good Friday. Lincoln had even invited the chief of the telegraph office, Major Thomas T. Eckert, a large man whom he had once seen bend an iron poker over his arm. Stanton grumbled that he needed Eckert that night, and warned the president once again about going to the theater, even in the company of men as strong as Eckert, if he could find any.

Finally, Mrs. Lincoln asked Clara Harris and her fiancé to accompany them. A month earlier, Clara, daughter of Senator Ira Harris of New York, had gone with the Lincolns to hear Mozart's *The Magic Flute.* Clara was a plain, full-figured woman of twenty, as short as Mrs. Lincoln, with a prominent nose and a weak chin. A clever girl, she had handled her father's correspondence during the war. She had just become engaged to her stepbrother, Major Henry R. Rathbone, heir to a banking fortune. The major, almost twenty-eight, with his receding hairline, mutton-chop whiskers, and droopy mustache, was as unprepossessing as his fiancée. It was considered a fine match where youth and beauty would not be squandered on either side, and the tidy fortune of Major Rathbone would be kept in the family. What Clara may have lacked in glamor she made up for in kindness and jollity; she made a good companion for the president's wife.

Despite the last-minute invitation, Clara Harris and her fiancé were delighted to accompany the president and his wife to see *Our American Cousin* at Ford's Theatre.

THIS DAY HAD been no different from many others during their twenty-two years of marriage except that they had spent more time together than usual, and Mr. Lincoln was in curiously high spirits. When two old friends from Illinois, Dick Oglesby and Isham N. Haymes, arrived just before mealtime, unannounced, Lincoln hailed them into the office to talk over old times. The president regaled them by reading aloud four whole chapters from the humorist Petroleum V. Nasby's book, and was so amused he nearly missed the supper with his family, having lost track of time.

In the carriage on the way to Ford's Theatre, Clara Harris "was struck with the uncommon hilarity of the President. He laughed & joked & he was evidently bent on having a jolly evening." She and Major Rathbone sat with their backs to the coachman, facing the Lincolns and their valet. Mrs. Lincoln wore a bonnet with little pink flowers. Fog had settled on the dark streets, making halos around the streetlamps. Francis Burns, the coachman, knew they would be late for the curtain, but he would not hurry. It was safest if the president's arrival was unpredictable.

The curtain had gone up on Act I of *Our American Cousin* when the presidential party pulled up in front of the theater. It was 8:25. The doorkeeper came out to greet them as Burns drove the vehicle onto a wooden ramp that kept the ladies' skirts above the mud. Beneath the streetlamps, they were aware of being watched. The papers had announced that not only the president, but General Grant would be attending the play, so now in front of Ford's Theatre groups of citizens stood waiting and peering— soldiers, idlers, patrons standing in line for tickets, and pedestrians on their way to taverns. Across the street in the lighted windows and doorways of the row houses, people scanned the shadowy street, looking for the coach that would bring the president and General Grant.

The president's bodyguard for the evening, John F. Parker, stood against the wall near the main entrance. As Lincoln's valet, Charles Forbes, leaped down and opened the door of the coach, a group of bystanders surged forward, and a policeman opened his arms to hold them back. Parker came forth to lead the president and Mrs. Lincoln into the theater, followed by Miss Harris. Major Rathbone came last, with Forbes, who carried the president's plaid shawl.

News passed from row to row that the president was leading his party to the prominent box draped with flags just above the stage on the right side of the theater. People turned their heads. The Lincolns walked through the lamplit lobby, climbed the dim, winding staircase, and crossed the first balcony on the way to their box. A few people in the dress circle stood, clapping, and soon the entire audience was on its feet, applauding the president. Onstage, Laura Keene broke character and joined in the applause as the Lincolns and their guests entered the state box and the orchestra struck up "Hail to the Chief."

A month had gone by since the Lincolns had enjoyed the sort of ovation that can rise only in a theater full of adoring countrymen. The people had come to Ford's not just to see a play, but to celebrate the Union victory and applaud the heroes. In the ecstatic moment of a heartfelt ovation, the audience and the actors become one, in a unique sort of intimacy. Mrs. Lincoln wore a black-and-white striped dress cut low in the neck and held a fan made of ivory and white feathers. She smiled and curtsied, and it was clear that she was both delighted by and grateful for the applause. Next to her, Mr. Lincoln, all in black except for his white kid gloves, bowed solemnly.

When the audience had had their fill of cheering, they took their seats to enjoy the play. Miss Harris sat on a cane chair at the right side of the box, nearest the stage, while Major Rathbone lounged on a sofa just behind her. The president took his seat in his favorite rocker, of black walnut upholstered in red damask. It was the manager's, and had been installed especially for the president's comfort. The rocker was placed near the left wall of the box, so that Lincoln was partly concealed by the state box curtain. Mrs. Lincoln sat on a straight chair to his right.

The president had been in a humorous mood for most of the day, relieved by the war's end and uplifted by the prospects of peace. After the warm welcome here, he was looking forward to the kind of entertainment that had transported him time and again during his darkest hours. Miss Harris later recalled, "Mr. Lincoln laughed heartily at the comical situations & dialogue of the play, and paid close attention to it." In a moment of spontaneous affection he reached out for his wife's hand and held it on the padded arm of the rocker. Absorbed in the action onstage, he held his wife's small hand, forgetting to let it go, until she whispered teasingly, "What will Miss Harris think of my hanging onto you so?" He replied, smiling, "She will think nothing about it." There the conversation ended.

At about 10:15 the comedian Harry Hawk was onstage delivering the line, "Don't know the manners of good society, eh? Well, I guess I know enough to turn you inside out, old gal—you sockdologizing old mantrap!" It was a laugh line, and the president, leaning forward in the box, his hand on the rail, was laughing along with everyone else when John Wilkes Booth used the cover of laughter to open the door to the state

box unnoticed, point his derringer at the president's head, and fire, lodging a bullet in Lincoln's brain behind his right eye. *In the midst of life we
are in death.* The dull sound of the pistol, like the popping of a child's
balloon, was noticed by only a few people in the noisy theater.

THE ACRID SMELL of gunpowder and a little cloud of gray smoke fill the
theater box. She sees her husband's head tipped forward on his chest as
if he has fallen asleep. Major Rathbone stirs on the sofa, turns, and lunges
toward the president. The black-coated intruder steps past her, drops the
pistol to the floor, and pulls out a knife. He raises the blade and swings it
in a high arc meant to drive the blade into Rathbone's heart, but the major
raises his arm to block the attack.

Blood is running from the long wound in Rathbone's upper arm. She
is confused, frightened, rubbing her cheeks as if trying to awaken from a
nightmare. The strange man with the knife leaps onto the stage while the
major howls in pain. He stands beneath the proscenium arch shouting
something unintelligible, then runs away into the wings. She turns to her
husband to wake him from his nap. "Father. Father?" Then she shouts
into his ear. She cannot rouse him. She lifts him into an upright position
in the rocker, and he is limp, heavy. Terrified, yet unsuspecting, she holds
his body upright in the chair. His eyes are closed.

"Stop that man!" cries the major. "Will no one stop that man?" There
is blood all over the state box, gushing from the wound in Rathbone's
arm, soaking Clara's dress. "He has shot the President!" Everyone in the
theater seems to be shouting at once. Maybe no one can hear her moaning, or the scream that involuntarily escapes her throat. There is no blood
on his white shirt or his peaceful face.

They are pounding on the door, trying to break it down with their fists
and shoulders. "For God's sake open the door!" At last they enter and a
man in front introduces himself. It is Dr. Charles Leale, a young army surgeon. She lifts her head from her husband's chest and reaches out for the
doctor's hand. "Oh, doctor, is he dead? Can he recover? Will you take
charge of him? Do what you can for him. Oh, my dear husband." The
doctor assures her he will do all he can. An older doctor arrives. Her tears
come in a torrent. Someone leads her to the sofa. The house lights come
up, illuminating the bedlam below. People are yelling for water, for ropes,
for a ladder. More than a thousand people are on their feet screaming,

pushing, jamming aisles, trying to get out of the theater or onto the stage or to climb up into the box. "Burn the theater! Kill the murderer!"

The doctors lift the president from the rocker and lay him flat on the carpet. Dr. Leale raises the head, probing, then gently lowers it to the floor. They cut away the coat to look for wounds. Laura Keene has come into the box, bearing water in a pitcher. She sits next to her on the sofa as she rocks back and forth, shaking, dazed, chilled. Then the actress is cradling the president's head on her lap, stroking his hair. A bloodstain spreads on her dress. Men are bending over Mr. Lincoln so she cannot see him. Laura Keene sits on one side of her, Miss Harris on the other. All the dresses are bloodstained.

"Wouldn't it be possible to carry him to the White House?" somebody asks.

"No," Dr. Leale replies. "His wound is mortal. It is impossible for him to recover."

Blood on her dress, the smell of gunpowder on her fingers, in her hair.

Then the men are carrying him out the door headfirst. Where are they taking him? Someone shrieks. She is screaming. They are taking him away, across the street. Soldiers surround them, the clanking of swords, more shouting and swearing in the crowd on the stairs, in the glaring lobby, mobs, mobs in the street trying to glimpse the president. A captain is swinging his sword, shouting, "Out of the way, you sons o' bitches!" She loses sight of Mr. Lincoln. "Where is my husband!" she cries. "Why didn't he kill me? Why was I not the one?"

It takes an eternity to cross the muddy street, even surrounded by the soldiers. He is still breathing as they carry him up the winding staircase to a boardinghouse owned by Mr. Peterson. Someone helps her, a major and a captain, for she cannot see where she is going. Guards are at the door shouting, pushing people aside, pulling others through the narrow entrance to the shabby house, through the dim hall. "There she is. Mrs. Lincoln. The President's wife."

He is lying diagonally across the small bed with spindle posts, in a little chamber wallpapered in a pattern of vines. The room is under the stairway. The doctors stand at the head of the bed, their backs to the door—young Dr. Leale and Dr. Charles Taft and Dr. Albert King. Mr. Lincoln's head is propped with pillows, against the wall, and his long legs hang off the end toward the window. "Open a window," a doctor commands.

A man is holding a lamp above them as Dr. Leale arranges the president's limbs on the small bed. She is standing in the doorway as someone turns up the gas jet on the wall, filling the low room with an eerie golden light. She reaches for him, calls out *Father, Father,* again and again, moving toward him, thinking as long as he breathes he must answer her. With so many doctors, surely he cannot die. She touches his matted hair, his hollow cheeks. He sighs. Dr. Leale gently holds her back, pulls her away. She must go for now while the doctors do their work. She must go and sit in the parlor. They will call her when Mr. Lincoln is settled.

She wants Robert. She begs them to call her son.

Like a woman in a trance she allows Miss Harris and Miss Keene to lead her to the parlor as the doctors remove her husband's clothes, looking for knife wounds. Dr. Robert Stone has arrived. She is seated on a sofa across from the fireplace, staring at the glowing coals. How must longer must she wait before they let her join him?

People are coming and going; they are coming from all over the city. Here are Stanton and Welles, General Meigs, General Halleck, Major Eckert. They look at her and mutter, then go into the room where her husband lies. They will not let her follow. Miss Harris pets her, whispering words of comfort. But look! Her dress is soaked with blood! "My husband's blood!" she cries, though it is not his but the blood of Major Rathbone, who grappled with the assassin, who lies unconscious on the carpet at their feet.

She cannot keep her hands still but rubs her cheeks, rubs her hands together, cries involuntarily, "Why didn't he shoot me? Why didn't he shoot me?" They must allow her to see her husband. He is in a room full of men and she is forbidden to enter. In a chamber between the parlor and the sickroom Stanton has set up a war room. Ah, here at last is Robert, her son, standing over her. Charles Sumner is with him. Thank God! Her son, Robert. Tears stream down his cheeks. He sits beside her and takes her hand in both of his. Why is he crying? Robert sits with her, and then he leaps up to see the chamber where his father lies.

They must allow her to see her husband. They must take her to see him. At last they lead her down the hall where someone has spread an oilcloth. The cloth is dabbed with drops of blood. The room is full of doctors and other men. She sees her husband still asleep upon the bed, the covers pulled up to his whiskers. His head is resting on a clean napkin covering the pillows. There is a chair for her. She sits next to him, kisses his forehead and cheek, imploring, "Love, live for one moment to speak to me once—to speak to our children." Silence. Robert stands at the foot of the bed, weeping. The room is silent while outside in the street rises the terrible animal cacophony of the crowd.

Unable to rouse him, she puts her head down next to his, sobbing, begs him to take her with him. The white napkin beneath his head begins to bleed. A hand touches her shoulder. It is Mrs. Dixon, the senator's wife. Hands are lifting her up, pressing a handkerchief to her eyes, leading her away, back down the corridor to the airless parlor.

A man stands above her, whispering words of comfort and encouragement. It is the Reverend Dr. Phineas Gurley, who surely must understand that God in his infinite mercy will not allow so good a man as her husband to die and leave her alone. Thank goodness the Reverend is here. She is quiet for a while, if not calm, in the presence of the clergyman.

The clock pendulum measures the minutes, the hours. She rises from the sofa again, nervously, as if she had misplaced something important, left it behind in the theater box. An hour has passed since she has seen him. She rises and sleepwalks down the crowded corridor to the sickroom full of weeping and whispering. She calls to him again and again, every hour, her own clock tower of grief tolling the hours, her tears and face powder clinging to his face and beard. He still looks like a sleeper who might awaken. *What about Taddie? Bring Taddie here! Oh, please, I'm sure he'll talk to Tad, he loves him so.* The white napkin is bleeding, the sign that she must go. A hand wipes her face, lifts her, leads her away for another hour or two until dawn is near.

In the dimness of the parlor she nods, forgetting not to sleep. If he is not quite alive nor dead, then she is neither awake nor asleep. It is all some terrible dream.

They should never have come to this place.

Someone hands her a cup of water. *Drink. You must drink.*

Slowly the room grows larger with the light. The April days are long. Hold back the light. Let the day never dawn that looks upon his death. As if in sympathy the dawn is suspended. The sun struggles with the clouds of night and the morning drizzle of rain. Dawn is delayed and comes in a dark cloak.

They call her and she goes, once more down the hallway to the bedroom under the stairs. In the low-pitched room, there are more men now than ever: Robert Lincoln, Sumner, Speed, Welles, Dr. Gurley, Usher, the doctors, generals, twenty men around the bed, many of them in tears, listening to Mr. Lincoln's hoarse breathing. Now his right eye is swollen, his face bruised, ghastly. She kisses his head, his lips. Now if she can put her head down next to his, like this, perhaps she might sleep as he is sleeping.

But suddenly a noise comes from his throat, a horrible choking, rasping sound. She jumps up, screaming, spins, and falls to the floor fainting or about to faint. Someone lifts her.

Hearing the piercing cry, the secretary of war, Stanton, rushes into the room, his hands raised, imploring someone above or below, "Take that woman out and do not let her in again."

Banished, broken, she turns away. Leaning upon the shoulder of Mrs. Dixon, she moans, "Oh, my God, and have I given my husband to die?"

She sits in the gray light of the parlor. Twenty minutes pass, and all the clocks and watches that tell the time say it is 7:22 A.M. Commotion and a cry from the bedroom and the sound of footsteps in the hallway, then the sad messengers:

"It is all over! The President is no more."

AFTERWORD

Mrs. Lincoln's history from April 15, 1865, until her death of apoplexy on July 15, 1882, is so singularly tragic that it has warped most views of her marriage. The human tendency to see the distant past through the lens of the more recent past is so natural as to be almost inevitable.

Therefore I have chosen to end the story with the death of Mr. Lincoln and not to go on a minute longer, in keeping with common sense and the *Book of Common Prayer*'s injunction, "till death us do part." The widow Mary Lincoln had nothing to do with the courtship of Abraham Lincoln and Mary Todd, their wedding, their life together in Springfield rearing children, or their terrible years in the White House. Life was cruel to Mary Lincoln, and the more she saw of life, from 1861 until her death, the crueler it became. Anyone who is interested will find half a dozen books that chronicle the widow's journey to its pathetic end.

The broken cords of several hundred kinships, friendships, and associations left by the untimely death of the great man lie in a hopeless tangle. Another book of this length, or longer, would be required to address the aftermath of the assassination, and how the principal friends and relations of Abraham Lincoln went about picking up the pieces of their broken lives. The nation itself suffered a brutal wound that has yet to heal entirely. Where one cannot do justice to a subject, above all a human subject, it is better—kinder certainly—to be silent.

The pittance of joy left in Mrs. Lincoln's life lay in her devotion to her sons, Tad and Robert; and much of Robert's youth and middle age were consumed with caring for his mother and brother. Tad grew up and learned to read and write, and showed promise. He died of pneumonia in 1871 at the age of eighteen, in Chicago, while he was still living with his mother. Over the next four years Mrs. Lincoln's physical and mental deterioration were so precipitous that it made Robert's task of caring for her virtually impossible. They became estranged. She traveled for a while in Europe on her government pension, and died in Springfield in the house where she was married, living with her sister Elizabeth.

John Wilkes Booth fled Washington on horseback and hid in a Maryland pine thicket for nearly a week before crossing the Potomac into Virginia. Racked with pain from his broken fibula, dismayed by the satanic image of himself in the newspapers, for twelve days he dodged manhunters. Asleep in a barn near Port Royal, Virginia, on the night of April 26, he woke to the shouts of Federal soldiers. When Booth refused to surrender, the soldiers set fire to the barn; by the light of the flames, Sergeant Boston Corbin killed Booth with a single shot from his pistol.

Robert Lincoln married Mary Eunice Harlan in 1868, and they had three children. He became a successful lawyer in Chicago, and although his name was put forward from time to time as a presidential candidate in the 1880s, he was never a serious contender. He called the office "a gilded prison." Under President Benjamin Harrison he served from 1889 to 1893 as ambassador to England, and from 1897 to 1911 he prospered as president of the Pullman Palace Car Company in Chicago. He died in his sleep in 1926 at his summer home in Manchester, Vermont.

ACKNOWLEDGMENTS

I would like to record my gratitude to my agent, Neil Olson, and my former editor, Elisabeth Dyssegaard, for their faith in this project from its inception, and to Susanna Porter, my present editor at Random House/Ballantine, for her encouragement and advice as the book has evolved.

I thank Thomas Schwartz, the Illinois State Historian, for the hours he spent working with me in the Illinois State Historical Library (now the Abraham Lincoln Presidential Library) when it was moving from its old quarters to the new. His advice and enthusiasm have been invaluable; much that is new in this book is owing to my work in the Springfield library. I am grateful to the collections manager, Cheryl Schnirring, and librarian Glenna Schroeder-Lein, who helped me find and copy documents there, and also to Dennis Suttles, who located and copied an 1860s map of Springfield.

Also in Springfield, Lincoln curator Kim Bauer was very helpful in showing me artifacts and photos that were not then on display. Susan M. Haake, curator of the Lincoln Home National Historic Site, was generous with her time, spending half a day with me touring the Lincoln home, answering my questions, and showing me precious artifacts that were then in storage. Stacey McDermott, assistant editor of the papers of Abraham Lincoln, provided important information concerning Lincoln's legal practice.

Dr. Alice Birney, the literary manuscript historian at the Library of Congress, and Dr. John Sellers, Civil War specialist of the Manuscript Division, helped me to locate materials in the many Civil War period collections there, as did librarian Jeffrey M. Flannery. Dr. Sellers was especially helpful in keeping me abreast of the most recent scholarship and discoveries in the Lincoln field. Clark Evans of the Rare Book and Special Collections Division assisted me in locating period materials, particularly regarding Chicago, Washington, D.C., and home economics during the nineteenth century. In the Newspaper and Current Periodical Room I particularly valued the assistance of librarians Travis Westly and Gary Johnson, who helped me find articles in nineteenth-century newspapers and magazines; and in the Map Division, I had the excellent advice of John Hebert.

Jane Westenfeld from the Allegheny College Library sent me documents I needed from the Ida M. Tarbell Lincoln Collection. I am also grateful to the staff of the Special Collections Division of the Sheridan Libraries of The Johns Hopkins University, and to the staff of the Peabody Library in Baltimore, a repository of many rare books.

Among the many generous scholars with whom I have had the privilege to converse about the Lincolns over the past seven years, I want especially to thank Dr. Catherine Clinton, who shared with me some insights into the life and character of Mary Lincoln, and who has also given me books and articles; Michael Burlingame (author of *The Inner World of Abraham Lincoln,* and editor of indispensable diaries and letters of John Hay, John Nicolay, William O. Stoddard, and others), who has worked side by side with me in the Library of Congress and has always found the time and good humor to answer my endless questions; and Wayne Temple, to whom I am indebted not only for his fine writings, but also for his illuminating conversations about Lincoln off the record. David Herbert Donald granted me access to the restricted Randall Papers at the Library of Congress. Author Harold Holzer has been extremely encouraging and supportive, and has introduced me to many Lincoln authorities. Lincoln's character is stamped upon this community of historians.

Because of the length and scope of this book, I am more than usually beholden to my friends and editors who have read and corrected the manuscript in various stages of development: Rosemary Knower, David Bergman, Michael Yockel, and Neil Grauer. In addition to commenting upon the entire manuscript, Ms. Knower, who is herself an authority on the life of Mary Lincoln, assisted with the research, and helped me to form an understanding of Mrs. Lincoln's character.

My debt of gratitude to the many historians who have written about the Lincolns will be clear from my endnotes. In addition, I want to call attention to the work of Douglas L. Wilson, who, with Rodney O. Davis, edited *Herndon's Informants*—arguably the most useful single resource for Lincoln scholars to have emerged since Earl Schenck Miers's *Lincoln Day by Day* in 1960. Mr. Wilson is also the author of the insightful *Honor's Voice,* a book concerning Lincoln's life from 1831 until 1842, the year my book begins.

Finally, I would like to thank my wife, Jennifer Bishop, and my children, Ruth, Benjamin, Theodore, and Nathaniel, without whose support during an eventful time, the book would never have been finished.

SOURCES AND NOTES

Abbreviations and Short Titles Employed in the Notes

EMS	Edwin M. Stanton	MTL	Mary Todd Lincoln
JGN	John G. Nicolay	WHH	William H. Herndon

Baker: Jean H. Baker, *Mary Todd Lincoln: A Biography.* New York: W. W. Norton, 1987.

Brooks: Noah Brooks, *Washington in Lincoln's Time.* New York: Rinehart, 1958; reprint of 1895 edition.

Browning Diary: Orville H. Browning, *The Diary of Orville Hickman Browning.* Ed. Theodore C. Pease and James G. Randall, 2 vols. Springfield: Illinois State Historical Library, 1925–1933. Unpublished supplements courtesy of ISHL.

CW: Abraham Lincoln, *The Collected Works of Abraham Lincoln,* ed. Roy P. Basler, 8 vols. New Brunswick, N.J.: Rutgers University Press, 1953.

Day by Day: Earl Schenck Miers, ed, *Lincoln Day by Day: A Chronology, 1809–1865,* 3 vols. Washington, D.C.: Lincoln Sesquicentennial Commission, 1960.

DLC: Document in the Library of Congress.

French: Benjamin Brown French, *Witness to the Young Republic: A Yankee's Journal, 1828–1870,* ed. Donald B. Cole and John J. McDonough. Hanover and London: University Press of New England, 1989.

Hay Diary: John Hay, *Inside Lincoln's White House: The Complete Civil War Diary of John Hay,* ed. Michael Burlingame and John R. Turner Ettlinger. Carbondale: Southern Illinois University Press, 1997.

Hay Letters: John Hay, *At Lincoln's Side: John Hay's Civil War Correspondence and Selected Writings,* ed. Michael Burlingame. Carbondale: Southern Illinois University Press, 2000.

Helm: Katherine Helm, *The True Story of Mary, Wife of Lincoln: Containing the Recollections of Mary Lincoln's Sister Emilie.* New York: Harper & Brothers, 1928.

Herndon's *Lincoln:* William H. Herndon and Jesse W. Weik, *Herndon's Life of Lincoln.* New York: Da Capo Press, 1983; reprint.

Herndon Letters: William H. Herndon. *The Hidden Lincoln: From the Letters and Papers of William H. Herndon,* ed. Emanuel Hertz. New York: Blue Ribbon Books, 1938.

HI: *Herndon's Informants: Letters, Interviews, and Statements About Abraham Lincoln,* ed. Douglas L. Wilson and Rodney O. Davis. Chicago: University of Illinois Press, 1998.

IJ: Illinois Journal, Springfield, Illinois.

ISHL: Illinois State Historical Library, Springfield.

Keckley: Elizabeth Keckley, *Behind the Scenes.* London: Penguin Books, 2005, reprint of 1868 ed.

Lincoln's Footsteps: Ralph Gary, *Following in Lincoln's Footsteps.* New York: Carroll & Graf, 2001.

MTL Letters: *Mary Todd Lincoln: Her Life and Letters,* ed. Justin G. Turner and Linda Levitt Turner. New York: Alfred A. Knopf, 1972.

Nicolay: John G. Nicolay, *With Lincoln in the White House,* ed. Michael Burlingame. Carbondale: Southern Illinois University Press, 2000.

NYT: The New York Times.

Randall: Ruth Painter Randall, *Mary Lincoln: Biography of a Marriage.* Boston: Little, Brown, 1953.

Ross: Ishbel Ross, *The President's Wife: Mary Todd Lincoln.* New York: G.P. Putnam's Sons, 1973.

Taft Diary: Horatio N. Taft, *The Diary of Horatio Taft,* DLC.

Tarbell Papers: Ida M. Tarbell Lincoln Collection, Allegheny College,

All quotes from Lincoln's speeches and correspondence are from Basler's edition of *The Collected Works of Abraham Lincoln,* and quotes from Mary Lincoln's correspondence are from *Her Life and Letters,* edited by Turner, unless otherwise noted. These are numerous and easy to locate in those collections by date and recipient, so they are not cited unless the context is unclear.

Where a section or subject relies heavily upon a single source, such as Wayne Temple's excellent thirteen-page monograph on Anson Henry, I will cite it once to apply passim or throughout the section, rather than repeating the citation opus citatum or ibid. with page numbers.

The details of the Civil War's progress I include are so numerous and well established that I have not annotated them. My chief reference for military matters is E. B. Long's *The Civil War Day by Day.* Details of Lincoln's law practice and schedule will be found in *Lincoln Day by Day* unless otherwise noted. All Springfield purchases have been checked against Harry E. Pratt, *The Personal Finances of Abraham Lincoln* (Springfield, Ill.: Abraham Lincoln Association, 1943).

Sources clearly cited in the text are not listed below. The notes are restricted to citations necessary for locating obscure and important sources and to acknowledge the work of other scholars. I have tried to avoid redundancy and annotating the obvious. As David Herbert Donald wrote in his introduction to the Sources and Notes of his monumental biography, *Lincoln,* "If I were to cite all the books and articles consulted in the preparation of his biography, I would have a book at least twice as long as this one."

THE TRYST: SPRINGFIELD, 1842

3 *"could then be studied"*: Brooks, 266.

3 *"the tree is the real thing"*: Ibid.

6 *"Abraham's bosom"*: Mrs. B.T. Edwards, interview, Tarbell Papers.

6 *"The very creature of excitement"*: James C. Conkling to Mercy Ann Levering, Springfield, September 21, 1840. ISHL.

6 *"forget his prayers"*: Helm, 81.

6 *"a brilliant woman"*: Herndon Letters.

7 *"crazy as a loon"*: HI, 133.

7 *"William Riley"*: Elizabeth Crawford to WHH, Herndon Letters, 293; verses, traditional.

8 *"best blood of Virginia"*: Herndon Letters, 412.

9 *a small town:* Main sources for Springfield history are Paul M. Angle, *"Here I Have Lived": A History of Lincoln's Springfield* (Chicago: Abraham Lincoln Book Shop, 1971; reprint) and *Lincoln's Footsteps.*

9 *first visit . . . spring of 1835:* Thomas Schwartz, "Mary Todd's 1835 Visit to Springfield," *Journal of the Abraham Lincoln Association,* winter 2005, vol. 26, no. 1.

9 *daughters of the Honorable Robert Todd:* Source for MTL's early life is William H. Townsend, *Lincoln and His Wife's Home Town* (Indianapolis, Ind.: Bobbs-Merrill, 1929).

11 *"enabling you to support a family"*: Letter from Ninian Edwards to his son Ninian Edwards, Jr., 1832, ISHL.

12 *"to hate holy water"*: Usher F. Linder, *Reminiscences of the Early Bench and Bar of Illinois* (Chicago: Legal News Co., 1879), 280.

13 *"Turkish splendor"*: Angle, *"Here I Have Lived,"* 88.

13 *a fine piano:* Frances Todd Wallace, newspaper interview, September 2, 1895, quoted in William A. Barton, *The Women Lincoln Loved* (Indianapolis, Ind.: Bobbs-Merrill, 1927), 244.

14 *"some Superior power"*: HI, 443.

15 *"A lovelier girl I never saw"*: MTL Letters, 20.

16 *"Without censuring . . . on its cost"*: Sangamo Journal, December 22, 1840.

17 *"Woe is me"*: HI, 475.

17 *They kissed and parted:* This story is told, with variations, by both Elizabeth Edwards, 443, and Joshua Speed, 474–75, in *HI.*

REMEDIES

19 *mercury pills:* Norbert Hirschhorn, Robert G. Feldman, and Jan A. Greaves, "Abraham Lincoln's Blue Pills: Did Our 16th President Suffer from Mercury Poisoning?" *Perspectives in Biology and Medicine,* summer 2001, vol. 44, no. 3, 315–32. The argument that Lincoln took blue mass pills for syphilis, real or imagined, is proposed by the authors. They do not, and I do not, attempt to prove that Lincoln had the disease.

19   *"caught the disease"*: Herndon Letters, 259.

20   *"excess of venery"*: Hirschhorn et al., as above.

20   *Speed wondered: HI,* 431.

20   *"as Speed supposes"*: Herndon Letters, 259.

20   *"a personal interview"*: *HI,* 431.

20   *Dr. Anson Henry:* Data passim, Wayne C. Temple, *Dr. Anson G. Henry: Personal Physician to the Lincolns,* Bulletin of the 44th Annual Meeting of the Lincoln Fellowship of Wisconsin, Milwaukee, 1987. 13 pages.

23   *"The Suicide's Soliloquy"*: Richard Lawrence Miller, "Lincoln's 'Suicide' Poem: Has It Been Found?" *For the People: A Newsletter of the Abraham Lincoln Association,* vol. 6, no. 1, spring 2004, Springfield, Illinois, 1–6.

25   *"Lincoln went crazy . . . remember that he had lived"*: *HI,* 197.

26   *"Is it true?"*: Martinette Hardin to John J. Hardin, January 22, 1841, Hardin Papers, Chicago Historical Society.

27   *"To love and not be loved again"*: Conkling to Levering, ISHL.

27   *"not knowing what he was doing"*: John G. Nicolay, *An Oral History of Abraham Lincoln,* ed. Michael Burlingame (Carbondale: Southern Illinois University Press, 1996), 2.

27   *at home with Anson Henry:* H. W. Thornton to Ida Tarbell, December 21, 1895, Tarbell Papers; Douglas L. Wilson's *Honor's Voice* (New York: Alfred A. Knopf, 1998) provides excellent background on these events, although I do not agree with his conclusions.

A YEAR OF WAITING

29   *"Swarms of strangers . . . perplexities of the law"*: Conkling to Levering, March 7, 1841, quoted in Carl Sandburg and Paul M. Angle, *Mary Lincoln: Wife and Widow* (New York: Harcourt Brace and Company, 1932), 180–81.

29   *"sanguine temperament only can love"*: Henry quoted in Ross, 47.

29   *"this affair of hers with Mr. Lincoln"*: Nicolay, *Oral History,* 2.

32   *"a misfortune not a fault"*: *CW* I, 261.

32   *"I think it reasonable . . . expect it?"*: *CW* I, 265–66.

33   *"that trouble is over forever"*: *CW* I, 269.

33   *"jealous of both of you now"*: *CW* I, 281.

36   *"enjoyed the trip exceedingly"*: *CW* I, 282.

37   *"Eliza told them to be friends"*: Baker, 93.

38   *"never think of the Subject again"*: *HI,* 444.

39   *"pinning"*: sources for this incident are an interview with a Mrs. Bradford, Tarbell Papers; Clyde C. Walton, *An Illinois Reader* (DeKalb: Northern Illinois Press, 1973), 255; and William A. Clark, news clipping from Blakeslee Scrapbook (Lincoln National Life Foundation, Fort Wayne, Indiana).

43   *"settle their personal differences on the field"*: Randall Parrish, *Historic Illinois* (Chicago: A. C. McClurg, 1905), 337.

43   *"Rebecca letters"*: the first letter is in *CW,* 293–96; the second is in the *Sangamo Journal,* September 9, 1842.

FAME

45 Chief sources for the account of the duel are Walter Stevens, *A Reporter's Lincoln* (Lincoln: University of Nebraska Press, reprint of 1916 edition), 15–20; Ida M. Tarbell, *The Life of Abraham Lincoln* (New York: Lincoln Memorial Association, 1900), vol. 1, 189. Newpaper accounts, originally appearing in the *Sangamo Journal,* October 1842, are collected in Herndon's *Lincoln.*

46 *"to guide us erring wanderers, home": Sangamo Journal,* October 7, 1842.

48 *"I feel impatient to know" CW* I, 303.

50 *"I want to get hitched tonight":* Octavia Roberts, "We All Knew Abr'ham," *Abraham Lincoln Quarterly,* March 1946, 27–28.

50 *"to be married out of my house":* Eugenia Jones Hunt quoting Francis Todd Wallace, *"Personal Recollections," Abraham Lincoln Quarterly,* March 1945, 237.

50 *"it must be from my house":* Helm, 94.

51 *"shall have to marry that girl": HI,* 251.

51 *"To Hell, I suppose":* Hunt, "Personal Recollections," 238.

51 *to witness the nuptials:* for the details of the ceremony I am indebted to Wayne C. Temple, *Abraham Lincoln: From Skeptic to Prophet* (Mahomet, Ill.: Mayhaven Publishing, 1995), 26–32.

53 *"the Statute fixes all that":* Metheny to Weik, in *HI,* 665.

NEWLYWEDS

54 *"exuberance of flesh":* MTL Letters, 22.

54 *"a matter of profound wonder": CW* I, 305.

55 *got Truett acquitted:* Kenneth J. Winkle, *The Young Eagle: The Rise of Abraham Lincoln* (Dallas: Taylor Trade Publishing, 2001), 211.

57 *Lincoln had night terrors:* Henry C. Whitney, *Life on the Circuit with Lincoln* (Caldwell, Id.: Caxton Printers, 1940, reprint of 1892 edition), 68.

58 *"as though her heart would break":* Ross, 52.

58 *hot coffee into her husband's face:* Judith Peterson, "Secret of an Unhappy Incident," *Illinois Junior Historian,* vol. 5 (February 1952), 91; Dale Carnegie, *Lincoln the Unknown* (New York: Perma Giants, 1932), 71–72. See also Michael Burlingame, *The Inner World of Abraham Lincoln* (Urbana: University of Illinois Press, 1994), 277, re this incident and MTL's temper.

59 *"hug it the tighter": CW* I, 280–81.

59 *"over which he has no control": Day by Day,* 198–99.

60 *the Mormon prophet Joseph Smith:* Circuit Court of the United States for the District of Illinois, December term A.D. 1842, vol. IV, no. 5, City of Nauvoo, Ill., January 16, 1843 [Whole NO-65].

61 *"Prophet of the Lord!":* Angle, "Here Have I Lived," 126.

61 *"so grateful to your mother":* Helm, 164.

A RUN FOR CONGRESS

63 *Edward Dickinson Baker:* Harry C. Blair and Rebecca Tarshis, *Lincoln's Constant Ally: The Life of Colonel Edward D. Baker* (Portland: Oregon Historical Society, 1960). Except as noted, data concerning Baker is from this source.

64 *exuberant "glees": Sangamo Journal,* February 24, 1843. Springfield social events, weather, commerce, etc., except where otherwise noted, are documented in this newspaper, later called the *Illinois Journal (IJ).*

64 *General William Fitzhugh Thornton:* "Petition of Support for William F. Thornton," July 20, 1837, signed document, ISHL.

65 *"the Convention System of nominating candidates": CW* I, 308.

66 *was not an avid reader of his prose:* See Mrs. B.S. Edwards (Ninian's daughter) in an interview in the Tarbell Papers (doc. #38090001, p. 5), for evidence of MTL's constant interest in Lincoln's writings and speeches. And Helm, passim.

67 *"whispering campaign":* David Herbert Donald, *Lincoln* (New York: Simon & Schuster, 1995), 111.

68 *"Yet so chiefly it was": CW* I, 319–20.

69 *"to secure party harmony": Sangamo Journal,* March 16, 1843.

70 *James Kierschner:* Ibid., March 24, 1843.

72 "A WORD TO OUR FRIENDS": Ibid., April 6, 1843.

73 *"to violate the instructions of the meeting": CW* I, 321.

74 *James Conkling's account of the journey:* Conkling's letter to his wife, April 18, 1843, ISHL.

A HOME AT LAST

77 *Albert Bledsoe:* Sophie Bledsoe Herrick, "Personal Recollections of My Father and Mr. Lincoln and Mr. Davis," *The Methodist Review* (Nashville), vol. 64, no. 4, October 1915, 665–70. All quotes from Sophie passim are from this source.

79 *"as good a wife as she has a husband":* Mary Edwards Brown, "Abraham Lincoln Married 78 Years Ago Today," *Illinois State Register,* November 4, 1920, quoted in Randall, 83.

79 *"in payment of notes": Day by Day,* 208.

80 *One day Lincoln would remark:* Rufus Rockwell Wilson, *Intimate Memoirs of Lincoln* (Elmira, N.Y.: Primavera Press, 1945), 61.

80 *"with such love and tenderness":* MTL Letters, 536.

81 *named for him:* According to Helm, 97, and other biographers of MTL, Robert Todd visited soon after Robert's birth.

81 *a $20 gold piece:* Baker, 103. Baker speaks of a $25 coin, but this must have been a $20 coin, as the U.S. mint made no $25 gold piece.

85 *the domestic economist Catherine Beecher:* Catherine E. Beecher, *Treatise on Domestic Economy* (New York: Harper and Bros., 1845).

90 *"not really necessary that I Should":* Harriet Hanks Chapman, letter to Herndon, in *HI,* 407. All quotes from Harriet Hanks passim come from letters and interviews with her, published in *HI.*

91 *"a sweet child but not good looking": HI,* 646.

91 *"smarter at about five than ever after"*: *CW* I, 391.

91 *"making any reply to his wife"*: *HI*, 407.

92 *"especially to a newcomer"*: Herndon's *Lincoln*, 166.

93 *"would keep things in order"*: Henry Clay Whitney, n.d., photostat, Hertz Collection, quoted by David Donald, *Lincoln's Herndon* (New York: Alfred A. Knopf, 1948), 21.

95 *"he would say so publicly in any manner"*: *CW* I, 350.

96 *"than you seem to now"* *CW* I, 361.

100 *"so desperately in love"*: Ross, 222.

THE ROAD TO WASHINGTON

104 *"to die by degrees"*: *CW* I, 391.

105 *"banished my fear of the giant"*: Helm, 99–100.

106 *"swell his coffers"*: Ross, 25.

107 *"to settle a judgment against him"*: Townsend, *Wife's Home Town*, 151.

108 *made the greatest impression*: Ibid., 156.

109 *"The day is dark and gloomy . . . direful and fatal"*: Henry Clay, *The Papers of Henry Clay*, ed. Melba Porter Hay (Lexington: University Press of Kentucky, 1991), vol. 10, 361–76.

111 Background sources for Washington in 1847 include Paul Findlay, *The Crucible of Congress* (New York: Crown Publishers, 1979), 61–132; Donald W. Riddle, *Congressman Abraham Lincoln* (Westport, Conn.: Greenwood Press, 1979), 12–15, 170–75; and Albert Beveridge, *Abraham Lincoln, 1809–1858* (Boston: Houghton Mifflin, 1928), 398–407.

112 *"rambling, scrambling village"*: Beveridge, 399.

115 *Lincoln's desk was number 191*: Ibid., 405.

115 *"a voice like [Stephen] Logan"*: *CW*, 448.

117 *the "mess" as it was called*: Descriptions of the members of Mrs. Sprigg's mess are based upon numerous sources—biographical dictionaries (nineteenth century and contemporary), data supplied by the U.S. Congress (online at bioguide.congress.gov), and census records.

118 *"puddings, pies, cakes, etc."*: Weld quoted in Findley, 88.

119 *"during its delivery"*: Samuel C. Busey, *Personal Reminiscences and Recollections* (Washington, D.C.: privately printed, 1895), quoted in Findley, 93.

119 *"The wanton violation . . . on our own soil"*: *Washington Intelligencer*, December 11, 1847.

120 *"see-sawing his person whilst reading"*: *The Whig*, December 22, 1847.

123 *a lavish dinner at the Fuller Hotel*: *National Intelligencer*, January 3, 1848.

123 *"required by law, of the incumbent"*: William D. Haley, *Philp's Washington Described* (New York: Rudd and Carleton, 1861), 196.

124 *"settles down on us at night"*: *The Whig*, December 11, 1847.

124 *"smoking opium"*: *National Intelligencer*, December 4, 1847.

124 *The boy would never forget it*: Robert Todd Lincoln, "Autobiographical Sketch," 1864, Harvard Archives.

124 *"sacrifice their lives"*: *Day by Day*, 300.

125 *"revilers of their own country"*: quoted in *The Lincoln Reader,* ed. Paul Angle, 138.

125 *" 'strike in,' and carry him off"*: Ibid.

125 *"Southern markets openly maintained"*: Findley, 125.

125 *"a free circulation of air"*: Findley, quoting a Mr. Abdy, 125.

126 *Ober de ribber: "Coralie"*: A New Ethiopian Song Written and composed by Harry & Lucy, Arranged for Dumbolton's Ethiopian Serenaders by Frank Howard (Pseudonym for Delos Gardner Spaulding) (New York: William Hall & Son).

126 *"Master Juba"*: data from various sources, including *People play UK–Juba Online,* www.peopleplayuk.org.uk/guided_tours/dance_tour/black_dance/minstrels.php.

128 *"known to members of this House"*: The source for the entire incident is the *Intelligencer,* January 18, 1848.

129 *a "manager"*: *Intelligencer,* February 22, 1848.

129 *"Chatham, in the Senate House"*: Ibid.

130 *"the postponement and its mournful cause"*: *Intelligencer,* March 3, 1848.

131 *"In the midst . . . American Freeman"*: *The National Era,* Washington, D.C., September 2, 1847.

132 *"any theatre of its size in the country"*: Advertisement in *Intelligencer:* December 20, 1847.

133 *"yet so audible"*: *Notable Women in the American Theatre,* ed. Alice M. Robinson (New York: Greenwood Press, 1989), 197–98.

SEPARATION

145 *"since the opening of the campaign"*: *Chicago Journal,* October 7, 1848.

147 *Lincoln's hat . . . has assumed iconic status*: Allen Thorndike Rice, ed., *Reminiscences of Abraham Lincoln by Distinguished Men of His Time* (New York: North American Review, 1886).

150 *"appointed to any high office"*: CW II, 48–49.

151 *"crumb of patronage which Illinois expects"*: Ibid.

151 *"appointed to that office"*: Ibid., 51.

151 *According to William Herndon*: HI, 349.

152 *"send me an answer by the bearer"*: Thomas Ewing, "Lincoln and the General Land Office, 1849," *Journal of the Illinois State Historical Society,* vol. XXV, no. 3, October 1932, 142–43.

152 *"he could not accede to it"*: Ibid.

152 *"the backers of Lincoln give slight odds"*: *Illinois Register,* June 14, 1849.

152 *95 degrees in the shade*: The weather in D.C. is chronicled in the *Daily National Intelligencer,* June 18–22, 1849.

153 *"similarly draped"*: *National Whig,* June 20, 1849.

154 *"some use to put me to yet"*: Ewing, 153.

THE SHADOW OF DEATH

155 The account of Robert S. Todd's death is drawn primarily from Townsend, 199–230.

159 *"one hair at a time from her head"*:

Tarbell Papers, interviews with John S. Ritter and Howard Dyson.

160 *"bursting into tears left the room"*: Ibid., interview with B.S. Edwards, Doc. 38090001, 9.

160 *"Eat, Mary, for we must live"*: Octavia Roberts, quoted by Randall, 141.

161 *"even if it should be offered to him"*: *IJ*, November 20, 1850.

163 *"signing the deed"*: CWII, 108–9.

163 *"Mrs. Lincoln often struck"*: HI, 597.

164 Elizabeth Black and her sister-in-law Mary Reman: "Took Tea at Mrs. Lincoln's: The Diary of Mrs. William M. Black," *Journal of Illinois State Historical Society*, vol. XLVIII, spring 1955, 59ff. All Black quotes are from this source.

164 *"the fellowship of the church"*: Temple, *Skeptic to Prophet*, 47.

164 *"every woman ought to have"*: Ibid.

165 *"the great national bereavement"*: *IJ*, July 9, 1852.

166 *"birth of my youngest son"*: MTL Letters, 475.

AT HOME IN SPRINGFIELD

167 Early Engagements: Mary Frazaer, *Early Engagements and Florence (A Sequel)* (Cincinnati: Moore, Anderson, Wilstach & Keys, 1854).

167 *"greatly interested in it"*: CW II, 210–11.

168 *"ambition could not tempt him"*: Howells quoted in Donald, *Lincoln*, 160.

168 *"criminal betrayal of previous rights"*: Ibid., 168.

168 *"thunderstruck and stunned"*: CW II, 282.

169 *"The Rotunda . . . Commissioners"*: *IJ*, July 11, 1848.

169 *"superior to such meanness as that"*: Townsend, 252 and passim for Clay quotes.

170 *"the destruction of his country"*: *Illinois State Register*, July 12, 1854.

170 *"a Great Heroic Speech"*: *IJ*, July 11, 1854.

170 *"do better somewhere else"*: *IJ*, July 11, 1854.

171 *"sad and homely face"*: Rice, *Reminiscences*, 232.

172 *"he did not promise to run"*: Donald, *Lincoln*, 171.

173 *"of the Illinois Legislature"*: HI, 266.

174 *"my six months visit to Springfield"*: Helm, 106. All Helm quotes infra are from this source.

177 *"She could love him better"*: HI, 453.

177 Mary always had a terrible temper: Burlingame, *Inner World*.

177 Both of the Lincolns . . . make snowmen: The weather in Springfield is chronicled in the *Illinois Journal*.

179 *"elect Lincoln on the first ballot"*: Letter of April 22, 1880, to *Globe Democrat*, Joseph Gillespie, Tarbell Papers.

179 Mary Lincoln climbed the grand wooden staircase: Baker, 149–50; Helm, 107–8.

180 *"the fate of any individual"*: Horace White, *The Life of Lyman Trumbull* (Boston & New York: Houghton Mifflin, 1913), 38.

182 *"he transferred his vote to Trumbull"*: White, 44.

182 *"wounded in the house of his friends"*: Gillespie letter, Tarbell Papers.

182 *"to congratulate my friend Trumbull"*: White, 45.

183 *"pretended not to see me"*: Letter from Julia to Lyman Trumbull, April 14, 1856, Trumbull papers, DLC, quoted in Baker, 150.

185 *"seldom ever uses what she has"*: quoted in Thomas Dyba and George Painter, *Seventeen Years at Eighth and Jackson* (Lisle, Ill.: IBC Publications, 1985), 27. This work is the chief source of background information about the Lincolns' home.

185 *"the most indulgent parent I have ever known"*: Herndon, *Lincoln*, 344.

186 *"couldn't walk good"*: Ruth Painter Randall, *Lincoln's Sons* (Boston: Little, Brown, 1955), 37.

188 *"fire and energy and force"*: Herndon, *Lincoln*, 312.

188 *"poor white men?"*: Carl Sandburg, *Abraham Lincoln: The Prairie Years and The War Years,* one-volume edition (New York: Galahad Books, 1993), quoting Whitney, 122.

189 *"on the track for the Presidency"*: Henry Clay Whitney, *Life on the Circuit with Lincoln* (Caldwell, Id.: Caxton Printers, 1940), 94.

189 *"a continual torment . . . loving liberty"*: *CW* II, 320–23.

190 *"hear me this time"*: Herndon Letters, 141.

190 *The maidservant Margaret Ryan: HI,* 597.

191 *"before the Eyes of the world"*: Ibid., 722–23.

191 *"Rubbing the blood off his face"*: Ibid., 692.

192 *"all the world gone to sleep"*: Herndon, *Lincoln*, 348–49.

193 *"the world of business and politics"*: *HI,* 729.

193 *"Mary would write"*: Norman Judd interview, Tarbell Papers.

194 *"anything to eat here"*: Henry G. Little, "Personal Recollections of Abraham Lincoln," Randall Collection, DLC.

195 "evasively": *CW* II, 389–90.

195 *"clean to the roots"*: P.P. Enos, *HI,* 449.

196 *Nelson's Handbook for Tourists: Falls of Niagara* (Toronto: James Campbell, 1860).

197 *"ten thousand years ago"*: *CW* II, 10–11.

198 *"set upon by garrotters . . . monotony of our existence"*: *New York Times,* July 29, 1857.

199 *"my next Husband shall be rich"*: MTL Letters, 50

200 *"the old man"*: Henry B. Rankin, *Intimate Character Sketches of Abraham Lincoln* (Philadelphia & London: J. B. Lippincott, 1924), 100.

ANOTHER RUN FOR THE SENATE

205 *"in the U.S. Senate"*: *Chicago Journal,* May 22, 1857.

207 *"making political speeches"*: Randall, *Lincoln's Sons,* 40.

207 *"brought Tad home on his shoulders"*: Philip Wheelock Ayres, "The Lincolns and Their Neighbors," from *Lincoln Among His Friends,* ed. Rufus Rockwell Wilson (Caldwell, Id.: Caxton Printers, 1942), 84–85. Quotes from Ardelia Wheelock passim are from this source.

208 *"By wagon, by rail . . . stone Stephen"*: *Lincoln's Footsteps,* 103.

209 *"threw them into ecstasies"*: Joseph Gillespie, "Memoir," ISHL.

211 *"Master of the Bath"*: *Lincoln's Footsteps,* 71.

315 *"without parade or fuss"*: Gustave Koerner's *Memoirs,* as quoted in Angle, *Lincoln Reader,* 246–47. Koerner quotes below are from this source.

214 *"Southern support for the Presidency in 1854"*: Neeley, 175.

215 *The panoramic setting:* Walter B. Stevens, *A Reporter's Lincoln,* ed. Michael Burlingame (Lincoln: University of Nebraska Press, 1998), pp. 56-59. Background, and many quotes infra come from Stevens.

215 *"just as he does physically"*: Helm, 140.

218 *"any impression on these people?"*: Stevens, 59.

218 *"such a residence very soon"*: Ibid.

THE PLEASURES OF 1859

221 *"and others of your family"*: *CW* III, 339-40.

222 *"he had his descent"*: Mark E. Neeley, Jr., *The Abraham Lincoln Encyclopedia* (New York: DaCapo Press, 1983), 91.

223 Farni *v.* Tesson: Letter from Stacy Pratt McDermott, assistant editor, *Papers of Abraham Lincoln,* to author, January 5, 2006, summarizing the case.

224 *"fly over my head"*: Chicago *Press & Tribune,* June 1, 1859.

224 *"Oriental Costumes"*: Ibid.

224 *"here in this town"*: to Remann, June 6, 1859, in Randall, *Lincoln's Sons,* 43.

225 a *"chalked hat"*: *Lincoln's Footsteps,* 40.

229 *"as submissive as possible"*: MTL Letters, 57.

229 *"on the side"*: *HI,* 597.

229 *Mary's shopping . . . was becoming compulsive:* Baker, 156.

TRAVELING TOGETHER

232 *tax assessment was in dispute:* Chicago *Tribune,* July 20, 1859, "Assessment of the Illinois Central Railroad."

234 *"a fine type of that race"*: Daily Commercial (Cincinnati), September 17, 1859.

236 *"as a remembrance for his Columbus friends"*: Ohio Statesman, September 17, 1859.

236 *"but never a pretty one"*: Lincoln's Footsteps, 278.

237 *"this is the short of it"*: Daniel J. Ryan, *Lincoln and Ohio* (Columbus: Ohio State Archaeological and Historical Society, 1923).

238 *"well worth hearing"*: Cincinnati Commercial, September 17, 1859 (and infra).

238 *"Champion of Freedom"*: Cincinnati Daily Gazette, September 18, 1859.

238 *"took his tea in very great haste"*: Ryan, 72.

242 *"and who gladly paid it"*: Cincinnati Commercial, February 16, 1861.

243 *"proceeded to his residence"*: Illinois State Journal, October 18, 1859.

THE NOMINATION

246 *broadening his political prospects:* Harold Holzer, *Lincoln at Cooper Union* (New York: Simon & Schuster, 2004), 10–27. Background on Cooper Union is from this source.

246 *"perfectly satisfactory"*: J.M. Pettengill, quoted in Holzer, 16.

247 *"temperate in tone"*: Herndon, *Lincoln,* 368.

247 the critical *New York audience:* Carl Sandburg, *Abraham Lincoln: The Prairie Years,* vol. 2 (New York: Harcourt, Brace, 1926), 214.

248 *"in the canvass for President"*: Holzer, 147.

248 *"in his usual spirits"*: *Day by Day,* II, 276.

249 *"place than yourself"*: Hay, quoted in Benjamin P. Thomas, *Abraham Lincoln* (New York: Alfred A. Knopf, 1952), 205.

250 *"to vote as a unit for him"*: William E. Baringer, *Lincoln's Rise to Power* (Boston: Little, Brown, 1937), 186.

251 *"brace your nerves for any result"*: Thomas, 210.

251 *"Game of Fives"*: Andrew M. Brooks, "Lincoln and the Game of Fives," Tarbell Papers 3807.0020.

251 *"Make no contracts that will bind me"*: *CW* IV, 50.

251 *"what we have to meet"*: Thomas, 210.

251 *"intensely excited"*: *HI,* 438.

252 *"the sight of General Washington"*: Ibid., 174.

252 *"Let's go to the telegraph office"*: Ibid., 438.

252 *"let her see it"*: Ibid., 491.

253 *"upon his nomination" and passim:* *IJ,* May 19, 1860.

255 *"I'm a Lincoln too!"*: *New York Tribune,* May 22, 1860.

256 *"seemed to be looking far away" and passim:* Ibid.

257 *"into the backroom, which he did"*: *Memoirs of Gustave Koerner,* ed. Thomas J. McCormack (Cedar Rapids, Iowa: Torch Press, 1909), 93–94.

258 *"deport yourself accordingly"*: Browning to Lincoln, April 4, 1860, DLC.

258 *"other company had retired"*: Browning, 415.

260 *"the most irreproachable of citizens"*: Cor Utica (New York) *Herald,* June 21, 1860, reprinted in *Sacramento Daily Union,* August 15, 1860.

262 *"to please Mrs. Lincoln"*: all quotes above are from Frank Fuller, "A Day with the Lincoln Family," address printed by Hotel Irving, New York City, ca. 1905, ISHL.

263 *" 'God bless you' "*: Elizabeth Lushbaugh Capps, "Early Recollections of Abraham Lincoln," files of Abraham Lincoln Association, copy in Randall Collection, LC.

264 *"back to a hotel in the city"*: Ibid.

265 *"exhibitions of regard were so terrible"*: Gillespie memoir, ISHL.

"MARY, WE ARE ELECTED"

267 "We are elected": Henry Bowen of *The Independent,* quoting Lincoln, in *Abraham Lincoln: Tributes from His Associates,* ed. William Hayes Ward (New York: Thomas Y. Crowell, 1895), 32.

268 *"infamous purpose"*: *IJ,* November 22, 1860.

268 *"the daily observer"*: Henry Villard, *Lincoln on the Eve of '61* (collected columns from the *New York Herald*) (New York: Alfred A. Knopf, 1941), 38. All quotes from Villard below are from this collection.

268 *"in fine spirits"*: Mrs. Conkling to Clinton, November 12, 1860, Conkling papers, ISHL.

268 *"I verily believe"*: H. Quigley to J.A.

McClernand, Springfield, December 8, 1860, McClernand Mss. ISHL; also quoted in Randall, 191.

269 *"his capacious mouth"*: Donn Piatt in Rice, *Reminiscences,* 479.

271 *"some* new clothes!":* Francis Bicknell Carpenter, *Six Months at the White House* (New York: Hurd and Houghton, 1866), 113.

273 *"a good motherly kind of woman"*: Edward Needles Kirk to his wife, January 6, 1861, ISHL.

273 *"the present state of political affairs"*: Mrs. Conkling to Clinton, January 19, 1861, ISHL.

274 *"looked upon as very shocking"*: Kreisman to Charles Henry Ray, manuscript in Huntington Library, quoted in Randall, 193.

274 *"she might not be mentally 'right' "*: W.A. Evans, *Mrs. Abraham Lincoln: A Study of Her Personality* (New York: Alfred A. Knopf, 1932), 158.

275 *"secured against bursting by iron hoops"*: Donald, *Lincoln,* 271.

276 *"witnessed here in many years"*: Villard, 63.

277 *"do honor at the White House"*: Helm, 156.

277 *"no place for a dog"*: Dorothy Meserve Kunhardt, "Lincoln's Lost Dog," *Life* magazine, February 15, 1954.

279 *"Where is that* bad *boy?"*: Lincoln's Sons,* 35.

279 *Then there was Mary Reman . . . until the child was asleep:* The Reman and Dallman incidents are recounted in William Dodd Chenery, "Mary Todd Lincoln Should Be Remembered for Her Many Kind Acts," *Illinois State Register,* February 27, 1938.

280 *"which he uttered"*: address of Senator Fred T. Dubois, February 16, 1906, at the Leland Hotel, Springfield, Ill., ms. in ISHL.

JOURNEY THROUGH OVATIONS

283 *"before he reached his hotel" and quotes from Villard passim: Lincoln on the Eve of '61.*

285 *"such an enthusiasm as has never been witnessed"*: David Davis Papers, ISHL.

285 *"pushing and yelling around us"*: Nicolay to Bates, February 15, 1861, DLC.

288 *the actor cursed the presidential party: Lincoln's Footsteps,* 264.

290 *"the advice and counsel of his wife"*: *NYT,* February 19, 1861.

291 *no promises about conciliatory measures: Chicago Tribune,* February 21, 1861.

291 *"smooth their wrinkled attire"*: quotes from *NYT* and Baltimore *Sun,* February 21, 1861.

292 *"no silly airs"*: Shepard to nephew and niece, February 21, 1861, Burton Historical Collection, Detroit Public Library, copy in Randall Collection, DLC.

293 *"insulting to Mr. Lincoln"*: *NYT,* February 25, 1861, dateline Harrisburg, February 23, 1861.

294 *"Pinkerton informed me . . . in existence"*: Lincoln's statement to Benson J. Lossing in 1864, quoted in Norma Barrett Cuthbert, *Lincoln and the Baltimore Plot, 1861* (San Marino: The Huntington Library, 1949), xv.

295 *"her intentions are correct"*: *NYT*, February 25, 1861, 8.

296 *going secretly on a separate train:* Ward Hill Lamon, *Recollections of Abraham Lincoln* (Chicago: A.C. McClurg, expanded 2nd edition), 41–42.

297 *"required the utmost secrecy"*: Alexander K. McClure, *Abraham Lincoln and Men of War-Times* (Philadelphia: Times Publishing Co., 1892), 52.

298 *"announced, rather vaguely"*: February 26, 1861.

298 *"expected to arrive"*: February 25, 1861.

298 *"the lives of all on board"*: Ibid.

299 *"indications of real danger"*: *Chicago Tribune*, February 26, 1861.

299 *"you bloody black Republicans"*: *NYT*, February 24, 1861.

300 *"the order of the day"*: *NYT*, February 26, 1861.

300 *"going to Washington as he did"*: *NYT*, February 24, 1861.

301 *"under a bodice"*: *Sun*, February 25, 1861.

DEBUTS

307 *"let all come that could . . . sustained the infliction"*: *NYT*, February 25, 1861.

308 *"an insult in these times"*: *Chicago Tribune*, March 2, 1861.

308 *"the Presidential mansion"*: Ibid., February 21, 1861, dateline February 18, 1861.

308 *"gaiety and flowers"*: www.whitehouse.gov/history/first ladies.

308 *"brought in by the first President"*: Elizabeth Todd Grimsley, "Six Months in the White House," *Jour-*

nal of the Illinois State Historical Society, vol. XIX, nos. 3 & 4, October 1926–January 1927, 43–73. All quotes from Mrs. Grimsley below are from this source.

310 *"not welcome in the capital"*: Julia Taft Bayne, *Tad Lincoln's Father* (Lincoln and London: University of Nebraska Press, reprinted 2001), 6.

311 *"claiming to be the rightful President"*: *Chicago Tribune*, March 8, 1861.

312 *"covered acres of ground"*: Ibid.

313 *"any sign of hauteur"*: Ibid., March 9, 1861.

313 *"the belle of the evening"*: Baltimore *Sun*, March 6, 1861.

314 *"sent to their relief"*: John G. Nicolay, "Memorandum, July 3, 1861," John G. Nicolay Papers, DLC.

314 *"engaged in animated conversation"*: *Washington Star*, March 8, 1861.

315 *"nothing to wear"*: Keckley, 38.

316 *"North and South mingled freely"*: Harry E. Pratt and Earnest E. East, "Mrs. Lincoln Refurbishes the White House," *Lincoln Herald*, February 1945, vol. 47, no. 1, 15.

317 *"called to fill"*: *NYT*, March 11, 1861.

317 *"the most successful ever known there"*: Nicolay, p. 30. All quotes from Nicolay below are from this source.

317 *"happiest man in this country"*: Carl Sandburg, *Abraham Lincoln: The War Years*, vol. 1, 137–38.

318 *"he disapproved"*: HI, 331.

319 *"to the joy of all the domestics"*: Harriet Lane Johnston Papers, DLC.

321 *"scarcely have been founded on fact"* and quotes passim: William Howard Russell, *My Diary North and South*,

ed. Fletcher Pratt (New York: Harper and Brothers, 1954), 23–29.

322 *"Gainsborough or Reynolds"*: Doris Kearns Goodwin, *Team of Rivals* (New York: Simon & Schuster, 2005), 339, quoting Thomas Belden and Marva Belden, *So Fell the Angels* (Boston: Little, Brown, 1956), 5–6.

323 *"call on me at any time"*: Ibid., quoting Belden and Belden, 4.

323 *"politician and not general"*: Montgomery Blair to Gideon Welles, May 17, 1873, Welles Papers, DLC.

324 *"the Beggar's Opera"*: Mr. Lincoln's *Whitehouse*, 8, at http://www.mrlincolnswhitehouse.org (The Lincoln Institute, 2005).

324 *"because of public business"*: *New York Herald*, April 6, 1861.

324 *"ill at ease, and not self-possessed"*: Comdr. Dahlgren quoted, J.G. Nicolay, Extracts from Dahlgren, DLC.

324 *"close application and study"*: John Hay, *At Lincoln's Side: John Hay's Civil War Correspondence and Selected Writings,* ed. Michael Burlingame (Carbondale: Southern Illinois University Press, 2000), 135.

325 *"the chartered libertine of Executive Mansion"*: Ibid.

325 *"on a bright windy day in March, 1861"*: Julia Taft Bayne, *Tad Lincoln's Father*, 1. All quotes from Julia below are from this source.

327 *"dominated Washington society"*: Grimsley, 51.

327 *"He quietly grinned"*: Hay Diary, 2.

328 *"seemed to enjoy the music vastly"*: *National Republican*, April 29, 1861.

328 *"not half are here yet"*: *Diary of Horatio Nelson Taft, 1861–65,* vol. 1, January 1, 1861–April 11, 1862, DLC.

All quotes from Taft (Julia's father) are from this source.

HOUSEKEEPING

331 *"with Arms of the United States on each piece"*: Pratt and East, "Mrs. Lincoln Refurbishes the White House." Most of the following details of Mrs. Lincoln's purchases, and the receipts, are in this article, cited above.

332 *"consented with some misgivings"*: Julia Taft Bayne, 42.

334 *"it has unnerved me"*: Ruth Painter Randall, *Colonel Elmer Ellsworth: Lincoln's Friend and First Hero of the Civil War* (Boston: Little, Brown, 1960), 262.

336 *"save the Capitol"*: Nicolay, 52.

336 *"I will not leave you at this juncture"*: Grimsley, 67.

337 *"her rural home in Illinois"*: Turner and Turner, *Her Life and Letters,* 88, quoting *The Crisis,* May 30, 1861.

338 *"in your most vital part"*: "Union" to Lincoln, June 26, 1861, ISHL.

338 the *"war"* the Lincolns had over *Wood:* Colfax to Nicolay, July 17, 1875, Nicolay Papers, DLC.

338 *"almost a monomaniac . . . duplicity of others"*: Keckley, 57–66.

338 *"I feel it to be my duty"*: Ibid., 65.

338 *"read the man correctly"*: Ibid., 58.

339 *"aided her in doing so"*: Browning, March 3, 1862.

340 *"the profanation of vulgar eyes"*: Nicolay, 54. All Nicolay quotes are from this source, *With Lincoln in the White House.*

340 *"seem almost regal"*: *New York Herald,* August 8, 1861.

341 *"Manure Fund"*: Burlington *Hawk-Eye,* February 8, 1862.

342 *"to pay more as less"*: Hay Letters, Appendix 2, Burlingame quoting Samuel Hopkins testimony to Congress, August 30, 1861, 192.

342 *"the papering of the President's House"*: National Archives, Outgoing Letters of the Commissioner of Public Buildings, vol. 14, 18, cc. In Randall Collection, DLC.

344 *"sorrow was equally poignant"*: Russell, *Diary North and South,* 258.

345 *"wither together"*: Blair, *Life of Baker,* 157.

345 *"deliberate collusion:"* Hay Letters, 194.

346 *"impelling to it"*: Lincoln to French, October 14, 1861, "Unpublished Lincolniana," *Journal of the American Lincoln Association,* vol. 17, no. 1, winter 1996, 51.

346 *"as will settle the matter"*: Caleb Smith to Seward, October 27, 1861, Seward Mss., University of Rochester Library, photo DLC.

347 *"struck with lightning"*: Hay Letters, 14.

349 *"She was in much tribulation . . . attend to everything"*: French, 382.

DARKNESS DESCENDING

352 *"than I have ever done in the past"*: Browning, 521.

353 *"vile creature . . . monstrosity . . ."*: John Hay, *Lincoln's Journalist: John Hay's Anonymous Writings for the Press, 1860–64,* ed. Michael Burlingame (Carbondale: Southern Illinois University Press, 1998), 120.

353 *"in her salon and on her drives"*: Margaret Leech, *Reveille in Washington: 1860–1865* (New York: Harper & Row, 1989), 319.

354 *"pull me in pieces"*: William O. Stoddard, *Inside the White House in War Times,* ed. Michael Burlingame (Lincoln: University of Nebraska Press, 2000), 98.

354 *"cannot invite to our dinners"*: Keckley, 43.

356 *"feasting and dancing"*: Leech, *Reveille,* 323.

356 *"every Street in the city" and Taft quotes below:* Taft Diary, January 11, 1862.

357 *"pronounced Willie better . . . no immediate danger"*: Keckley, 45.

358 *"before they have any"*: Randall, *Lincoln's Sons,* 97.

358 *"than any boy of his age"*: Taft Diary, February 20, 1862.

358 *"gentle-mannered"*: Bayne, 3.

358 *"a fine little fellow"*: Howard Glyndon (pseudonym of Laura Catherine Searling), "The Truth About Mrs. Lincoln," *The Independent,* New York, vol. XXXIV, no. 1758, August 8, 1882, 4–5.

359 *"no cause for alarm"*: Keckley, 45–46.

360 *"a look of offended dignity"*: Ibid.

361 *"imbecility of commanders"*: The account of the dinner, and all quotes, are from *The Washington Star,* February 6, 1862, except as noted.

361 *"struck with admiration . . . dazzling splendor"*: Kenneth A. Bernard, "Lincoln and the Music of the Civil War," *Lincoln Herald,* spring 1963, vol. 64, no. 1, 3–8.

362 *"blended in confusion"*: *Chronicle,* February 9, 1862.

362 *bilious fever: New York Herald,* February 10, 1862.

363 *Greenhow . . . Morris:* See Ross, 136–37.

364 *"scandalous insinuations":* Leech, *Reveille,* quoting *New York Herald,* 329.

365 *"adjourned for the day":* E.J. Edwards, untitled clipping in Randall Papers, DLC, with Jesse Weik's stamp, ca. 1880. Edwards is quoting the senator's testimony to General Thomas L. James, the postmaster general.

366 *"past all hope of recovery": New York Herald,* February 17, 1862.

366 *"he is actually gone!":* Nicolay, 71.

367 *"paroxysms of grief" and passim:* Keckley, 46–48.

368 *"great satisfaction to all present": Washington Star,* February 22, 1862.

368 *"I did not see Mrs. Lincoln at all":* French, 389.

369 *"the beloved youth . . . because they were not":* For an account of Gurley's oration, see Temple, *From Skeptic to Prophet,* 186–89.

370 *at a cost of $4,420:* National Archives Files of General Accounting Office, "Appropriation for Introducing the Potomac Water into the Pres. House," approved, February 20, 1861.

370 *"a judgment for her party":* Baker, 215.

371 *"Delilah . . . gluttony":* Ross, 175.

371 *"violent grief":* Elizabeth Edwards to Julia, March 12, 1862, Randall Collection, DLC.

372 *"gave it back to Defrees":* Browning, March 3, 1862.

372 *"to Mr. L's also:"* Elizabeth Edwards to Julia, late March 1862, as above.

372 *"I hope they are either dead, etc.":* Rev. Noyes Miner's *Personal Reminiscences of Abraham Lincoln,* ISHL.

372 *"My very brain feels palsied":* Elizabeth to Julia, April 1, 1862.

1863: A NEW YEAR

374 *"since last we stood here":* French ms. in Brown University Library, in Randall, 320.

375 *"the dignity of official position": NYT,* October 26, 1862.

376 *his new friend Captain David Derickson:* Lincoln's friendships with Derickson and the other officers at the Soldier's Home are discussed in Matthew Pinsker, *Lincoln's Sanctuary: Abraham Lincoln and the Soldier's Home* (New York: Oxford University Press, 2003), 84–85.

377 *"His Excellency's night-shirts!":* Thomas Chamberlin, *History of the One Hundred and Fiftieth Regiment Pennsylvania Volunteers, Second Regiment Bucktail Brigade* (Philadelphia: F. McManus, 1905), 27.

377 *"What stuff!":* Fox, quoted in Pinsker, 85.

377 *"Capt. D. and his company": CW* V, 484–85.

378 *"retire to private life":* Burnside to Lincoln, January 1, 1863, in *CW* VI, 32.

379 *"her little son Willy":* Browning Diary, 608.

381 *"must not leave Washington":* Temple, *Skeptic to Prophet,* 199.

382 *"details of the nefarious practice":* William P. Wood, *Washington Gazette,* January 16, 1887.

382 *"the result of partial insanity":* Ibid.

382 *"no time for personal affairs":* Pratt,

Personal Finances, 129. The ensuing anecdote is told in Pratt, 124–30.

384 *"could be discovered"*: Stoddard, *Inside the White House,* 33.

385 *"walls and furniture" and passim:* Brooks 66–68.

386 *"choice spirits themselves"*: Speed to Lincoln, DLC.

387 *"after 8 o'cl"*: Henry to his wife, February 17, 1863, ISHL.

387 *"in high spirits"*: *Day by Day* III, 169, quoting Fox, *Diary.*

388 *"Julie and her don't visit"*: Henry to his wife, February 17, 1863, ISHL.

388 *"best and dearest friend"*: MTL Letters, 271.

388 *"they were the aggressors"*: Henry to his wife, February 18(?), '63, ISHL.

388 *"open family rupture"*: Ibid.

389 *"to anybody else"*: Ibid.

389 *"you have no more father"*: Jean Paul Richter, *Flower, Fruit, and Thorn Pieces* (London: William Smith, 1845).

389 "a pretty hard life for him": French, 416–17.

390 they made him feel *"cross"*: H.C. Whitney to Herndon, *HI,* 631–32.

391 *"nervous and uneasy"*: *Day by Day* III, 172.

391 He drolly *"ordered"* his friend: Henry to his wife, April 12, 1863, ISHS.

391 *"in the most free and easy way" and passim:* Brooks, 51–59.

THE WAR COMES HOME

394 *"What will the country say!"*: Ibid., 60–61.

395 *"where certain destruction awaits*

him": *Washington Evening Star,* May 5, 1863, 2nd ed.

396 *"it is not in my power to prevent"*: Hooker to Lincoln, June 15, 1863, *CW* VI, 276.

397 *"in bed with his wife"*: Pinsker, 107.

398 *"blood flowed freely" and passim:* *Washington Star,* July 2, 1863.

399 *"dejected and discouraged"*: Welles, *Diary,* quoted in *Day by Day* III, 197.

399 *"on the desk in front of him"*: Nicolay, *Oral History,* 88.

399 *"whipped them myself"*: Hay Diary, 63.

399 *"since you left"*: Hay, *At Lincoln's Side,* 45.

400 *"so would my father"*: Helm, 250.

400 *"all at once"*: Hay, *At Lincoln's Side,* 49.

401 *"death of Absalom"*: Helm, 216–17.

403 *"telegraph the President of your decision"*: Ibid., 220–21.

404 *"dined intimately, alone"*: Ibid., 221.

404 *"did not wish it known"*: Browning, 651.

404 *"the scape-goat for both North and South!" and passim:* Helm, 225–27.

407 *"not of her own volition"*: Helm, 231.

FIRE AND ICE

411 *"We did not try to enter"*: Browning, 653.

411 *"her usual ease and urbanity"*: French, 443.

412 *"usual good nature"*: Ibid.

413 *"promote that object"*: John C. Waugh, *Reelecting Lincoln* (New York: Crown Publishers, 1997), 114.

413 *"you do him an injustice" and pas-sim:* Keckley, 57–67.

415 *"awful sublimities of nature":* Nico-lay, 124.

415 *"forms of expression" and passim:* Stoddard, *Inside the White House,* 32–33.

416 *"a cerebral disease":* Herndon's *Lincoln,* 351.

417 *"shall not live to see the end": Day by Day* III, 238.

417 *"accumulated upon its hands" and passim:* Browning, 659.

419 The Sea of Ice: Adolphe P. Dennery (London: Thomas Hailes Lacy, n.d.).

421 *"Put crepe on your hat":* Nicolay, 126.

421 *"the cry of fire":* Elizabeth Blair Lee, *Wartime Washington: The Civil War Letters of Elizabeth Blair Lee,* ed. Virginia Jeans Laas (Urbana: University of Illinois Press, 1991), 346.

421 *"gone where the good horses go":* Nicolay, ibid.

422 *"to beat the Tycoon":* Nicolay, 127.

423 *"he needed rest":* Angle and Sand-burg, *Mary Lincoln: Wife and Widow,* 111.

424 *"sink and let me go through":* Ibid., 112.

425 *"as I ever saw him":* French, 447.

426 *"several ladies fainted" and passim: Philadelphia Dispatch,* April 25, 1864.

428 *"a few private friends": New York Herald,* May 2, 1864.

428 *"whatever money I require":* Keck-ley, 67.

429 *"occurrences of the day":* MTL Let-ters, 186.

429 *a little theater . . . gave up the latchkey:* The account of Tad's play

theater and the photography inci-dent is from Carpenter, 91–92.

431 *"any general has been tried":* Keck-ley, 59–60.

432 *"saddest face I ever knew":* Carpen-ter, *Six Months,* 30.

432 *"sent gifts to the older people":* "Aunt Mary Dines, the Contraband Singer," quoted in John E. Washing-ton, *They Knew Lincoln* (New York: E.P. Dutton & Co., 1942).

433 *"so glad to see you":* Dr. Darius Orton, "An Eyewitness Account," *Lincoln Herald,* spring 1975, vol. 77, no. 1, 68.

434 *"knew most of them by heart" and passim: They Knew Lincoln,* 84.

ONE MORE ELECTION

437 "to his own territory": Lee quoted in Benjamin Thomas, *Abraham Lincoln* (New York: Alfred A. Knopf, 1952), 432–33.

438 *They moved on Independence Day:* See Pinsker, *Lincoln's Sanctuary,* 127

438 *Jubal Early had swept down:* Back-ground on the "invasion" of Wash-ington and Jubal Early's defeat comes from E.B. Long, *The Civil War Day by Day* (New York: Dou-bleday, 1971), 532–38, and John Henry Cramer, *Lincoln Under Enemy Fire* (Baton Rouge: LSU Press, 1948).

440 *"within five miles":* Hay Diary, 221.

440 *"period of excitement":* Long, 538.

442 *"I am inconsolable":* Donald, *Lin-coln,* 512.

442 *"travel around the defenses":* Hay, as above.

443   *"in a perfect maze, bewildered"*: Welles, *Diary,* quoted in *Day by Day* II, 69–70.

443   *"the occasion of much censure"*: Carpenter, *Six Months,* 301.

444   *"unattended except by their coachman"*: Cramer, *Enemy Fire,* 28.

445   *"supposing he would accept"*: Ibid., 28–29.

445   *"in full retreat"*: Bull letter quoted in Cramer, 26–27.

446   *"one-half of his tall form"*: Wright, *Washington Times,* June 15, 1900.

446   *"towards the enemy"*: Welles quoted in Cramer, 54.

446   *"Peace appeared to be a distant dream"*: Thomas, *Abraham Lincoln,* 440.

447   *"ever known in this country"*: Long, quoting "a southern soldier," 548.

448   *"the political cloud that hung over him"*: McClure, *Men of War-Times,* 113–15.

449   *"forsaken us yet"*: Brooks, p. 165

450   *"scandalized nation no longer"*: *IJ,* quoted in Ross, 210.

450   " *'you must bear the disappointment'* ": Hay Diary, n. 297, 366, Burlingame quoting "Some Incidents in the Life of Mrs. Benjamin S. Edwards, " ed. Mary Edwards Raymond (n.p. 1909), 16.

451   *"the only path of patriotic duty"*: Gideon Welles, "Lincoln's Triumph in 1864," *Atlantic Monthly,* March 1878, 464.

451   *"clerks of the telegraph"*: Hay Diary, 244.

451   *"more anxious than I"*: Ibid.

452   *"blow his own horn"*: the looking glass incident is from Brooks, 198–200.

453   *"not get through the next four years"*: Keckley, 70.

GHOSTS IN THE MIRROR

457   *"with critical curiosity"*: Keckley, 66.

457   *"asks a great many questions"*: Taft Diary, December 14, 1864.

459   *"in your husband, and you and me"*: Stanton, quoted in "The Late Secretary Stanton," *Army and Navy Journal,* January 1, 1870, quoted in Randall, 360–61.

459   *"without any serious damage"*: Nicolay, 167.

460   *"her position and her heart"*: French, 463.

461   Indianapolis Sentinel: December 3, 1864.

461   *"are to their mothers" and passim:* Keckley, 54.

462   *"by even General Taylor"*: Stoddard, 3.

463   *"wounded him deeply"*: Keckley, 65.

464   *"for the present"*: Washington *Chronicle,* February 19, 1865.

464   *"since he became President"*: Browning, vol. 2, 7.

465   *"without the slightest effort"*: de Pineton, quoted in *Day by Day* III, 315.

465   *"for I know"*: Temple, *Dr. Anson Henry,* 11.

466   *"in a dazed hap-hazard sort of way" and passim: Washington Star,* March 4, 1865.

467   *"A sea of faces"*... *"very brilliantly"*: *New York Herald,* March 6, 1865.

468   *"of him who took it"*: Salmon Chase to MTL [with endorsement by Lincoln], April 4, 1865, DLC.

CITY POINT

469   Philip Van Doren Stern's *An End to Valor* (Boston: Houghton Mifflin,

1958) provides valuable background for this chapter.

470 *"My husband's first wife"*: Sandburg, *Abraham Lincoln: The War Years,* vol. 4, 118.

471 *"was properly cared for"*: Baltimore American, "A Day at the White House," March 23, 1865.

472 *"possessed her to do it?"*: Benjamin French to Sister Pamela, May 21, 1865, French papers, DLC.

473 *"so easily assailed"*: John S. Barnes, "With Lincoln from Washington to Richmond in 1865," *Appleton's Magazine,* vol. IX, no. 5, May 1907, 519. Quotes passim from Barnes are from this source.

474 *"the most anxious"*: Grant, quoted in Sandburg, *The War Years,* 139.

474 *"covers enough on him"*: MTL, quoted in William B. Crook, *Through Five Administrations* (New York and London: Harper and Brothers, 1910) 4.

475 " *'a little further off' "*: Stanton to Lincoln, March 25, 1865, in *CW* VIII, 374.

475 *"Mr. Lincoln expressed"* . . . *"for the President"*: Barnes, "With Lincoln," 521.

476 *"the fight was still going on"*: Barnes, ibid. All quotes from Barnes below are from this source, 521–24.

476 *"glad to be at rest"*: Lincoln, quoted by Barnes, 521.

476 *"were in contemplation"*: Adam Badeau, *Grant in Peace* (Hartford, Conn.: S.S. Scranton, 1887), 356–57. All quotes below from Badeau are from this source, 356–62.

477 *"The Secretary of War"*: MTL quoted in Badeau, 357.

478 *"saw no one again that evening"*: Barnes, 522.

478 *"neither of us must ever mention it"*: Badeau, as above.

478 *"there will be no pause"*: Stanton to Lincoln, March 31, 1865, in *CW* VIII, 378.

478 *"in the same condition"*: Stanton to Lincoln, April 3, 1865, ibid., 384–85.

479 *"in his native town"*: Barnes, 522.

481 " *'Tis very nice"*: Badeau, 359.

484 *"witnessed the failure"*: Barnes, "With Lincoln," Part II. "The President Enters the Federal Capital," *Appleton's Magazine,* June 1907, 743.

484 *"arm in arm in the woods"*: Barnes, Ibid. All quotes from Barnes below are from this source, 743–51.

485 *"a long married life like theirs"*: Lee, *Letters,* April 19, 1865, 497.

485 *"exertions that will bring Richmond"*: Stanton to Lincoln, March 31, 1865, in *CW* VIII, 378.

486 *"killed by an assassin!"*: Ward Hill Lamon, *Recollections of Abraham Lincoln* (Chicago: A.C. McClurg & Co., 1895), 117.

486 *that the White House was on fire*: Stern, *An End to Valor,* 49.

487 *As they walked into Richmond*: An important background source is Edward H. Ripley, "Final Scenes at the Capture and Occupation of Richmond," *New York MOLLUS,* vol. III, 1907.

488 *"the first sweet blossoms of spring"*: Keckley, 73.

489 *"deserted banquet hall?"*: MTL Letters, 213.

490 *"Everything bespoke desolation"*: Adolphe de Chambrun, "Personal

Recollections of Mr. Lincoln," *Scribner's Magazine*, vol. 13, 1893, 26–38. All quotes from Chambrun are from this source.

490 *"could go to bed now"*: Keckley, 76.

NO WORD OF FAREWELL

491 *"We must never speak of that"*: Chambrun, "Personal Recollection," 35.

492 *"a sudden and violent end"*: Keckley, 79.

492 *"dangerous thing to do" and passim*: Ripley, as above.

495 *"sea of hats, faces, and arms" and passim*: Brooks, 224–25.

496 *illumination fitting the people's festive mood*: See Leech, 421.

498 *"assenting by silence"*: MTL Letters, Turner quoting letter from Sumner to Chase, 217.

499 *Field later recalled*: Maunsell B. Field, *Memories of Many Men and Some Women* (New York: Harper & Brothers, 1874), 321.

500 *"above the tumultuous throng"*: *Washington Star*, April 14, 1865.

500 *"by ourselves to day"*: MTL Letters, 284.

501 *"very miserable"*... *"deeply engraven"*: Ibid., 285.

502 *"I do not visit Mrs. Lincoln"*: Badeau, *Grant in Peace*, 360.

502 *Major Thomas T. Eckert*: David Homer Bates, *Lincoln in the Telegraph Office* (New York: Century, 1907), 367.

503 *"bent on having a jolly evening"*: Letter of A.J. Bloor to Walt Whitman, June 7, 1879, DLC.

503 *The curtain had gone up*: Of the vast literature on the assassination,

for background I have relied most heavily upon Jim Bishop, *The Day Lincoln Was Shot* (New York: Harper & Brothers, 1955); W. Emerson Reck, *A. Lincoln, His Last 24 Hours* (Jefferson, N.C.: McFarland, 1987); Edward Steers, Jr., *Blood on the Moon* (Lexington: University Press of Kentucky, 2001); and James L. Swanson, *Manhunt* (New York: William Morrow, 2006).

504 *"paid close attention to it"*: A.J. Bloor letter, as above.

504 *"think nothing about it"*: Anson Henry to his wife, April 19, 1865, ISHS.

505 *"Stop that man!... shot the President!"*: Swanson, *Manhunt*, 49.

505 *"For God's sake open the door!"*: Ibid., 73.

505 *"Oh, my dear husband"*: Charles A. Leale, "Lincoln's Last Hours," *Harper's Weekly*, February 13, 1909, vol. 53, 7–10. Leale quotes passim are from this source.

506 *"you sons o' bitches!"*: Bishop, 564.

506 *"Why was I not the one?"*: *Chicago Tribune*, April 15, 1865. See also Field, *Memories of Many Men*, 322. Several witnesses testify that Mrs. Lincoln repeated the phrase throughout the night.

507 *"My husband's blood!"*: Swanson, 108.

507 *"Why didn't he shoot me?"*: *Tribune*, as above.

508 *"to speak to our children"*: Charles Sabin Taft, "Abraham Lincoln's Last Hours," *Century Magazine*, vol. 45, February 1893, 635.

508 Bring Taddie here: J.P. Usher to his wife, April 16, 1865, Randall Collection, DLC.

509 *"do not let her in again"*: Stanton,
     quoted by Leale.

509 *"given my husband to die?"*: Letter
     from James Tanner to Mr. Watch,
     April 17, 1865, reprinted in William
     E. Barton, *The Life of Abraham*

Lincoln (Indianapolis, Ind.: Bobbs-
Merrill, 1925), vol. 2, 472.

509 *"The President is no more"*: Letter
     from Elizabeth Dixon to Louisa
     Wood, May 1, 1865, *The Collector,*
     March 1950, 49–50.

INDEX

ABOUT THE AUTHOR

DANIEL MARK EPSTEIN is a biographer, poet, and dramatist whose work has been widely published and performed. His writings have appeared in *The Atlantic Monthly, The New Yorker, The New Republic,* and many other magazines and anthologies. He is the author of seven prize-winning books of poetry and five highly acclaimed biographies. His *Nat King Cole* was a 1999 *New York Times* Notable Book, and his biography of Edna St. Vincent Millay was a New York Public Library Honoree "Books to Remember" for 2001. His honors include the Rome Prize in 1978, a Guggenheim Fellowship in 1984, and an Academy Award in Literature from the American Academy of Arts and Letters in 2006. He lives in Baltimore, Maryland.

www.danielmarkepstein.com